"Yong's work brilliantly articulates what the world of Christian theology is fast becoming: the dawning reality that the 'regions beyond' have become the new center of Christianity. *Renewing Christian Theology* is a twenty-first-century expression of what it means to have 'good news for all people!'"

—*Byron D. Klaus, President, Assemblies of God Seminary*

"This remarkable book introduces  ecostal summa in sympathetic and critical c heritage. No one interested in Pentecost gnore this work."

—*Veli-Matti Kärkkäinen, Professor of Systematic Theology, Fuller Theological Seminary and Docent of Ecumenics, University of Helsinki*

"Yong reprioritizes the order of classic theological reasoning, beginning with eschatology, in order to emphasize Christ-centered and Spirit-empowered Christianity."

—*Don Thorsen, Professor of Theology, Azusa Pacific University*

"Here at last is a vibrant theological text that systematically addresses the big intellectual challenges confronting twenty-first-century Pentecostals and charismatics. Every chapter bursts with constructive ideas, bringing biblical exposition and theological themes to bear on the doctrinal statements that define the Church's long renewal."

—*William K. Kay, Professor of Pentecostal Studies, University of Chester*

"Amos Yong delivers a forward-looking and pneumatologically grounded systematics of Renewal demonstrating its contribution to the wider theological academy and the global church."

—*Sammy Alfaro, Assistant Professor of Theology, Grand Canyon University*

"No doubt this book will be a landmark work in Renewal Theology and spark a spirited conversation about the role of Pentecostal theology in ecumenical and interreligious dialogue."

—*Peter C. Phan, The Ignacio Ellacuria Chair of Catholic Social Thought, Georgetown University*

Renewing Christian Theology
Systematics for a Global Christianity

AMOS YONG

with artistic images and commentary by
JONATHAN A. ANDERSON

BAYLOR UNIVERSITY PRESS

Cover Design by Nicole Holmes, Zeal Design Studio
Cover Image: Sadao Watanabe (Japanese, 1913–1996), *Oikoumene*, 1991, traditional Japanese colors on washi paper. Courtesy of Tatsuo Watanabe. Select public domain images courtesy of Wikimedia Commons, http://commons.wikimedia.org / Eitan f. (fig. 6.2), IT1315922 (fig. 6.3), Gunnar Bach Pedersen (fig. 9.1), Sitiens lucem (fig. 9.4), Marie-Lan Nguyen (fig. 12.2), and Caroline Léna Becker (fig. 12.4).
Book Design by Diane Smith

Library of Congress Cataloging-in-Publication Data

Yong, Amos.
  Renewing Christian theology : systematics for a global Christianity / Amos Yong; with artistic images and commentary by Jonathan A. Anderson.
  477 pages cm
  Includes bibliographical references and index.
  ISBN 978-1-60258-761-8 (pbk. : alk. paper)
  1. Assemblies of God--Doctrines. 2. Pentecostal churches--Doctrines. 3. Theology, Doctrinal. 4. Pentecostalism. I. Title.
  BX8765.5.Z5Y66 2014
  230'.994--dc23
                                        2013049573

To our colleagues in the Biola University Art Department
and in the Regent University School of Divinity
for your friendship, laughter, prayers, and common labor
that is the outworking of a Spirit-filled life of the mind we all desire,
for the sake of the gospel, in anticipation of the coming reign of God

~ 1 Corinthians 13:12 ~
~ 1 John 3:2 ~
~ Romans 11:33-36 ~

Contents

Figures and Permissions   xiii

Acknowledgments   xix

Preface   xxiii

1   Introduction   1
Renewing Christian Theology—The Contemporary Task in Global Context

2   The Last Days and the End of Time   29
Christian Hope Then and Now

3   The Gifts of the Holy Spirit   57
Christian Ministry and the Mission of God

4   The Baptism in the Holy Spirit   81
A Salvation-Historical Perspective

5   Sanctification and Holiness   103
In the World but Not of It

6   Ordinances and Sacraments   131
Practicing the Christian Life

7   The Church and Its Mission   161
The Spirit of the Reconciling God

8   Divine Healing   193
Salvation of the Body and Redemption of the World

9   Salvation in Christ through the Spirit   223
An Eschatological Soteriology

10   Creation and Fall   255
     Natural History and the Redemptive Ends of God

11   The Eternal Godhead   293
     The Mystery of the Triune God in a World of Many Faiths

12   The Spirit-Inspired Scriptures   327
     Biblical Authority and Theological Methods for Us and Our Salvation

Epilogue   357

Appendix 1   359
     The World Assemblies of God Fellowship Statement of Faith

Appendix 2   363
     Early Ecumenical Creeds

Glossary   365

References   371

Scripture Index   421

Index of Names   437

Subject Index   440

Expanded Table of Contents

Figures and Permissions   xiii

Acknowledgments   xix

Preface   xxiii

1   Introduction   1
    Renewing Christian Theology—The Contemporary Task
    in Global Context
    1.1   World Christianity: An Overview
    1.2   Christian Theology: One Faith—Changing Contexts
          and Forms
    1.3   Renewed and Always Renewing: A Way Forward
          for Christian Theology
    1.4   An Overview and Road Map for the Book

2   The Last Days and the End of Time   29
    Christian Hope Then and Now
    2.1   Paul the Apocalyptic Apostle
    2.2   What and When? Contextual Considerations
          2.2.1   Millennialism: Historical Developments
          2.2.2   Final-State Eschatologies: Disputed Possibilities
          2.2.3   Contemporary Challenges in Global Context
    2.3   Apostolic Anticipations: Lukan Eschatology
    2.4   Christian Hope Today and Tomorrow

3   The Gifts of the Holy Spirit   57
    Christian Ministry and the Mission of God
    3.1   Elizabeth as Prototype of the Spirit-Filled Life
    3.2   The Spiritual Gifts: Historical Considerations
          3.2.1   Patristic and Medieval Developments
          3.2.2   Reformation and Early Modern Disputes
          3.2.3   Global "Charismania"!?

    3.3   Pauline Charismology: A Dialogue with the Corinthians

    3.4   Surprised by the Holy Spirit!

4   The Baptism in the Holy Spirit   81
    A Salvation-Historical Perspective

    4.1   Peter's Journey in the Spirit

    4.2   Spirit Baptism: Quests for Understanding
        4.2.1   The Puritan and Reformed Quest for Assurance
        4.2.2   The Wesleyan-Holiness Search for Perfection
        4.2.3   Signs and Interpretation: Spirit Baptism in
               Ecumenical and Global Contexts

    4.3   Apostolic Fragments: The Many Tongues of Acts

    4.4   Be Filled with the Spirit!

5   Sanctification and Holiness   103
    In the World but Not of It

    5.1   Mary: Set Apart by the Spirit

    5.2   Christian Perfection: Historical Trajectories
        5.2.1   The Quest for Perfection in the Christian Tradition
        5.2.2   Perfect Love in the Wesleyan-Holiness Movement
        5.2.3   Sanctification in Ecumenical and Global Perspective

    5.3   Johannine Sectarianism—and Sanctification

    5.4   Be Holy and Being Made Holy!

6   Ordinances and Sacraments   131
    Practicing the Christian Life

    6.1   John the Baptist: In Water—and the Spirit?

    6.2   The Great Tradition and Its Sacramental Tributaries
        6.2.1   Christian Initiation and Baptism
        6.2.2   The Eucharist/Supper as Sacrament and/or
               Ordinance?
        6.2.3   Renouncing the Devil: Deliverance and Discernment

    6.3   The "Sacramentalism" of the Fourth Gospel

    6.4   Repent, Renounce, Be Baptized, Eat, and Drink:
           Practicing the Christian Life

7   The Church and Its Mission   161
    The Spirit of the Reconciling God

    7.1   Stephen's Eschatological Vision of the People of God

    7.2   Contestations among/about the People of God
        7.2.1   Israel and the Church: Whence the Temple
               of the Spirit?
        7.2.2   Reformist, Restorationist, Renewalist: What Body
               of Christ?

7.2.3   Between Israel and the Reign of God: Whither Global Christianities?

7.3   An Ephesian Ecclesiology

7.4   Into All the World! The Church as *Missio Spiritus*

8   Divine Healing   **193**
Salvation of the Body and Redemption of the World

8.1   Legion: Deliverance and Healing

8.2   Healing, Miracles, and Disability: The Broader Conversation

    8.2.1   Healing and Miracles: Unpredictable Traditions?

    8.2.2   Healing and Modern Science: Challenges or Opportunities?

    8.2.3   Disability: Renewal Christianity's "Thorn in the Flesh"?

8.3   Wholeness and Salvation in Mark

8.4   Be Healed! Saving the Church, Redeeming the World

9   Salvation in Christ through the Spirit   **223**
An Eschatological Soteriology

9.1   Zacchaeus and the Salvation of the Children of Abraham

9.2   Salvation Histories and Christian Traditions

    9.2.1   The Many Encounters with the Saving Christ

    9.2.2   The Many Theories of the Work of Christ

    9.2.3   The Many Face(t)s of the Person of Christ

9.3   Once-and-for-All through Christ and the Spirit: Salvation for Hebrews and Gentiles

9.4   "Today If You Will Hear His Voice . . .": Receiving the Gift of Salvation

10   Creation and Fall   **255**
Natural History and the Redemptive Ends of God

10.1   Judas, the Son of Perdition

10.2   Creation and Fall: So What Is the Problem?

    10.2.1   Creation and Modern Science: The Problem of Providence

    10.2.2   Evolution and Death: The Problem of Evil

    10.2.3   The *Imago Dei* and the Fall: The Problem of Sin

10.3   The Groaning of the Spirit: Romanizing Creation and Fall

10.4   Renewing the Cosmos: A Trinitarian Theology of Creation, Cross, and Culmination

11   The Eternal Godhead   **293**
The Mystery of the Triune God in a World of Many Faiths

11.1　Cornelius the Just

11.2　The Triune God: Pentecostal, Ecumenical,
and Interreligious Perspectives

　　11.2.1　Oneness and Trinity: Foundational Issues

　　11.2.2　Toward a Twenty-First-Century Trinitarian Faith

　　11.2.3　Renewal Theology in a Pluralistic World

11.3　From Israel to the Nations: Matthew's Narrative
of the Triune God

11.4　Worshipful Witness to the God of Jesus Christ in the Spirit

12　The Spirit-Inspired Scriptures　　　327
Biblical Authority and Theological Methods for Us and Our Salvation

12.1　John—One Name, Many Voices

12.2　Divine Revelation/s: Many Interpretations

　　12.2.1　*Sola Scriptura* and the Word of God: Reformed
and Always Reforming

　　12.2.2　Christ and/as Divine Revelation: From Canon to
Tradition

　　12.2.3　The Spirit and Theological Method: Renewed
and Always Renewing

12.3　The Apocalyptic Revelation: One Christ, Many Images
and Resonances

12.4　Knowing, Loving, and Serving God: One Spirit,
Many Tongues

Epilogue　　　357

Appendix 1　　　359
The World Assemblies of God Fellowship Statement of Faith

Appendix 2　　　363
Early Ecumenical Creeds

Glossary　　　365

References　　　371

Scripture Index　　　421

Index of Names　　　437

Subject Index　　　440

Figures and Permissions

Figure 1.1   Anonymous (Roman), *The Good Shepherd*, ca. 300–325,   3
             marble, from the Catacomb of Domitilla, Rome, Italy.
             Museo Pio Cristiano, Vatican Museums, Vatican City State
             / Scala / Art Resource, NY.

Figure 1.2   Anonymous (Indian), *The Christ Child as the Good Shep-*   3
             herd, ca. 1600–1650, ivory, from Goa, India. The Walters Art
             Museum, Baltimore, Maryland.

Figure 1.3   Andrej Rublev (Russian, 1360–1430), *The Three Angels at*   13
             Mamre (*The Holy Trinity*), ca. 1408–1427, tempera and gold
             leaf on wood. State Tretyakov Gallery, Moscow, Russia.

Figure 1.4   Hubert (ca. 1370–1426) and Jan (1390–1441) van Eyck   16
             (Flemish), *The Adoration of the Mystic Lamb*, interior lower
             central panel of the *Ghent Altarpiece*, 1432, oil on wood. St.
             Bavo Cathedral, Ghent, Belgium / © Lukas—Art in Flan-
             ders VZW / The Bridgeman Art Library.

Figure 1.5   P. Solomon Raj (Indian, 1921–), *The Vine and the Branches*,   20
             2009, woodcut color block print / Courtesy of the artist.

Figure 2.1   Michelangelo Merisi da Caravaggio (Italian, ca. 1571–1610),   31
             The Conversion of Saint Paul, ca. 1600–1601, oil on canvas.
             Cerasi Chapel in Santa Maria del Popolo, Rome, Italy.

Figure 2.2   Attributed to Coppo di Marcovaldo (Italian, ca. 1225–ca.   39
             1276), *The Last Judgment*, ca. 1265–1270, mosaic, from the
             octagonal dome of the Baptistery of San Giovanni, Florence,
             Italy / Photo by Jonathan Anderson.

Figure 2.3   Anonymous (Syriac), *The Ascension of Christ*, fol.13v of the   46
             Rabbula Gospels, 586, tempera on vellum, from the Mon-
             astery of St. John, Beth Zagba, Syria. Biblioteca Mediceo
             Laurenziana, Florence, Italy / De Agostini Picture Library /
             The Bridgeman Art Library.

Figure 2.4   Mandy Cano Villalobos (American, 1979–), *Undone*, 2006,   54
             unraveled sweaters / Courtesy of the artist.

Figure 3.1   Rogier van der Weyden (Flemish, 1400–1464), *Visitation of*   59
              Mary to Elizabeth, ca. 1435–1445, oil on wood. Museum der
              Bildenden Künste, Leipzig, Germany.

Figure 3.2   Sawai Chinnawong (Thai, 1959–), *Pentecost*, 1997, acrylic   66
              on canvas / Courtesy of the artist. Special thanks to Paul de
              Neui.

Figure 3.3   Anonymous (Russian), *The Descent of the Holy Spirit*, 15th c.,   70
              tempera and gold leaf on wood, from the Cathedral of St.
              Sophia, Novgorod, Russia. Museum of Art, Novgorod, Rus-
              sia / The Bridgeman Art Library.

Figure 3.4   Anthony van Dyck (Flemish, 1599–1641), study for *Pente-*   79
              cost, 1620–1621, ink on paper. State Hermitage Museum, St.
              Petersburg, Russia / The Bridgeman Art Library.

Figure 4.1   Gerrit van Honthorst (Dutch, 1590–1656), *The Denial of*   83
              Saint Peter, ca. 1623, oil on canvas. Minneapolis Institute of
              Arts, Minneapolis, Minnesota / The Putnam Dana McMil-
              lan Fund / The Bridgeman Art Library.

Figure 4.2   Tim Hawkinson (American, 1960–), *Pentecost*, 1999, poly-   90
              urethane, foam, sonotubes, mechanical components / Cour-
              tesy of the artist and Pace Gallery.

Figure 4.3   Anonymous (German), *The Trinity and the Apostles*, fol. 73 of   94
              Codex 132 illumination of Rabanus Maurus, *De universo*,
              1023. Library of the Abbey, Montecassino, Italy / BPK, Ber-
              lin / Alfredo Dagli Orti / Art Resource, NY.

Figure 4.4   Anonymous (English), *Pentecost*, fol. 29v of MS 369 (Y-7),   99
              the *Winchester Pontifical*, late 10th–11th c., tempera and gold
              leaf on vellum. Bibliotheque Municipale, Rouen, France /
              Giraudon / The Bridgeman Art Library.

Figure 5.1   Fra Angelico (Italian, ca. 1387–1455), *The Annunciation*, ca.   105
              1430–1432, tempera and gold leaf on wood. Prado Museum,
              Madrid, Spain.

Figure 5.2   Michelangelo Merisi da Caravaggio (Italian, ca. 1571–1610),   111
              The Calling of Saint Matthew, 1599–1600, oil on canvas. Con-
              tarelli Chapel in San Luigi dei Francesi, Rome, Italy. Scala /
              Art Resource, NY.

Figure 5.3   Michelangelo Buonarroti (Italian, 1475–1564), *The Cre-*   111
              ation of Adam (detail), ca. 1511, fresco. Sistine Chapel, Vatican
              Museums, Vatican City State.

Figure 5.4   Anonymous (German), *The Tree of Vice* and *The Tree of Virtue*,   120
              fol. 25v/26r of MS W72 illumination of Conrad of Hirsau,
              Speculum Virginum, early 13th c., ink on parchment. Private
              collection / The Walters Art Museum, Baltimore, Maryland.

Figure 5.5   Jean Fouquet (French, ca. 1420–1481), *The Right Hand of*   127
              God Protecting the Faithful against the Demons, or *Descent of the*

Holy Spirit upon the Faithful, from the *Hours of Étienne Chevalier*, ca. 1452–1460, tempera and gold leaf on parchment. Robert Lehman Collection, The Metropolitan Museum of Art, New York, New York / © The Metropolitan Museum of Art, New York, New York / Art Resource, NY.

Figure 6.1   Andrej Rublev (Russian, 1360–1430), *The Baptism of Christ*,   133
1405, tempera and gold leaf on wood. Cathedral of the Annunciation, Moscow, Russia.

Figure 6.2   Cruciform baptismal font in a 5th c. church in Shivta, Israel.   138

Figure 6.3   Octagonal baptismal font in a 5th c. church at Costa Balenae   138
in Riva Liguria, Italy.

Figure 6.4   He Qi (Chinese, 1950–), *The Risen Lord*, 2001, gouache on   143
paper / Courtesy of the artist, He Qi © 2013 | www.heqi
gallery.com.

Figure 6.5   Anonymous (Egyptian), *The Washing of the Feet*, 8th c., tem-   152
pera and gold leaf on wood. Monastery of Saint Catherine, Sinai, Egypt / Gianni Dagli Orti / The Art Archive at Art Resource, NY.

Figure 7.1   Giorgio Vasari (Italian, 1511–1574), *The Stoning of Saint Ste-*   163
phen, with the Trinity Above, 1571, chalk and ink on paper. Private collection / Photo © Christie's Images / The Bridgeman Art Library.

Figure 7.2   Sadao Watanabe (Japanese, 1913–1996), *Oikoumene*, 1991,   171
traditional Japanese colors on washi paper / Courtesy of Tatsuo Watanabe. Special thanks to Sandra Bowden and Junko Watanabe.

Figure 7.3   Anonymous (English), *The Seven Churches of Asia Minor*, fol.   177
2v (detail) of MS Ludwig III 1 (*Dyson Perrins Apocalypse*), ca. 1255–1260, tempera, gold leaf, and ink on parchment. The J. Paul Getty Museum, Los Angeles, California.

Figure 7.4   Tim Hawkinson (American, 1960–), *Untitled*, 2003, unique   185
photographs on foamcore on panel / Courtesy of the artist and Pace Gallery.

Figure 8.1   James Jacques Joseph Tissot (French, 1836–1902), *The Swine*   195
Driven into the Sea, illustration for *The Life of Christ*, ca. 1886–1894, watercolor and gouache on paperboard. Brooklyn Museum of Art, Brooklyn, New York / The Bridgeman Art Library.

Figure 8.2   Tim Lowly (American, 1958–), *Temma on Earth*, 1999,   205
acrylic gesso with pigment on panel / Courtesy of the artist.

Figure 8.3   Anonymous (Italian), *Christ Healing the Man Born Blind*, ca.   212
1075–1100, fresco. Sant'Angelo in Formis, Capua, Italy / Hirmer Fotoarchiv / The Bridgeman Art Library.

Figure 8.4 Matthias Grünewald (German, ca. 1480–1528), *Crucifixion*,   217
closed central panel of the *Isenheim Altarpiece*, ca. 1512–1515,
oil on wood. Musee d'Unterlinden, Colmar, France / The
Bridgeman Art Library.

Figure 9.1 Niels Larsen Stevns (Danish, 1864–1941), *Zacchaeus*, 1913,   225
oil on canvas. Randers Museum of Art, Randers, Denmark.

Figure 9.2 Cristovao Canhavato (Kester), Hilario Nhatugueja, Fiel dos   231
Santos, and Adelino Serafim Maté (Mozambican art group
Nucleo de Arte), *The Tree of Life*, 2004, welded recycled fire-
arms. British Museum, London, United Kingdom. Photo
credits: left, © Kati Byrne; and right, © David Rose (www.
davidrose.co.uk).

Figure 9.3 Anonymous (Byzantine), *Anastasis*, 1310–1320, fresco. The   236
Parecclesian apse vault of Kariye Camii (Chora Church),
Istanbul, Turkey / Photo © Tarker / The Bridgeman Art
Library.

Figure 9.4 Anonymous (Italian), *The Tree of Life*, 12th c., mosaic. The   248
apse of the Basilica of San Clemente, Rome, Italy.

Figure 10.1 Domenico Morelli (Italian, 1826–1901), *The Repentance of*   257
Judas, illustration from the Amsterdam Bible, 1895. Galleria
Nazionale D'Arte Moderna, Rome, Italy / De Agostini Pic-
ture Library / A. Dagli Orti / The Bridgeman Art Library.

Figure 10.2 Rembrandt Harmenszoon van Rijn (Dutch, 1606–1669),   264
Adam and Eve, 1638, etching. Private collection / The
Bridgeman Art Library.

Figure 10.3 Anonymous (Egyptian), *Mummy Portrait: Head of a Woman*,   270
130–160, encaustic and gilded stucco on wood, from Fayum,
Egypt. Detroit Institute of Arts, Detroit, Michigan / Gift of
Julius H. Haass / The Bridgeman Art Library.

Figure 10.4 Attributed to Allan Ramsay (Scottish, 1713–1784), *Portrait*   270
of an African, ca. 1757–1760, oil on canvas. Royal Albert
Memorial Museum, Exeter, Devon, United Kingdom / The
Bridgeman Art Library.

Figure 10.5 Laura Lasworth (American, 1954–), *Lily among the Thistles*,   280
2001, oil on panel / Courtesy of the artist.

Figure 10.6 Craigie Aitchison (Scottish, 1926–2009), *Crucifixion*, 1999–   280
2000, oil on canvas. Private collection / The Bridgeman Art
Library.

Figure 11.1 *Peter's Vision on the Housetop*, illustration from Henry Daven-   296
port Northrop, *Charming Bible Stories Written in Simple Lan-*
guage, 1893 / © Florida Center for Instructional Technology,
University of South Florida, Tampa, Florida.

Figure 11.2 Matfre Ermengau of Béziers (French, active 1288–1322), 303
The Holy Trinity (detail), fol. 16r of the Provençal codex
Bréviaire d'Amour (*Breviary of Love*), late 13th to early 14th c.
Real Biblioteca de lo Escorial, Madrid, Spain / Gianni Dagli
Orti / The Art Archive at Art Resource, NY.

Figure 11.3 Anonymous (Peruvian–Cusco School), *The Holy Trinity*, 303
ca. 1750–1770, oil on canvas. El Museo de Arte de Lima
(MALI), Lima, Peru.

Figure 11.4 Anonymous (Ethiopian), *The Virgin and Child with Arch-* 313
angels, Scenes from the Life of Christ, and Saints, early 17th
c., tempera on wood. The Walters Art Museum, Baltimore,
Maryland.

Figure 11.5 Laura James (American, 1971–), *Christ Enthroned*, 2002, 322
acrylic on canvas. Private collection / The Bridgeman Art
Library.

Figure 12.1 Maius (Spanish, 10th c.), *Vision of the Heavenly Jerusa-* 330
lem, fol. 222v of MS M.0644 illumination of Beatus of
Liébana, *The Commentary on the Apocalypse*, ca. 940–950,
tempera on vellum. The Pierpont Morgan Library, New
York, New York / The Pierpont Morgan Library / Art
Resource, NY.

Figure 12.2 Jacob Jordaens (Flemish, 1593–1678), *The Four Evangelists*, 333
ca. 1625, oil on canvas. Louvre, Paris, France.

Figure 12.3 Eastman Johnson (American, 1824–1906), *The Lord Is My* 340
Shepherd, ca. 1863, oil on wood. The Smithsonian American
Art Museum, Washington, D.C. / The Smithsonian Ameri-
can Art Museum / Art Resource, NY.

Figure 12.4 Anonymous, previously attributed to Artus Wolffort (Flem- 348
ish, 1581–1641), *Saint Jerome Reading*, ca. 1630, oil on canvas.
Musée des Beaux-Arts de Caen, Caen, France.

Acknowledgments

This volume presents a culmination of sorts at this point of my thinking as a pentecostal theologian, which vocation was initiated during my doctoral studies in the mid-1990s. First and foremost, my wife's patience, love, and encouragement must be recognized as allowing for the germination over the last two decades plus of whatever insights are valuable in this book. For this I can only say, "Thank you, Alma!" As this manuscript goes to the publisher, we are both looking forward to so much together in this new "empty nest" chapter of our lives.

I am sure that some of the thoughts here go back to my undergraduate days and even behind that to my growing up as a pentecostal pastor's kid and missionary kid. Yet the best I can do for those interested in the foundational ideas summarized herein is to direct attention to the notes and references in the more than a dozen of my own monographs and another dozen-plus edited volumes that precede this work, some of which are mentioned in what follows. The references collected at the end of this book, of course, also provide important pointers. Needless to say, my debts are endless, given the help I have received over the years.

I must include the librarians who have supported my research, starting at Bethel University in St. Paul, Minnesota (1999–2005); Xavier University in Cincinnati, Ohio (fall 2004); and now Regent University (since 2005). Patty Hughson in the interlibrary loan department here at Regent has been more than efficient, courteously collegial, and always helpful. Bob Sivigny, who retired right about the time that the initial draft of this manuscript was being undertaken, was also always diligent in acquiring books and resources in the growing field of pentecostal-charismatic or renewal studies that have been indispensable for this work.

Former Regent University School of Divinity dean and now colleague Michael Palmer supported my sabbatical year that allowed this book to be written. My former graduate assistant and doctoral student Vince Le helped with research, bibliography, proofreading, and drafting the glossary. Enoch Charles, my present graduate assistant, assisted with the indexing. Regent University has been a unique laboratory for thinking about renewal studies in general and renewal theology especially.

My yearlong sabbatical (2012–2013) was generously funded by a Henry Luce III Theological Fellowship. Thanks to Stephen Graham at the Association of Theological Schools for his role in chairing the fellowship selection process and to Frances Pacienza for her administrative assistance. Some of the Luce funds along with a research grant from Biola went to offset the production costs for the artwork with Baylor University Press.

I received encouragement and important feedback on my Luce proposal from Peter Althouse, Johnathan Alvarado, Klaas Bom, Shane Clifton, Byron Klaus, Waldemar Kowalski, Larry Hart, Louis "Bill" Oliverio, Opoku Onyinah, David Ricci, Tony Richie, Ed Rybarczyk, Charlie Self, Christopher "Crip" Stephenson, Karl Inge Tangen, and Jack Wisemore. I appreciate the support of Peter Phan, Mark Cartledge, and Alan Padgett for my Luce application. Peter Phan also went above and beyond the call of duty in reading my manuscript, contributing to the improvement of the text with his helpful observations, and graciously serving as my conversation convener at the Luce fellows conference in November 2013. Discussions at this conference in response to my project description and presentation, particularly with Peter Phan, Chloë Starr, and Paul Chang-Ha Lim, resulted in important tweaks in the first chapter on the creed during the copy-editing stage of book production.

Perspective on the World Assemblies of God Fellowship (WAGF) Statement of Faith (SF) was provided by archival materials from the Flower Pentecostal Heritage Center in Springfield, Missouri. Center director Darrin Rodgers went out of his way to facilitate my consultation of important WAGF minutes. Reference archivist Glenn Gohr and special projects coordinator William Molenaar both also shared important background material on the SF with me. Thanks to Assemblies of God general superintendent George O. Wood and WAGF administrative assistant Joy Wooten also for their help in accessing the relevant documents.

The following read and commented variously on the first draft of the manuscript: Anne Dyer, Vince Le, Louis "Bill" Oliverio, Tony Richie, Michael Rakes, Ed Rybarczyk, Christopher "Crip" Stephenson, and Stephen Tourville. Words cannot express how grateful I am for the time these friends have invested in helping me improve this text. Néstor Medina and Wolfgang Vondey also sent initial comments on the introductory chapter, which strengthened it, and Bev Mitchell gave me incredibly valuable feedback on chapter 10 from his perspective as a biologist. I also received substantial input and encouragement from Trinity Western University (TWU) and Associated Canadian Theological Schools' graduate students—especially Tyler Harper, Jason Lavergne, Park Lim Jung, Danny Stebeck, and Larry Young—and other participants in the Theology and Global Renewal Christianity seminar in May 2013, where much of the text was presented. Thanks to Michael Wilkinson for the invitation to TWU, for organizing the lectures, and for his own responses to the manuscript and discussion of it. My gratitude extends also to Dennis Lum and Joseph Tang of TCA College in Singapore for inviting me to talk about the manuscript with the TCA faculty (on 22 July 2013), which initiated vigorous discussion and led to some revising and nuancing of the text.

Needless to say, the deficiencies of the book remain my own responsibility.

Carey Newman, my editor at Baylor University Press, has been enthusiastic from the start about this book. I am grateful for his efficiency, professionalism, and most importantly, his humor—the last immeasurably helpful during the long process during which the book was conceptualized, developed, written, and then produced. Thanks to the anonymous reader for his or her important comments. Baylor University Press staff at all stages from contract through to production has also been at their typically excellent best.

Last but not least, it was providential to have met Jonathan Anderson when I was on research leave during the inaugural semester of Biola University's Center for Christian Thought (spring 2012). Jonathan is one of the few artists I know who actually understands theology, and I consider it an unexpected blessing of the Holy Spirit that he has emerged as collaborator on and contributor to this volume. He read the full manuscript and provided his interpretive gloss on the text through choice of the images (for which he also arranged for and secured permission to use) and commentary on them. The result is a richer theological experience, one that enlivens what words alone fail to adequately convey. I am deeply touched by his investment of time and persistent efforts. It has been a joy to have worked with him, and I commend his theological work as a theologian-artist to you the reader.

Jonathan and I dedicate this book to our faculty colleagues at Biola and Regent for all they have contributed to our lives and thinking. Although this book goes to press on the eve of the public announcement that I am transitioning to Fuller Seminary, my friends at the Regent School of Divinity will always have a place in my heart and will always be in my prayers.

Preface

This textbook seeks to provide a summary exposition of central teachings of the Christian faith relevant to the twenty-first-century global renewal context (to be defined more carefully in the introductory chapter) for second-year theology students taking quarter- or semester-long courses, whether at the undergraduate or graduate level. Given that the vanguard of world Christianity is itself increasingly shaped by renewalism, if not becoming renewalist in orientation, it is hoped that this volume will also be found useful in broader evangelical and ecumenical educational contexts. Its major goal is to faithfully articulate key Christian doctrines in ways that nevertheless engage the demands of the present time from a renewalist perspective.

I am fully aware that much of what is covered in these pages begs for further elucidation. Each section, as well as each subsection of the historical and contextual considerations of each chapter, deserves its own book-length treatment from a renewal vantage point. Perhaps this one-volume introduction to theology is a preliminary installment of a multivolume theological work that will have to come later. So without any claims to being exhaustive and with full awareness of the many shortcomings of what are in some cases rather superficial analyses, I still am hoping that renewalists and other Christians will find this a helpful primer on how to think theologically in the twenty-first-century global Christian context.

The sequence of the text reverses the order of the WAGF's SF. As will be explained more thoroughly in the introductory chapter, eschatology provides the initial thrust and orientation for renewalist thinking rather than being relegated, as historically, to an afterthought, while scripture is understood less as a formal "foundation" for theology, as in the classical tradition of systematic theology, and more as an overarching framework for faithful reflection on things divine. Yet while the flow of the text does presume the building of the argument, it may also be possible for instructors to assign specific chapters at different points of the semester correlated with when related topics are engaged from other main theology texts. Regardless of what approach is adopted, beginning students will benefit especially from instructor guidance through the first chapter in order to appreciate the methodological commitments undergirding the form and argument of each chapter under consideration. Those who opt to skip chapter 1 up front can always return to consult it at any point.

For instructors and students, each chapter also concludes with some discussion questions plus a further reading list. Those interested can follow up on the references in the text, which are combined and gathered at the end of the book. There are also images distributed throughout the text. These are intended to engage readers visually in order to inspire imaginative thinking about and with the text. Renewal spirituality insists that theology functions not only at the abstract cognitive level but also at the imaginative, affective, and embodied level of human life. The artwork provides alternative windows into the material and is designed to complement, enrich, and perhaps expand on what is otherwise discursively communicated. It was at one point a hope for the book that an interactive website could be constructed that would include musical pieces correlated with each chapter to facilitate the oral, aural, and audible aspects of renewal thinking (see Ingalls and Yong, forthcoming). For now, however, that remains a dream . . .

Introduction

*Renewing Christian Theology—The Contemporary Task
in Global Context*

What does it mean to talk about renewing Christian theology? This introductory chapter will clarify what is involved, first, by providing some historical and contemporary perspective on world Christianity; second, by examining the development of the kind of theological writing to which this book contributes; and third, by summarizing how the book's distinctive approach hopes to renew Christian theology in the present time. The fourth and final section will orient the reader to the structure of the main chapters of the book.

1.1 World Christianity: An Overview

From its beginnings, Christianity has been a missionary religion. The vast majority of those who initially were convinced that Jesus of Nazareth was the promised Messiah of Israel were Jews. Yet within the first two decades, many God-fearing Gentiles also became his followers. Saint Luke reports that it was at Antioch, located in what is modern-day Turkey, where believers in Jesus, Jews and Gentiles alike, were first called "Christians" (Acts 11:26). This epithet was meant originally as a derisive term (cf. 1 Pet 4:16). But even then, this messianic movement was quickly gaining a reputation for seeking converts (see Acts 26:28).

Within a generation of the death of Christ, Christians had spread far beyond the region of Judea. Some were forced to emigrate from the region due to persecution, while others took advantage of the travel made possible by the Peace of Rome. By the late 50s or early 60s, Paul the apostle brought the gospel message to the city of Rome, the heart of the Roman Empire. From the Jerusalem-centered worldview of the early Christians, Rome was seen also as being on the way toward the ends of the earth (see Acts 1:8b). Before the end of the first century, the Christian presence would extend even further west to Gaul (now France) and

Spain, south to Egypt and to North and East Africa, and east to Mesopotamia and Persia.

This missionizing mentality did not subside, and Christian expansion
continued over the next few hundred years through a variety of means
(Chidester 2000; Irvin and Sunquist 2001). Missionaries first arrived in
Britain by the middle of the second century CE, and in India by the
late second century. By a little later than the middle of the first Christian millennium, Christians had also made it further east in Central Asia
and to what is now called China. Then the conversion to Christianity
of Emperor Constantine in the early fourth century resulted in a gradual "Christianization" of the Western world. The emperor established a
precedent for other kings in other regions within and beyond the Holy
Roman Empire, which also contributed to the spread of Christian faith.
Christianity was a very transportable religion. Arguably its mobility lay in
its capacity to accommodate itself to many different cultures, languages,
and people groups.

The next great missionary movements were launched in the mid- to
late fifteenth century in Africa and in the Americas. The former was
into what is now called sub-Saharan Africa, initially focused on the west
African coast but then increasingly moving south and then inland. While
North Africa and even East Africa have had Christians since the first
century (remember that the Ethiopian eunuch was converted on his way
home; see Acts 8:26-40), missionary endeavors to the rest of the continent were checked initially by the Sahara and then later by the emergence
and spread of Islam. Unfortunately, many of the missionary achievements
in the heart of Africa after 1492 would be tainted by the slave trade to the
"New World." Over the next few centuries, the Christian mission to the
Americas was severely tarnished by the forced migration of Africans as
slaves of New World landowners (Carter 2008; Jennings 2010).

The organized Christian missionary movements of the eighteenth
and nineteenth centuries remain deeply intertwined with the history of
Euro-American colonialism (Merk and Merk 1963; Walls 1996; Robert
2008). Motivated by technological, scientific, and other Enlightenment
advances, missionaries often sought conversion not only to Christ but
also to Western culture. While no one should minimize the contributions of Christian missionaries, especially in preserving the languages of
indigenous cultures (Sanneh 1989), we also should not turn a blind eye
toward the many ways in which non-Western ways of life were devalued.
Contemporary Christians continue to wrestle with this ambiguous legacy
of the missionary movement. On the one hand, the fruits of this enterprise are now being enjoyed due to the fact that Christians in the majority

world who were once the objects of missionization are now engaged in massive efforts to reevangelize the Western world (e.g., Währisch-Oblau 2009). On the other hand, there is also the sense that Christianity's contemporary theological formulations remain dominated by Western cultural forms and expressions perpetuated by the missionary movement (Rah 2009).

FIGURE 1.1 FIGURE 1.2

Christian histories of the arts (visual or otherwise) readily demonstrate that Christianity has no fixed language, image, or cultural format: from the beginning, translation has been intrinsic to the announcement of good news for "all nations" (Matt 28:19; Luke 24:47; Rom 16:26). As Andrew Walls has argued, Christianity's "pilgrim principle," which calls disciples into a life not at home in received social norms, coexists with an "indigenizing principle" by which the gospel is apprehended and embodied in ways thoroughly at home within pre-existing languages, thought patterns, and cultural contexts (Walls 1996: 7–9). This dynamic is glimpsed in these images of the Good Shepherd. This densely meaningful biblical image draws together references to God as the shepherd of his people (Gen 49:24; Ps 23:1; 28:9; Isa 40:11; Jer 31:10) and Davidic kings as vice-regent shepherds (Ps 78:70-71; Jer 23:1-8; Ezek 34; Zech 10:2-3), ultimately converging in Jesus, Son of God and son of David: the shepherd who calls, leads, rescues, heals, and gives his life for/to his flock (Matt 18:12-14; Luke 15:3-7; John 10:1-21; 1 Pet 2:25; Heb 13:20; Rev 7:15-17).

Yet when these sculptors take up this biblical image, they do so within very different cultural frames. The first is a Roman carving fully characteristic of Greco-Roman sculpture: a handsome, beardless Christ stands in a carefully proportioned contraposto pose reminiscent of Hermes Kriophoros, Apollo, Orpheus, or Tityrus. He pulls a rescued lamb tightly to his shoulders while looking attentively toward his left (associated with evil in Roman culture), enabling the lamb to look toward what is "right." By contrast, the second carving inhabits the ivory carving traditions of Goa, India. Here a youthful Christ (too young for Roman respectability) holds the lamb on his lap and demonstrates power not through physical prowess but through enthroned restful meditation as his flock peacefully gathers around "springs of the water of life" (Rev 7:17). At the bottom, Mary Magdalene (representing penitence) meditates over the Scriptures, learning to embody the same posture as her Shepherd.

Both artists present the biblical image in ways that maximize local intelligibility, situating it within the histories and grammars of their own visual cultures. Just as Christ's parables—of a shepherd searching for a lost sheep, for instance—take particular form in his own cultural context, so these carvings translate them into further contexts. And this seems an appropriate witness to the Shepherd who pursues his sheep into the diverse cultural-historical situations of human life—even "to the ends of the earth" (Acts 1:8; cf. Isa 49:6; Acts 13:47). ✦

The problem of a Western-dominated theology is exacerbated when we consider that Christianity is increasingly becoming a non-Western religion (Jenkins 2002; Sanneh 2008). Many of the reasons for the shifting of the center of gravity from the West to the South can be traced to the emergence of pentecostal and charismatic forms of Christianity over the course of the twentieth century (Shaw 2010). Pentecostal and charismatic renewal movements have always emphasized the ongoing work of the Holy Spirit

in the life and mission of the church. If the nineteenth century was designated the "great century of foreign missions" (Latourette 1941), the twentieth has been dubbed "the century of the Holy Spirit" (Synan 2001). The
roots of pentecostal-charismatic Christianity at the turn of the twentieth
century are just as much in the West as they are around the world (Hollenweger 1972, 1997). But it has been the recent explosion of precisely
such churches and movements in Asia, Africa, and Latin America that has
shaped Christianity as a world religion (Martin 2002; Anderson 2004). At
least three characteristics of contemporary global Christianity stand out.

First, the pentecostal churches and denominations birthed out of
the Azusa Street revival in Los Angeles from 1906 to 1908 were thoroughly committed to the missionary task (Robeck 2006). Over the last
one hundred years, these churches have sent many missionaries abroad
and engaged intensely in world evangelization (Anderson 2007; Bundy
2009). While they have extended the colonial paradigm of missions in
some ways, they have also recognized the importance of an "indigenous
principle" that empowers local church leaders to develop Christianity on
their terms rather than on the terms of the missionary (Dempster, Klaus,
and Petersen 1991). So on the one hand, forms of uniquely North American pentecostal Christianity have been "exported" to the rest of the world
(Gifford, Brouwer, and Rose 1996; cf. Noll 2009). On the other hand,
as pentecostal churches in the global south also have matured, they have
begun to develop their own missionary vision and initiated their own
programs of world evangelization (Ma and Ma 2010).

Yet besides the pentecostal churches, charismatic forms of Christianity also have emerged across the Christian world. Beginning in the late
1950s in North America and continuing around the world since (Hunt
2009), charismatic renewal movements have reinvigorated segments of
the mainline Protestant denominations and also the more established
Roman Catholic and Eastern Orthodox churches (see also McDonnell
1980: esp. vol. 3). While shifts in church membership are common, many
charismatic Christians have chosen to remain involved in the work of
renewing their churches. These established churches have been revitalized
as a result. Up to 25 percent of more than one billion Roman Catholics
around the world, for instance, belong to those involved in the charismatic renewal (Cleary 2011). Further, large swaths of Protestant churches
throughout the global south are being increasingly "pentecostalized" or
"charismatized" (e.g., Vähäkangas and Kyomo 2003; Asamoah-Gyadu
2005; Omenyo 2006). In short, the historic churches and Christian traditions around the world are slowly becoming dominated by pentecostal
and charismatic forms of spirituality.

These "pentecostalizing" and "charismatizing" trends can also be observed outside the established churches and traditions. Indigenous churches have always arisen in reaction to the Western missionary movement, but these have taken on a more distinctively pentecostal and charismatic flavor in the twentieth century. Especially in the African context, these local expressions of Christianity have come to be labeled not only as independent churches, but also as "Spirit-type" Christian movements (Anderson 2001). While these developments have been unfolding in the southern part of the world, the charismatic renewal in the northern hemisphere has also spawned its own mutations. Independent churches fully charismatic in their spirituality and practice but distinct from pentecostal and charismatic movements have been identified as a "third wave" of renewal Christianity (Hummel 1994). These continue to proliferate in various independent congregations, nondenominationally affiliated churches, and "apostolic networks" that feature centrally in what is increasingly seen as a postdenominational landscape (Walker 1985; Kay 2007; Hirsch and Catchim 2012). Pentecostal and charismatic forms of Christianity are thus exploding around the world, albeit increasingly going by other (than "pentecostal" or "charismatic") names.

The preceding has only highlighted both the inherently missionary character of Christianity and its increasingly charismatic form of spirituality into the third Christian millennium. Demographers anticipate an even further pentecostalization and charismatization of global Christianity at least through the middle of this century (Johnson and Ross 2009). Because of these trends, researchers have begun to take notice. A recent Pew Forum study of contemporary pentecostal and charismatic Christianity (see www.pewforum.org/Christian/Evangelical-Protestant -Churches/Spirit-and-Power.aspx) observed that while various labels exist, pentecostal and charismatic types of spirituality are renewing existing churches and charting new frontiers. Thus has the nomenclature of "renewal Christianity" come into prominence. Following such conventions, we will use the label of "renewal" all-inclusively in this book to refer to the pentecostal and charismatic forms of Christianity around the world, including independent and indigenous church expressions, as well as those established ecclesial bodies that are increasingly impacted by such tendencies.

This volume reflects theologically on the basics of the Christian faith as informed by global renewal Christianity as herein described. While the writing of global theology is emerging (e.g., Ott and Netland 2006; Tennent 2007; Bevans 2009; Greenman and Green 2012), even within the renewal movement (e.g., Warrington 2008), a conversation between renewalists and Christians theologians at large is just beginning. At this juncture, the looming question is this: What kind of theological discourse will follow from such conversations instigated by the global renewal movement that is reshaping religion in the twenty-first century?

1.2 Christian Theology: One Faith—Changing Contexts and Forms

The first Christian letters provide insight into the one faith (Eph 4:5) proclaimed by the earliest followers of the Messiah. In that sense, the good news of the Christian faith is timeless: God has reconciled himself to the world in the incarnate, crucified, and risen Christ and by the Holy Spirit so that human beings can participate in the task of reconciling the world to God. This message is most fundamentally embodied in human lives and deeds, as Jesus himself did by welcoming children as a sign of the impending reign of God. Yet it also has been and should continue to be communicated in words. In their preaching and teaching, Christians perennially have attempted to summarize the content of this gospel as they understand it in their places and times.

This book can be understood as such a theological and doctrinal summary of global Christian faith at the beginning of the twenty-first century. To appreciate its distinctive shape, it is helpful to have some perspective on the various forms of Christian faith summations. For many Christians throughout the centuries, the Apostles' Creed and the Nicene Creed have served this purpose (see appendix 2). Some renewalists also recite these ancient creeds. Others are noncreedal, with some even being anticreedal and suspicious that such summations compromise commitment to the biblical message.

For our purposes, we can begin with the "summaries" of Christian faith intended as more or less comprehensive and produced in the second millennium. The scholastics were at the forefront of this development, motivated in particular to give an account of Christian faith in light of the rediscovery of Aristotelian philosophy. The most impressive of these works by far was the *Summa theologica* by Thomas of Aquinas (1225–1274), which utilized the method of disputation popular during the medieval period. The three parts of the *Summa* discuss topics related to theology proper (the doctrine of God), theological anthropology (the doctrines related to human nature), and Christology and ecclesiology (the doctrines of the person and work of Christ and of the church). Thomas was canonized by the Catholic Church (in 1323), and his theological writings remain authoritative especially for Roman Catholic students of theology, even almost a thousand years later.

On the Protestant side, one of the first great summations was provided by the Reformer John Calvin (1509–1564). His *Institutes of the Christian Religion* went through six editions in his own lifetime. There were four parts to at least the later and more mature editions of the *Institutes*: (1) on the knowledge and doctrine of God; (2) on the fall of humanity and on God's response in the person and work of Christ; (3) on the doctrine of salvation in all of its complexity; and (4) on the church and the role of the church in relationship to the world. The structure of the *Institutes* was basically adapted over two hundred fifty years later by Reformed theologian Friedrich Schleiermacher (1768–1834) in his *The Christian Faith* (rev. ed., 1830–1831). But Schleiermacher opted as a modern thinker to begin with human experience and thus relegated the doctrine of the Trinity to the end. He felt this idea was derived not primarily from Christian consciousness but was inferred from more primordial theological statements.

The twentieth century has seen the full flowering of Christian faith summary in the form of systematically organized theologies. The greatest twentieth-century Protestant theologian, Karl Barth (1886–1968), wrote fourteen volumes called the *Church Dogmatics* because he was convinced that theological writing ought to be done by those nurtured by the church for the purpose of edifying the church. Barth's "system" was framed by his understanding of Christ as the living word of God, and this provided a christological shape for the *Dogmatics*. In contrast to Schleiermacher, then, a trinitarian framework for theology was foregrounded: God revealed himself in Christ by the Spirit.

Protestant theologians during and after Barth, including such luminaries as Paul Tillich (1886–1965), Wolfhart Pannenberg (1928–), and Thomas Oden (1931–), have followed Barth's trinitarian lead. The difference might be that these post-Barthians, while not dismissing Barth's christological orientation, have also attempted to frame their reflections in a more explicitly trinitarian manner, following the three articles of the Nicene Creed (see appendix 2). The first article of faith is devoted to the doctrine of God as Creator; the second to Christ as Redeemer; and the third to the Holy Spirit, the church, and the last things. This triadic structure, exposited in three volumes, was anticipated already by nineteenth-century Reformed theologian Charles Hodge (1797–1878). More recently, three-volume theologies also have been written by contemporary North American evangelicals such as Millard Erickson and (writing jointly) Gordon Lewis and Bruce Demarest.

Within the renewal movement, the two theologians who have produced a multivolume theological work are J. Rodman Williams

(1918–2008) and French Arrington (1931–). With a Ph.D. from Columbia University and deeply shaped by the charismatic renewal in the Presbyterian Church, Williams was a prolific author. While teaching at Regent University School of Divinity—which locates itself within the charismatic movement—he wrote *Renewal Theology: Systematic Theology from a Charismatic Perspective* (three vols. 1988–1992, one vol. ed. 1996). Rather than being shaped according to the trinitarian structure of the creed, however, Williams' *Renewal Theology* is more topically organized. The initial volume is devoted to God, the world, sin, and redemption (including Christology and atonement); the second focuses on the human experience of salvation, the Holy Spirit (pneumatology), and the Christian life; and the third discusses the church (ecclesiology), the coming reign of God, and the last things (eschatology).

French Arrington's Ph.D. from St. Louis University was actually in New Testament studies (focused on the Corinthian letters). His teaching of theology at Lee University (of the Holiness Pentecostal Church of God denomination, headquartered in Cleveland, Tennessee) over the years led him to write a three-volume *Christian Doctrine: A Pentecostal Perspective* (1992–1994). The fact that it is only about half the length of Williams' *Renewal Theology* probably reflects Arrington's intended audience: first- and second-year undergraduate students, many still in their teenage years. The three books are organized classically in the post-Barthian trinitarian manner. The first discusses the doctrines of revelation, God, creation, and humanity; the second explicates the doctrines of Christ, sin, and salvation; and the last elucidates the doctrines of the Holy Spirit, the church, and the last things.

Like other evangelical approaches to the theological task, both Williams' and Arrington's methodologies are biblically inductive. Each doctrinal topic is discussed by collecting what the Bible has to say and then organizing this material as coherently as possible. It is not so surprising for Arrington, a New Testament scholar, to approach the traditional doctrines of systematic theology in terms of the scriptural witness. Both theologians do provide more expansive pneumatological commentary across some of the theological topics (like Spirit Baptism, the spiritual gifts, and healing). However, there is little else that is distinctive in the ordering and methods of their theologies, especially as compared with their more evangelical counterparts. Still, the legacies of Williams and Arrington provide a rich resource of biblically informed reflection for students across the various streams of the renewal movement. Both wrote at a time when seminary curricula often devoted three semesters to introduce students to systematic theology. As few divinity schools or even Bible colleges retain that many credit hours for systematic theological instruction, shorter treatments are needed.

In part for this reason, one-volume summaries are now much more in vogue. Deserving of mention here is Wayne Grudem's *Systematic Theology* (1994), especially because of his longtime involvement in charismatic renewal in evangelical and Reformed circles. But Grudem's book is still far too long (at over 1200 pages!) to be used in a single semester as an introductory text. He does engage with many topics—often neglected by evangelical systematic theologians but of interest to renewalists—related to the person and work of the Holy Spirit, such as miracles, spiritual beings (angels and demons), the baptism in the Spirit, and spiritual gifts. Yet discussion of these charismatic topics throughout is set within the broader Reformed theological framework to which Grudem is committed.

Another single-volume systematics text that covers much of the same territory in almost half the space is a multiauthored collection edited by Stanley Horton (1995), commissioned by a classical pentecostal denomination. Although the chapters were written by twenty scholars and theologians from the American Assemblies of God Church, this volume otherwise differs little from the works of Grudem, Arrington, and Williams. The ordering of the theological doctrines follows the standard sequence, beginning with the foundations of knowledge and the doctrine of Scripture and moving through the doctrines of the triune God, creation, the fall into sin, and salvation through Christ. There is a shift then to the expected pentecostal themes of the Holy Spirit, sanctification, Spirit Baptism, the spiritual gifts, and divine healing. The volume ends with treatments of the church, its mission, and the last things. Beyond these structural similarities, most of the authors of the various chapters adopt the inductive methods of biblical study characteristic of other evangelical systematic theologies.

Last but not least is Larry Hart's six-hundred-page *Truth Aflame: Theology for the Church in Renewal* (2005). A Baptist charismatic theologian at Oral Roberts University, Hart follows the same basic sequence as both Grudem and Horton, but his eschatology is the penultimate chapter, followed by his ecclesiology. While more explicitly evangelical (with Grudem) rather than pentecostal (with Horton), he is also, interestingly, more consistently charismatic throughout the volume (certainly more so than Grudem and maybe even more than Horton and Williams). Yet the net effect is that these three single-volume renewal texts can be characterized as "evangelical theologies plus." Each follows a basic evangelical theological pattern and methodological approach and, especially with Williams and Hart, is devoted explicitly to few topics related to pneumatology and recognized as central to renewal spirituality.

The result, however, is that the radicality of renewal Christianity is muted, at least in two respects. First, across the twentieth century, renewal Christianity has flourished precisely as a countercultural phenomenon, especially when contrasted with the established churches. This is not to say that renewal Christianity has been anti-ecclesial. It is to say that its major contributions have been to renew the churches by providing alternative perspectives. Yet its systematic theology textbooks, as we have seen, tend more to follow the established patterns than to reflect the distinctive features of renewal spirituality.

But second, it should be clear from the preceding that the dominant strands of Christian theological discourse that have been feeding renewal streams have been in the Western tradition. This means that the various non-Western theological perspectives (e.g., Coakley and Sterk 2004), already minority voices in the Christian tradition, have been little considered so far. The fact is, of course, that even from its origins, Christianity has been constituted by a plurality of languages, cultures, and traditions. The one faith in Jesus Christ has taken on many forms from the first to the present century. Christian doctrinal, dogmatic, and systematic theology, at least in their written and elaborated forms, however, have been the preserve of the West. Part of the goal of this volume is to extend this conversation so as to engage global voices and perspectives.

Yet any systematically organized consideration will adopt some set of parameters or other. The question is how such organizational principles can orchestrate the many voices into a harmonious whole. More precisely, are there any theological frameworks that can facilitate the many tongues and languages into a cohesive yet faithful proclamation of the wondrous works of God for the globalizing world of the twenty-first century?

There is no other way to answer this question than to take a risk and make an effort. This book uses the World Assemblies of God Fellowship's (WAGF) Statement of Faith (SF) as the template for systematic theological reconsideration. There are two basic reasons for this choice. First, the WAGF constitutes one of the largest fellowships of renewal churches internationally, with over 350,000 congregations and sixty million adherents worldwide. It is an organization of Assemblies of God national councils around the world formed in 1989 to facilitate mutual support for missions and evangelism, to promote fellowship among the various churches, and to be a cooperative voice regarding issues of faith, social justice, and the persecution of Christians. There is far too much diversity within the global renewal movement to claim that the WAGF is representative of contemporary renewal Christianity. Yet as one of the most established of renewal organizations and networks, the WAGF is often viewed by other renewal denominations and churches as being in the vanguard internationally in providing missional and educational leadership.

Second and more importantly, Christian theologians working and writing in the wake of Barth's *Church Dogmatics* need to give careful consideration to how theological reflection should be nurtured by and intended for the edification of the church. There are those in a postdenominational world, especially in the Free Church stream, who will question the usefulness of binding the theological task to ecclesial traditions. Others will say there is a big difference between being rooted confessionally (for instance in the Westminster or Augsburg confessions) and being dependent upon something like the WAGF SF. The latter functions more pragmatically to consolidate missional endeavors than as a dogmatic bulwark for the WAGF's ecclesial and theological self-understanding. These are legitimate concerns that will need to be heeded. Suffice it to say that this text's adoption of the WAGF SF is meant to signal a commitment to historic Christian orthodoxy. It is also meant to serve as a case study for how renewalists in particular and Christians in general in the twenty-first century might engage their various traditions in faithful and yet creative ways in order to address contemporary challenges. This means that renewalists from across the breadth of churches and movements, not to mention nonrenewal Christians, can retrieve and ought to reappropriate their distinctive treasures in quest for a Christ-centered and Spirit-empowered theology relevant for the present age.

Yet the choice of adopting the WAGF SF as the basic structure for theological reflection brings with it the SF's fundamentally evangelical theology–plus pattern—common to most conservative Protestant statements of faith, actually—and raises critical questions for this book. Is renewal theology best formulated within such a Western-oriented paradigm? Does not renewal Christianity's orientation toward the charismatic and Spirit-filled life invite more than just a few middle chapters devoted to pneumatological topics? In short, how, if at all, might Christian theology undergo renewal within such a configuration?

1.3 Renewed and Always Renewing: A Way Forward for Christian Theology

The wager of this volume is that the Christian theological tradition as a whole has something to gain from engaging especially with renewal voices and perspectives and may even be revitalized in such a discussion. Three features of renewal beliefs and practices hold promise for renewing Christian theology.

FIGURE 1.3

Rublev's icon of the Holy Trinity derives from that enigmatic scene in Genesis 18 in which "The Lord appeared to Abraham by the oaks of Mamre" (18:1ff.) in the form of three visitors—which often led Christians to interpret the passage in trinitarian terms. Rublev adopts this interpretation, structuring his image as a theological meditation on trinitarian relationality. The figure furthest left represents God the Father, whose heavenly blue tunic is covered with a garment of iridescent light (1 Tim 6:16; John 1:18; Matt 6:6); above and behind him stands a great house "not made with hands" (2 Cor 5:1; cf. John 14:2). The Father's eyes are fixed on the Son, who sits in the center of the image looking back at the Father: the icon is resolutely christological, centered on the incarnate "image of the invisible God" (Col 1:15; Heb 1:3), the only exegete of the Father (John 1:18). The Son's blue garment is worn over an earthy crimson with a royal gold band over his right arm ("authority rests upon his shoulders," Isa 9:6). His right hand rests on the table-altar with outstretched fingers, signifying the two natures of Christ (fully God, fully human), pointing to the chalice containing either a roasted calf (Gen 18:7-8) or lamb (Eucharist). Behind the Son a tree reaches into the golden background, alluding to Mamre but also to the cross (Gal 3:13; 1 Pet 2:24) and the tree of life beyond the cross (Rev 2:7; cf. fig. 9.4).

The Christology of this image immediately moves into pneumatology. The Son looks at the Father while directing his posture toward the Spirit, who sits in near symmetry to the Father. The Spirit wears the same brilliant blue but over it a vivid green, giving life to the church (green is the liturgical color of Pentecost in Russia) and to creation (note the same green beneath the thrones; cf. Ps 104:30). Above and behind him a mountain bends toward the Son's tree and the Father's house. Indeed, the Spirit exerts tremendous semicircular pressure in the composition, directing the viewer upward along the mountain or downward along the ground—both routes leading to the Father. The composition is a great circle: the Father sends the Son, who sends the Spirit, who directs us back toward the Father "from whom are all things and for whom we exist" (1 Cor 8:6). Thus the christological and pneumatological content of the image is also ultimately eschatological, ushering us into the trinitarian love of God who is making all things new. ✦

First, at the heart the renewal movement is a spirituality characterized by relational encounter with the living Christ through his Holy Spirit. While the Christian faith has always affirmed God as Creator and Christ as Redeemer, there has been by comparison virtually no sustained theological and doctrinal development on the person and work of the Spirit (Bruner and Hordern 1984). Over the course of the twentieth century, in part in response to the revival of trinitarian theology inaugurated by Barth, there has been a gradual recognition that Christian theological reflection inspired by the first and second articles of the Nicene Creed (on the Father and the Son, respectively) needed to be augmented by theologies of the third article on the Spirit (see Van Dusen 1958; Taylor 1972). The result, however, ought not merely to be theologies of the Holy Spirit (although there should be and are a growing number of these). Rather, they should be pneumatological theologies, that is, theologies systematically reconsidered from a third article perspective (e.g., Pinnock 1996). And given the relational character of the Holy Spirit—who is both the Spirit of God and the Spirit of Christ—a pneumatological approach ought also to open up to a relational and trinitarian theology.

Renewalists seem to be in prime position for participating in such theological work. What might it look like to rethink the various theological doctrines if we began with the Spirit of Christ (e.g., Yong 2005;

Lederle 2010)? More to the point, as noted by scholars of renewal Christianity (e.g., Dayton 1987; Faupel 1996), the pneumatological spirituality of at least the classical pentecostal movement in North America was thoroughly eschatological as well, oriented in hope toward the second coming of Christ and the impending reign of God. If so, then a renewal approach to Christian theology is not only pneumatological and christological but also eschatological. This is in keeping with the intricate connection in the New Testament between the Holy Spirit and the (already-and-not-yet) coming reign of God. Hence, as shall be seen, such an emphasis on the "last days" does not need to be otherworldly or escapist. Instead, it can be appropriately this-worldly in terms of what the gospel requires.

The proposal of this volume, then, is that starting with the Spirit also involves starting not at the beginning with the doctrine of creation but at the end with God's redemptive work culminating in the last things. This invites us, then, to reverse the order of the WAGF SF, precisely so we begin in the next chapter with eschatological matters (article 12 of the SF). This presumes, as will be argued soon, that the fifth aspect of the classical pentecostal fivefold gospel, Jesus the coming king, is not just an add-on but is actually central to an understanding of Jesus as the Christ and that this even sheds new light on how to understand the other four faces of Jesus as savior, healer, sanctifier, and Spirit Baptizer (see McQueen 2012). The point to be emphasized is that the renewal of Christian theology ought to allow the Christian hope to inform and perhaps reform Christian theological reflection as a whole (e.g., Moltmann 1967; Phan 1985; Finger 1985, 1989; Peters 2000; Knight 2006; Rausch 2012). Such a reversal of the usual order of systematic theology leads to a second important feature of renewal Christianity, with implications for contemporary theology.

Starting with the Spirit suggests linking human hope with human hearts, because, as the Apostle Paul wrote, Christian "hope does not disappoint us because God's love has been poured into our hearts through the Holy Spirit that has been given to us" (Rom 5:5). Thus a pneumatological and eschatological theology is not only a theology of hope but also a theology of the heart. The heart, in the biblical traditions, signifies the whole human person, calling attention to the desires, affections, and emotions that so centrally define what it means to be human. On such a pneumatological register, human beings are affectively rather than only cognitively oriented, motivated more by holistic-charged desire than merely by abstract ideas (see Yong 2012). Further, however, such an eschatological orientation both invites recognition of the historicity and partiality of theological knowledge and urges embrace of the dynamic task of theological reflection, which celebrates the salvation inaugurated in the incarnational and pentecostal events but not yet culminated until the restoration of all things in the age to come (Acts 3:21). Hence, our eschatological sensitivity can be enthusiastically bold in bearing witness to Christ in the power of the Spirit, but yet also appropriately humble in acknowledging we now have only glimpses of "the depth of the riches and wisdom and knowledge of God! How unsearchable are his judgements and how inscrutable his ways!" (Rom 11:33).

FIGURE 1.4

The van Eycks' masterful Ghent Altarpiece *is a striking articulation of trinitarian theology that is at once pneumatological, christological, and eschatological. The entire cycle of images in this massive polyptych (twenty-four panels total) is organized around the panel reproduced here. This image amalgamates several scenes in the book of Revelation in which "a Lamb standing as if it had been slaughtered" (Rev 5:6) appears in front of or even "at the center of" (7:17) the throne of God. In the center of this composition the Lamb stands enthroned upon an altar as a wound in his chest pours blood into a chalice, thus identifying the body and blood of the Lamb with the eucharistic meal of Christ (1 Pet 1:19). This christological centerpiece of the image is set in eschatological perspective:*

immediately in front of the altar (and visually connected to it) an octagonal foun-
tain streams with the (baptismal) waters of life (Rev 22:1, 17; cf. fig. 6.3).
Multitudes gather from the "four corners" of the composition to offer their hearts,
bodies, and minds in adoration of the Lamb: "by your blood you ransomed for
God saints from every tribe and language and people and nation; you have made
them to be a kingdom and priests serving our God, and they will reign on earth"
(Rev 5:9-10; cf. 7:9-17).

This painting seems insistent that this reign will in fact be "on earth." In
contrast to the stylized flatness of Orthodox icon painting (fig. 1.3), the van
Eycks rigorously depict every last detail of the landscape: every ripple in the
water; every fold of fabric; every piece of embroidery; every architectural detail of
the New Jerusalem in the background; and indeed every leaf, flower, and blade
of grass (the vegetation is so specifically rendered that particular plant species are
identifiable, many not native to Europe). This way of envisioning the Christian
eschatological hope is itself a declaration that the goodness of creation (and culture)
is the subject of this hope.

We must notice, however, that this eschatological-christological vision is also
pneumatological in organization. From the top central position in the compo-
sition, the Spirit presides over and enlightens the entire scene. The Spirit is
depicted as a dove, which comes not from Revelation but from the gospel accounts
of Christ's baptism (cf. figs. 3.4, 4.3, and 6.1), thus drawing a line of intertex-
tual continuity from the Spirit's baptismal anointing of Christ (and the outpour-
ing at Pentecost) to the Spirit's eschatological blessing of creation. ✦

To be eschatological, then, is to be pneumatological and christological, and hence trinitarian. Similarly, to be pneumatological is to be
eschatological and christological, and again, trinitarian, and to be christological, as I shall argue, can only be possible when one is pneumatological
and eschatological, or fully trinitarian. Thus, a fully trinitarian theology
has to be pneumatological, christological, and eschatological, precisely
what is aspired to in this book.

Yet taking up the task of renewing Christian theology by reversing
the order of the loci means not only that this volume begins with eschatology (which concludes the SF) but also that it ends with the doctrine
of Scripture (which is article 1, but which will be ch. 12 at the end of
our book). The one minor exception will be that chapter 9 (on article
4) will also discuss a subsection of the lengthy article 2, for reasons to be
elaborated then. How large of a shift will this be, and what further reasons

justify what for some will be a rather radical reorganization of the classical theological loci?

As the preceding discussion shows (section 1.2), there are historical factors behind the conceptualizing and writing of doctrinal and systematic theologies. One way to understand the logic behind the dominant forms is to observe how they do follow the logic of the scriptural narrative, which begins with creation (Genesis) and ends with eschatological matters (Revelation). Within this framework, Reformation traditions especially have emphasized that the good news of Christ cannot be appreciated apart from an understanding of the despair of the fallen human condition—hence the doctrines of creation and fall ought to precede that of Christ and salvation. Then, the pluralization of theological systems during the modern period led to arguments regarding epistemic warrant and justification: What are the authoritative sources of rationales for making theological claims? The answers—whether the Bible (for Protestants) or Scripture in relationship to tradition (Catholic and Orthodox churches)—also moved to the forefront discussion of norms, methods, and the doctrine of revelation (Scripture and tradition). Seen in this light, starting with eschatology, and then treating creation and fall and even the theology of Scripture close to or at the end, constitutes a major paradigm shift for doing theology in the twenty-first century.

There is a greater than modernist concern, however, that will be worrisome especially to renewalists from creedal traditions, like charismatic Anglicans, Orthodox, and Roman Catholics, not to mention those in such churches without a stake in the renewalization of contemporary Christianity. This concerns the logic not just of the salvation history narrative of Scripture but of the creed, in particular the Nicene confession (see appendix 2). Christian faith has for the last 1700-plus years been structured by the three articles of confession—of God the Father, God the Son, and God the Spirit—with the last article connected to matters eschatological. Would not beginning with the Spirit and with the end not just upset but even unravel the structure of historic Christian faith? This is an important question for which there is no simple response. Most importantly, it should be said, the present project and set of proposals is not meant to displace the orthodox tradition. Instead, however, the goal is theological renewal, with perhaps even the aspiration for doctrinal or dogmatic renewal. Toward this end, then, perhaps the sojourn initiated in the pages of this volume will allow return to the tradition in currently unpredictable ways that retrieve, reinterpret, and reappropriate the creed for a twenty-first century global Christianity.

In effect, a full justification for such a reconceptualization can only emerge, if in fact at all, no sooner than the end of this book, and perhaps even quite some time after its possible reception. Preliminarily, however, a renewalist perspective would emphasize that the ultimate authority comes from the word of God and the creedal traditions made alive in and through the Holy Spirit. Texts can be quoted, but this oftentimes leads to arguments about meaning and application. Christian faith, however, concerns a living relationship between the people of God and the living Christ, made possible by the Holy Spirit. Pentecost thus becomes not an appendage to Christian life, but its point of entry. People come into reconciliation with God in Christ through the work of the Holy Spirit. Theology is, similarly, thus also pneumatologically enabled and mediated (see Yong 2002). From this scripturally authorized day of Pentecost starting point, then, the many tongues and languages of the many cultures within which the church has developed and flourished become potential conduits for theological reflection and even doctrinal formulation.

The preceding thus invites reconsideration of the form of the traditional structure itself. Both modern statements of faith and the form of systematic theology have begun with the doctrine of Scripture and of revelation due to the crisis of authority that emerged during the Enlightenment (see Farley 1982). Almost without exception, theologians have had to begin by establishing the epistemological foundations for Christian doctrine: How do we know what we know theologically? As one of the by-products of the Enlightenment's rationalism has been the reduction of religion, including Christian faith, to its doctrinal propositions, then starting with the Bible made sense, because that has always been understood as God's self-revelation in human words. From this perspective, the important thing about word-centered religiosity is its beliefs, and the need to secure the epistemic warrants of such beliefs led to identification, valuation, and prioritization of their authoritative sources.

But if the intellect is only one important dimension alongside others symbolized by the human heart, then starting with the Spirit demands that we pay attention not just to abstractly stated ideas but to desires shaped over time (narratives), feelings (affections), and practices (missional engagement). Theological orthodoxy (right beliefs) is now important, because it includes orthopathy (right feelings) and orthopraxy (right behaviors). Two implications follow. First, we shall see that reversing the traditional order of the loci requires discussion of the more concrete doctrines before concluding with those which, at least since the early modern period, have become more abstract. In effect, orthopraxy thus informs orthodoxy as we progress through the volume. Second, foregrounding orthopathy motivates the inclusion of artwork in this book. Images engage different parts of the brain, often fostering imaginative modes of engaging with the world. It is also hoped that the historical depth and global provenance of many of the accompanying images will provide different windows into the ideas than those afforded merely by words and propositions. Just as importantly, the latter are now also informed by the artwork, even as the artwork is complemented by the text.

FIGURE 1.5

Theologian and artist Solomon Raj created this image as a visual exegesis of John 15, wherein Jesus charges his disciples to "Abide in me as I abide in you. Just as the branch cannot bear fruit by itself unless it abides in the vine, neither can you unless you abide in me" (John 15:4). This theme has been depicted in many ways over the past two millennia, but in most cases Christ is pictured enthroned in or sometimes growing out of the top of the vine—thus presenting him as the "true vine" (15:1) in the sense of being the culmination and telos of the vine of Israel (cf. Ps 80:7-19; Jer 2:21; Hos 10:1-2). Much more rare is Dr. Raj's choice to depict Jesus as the root and trunk of the vine itself, out of which everything else in the image grows. When Christ is placed at the crown of the vine his hands are usually shown offering signs of blessing to his disciples; in Raj's less traditional imagery Christ's hands are also blessing, not through hand signs but by giving form and life to all the branches. Here the branches are continuous with—or simply are—Jesus's hands (cf. fig. 7.4): His activity in the world is manifest in and through disciples who are alive in him.

This image highlights the way that John's Gospel articulates the logic of Christian discipleship in terms of a holistic fruitfulness rooted in the One who truly has "life in himself" (John 5:26; cf. 1:4; 10:10). The Fourth Gospel's notion of faith is not simply a matter of holding true beliefs or assenting to precise doctrines (orthodoxy), as important as that may be; it also includes faithful affections, longings, and trust (orthopathy), as well as a faithful willingness to enter into the life-giving activity of Jesus (orthopraxy). Being a disciple is a holistic abiding "in Christ" (cf. 2 Cor 5:17; Rom 6:11; Gal 3:27) such that his life flows fruitfully through a person's patterns of mind, heart, and body (cf. fig. 5.4). At its most fundamental level the life of Christ issues through love: "As the Father has loved me, so I have loved you; abide in my love" (John 15:9). Love orients and manifests itself in activity—"If you keep my commandments, you will abide in my love" (15:10)—but here praxis and doxa are once again united in orthopathy: "This is my commandment, that you love one another as I have loved you" (15:12, 17). ✦

Of course, the Bible is essential for renewing Christian theology. However, the Bible now not only provides us with propositions about what happened before but opens up to a range of genres that invite imagining a new world reconciled to God in Christ by the Spirit and participation in that reconciling work. Hence Scripture is seen to function authoritatively to shape human hearts (desires) and hands (behaviors) and not just to fill human minds (with ideas). We will return to this in the last chapter of the book.

Renewal spirituality has the potential to inspire just such a triadic (orthodoxy–orthopathy–orthopraxy) reformulation of Christian theology (see Land 1993; Solivan 1998), in part due to its pietistic predispositions (which are allergic to merely abstract speculation) and in part due to its pragmatic inclinations (see Wacker 2001). Further, reversing the order of the loci foregrounds precisely those doctrines that are distinctive to renewal spirituality (e.g., the charismata and Spirit Baptism) rather than relegating them to being mere add-ons to the Christian theological vision. This then invites review of established Christian theological themes (the later chapters of the volume) in light of sensibilities (developed in the first part) that have the potential to renew the systematic and dogmatic tradition, precisely the task of this volume. To be sure, these tendencies and aspirations can also potentially skew important and essential theological notions, as much as enhance them. This book presumes that a robustly trinitarian theological method (e.g., Yong 2002) will procure the necessary checks and balances to guide the tasks at hand.

Last but not least, renewal Christianity can catalyze theological revitalization precisely because of its global presence. The church universal is certainly global in reach, as is the Roman Catholic Church. Yet as the discussion in the first part of this chapter has highlighted, renewal Christians can be found across the spectrum of Christian churches, traditions, and movements, even in those postdenominational and independent tributaries of world Christianity. It is in part for this reason that renewal spirituality has the capacity to inspire a truly global theology, one that is geographically expansive in scope and ecumenically rich in character (Yong 2005, Vondey 2010a).

The implications of a dynamic global Christianity for renewing Christian theology are significant. Much of what has been codified in systematic texts derives from Euro-American models of theological reflection. The present ferment in theological studies is marked by a post-Western, post-Enlightenment, and post–Euro-American set of sensibilities. Postmodern approaches highlight the diversity of perspectives that ought to be attended to in any discussion, while postcolonial analyses insist that issues of race, gender, and class need to be factored in. Further, science has become a contemporary international lingua franca, and this challenges theology to be attentive to the questions that science raises. On top of all this, theology is increasingly aware it has to account for and engage with the pluralism of cultures, ideologies, and also religious traditions (e.g., Smart and Konstantine 1991). While more and more theologians are calling for a reconsideration of the theological tradition as a whole in light of such global realities, all too often these latter contributions are thought to be no more than contextual variations of what has been handed down in the doctrinal tradition that is relevant only for local communities. The renewing of Christian theology envisioned in this book does not deny that there is one gospel for many places and times. But it does imagine that the one gospel remains richer than what has so far been articulated by the tradition, and that attending to the dynamics of contemporary global life and the many different ways that the gospel has been imagined in these various locales will reinvigorate Christian thinking about and revitalize Christian living in the twenty-first century.

1.4 An Overview and Road Map for the Book

The eleven chapters following each expand on one of the eleven statements in the WAGF SF, but do so in the reverse order of the SF (see appendix 1). As already noted, this might be jarring for those who have read and approached systematic theological texts in their more traditional formats. This means, for instance, that we begin with eschatology and move through the charismatic, pneumatological, sacramental/ecclesiological, healing, and soteriological/christological loci before winding down, toward the end of the book, with considerations of the doctrines of creation, God/Trinity, and Scripture/revelation. I can only beg the reader's indulgence to withhold judgment until having completed the book on whether such a reversal of the traditional logic of renewal theology is finally coherent.

My wager is that moving in this direction is actually more consistent with Christian life and experience. Neophytes in the faith or children begin not with abstract doctrines of creation, Trinity, and revelation, but with the daily realities related to human flourishing, relationships, and health. How might gaining theological fluency in these more practical arenas equip beginning theological students to encounter and engage with other topics that are a bit more removed from their daily lives? People encounter God in Christ through the (ecclesial) fellowship of the Holy Spirit first, and then are launched on the path of purification, long before they begin theologizing about soteriology and the fall; so why not approach these latter theological topics after dealing with the doctrines of the church and sanctification? In renewal circles, people often first encounter God the savior as their healer before they understand what it means that Christ died for their sins; so why not deal first with the doctrine of healing (ch. 8) before soteriology proper (ch. 9)? In all of these ways and more, I believe that such a reversal of the traditional sequence warrants consideration. My hope is that working through the doctrines in this way will open up new perspectives on what have been traditionally considered the foundational doctrines of Scripture, Trinity, and creation (chs. 12, 11, and 10, respectively).

Each of the following eleven chapters follows a similar format of four major sections, beginning with a short narrative reflection on a scriptural personage. Such a narrative point of entry befits the oral character of much of global renewal spirituality, even as it invites readers to enter into the theological task by reflecting on how human stories and life narratives interface with God's salvation history (see McClendon 1974). However, due to space and other constraints, we will be unable to go deeply into historical, cultural, contextual, and hermeneutical issues related to these narrative retrievals. The goal of this section is less to conduct an in-depth exegesis of relevant biblical texts or get at historically justifiable details of these figures than to explore how scriptural characterizations provide windows into the dogmatic themes that we will be considering.

The second section is the longest in each chapter, because in general it seeks to achieve three objectives: (1) locate the historical context of the statement from the SF that is being considered; (2) provide broader ecumenical perspective on some of the major elements of the statement; and (3) sketch some of the contemporary and global issues relevant to understanding the statement and its implications. We do not always proceed in this order. There are also a few chapters that do not follow this division of labor exactly. In some cases—especially after chapter 6—the approach is thematically demarcated, although even each motif is still situated historically, ecumenically, and in a global context in some respect or other. Much of the discussion proceeds descriptively. In many cases, my discussions here selectively highlight what I presume to be normative of the orthodox Christian tradition and upon which our constructive responses build. In all cases, though, the challenges and opportunities delineated provide parameters that inform our constructive reflections in the second half of each chapter.

The various section threes explore the Scriptures in relationship to the statement under consideration. Our reading of the Bible, however, will deploy a more literary and thematic hermeneutical approach, albeit one informed by the contemporary global horizon (e.g., Patte 2004; Segovia and Sugirtharajah 2007; DeYoung et al. 2010), including evangelical feminist and postcolonial perspectives (e.g., Kroeger and Evans 2002; Blount 2007; Adeyemo 2005). Proceeding hermeneutically in this way, we will also be focusing almost each chapter on a separate book or letter of the New Testament. Hence historical criticism, while important, will be of secondary priority. For instance, rather than having to wade into questions of authenticity, we will follow the canonical or received tradition with regard to the authors of the New Testament writings. Historical-critical perspective will be drawn upon where relevant.

The hermeneutical approach deployed here is undergirded by a three-fold rationale. First, in order to avoid proof-texting the Bible, we will seek to interpret the relevant Scriptures within their broader narrative, literary, and canonical contexts. Christian doctrine is increasingly being approached first and foremost narratively (e.g., Fackre 1984) rather than dogmatically or propositionally. This orientation is also congenial to, not to mention consistent with, the oral and testimonial sensibilities of renewal Christians, especially in the majority world.

Second, while many of the doctrines to be discussed can be found or are at least alluded to if not mentioned across the New Testament, focusing our scriptural horizons in each case enables delving further into various biblical texts as whole documents. Inductive approaches inevitably cover more ground but reside more on the surface of the biblical material. Our approach is narrower in scope but drills deeper into a source text and thereby attains better traction on and contextualization of its communicative aims. The result, by the end of the book, will be a series of theological commentaries on eleven different New Testament writings. Of course, none of these will be exhaustive, because they are dictated by the theological and doctrinal topics under discussion; informed by our own renewal, pneumatological, eschatological, and trinitarian principles; and motivated by the global contexts of renewal and world Christianity. Still, theological students will be introduced to one way of bridging the divide between biblical and systematic theology (see Green and Turner 2000). They can apply this strategy next to reading the whole of the First or Old Testament theologically, if they are so inclined.

Finally, then, the decision to focus on New Testament writings rather than on the First Testament is not because the latter is deemed of secondary importance. There are constraints of space and the challenge of writing a short introductory systematics text that can be accessible to beginning theological students. Much more can be said scripturally about each doctrine than what is said from the discussed New Testament text. Further, much more also can be said about each of the gospels or letters than is said. Yet as already indicated, the method adopted here is replicable. Those interested can dig deeper into the biblical writings from other doctrinal or theological vantage points. They also can explore these eleven or even other dogmatic themes by engaging other scriptural writings and by doing more exhaustive biblical studies in each case.

The preceding means that our scriptural analysis follows a theological and thematic logic rather than any other organizational or chronological one. We shift from Lukan to Pauline or Johannine or Petrine, and so on, documents not because we are following any historical ordering but because they are deemed to be more appropriate to addressing the doctrinal themes and topics introduced by approaching the WAGF SF articles in reverse order. Within each chapter, we also try to connect the narrative introduction in the first section with the wider scriptural considerations in section three, although this does not happen in every case. The goal is not to provide a biblical theology of this or that, but to elucidate doctrinal loci through sustained engagement with select scriptural material. Thus we deploy a more narrative and literary rather than an inductive approach to the biblical material, albeit this is done within a wider strategy of reading Scripture in light of selected doctrinal and theological themes.

In anticipation of the fuller explanation in the final chapter, the rationale for discussing the scriptural horizons for each doctrinal locus (section 3 of each chapter) after the historical, ecumenical, and global framing of the topic (the second section) also deserves a brief comment. Older or more classical evangelical approaches opted to foreground the scriptural horizon, although almost always proceeding inductively rather than exegetically in terms of collating all relevant biblical references to the matter and then organizing them according to whatever systematic principle or orientation adopted. Our model also proceeds in a type of a posteriori manner, but by privileging renewal perspectives, experiences, and commitments. Hence the following chapters attempt to situate reflection on the scriptural material within the broader historical, ecumenical, and global contexts rather than presume that a kind of objective or neutral reading of the Bible is possible. At the same time, the normativity of Scripture is assumed: we turn from contextual considerations in section 2 to biblical reflection in section 3 precisely because the third section proceeds to lay the scriptural foundation for the constructive theological tasks in the final section of each chapter.

Thus the fourth and final major section of each chapter also will seek to accomplish three interrelated objectives: (1) provide a constructive yet biblically informed restatement of the doctrine as it relates to the gospel; (2) proffer a contextual analysis that addresses some of the specific issues discussed in the second section about the contemporary global context; and (3) recommend a performative application of what it means to live out Christian faith in the twenty-first century, albeit not merely from human capacities but as inspired by the power of the Holy Spirit. The renewalist emphasis on Christian living charts the path for discussion in these parts of each chapter. Renewal theology is useless apart from empowering renewal praxis, while the latter also needs the former for proper orientation. The renewing of Christian theology and doctrine must mean that theological thinking can never be merely abstract but will have practical relevance, especially for the church's mission (see Yong 2014b).

Each chapter will conclude with a few discussion questions and a short further reading list related to the topics treated therein. A full list of references covering all twelve chapters concludes the volume.

In sum, the wager of this volume is that the WAGF's SF provides a springboard for renewing Christian theology that should be of interest to all Christians engaged in the task of theological reflection in global context. Renewalists outside the WAGF can generalize methodologically from this volume for their own churches and contexts. Members of churches with other confessions can approach this volume as a case study of how to think with and through any set of dogmatic commitments in global context. Christians in ecumenical and independent church environments ought also to be able to appreciate the goal of renewing Christian doctrine and theology in light of classical and contemporary concerns. Of course, those sympathetic with or even committed to the WAGF or its national fellowships have in this volume one perspective on how to interpret, understand, and embrace its fundamental doctrines despite the many questions that persist.

Christian theology today, no less than in times past, is complicated. Yet to the degree that all Christians have ideas about God and God's relationship to the world, all are theologians. Beginning theological students reading this book are invited upon a path of intentional theological reflection. Learning and doing theology should be a joy, done by Christians as with all other things, "in the name of the Lord Jesus, giving thanks to God the Father through him" (Col 3:17). Welcome to the journey.

2

The Last Days and the End of Time

Christian Hope Then and Now

World Assemblies of God Fellowship Statement of Faith
—Article 11: The End of Time

We believe in the premillennial, imminent, and personal return of our Lord Jesus Christ to gather His people unto Himself. Having this blessed hope and earnest expectation, we purify ourselves, even as He is pure, so that we may be ready to meet Him when He comes (John 14:1-3; Titus 2:13; 1 Thessalonians 4:15-17; 1 John 3:2-3; Revelation 20:1-6).

We believe in the bodily resurrection of all humanity, the everlasting conscious bliss of all who truly believe in our Lord Jesus Christ, and that everlasting conscious punishment is the portion of all whose names are not written in the Book of Life (John 5:28-29; 1 Corinthians 15:22-24; Revelation 20:10-15).

2.1 Paul the Apocalyptic Apostle

"The blessed hope" mentioned above first appeared in the Letter to Titus: "we wait for the blessed hope and the manifestation of the glory of our great God and Savior, Jesus Christ" (Tit 2:13). While some scholars question whether this letter was written by Paul, it is consistent not only with what he wrote elsewhere in the undisputed Pauline Letters but also with what is known about the details of his life. The latter is especially important for understanding why Paul and other early Christians anticipated the return of Christ both as a blessed hope and as their "hope of glory" (Col 1:27).

Paul was a fervent Jew. In his own words, he was "circumcised on the eighth day, a member of the people of Israel, of the tribe of Benjamin, a Hebrew born of Hebrews; as to the law, a Pharisee; as to zeal, a persecutor of the church; as to righteousness under the law, blameless" (Phil 3:5-6). He was trained under a respected doctor of the Pharisee party,

Gamaliel (see Acts 5:34; 22:3), and later worked with other Hellenistic Jews associated with the Synagogue of the Freedmen (6:9) against the early messianic believers. This led him to initiate "a severe persecution" (8:1) against the fledgling group, beginning in Jerusalem and spreading outward from there. Fully intending to eradicate this heresy, Paul, then called Saul, obtained permission to find and arrest followers of Jesus up the coast toward Damascus. His methods, as he indicates, were radically punitive rather than restorative: "I was violently persecuting the church of God and was trying to destroy it" (Gal 1:13; see also 1 Tim 1:13; Acts 9:13, 21; 22:4; 26:10-11). Saul was a man on a mission dedicated to stem the tide of messianic heterodoxy before it got out of control. Those who opposed him would be put to death if necessary, as Stephen was (Acts 7:57-60).

Yet on his way to Damascus, Saul encountered Jesus, who he thought was dead. Luke recounts Paul's testimony: "While I was on my way and approaching Damascus, about noon a great light from heaven suddenly shone about me. I fell to the ground and heard a voice saying to me, 'Saul, Saul, why are you persecuting me?' I answered, 'Who are you, Lord?' Then he said to me, 'I am Jesus of Nazareth whom you are persecuting'" (Acts 22:6-8; see also 26:12-15). Perhaps Stephen's cries—"I see the heavens opened and the Son of Man standing at the right hand of God" (7:56)—right before his demise at the hands of the Freedmen mob had haunted Saul, and he now saw that he had participated in an egregious act of murdering an innocent person. Yet the living Christ did not hold this against Saul but instead invited him to be the apostolic witness to the Gentiles that perhaps Stephen had been called to be.

Saul, now Paul, assented to the call in part because he had experienced Jesus' forgiveness of his sins, including his participation in Stephen's execution. This decision charted the rest of his life's course. Paul therefore preached the forgiveness of sins (Acts 13:38; cf. 26:18), just as the apostles did (2:38), calling for repentance and reconciliation to God through the risen Christ (2:29-36; 13:26-37). Thus was the salvation of God tied in with the resurrection of Jesus, and thus did Paul preach not just Christ but his resurrection (e.g., 17:3, 18, 31; 26:23; see also 1 Cor 15:12-19). As it turned out, Saul the persecutor of messianic believers became Paul the one persecuted as a messianist himself. He was imprisoned and tried a number of times, not only because he proclaimed Jesus' resurrection but also because he linked that to the Jewish hope in the coming Messiah (Acts 23:6; 24:15, 21; 25:19; 26:6-8; 28:20).

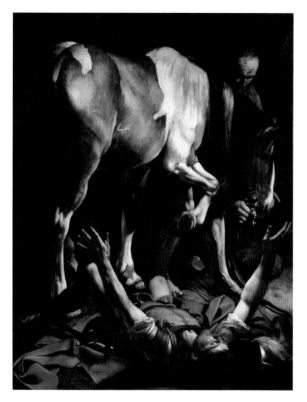

FIGURE 2.1

The book of Acts repeatedly recounts Saul's encounter with the risen Jesus as taking place at "about noon" (Acts 22:6; 26:13), at the height of the sun's position in the sky. When Caravaggio represents this scene, however, he sets the scene in a deep darkness (cf. fig. 5.2). The artist is not merely ignoring the text; he is making an interpretive move, emphasizing that the "very bright light" from heaven overwhelms not only the natural light of the sun but also (and more to the point) Saul's interior darkness—a blindness that persists even in the midst of his midday journey. A flash of light from somewhere beyond the limits of the image pierces into Saul's blackness and leaves him lying on the ground, blindly reaching toward the source of the light. And in relation to this Light, the rest of the world—including the midday sun—appears as darkness.

One might understand this painting as the inversion of conventional depictions of conquering heroes on horses. All of the same components are here: Saul is rendered as a warrior—complete with armor, a sword, a valiant horse—and up to this moment he was engaged in what he considered the morally heroic act of defending his faith. Yet here we find him at the bottom of the frame, lying flat on his back on the road he was previously journeying along, beneath the horse that he might otherwise be mounted upon with dignity and stature. In the grammar of heroic history painting, this is the image of a debased man, a defeated warrior in a state of utter submission before his opponent. And perhaps that is exactly right. Saul is overthrown and unraveled by this experience, indeed blinded by it, but it is also a moment of great glory, the beginning of his reconstitution: he will eventually emerge from it as a new man—an eschatological man—Paul, "an apostle of Christ Jesus by the will of God" (see the first verse of each of his epistles). He will live the rest of his life following one whose "power is made perfect in weakness" (2 Cor 12:9). So this is perhaps precisely what a Christian hero painting looks like. ✦

Paul can therefore be understood as an apocalyptically inspired preacher (Beker 1982; Plevnik 1997). While sometimes *apocalyptic* includes notions of catastrophic and cataclysmic destruction, here it means both that the travails of the present age are giving way to a new time and that God's plans for this transitional period have been unveiled to those able to discern it. Paul believed and proclaimed that God's messianic revelation had been hidden until the life, death, and resurrection of Christ, and that association with Christ provides access to the eternal life he makes available. If Christ had been raised, then death itself had been defeated, God's triumph over the forces of evil guaranteed, and human hope secured (1 Cor 15:50-56). Paul could witness to this because he himself had experienced new birth toward a higher calling in his encounter with the living Christ.

So yes, on the one hand, believers in Jesus eagerly anticipated and hoped for his imminent return, particularly given the trials and even persecutions that many were experiencing (1 Cor 1:7; 7:29; 1 Thess 1:10; 3:13; 4:13-18; see also Heb 9:28; James 5:7; 2 Pet 3:11-12). On the other hand, the resurrection of Jesus meant this would be a future hope for all (1 Cor 6:14; 2 Cor 4:14; Phil 3:20-21), and his followers could experience that resurrected life in the here and now (Rom 6:4-5; 7:4; 8:11; 2 Cor 5:15). Such confidence provided needed inspiration for messianists who felt assailed on every side. Thus living in light of the end, on the brink of the Parousia (the return of Christ), involved not only the hope of the coming age but also a resolute and responsible steadfastness amid the challenges of life (e.g., Evans 1968; Mason 1993; Luckensmeyer 2009).

As Paul wrote: "I want to know Christ and the power of his resurrection and the sharing of his sufferings by becoming like him in his death, if somehow I may attain the resurrection from the dead" (Phil 3:10-11). Jesus would return indeed, but the blessed hope included the promise that new life in Christ began in this life and opened up new possibilities for the present.

2.2 What and When? Contextual Considerations

The WAGF article 11 is titled "The End of Time," which is called "eschatology." This derives from the Greek combination of *eschaton*, referring to last things, and *logos*, meaning reason, teaching, or doctrine—thus *eschatologia* or the doctrine of the last or final things. As the WAGF SF indicates, there are at least two major aspects to the Christian hope: the return of Christ and the final resurrection. These relate to historical eschatology (the return of Christ and the millennial reign of God) and final-state eschatology (what happens after death and after the end of this world), respectively. In its immediate context, the statement opposes understanding eschatological doctrines (the millennium, the return of Christ, heaven, and hell) in spiritual, metaphorical, or symbolic terms only. The clause on "everlasting conscious punishment" also rejects the annihilationist alternative (that hell is of temporal rather than eternal duration) and, implicitly, the doctrine of universalism (that all shall be saved). Needless to say, all of these ideas have had variegated histories that need to be clarified in order to appreciate the eleventh article.

Interestingly, while certain renewal streams have converged upon and are steadfast promoters of particular eschatological visions—especially a premillennial return of Christ (as seen in this SF)—there has never been any consensus across the renewal spectrum. Many early modern Pentecostals were certainly premillennialists, although there were also wide-ranging differences and emphases across the movement (see McQueen 2012: chs. 3–4). There are even some contemporary renewalists who abstain altogether from advocating any millennial position (e.g., the Elim pentecostal churches of Britain; see Kay 2002: 133). What is undeniable is the overall eschatological orientation: early modern pentecostal believers were resolutely focused on the imminent second coming of Christ to bring about a culmination of the reign of God inaugurated in the life and ministry of Jesus and in the day of Pentecost event. So emphatic is this eschatological emphasis that even to the present day, the North American Assemblies of God's Statement of Fundamental Truths, which totals sixteen affirmations, includes four eschatological assertions (collapsed to one in the WAGF): on the blessed hope, on the millennial reign of Christ, on the final judgment, and on the new heavens and the new earth.

The following discussions will focus especially on the development of the doctrine of the millennium, summarize some of the contested views across the spectrum of final-state eschatologies, and briefly explore some of challenges encountered when the issues are considered in global perspective. The multiplicity of views can be seen to derive from the disparate data across the New Testament. But the next few pages will help us understand how Paul's apocalyptic testimony remains meaningful for renewing Christian eschatology in the present time.

2.2.1 Millennialism: Historical Developments

There is space only to highlight briefly some of the major historical shifts in Christian eschatological thinking over the centuries (see, e.g., Grenz 1992: ch. 2). The first few hundred years of the early church were dominated by what is now called classical premillennialism: that Christ returns to reestablish God's rule on the earth (e.g., Rev 19) and that this is what inaugurates the thousand-year (millennial) reign of God (Rev 20). The plot line of the book of Revelation indicates that the events of the end will be cataclysmic, with the world reeling from sin and crying out for divine judgment. This appears to be consistent with Jesus' sermon on the Mount of Olives (Matt 24), especially that "because of the increase of lawlessness, the love of many will grow cold" (Matt 24:12). The numerous persecutions of Christians during the first three centuries confirmed for many that the end times were near, that the return of Christ would be the only hope for vindication of the martyrs and the witness they bore.

The conversion of Constantine the Great (272–337) near the beginning of the fourth century and the subsequent Christianization of the empire, however, made possible acceptance of a more allegorical approach to the scriptural witness that minimized, if not rejected, the literal references of apocalyptic and symbolic texts such as the book of Revelation. Over the next century, the relatively small group of persecuted and martyred Christians now came into institutional power, prominence, and privilege, and the world appeared to be getting better rather than worse. In line with the allegorical interpretations of theologians in the Alexandrian school, St. Augustine (354–430) and others rejected notions of literal millennial pleasures enjoyed by the righteous as depictions of carnally minded Christians. They also found it more persuasive to understand the book of Revelation as mapping the unfolding history of the church itself. This led to at least two interpretations of the Augustinian legacy: either the millennium itself was to be understood symbolically to refer to

Christ's reign over the work of the church, or if taken literally, Christ's return would occur a thousand years after his initial appearance.

The latter view set up the church for millenarian fervor, especially at the end of the first thousand years after Christ, and even frequently thereafter at the turn of almost each new century. Yet it has been the former, since known as amillennialism, that has become the unofficial position of the Roman Catholic Church, not to mention being attractive to many Protestants also. The combination of the immense stature of Augustine with the new sociopolitical arrangements brought about by the emergence of Christendom in the Latin West effectively minimized millennial speculation in the mainlines of the Western theological tradition for the next thousand years. For many, amillennialism renders unnecessary conjecture about the future, holding only that Christ will return in God's good time to judge the living and the dead. And that is all that matters for Christian faith and life.

The major Reformers also followed in the Augustinian trajectory, motivated in part by resistance to the millenarian activities of the Radical Reformation (involving the Anabaptists and other groups). These contrary eschatological visions anticipated alternative modern trajectories. The founding of the New World and the Great Awakening revivals led important theologians within the dominant Reformed Puritan tradition, such as Jonathan Edwards (1703–1758), to adjust the Augustinian view in a postmillenarian direction. Extended into the nineteenth century and early twentieth century, the "manifest destiny" of earlier Puritan evangelization among the indigenous peoples was extended by other emerging denominations, first across the Americas and then into the heart of Africa and around the world. So even if it were incorrect to read Augustine as asserting Christ's return at the end of the first thousand years, perhaps the great North African theologian was right at least in this respect: Christ's return will take place *after* the church has, even if very gradually, accomplished its task of evangelizing the world (see Matt 13:31-33). Was this not what Jesus himself foretold: "this good news of the kingdom will be proclaimed throughout the world, as a testimony to all the nations; and then the end will come" (Matt 24:14)? Yet postmillennial aspirations were then seriously dampened over the course of the world wars of the twentieth century.

Despite the long history of at least semiofficial amillennialist inclinations in the church and the growth of postmillennial optimism during the early modern period, classical premillenialism never completely abated. Assuredly, occasional millenarian enthusiasm, including that promulgated by the Radical Reformers, ended tragically on enough occasions (Cohn

1977; Weber 1999), so these views were frequently dismissed by the theological tradition. Yet if amillennialism questioned the propriety of a literal thousand-year reign of God and if postmillennialism affirmed that Christ's return would be followed at the end of the church age (no matter how long it lasted), then premillennialism insisted that it is precisely the second coming of Jesus that will initiate the final divine rule on earth and in heaven.

In the last two hundred years, however, a distinctive strain of premillennialism, known as *dispensationalism* (see Pentecost 1958), has gathered quite a following across the evangelical-renewal spectrum. While the notion that God's salvation history could be divided into different administrative stages, each with distinctive criteria for how God both rules and redeems the world, has had various iterations and proponents, dispensationalism emphasizes that the present church age will be superseded by a coming period during which God will return to fulfill the covenant with the Jews and when "all Israel will be saved" (Rom 11:26). If amillennialism tends to spiritualize the people of God through the church's inheritance of the promises made to Israel, dispensationalism insists on maintaining the present distinction between the church and Israel. (Chapter 7 will explore in more detail the range of renewal views on Israel.) Further, postmillennial optimism is challenged by dispensational pessimism, in particular its emphasis on the devolution of world history into a period that the King James Version (KJV) calls the "great tribulation" (Matt 24:14; Rev 7:14). And last but not least, historic premillennialism urges reconsideration of the broad scope of New Testament eschatological texts that suggest two future returns of Christ: initially *for* the church, to rapture or remove its members from the coming ordeal (e.g., 1 Thess 4:14-17; Rev 3:10), followed by a second return *with* the church after the tribulation to establish the millennial rule and reign of God. The doctrine of the tribulation raises an intradispensationalist debate: whether Christ returns for the church before, in the middle of, or after, the time of trouble (Archer 1996). This is a dispute that does not need to be adjudicated for our purposes—as it is not addressed in the SF—although there are minority renewalist voices advocating for a posttribulational rapture (e.g., Hart 2005: 509–13) against the predominant pretribulationist mentality.

Dispensationalist premillennialism has become popularized over the course of the twentieth century, in part due to the turmoil and upheaval of the last hundred years but also in part in anticipation of the end of the second millennium (Boyer 1992). In its popular manifestations, dispensationalism, like many of the varieties of millenarian fervor in Christian history, has questioned, even resisted, the ecclesial and sociopolitical status quo. The early modern pentecostal embrace of dispensationalist eschatology buttressed pentacostalists' apocalyptic fervor, but in many cases what remains now are the charts of end-time speculation without the missional fervor of the blessed hope (Yong 2010: ch. 8.1).

2.2.2 Final-State Eschatologies: Disputed Possibilities

The following focuses on the doctrines of the resurrection, heaven, and hell referred to in the second paragraph of article 11 of the SF. The doctrine of the resurrection probably has fewer twists than most others in the Christian tradition. Paul's vigorous defense of the resurrection of Jesus in the first Corinthian letter as "the first fruits of those who have died" (1 Cor 15:20) has preempted most efforts to deny it. Even the early gnostics, who spiritualized or allegorized Jesus' resurrection, did so fundamentally because they subordinated material existence to the spiritual life not because they were incredulous toward the idea as such. It is difficult, well-nigh impossible perhaps, to read the New Testament in any other way, except as presuming its authors were convinced Jesus rose from the dead. Of course, faith is certainly still needed to embrace this claim, because the empty tomb and the eyewitness accounts invite rather than force belief (see Pannenberg 1977: esp. ch. 3). At the same time, it may take a "will to disbelieve" to remain doubtful about New Testament claims. Only those predisposed for whatever reason against Jesus' rising from the dead will question its centrality to and constitutive character for Christian faith. Jesus' resurrection in effect establishes the plausibility structures not only for belief in the final resurrection at the end but also for the Christian gospel as a whole. In fact, that Jesus is raised from the dead suggests that the end of time has invaded the history of the world. Thus believers in Jesus live in anticipation of their own future resurrections, even as they participate now in the work of the Spirit poured out upon them by the resurrected Christ.

One way in which early Christian understandings of the doctrine of the resurrection differ from contemporary views concerns the underlying metaphysical presuppositions. Patristic and medieval inflections of the doctrine were formulated against the backdrop of a neoplatonic hierarchical worldview that valued the spiritual or ideal dimensions of reality and tolerated (at best) or despised (at worst) the materiality of the created order. Within this framework, the resurrection of creaturely bodies was affirmed, albeit what was privileged was a presumed eternal soul or spirit that, during the intermediate state, awaited to be clothed with the resurrection body at the end of the age (according to some readings of 2 Cor 5:1-5). While such dualistic construals of the human constitution—as consisting of souls in bodies, for instance—remain compelling for various reasons, contemporary theological anthropologies are less dependent on neoplatonic philosophical assumptions and more inclined toward holistic and relational accounts. The resurrection of the body is herein less a secondary add-on to eternally existing souls or spirits than it is the necessary destiny of creatures defined essentially in part by their embodiment. This is why the resurrection at the end of the age will involve all who have ever lived: "those who have done good, to the resurrection of life, and those who have done evil, to the resurrection of condemnation" (John 5:28-29; see also Dan 12:2). Resurrection becomes the lot of all, for those who receive everlasting life and those who suffer everlasting damnation.

The traditional doctrine of everlasting punishment is based in part both on Jesus' reference to hell, "where their worm never dies, and the fire is never quenched" (Mark 9:48; see also Matt 25:41, 46), and on the vision of the Apocalypse that the torments associated with the lake of fire will persist "day and night for ever and ever" (Rev 20:10b; see also Rev 14:11; Jude 6). It presumes also that God has given certain creatures such as human beings sufficient freedom to shape their own destinies (see Walls 1992: ch. 5) and that persistence on the path of sinful rebellion leads away from rather than to union with God. So to those who are uneasy with an infinite punishment imposed for finite wrongdoings, the counter is at least twofold. One response is that the doors of hell are more locked from the inside by sin and self-centeredness than they are from the outside (e.g., Jenson 2006). Another is that there are those whose life trajectories leave them with the inability to enjoy, much less respond, to God's love and goodness. Perhaps in eternity these who have followed a life of wickedness will devolve from any semblance of beings created in the image and likeness of God (see Wright 2008: 182–83).

Yet the Christian teaching about eternal reprobation has spawned a variety of alternatives. The two most pertinent for our consideration are the annihilationist and purgatorial views. The former, also called conditional immortality, insists first that the idea of human souls being inherently unending is more of Hellenistic than biblical provenance (which says that only God is immortal; 1 Tim 6:16). Annihilationists also wonder how an essentially loving God can be everlastingly confronted with the unrelenting suffering of creatures. Does not this stain the ultimate divine victory when God is supposed to "be all in all" (1 Cor 15:28b)? This suggests that the wicked will undergo a final and ultimate destruction rather than endure incessant punishment. Thus the end-time judgment is necessarily terminal, as "God is a consuming fire" (Heb 12:29; see also Heb 6:8; 10:27; cf. Matt 7:19; 13:40; John 15:6). For Paul the apostle, the unrighteous "will suffer the punishment of *eternal destruction, separated* from the presence of the Lord and from the glory of his might" (2 Thess 1:9 [emphasis added]; see also Phil 1:28; 3:19; Matt 10:28b; John 3:16b; Col 3:17; Heb 10:39; 2 Pet 3:7). If creatures exist as sustained by God's loving presence, what can the divine withdrawal mean except their once-and-for-all evaporation, extinction, and even obliteration? While many traditional Christians do not believe these considerations overturn traditional understandings of the doctrine of hell (see Moore 1995), an increasing number are rethinking the scriptural witness (see Fudge and Peterson 2000).

FIGURE 2.2

This massive, glittering mosaic of the last judgment presides over the octagonal cathedral baptistery in Florence, Italy (cf. fig. 6.3). On the western half of the ceiling (associated with the sunset at the "end" of the "day") is an enormous image of the resurrected, ascended Christ enthroned on the celestial spheres containing all the stars and planets. His feet rest on the earth, identified by a geometric pattern that is visually rhymed in the tilework on the floor of the baptistery:

"Thus says the Lord: Heaven is my throne and the earth is my footstool; what is the house that you would build for me?" (Isa 66:1).

Below Christ, along the very bottom of the image, naked human bodies emerge from tombs in a universal resurrection of the dead. As they emerge, they peel away from the centerline toward the right and the left. Those who go toward the left (Christ's right) are clothed and ushered through a doorway into a paradisical garden, where they are embraced by Abraham, Isaac, and Jacob. Those on the right (Christ's left) are met by demonic beasts, who fling them into a terrifying burning pit, at the center of which is the Satan carnivorously devouring everyone it can get its hands on. This provocative visualization of hell understands evil as fundamentally consumptive: it viciously devours God's good creation, even the very creatures made in the image of God. Over against this, the resurrection unto life is understood here as fundamentally loving: a peaceful, holistic communion with others.

As resurrected people run from their graves to their respective ends, Christ holds out his wounded hands in the articulation of judgment: he opens his right hand to those who receive his mercy and shows the back of his left hand to those hurtling toward the belly of the beast. Christ is judging here, but it is ambiguous whether his gestures should be interpreted as forceful or revelatory. In other words, showing the back of his hand is surely a "depart from me" (Matt 25:41), but it is unclear whether this is a violent casting out or a letting go—a terrifyingly final instance of his willingness to look upon the creatures He loves and, even so, to give them over to the sinful, self-consuming desires of their hearts (cf. Rom 1:24). ✦

The purgatorial view has had a long history in the Latin West, especially within the Roman Catholic tradition. Yet a number of evangelicals are reexamining the issues, even if they are reluctant to embrace the traditional Catholic teaching (e.g., Baker 2010; Jersak 2010). Direct scriptural evidence for this teaching is slim indeed—most explicitly in 1 Corinthians 3:

> If anyone builds on the foundation with gold, silver, precious stones, wood, hay, straw, the work of each builder will become visible, for the day will disclose it, because it will be revealed with fire, and the fire will test what sort of work each has done. If what has been built on the foundation survives, the builder will receive a reward. If the work is burned, the builder will suffer loss; the builder will be saved, but only as through fire. (vv. 12-15)

However, the more overarching set of presuppositions is that divine punishment is restorative rather than punitive (e.g., Heb 12:5-11). Hence, divine wrath and judgment are real and consequential, possibly although not necessarily everlasting, depending on how individuals respond. The major challenge to this view is that it requires postmortem opportunities for both purification or sanctification and then response to the gospel. The biblical witness to this is also scant and ambiguous: i.e., Paul's almost parenthetical reference to Christ's descent to hell (Eph 4:7-10) and Peter's abstruse account of Jesus' proclamation to the dead (1 Pet 3:18-20; 4:6). But these seem to refer more to events related to Christ's incarnation and death rather than to the second coming or the end of time. However, although the Bible says, "just as it is appointed for mortals to die once, and after that the judgement" (Heb 9:27), when, how long, and what relationship this judgment has to the final judgment is unclear. Some Catholic theologians are exploring now how Christ's descent into hell can be understood eschatologically so that purgatory both provides epistemic clarity for and confirms trajectories established in the present life without necessarily providing for postmortem "conversions" (D'Costa 2009: part 4; cf. Ratzinger 1988: 228–33). Evangelicals may be sympathetic to such arguments, as this would neither require denial of hell, understood as everlasting punishment, nor affirmation of universalism, the final salvation of all (Walls 2012).

Universalism has never been more than a minority strand within the Christian tradition. Nevertheless, significant Christian voices throughout the centuries have urged its consideration (see G. MacDonald 2011). While the Unitarian and more liberally inclined proposals have never been persuasive to evangelicals, more resolutely christological arguments have not been as easily dismissed. Karl Barth, for instance, argued that the Pauline rhetoric in Romans 5:12-21 that counters universal death introduced by the sin of Adam through the eternal life offered in Christ leads, if not to universal salvation, at least to a posture of appropriate biblical hope for all (see Parry and Partridge 2004; cf. de S. Cameron 1992). Thus Paul can write in the same epistle that nothing "in all creation, will be able to separate us from the love of God in Christ Jesus our Lord" (Rom 8:39b); that "For from him and through him and to him are all things" (Rom 11:36; cf. Eph 1:10, 21-23; Col 1:20); and, quoting the prophet Isaiah (49:18, 45:23), that "[a]s I live, says the Lord, every knee shall bow to me, and every tongue shall give praise to God" (Rom 14:11; cf. Phil 2:10-11).

Barth was careful, though, to acknowledge that the scriptural warnings regarding eternal perdition ought to caution Christians about being presumptive regarding universal salvation. The logic of heaven and of eternal joy (Walls 2002), for instance, hopes for divine redemption of all that is tragic, terrible, and even evil. But it also assumes creaturely identities are shaped virtuously and given meaningful orientation over the course of life's decisions. If so, then we cannot overlook the possibility, even probability, that some or even many creatures will follow an alternate path of sinfulness into the eternal abyss. The warnings throughout the Scriptures about the judgment of God on sin and evil ought to be heeded as such.

2.2.3 Contemporary Challenges in Global Context

There are three further distinctive challenges to the preceding historical and theological issues that any contemporary effort to reconsider Christian eschatology mindful of the global context ought to engage: the eschatologies of the world religions, especially contrasting eschatological visions; indigenous views of time that have impacted global Christian thinking; and modern science and its impact on present understandings of space and time. We will briefly comment on each in order.

Christians among the world religionists or people of faith are, of course, not the only ones who believe in an afterlife. Millenarian themes in particular, as well as other eschatological ideas, abound in the major religious traditions (e.g., Bowie and Deacy 1997; Ashton and Whyte 2001). Many of these are debated, as they are within the Christian tradition. Some might think that the similarities across religious lines are indicative of common visions regarding the end of the world and what comes after that. However, we ought to proceed very cautiously before reaching such conclusions. Most religious traditions also prescribe divergent sets of practices designed to achieve specific ends.

The distinctiveness of other religious eschatologies and their associated practices is most clearly seen when Christian eschatology is set alongside notions of reincarnation and liberation prevalent especially in the Indian subcontinent. Both Hindu and Buddhist traditions are based on karmic understandings of causality and history, wherein individuals are, paradoxically, expressions of the seeds sown in prior actions and lives. (In this view, the continuity and discontinuity between lives is analogous to the continuity and discontinuity of waves in the ocean or of flames passed on by candles.) The goals of liberation—*moksha* for Hindus and enlightenment or awakening for Buddhists—are attainable, if only over many "lifetimes" (see Häring and Metz 1993). What is perhaps more important, however, is how these aspirations shape, or ought to impact, human life in the here and now. Meditation is central to Indian religious traditions. It nurtures—or ameliorates, as the case may be—the hopes, desires, and expectations of devotees. The ultimate point about *moksha* or enlightenment is to overcome attachment to greed or lust and to experience liberation from the negative forces of karma in the present life (Bigger 2010). The contrast to the Christian vision of entering the presence of God cannot be more starkly noted. Christian prayer and meditation is designed to nurture, not dampen or squash, the longing for reunion with Christ and union with the triune God through the eternal Spirit.

The currents tapped into by these Indian-based traditions, however, include indigenous sensibilities regarding the cyclical nature of time, shaped at least in part by nature's rhythms (Hong 1976). In contrast to Christianity's more linear notion of temporality, indigenous cultures around the world are organized around seasonal and agricultural activities and intuitively discern that life emerges out of death, which in turn follows life, and so on. Within this framework, there are also views of ancestral reincarnation that posit a solidarity (rather than strict personal identity) between deceased individuals and every generation. These views signal how human intuitions regarding life after death are deeply organic, relational, and even interpersonal. Thus many premodern societies lack teleological notions of time that transcend the human or historical sphere. Christian theologians sensitized to these more biocentric and environmentally rooted cosmologies thus feel the urgency of reappraising eschatological ideas in the Bible (e.g., Mbiti 1971). Some are even revisiting the question of to what extent the Christian doctrine of resurrection is commensurable with folk or popular views of rebirth prevalent around the world (e.g., Obilor 1994; see also MacGregor 1992).

If global and local religious traditions bring with them a pluralism of eschatological possibilities, modern science has further complicated the theological and eschatological task. On the one hand, technological advances since the early modern period have done their part in ushering in a new age of optimism regarding what human beings can accomplish (see Sampson 1956). This, among other developments, has fueled postmillennial visions regarding the task of world transformation, if not Christianization. On the other hand, the splitting of the atom has also fostered a more recent awareness that scientific and technological breakthroughs could lead just as well to the end of life on earth as we know it. Beyond these possibilities, however, the astrophysical and cosmological sciences now are capable of peering into the distant past of our cosmic origins and of anticipating a number of possible eschatological endings for the universe as a whole.

Briefly and nontechnically put, based on statistical models applied to what is known about the laws, constitutive elements, and history of the universe, the cosmos will either continue to expand forever or it will at some point begin to contract (e.g., Polkinghorne and Welker 2000). The latter development will result in what has been called a "big crunch," a fiery collapse of the universe into a dimensionless singularity symmetrical to the big bang that many scientists agree set the world in motion. If universal expansion is uninhibited, however, then the fate of the cosmos will be either a gradual "big freeze," related to temperatures descending to absolute zero, or a "big rip," a final singularity caused by the expansion rate of the world reaching infinity. In the case of either singularity, physical cosmologists are thereafter divided about what, if anything, might happen. Here, metaphysical intuitions take the lead. Some hypothesize a "big bounce," one of perhaps an infinite number that includes the big bang launching our own universe. Others suggest that even if nothing else happens, our world might be part of a "multiverse" involving an innumerable number of big bangs. Needless to say, these guesses are neither scientifically grounded nor testable.

Nevertheless, Christian theological thinking about the end of the world ought to ignore neither other religious eschatologies nor scientific prognostications regarding the far-off future of the world (see Peters, Russell, and Welker 2002). This contemporary milieu potentially constrains how Christian might think about the millennium, resurrection, and the afterlife in the twenty-first century. Contemporary astrophysical cosmology, for instance, is consistent with the biblical and theological traditions' claim that the salvation of the world rests not in creaturely hands but in the redemptive and renewing work of God. Yet having said that, how else might we further understand Paul, whose apocalyptic eschatology opened this chapter, and his apostolic colleagues in the present global context?

2.3 Apostolic Anticipations: Lukan Eschatology

Attention to the Apostle Paul's apocalyptic gospel, centered on the resurrected Christ, anchors Christians in the messianic hope of the early believers. Above we followed Paul's narrative as unfolded in the book of Acts. Given the centrality of the Acts account historically in renewal spirituality, theology, and praxis, it may be beneficial to remain with the Lukan materials in thinking about apostolic eschatology. Such an approach is further warranted in light of the fact that the last generation of Lukan scholarship (initiated in part by Conzelmann 1961) has wrestled with the question about the extent to which eschatological themes are central to both of his books. This suggests that a more in-depth interaction with the author of the Third Gospel and Acts could be beneficial for Christian thinking about the last days and the end of time.

As already indicated, Paul's preaching the forgiveness of sins based on the resurrection of Jesus is in line with the apostolic proclamation. On the day of Pentecost, Peter urged repentance and promised the forgiveness of sins to the crowd (Acts 2:38), because he knew "with certainty that God has made him both Lord and Messiah, this Jesus whom *you* [his listeners] crucified" (2:36 [emphasis added]; also 3:15a). And the early believers were convinced about the latter, in part because the messianic expectations included the Davidic promises regarding salvation from the corruption of death (2:27, 31), and there could be no doubt that these had been fulfilled in Jesus, whom "God raised up, and of that all of us are witnesses" (2:32; also 4:2, 10, 33). If this was the case, then God had vindicated Jesus' life and message, and done so at least in part by graciously offering a second chance, even to those implicated in Jesus' unjust execution. If this most heinous sin could also be forgiven, then what could not be (cf. Luke 1:77; 24:47; Acts 3:19; 5:31; 10:43)?

From a renewal perspective, there are two further pneumatological aspects to the eschatological or end-time events related to Jesus' life and ministry. First, Jesus' resurrection is itself a work of the Spirit (Brodeur 1996). He "was declared to be Son of God with power according to the spirit of holiness by resurrection from the dead" (Rom 1:4; see also Rom 8:11a; 1 Tim 3:16; 1 Pet 3:18). Second, Jesus' resurrection in Luke's account is also followed by his ascension to heaven (Luke 24:50-51; Acts 1:9; 7:55-56), from where, "exalted at the right hand of God, and having received from the Father the promise of the Holy Spirit, he has poured out this that you both see and hear" (Acts 2:33). This outpouring of the Spirit, however, is not merely a historical event but an eschatological one, part and parcel of the inauguration of the "last days" (2:17) that is usually thought about only in futuristic terms.

Hence, within the broader two-volume Lukan narrative, we should consider that what the Spirit had been given to accomplish in the apostolic community (recorded in Acts) ought to be consistent with what the Spirit had already begun to achieve in the life of Jesus (explicated in the gospel of Luke). If so, the last days ministry of the Spirit upon and through all flesh—sons and daughters, young and old, slave and free (Acts 2:17-18)—had been anticipated in Jesus' Spirit-anointed accomplishments, his Spirit-filled life, and his Spirit-enabled arising from the dead. His preaching, teaching, and healing under the power of the Spirit (Luke 4:18; Acts 10:38) were all signs announcing the impending reign and rule of God. So also were his exorcisms; as Jesus said, "If it is by the Spirit of God that I cast out demons, then the kingdom of God has come to you" (Matt 12:28; see also Luke 11:20). So for those who were wondering "when the kingdom of God was coming," the answer was: "The kingdom of God is not coming with things that can be observed; nor will they say, 'Look, here it is!' or 'There it is!' For, in fact, the kingdom of God is among you" (Luke 17:20-21). Unsurprisingly, then, Jesus had already begun to commission his disciples to broadcast, "The kingdom of God has come near to you" (10:9; also 10:11).

FIGURE 2.3

In Christian art, as in theology, images of the ascension are deeply connected to both Pentecost and the eschatological judgment of Christ. One way to (artistically) make this connection is to say that the ascension "places" Christ in the (pictorial) position from which the Spirit is poured out and from which Christ alone has the authority to judge the earth. In the Acts account "suddenly two men in white robes" appeared with the disciples, assuring them, "This Jesus, who has been taken up from you into heaven, will come in the same way as you saw him go into heaven" (1:11). So too, images of Jesus' ascension and return might be depicted "in the same way" and might mutually imply one another.

This sixth-century illumination densely packs numerous biblical allusions together in order to portray Christ's ascension as a divine enthronement. Here Christ ascends not simply into the sky but into heaven—the space "beneath," "above," and "behind" the visible spheres of earth and sky—depicted here as a sapphire throne encircled by a rainbow (Ezek 1:26-28; Rev 4:2-3; cf. Exod 24:10). This enthronement is attended not only by angels bringing crowns but also by the mysterious "four living beings" who surround the throne of God in Ezekiel's visions—each with the faces of a man, lion, ox, and eagle and accompanied by "a wheel within a wheel" (Ezek 1:4-28)—who then reappear in Revelation (4:6–6:8; 7:11; 14:3; 15:7; 19:4).

By synthesizing the ascension of Jesus, described at the end of Luke and beginning of Acts, with the apocalyptic visions of the throne room of God in Ezekiel and Revelation, this image theologically interprets the ascension not as Christ "leaving" but as inhabiting the position "at the right hand of the power of God" (Luke 22:69; cf. Matt 26:64; Acts 7:56; Rom 8:34; Eph 1:20; Col 3:1; Heb 8:1; 12:2; 1 Pet 3:22). And it is precisely this position from which he has "all authority" over the church and the world (Matt 28:18), from which he is currently present to the world through the Spirit, and from which he will return again to initiate the marriage of heaven and earth (Rev 21:2-5). And as with depictions of Pentecost (cf. fig. 3.3), this image does not simply depict the historical event of Christ's ascension (e.g., Paul is portrayed here, even though the ascension occurred years before his conversion); it also symbolically depicts Christ's ongoing relation to the church. ✦

Yet it would be a mistake to conclude from this that Luke held only to what scholars have called a "realized eschatology" (C. Sullivan 1988). There is certainly a future dimension to the Lukan horizon of which believers could be assured, even if the divine timeline was only dimly discernible. Thus did Jesus diffuse notions "that the kingdom of God was to appear immediately" (Luke 19:11) by telling the parable of the Ten Pounds, inviting patient and faithful service. He also cautioned those who operated only according to an imminentism that declared, "The time is near!" (21:8), by providing signs of the end of the age and exhorting moral and spiritual vigilance (see Ellis 1972). Yes, his followers "must be ready, for the Son of Man is coming at an unexpected hour" (12:40; cf. 12:46), but the end will not come "until the times of the Gentiles are fulfilled" (21:14). In other words, this time of Jesus' absence in heaven is the time of the Spirit's work among all who believe, but especially among the Gentiles, "all who are far away, everyone whom the Lord our God calls to him" (Acts 2:39). After all, the covenant promised to Abraham was that, "in your descendants all the families of the earth shall be blessed" (Acts 3:25; see also Luke 2:32; 3:6).

All are thereby urged to repent, "so that times of refreshing may come from the presence of the Lord, and that he may send the Messiah appointed for you, that is, Jesus, who must remain in heaven until the time of universal restoration that God announced long ago through his holy prophets" (Acts 3:20-21). Jesus' future return from heaven (Acts 1:11) would then both accomplish the coming judgment upon sin and wickedness (Luke 17:28-35) and achieve the final salvation of Israel and the world (Luke 2:38; 13:28-30; 14:15-24; Acts 15:16-17; see also Chance 1988, Bridge 2003, Lennartsson 2007). For this reason there are repeated warnings of the judgment and wrath to come (Luke 3:7; 10:12-16; 11:31-32; 12:5; 21:23; cf. Acts 17:31; 24:25), even as there is also encouragement about reward for those who persevere (Luke 10:20; 21:28; 22:28-30). The key, however, is that eschatological redemption is conceived of more in terms of a this-worldly (resurrected and embodied; Luke 14:14; 20:35-36) messianic day of the Lord (Luke 4:19; Acts 2:20) involving Jews and Gentiles than in otherworldly terms. The last days or ends of time (2:17), after all, include also the ends of the earth—which is ἐσχάτου τῆς γῆς (escatou tes ges) in Acts 1:8—because the outpouring Spirit has broken into and begun the transformative redemption of creational time and space (see Westhelle 2012: 132).

In broad strokes, the preceding picture of Luke's eschatology is consistent with what is found in the rest of the New Testament, including Paul's letters (Witherington 1992; cf. Wright 2008: part 2). For Paul, the present work of the Spirit was intimately intertwined with that of the resurrected Christ, so his pneumatology and his eschatology were mutually informing (see Fee 1994: 801 passim). Hence although Paul's apocalypticism is not bereft of cosmic cataclysmic events, it is more deeply shaped by the new world unveiled, depicted, and envisioned through the resurrected Christ. Thus Paul, and believers in Christ after him, live now in Christ by the Spirit, and yet in anticipation of the full reign of God to come. Pauline and Lukan eschatologies parallel one another on these matters.

What still needs to be highlighted, however, is Luke's explicit warning against any efforts to correlate contemporary events with the divine timetable. When the disciples "asked him, 'Lord, is this the time when you will restore the kingdom to Israel?' He replied, 'It is not for you to know the times or periods that the Father has set by his own authority'" (Acts 1:7). Instead of date setting, believers ought instead to live by and in the Holy Spirit, who was given to Jesus and who Jesus has poured out in turn. As he promised his eschatologically curious followers, "You will receive power when the Holy Spirit has come upon you; and you will be my witnesses in Jerusalem, in all Judea and Samaria, and to the ends of the earth" (1:8). In short, those genuinely interested in the coming divine rule were redirected to live in the Spirit of Jesus instead and witness to the reign of God manifest in his life and teachings by the power of his Spirit. Praying to the Father, "Your kingdom come" (Luke 11:2b) brings about nothing less than the gift of the Holy Spirit (11:13), so the reign of God may flourish (13:18-21). This is not to say that believers will establish the reign of God through their own efforts, because "[i]t is through many persecutions that we must enter the kingdom of God" (Acts 14:22; Luke 21:12). It is to say that living in light of the resurrection not only brings hope for the life to come but also participates in God's salvific work in the present.

Much more can and should be said about Luke's eschatology, not to mention the last things as a whole, than what is so quickly covered here. But recall that each chapter's third section explores the particular doctrine under consideration focused through a specific author or writing in the New Testament and that this provides a model for doing something similar on that topic with other parts of Scripture. Further, while we will here provide some summary remarks about eschatological matters, we have also the rest of the volume to fill out the details as they interface with other doctrines. So the preceding, as well as this whole chapter, is only a point of entry into an eschatological theology. But focusing on the apostolic proclamation highlights how later ruminations (summarized above) are often divorced from vital Christian praxis. With this in mind, we cautiously proceed to revisit the WAGF SF on the "end of time" and proffer how it might invite eschatological beliefs and practices suitable for the present global context.

2.4 Christian Hope Today and Tomorrow

Nothing in the SF article 11 as it stands hearkens to anything distinctive about renewal Christianity. Yet our task here is not to conduct an exegesis of the SF but to use it as a springboard for theological reflection in a global context that is increasingly renewalist in orientation. So the question here is, at least in part, what a renewal theological approach might contribute to eschatology. The answer is not obvious given the diversity of renewal perspectives on eschatology both historically and in the present (Althouse and Waddell 2010).

Now the fivefold gospel was adopted and adapted from the beginning by large swaths of the classical pentecostal movement, and this included emphasis on "Jesus the coming King" (see Yong 2010: ch. 8). Yet even as a central motif in renewal Christianity, when not integrated with the specifically renewalist elements—for example, "Jesus the healer" and "Jesus the Spirit Baptizer"—Jesus the coming blessed hope has more often than not degenerated in some circles to an escapist mentality. The latter is especially prevalent amongst those influenced by the dispensationalist teaching regarding the secret rapture of the church prior to the tribulational period (Prosser 1999). Contemporary renewal theologians sensitive to these developments have thus labored to formulate eschatologies that are more attentive to the embodied holism presumed in renewal spirituality. Many have helpfully urged a more explicitly this-worldly and transformational understanding of the last things (Althouse 2003; Thompson 2010). This includes conceiving of human destinies in relational rather than merely individualistic terms and therefore also as part and parcel of the restoration and renewal, rather than the destruction, of the cosmos so that the new heavens and earth can be the dwelling place of God and God's creatures (also Macchia 2010).

In line with these recent contributions, four aspects of the SF can potentially renew Christian thinking about eschatology in the present time. First, it should not be understated that the Christian expectation is locked in on the "personal return of our Lord Jesus Christ." This presumes, of course, the apostolic witness to the resurrection of Jesus. Yet beyond this is the *personal* character of what is desired. Christians anticipate not first and foremost events of this or that nature, but a personal rendezvous with their Savior, who is also characterized across the pages of the New Testament as the departed groom for whom the church-bride longs (Matt 25:1-13; Luke 5:34-35; Eph 5:22-33; Rev 19:7-8; 21:2, 9). The Christian hope is not about (arriving at) a place, but is about everlasting life with a person, the divine person revealed in Jesus by the Spirit. Christ after all is "the Alpha and the Omega . . . who is and who was and who is to come . . . the first and the last, the beginning and the end" (Rev 1:8; 22:13).

Second, this leads to a sense that any speculations about the premillennial timing of the return of the Lord ought to be subservient to emphasizing the imminence of Christ's return. That Christ's return has been delayed was recognized as problematic even in the pages of the New Testament (e.g., 2 Pet 3:3-9). Yes, the christological delay is part and parcel of a much longer history of messianic delay intrinsic to ancient Judaism (Holman 1996). The proper response is to recognize the conditional nature of the divine timeline (Allison 1985: 174–78) and cultivate the appropriate posture of yearning. The latter focuses not on messianic events but on the Messiah himself. Thus spouses longing for one another can anticipate in the present what the future event will be, because they are already keenly attuned to the personal characteristics of their beloved. We "know" our spouses not just cognitively but affectively, imaginatively, and personally. Thus even during periods of physical separation, we are reminded of those we love by sights, smells, sounds, and other palpable even if fleeting perceptions. They remain present to us in these moments, stirring desire and deepening anticipation. Similarly, then, the Christian expectation of the imminent return of Christ highlights how the yearnings of messianic hearts are oriented toward reunion with the groom. Christians realize Jesus is also paradoxically never far from them, as when they meet him in the Supper, or in prayer and meditation, or in any other events wherein the Spirit of Jesus is present and active in a discernible way. The imminent return of Christ thus points to his being literally at the door (James 5:9; Rev 3:20); absent still in the body yet also present in some sense through his Spirit. And Christ's followers are sensitive to his spiritual presence even as they anticipate full personal union with him.

Yet third, the premillennial nature of renewalist eschatology has some content. It points to the belief that however else the millennium ought to be understood, the bride, or the people of God, will be at work in the time to come under the oversight of the coming regent. The return of Jesus before the millennium in this case ought to be understood as enabling the participation of believers in the coming reign of God. The actual nature of the thousand years may not be resolvable on this side of the eschaton, but Christians across the evangelical-ecumenical spectrum ought to be able to agree that eschatological salvation includes creaturely involvement in the divine rule (Luke 22:29-30; 1 Cor 6:2).

Most importantly, such activity is not only part of the not yet future, but also central to the already present (see also Ladd 1974). The last days initiated with Jesus' outpouring of his Spirit upon all flesh empowers human sharing in God's work of reconciling all creation to himself. That is why the SF goes beyond pointing to the objects of Christian commitments (that Christ will return personally) and touches importantly on the present posture and priorities of believers: "we purify ourselves, even as He is pure, so that we may be ready to meet Him when He comes." Eschatological doctrines thus ought not to be primarily speculative ideas about what will come to pass but should reflect believers' aspirations and order their practical lives on this side of the Parousia (Rook and Holmes 2008). One of the important aspects of any doctrine, including that regarding the last things, is what kind of attitudes it engenders and what kinds of behaviors it fosters. Article 11 indicates that the goal of contemplating eschatological matters is finally performative: to inspire followers of Christ to live into the purifying work of the Spirit in the present life. Yet Christians do not bring about the end; rather, they participate in the eschatological work of God manifest in Christ and poured out in the Holy Spirit.

This emphasis on present implications is especially important when considering the clauses regarding everlasting bliss and punishment in the second paragraph of article 11. Those blessed with the beatific vision are those who "truly believe." This involves not only intellectual assent (the head) but also the placing of faith and trust in the Lord, which involve as much the affections (the heart), habits, and way of life (the hands). On the other hand, those who trust in themselves and are misshapen by evil deeds and misdirected by evil desires also will have to suffer the consequences of their misguided lives. The final judgment will expose the sins and evils of the world (see also section 10.4) while sanctifying the goodness, truth, and beauty that is also manifest. Those who are irredeemable because of their sin and rejection of God will be left to their own demise and fate; others will anticipate worshipping the triune God in the presence of the community of saints (see also section 11.4). It is a mystery and thereby an article of faith how the cosmic lordship of Christ can coexist with an eternally persisting damnation, a theme to which we shall return in later chapters.

Thus God will judge justly and rightly in determining which names are included in the Book of Life. A person with profound intellectual disability who may not have the capacity to cognitively confess Christ as Lord may still be capable of believing in terms of trusting in God through his or her community of support (see also the discussion of disability in ch. 8 of this volume). But others who may know how to call out to God by name may nevertheless be evildoers (see Matt 7:21-23) left out of the Book of Life. Yes, there is assurance for those who place their hope and trust in Christ. But grace is not cheap, and the point about everlasting bliss and punishment is not about guesses concerning others who are "in" or "out" but about how human beings respond to what is given them.

Even for religious traditions that postulate reincarnation rather than resurrection, the central point concerns transcending through *moksha* or final liberation the karmic consequences of actions in this life. So in these traditions, rebirth is at its best a further opportunity to fix accrued negative karma rather than being an eternal destiny. Christian faith already affirms that the present life has important repercussions and unavoidable consequences: "Do not be deceived; God is not mocked, for you reap whatever you sow. If you sow to your own flesh, you will reap corruption from the flesh; but if you sow to the Spirit, you will reap eternal life from the Spirit. So let us not grow weary in doing what is right, for we will reap at harvest time, if we do not give up" (Gal 6:7-9). Even eschatologically, divine judgment is meted based on what people do (Matt 25:31-46; Rev 20:12; 21:8, 27; 22:14-15). Yet without diminishing the severity of present decisions and actions, the Christian gospel also announces that forgiveness is available because of the living Christ, with salvific relevance for both this life and the one to come. Herein is the Christian doctrine of resurrection most starkly distinguished from notions of reincarnation found in other traditions.

The last point to be made concerns the bodily nature of eternal life. Christ's resurrected body maintained some continuity with his earthly body (although there are indications that he was not easily recognizable). But his capacity to appear in and disappear out of closed rooms (John 20:26) suggests that the character of everlasting life transcends space and time as conventionally known. However, such bodily transcendence of space and time does not mean that the new heavens and new earth are dematerialized final states. Rather, it points to the fact that God's redemptive work intends to renew and restore the present physical world, originally created good but now tarnished by sin. The new Jerusalem will descend from heaven (Rev 21:10) and sanctify and renew the earth (cf. Rom 8:18-28). The resurrection of the body therefore involves a new valuation not only of human persons as embodied but of the material world as the home given by God. The spiritual dimension of human life is thus intimately interrelated with human bodies and their embeddedness in the created world. The doctrine of the resurrection thus invites Christians to care not only for themselves but also for this world in all of its dimensions (environmentally, ecologically, and even cosmically). For these domains of human responsibility (recall the mandate to care for the creation in Genesis 1:26-28), scientific advances need to be combined with the knowledge and wisdom of indigenous cultures.

Mention of modern science, however, recalls our earlier observations about its predictions regarding the end of the world. Yet even as contemporary cosmology continues to grapple with these inevitabilities, understood naturally, it also continues to struggle with the nature of time and, relevant for our purposes, the connectedness between time and space. Contemporary theories of space, time, and the space–time continuum indicate that our existential and conventional experience of temporality masks many mysteries about the nature of time that confirm Paul's intuition: "For now we see in a mirror, dimly" (1 Cor 13:12a). This pertains to our understanding not only of resurrected bodies (see also 1 Cor 15:35-49) but also of the nature of eternal life and everlasting punishment. Is such eternity timeless yet somehow subsistent in consciousness? Or perhaps the new heavens and new earth are characterized by a kind of relative duration, wherein resurrected bodies have the capacity to transcend various dimensions of space and time? Regardless of how we respond to such questions, theology can affirm that the power of the resurrection defeats the death that holds the world in its grip. So maybe the new heavens and earth will be the result of a divine work, such as was seen in the resurrection of Jesus. Or maybe the resurrection will come to be seen as the operation of other dimensions of divinely enacted laws that will also, in due course, bring about the new creation (Haire, Ledger, and Pickard 2007). The point to be made here is that our present knowledge of the world is as inexhaustible as the one to come is mysterious, which reflects the character of the triune God who remains hidden amid the divine creative and redemptive activities.

FIGURE 2.4   FIGURE 2.4 (DETAIL)

The sculptural artworks of Mandy Cano Villalobos constitute an extended meditation on the passage of time and the enduring sense of loss that often accompanies our experience of time. The objects she makes are objects of and about memory—sometimes contested public memories, sometimes deeply personal family memories (as is the case in this work). Undone consists of a wooden cabinet that stores and presents sweaters and other articles of clothing that have been unraveled and tightly wound into balls of thread and yarn. Each piece of unraveled cloth-ing, by virtue of the fact that it has been worn and used, is strongly associated with particular persons, events, and stages of life—associations made somewhat more specific by the labels that accompany these artifacts: "Big Daddy's favorite sweater," "Tim's gloves," "The sweater nobody wanted to wear anymore." All of the materials remain, but the original forms and functions of these objects are lost, existing only as memories (imagined memories for most of us), such that each ball of yarn represents both irretrievable loss (an unraveling of what once was) and hopeful potential (the reknitting of something new).

Undone is thus an emblem of longing both for what has passed and for some sort of reconstitution still in the future. And the scope of this longing quickly expands: unraveled sweaters suggest not only unraveled moments but also unrav-eled bodies (or lives)—which are here held in the embrace of a large cabinet whose dark interior functions as a place of the dead, a spacetime in which these undone garments are suspended in a "formless" state. Do we venture to imagine these bodies knitted anew? Can these remembered persons be clothed again? When St. Paul articulates Christian eschatological longing ("groaning"), his orientation is ultimately not toward disembodiment but resurrection, which he describes in terms of being reclothed: "we wish not to be unclothed but to be further clothed, so that what is mortal may be swallowed up by life" (2 Cor 5:4; cf. 1 Cor 15:54).

Cano Villalobos' Undone does not attempt to envision the eschaton, but it does voice a human longing and anticipation for it: that somehow the world might be knit back together. And we should note the interpersonal, embodied character of this anticipation: these are not abstract or impersonal nobodies; these are indi-viduals known by the artist in all the particularities of life—particularities fully known by the One who is "making all things new" (Rev 21:5). ✦

The more important matter thus concerns how eternity's beckoning cuts into each present moment of existence. Jesus' and the Spirit's calling from heaven (e.g., Rev 22:17) can in that sense be seen as intersecting with each instant of the space–time continuum in an equally relevant manner. Thus every breath is an opportunity to shape an eternal path. And we begin here with the end, because as hopeful, desiring, and loving creatures, human beings live ultimately for what they hope for, what they desire, and what they love, even as they perceive all of this through a mir-ror, dimly. Jesus' resurrection promises that the God who loves the world will neither abandon his people nor ignore their corruption. Rather, his plan is to redeem what is corruptible as part of an overall renewal of the creation. Thus Christian believers prayerfully purify themselves in eager expectation of embracing the Lord Jesus upon his return.

Discussion Questions

1. What are some aspects of your church's teachings about eschatology that are different from the preceding discussion? Are these differences complementary or are they contradictory, and if the latter, what are possible responses to these divergent views?

2. How might starting with the doctrine of eschatology orient us toward theological studies? How does focusing on Luke and the book of Acts provide a helpful perspective on the last days and the end times in comparison with what you see in other parts of the Bible?

3. What are the most important ideas about eschatology that you think we ought to come away with from this chapter? How might these ideas have practical consequences for Christian living?

Further Reading

Bloesch, Donald. 2004. *The Last Things: Resurrection, Judgment, Glory.* Downers Grove, Ill.: IVP Academic.

Clouse, Robert G., ed. 1977. *The Meaning of the Millennium: Four Views.* Downers Grove, Ill.: IVP Academic.

Crockett, William, ed. 1992. *Four Views on Hell.* Grand Rapids: Zondervan.

Landes, Richard. 2011. *Heaven on Earth: The Varieties of Millennial Experience.* Oxford: Oxford University Press.

Moltmann, Jürgen. 1995. *The Coming of God: Christian Eschatology.* Margaret Kohl, trans. Minneapolis: Fortress.

Pate, C. Marvin, ed. 1998. *Four Views on the Book of Revelation.* Grand Rapids: Zondervan.

Walls, Jerry L., ed. 2008. *The Oxford Handbook on Eschatology.* Oxford: Oxford University Press.

Wright, N. T. 1999. *The Millennium Myth.* Louisville, Ky.: Westminster John Knox.

The Gifts of the Holy Spirit

Christian Ministry and the Mission of God

World Assemblies of God Fellowship Statement of Faith
—Article 10: The Gifts of the Holy Spirit

We believe in the present day operation of the nine supernatural gifts of the Holy Spirit (1 Corinthians 12) and the ministry gifts of Christ (Ephesians 4:11-13) for the edification and expansion of the church.

3.1 Elizabeth as Prototype of the Spirit-Filled Life

Article 10 includes two references to the Pauline Letters. However, most renewalists look to St. Luke for insight into the charismatic nature of the church (e.g., Stronstad 1984; Menzies 1994), because they view the book of Acts as providing the standard for Christian life. Our character vignette introducing this chapter, then, derives from St. Luke. But we will be starting at the beginning of the Lukan story, in the infancy narratives of the gospel, rather than with the day of Pentecost's outpouring of the Spirit.

We focus on the initial Lukan volume, because as indicated in the preceding chapter, the life of Christ is paradigmatic for what Spirit-filled and Spirit-empowered ministry ought to be. Hence, the apostolic mission can also be understood as being Spirit-led in the footsteps of Jesus. What is interesting for our purposes, however, is that in the Lukan account, the charismatic ministry of the Spirit predates even Jesus himself. One of the first persons filled with the Holy Spirit and responsive to the Spirit's empowering witness is not a man, but a woman!

To be sure, the prophecy is given first that it is John, Elizabeth's son, who "even before his birth . . . will be filled with the Holy Spirit" (Luke 1:15). Further, to Elizabeth's niece Mary it was said: "the Holy Spirit will come upon you, and the power of the Most High will overshadow you; therefore the child to be born will be holy; he will be called Son of God" (1:35). We will return in chapter 5 to Mary's story. For now, it is noteworthy that when Elizabeth is about six months pregnant with John, at Mary's visitation and greeting, "the child leapt in her womb. And Elizabeth was filled with the Holy Spirit" (1:41). So who was Elizabeth, and why ought we to begin consideration of the charismatic life with her?

Elizabeth was the wife of Zechariah, a priest who served regularly in the temple. "Both of them were righteous before God, living blamelessly according to all the commandments and regulations of the Lord" (1:6). But they were "getting on in years" (1:7; also 1:18), and, "they had no children, because Elizabeth was barren" (1:7). It is clear that their childlessness was something over which they grieved and about which they prayed to God (1:13). Yet up until now, their prayers had not been answered. As a woman whose role in life was to bear and nurture children, Elizabeth had long lived with the stigma of infertility. (In all likelihood, Elizabeth bore the brunt of the responsibility for the couple's sterility, because the ancient world had fewer resources to identify male impotency, especially in the case of faithful lifelong spouses.) Her prayer of thankfulness upon conception according to the promises of the angel Gabriel captures the pain and anguish she had experienced over the years: "This is what the Lord has done for me when he looked favourably on me and took away the disgrace I have endured among my people" (1:25).

So, one of the first of the new charismatic or Spirit-filled people of God is not Peter, James, John, or even Jesus. Instead, it is an older, even aged, childless and desolate woman, one surely despised because of her physical condition (Reid 1996: ch. 4). Thus, Elizabeth presages the exaltation of the lowly in Luke (1:48-52), being one of the first instantiations of a world turned upside down according to God's new world order (Acts 17:6). Luke could preserve Peter's explanation of the day of Pentecost event (drawn from the prophet Joel), because the promise of the Spirit's outpouring upon women, the elderly, and slaves (2:17-18) was in effect foreshadowed in Elizabeth's experience of the salvation-historical events surrounding the coming of the Messiah. Here according to society's conventions was an expendable person, one who had failed to fulfill her role as a wife and mother. But Elizabeth was now a witness to the fact that "God shows no partiality" (10:34), and God's gifts, including the gift of his Spirit, are liberally dispensed "to each one individually just as the Spirit chooses" (1 Cor 12:11).

And what happened when Elizabeth was filled with the Spirit? She exclaimed to Mary, "Blessed are you among women, and blessed is the fruit of your womb. And why has this happened to me, that the mother of my Lord comes to me? For as soon as I heard the sound of your greeting, the child in my womb leapt for joy. And blessed is she who believed that there would be a fulfilment of what was spoken to her by the Lord" (Luke 1:42-45). Three brief comments suffice. First, the gift of the Spirit produces joy, but one that is embodied rather than disembodied. The arrival of the Spirit is thus never a merely "spiritual" occasion. Rather, Elizabeth receives the Spirit in the very depths of her being, touching even upon the child she is carrying in her womb. Hence the charismatic life is palpable, tangible, and kinesthetic, at least as Elizabeth experienced it.

FIGURE 3.1

Luke places the greeting between Mary and Elizabeth inside the home of Zechariah and Elizabeth (1:40). When Rogier van der Weyden depicts the scene, however, he places it outside at quite a distance from the house, seemingly playing up Elizabeth's sense of anticipation for Mary's arrival. The deep landscape behind Mary suggests the great distance she has traveled to visit Elizabeth, who has in turn run down the road to meet her. And as they greet each other, the women's pregnant bellies meet in the center of the composition, each placing a hand of blessing on the other. At the center of this image (compositionally and conceptually) is pregnancy, evoking anticipation for the redemptive narratives that will unfold from these two mothers.

A silent but complex exchange ensues between the women. This aunt and niece knowingly glance at each other: a weighty significance permeates their meeting. The older Elizabeth blesses the young Mary and looks at her with a complex mixture of affection, concern, and reverence: "why has this happened to me, that the mother of my Lord comes to me?" (Luke 1:43). And Mary glances back with an equally subtle mix of affection, fatigue, and probably fear (cf. fig. 5.1). Mary lifts her brilliant blue mantle to reveal a lavishly embroidered royal tunic underneath: she has been called to bear "the Son of the Most High" to whom belongs "the throne of his ancestor David" (1:32-33)—a fearful and mindbending calling indeed. And immediately alongside the arm that reveals this royal tunic a young tree conspicuously stretches its branches into the sky, alluding to a future in which her son will paradoxically offer "permission to eat from the tree of life" (Rev 2:7; 22:14) specifically by way of bearing "our sins in his body on the cross" (1 Pet 2:24; cf. Gal 3:13; Acts 5:30; 10:39). And it is the child leaping in the womb of Elizabeth who will be "one crying out in the wilderness: 'Prepare the way of the Lord' " (Luke 3:4).

The scene leads off toward Elizabeth's home, which towers like a cathedral in the background. This conflation of the home of Zechariah and Elizabeth with a church (and a first-century Judean setting with a fifteenth-century Flemish one) is intentional, allowing Elizabeth to serve as a model for all generations of the church: filled with the Spirit in joyful anticipation of the Redeemer who is coming. ✦

But second and more importantly, the filling of the Spirit focuses attention outward, to others, for their edification. Thrice Elizabeth pronounced blessing on Mary and upon her child to come. Here the older woman affirms, nurtures, and confirms the faith of the younger (probably) teenage girl. Even in her time of joy, she is sensitive to the needs of others. The reception of the Spirit is not first and foremost for the building up of the self but for the encouragement of others. In this case, Elizabeth's exhortation came through blessings inspired by the Spirit.

Last but not least, the charismatic encounter is nevertheless predicated on believing, encountering, and living out "what was spoken . . . by the Lord." The work of the Spirit is thus intimately connected to the fulfillment of the promises of God as they mark God's faithfulness even to those who have felt forsaken (as did Elizabeth and the people of whom she was a part, living as they were under the Roman occupation). How might the Spirit-filled utterance and response of this older woman, neglected and marginalized perhaps for decades, now inform our own considerations of charismology, the theology of the charismatic life?

3.2 The Spiritual Gifts: Historical Considerations

Article 10 of the SF mentions two sets of gifts: the supernatural and the ministerial. The former is the one most renewalists focus upon, derived from Paul's list of nine charismata (χαρισμάτων/*charismaton*; 1 Cor 12:4) or manifestations (φανέρωσις/*phanerosis*; 12:7) of the Spirit (12:8–10): utterance of wisdom, utterance of knowledge, faith, gifts (plural in the original) of healing, working of miracles, prophecy, discernment of spirits, various kinds of tongues, and the interpretation of tongues. The ministry gifts denote what in renewalist circles is often dubbed the fivefold ministry (Eph 4:11): apostles, prophets, evangelists, pastors, and teachers. They are often seen as offices (with some grammatical justification to link the last two, pastors and teachers, into one office), while the manifestation gifts are often understood as person relative: they are given by the Spirit, "who allots to each one individually just as the Spirit chooses" (1 Cor 12:11b). Interestingly, after enumerating the manifestation gifts in his Corinthian letter, Paul launches into a consideration of the one body of Christ and its many members, amid which he mentions both ministries (apostles, prophets, and teachers) and an even wider array of manifestations—"deeds of power, then gifts of healing, forms of assistance, forms of leadership, various kinds of tongues" (1 Cor 12:28)—*together* as gifts (12:31). While there is a valid sense in which all of the gifts can be understood as ministerial in that they build up and edify others (e.g., Berding 2006), we shall also see that there are even more gifts than those listed above and that the diverse forms also deserve attention.

This chapter focuses on the gift of prophecy in particular and the manifestation (also known as charismatic or spiritual) gifts in general. For reasons that will become more evident as we proceed, discussion of tongues and interpretation will be reserved for the next chapter, and the triad of healing, miracles, and discernment of spirits for later chapters. In order to appreciate the core affirmation of article 10, some historical perspective will be beneficial. The following discussion will be divided into three eras—the early medieval, the Reformation and early modern, and the contemporary (roughly since the twentieth century)—with each one focusing on the distinctive challenges confronted. We shall see why the spiritual gifts have been controversial, but also why they demand our considered attention in an era of global Christianity.

3.2.1 Patristic and Medieval Developments

While there is growing scholarly evidence that prophecy and charismatic manifestations have been ongoing throughout the history of Christianity (e.g., Robeck 1984; Cartledge 2007: ch. 2; Burgess 2011), there is no question that they have waxed and waned, appeared in various guises, and been contentious and even notorious. The author of the Letter to the Hebrews seems to at least distinguish between the prophetic utterances of ancient Israel and God's revelation in the Son (Heb 1:1-2), if not suggest that the latter had displaced the former. So also did other Jews during this period of time feel as if prophecy had been at least suspended, if not abrogated, perhaps because it was no longer needed, as Israel did not remain in idolatry and the writings of the prophets were now accessible (Cook 2011: part 2). Yet even such suspension did not exclude divine pneumatic presence amid Israel. The apocalyptic community at Qumran, for instance, believed that the Spirit of the Lord was also the Spirit of truth who sanctified community members and nurtured communal life (Montague 1976: ch. 11).

Although the charismatic gifts remained prevalent throughout much of the first two centuries of the Christian era, extant records indicate a diminishment during the third century (Kydd 1984). The gifts seemed to become less important in the life and thinking of the church as it became more organized. Yet it was amid this process of institutionalization during the late second and early third centuries that the Montanist revival broke out in Asia Minor (Robeck 1992). Montanus (a local priest) and his followers, including two prominent women, believed that their experiences of the Spirit fulfilled Jesus' promises regarding the coming Paraclete (in John's gospel) and that the spiritual revelations they received were for the chastisement and revitalization of a spiritually languishing and ethically lax church. The ecstatic and frenzied character of the Montanist prophets no doubt cast further suspicion on their character. Synodic and other condemnations appeared; the prophecies, oracles, and writings of the Montanists came to be regarded as heresy; and the movement was eventually rejected as unorthodox. Yet it is arguable that the main reasons for their rejection may have been related to the charismatic authority with which they challenged the progressively institutionalized church and to the prominent roles granted to women in what was becoming a predominantly male ecclesial hierarchy (Trevett 1996). In addition, their message of moral rigor proclaimed against an increasingly comfortable clerical leadership was surely unpopular among that audience.

The Montanist episode augurs what will happen with charismatic movements throughout much of the history of Christianity. On the one hand, the ever-growing institutional dimensions of Christianity and the church either are suspicious about or threatened by charismatic manifestations and movements (von Campenhausen 1969). Particularly after Christianity becomes the religion of the empire during the fourth century, and certainly after the emergence of a fully developed papacy, including the development of papal–imperial relationships throughout the medieval period (Russell 1968), charismatic authority was thought to be vested in the ecclesial hierarchy rather than among the laity. If the gifts of the Spirit were emphasized at all within this ecclesial-hierarchical framework, they were those the prophet Isaiah promised would be dispensed to the Messiah of Israel (Isa 11:2) and passed on to the church's leadership through apostolic succession. Not without reason, histories of Christianity told from the ecclesial point of view inevitably labeled charismatic movements as sectarian, schismatic, and heretical. They were to be resisted because of their (alleged) unorthodox expressions, and perhaps more so because on occasion their prophetic claims either exceeded the scope of Scripture or even contradicted the Bible altogether. But more pointedly, charismatic prophets acted as if their authority derived directly from the Holy Spirit, and this undermined the priestly authority of the church.

Yet on the other hand, prophecy and charismatic movements would not be subdued (Hvidt 2007). Earlier on, confessors, martyrs, and other saints were viewed as having charismatic powers. During the medieval period, founders of monastic movements appeared as charismatic leaders whose achievements served to renew and revitalize the church. Mystics across the centuries, no less the women mystics in the medieval era, experienced dreams, visions, and other apparitions that inspired them and others. In most of these cases, the prophet, charismatic leader, and even mystic did not claim to rival the authority of the Bible, the church, or the received tradition. In fact, more often than not, prophetic messages and the content of visions or dreams had to fit the mold of what was acceptable in the tradition, with some negotiation possible at the edges, if these were to have any chance of wider promulgation (Voaden 1999). Yet just as often, once authorized by the church hierarchy, these divine "revelations" would inspire the masses, and so aroused, the practical and theological results on the ground would be unpredictable, not to mention uncontrollable in some instances.

3.2.2 Reformation and Early Modern Disputes

By the sixteenth century, the magisterial Protestant Reformers felt the pressure of prophecy and charismatic manifestations on two fronts. On the one side was proliferation of medieval mysticism and, by extension, the Roman Church's implicit sanctioning of such experiences, visionary apparitions, and other forms of "private" revelations. On the other side were pockets of Radical Reformers—*Schwärmer* (enthusiasts or fanatics), they were called—who insisted they were following the "inner word" of the Holy Spirit, but whose actions and demands went well beyond the major Reformers' comfort zone. While all Reformers sought to keep together both the "inner word" of the Spirit and the "outer word" of Scripture, commitments to *sola scriptura* were honed in part in response to perceived excesses on both fronts. So if the church catholic's polemic against Montanism and other charismatic movements led to the minimizing of prophecy, the Reformation reaction to medieval Catholicism and its miracles further fueled the cessationist argument that such phenomena dissipated with the end of the apostolic age. Thus John Calvin was reluctant to affirm the ongoing propriety of various supernatural or ministerial gifts (especially of apostles and prophets in the latter group) unless they were promulgated among "duly constituted churches" (Calvin 1965: §4.3.4), that is, those of the Reformation movement.

Within the next century, predicated on the conviction that "those former ways of God's revealing his will unto his people being now ceased" (Westminster Confession of Faith 1.1), the divines convocating at Westminster in England (in the 1640s) began their confession affirming the absolute priority of Scripture. "Those former ways" for the divines referred to whatever was claimed to arrive *immediately* to individuals, rather than *mediately* through the Scriptures. Their concerns revolved around alleged charismatic or supernatural revelations of the Spirit. Thus dreams, visions, direct prophecies, and so on were no longer sent by God nor needed in light of the scriptural witness. Those in the Reformed tradition either limited such immediate forms of revelation to the apostolic community, or they interpreted scriptural texts like Acts 2:17-18—about the ongoing relevance of prophecy, visions, and dreams for the eschatological age—as being fulfilled analogically or typologically in the postapostolic period, for instance, through the church's capacity to understand Scripture correctly (Milne 2007: 133–40).

This cessationist strand of the Reformed tradition provided the impetus for developments in the next two centuries. Streams of thought unfolding the tradition of Protestant scholasticism and Enlightenment rationalism both presumed the cessationist thesis, albeit for different reasons. The former were committed to the absolute norm of Scripture and would not allow for ongoing subjective "manifestations" of the Spirit that could and would (it was believed) compromise the objectivity of divine revelation. The latter came to include, in the eighteenth century age of reason, free-thinkers and skeptics who were comfortable with a deistic deity, who was aloof from the mundane affairs of the world and thus neither intervened in human activities nor provided special revelatory messages. For these rationalists, religious supernaturalists were those engaged in fanatical, zealous, sectarian, and even antinomian (unlawful) behavior.

Pietism in its various guises across Europe and North America emerged at least partly in response to Protestant scholasticism (Lindberg 1983: ch. 3), even as revivalism erupted alongside if not squarely amid Enlightenment deism. The Methodist movement nurtured a heart religiosity (Mack 2008) while the Great Awakening revivals featured a range of ecstatic behaviors, if not charismatic manifestations (De Arteaga 2002: ch. 7). From the so-called French Prophets to the Quakers and Shakers, among other movements, heart religionists resisted the cognitivisim advocated by scholasticism and rationalism (Michaels 2003). These were pejoratively labeled as "enthusiasts"—from the Greek, literally meaning "possessed by a god" (Knox 1950)—because of their beliefs that God's Spirit was at work in their lives, even within their bodies, quite apart from the institutional mechanisms of the church.

By the nineteenth century, such enthusiastic forms of religiosity had burgeoned rather than been disciplined. In England and North America, there were Mormons claiming to speak in tongues as discussed in the Bible, Catholic apostolics (also known as Irvingites) who practiced almost the full range of charismatic manifestations, and Christian Science and other faith-cure movements that believed in divine or spiritual healing, among many other groups featuring charismatic-type occurrences. Princeton theologian Benjamin B. Warfield (1851–1921) was motivated at the turn of the twentieth century to polemicize against such presumptiveness. Warfield's *Counterfeit Miracles* (1918) reasserted the cessationist argument not only against these phenomena (as an extension of the Reformation response to medieval and Catholic miracles), but also against the newly emerging pentecostal manifestations that had begun to appear on the horizon during the first decade of the twentieth century.

3.2.3 Global "Charismania"!?

In hindsight, one can see that Warfieldian cessationism did not stand a chance against the global expansion of pentecostal-charismatic renewal occurring over the last century (see Ruthven 1993; Deere 1996). Assuredly, there remain those who for a wide range of reasons are cautious about charismatic spirituality, if not downright skeptical about claims regarding the ongoing manifestations of the Holy Spirit. That is why there are critical analyses of charismatic renewal from both fundamentalist (e.g., MacArthur 1992) and progressive/liberal perspectives (e.g., Cotton 1996). And there is reason to be hesitant, particularly with respect to the extreme subjectivism and excesses present in various quarters of the movement. In the contemporary global context, however, three sets of questions are especially important in light of the preceding historical sketch.

FIGURE 3.2

Thai artist Sawai Chinnawong imagines the outpouring of the Spirit on Pentecost in the visual vernacular of traditional Thai Buddhist painting. As such, the bright red and gold colors and the triple-peaked blue trim at the top identify this as a holy space. It is common to see this same format framing the seated Buddha, whose head is often surrounded by a stylized holy fire similar to the one filling the center of this image. These pictorial elements are simply the grammar of holiness and spiritual enlivenment in Thai visual culture, and thus Chinnawong's deployment of these elements in depicting the outpouring of the Holy Spirit is already highly charged in his cultural context (see ch. 11 for further discussion of renewal Christianity in a religiously pluralistic world). But where one would expect in a Buddhist painting to find a singular figure, we see a community organized around—and organized by—the massive holy flame in the center of the image. This body of fire is visually rhymed in the tongues of fire burning above the disciples' heads. And as they circle around this fire, the disciples dance with a joy that is striking both in its individuality (glimpsed in a diversity of colorful patterns and gestures) and its commonality: they are vitalized and unified in the movement of one Spirit. As the fire fills the space (and the disciples), it burns but does not consume.

While the triple-peaked blue line at the top of the image (known in Thai as a sinthao) commonly connotes holy space in Buddhist art, we might also wonder if in this context it might serve as a kind of stylized mountain range—a possibility that is interesting to the extent that it amalgamates an interior space and a landscape into one structure. After all, this event opens ever-outward: The singular event of Pentecost at a particular time and "in one place" (Acts 2:1) immediately has worldwide implications articulated in many times and places and sociocultural forms, as evidenced by the very existence of this painting (and this book). This is further alluded to in Chinnawong's depiction of the disciples: he has not rendered twelve Jewish apostles but a community of eleven Thai Christians, including both men and women and even one child. This is an icon of the outpouring of the Spirit reiterating "in Jerusalem, in all Judea and Samaria, and to the ends of the earth" (Acts 1:8). ✦

First, the charismatic explosion around the world has led scholars to ask why this form of Christianity has emerged at the vanguard of the religion's transition from the Euro-American north to the global south (Poewe 1994). While various political, economic, and social theories have been suggested to explain renewalism's phenomenal growth, the specifically religious character of the movement begs for further consideration. Might it be that the enthusiastic dimensions of charismatic renewal map well onto indigenous religious traditions worldwide? This is the thesis of Harvard religion professor Harvey Cox (1995): renewal spirituality is multiplying because it participates in what he calls a "primal spirituality" constituted by embodied encounters with the divine, ecstatic speech (like speaking in tongues), and wondrous healing. While renewalists themselves have long been quick to deflect any observations about similarities with shamanic practices and cultures—Spirit Baptism has been compared to spirit-possession; visions and dreams to shamanic flight; pentecostal healing to traditionalist practices of healing; and pentecostal blessing to indigenous religious rites of prosperity—the phenomenological similarities are noticeable (cf. Murphy 1994). So even as the theological differences are stark, is it possible that charismatic spirituality opens up windows into transcendence similar to what has been claimed by indigenous religions for millennia?

Second, even if one were to resist the comparison with shamanist traditions, there is no denying that the dreams and visions at the heart of historic charismatic spirituality also have played prevalent roles in indigenous cultures. Dreams and visions are woven throughout the scriptural traditions and have long been a staple of encounters with the divine in the Christian tradition (Kelsey 1974; Pilch 2004). Globalization trends have brought to awareness the religious aspects of dreams and visions around the world (Bulkeley 2008). The prominence of spirituality, even among the non- or less-religious folk in the modern West, has prompted a range of analytic approaches, especially to the phenomenon of dreams (e.g., Strickling 2007). Renewalists might say that it is the one true God who appears to them in their dreams, while it is deceiving demons that appear to non-Christians in theirs. This too simplistic response begs for alternative theological explanations.

Third, following on these two points, what about the renewalist claim in the late modern world that God speaks, reveals himself, and interacts with people in a very personal way? In effect this is the fundamental conviction at the heart of charismatic spirituality: that God is involved in the daily routines of people's lives. Even those who are open to the idea are skeptical that much can be known about *how* God engages the world, particularly given what is known about how the world works as illuminated by modern science. When the renewalist relationship with God is scrutinized, what emerges is a deep communal ethos, extensive mentoring relationships, distinctive embodied practices, affective and psychological dispositions, and, at a more structural level, specific neurophysiological capacities enacted, among other factors that facilitate charismatic spiritual intensity (see Luhrmann 2012). There is a tendency, then, among those who are more scientistically inclined, to reduce renewalism to socioeconomic forces, personality types, or even neurological correlates.

Hence, if by and large the history of renewal spirituality ought to be understood in terms of the tensions between the charismatic and institutional dimensions of the church ecumenical, the contemporary global context raises interreligious and even interdisciplinary scientific questions about how to develop a theology of the spiritual gifts. Our reconsideration of what the New Testament says and the constructive formulations following ought to keep these elements in mind. It is perhaps uncanny, then, to find Paul's admonitions to the Corinthian congregation relevant to a very different global context almost two thousand years later.

3.3 Pauline Charismology: A Dialogue with the Corinthians

We begin with 1 Corinthians 12, both because it is what is referenced in article 10 and it is where Paul's own thoughts about the charismata are more comprehensively detailed. Most obviously, the charismata are dispensed to individuals in a sense sovereignly by the one Spirit of God (12:4-6, 11). Yet the workings of the Spirit are framed both christologically and ecclesiologically. We proceed first to the latter, following out Paul's argument in the rest of the epistle, before returning to the former, more fundamental motif.

In light of the contested history of ecclesial responses to renewal movements, it is noteworthy that Paul's own discussion of the operation of the charismata is set within his broader concerns about the health of the church as the people of God (Martin 1984). What Paul insists on is that the one Spirit who dispenses many gifts does so to many members of the one body of Christ. In effect, then, the many gifts define the many members, even as the many members are recipients and conduits of the diverse charismata. But more pointedly, there is no hierarchy to the gifts of the Spirit—except insofar as they are motivated by and manifest in love (1 Cor 12:31–13:3)—so there is none also with respect to the members of the body. This undermined the exalted self-understanding of certain members of the Corinthian congregation as it related to their giftedness, knowledge, reputation, and social standing within the wider community (see also 1:26). Rather, "God has so arranged the body, giving the greater honour to the [apparently] inferior member" (12:24b). In other words, each member, given distinct gifts, makes essential and unique contributions to the body, and should be recognized and appreciated as such.

FIGURE 3.3

Images of Pentecost always refer in at least two directions at once. Not only do they depict and remember the historical events of Acts 2, they also celebrate and anticipate a present and hoped-for reality: the active presence of the Holy Spirit in the church. For this reason, Pentecost icons often deliberately conflate multiple events into one image. For instance, St. Paul often appears in these images (here at the top right of the apostolic semicircle, opposite Peter), even though his conversion does not happen until Acts 9—four to six years after the events of Acts 2 (cf. fig. 2.3). Similarly, Luke and Mark are sometimes also included, although they are not named as being present in Acts 1–2. The gathering shown here is thus not a synchronic representation of the early church, which is why it is often titled The Descent of the Holy Spirit *rather than simply Pentecost. The implication is that the Holy Spirit's filling is not isolated to a single event but is potentially repeated at any time and place, a concept visually reinforced by the arrangement of the apostles into a semicircular shape, inferring that Christians of every era are to perpetually complete the circle.*

At the bottom of the image—in another semicircle—an elderly king stands against a dark background. Iconographic traditions often refer to him as

"Cosmos": he represents the nations of the earth (the "world" of human power structures), not creation per se. He wears a crown of earthly authority, but he resides "in darkness and in the shadow of death" (Luke 1:79; cf. Isa 9:2), and he is aged with the corruptibility of the world. He also holds a cloth containing twelve sealed scrolls of apostolic teaching. Though he currently stands in darkness, the entire composition is organized around him and directed toward him. The descent of the Holy Spirit has not only reached individuals; it turns the apostles toward one another and toward the "cosmos." Indeed, this event will propel them into every corner of the earth, ultimately to the effect that "in our own languages we hear them speaking about God's deeds of power" (Acts 2:11). ✦

Thus while not minimizing the role of the charismata, Paul nevertheless subordinates them to "a still more excellent way" (12:31b), the way of love. Not only are the manifestations nothing without love (13:2-3), but love neither ends nor fails (13:8), and it remains the greatest (13:13b) expression of church. So desires for the gifts could be encouraged only if the members of the body follow and pursue after the way of redemptive love (14:1; see also Arrington 1978a: ch. 8). Hence also in his Letter to the Romans, Paul's discussion of the gifts of grace—"gifts that differ according to the grace given to us: prophecy, in proportion to faith; ministry, in ministering; the teacher, in teaching; the exhorter, in exhortation; the giver, in generosity; the leader, in diligence; the compassionate, in cheerfulness" (Rom 12:6-8)—occurs in the broader context of his exhortation that love must be genuinely and sincerely expressed (12:9). The whole point about the charisms is that they are given to individuals in the body of Christ who "are members one of another" (12:5b). As such, members will or ought to use their gifts to love and bless others (12:10-21).

While we will say more about the gift of the Spirit as the baptism of love in the next chapter, for now it is important to highlight that the charismata does not exalt the spiritually gifted member but will instead build up, encourage, and console others (1 Cor 14:3; also Schatzmann 1987). So, for instance, Paul spends a good deal of time discussing prophecy and tongues, all in order to emphasize "that the church may be built up" (14:5b; also 14:12b, 17, 26b, 31b). Elizabeth becomes prototypical in her being filled with the Spirit and immediately blessing Mary, her visitor. Similarly, the ministry gifts in Ephesians are not designed for ministerial acclaim but "to equip the saints for the work of ministry, for building up the body of Christ" (Eph 4:12).

If so, then assessment of the veracity of the gifts—either the charismata (in 1 Cor 12) or the ministerial (in Eph 4)—is the prerogative of the body that receives them. "If anyone speaks in a tongue, let there be only two or at most three, and each in turn; and let one interpret" (1 Cor 14:27), and "Let two or three prophets speak, and let the others weigh what is said" (14:29). The point is that attention is not to be placed on the conduits of the gifts but on whether they are uplifting, and the latter can only be discerned by the members of the body. When this happens, the charismata serve the congregation, and the church flourishes so as to provide a healthy context for charismatic expression (see Njiru 2002).

Part of the challenge related to the misuse and perhaps even abuse of prophecy and tongues at Corinth may have had to do with how some congregants had a false sense of superspirituality given their giftedness in certain areas. To revert to the language introduced in the last chapter, certain Corinthian members may have misunderstood that their not lacking in any of the spiritual gifts (1 Cor 1:17) signaled the eschatological age was being fully realized in their midst and that this left little or no room for future eschatological fulfillment. Paul was thus concerned to emphasize that the times of completion and perfection remained in the future and that "now we see in a mirror, dimly, but then we will see face to face" (13:12a). In this vein, he corrected the Corinthian misunderstanding that the resurrection had already occurred or that there would be no future resurrection (15:12), and he expended a great deal of effort showing the importance of this perspective (1 Cor 15). The charismata are not signs that the end of the age has fully arrived. Rather, they are present indicators that point to the coming age (Arrington 1978b). Note in this regard also that the brief reference to the charisms in 1 Peter 4:10-11—"Like good stewards of the manifold grace of God, serve one another with whatever gift each of you has received. Whoever speaks must do so as one speaking the very words of God; whoever serves must do so with the strength that God supplies"—also occur within an eschatological context. They are to be worked out during that time when the "end of all things is near" (1 Pet 4:7), in a sense anticipating and heralding the age to come.

Such was also the case with the ministry of Jesus, whose signs and wonders touched others and announced the reign of God was at hand. Comparison with the signs performed by Jesus invites Christians to revisit the christological dimension of the charismata that Paul commended. The manifestations of the Spirit build up the body of Christ under the lordship of Christ (1 Cor 12:3). But note that Christ's lordship was not only of worldly or conventional power. Rather it involved the salvation of others even as it involved his self-effacement, ultimately leading to his death (Phil 2:5-8). This invites consideration about the gifts of the Spirit as the gifts of Jesus himself, and thus as representative of his person. After all, as seen in the previous chapter, the Spirit's outpouring is itself a work of the ascended Christ. With this turn, the christomorphic and even cruciform character of the gifts looms larger.

The Corinthian letter itself suggests this as most appropriate for developing a theology of the charismata. After all, as already noted, the congregants' major problems were self-elevated perspectives regarding their wisdom, giftedness, and social standing. All of this contributed to a factious, individualistic Corinthian Christianity that lacked christological focus and displayed misguided eschatological sensibilities (see Furnish 1999: 11–12). Paul's corrective was to talk not of the exploits, gifts, and capacities of the Corinthians but about Christ and his cross (1 Cor 1:18–2:5; also Brown 1995). Rather than affirming the Corinthian theology of glory, what was needed was a theology of the cross. This perspective makes better sense, then, of Paul's linking the charismata to ecclesiology, in particular his emphasis on the diversity of members as including the indispensability of those who are thought to be weaker (1 Cor 12:22). In fact, not only are these presumably weaker members essential, but they are to be "treated with greater respect" and honor (12:23b, 24b) and all members ought to "have the same care for one another" (12:25b). Notice here two important truths. First, the apparently weaker members also have gifts, and thus gifts are not signs of superiority as defined by the world's conventions. Second, any expression of the gifts, even by those deemed more honorable, are not for their own commendation but for the sake of others.

Such a charismatic theology of the cross is consistent with Paul's theology of weakness articulated across both Corinthian letters (Savage 1996). He is particularly clear that believers ought not to boast except in their weaknesses (2 Cor 11:30; 12:5; also 1 Cor 1:31) and that the power of Christ's strength is to be found in his weakness (2 Cor 12:9-10; 13:9). More precisely, Christ "was crucified in weakness, but lives by the power of God" (13:4a). Within this crucicentric perspective, the spiritual gifts are not to be elevated as signs of the divine glory. Instead they ought to be seen as invitations to bear witness the coming reign of God, perhaps even to the point of martyrdom (Acts 1:8) and death, in ways that turn this world upside down (17:6). Recipients of the charismata, in other words, become servants who build up, edify, and encourage others, even if that involves their own self-diminishment. We shall see later (ch. 10, this volume) that even the rhythms of creation are driven by this cruciform reality. But for now, it is sufficient to insist that the people of God are most authentically the body of Christ if they follow in the footsteps of Christ's weakness, living not in human strength but in the power of the Spirit of the crucified lord (Dawn 2001).

In sum, the charismata and other gifts of the Spirit, at least in light of the Pauline witness, are ecclesiologically funded with both a christological focus and an eschatological horizon. Such an ecclesial foundation does not mean that only those who are within the church are edified. As shall be seen, the common good of the church inevitably spills out into the wider community, and in that sense the eschatological character of the gifts provides a foretaste of the coming age. Yet the cruciform character of the gifts means that they serve not to magnify their recipients but to bless others. Of course, the fallen character of the members of the body of Christ means that the church often does not live up to this Pauline ideal (e.g., Ndubuisi 2003). So what are the steps to take from here toward formulating a constructive theology of the charismata in a global context?

3.4 Surprised by the Holy Spirit!

The following triangulates toward a contemporary charismology by moving from theology to ecclesiology-anthropology and then to missiology. Any contemporary theology of the charismata ought to begin with the Spirit of God and end with the purposes of God. Along the way we will take up the most important historical issues previously discussed, especially in the central part of this fourth section.

The first thing to say about a theology of the charismata is to reiterate that they derive from the Spirit of God in and from Christ. Their operation according to the divine economy means that their appearance may confound human expectations normed according to the world's standards. Thus charismatically inspired prophecy, words of wisdom, and words of knowledge will illuminate the world in ways inaccessible to natural human minds (see 1 Cor 2:9-16). In large part for this reason, the workings of the Spirit's manifestations will often surprise, if not confound. There will be elements of ambiguity and unanticipated novelty in what the Spirit achieves (see Suurmond 1994). When the Spirit "shows up," the impossible becomes possible, and the dead end opens up to a new beginning (see Wariboko 2012). Christians therefore engage with the charismatic life only if they become docile and vulnerable to the unanticipated character of the Spirit whose wind blows "where it chooses, and you hear the sound of it, but you do not know where it comes from or where it goes" (John 3:8).

Any discussion of the "new" accomplished by the charismata will need to address the nature of such novelty. Most pressing for cessationists are claims regarding "new revelations" of the Spirit. While fuller discussion of this important matter will have to wait until the final chapter on the doctrine of revelation, suffice it to say for now that the eschatological reign of God toward which the redemption and renewal of creation is called involves genuinely new things that God is seeking to accomplish, beyond any restoration to a primordial garden of Eden. In fact, human maturation into the image and likeness of the second Adam dictates that the abode of the first Adam (in the Genesis narrative) also undergoes a kind of cosmic refurbishing (in Rev 21–22) such that the primeval garden is now set within the heavenly city. If that is the case, then not only do we now see in part, but "what we will be has not yet been revealed. What we do know is this: when he is revealed, we will be like him, for we will see him as he is" (1 John 3:2). So if God's redemption in Christ by the Spirit involves what has not yet been fully disclosed, then there is no reason to think that the charismatic work of the Spirit will also not unveil that mystery with ever greater clarity.

Of course, Christ remains the material and concrete climax of revelation, and the apostolic tradition as preserved in the canon of Scripture constitutes the normative criterion of that revelation. Hence anything that contradicts the image of God in Christ as asserted by the scriptural witness cannot be of the Spirit, who enables confession of Jesus' lordship. However, what does not clearly controvert the biblical testimony to the living Christ will need to be discerned in an ongoing way. It may be that in the end, such will illuminate glorious aspects of God in Christ now only dimly understood; it may also be that in that day, even some who say "Lord, Lord," will be exposed for the deceptive lie that they are, because they mouth but do not embody his cruciform life (see Matt 7:21-23).

The second set of considerations regarding the charismata concerns their ecclesial and anthropological dimension. As already seen, an understanding of the spiritual gifts cannot be gained apart from the diversity of the body and its many members. Arguably, the many gifts of the Spirit empower the healthy parts and roles that constitute the one body. Three corollary theses present themselves within such an ecclesiological charismology.

1. There is a sense in which the gifts of the Spirit operate under proper ecclesial authority (e.g., Carson 1987: ch. 4). After all, "God is a God not of disorder but of peace" (1 Cor 14:33), and hence "all things should be done decently and in order" (14:40). Simultaneously, the ministerial leaders (or servants)

of the body of Christ facilitate rather than control the manifestations of the Spirit. Proper discernment and judgment of whatever charismata appear remain the responsibility of the body as a whole (14:29-31). As God is no respecter of persons (see Acts 10:34), not only are the gifts not signs of privilege they are also not arbitrarily limited in their dispensations. Men and women, sons and daughters, young and old, rich and poor—all are potential recipients and all have responsibility to be channels of the Spirit's ministry through the body of Christ (see Stronstad 1999). The charismatic life thus has to be lived within, without collapsing into, this tension of hierarchically ordered democratic giftings, or (to put it another way), of democratically empowered hierarchical authorities.

2. Under the preceding rule, none, neither male nor female, should provoke disorder, indecency, or indecorousness. This is the best way to understand the specific reference to wives in the Corinthian congregation, especially the ways in which their ecclesial behaviors shamelessly exhibited unruliness and insubordination (14:34-35). When operative according to the Spirit of Christ, however, women are among those whom the Spirit fills (e.g., Acts 2:17-18) and empowers to bless and build up others (as our discussion of Elizabeth above illuminates). After all, the Spirit dispenses the charismata as the Spirit wills, even upon those members of the body who are perceived as lacking honor. There is no indication that women are excluded in the various roles that constitute the ministry of the body of Christ. (This important issue will be touched upon further later.)

3. That the gifts derive from God and are graciously dispensed does not mean that they are supernatural in the modernist sense (see Yong 2005: ch. 7). Enlightenment rationalism distinguished what behaved according to natural laws versus what was thought to happen "supernaturally" due only to divine activity. The earliest Christians did not operate according to such a dichotomous understanding of the natural and the supernatural. Rather there are various spiritual gifts, some more charismatic (such as those in 1 Cor 12) and others less so (as in Rom 12; Eph 4; 1 Pet 4)—yet the latter are no less gracious endowments of God's Spirit. On the other hand, once the natural–supernatural dichotomy is rejected, there is a special but no less real sense in which the charisms

of the Spirit can be nurtured. This is the point of discipleship within charismatic communities: those more mature in
the faith are able to mentor novices, with the latter learning
from their exemplars in relational apprenticeships (see Mühlen 1978). In other words, there are basic human processes
through which the gifts can be developed and cultivated, and
these are open to study via the human sciences. This anthropological dimension does not require a reductionist view of
the charismata. Instead, it challenges believers to see how
God both transcends and yet works within and through the
historical processes of the world God has made. Life in the
Spirit unfolds organically in a divinely ordered incubation
that is the church, or to put it otherwise, in the body of Christ
and through the fellowship or communion of God's breath.

We will return in chapter 8 to further discuss the notions of miracles
in ways that go beyond the natural–supernatural duality. For the moment,
however, the important point to be made is that in a post-Enlightenment
world, we can accept both that God works charismatically by the Spirit
and that this does not eliminate the integrity of creation's processes, themselves provided for by God. This means that people of no or other faith
may also be tapping into the potentiality inherent in humankind made
in the image of God and resident in the creation imbued by the power of
God. Thus shamanist, indigenous, and even other religious traditions may
in one or another respect participate in the cosmic work of God, even if
they may not interface with Christ's saving character. Even Corinthian
prophecy, it has been shown, exhibits both continuity and discontinuity
with its surrounding first-century environment. While not rooted substantially in Hellenistic parallels, a degree of phenomenological and even
experiential similarity can be discerned (Forbes 1995). Yet the purposes of
Christian prophecy—not to mention tongues and interpretations, as well
as dreams and visions—were different, designed as they were to bring
about repentance and conversion to Christ (1 Cor 14).

This leads to the ministerial and missiological dimension of charismology. The spiritual gifts are bestowed by God upon and exercised by the
body of Christ and its members for the common good of both the church
and the world. The charismatic manifestations of the Spirit are never for
the self-aggrandizement of those so equipped but are rather intended to
accomplish God's mission of renewing, restoring, and redeeming the
world amid its brokenness. This extends the thesis regarding the pentecostal outpouring of the Spirit in Acts 2 as directed toward the renewal and

restoration of Israel, the concern of both Lukan volumes (see Turner 1996; Yong 2011a). The point to be made is that the gift of the Spirit himself and the Spirit's gifts in each instance are intended to enhance faith in the living Christ. The overarching goal is practical and teleological: to announce, initiate, and inaugurate the reign of God in Christ, which is what heals, transforms, and saves the world. That which builds up the many members of Christ's body also in turn serves the wider common good—the world, in which the church exists, albeit of which it is not. Thus even as the world may already participate in the Spirit's gifts in some respect, there is no minimizing of the church's charismatic mission and evangelical witness to illuminate the mystery of Christ that fulfills the world's longings. In all of this, Spirit-filled believers act not on their own initiative but under the guidance and enablement of the divine breath.

In the end, then, the gifts of the Spirit are less abstract ideas to be debated than they are divine instruments accomplishing God's renewing, redemptive, and salvific purposes. This is precisely what article 10 of the SF communicates. The point of expecting God to accomplish something new is not so human beings can receive the glory that belongs to God alone, but so they may participate more and more fully in the unpredictable nature of God's saving the cosmos. The degree to which the charisms transcend the world highlights the discontinuity between the present fallen order and the future redeemed cosmos. Yet the degree to which the charisms are Spirit-initiated irruptions from within the present order of things reflects the continuities between the world understood as divinely created and the renewed cosmos of God. There is therefore assurance both that the works of the Spirit of order will check, even judge, the chaos of the present fallen world and that the surprises of the Spirit will rightly reorder the world in anticipation of the coming rule of God. Such a charismology may also open up new vistas for understanding the classical pentecostal theology of Spirit Baptism and its initial sign of speaking in other tongues.

FIGURE 3.4

This depiction of the Pentecost event follows many of the standard formulae: the Holy Spirit (depicted in the form of the dove that appears in Christ's baptism; cf. figs. 1.4, 4.3, and 4.4) descends with beams of light onto a tightly grouped early church, which turns its attention heavenward. This particular portrayal is unusual, however, in its strong visual parallels with depictions of the nativity. As with most nativity scenes, Mary sits centrally in the composition with her head turned downward, thankfully meditating on what God has done. Traditionally, nativity scenes make at least two significant points: (1) God has come among us in the radically particular form of a lower-middle-class Jewish Palestinian child (who temporarily takes up residence in a feeding trough), and (2) it seems that only those on the margins (or even entirely outside) of Christ's own first-century Jewish culture—shepherds and foreign astrologers—seem to recognize the tremendous gravity of what is happening. When van Dyck visually rhymes Pentecost with nativity he beckons us to interpretively connect the two events, seeing intertextual similarities, continuities, and mutual implications.

On the one hand, this prompts us to consider the giving of the Spirit in Acts 2 as parallel to and a direct extension of the incarnation. Gabriel's words of annunciation to Mary are directly echoed in Jesus' postresurrection words to his disciples: in both cases the Holy Spirit will "come upon you" (Luke 1:35; Acts 1:8). Further, the anointing baptism of the Son is directly connected to the anointing baptism of the church in the Spirit (Luke 3:16; Acts 1:5)—a connection made in this image by rendering the Spirit in the form of a dove. On the other hand, in the same way that the nativity features those on the margins of Jewish culture who are welcomed into adoration of the Christ child, so too Pentecost represents a radical opening up toward and inclusion of people from all nations and languages into the people of God and into adoration of the risen Christ. ✦

Discussion Questions

1. What are some aspects of your church's teachings about the spiritual gifts, different from the preceding discussion, that attempt to understand the gifts eschatologically, ecclesiologically, christologically, and missionally? Are these differences complementary or are they contradictory, and if the latter, what are possible responses to these divergent views?

2. Are the various lists of gifts in the New Testament exhaustive or representative of the Spirit's gifts? What are the implications for doctrine and practice of our response to this question?

3. Have you or people you know had personal experiences of prophecies, dreams, visions, and other charismata? How does the preceding chapter help you to understand such and perhaps interact with such going forward?

Further Reading

Cordes, Paul Josef. 1997. *Call to Holiness: Reflections on the Catholic Charismatic Renewal.* Collegeville, Minn.: Liturgical.

Grudem, Wayne A. 1988. *The Gift of Prophecy: In the New Testament and Today.* Westchester, Ill.: Crossway.

Koenig, John. 1978. *Charismata: God's Gifts for God's People.* Philadelphia: Westminster.

Lovelace, Richard F. 1979. *Dynamics of Spiritual Life: An Evangelical Theology of Renewal.* Downers Grove, Ill.: InterVarsity.

Turner, Max. 1998. *The Holy Spirit and Spiritual Gifts in the New Testament Church and Today.* Rev. ed. Peabody, Mass.: Hendrickson.

4

The Baptism in the Holy Spirit

A Salvation-Historical Perspective

World Assemblies of God Fellowship Statement of Faith
—Article 9: The Baptism in the Holy Spirit

We believe that the baptism in the Holy Spirit is the bestowing of the believer with power for life and service for Christ. This experience is distinct from and subsequent to the new birth, is received by faith, and is accompanied by the manifestation of speaking in tongues as the Spirit gives utterance as the initial evidence (Luke 24:49; Acts 1:8; 2:1-4; 8:15-19; 11:14-17; 19:1-7).

4.1 Peter's Journey in the Spirit

The baptism of the Holy Spirit and its accompanying evidential sign of speaking in tongues (glossolalia) has been long recognized as the distinctive "crown jewel" or most important feature of pentecostal teaching and practice (see Macchia 2006: 20). This is one of the chief, if not sole, elements historically setting apart classical Pentecostalism from charismatic and other renewal expressions of Christianity. This chapter thus begins by sketching the life of Peter embedded in the gospel accounts, because Peter's experience illuminates the major thrusts of this article and more. We shall see that Peter's infilling with the Spirit enabled his powerful, even if imperfect, witness to the risen Christ even as we also can come to appreciate the richness and range of testimony to a Spirit-baptized life.

In many respects, Peter's was an ordinary life for his place and time (Foakes-Jackson 1927; McBirnie 1973: ch. 3). His father, John (Matt 16:17; John 1:42), named him Simon, and he grew up with at least one brother, Andrew (Matt 4:18; John 1:40; 6:8), in the adjacent towns of Capernaum and Bethsaida (Mark 1:21, 29; John 1:44) near the Sea of Galilee (also called the Lake of Gennesaret—Luke 5:1). As the brothers earned their living as fishermen (Luke 5:2-3; John 21:3), we are not surprised to find out about their lack of formal education (Acts 4:13). Later,

Peter married, and his mother-in-law stayed with him (cf. Matt 8:14-15; Mark 1:29-31; Luke 4:38-39), although we know little else about his family and children (Hengel 2010: 103–10). By the time of the beginning of his public ministry, he does not appear to be affluent (Acts 3:6), although there is no way to know if this is because he had voluntarily divested himself of his home or other accumulations to follow Jesus (see Matt 19:27; Luke 18:28; cf. Matt 26:33-35).

Later, his life of ministry brings him to the Mediterranean coastal town of Joppa, where he is hosted in the home of one Simon the tanner (Acts 9:43; 10:6, 32). There is no indication of how long this arrangement persisted, whether or not it included his family, or the degree to which Simon supported Peter's ministry. If throughout he appears to have lived a faithful Jewish life, at least as understood in terms of following its dietary laws (see Acts 10:14), his willingness to stay with a tanner who processed dead animal hides into finished leather indicates he may already have been willing to rethink previous taboos. Tradition—of which there are various sorts regarding Peter, some of which were rightly rejected by the early church—reports that the end of his life was marked by suffering and eventually martyrdom in Rome (perhaps intimated in Luke 22:31-32 and John 21:18-23).

Peter is also known to have been with the Twelve (now minus Judas) and other believers in the Upper Room when they were all "filled with the Holy Spirit and began to speak in other languages" (Acts 2:4; also 4:8). He was certainly empowered to bear witness to the living Christ, beginning with his sermon to the onlookers in Jerusalem on the day of Pentecost, which resulted in 3,000 baptisms. Up until Acts 15, Peter emerges as the key leader of the young messianic movement, manifesting the gifts of the Spirit, including the word of knowledge (vis-à-vis Ananias and Sapphira in 5:1-11 and Simon Magus in 8:20-23) and faith, healing, and miracles on various occasions (3:1-6; 5:15; 9:32-42). From a classical pentecostal perspective, Peter's boldness on the day of Pentecost contrasts with his earlier cowardice, in particular his threefold denial of Christ.

Yet there is no need to overemphasize the discontinuities between the pre- and post-Pentecost Peter. The gospel accounts give plenty of evidence of Peter's impetuous and bold personality before his Spirit Baptism. Peter is not reticent to speak out from, if not for, the group of disciples (e.g., Matt 15:15; 18:21; Mark 13:3; Luke 8:45; 12:41). He appears to have established himself, perhaps along with James and John, as a leader among the Twelve (Mark 16:7; Acts 1:15), as evidenced also by how Jesus treats and interacts with him vis-à-vis the other disciples (e.g., Matt 26:40; Luke 8:51) and by his accompanying Jesus to the Mount of Transfiguration and the garden of Gethsemane. And this prominence seems to have been recognized by outsiders as well (Matt 17:24; John 20:2). Perhaps in part for these reasons, plus his recognition of Jesus' messiahship, Jesus renames him Cephas—Greek, meaning "the rock"—and says that "on this rock I will build my church, and the gates of Hades will not prevail against it. I will give you the keys of the kingdom of heaven, and whatever you bind on earth will be bound in heaven, and whatever you loose on earth will be loosed in heaven" (Matt 16:18-19). In short, while there is no denying that Peter, as with the others in the Upper Room, was indeed "clothed with power from on high" for his apostolic ministry as Jesus promised (Luke 24:49b), this empowerment worked with the character and dispositions that were already obvious in the years leading up to the Pentecost event.

FIGURE 4.1

The primary source of light in this otherwise dark image emanates from a single candle in the very center of the composition. The servant girl of the high priest holds this candle as she stands on the central axis of the painting interrogating

Peter: "You also were with Jesus, the man from Nazareth" (Mark 14:67). By centralizing this servant girl (rather than Peter) and illuminating her throat and mouth, the artist allows this accusation to ring out, suspending us in the moment before Peter is able to muster an answer. He is panicking, scrambling for a response as soldiers begin to close in around him. One of these soldiers reaches toward Peter in accusation, obscuring and negating (from our point of view) the fragile light of the candle.

In the moments that follow Peter will lie: "I do not know or understand what you are talking about" (Mark 14:68). In fact, in the face of further scrutiny, he will go so far as to curse and swear an oath: "I do not know this man you are talking about!" (14:71). The significance of artistically isolating this moment—the moment of panicked deliberation before he lies—is twofold: On the one hand, it places us in greater sympathy with Peter's situation, prompting us to question the depth of our own faithfulness in the midst of radical instability, danger, and fear. On the other hand, however, by suspending Peter in a moment of speechlessness, van Honthorst creates a stronger and more direct contrast to Acts 2, where we will see this same man filled with speech. We might even reimagine the scene of Acts 2 in this same compositional format—only now the light is of an entirely different quality (perhaps a tongue of fire), and Peter speaks without hesitation: "Men of Judea and all who live in Jerusalem. . . . Let the entire house of Israel know with certainty that God has made him both Lord and Messiah, this Jesus whom you crucified" (Acts 2:14-36).

The liminality inherent in this image brings one of the central thrusts of this chapter further into view: baptism in the Holy Spirit (as exemplified in Acts 2) is divinely initiated, but it also includes and demands real human reception and response. Peter's wavering in this image is not final, but it powerfully embodies the betwixt and betweenness that we all experience and must act within. ✦

On the negative side of the ledger, being filled with and empowered by the Spirit to witness neither turns people into something they are not nor guarantees the infallibility of their testimony. Peter recognized he was a sinner when he met Jesus (see Luke 5:8), and his shortcomings were plain to see both before and after the Pentecost event. Perhaps his denial of Jesus could have been prevented if he had persevered in watchful prayer the evening before in the garden with Jesus rather than being weak in spirit and sleepy in body. Yet even after being filled with the Spirit and realizing that "God has shown me that I should not call anyone [even Gentiles] profane or unclean" (Acts 10:28), he failed to follow through on this newfound understanding of what it meant to be the people of God.

Apparently staying with a Jewish tanner was all right, but eating with Gentiles who were strangers was not, even if they were followers of Jesus the Messiah. His hypocrisy of not sharing table fellowship with Gentiles was confronted by Paul at Antioch (Gal 2:11-14). Clearly being filled with the Spirit empowered his witness, but that neither negated his personal dispositions nor rendered him immune to the fears, anxieties, and concerns of life. Peter the "rock" was also Peter the hypocrite. Yet his course of ambiguity (see Perkins 1994) can also be considered as part and parcel of the Spirit-filled life.

4.2 Spirit Baptism: Quests for Understanding

There are at least three aspects of article 9 that ought to be addressed before the end of this chapter. First, what is the nature of the baptism in the Holy Spirit, and what purposes does it serve? Second, is baptism in the Spirit "distinct from and subsequent to the new birth," and if so, how ought such distinction and subsequence be understood? Finally, how should the evidential character of speaking in tongues in relationship to Spirit Baptism be comprehended? The following more historical overviews, in particular case studies in the Puritan and the Wesleyan-Holiness traditions, provide some background for appreciating how renewalist approaches to evidential tongues and being filled with the Spirit are both continuous with the broader Christian tradition on the one hand, but novel on the other hand.

Yet the narrative approach to the topic through the life of Peter calls attention to the fact that doctrinal statements are always more generalized summaries of human experiences that usually resist neat systematization. Hence the following historical, biblical, and theological reflections are efforts to make sense of the apostolic revelation and how that has given shape to the Christian tradition and its various permutations. Within this larger scheme of things, the doctrine of Spirit Baptism ought not to be abstracted from the broader Christian life (see Menzies 2013). In that sense, this exploration both presumes the preceding two chapters even as it anticipates the rest of this book.

4.2.1 The Puritan and Reformed Quest for Assurance

The notion of tongues-speech (or glossolalia) as evidence of Spirit Baptism would be anomalous at best and indecipherable at worst if not situated within the Christian tradition, particularly as played out in the New World. An antecedent that can provide some perspective is the Puritan quest for assurance of divine election. This Puritan preoccupation needs to be understood against the backdrop of a seventeenth-century colonial theology that defined the North American experiment as fulfilling and completing the Protestant Reformation, which was by then fragmenting and breaking down in the Old World (see Stoever 1978). Within this anxiety-laden context, Calvin's doctrine of assurance, centered on the inner witness of the Holy Spirit in the soul to the trustworthiness of Scriptures' promises about God's preserving grace, was not quite sufficient. The need to provide a greater sense of confirmation was heightened especially in light of the assumption that those who did not show clear signs of persevering to the end evidenced ultimately that they had not been among the company of the elect.

For the Puritans, such concerns were exacerbated by the fact that succeeding generations of children raised by Christian parents more often lacked the inner witness their parents received with their own conversion experience. But could the children of these children (the grandchildren) be baptized? Theologically and ecclesiologically, adjudication of such matters resulted in various measures, including the Halfway Covenant enacted in New England in the latter half of the seventeenth century, which allowed for the baptism of such children so long as the parents submitted themselves to the discipline of the church. Part of the result was a revitalization of ecclesial life and commitments (see Pope 1969), including the understanding that the inner witness of the Spirit was now expanded to include outward exhibitions of holy living. This helped to check any antinomian tendencies that dissociated election from moral living. Yet simultaneously, these Spirit-wrought outward displays—understood theologically as manifestations of the "seal of the Holy Spirit" (Eph 1:13)—also provided communally recognized assurances of divine election that prevented some from despairing about their salvific status before God (see Lederle 1988: 5–9). The Great Awakening revivals of the next two centuries were unconventional ecclesial contexts that facilitated conversion experiences and invited further communal discernment regarding the signs of assurance.

Developments during the middle to the late nineteenth century opened up a number of other venues in the Reformed tradition that anticipated the pentecostal revival. Controversial revivalist Charles Grandison Finney (1792–1875) reacted to the Old School Presbyterian theology but yet remained within the Reformed orbit. Important for our purposes is Finney's teaching that the baptism of the Holy Spirit was a repeated experience subsequent to salvation that enabled sanctification and empowered believers for Christian service (see Gresham 1987). Reformed evangelical successors of Finney's revivalism such as D. L. Moody (1837–1899), A. J. Gordon (1836–1895), and R. A. Torrey (1856–1928) would minimize sanctification and emphasize Spirit Baptism in terms of its empowerment for testimony and service (see Dayton 1985). Meanwhile, the Higher Life movement promoted after 1875 through conventions at Keswick, England, was more concerned about connecting the work of the Holy Spirit to holiness than were the Reformed evangelical revivalists, albeit without neglecting the theme of empowerment. Toward the end of the century, Higher Life ministers were advocating a postconversion "second blessing" that fostered faith, godliness, piety, and Christian service (e.g., Murray 1898: 168–72), as well as a baptism in the Holy Spirit that sets apart and enables sanctified lives for the task of world mission and evangelization (see Gilbertson 1993).

This all-too-quick review of strands of Reformed Puritanism and evangelical Christianity in North America demonstrates that the descendants of Calvin did not rest content with the notion of salvation as merely a single work of grace. At least in practice, if not theologically, the quest for assurance pressed the question of what signs, if any, could provide indications of God's saving work. This in turn invited further consideration about postconversion experiences of God, whether related to assurance, sanctification, or empowerment of the Christian life.

4.2.2 The Wesleyan-Holiness Search for Perfection

Many of the nineteenth century developments in the revivalist and Keswickian streams of the Reformed tradition intersected with Wesleyan-Holiness trajectories both in England and in North America. We turn now to pick up on especially the American Holiness tradition of the second half of the nineteenth century because of its key contributions to the distinctive pentecostal doctrine (see Dayton 1987). In the wake of Finney's influence, Holiness preachers and writers would tighten the connection between baptism in the Holy Spirit and sanctification. William Arthur's (1819–1901) *The Tongue of Fire* (1856), Phoebe Palmer's (1807–1874) *Promise of the Father* (1859), and Asa Mahan's (1799–1889) *The Baptism of the Holy Ghost* (1870) are representative of Methodist and Holiness works during this time that explicated the sanctifying work of the Spirit as a postconversion work of grace.

The roots of this Holiness theology of Spirit Baptism can be traced back to the founding generation of Methodism. The important Holiness doctrine of entire sanctification is rooted in John Wesley's (1703–1791) teaching that Christian conversion ought to be followed by purification and perfection. If sins were remitted in the former experience, the sinful nature itself was eradicated in the latter, and this enabled believers to pursue lives of holiness in accordance with the commandments of God (e.g., Matt 5:48; Heb 6:1; 1 John 4:12, 17). What is important to note at this juncture is that Wesley's confidant, the Englishman John Fletcher (1729–1785), made explicit the connection between the sanctifying work of God and the gift of the Holy Spirit. This pneumatological link was picked up a century later, especially in the American Holiness movement. For some, the baptism of the Spirit brought with it both sanctifying purity and empowerment for the Christian life. For others, Spirit Baptism as a second work of grace effected the cleansing of the heart, meaning an even further work of the Spirit that brought power for witness could be expected to follow.

We will return in the next chapter to unpack in more detail debates about sanctification in the Wesleyan tradition. The point to be emphasized here, however, is that Holiness thinkers continuously asked about the nature of such postconversion experiences. At one level, indications of the Spirit's sanctifying work were most obviously displayed in holy lives. Yet at another level, were there other more tangible experiences that bore witness to the Spirit's purifying or empowering works in the lives of those tarrying, waiting, and praying for them? One could easily understand why Reformed evangelical revivalists distanced themselves from associating the baptism of the Spirit with full sanctification: Christian perfection would be attained only in the coming age; hence it was pointless to look for signs of such a work of the Spirit in the present era. But for Holiness believers, if conversion as a first work of grace was apparent with repentance (among other signs), then what was sanctification (and empowerment) as a second (or third) work of grace evidenced by?

It is in this context that we can better appreciate how Holiness preachers like Charles Fox Parham (1873–1929) were searching the Scriptures to identify the signs of the Spirit's sanctifying and empowering works. Parham and his students at Bethel Bible College in Topeka, Kansas, were led to study the book of Acts. With their observation that on three separate occasions the outpouring of the Spirit resulted in tongues-speech (Acts 2; 10; 19:1-7), the die was cast. The "Bible evidence of the baptism of the Holy Ghost" (Goff 1988: 66) was the ability to speak in other tongues as the Spirit gave utterance.

4.2.3 Signs and Interpretation: Spirit Baptism in Ecumenical and Global Contexts

While the Assemblies of God in its early years of formation adopted a statement regarding what Parham called the "Bible evidence" that is very similar in intent to article 9 of the WAGF SF, differing interpretations of glossolalia emerged within the first generation of the pentecostal revival. Parham himself not only affirmed the evidential character of tongues but also emphasized that this gift of the Spirit involved the ability to speak in other actual languages so as to hasten the last days missionary proclamation of the gospel around the world in terms understandable to non-English speakers. Within the broader classical pentecostal movement there have been various formulations of how tongues functioned evidentially. Some insist that glossolalia serves only as *a physical sign* of Spirit Baptism (implying both that it may be only one of many or that other nonphysical signs may also be detected), while others debate whether it always happens immediately (as asserted by those who insist on its "initial" character) or if it could occur after an indeterminate period of time. Most radically, oneness Pentecostals, whom we shall discuss further in chapter 11, see (or hear) tongues as a sign not only of Spirit Baptism but also of the new birth, because the culmination of the latter is the infilling of the Spirit.

While most, although not all, classical pentecostal churches and denominations have embraced the evidential character of glossolalia at some level of doctrine or other, the opposite is the case for most groups associated with the charismatic renewal (see Lederle 1988). This should be expected, given the presence of the renewal in churches that have had established doctrinal traditions—mainline Protestant, Roman Catholic, and even Orthodox communities (see Stephanou 1997; Martin 1998). Roman Catholic and other charismatic theologians affiliated with historic forms of Protestantism have been drawn toward more sacramental interpretations of Spirit Baptism. While there are isolated views of Spirit Baptism as nonsacramental and repeated pneumatic impartations among Roman Catholic theologians (e.g., Sullivan 1982: ch. 5), much more prevalent is the understanding of the Spirit as given at Christian initiation (about which more in ch. 6), followed by repeatable subsequent releases, infusions, and even intensifications. Yet even others see Spirit Baptism as more or less related to what in classical terms is called the sacrament or rite of confirmation (see Wood 1980: ch. 7; Jungkuntz 1983; cf. Austin 1985). There are also a range of nonsacramental interpretations of Spirit Baptism across the charismatic renewal spectrum, although many of these are integrated in some respect with the reception of the Spirit in Christian initiation. What is widely agreed upon is the normativity of glossolalia and the other spiritual gifts for vibrant Christian life—with the notion of subsequence being interpreted in greater or lesser continuity with Christian initiation—along with the rejection of the classical pentecostal teaching of evidential tongues. Inevitably for most theologians in the charismatic renewal, the horizons and parameters of their own dogmatic traditions frame the constructs of Spirit Baptism they proffer (Yun 2003: ch. 7).

Figure 4.2

Tim Hawkinson's Pentecost *is a sprawling tree form constructed out of commonplace domestic building materials: air conditioning ducts, cylindrical sonotubes, house paint—the stuff of everyday suburban culture-making. Although painted to mimic the look of wood grain, this tree is hollow, built to conduct air, wind, "breath." Situated around the gallery are twelve humanoid figures, each hammering on the tree with a different mechanized body part—a kneecap, a toe, an ear, a nose, an Adam's apple—creating percussive sounds that reverberate through the sprawling hollow branches. And because these branches are of varying diameters, the sound each figure produces has a unique pitch in relation to all the others such that together they roughly comprise a musical octave. The individual rhythm of each figure is unremarkable, but the collective sound of all striking their respective branches creates complex rhythms that fill the tree and the space around it with a percussive glossolalia. And though not readily discernible, the compositional structures of these rhythms are all based on Christmas carols and hymns.*

This work is a startling image of the church at Pentecost: the diverse "voices" of the diverse members of the church body are enlivened and united into a single Christmas hymnody through the wind channels that comprise this pneumatological tree of life (cf. fig. 7.4). When this work was exhibited at the Whitney Museum of American Art in New York (2005), the pneumatological inflection was made even stronger, as the work was installed "upside down," such that the trunk was growing out of the ceiling, seemingly filled with a wind "from above." However, the work also helpfully embodies some of the strangeness and undecidability that attends Pentecost and the phenomena of glossolalia more generally. How, for instance, are we to interpret the whimsical materiality of this work? On the one hand, Hawkinson's use of home-improvement building materials situates the transformative movement of the Spirit in terms of the common (sub)urban structures and spaces of our lives (cf. fig. 5.5). On the other hand, the conspicuous constructedness of the work raises helpful questions about the social constructedness of tongues-speech. The content of the "speech" in this work is profound and particular—celebrations of Christmas (incarnation)—although not in a readily discernible form, leaving us feeling somewhat "amazed and perplexed, saying to one another, 'What does this mean?'" (Acts 2:12). ✦

The emergence of the charismatic renewal also motivated reexamination of the biblical data regarding the baptism of the Spirit. The most long-standing challenges to classical pentecostal interpretations have been arguments that the baptism of the Spirit occurs at conversion and regeneration, even if the spiritual gifts can be expected to follow an engaged Christian life (see Bruner 1970; Dunn 1970; cf. Fee 1991: ch. 7). Pentecostals, of course, have provided apologies for the subsequential nature of Spirit Baptism, utilizing various hermeneutical methodologies (e.g., Ervin 1987; Menzies and Menzies 2000; Hunter 2009). But for charismatics, even those who affirm the purpose of Spirit Baptism as empowering witness will often not go all the way in accepting the "crown jewel" teaching of evidential tongues (e.g., Shelton 1991).

Before taking up the more constructive tasks of this chapter, one more comment about glossolalia in global context needs to be noted. The heterogeneity of renewal especially across the global south means that no one understanding of Spirit Baptism has attained consensus. In fact, as will be shown later (ch. 8, this volume), healing may be more prevalent globally than glossolalia. But not only is there a diversity of interpretations, even the expressions of tongues-speaking are different. In many respects, Western renewal manifestations of tongues are rather tame and domesticated when compared to their expressions elsewhere. As renewal Christianity has been adapted in contexts largely dominated by indigenous religious traditions with their own rituals of spirit-possession, the phenomenological similarities between Spirit Baptism (baptism in the Holy Spirit) and spirit-possession have been striking. Marked by trance-like and dissociated states of consciousness, as well as vigorous kinetic behavior and rhythmic movements (Goodman 1972: 123–27), Spirit Baptism obviously varies in its form across cultures. How then ought we to think about the nature and purpose of baptism in the Spirit in light of these divergent beliefs and practices?

4.3 Apostolic Fragments: The Many Tongues of Acts

In contrast to prophecy, which, as seen in the previous chapter, had parallels in the wider Greco-Roman culture of the first century, glossolalia appears to be a phenomenon unique to the early Christian community (Hovenden 2002). Paul discusses it in his first Letter to the Corinthians (chs. 12 and 14), and it also appears episodically in the book of Acts. Classical pentecostal theology, however, has generally insisted that the function of tongues is different in these writings. The former provides guidelines in order to ensure that the manifestation of tongues is edifying to the congregation during worship. The latter reflects tongues as a sign of empowerment for witness. This classical pentecostal distinction is grounded in their unique doctrinal reading of the book of Acts (Stronstad 1995).

Article 9 of the SF identifies the three references to glossolalia in Acts. While nonpentecostal interpreters generally view these in relationship to Christian initiation, renewalists connect them to one or another aspect of baptism in the Holy Spirit. The first, on the day of Pentecost (Acts 2:1-4), is understood as initiating the fulfillment of Jesus' promise to the disciples: "You will receive power when the Holy Spirit has come upon you; and you will be my witnesses in Jerusalem, in all Judea and Samaria, and to the ends of the earth" (1:8). The second, when those in Cornelius's household spoke in tongues (10:44-45), is suggestive regarding the sign-character of glossolalia for the early believers. Notice the prepositional clause in Luke's account that highlights this evidential function: "The circumcised believers who had come with Peter were astounded that the gift of the Holy Spirit had been poured out even on the Gentiles, *for* they heard them speaking in tongues and extolling God" (10:44-45 [emphasis added]; cf. 11:15-17). The final reference concerns the reception of the Spirit, with tongues following, by the Ephesian disciples (19:6). What is additionally important about this passage is Paul's initial question to these Ephesian believers, which could be read in English as either "Did you receive the Holy Spirit when you became believers?" (19:2, NRSV) or "Have ye received the Holy Ghost *since* ye believed?" (KJV [emphasis added]).

The difference turns on the translation of the aorist or past-tense particle πιστεύσαντες/*pisteusantes*, which could mean either. The latter translation, of course, provides more explicit warrant for thinking about baptism in the Spirit as an experience subsequent to the new birth, a view deeply ingrained within the pentecostal tradition as derived from their Holiness forebears. This triad of texts together undergirds the pentecostal doctrine of Spirit Baptism.

But what if the inductive hermeneutical lens at work in the preceding were broadened beyond the book of Acts? Might a more capacious understanding of Spirit Baptism emerge that would include, albeit be irreducible to, the doctrinal claims highlighted in article 9? In the remainder of this chapter and across the next few chapters, just such a more all-inclusive theology of baptism in the Holy Spirit will be provided (see Yong 2005: ch. 2). In brief, baptism in the Spirit can be understood as a scriptural trope that points to a more holistic understanding of the work of God in Christ to save, sanctify, and empower the people of God to participate in the cosmic history of salvation. Let me now briefly explicate the scriptural horizons for such a claim.

My suggestion turns on the fact that the book of Acts is the second of two volumes written by St. Luke. If so, then the baptism of the Spirit in Acts ought to be understood also in light of what is said in the Third Gospel. There, Luke records the pronouncement of John the Baptist: "I baptize you with water; but one who is more powerful than I is coming; I am not worthy to untie the thong of his sandals. He will baptize you with the Holy Spirit and fire" (Luke 3:16). This reference to Jesus as the Spirit Baptizer is not only confirmed in Acts (e.g., 2:33), but also preserves a primordial understanding of the Baptist's message seen in the other gospels (Matt 3:11; Mark 1:8; John 1:33). If it makes sense to say for Luke that the Baptist's promise about Jesus' ministry was fulfilled in the second book, which is Acts, such an assertion would not hold up for Matthew or Mark, who did not write follow-up volumes. Yet rather than reinterpreting the Baptist's remarks in light of the Acts narrative, what about doing the reverse? We should consider baptism in Luke (both the gospel and Acts) in light of the broader synoptic witness. This ought not to be too contentious, because the only two explicit references to the baptism of the Holy Spirit in Acts (1:5, 11:16) hearken back to the Baptist's proclamation in Luke, which is paralleled in Matthew and Mark. So if we are to understand Spirit Baptism in the early church according to the synoptic accounts, what does it mean to affirm Jesus as the Spirit Baptizer and to understand such in light of his life and ministry?

FIGURE 4.3

Images of Pentecost often portray the Spirit in the form of a dove (fig. 3.4), and occasionally they also include the hand of the Father who gives the Spirit (fig. 4.4), but less commonly is Christ also depicted, as he is here. In fact this depiction of Pentecost presents the outpouring of the Spirit in overtly trinitarian terms. In the center of the apostolic semicircle (cf. fig. 3.3), Christ appears in the typical pose of the Pantokrator: he holds the Book of Life (or the Word) in his left hand while offering a blessing with his right (cf. fig. 8.3). The blessing he offers is the blessing of the Father, as pictorially communicated in the visual repetition of the Son's hand and the Father's hand above him. And the content of Christ's blessing in its most powerful form is the giving of the Holy Spirit, the giving of the very presence of God to dwell in people as the temple of God (1 Cor 3:16, Eph 2:22, Rom 8:11).

This clustering of imagery is significant on multiple levels. First, the representation of the Spirit as a dove explicitly connects the Spirit Baptism of the early church to the baptism of Christ. The same Spirit that anoints Christ in his baptism now proceeds from Christ to his disciples, creating a direct line of continuity between the life and ministry of Christ and the church: the church is now Christ's body on earth. Secondly, this image explicitly presents the outpouring of the Spirit as a work of Christ (Acts 2:33). The giving of the Spirit is a natural extension of, and in continuity with, the self-outpouring life of the Son. In fact, significantly (and unusually) the Spirit is depicted here with a cruciform halo complementary to Christ's: the Spirit fills the church with the cruciform life and ministry of the Son. In all of this, the Son offers the blessing of the Father in the offering of the Spirit for the purpose of saving, sanctifying, and empowering the people of God to participate in the cosmic history of salvation. ✦

Asking these questions leads to the observations that the same Spirit who is poured out upon the disciples and all flesh at Pentecost is also given in the gospel account of Jesus' birth, life, and ministry. The previous chapter looked at Elizabeth as the first person who was said to be filled with the Spirit—with her husband Zechariah following suit (Luke 1:67)—even as the next chapter will focus on Mary who conceived Jesus by the Spirit. What is noteworthy for our purposes here, however, is what is said of Mary—that "[t]he Holy Spirit will come upon you" (Luke 1:35a)—anticipates precisely what Jesus promised the disciples (Acts 1:8) would be fulfilled on the day of Pentecost. The point is that the baptism of and infilling with the Holy Spirit when understood across both Lukan volumes is not just a Pentecost or post-Pentecost experience. Rather, Spirit Baptism relates to and is the result of the work of Christ.

This means then that baptism in the Holy Spirit concerns the entire life and ministry of Christ. John's baptizing with water was one of repentance that anticipated Christ's baptizing with the Holy Spirit. Hence the entirety of God's saving work in Christ can be understood in terms of Spirit Baptism (see Macchia 2006). This includes Jesus' self-understanding of being anointed and empowered by the Spirit "to bring good news to the poor. He [the Spirit] has sent me to proclaim release to the captives and recovery of sight to the blind, to let the oppressed go free, to proclaim the year of the Lord's favour" (Luke 4:18-19). Within the Third Gospel, however, the ministry of Christ is focused on the renewal and restoration of Israel (1:16, 54). Baptism in the Spirit in this wider Lukan horizon is therefore multidimensional, involving individual lives as well as God's salvation history as a whole. The Acts portion simply highlights that the empowerment of the Spirit enables testimony to and participation in God's work manifest in Jesus, albeit now beyond the confines of Israel to the ends of the earth. In this sense, the pentecostal "crown jewel" teaching does not need to be denied. But it ought to be elaborated to include the witness of the first Lukan volume (and the rest of the New Testament).

We will keep returning to this thesis about baptism in the Holy Spirit in later chapters. Here, however, one more brief comment related in part to another portion of the New Testament needs to be registered. This also concerns clarification needed in relation to the classical pentecostal emphasis on empowerment for witness. More often than not, the focus on the power of the Spirit leads in the direction of a "theology of glory" (see Kärkkäinen 2002a: ch. 12), one that has been exploited and abused by theologies of health and wealth. This ignores the fact that the Greek word for "witnesses" in the central pentecostal text of Acts 1:8 is μάρτυρες/*martures*, from which the word "martyr" derives (see also Luke 11:48; 24:48; Acts 2:32; 3:15; 5:32; 7:58; 10:39; 13:31). The book of Acts also gives ample witness to the martyrdom suffered by those sent out to bear witness to the gospel (Stephen and James, for instance). There is a real sense that Spirit Baptism identifies believers with the life, ministry, and even fate of Jesus, the Spirit Baptizer, especially as culminating in the cross. Pentecostal power thus ought to be understood as much in terms of suffering as in terms of success (see Mittelstadt 2004).

This theme of suffering in relationship to the baptism in the Spirit is consistent with the testimony of Peter, whose life was looked at briefly at the beginning of this chapter. Even if the authenticity of the first letter of Peter remains disputed, its message given to a suffering church ought to resonate with Christians yearning for the visitation of the Spirit in contemporary global contexts of persecution (see 1 Pet 2:20-25; 3:14; 4:1, 12-19; 5:7-10). Here, Peter's greeting reconnects the renewalist emphases on the Spirit with the Holiness and Puritan quests for sanctification and assurance respectively: "To the exiles of the Dispersion in Pontus, Galatia, Cappadocia, Asia, and Bithynia, who have been chosen and destined by God the Father and sanctified by the Spirit to be obedient to Jesus Christ and to be sprinkled with his blood" (1:1-2). This may not be a popular message today. But the witness that Spirit Baptism enables is a life and message whose values run counter to the dominant conventions and structures of this world. Perhaps contemporary Christian life ought to be more marginal or exilic than mainstream, as it currently is in various parts of the world. In that case, Christian election is related to the sanctifying work of the Spirit that testifies to the saving work of God in Christ through a minority people of God (see McDonald 2010).

4.4 Be Filled with the Spirit!

This final section of the chapter registers three sets of comments related to the evidence of Spirit Baptism, its purpose, and its scope. My goal is both to interpret article 9 of the SF for a wider context and to use it as a springboard for renewing the global theological enterprise. As already mentioned, however, the full scope of such interpretation and renewal will stretch across the remainder of this volume. What follows can be understood as an initial reframing of article 9 for the latter wider task.

First, we begin with the most controversial claim that glossolalia is the "initial evidence" of baptism in the Holy Spirit. The language of "evidence" is a by-product of the formulation of this article of faith in the early twentieth century, at the height of modernist optimism about the empirically demonstrable nature of science as a way of knowing. Into this vortex the Puritan and Holiness quests for external signs were translated by Pentecostals into tongues as a physical, tangible, and palpable indication of their encounters with the Holy Spirit. Incorporation of such language into the church's confession runs the risk of reducing a rich set of experiences with God to both repeatable empirical observations and a finite and inflexible proposition. Yet every dogmatic claim and even confession, from the Apostles' Creed onward, is vulnerable to one or another form of reductionistic interpretation. What ought to be redemptive about the renewal affirmation of evidential tongues is its creating a horizon of personal expectation that whenever the Spirit descends, the gift of divinely inspired speech should be expected to manifest itself. Yes, such "tongues" can be learned sociologically (ecclesiologically), but that makes them no less enspirited (Yong 2011c: ch. 2). As is said even of the apostles, they "began to speak in other languages, as the Spirit gave them ability" (Acts 2:4b). Hence the human element does not cancel out the divine; rather a certain synergy enables human speaking amid divine inspiration (cf. Phil 2:12-13).

The point is that those filled with the Spirit *get* to speak in tongues, not necessarily *have to* speak in tongues right there and then. Understood in this sense, tongues-speaking is normative for Christian spirituality in general in terms of signifying the Spirit's presence and activity (see Keener 2001: ch. 9). Note therefore that while the earliest Pentecostals spoke a great deal about tongues as the "Bible evidence" of the infilling of the Spirit, their biblicist instincts ought instead to have led them to the scriptural language of signs. According to the latter approach, the semiotic or sign-character of glossolalia can be understood as normative without the scientistic baggage and empiricistic presuppositions that come with the rhetoric of "evidence." In this case, the Lukan sign of glossolalia heralds the pneumatological and eschatological in-breaking of the reign of God while empowering the mission of the people of God in hastening its inauguration.

But why tongues as a sign of the Spirit? James 3 provides some perspective on this question. James's concern has to do with bridling the tongue, especially of those who are teachers of the faith (3:1). The tongue and the words it utters have a destructive capacity (3:5-8); yet its potency to curse can be redeemed for the blessing of God (3:9-10) and the edification of others (1 Cor 14; see ch. 3 of this volume). The curse of Babel similarly can be viewed as redirected in the Pentecost event. What inhibited human pride is now being redeemed, so each different language can witness to God's saving deeds (Acts 2:11). The orchestration of the many tongues of Pentecost is a harbinger of the eschatological redemption in which "saints from every tribe and language and people and nation" (Rev 5:9b) are gathered before the throne of God. The new heavens and earth will be similarly "pentecostal," with the kings and peoples of the earth bringing into the heavenly city "the glory and the honour of the nations" (Rev 21:26). Whereas Babel dispersed, Pentecost reclaims for the glory of God, but by harmonizing rather than homogenizing the many tongues.

The key is that when left to its own devices, the tongue and its messages are destructive, full of the self and its machinations. Christ's gift of the Spirit, however, enables testimony to the wondrous works of God, beyond the capacity of human languages on their own terms. This is not to say that each instance of glossolalia or Spirit Baptism is mystical or ecstatic in character. But it is to say that the act of speaking in tongues *both* symbolizes the human openness to things divine that overrules worldly conventions, including those of human language (see Smith 2010: ch. 3) *and* signifies the presence of the Spirit of God as descending upon, or irrupting from within (cf. Rom 8:23)—depending on which directional metaphor is preferred—and dwelling in human bodies (temples) to achieve divine purposes.

The more important point to be made concerns the renewalist invitation, following the apostolic paradigm, to "be filled with the Spirit" (Eph 5:18). Article 9 identifies the purpose of such infilling as empowerment for witness to and service of Christ. The Lukan framework unfolded in the preceding section summons believers to the fullness of Christ's baptizing work, which involves participation in his ministry of heralding the coming reign of God. What for Jesus' own ministry involved the renewal and restoration of Israel is for his followers enlarged to include the eschatological redemption of the cosmos. The gift of the Holy Spirit thus includes the reception and sharing of God's saving work, initiated with the work of Christ. So yes, the baptism in the Spirit also involves a subsequent work of grace available to all. But it is also more than that, involving the full scope of the saving work of God so that each encounter with God—each infilling of the Spirit—deepens the Christian life and intensifies its witness. As Paul insisted: "If we live by the Spirit, let us also be guided by the Spirit" (Gal 5:25). Initial evidences or signs without a testifying life amount to nothing.

FIGURE 4.4

The book of Acts tells us that those gathered together on the day of Pentecost "saw what seemed to be tongues of fire that separated and came to rest on each of them" (Acts 2:3, NIV). Visual interpretations of this moment have thus usually associated these tongues of fire with the tops of the apostles' heads, although the text itself does not necessitate this convention. In this tenth-century image, however, the filling of the Spirit is directly associated with the disciples' mouths rather than the tops of their heads. This emphasis on the mouth—both the disciples' and the Spirit's (depicted here in the form of a dove; cf. figs. 1.4, 3.4, and 4.3)—carries two significant implications for the ways we might understand this event: (1) it better suggests that the outpouring of the Spirit is a more comprehensive filling of the disciples' entire bodies, not only their minds; and (2) it directly connects this filling of the Spirit with new speech, not just thoughts or beliefs. And this seems to fit extremely tightly with the narrative as a whole: after all, the tongues of fire that rest on each person are directly narratively paired with the apostles speaking "in other tongues as the Spirit enabled them" (2:4, NIV). And perhaps this coupling of the Spirit being on a people and in their mouths is a full realization of Isaiah's prophecy, in which the Lord describes his covenant in exactly those terms: "my spirit that is upon you, and my words that I have put in your mouth, shall not depart out of your mouth" (Isa 59:21).

This emphasis on the opening of the apostles' mouths is profoundly significant. The Pentecost event in Acts 2 produces speech and unexpected comprehension across cultural boundaries. Whereas "spirituality" is commonly associated with unspeakable mystery and ineffability, Christian Spirituality confesses that when the Spirit of God moves, interpersonal communication and understanding occur with power and freedom (Guthrie 2011). In other words, the deepest spiritual reality does not isolate people from each other but brings them into deeper interpersonal love and flourishing. ✦

What ought to be emphasized, then, is not necessarily the gift per se, not even its accompanying signs. Instead, Jesus' baptism in the Spirit inaugurates a Spirit-filled life, one that includes crisis moments understandable as initial and later works of grace. The disciples encountered the Spirit of God in a life-transforming way on the day of Pentecost, but they were also repeatedly thereafter filled with the Spirit (e.g., Acts 4:31; 7:55; 13:52). This is not to collapse Spirit Baptism into conversion and regeneration. It is to recognize the broader scope of Jesus' baptism in the Spirit, which includes but is not limited to initiation into faith (see also ch. 6 of this volume). On the one hand, this opens up possibilities for considering how classical pentecostal notions of Spirit Baptism may be more rather than less amenable to sacramental and charismatic interpretations across the ecumenical spectrum. On the other hand, whereas renewalists are likely to focus on these experiential highlights subsequent to the conversion experience (what they think article 9 says happens when they are baptized in the Spirit), the performative dimension of the doctrine of Spirit Baptism means that Christians also get to live out this reality as witnesses to the world (the function of Spirit Baptism). So even if the Puritan, Holiness, and Pentecostal quests for signs are understandable, such are misplaced if they devolve into a seeking after empirical assurances or evidences for their own sake. The goal of Jesus' outpouring of the Spirit is to save, sanctify, and empower for witness. Any more narrow or legalistic focus truncates what God desires to accomplish in the world rather than leads or lives into what the Spirit's gift opens up.

This is because the Spirit-filled life bears witness to nothing less than the love of God in Christ for the world. The early modern Pentecostals understood clearly that baptism in the Holy Spirit was also baptism in the love of God (Rom 5:5; cf. Yong 2012: ch. 5). The God who loves through the gift of the Spirit also redeems all things through the gift of the Son (John 3:16). To be filled with the Spirit is to be filled with the love of God that creates, sustains, and covers the world. Unknown tongues roll forth from the inner recesses of human hearts, primed by the Spirit (John 7:38), even as the love of the Father overflows into and penetrates the depths of the world. Baptism in the Spirit catches human beings up into a divine love intent on redeeming the cosmos.

My final point therefore concerns the scope of Spirit Baptism. In the Acts narrative, Peter's explanation was that such outpouring of the Spirit was not only "for all who are far away, everyone whom the Lord our God calls to him" (Acts 2:39b). But this was, as Peter adapted from the words of the prophet Joel, for all people, sons and daughters, young and old, slave and free (Acts 2:17-18). None were excluded from Jesus' baptism in the Spirit; all are invited to participate in God's work of salvation and reconciliation.

This egalitarian character of the baptism of the Spirit was central to the Azusa Street revival. Comment has already been made on its multiethnic character and how that has precipitated a global renewal movement that is at the vanguard of world Christianity. Chapter 3 also briefly discussed the reference to women in relationship to Corinthian worship. Here, further emphasis is given to the fact that God's saving and empowering work crosses gender boundaries as well. In Christ, "there is no longer male and female" (Gal 3:28). Women were central to the work of the Azusa Street mission, because the early twentieth-century renewalists believed that God was no respecter of gender (see E. Alexander 2005, 2008; Stephenson 2012). The role of women has been central to the growth of renewal Christianity ever since (see Billingsley 2008; Alexander and Yong 2009). These scriptural and historical observations have implications for Christian soteriology, for the outworking of Christian ministry (and ordination), and for considering theological anthropology in the contemporary global context.

We shall return to expand on many of these themes going forward. What ought to be clear from the preceding is how Spirit Baptism might inspire Christian rethinking about salvation, sanctification, and the whole work of God. The renewalist contribution is precisely to highlight how Jesus' gift of the Spirit facilitates witness to this full scope of God's cosmic purification, redemption, and perfection.

Discussion Questions

1. What is your own personal experience of being filled with the Spirit? Compare your experience with that of someone else. Is there room in the preceding construct for both, and even other, accounts?

2. What are some aspects of your church's teachings about the baptism in the Holy Spirit which are different from the preceding discussion? Does expanding the horizons of understanding Spirit Baptism help or hinder a clearer understanding of the scriptural message?

3. What is gained or what is lost when Spirit Baptism is connected to suffering and perhaps even martyrdom? How might this radical conception of witness be understood in times and places where Christians are in little danger of being persecuted for their faith? What are the implications of this link for renewing Christian theology in the twenty-first century?

Further Reading

Atkinson, William. 2011. *Baptism in the Spirit: Luke-Acts and the Dunn Debate.* Eugene, Ore.: Pickwick.

Brand, Chad Owen, ed. 2004. *Perspectives on Spirit-Baptism.* Nashville: B&H Academic.

Cartledge, Mark J., ed. 2006. *Speaking in Tongues: Multi-disciplinary Perspectives.* Milton Keynes, U.K.: Paternoster.

McGee, Gary B., ed. 1991. *Initial Evidence: Historical and Biblical Perspectives on the Pentecostal Doctrine of Spirit Baptism.* Peabody, Mass.: Hendrickson.

Mills, Watson E., ed. 1986. *Speaking in Tongues: A Guide to Research on Glossolalia.* Grand Rapids: Eerdmans.

5

Sanctification and Holiness

In the World but Not of It

World Assemblies of God Fellowship Statement of Faith
—Article 8: Sanctification

We believe that sanctification is an act of separation from that which is evil, and of dedication unto God. In experience, it is both instantaneous and progressive. It is produced in the life of the believer by his appropriation of the power of Christ's blood and risen life through the person of the Holy Spirit. He draws the believer's attention to Christ, teaches him through the Word and produces the character of Christ within him (Romans 6:1-11; 8:1-2, 13; 12:1-2; Galatians 2:20; Hebrews 10:10, 14).

5.1 Mary: Set Apart by the Spirit

Sanctification, as the article above indicates, is a work of the Holy Spirit designed to produce Christ-like holiness. Our character vignette into Mary, the mother of Jesus—even the "mother of God" (*theotokos*), as was affirmed by the early ecumenical Council of Ephesus (430)—as an "example of holiness" (Hickey 1988) illuminates this christocentric truth. This is in part because, for all that Mary has inspired in the Christian theological and even doctrinal tradition, what is most worthwhile concerns how her life is effectually set apart to exalt Christ and illuminate the gospel message. In what follows, our goal is not to adjudicate images of Mary disputed especially between Protestants and Catholics over the centuries (for an impressive effort, see Perry 2006) but to understand God's purifying and perfecting work.

What is known about Mary given the fairly scant scriptural data? We know she grew up, at least in part, in Nazareth (Luke 1:26) and had at least one sister (John 19:25); that she was provided at least a rudimentary education in the Jewish Scriptures (as reflected in her knowledge of Israel's story in the Magnificat—Luke 1:46-55); that Elizabeth (see section

3.1) was her relative in the region of Judea (1:39), with whom she stayed for about three months (1:50); that at a young age she was betrothed to Joseph, a carpenter, married him, and, while remaining a virgin, bore Jesus; that at least for the first two years of her motherhood, the family lived in Egypt for fear of Herod (Matt 2:13-20); and that she returned with Joseph to Nazareth, where they raised a large family of Jesus and at least six other brothers and sisters (Mark 6:3). While Mary remained connected to Jesus' brothers after his death (Acts 1:14), she appears not to have lived with them. The Fourth Gospel records that Mary was at the crucifixion site and that Jesus commended his mother to the disciple whom he loved. That the latter "took her into his own home" and cared for her (John 19:27) indicates that Mary was a widow by this time (Joseph is last seen or heard about in the Temple episode in Luke 2:41-50), perhaps still only in the forties of her life. And while we cannot be sure that all of Jesus' siblings were from Joseph's previous marriage (or more), as the Catholic tradition holds, this best explains Jesus' commendation and his mother's living circumstances later in life.

The preceding broad sketch sets in relief two more specific windows into Mary's journey in holiness. The first of course concerns her son's virginal conception through the Holy Spirit (Matt 1:18, 20; Luke 1:35). While Matthew's gospel is focused more on Joseph's character and actions in relationship to Jesus' birth, Luke's emphasis remains on Mary throughout. There is no reason to question that Mary's lowly stature (Luke 1:48) applies both to her spiritual posture and to her socioeconomic location (1:51-53). It is from this position of humility that Mary is "greatly troubled" (1:29, ASV) by the angel Gabriel's visitation and greeting, and also out of which she responds: "Here am I, the servant of the Lord; let it be with me according to your word" (1:38).

We ought here to pause and reflect on what Mary (and Joseph) had to endure and work through with her pregnancy coming to light. From a salvation history perspective, this was part of God's incarnational plan. From the perspective of being separated from the world and being dedicated to the work of God—central to the definition of article 8 above—this involved Mary's coming to terms with her giving of herself, literally and fully in her pregnancy, to the will of God. Elizabeth, of course, becomes her trusted confidante and ally, one whose own experience of God's miraculous intervention (in her barrenness) provided her with sufficient perspective on the angelic insistence, "nothing will be impossible with God" (Luke 1:37). The point is that Mary's passage to holiness involved an uncompromisingly profound surrender. Each day of morning sickness for this first-time mother; the many changes of her body; each movement and kick of the baby in her womb—these experiences, all undergone in a social climate of suspicion about the paternity of this child (see Matt 1:19), were tangible reminders of her commitment to and submission under God's mysterious will.

FIGURE 5.1

This version of Fra Angelico's Annunciation *is compositionally divided into thirds. In the central section the archangel Gabriel humbly crosses his arms in front of his chest, bows toward the young Mary, and delivers a surprising announcement: "And now, you will conceive in your womb and bear a son" (Luke 1:31). Mary's posture echoes that of Gabriel, but it has a greater complexity to it: Her gesture suggests not only a humility symmetrical to Gabriel's but also a deep inner conflict, a troubled wrestling with the weight of this announcement. In fact, Luke's account of the annunciation is anything but sweetly sentimental. Gabriel's opening words to Mary—"You who are highly favored! The Lord is with you"—cause her to become "greatly troubled at his words" (1:29, NIV)*

*and apparently quite fearful, given that Gabriel then implores her not to be afraid
(1:30). Mary ultimately presents herself as faithful and open to the movement of
the Holy Spirit: "Here am I, the servant of the Lord; let it be with me according
to your word" (1:38).*

*Angelico's visual exegesis of Luke's annunciation account takes a fascinat-
ing intertextual approach. He follows Christian tradition in picturing Mary with
a Bible opened to the book of Isaiah: "Look, the young woman is with child
and shall bear a son, and shall name him Immanuel" (Isa 7:14). (Mary almost
certainly would not have had a copy of the Prophets, and if she did, it would
not have been bound in codex form; but bare photographic factuality is not the
point in such images. The inclusion of the little Bible is simply a visual device
for prompting viewers to theologically interpret the scene within the whole biblical
narrative.) Further, and more unusually, Angelico also places the annunciation
in direct proximity to an image of Gabriel expelling Adam and Eve from Eden
(Gen 3:23-24). In this context, the announcement of the incarnation is understood in direct contradistinction to the relational rupture signified in the expulsion.
Mary appears as a "second Eve," and the reconciliation of the great ruptures
of Genesis 3 (cf. fig. 10.2) is enfolded in the angel's announcement that "the
power of the Most High will overshadow you" and "the holy one to be born will
be called the Son of God." This announcement both consecrates, purifies, and
sanctifies humanity (in the representative form of Mary) and inaugurates a new
Adam, a new humanity.* ✦

The second window into Mary's journey of holiness is better appreciated in kaleidoscopic terms, one that opens up to the full panorama of her
motherhood. Jesus' birth intensified a path of sanctification that already
goes beyond what everyone else is able to imagine, much less endure. At
Jesus' dedication in the temple, Simeon not only prophesies of what God
desires to accomplish through Jesus but also says to Jesus' mother that "a
sword will pierce your own soul too" (Luke 2:35). Thus is a trajectory
of motherhood charted that involves her pondering in her heart (2:19,
51b)—through the agonizing lifelong course of Jesus' thirty-year–plus life
that is spent waiting, wishing, praying—and anticipating the unavoidable
fulfillment of these words but still hoping for the best. The incident in the
temple when Jesus was twelve was a reminder that his was an unconventional life and mission, one not disrespectful of his mother or parents but
yet with even deeper allegiances to the heavenly Father (2:48-51a), whose
will for him was inscrutable in its details. Perhaps up to another twenty

years go by, and Mary is now older, probably widowed, but still wondering when the time of trouble will come (e.g., John 2:1-5) and how Jesus' mission would unfold. He becomes an itinerant preacher, with his mother no doubt worrying that he "has nowhere to lay his head" (Matt 8:20; Luke 9:58). And there would be no turning back. Her surrendering of her body, of her life as mother, of the fruit of her womb, would culminate inexorably through her own *via dolorosa* (Pelikan 1989: 18–19) at the foot of the cross. What she fears most finally comes to pass. Is this the path of sanctification?

Yet what is unfolded here is Mary's christocentricity. Of course, she is focused on Jesus also because she is his mother: What mother would not be? But it is also important to observe how Mary can be understood as being filled with the Spirit for her own life and witness, as well as sanctified by the Spirit for her own path in holiness. The promise that the disciples will be empowered when the Holy Spirit comes upon them (ἐπελθόντος/*epelthontos*, Acts 1:8) is anticipated by the Holy Spirit's coming upon Mary (ἐπελεύσεται/*epeleusetai*, Luke 1:35). Mary thus becomes a prototype of the Spirit-baptized life (Shelton 2015), one who carries and brings forth the Messiah himself. Yet she is also present in the Upper Room (Acts 1:14) and thereafter filled afresh, even anew, with Holy Spirit (2:4). Perhaps this second baptism or later infilling did not completely alleviate the pain of her sojourn, but it also no doubt empowered her own ongoing witness to the holy and sanctifying work of God.

5.2 Christian Perfection: Historical Trajectories

Central to the eighth article of the SF is not the *what* but the *how* of sanctification. Intriguingly, the life of Mary as an opening into holiness illuminates the article's claim that sanctification is both instantaneous and progressive. We will return to revisit the point about Mary later. However, historically, the Assemblies of God has emphasized the *process* of sanctification, with some even denying any instantaneous notion, at least as understood in Holiness terms. This was connected in part to the debate about the "finished work of Christ" that raged within the nascent pentecostal movement from about 1910 to 1912 (see Jacobsen 2003: ch. 3). Influenced by the Keswickian, Higher Life, and Reformed impulses at the turn of the twentieth century, finished work proponents insisted that conversion came about because the sinful nature was crucified with Christ. Fellowships like the Assemblies of God embraced the finished work teaching and hence taught that in typical Reformed fashion, sanctification was a lifelong process of learning to live out once-and-for-all regenerated hearts. This was in contrast to Holiness-Pentecostals, who insisted on retaining the Wesleyan distinction regarding initial and entire sanctification, and this effectively expanded into a three-stage Holiness-Pentecostal *ordo salutis*: initial salvation, entire sanctification, and baptism in the Holy Spirit with endowment of power to bear witness.

Appreciating what is at stake requires some understanding of the controversies in the Holiness movement, both those that preceded modern Pentecostalism and those that have run parallel to the growth and expansion of global renewalism. (In this section, we will very briefly trace developments up to Wesley, follow the debates within especially the North America Holiness movement, and resituate the contemporary discussion in global and ecumenical context. Our goal is to gain perspective for the task of renewing present Christian understandings of sanctification when notions of holiness and perfection sound quaint or are not easily intelligible.)

5.2.1 The Quest for Perfection in the Christian Tradition

The diversity of views about sanctification, it may be argued, is inspired by the variegated scriptural witness itself (e.g., Baxter 1973). A number of models of holiness have been derived from the Bible, including the moral (concerned with holy behavior), the eschatological (which anticipates a future realization of full holiness), the formal (a positional and even confessional holiness), and the mystical (based on unity with Christ) (see Du Plessis 1959: ch. 1). A related but different set of categorizations is to be preferred. Jesus' life and teachings and the general Epistles indeed do suggest a *moral orientation* that prioritizes the interconnectedness between loving God and neighbor. In contrast, the Pauline corpus defines sanctification oppositionally, in the *dualistic terms* of living after the flesh versus being in Christ and in the Spirit. This Pauline construct is deeply dependent also on what the Hebrew Bible, as well as the Letter to the Hebrews (see ch. 9 of this volume), consistently elaborates as a *cultic approach* to holiness that details how pervasively defiled bodies and lives need to be purified in order to approach the divine presence. Last but not least, sanctification as a motif in the New Testament as a whole also can be understood *ecclesiologically or socially* as demarcating solidarity in the body of Christ over and against "the world." Of course, these moral, dualistic, cultic, and ecclesial/social models are not discrete, as each presumes and involves the others in various respects. My point is that these threads represent permutations that get played out in various quests for holiness in the Christian tradition (Flew 1934; Deal 1978; Bassett 1997).

The monastic Christians of the fourth century onward, for instance, were intentional about retrieving the countercultural understanding of the earliest messianic followers in a time when the lines between the people of God and the world were in danger of being blurred. With the emergence of Constantine and the establishment of Christianity as the religion of the empire, the persecutions and martyrdom suffered by preceding generations dissipated. In this milieu, monasticism—from the Greek μοναχός/ *monachos*, derived from μόνος/*monos*, "alone"—gained impetus. Solitaries eschewed the comforts of institutionalizing Christianity and inculcated ascetic lifestyles that reflected their other-than-worldly conventions and allegiances. Monastic practices directed toward attaining communion with God presumed the Pauline distinction between flesh and spirit, thus disciplining the former in search of perfection and holiness. Here the intertwining of the social and spiritual models of biblical sanctification is manifest, even as the First Testament's emphasis on defilement is also evident in monastic views of the body.

Monastic perfectionism also presumed, in some quarters, the neoplatonic hierarchy of being. Christian perfection involved, in this view, a suppression of the human body and the nurturing of the human soul and spirit in its ascent toward the divine. This anthropological view took shape as it interfaced with the Alexandrian school during the patristic period (Lilley 1925), and the resulting convergence became a staple of medieval thought. Christian theological reflection was deeply influenced by this philosophical anthropology and even cosmology because of its parallels to, if not correlations with, the Pauline contrast of flesh and spirit. Thus Christian mystics spoke of sanctification and perfection in terms of the overcoming the flesh and the freeing of the spirit. Thus also did St. Augustine (354–430) react to the perfectionist teachings of Pelagius (354–420/440), a British monk, by developing a doctrine of original sin which condition and effects were perpetuated by human sexuality and lust. Human life, conceived as it is out of such carnality, is therefore perennially defiled (in keeping with the Hebraic cultic notion) and beset by sinfulness and imperfections. However, human hearts are restless until they find their rest in God and the heavenly city. Hence the path of salvation in this life includes glimpses of perfection that stoke the soul's desire for eschatological union with God (Bassett and Greathouse 1985: 87–108).

The "Angelic Doctor" of the Roman Catholic Church, Thomas Aquinas, by and large assumed the Augustinian and medieval hierarchy of being, even if he also managed to introduce one or two important Aristotelian ideas into the mix. Whereas the city of God was the goal of the

Christian life in the Augustinian register, the beatific vision was the fundamental telos or goal of sanctification in the Thomistic *ordo salutis*. This aim was consistent with the mystical tradition's prioritization of the contemplative over the active life. From Aristotle, however, Thomas learned to minimize the chasm separating the material and the spiritual domains. The grace of the latter elevated the capacities of the former, rather than suppressing or overwhelming them. In addition, the Aristotelian virtues provided language to further articulate how Christians can grow in sanctity and holiness in the present life (see Leies 1963), enabled by divine grace, even while anticipating final perfection in the life to come.

Reformation theologians developed the Augustinian idea of original sin into a more expansive doctrine of human depravity. For Martin Luther (1483–1546), Hebraic defilement and purity and Pauline flesh and spirit are translated into the theological categories of law and gospel. The condemnation of the former is dealt with christologically: faith, justification, and sanctification are available to believers not because of their own efforts (which are ineffective because of original sin and human depravity) but through the work of Christ. Hence it is Christ and his atonement that justifies and even sanctifies. For Luther, along with other magisterial Reformers like John Calvin, then, sanctification was more a position or state of being believers enjoyed through their incorporation into the work of Christ, rather than through their own merited achievement (the latter being associated with the Roman Catholic position they defined as works-righteousness). Practically speaking, however, sanctification was thus a lifelong process that followed, expressed, or manifested salvation understood in terms of justification, conversion, and regeneration (with election included, especially in the Calvinist tradition).

The next generation of Lutherans (and their descendants within and even beyond the Lutheran tradition), however, included pietists, who were not enthused about developments they felt took an overly intellectualist direction. For pietists, sanctification was important on its own terms and not just as a corollary to justification. In that case, holiness was not just a theological state of being in relationship to Christ but involved a living and dynamic pursuit. Hence belief *in* Christ involved the *imitation of* Christ, and vice versa. For many pietists over the next few centuries, then, Christ is savior in part because he is also a moral exemplar. Salvation includes the path of holiness in the footsteps of Christ, beyond the moment of conversion (see O'Malley 1995).

FIGURE 5.2

FIGURE 5.3

In Caravaggio's Calling of St. Matthew, *Jesus enters from the right with Peter and singles out a lavishly dressed tax collector named Matthew (Matt 9:9; 10:3). Jesus points at him and issues a terse request: "Follow me." And as Jesus points, further pointing ensues from many angles: Peter points, the light from a window points (casting a long shadow toward Matthew), and even Matthew finds himself pointing toward himself, albeit questioningly. And thus Christ's calling echoes through the church (Peter), nature (the window), and conscience, respectively.*

Those familiar with art history will soon recognize that Jesus' pointing hand is a loaded visual quotation from another extraordinary painting: Michelangelo Buonarroti's Creation of Adam *(near the center of the Sistine ceiling). Jesus' hand in Caravaggio's painting is a direct quotation of Adam's hand in Michelangelo's painting, thus subtly identifying Jesus as a new Adam—a truly human person fully bearing the image of God (Col 1:15; Heb 1:3). However, although Jesus points with the hand of Adam, he occupies the compositional position of God the Father; and like the Father, he reaches forward with an active, life-giving pointing. Caravaggio thus presents Jesus as the truly human one (the second Adam) who comes from the "position" of the Father, offering Matthew new life and forming him into a new creation (cf. 2 Cor 5:17).*

Responding to this pointing will entail a radical reordering of Matthew's identity, akin to what Paul refers to as being clothed with a "new self, created according to the likeness of God in true righteousness and holiness" (Eph 4:24; cf. Col 3:10; fig. 2.1). This is a call to abandon his life and to apprentice himself to one who is truly good: "as he who called you is holy, be holy yourselves in all your conduct" (1 Pet 1:15). And on this count, we might notice two details: (1) the way of Jesus includes the cross (note the subtle cruciform window grille immediately above Christ's hand), and (2) the call of Jesus cuts across eras, cultures, and geographical locations (cf. figs. 1.1 and 1.2). There is a kind of temporal-spatial rift in the painting: Jesus and Peter wear first-century tunics, whereas Matthew and his cohort don the clothes of seventeenth-century Italian culture. Jesus reaches across this rift and thus the pointing in this painting is directed not only toward a historical Matthew but toward the artist, his contemporaries, and toward every other person who sees this image: You too have been pointed at and called to follow. ✦

5.2.2 Perfect Love in the Wesleyan-Holiness Movement

The preceding chapter introduced John Wesley at the fount of the Holiness movement. Wesley himself was a member of the Church of England, and in that sense was firmly within the broader Reformation stream, albeit with catholic (not just Roman Catholic) sensitivities that inclined him to consider and appropriate patristic, Orthodox, and other sources available in the theological tradition (see Greathouse 1979). From these, as well as from his own encounters with God, Wesley came to a deep conviction about holiness as being central, not just incidental, to the Christian life.

Wesley's mature thoughts on the subject (Wesley 1872: 114–15) include the following highlights. First, the scriptural call to perfection, "as your heavenly Father is perfect" (Matt 5:48; cf. 2 Cor 7:1; 13:9; Heb 6:1; 1 John 2:5; Rev 3:2), suggests it is not only a possibility in the present life but an expected and even normative postconversion (subsequent to the experience of justification) work of grace. Second, however, scriptural perfection is neither absolute nor does it bestow infallibility on anyone; rather, it is a continuously improvable salvation from intentional sinning and a growth in grace motivated by "perfection in love" (1 John 4:18). Third, while Wesley recognized that the instantaneousness of such an experience of full sanctification was under dispute, he suggested that such merely might not have been perceived; but "if ever sin ceases, there must be a last moment of its existence, and a first moment of our deliverance from it" (Wesley 1872: 115). Regardless, those who "rejoice evermore, pray without ceasing, and in everything give thanks" (cf. 1 Thess 5:16–18, KJV), are living testimonies to the Spirit's work of entirely sanctifying grace.

Over the course of the last two-plus centuries, Wesley's legacy has spawned a range of contested interpretations. Reception of his teaching within the nineteenth-century North American Holiness movement emphasized not only the imputation of righteousness but also the impartation of the capacity to pursue holiness and perfection in love. Actual sins are not only forgiven, but the inbred sinning nature of the heart also is eradicated through the sanctifying work of the Spirit. And such a postregenerative encounter with God ought to be understood as a second or subsequent work of grace given the aorist or Greek past tenses used to describe the Spirit's baptizing, sealing, and sanctifying work. This has been the standard interpretation of "the distinctive doctrine of Wesleyanism" (the subtitle of Grider's 1980 volume).

Yet the debates of the nineteenth century have raged into the twentieth century, in part because the message of holiness in general and the claims regarding entire sanctification in particular are becoming increasingly indecipherable. Not only have standards of holiness changed dramatically from the heyday of the Holiness movement a hundred years ago (known for its "ascetic" rules and regulations that set "holiness folk" apart from the world), but fewer and fewer testimonies about entire sanctification threaten to render it a relic of the past. The lack of explicit witness to having experienced sanctification as a second work of grace might be related to the humility that such experience is supposed to bring, but that is not the only mitigating factor. More important is that the scriptural contrasts between flesh and spirit and between church and world are being reinterpreted away from earlier philosophical paradigms. Neither the dualism and hierarchicalism of neoplatonism nor Aristotelian notions of substantiality (as applied to things in general or to human beings specifically) are as foundational now as they were before. Part of the pressures exerted on these earlier paradigms relates to advances in the sciences. The Newtonian cosmology has been giving way to an Einsteinian one, and substances are now being reconsidered in terms of dynamic relations.

These broader cultural and philosophical currents have also led to shifts in the anthropological sciences, with concomitant implications for thinking about holiness. Whereas an Aristotelian ontology of persons and of sin undergirds the notion of a second work of grace eradicating the sin nature, such discourse sits uneasily within a relational anthropology. For the last one hundred years or more, psychologists have been opening up the developmental shape of human nature as well as the dynamic contours of religious ritual across the life cycle; sociologists in turn have been illuminating the sociohistorical and linguistic character of human religious projections even as these can also be seen, for theists, as reflecting human beings as image bearers of God; and cognitive scientists have increased our understanding of the neurophysiological bases of the mythic and ritual aspects of religious life. What is gradually emerging is a theological anthropology that is complex (rather than unambiguous about the nature of religious life or holiness), multidimensional (rather than dualistically framed), social (rather than individualistically attuned), dynamic (rather than statically divided into two or three basic religious states), and yet involving freedom and responsibility (rather than being deterministic either scientifically or theologically). These developments are leading Wesleyan theologians to rethink not only the tradition's doctrine of holiness but also Christian theology of sin and salvation in general (e.g., Mann 2006; Markham 2007).

Part of the result, then, is an emerging dilemma in the Wesleyan understanding of sanctification (Quanstrom 2004: ch. 7). On the one hand, there have been efforts to reassert the traditional American Holiness interpretations of the doctrine of entire sanctification (e.g., Taylor 1985). On the other hand, relational understandings of holiness understood as perfect love vis-à-vis both God and others are increasingly taking hold (e.g., Wynkoop 1972; Oord and Lodahl 2005). Within this latter frame of reference, Jesus' moral vision and exemplarity have reemerged and become an interpretive angle on the scriptural witness. Entire sanctification becomes a dynamic process of being made perfect in love according to the image of Christ by the power of the Holy Spirit so as to respond in kind to God and others. Most importantly, holiness is less a noun denoting a state of being than it is a verb indicative of the Christian way of life.

5.2.3 Sanctification in Ecumenical and Global Perspective

Yet, our path is not yet completely clear toward a constructive response. So far we have looked more broadly at developments in the overall Christian tradition as well as more narrowly and recently within the Wesleyan-Holiness stream. But the disputes within the latter are even further complicated were we to (again) broaden our horizons beyond Anglo-American confines. Here I briefly denote additional challenges in thinking about sanctification when our scope widens globally and with regard to the contemporary ecumenical landscape.

A couple of trends suggest themselves when we examine discussions of holiness in a global context. First, the focus on individual sanctification expands to encompass the socioeconomic and political orders (e.g., Runyon 1981). This is in keeping with the emphasis on the social dimensions of holiness, which have deep roots in the movement (Smith 1957; Magnuson 1977). The difference now is that Wesleyans are also engaging with liberation theological traditions more intentionally, and hence focus not just on works of mercy but on the need for structural transformation and political praxis (e.g., Hinchliff 1982; Sobrino 1988). Within the global context, this also involves development of a spirituality of persecution and martyrdom amid attentiveness to the struggle for human rights. Sanctification understood in anticipation of the coming reign of God now has implications also for holistic mission (see Miyamoto 2007).

Second, Wesleyan theological discussions across the Asian rim have also highlighted the need to think about holiness and sanctification within an even more expansive cosmic vista (e.g., Ackerman 2002). The Asian context already suggests that the doctrine of sin ought to be understood in relationship to a shame culture, and this requires a more communal anthropology. Beyond this, however, human relationships are situated not only in relationship to "heaven" (or God) but also to the "earth," with the latter imagined as a symbiosis between human beings, other creatures, and the planetary environment. Hence only a fully trinitarian—not just christological and pneumatological—theology can sustain the robustly theocentric, theological, and cosmological vision of holiness needed for such a task.

As if these challenges were not sufficiently daunting, we must not forget that our broader task in this volume is the renewing of Christian theology, ecumenically considered. Our approach has been, however, from the particular to the universal, especially from renewal perspectives toward the church catholic. In this chapter, we have sought to engage with the issues in some focused dialogue with the Wesleyan-Holiness tradition, in large part because at least in the North American scene, Holiness and pentecostal churches have long had a sibling, if sometimes one of intense rivalry, relationship (see Synan 1997; Sanders 1996). It has been illuminating to observe Wesleyan-Holiness theologians struggle to articulate their distinctive doctrines in ways that will strengthen their churches, while simultaneously trying to make a contribution to the wider Christian theological task. Yet the latter remains a distinctive challenge. Wesleyan understandings of sanctification remain one of a number of options, and a minority perspective at that.

Refocusing our ecumenical lenses suggests that the breadth of the biblical models for holiness have generated a range of theologies of sanctification (e.g., Alexander 1989). The dominant alternatives to Wesleyan views include Lutheran and Reformed articulations. The former emphasizes the simultaneity of being saints and sinners (reflecting the complex relationship between law and gospel in Luther's writings), while the latter defines sanctification christologically, achieved once-and-for-all through baptism by the Spirit into Christ and the body of Christ. Both therefore reject any subsequent work of grace, while insisting on the progressive character of the path to holiness. As already mentioned, the Reformed view has made its way into renewal circles, especially in the finished work perspective of early Pentecostalism. These various options (put positively) or impasses (put negatively) reflect only the level of formal ecumenical conversations about these matters. And we have not even begun to factor in Catholic notions of holiness (no more than touched upon above) or Orthodox views of sanctification as theosis or deification (union with God).

But what if we were to multiply our ecumenical interlocutors to include not only the dogmatic and systematic theological formulations of other Christian traditions but also a range of variegated religious practices, even those in the broader history of religion? There is neither space nor time here, of course, for any extensive or exhaustive query. However, the research of the Jewish scholar of religion Evan Zuesse (1979) on African religious life and spirituality is instructive for our purposes. Zuesse focuses on indigenous African rituals of space and time related to hunting and sacrifice and finds that historically, Africans have not spent much time intellectually elaborating on their significance. Instead, phenomenological analyses open up windows into the efficaciousness of such rites as performative exercises that address the existential, holistic, and communal needs of African societies. More precisely, sub-Saharan peoples are oriented through these agricultural but yet also religious rituals toward engaging with and navigating a divinely imbued cosmos. Ritual practices thus open up participatory paths toward self-transformation and self-knowledge within a more holistically perceived cosmic horizon. Zuesse suggests that the cyclical performance of these rites is the means through which African peoples have perennially affirmed their solidarity with the renewing nature of the cosmos evidenced in its seasonal rhythms. In terms of this chapter, indigenous and traditional African ritual practices are instruments of sanctification that purify and renew individuals within communities and in relationship to their ancestors, the environment, and other cosmic and even superterrestrial beings. Individual salvation and sanctification here is interrelated with the harmonious equilibrium of the whole (Rappaport 1999).

The preceding certainly has implications for Wesleyan-Holiness theological discussions unfolding across the Pacific rim, even as other connections can be drawn for thinking about an ecumenical and interreligious theology of holiness, sanctity, and even wholeness (cf. Kieckhefer and Bond 1988; Sharma 2000). While it is beyond the scope of this chapter (or this volume as a whole) to resolve fully the issues, Christian theology in global context cannot ignore these realities or the questions they prompt. In the rest of this chapter we will think constructively about sanctification and holiness, even if this will only chart important trajectories toward, rather than provide a full enunciation of, such an understanding.

5.3 Johannine Sectarianism—and Sanctification

As is the procedure in each chapter, we now turn to the New Testament, in quest of some scriptural guidelines for thinking about sanctification today. Of course, no appeal to the Bible is entirely neutral, as if one could develop an objective biblical theology of sanctification (or any other topic). We are motivated in our approach to understand more clearly what is being affirmed in article 8 of the SF. Our discussants thus far have been the conversations in the Wesleyan-Holiness tradition. Toward this end, we turn to the first Epistle of John.

Why 1 John? This relatively short letter deserves attention in part because it functioned for John Wesley himself as a "canon-within-the-canon" (see Wall 2011), in particular a lens through which to understand the scriptural message of holiness. Granted, pneumatology is not a prevalent theme in this missive, although the work of the Holy Spirit is more substantial here than commonly acknowledged (Yong 2012: ch. 8). But Wesley's own reading of this small epistle highlights the role of the Spirit in the perfecting work of God. Indeed, 1 John plays a central role both in Wesley's scriptural reflections on Christian perfection and his thinking about how the Spirit attests to such in the lives of believers (see Wesley's sermons on "Christian Perfection" and "The Witness of the Spirit I" in Outler and Heitzenrater 1991). In light of these considerations, let me venture three sets of comments toward what might be called a Johannine, Wesleyan, and renewal theology of perfection.

First, uninitiated readers of this letter might be taken aback first by what appear to be contradictory claims. On the one hand, the author—which tradition identifies as John, perhaps the apostle, although this does not need to be resolved for our purposes (see section 12.1)—asserts plainly: "If we say that we have no sin, we deceive ourselves, and the truth is not in us," and "If we say that we have not sinned, we make him a liar, and his word is not in us" (1 John 1:8, 10). But then not long thereafter, he also adds, "No one who abides in him [Christ] sins; no one who sins has either seen him or known him," and "Those who have been born of God do not sin, because God's seed abides in them; they cannot sin, because they have been born of God" (3:6, 9; also 5:18a). How might these be understood more consistently across the letter?

The immediate context of the first set of assertions includes the mediating claim that "[i]f we confess our sins, he who is faithful and just will forgive us our sins and cleanse us from all unrighteousness" (1:9). This is possible because of the work of Christ: "if anyone does sin, we have an advocate with the Father, Jesus Christ the righteous; and he is the atoning sacrifice for our sins" (2:1-2). Hence, while all are sinners, those who know Christ have their sins covered and forgiven and are purified from sin. More to the point, those who know Christ are born of God and as children of God cannot continue in sin, because to do so would be to perpetuate the devil's works (3:8-10). But the latter pair of claims regarding sinlessness in the third chapter then needs to be understood within the eschatological framework of this section: "we are God's children now; what we will be has not yet been revealed. What we do know is this: when he is revealed, we will be like him, for we will see him as he is. And all who have this hope in him purify themselves, just as he is pure" (3:2-3). In other words, absolute sinlessness is an eschatological achievement, rather than fully realizable in the present age (see Bogart 1977; Walters 1995: 155–82). Yet such eschatological anticipation makes sense only when present lives are empowered in Christ and by the Spirit not only to desire holiness but also to resist sin and discontinue sinning. In short, human beings are all sinners (to deny this is to be self-deceived) even as all are called toward present and yet also eschatological perfection in Christ.

Second, how is holiness of life evidenced in the lives of believers? While not minimizing the role of rules and regulations in guiding moral living, 1 John provides an ethical framework oriented around keeping God's commandments and loving others. The author writes: "but whoever obeys his word, truly in this person the love of God has reached perfection" (2:5; see also 5:2), and "this is his commandment, that we should believe in the name of his Son Jesus Christ and love one another, just as he has commanded us" (3:23). Those who do not obey the divine commandments and do not love others are liars (2:4; 4:20). And those who hate their brothers and sisters remain in darkness (2:9-11) and ultimately reflect they are neither children of God (3:11b) nor recipients of God's eternal life (3:15). After all, those who do not love others who are seen cannot love a God who is unseen (4:20b; cf. 5:1).

But put positively, those who keep the commandments and love their neighbors are those who walk in the light (2:10), abide in the eternal life of God (3:14), and are born of God (4:7) and abide in God (4:16). The most unmistakable acts of love follow in the footsteps of Christ: "We know love by this, that he laid down his life for us—and we ought to lay down our lives for one another" (3:16). Such love is manifest concretely in deeds of assistance to those in need (3:18). Because "God is love" (4:8b, 16), and "since God loved us so much, we also ought to love one another . . . if we love one another, God lives in us, and his love is perfected in us" (4:11-12). And such perfect love assures believers anticipating the day of judgment (4:17), because "There is no fear in love, but perfect love casts out fear; for fear has to do with punishment, and whoever fears has not reached perfection in love" (4:19).

Yet third, the believers' capacity to love derives not from themselves but from God: "We love because he first loved us" (4:19). More precisely, the ability to love and to keep the commandments comes from the gift of the Spirit of God: "All who obey his commandments abide in him, and he abides in them. And by this we know that he abides in us, by the Spirit that he has given us" (3:24). The Spirit not only enables believers to discern the truth (from error) and recognize and acknowledge Christ (as opposed to the antichrist), but is also the source of their abiding in that truth: "we know that we abide in him and he in us, because he has given us of his Spirit" (4:13; cf. 2:20-27, 4:1-6). As Wesley noted, then, it is the Spirit who bears witness to our new birth as children of God (see Outler and Heitzenrater 1991: 147–48). One could go further to also say that the Spirit enables and attests to our abiding in that perfection in love which is also the core of the Wesleyan doctrine of entire sanctification.

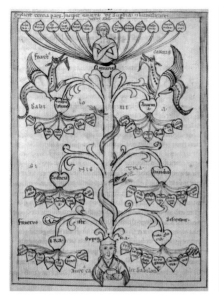

FIGURE 5.4

Throughout the Bible the human heart (and the human person in general) is often compared to and understood in terms of organic plant life (e.g. Deut 29:18; Ps 1:3, 52:8; Prov 11:28-30; Matt 7:15-19; James 3:12). The central principle is that the character and quality of one's daily actions are never simply a matter of isolated choices; rather, they are the "fruit" of an entire way of being, an integrated living system of body, heart, and mind that is organized in relation to one's environment in more or less healthy or unhealthy ways. This human-plant imagery not only prompts us to understand virtues or vices as systemically interconnected (and cultivated as such), it also characterizes fruitfulness as ultimately a matter of what kind of life is flowing through a person—what the heart is rooted in, dependent upon, and abiding in. There is a massive difference, St. Paul tells us, between living "in the flesh" and "in the Spirit" (Rom 8:5-6; Gal 6:8).

These ideas were thoughtfully systemized throughout the Middle Ages, as exemplified in the images above. The tree on the left schematizes the "fruit of the flesh" (fructus carnis). The princely figure at the base of this tree represents pride (superbia), which is the root of seven types of vicious fruit: wrath, vanity, sloth, envy, gluttony, greed, and ultimately lust (luxuria)—each of which gives way to further fruits of its own. Although pride is the root of these vices, the person formed at the culmination of this tree—the "old man" (vetus adam)— is naked, insecure, and self-protective. This organic system of vices is directly contrasted with the tree on the right, which produces the "fruit of the Spirit" (fructus spiritus), blossoming into the seven cardinal virtues: justice, prudence,

[handwritten margin notes:]
taking enjoyment in using things for your own good (rather than considering what's good for the other you're using)

*temperance, fortitude, faith (*fides*), hope (*spes*), and at its highest, love (*cari-tas*). And like the vices, each of these branches into seven further virtues, except for the crowning virtue of love, which sprouts into ten: harmony, generosity, compassion, piety, grace, peace, forgiveness, mercy, kindness, and meekness. The tree of virtue grows from the root of humility (represented by a scholar-monk) and culminates in the image of Christ, the "new man" (*novus adam*), who blesses the reader rather than protecting himself.*

Ultimately, these trees are not only associated with individual lives but with entire sociopolitical entities: Babylonia is inscribed across the tree of vices, whereas the virtues are identified with Jherusalem. The human life that abides in Christ and is alive in the Spirit is one that abides in the love of God and neighbor. ✦

The preceding is intended to lay some scriptural groundwork for our constructive reflections. The Johannine perfection in love involves a life-long process of abiding in God, hearkening to the commandments of Christ, and loving others. Yet this is irreducible to a gradualist view of holiness, because there is also a sense that the Scripture expects believers will at some point discontinue their sinful ways. This Wesleyan reading is consistent with what we see in the wider New Testament witness regarding sanctification. In particular it resonates with the idea that sanctification is definitively associated with Christ in ways that launch believers on a decisive path of renewal and transformation (see Peterson 1995).

But we are not yet ready to take leave of this Johannine material, as some comment on the social dynamics behind the text is important. This is not only because the historical realities in the background are evidenced in the text itself, but also because in other hands the sectarian and dualistic imagery and rhetoric motivated by such realities can become potent sources of in-group legitimization and out-group demonization (see Petersen 1993). The reception history of the Johannine literature—both the Epistles and the gospel, which many scholars see as related even if not authored by the same person, as well as postcolonial analyses of the text—has alerted us to how Johannine sectarianism can be used polemically in inappropriate ways (e.g., Segovia and Sugirtharajah 2007: 413–18). Of course, this is not a challenge only for 1 John or even for the Fourth Gospel, because binary modes of thinking can be detected across the Christian Testament. However, this is an apposite place to observe these rhetorical dynamics, because our topic is sanctification, and this has often involved separation from the world and consecration for divinely sanctioned initiatives.

While a complete response is impossible, the beginnings of any adequate answer ought to also observe that each of the four models of holiness delineated above—the cultic, the moral, the spiritual, and the social—can be discerned within the Johannine community. This comes into greater focus when the first letter is read against the backdrop of the Fourth Gospel. The cultic dimensions of holiness are manifest in the footwashing rite of cleaning, and this is part and parcel of the numerous strategies adopted within the Johannine community to nurture bonds of solidarity against an outside world that hates and despises them and the God they serve in Christ (see Bauckham 2007: ch. 12). When combined, these various designs to cultivate holiness within the community worked to preserve communal cohesiveness amid threats both external (from Jews who had rejected messianic believers and cast them out of the synagogue; see John 9:22; 12:42; 16:2) and internal (those within the community who held, for instance, a docetic view of Christ that minimized if not denied his full humanity). The rhetorical sharpness of the contrasts deployed is also designed to motivate and encourage readers to embrace the ways of God rather than apostasize.

Having said this, it is essential to note that even within the Johannine literature there is a global horizon, one in which those outside of the community might yet find inclusion. The writer of the first letter says clearly, for example, that Christ "is the atoning sacrifice for our sins, and not for ours only but also for the sins of the whole world" (1 John 2:2), even as the Fourth Gospel also pronounces the well-known saying, "For God so loved the world that he gave his only Son, so that everyone who believes in him may not perish but may have eternal life" (John 3:16). We have already seen the central role of love in the first letter, and this motif is just as palpable in John's gospel. The Johannine tradition thus has built within its own discursive framework the love commandments that, although focused on the body of believers, is or should also be open to, precisely because of God's expansive love, the world. Further, even the Christ in whom the community is urged to abide reached out to those outside the community, arguably believing that his holiness was contagious and could rub off on sinners (see Blomberg 2005). Is it not possible, even mandatory, that any contemporary theology of holiness nurture a christic and ecclesial identity that sets the church apart from the world even while releasing its fragrance to the same world about the redemptive possibilities of the gospel? Is it not possible to love God and fellow believers in a distinctive way that yet bears witness to the world? Jesus himself said: "I give you a new commandment, that you love one another. Just as I have loved you, you also should love one another. By this everyone will know that you are my disciples, if you have love for one another" (John 13:34–35).

5.4 Be Holy and Being Made Holy!

This final section responds to three questions that have percolated in the discussion above. (1) What is holiness? (2) How is holiness given, received, or accomplished? (3) What is holiness for? Our provisional thesis in response, to be elaborated in the rest of the chapter, is that holiness is a gift of sanctity received in (the body of) Christ and empowered by (the fellowship of) the Spirit as a way of embodying and living out God's perfect love for the world. While the parenthetical clauses may suggest these notions are incidental to holiness, we shall see why this is not the case. We begin our exposition of this working definition by returning to our discussion of the Virgin Mary with which this chapter opens to see how she as an exemplar of holiness illuminates aspects of the WAGF SF.

In the first place, what is holiness? The article calls attention to sanctification as derived from the person and work of Christ (Heb 10:10-14) and involving formation in and by Christ's character. This is consistent with the christological character of holiness, which has always been central to catholic—both Roman and ecumenical—understandings of Mary. Mary's sanctity derives from her being set apart to be the *theotokos*, the mother of the Lord Jesus Christ. This meant her separation from the normal affairs of the world in order to be consecrated as the mother of Christ. John's first letter also asserts that sinlessness consists in rejecting the darkness, hatred, and the ways of the flesh and the world, and chiefly in abiding in Christ, in his love, and in his commandments, and allowing these also to abide with the believer in turn. Hence holiness involves being separate from the world (and all of the sinfulness that it embodies) and being joined to God's love in Christ. Yet the setting apart of those who are being sanctified can never be merely an individualistic affair. Mary, we have seen, first comes to find part of her way with the help of her older cousin Elizabeth. Later, Mary finds the fulfillment of her Spirit Baptism in the company of the one hundred twenty in the Upper Room, and together they are baptized into the fellowship of the Spirit (see also 2 Cor 13:13).

But, second, how is holiness accomplished? The article contends this happens both instantaneously (theologically) and progressively (existentially). We have seen above that Wesley also recognized both aspects of the divine work of sanctification. When we turn to Mary's life, we can see her journey in holiness also reflects significant moments of divine visitation. Two instants have already been noted: the Spirit's coming over her in the conception of Jesus and on the day of Pentecost in the Upper Room. Both are theological encounters. Neither of these occurrences, however, undermines the progressive character of Mary's growth in grace, natural for human beings. Now some Roman Catholic interpreters might, in view of the dogma of Mary's "immaculate conception," insist that from the beginning Mary had been preserved from the stains of original sin for her Christ-bearing vocation (see Gentle and Fastiggi 2009: ch. 1). The argument is that the perfect passive tense of the angelic greeting of Mary as highly favored or, literally, full of grace (κεχαριτωμένη/*kecharitoméne*; Luke 1:28) indicates her sanctification had been completed in the past (with present and ongoing effects), thus denying any need for a more dynamic view of her holiness. (Formal Roman Catholic teaching would still insist that Christ is the Redeemer of all, including Mary, in the sense that it is only in light of his life and work that she was both preserved from sin and consecrated toward God in a fallen world [see Bonnefoy 1967: 58].) For such Roman Catholics, then, Mary's separation from evil was divinely ordained from her own conception, rather than achieved during her life, as would be understood by most renewalists. Yet even Protestants, including non-Catholic renewalists, who do not see sufficient biblical warrant for such a doctrinal affirmation, can appreciate the scriptural witness regarding Mary's docility to the work of the Spirit and commitment to the divine mandate. And there is no reason that Roman Catholics cannot view Mary's obedience as also emerging in a process of spiritual maturation. The point to be made is that crisis moments of encountering the divine love can have instantaneous effects, and these do not minimize the dynamic nature of coming to understand, embracing, and then living into or out of these foundational experiences. The latter processes are clearly communal, ecclesial in fact, involving being conformed in mind, body, and soul to the image of Christ in the company, communion, and fellowship of others by the Spirit (see Rom 12:1-2).

In the end, third, toward what end is holiness? Mary's holiness is not her own but designed to achieve the purposes of God. The lacuna in article 8 has to do with its relative silence regarding the telos of holiness.

Sanctification separates believers from something (the darkness of sin and the ways of the world) and consecrates and dedicates them to something (the resolutions of God)—and in this sense, there is an ecclesiological dimension that registers the countercultural difference that holiness is supposed to make to distinguish the people of God from those of the world. Yet the Johannine witness indicates that the ultimate purposes of the outworking of God's perfection in human lives involve their participation in the love of the Father for the Son and vice versa so that the world can be saved. Mary's sanctification involved her own baptism in divine love, an immersion in the love of the Father and the Son to the point of carrying the Son in her womb, delivering the Son into the world, raising the Son in the world, and then releasing him for the world.

The preceding explication highlights the deeply christological and pneumatological, and hence trinitarian, character of holiness. Central here is Wesley's understanding of sanctification as including God's purification and consecration of human hearts and lives. After all, human beings who are "dead through the trespasses and sins" (Eph 2:1) are unable to live holy lives on their own accord. Indeed, "all have sinned and fall short of the glory of God" (Rom 3:23). Thus the atoning work of Christ, who is indeed the perfect one in the New Testament (Heb 5:9), allows for the forgiveness of sin, while the renewing work of the Spirit accomplishes the eradication of such tendencies and proclivities in human hearts (cf. Ezek 36:24-27; Heb 8:8-13; 9:14). While these could be conceived as two separate works of grace—for Wesley, as initial and final sanctification—this is a theological rather than experiential distinction. A more relational and dynamic perspective realizes that the human progression with God is marked by any number of concrete encounters—distilled, this forms the core of the testimony prominent in renewal circles—even while these encounters do not undermine the processes through which individuals are finally conformed to the image of God in Christ.

More pointedly, sin itself is undeniably social in character (see Niebuhr 1934). Being born into sin is biological not in the sense of the older traducianist notion that the sinful nature is passed on to each person through the lustful act of sexual intercourse. Rather (and as we shall see further in ch. 10), because all creation labors under the bondage of sin (see Rom 8:18-22), human creatures struggle with sinful relationships, life systems, and environments from their conception. But if sin has this inextricably social dimension, then so has sanctification. The purification from sin and the consecration to holiness therefore inevitably have to involve the reconciling of alienated relations, the redemption and renewal of social structures, and the healing of the world. Hence to admit that holiness from this experiential perspective is a lifelong course of learning how to walk in the Spirit is not to minimize the handful (or more) of important points in the journey that are appropriately tabbed in theological terms as "salvation," "regeneration," or "sanctification." Instead it is to say that growth in sanctifying and perfecting grace involves people in community, in particular in the body of Christ empowered by the fellowship of the Spirit (see Rabens 2010: part 2), to bear witness to the possibilities of realizing the divine holiness in a still sinful world.

From here it is important to fill out the performative dimensions of the doctrine of sanctification, in effect following in the footsteps of Mary as she illuminates those of Christ. This consideration should be augmented at three interrelated levels: the personal, the ecclesial, and the social/cosmic. Personally, holiness is a spiritual matter touching on human hearts and lives. The first Johannine epistle describes this in the intimate terms of abiding in Christ by the Spirit. Hence there is a cruciform and christomorphic character to holiness (note article 8 refers to Gal 2:20), one that is pneumatologically infused, and thereby trinitarianly oriented. Holiness involves having the depths of sin rooted out of human hearts by the power of the Spirit, so they can participate and abide in the love of the Father and the Son. This is fundamentally a spiritual transformation that purifies what John calls "the desire of the flesh, the desire of the eyes, the pride in riches" (1 John 2:16) and involves a daily putting to death of the sinful self (1 Cor 15:31; Col 3:5). What emerges are new creatures remade in the image and likeness of the second Adam (1 Cor 15:45-49; 2 Cor 5:17) whose lives are redirected toward the city of God (Augustine) and the beatific vision (Aquinas). Yet this deeply interior and renovative work of grace is not merely spiritual or otherworldly. Purification of the flesh, renewal of the heart, and reorientation of hopes and desires enables humans to love God as they love themselves in the present life. This love of God is also worked out as love of neighbor and thus is irrevocably intertwined with the other two ecclesial and cosmic dimensions.

Ecclesially, holiness is a cultic and moral matter touching on the relationships that followers of Christ have with one another in the Spirit. Central here is embodiment of, participation in, and being a conduit for the love of God to others. There ought thus to be a distinctive form of loving relationality that defines ecclesial life. The cultic dimension of the scriptural witness here provides a template not only for the liturgical expression of Christian love (most concretely manifest in the Lord's Supper—see ch. 6 of this volume), but also nurtures a distinctive type of ritualized interactions. These involve meeting one another's needs (1 John 3:16-17); taking responsibility for one another's spiritual and moral lives (1 John 5:16-21); showing hospitality to one another (e.g., 3 John 5-8); and even deferring to one another appropriately, to the point of greeting each other with a kiss of love (1 Pet 5:14)—these are the interpersonal rites and moral behaviors that bind the church together in the love of God and that nurture the virtues that sustain holy living (Castelo 2012: ch. 3). So yes, holiness involves the reshaping of human behaviors in anticipation of the purifying judgment to come (1 Cor 3:12-15; see also ch. 10 of this volume). Yet sanctified perfection at this level is still less a series of dos and don'ts or culturally defined conventions or moralisms—although it is and often also will be at least this—than a set of ecclesially and trinitarianly shaped relationships. The ritual and relational interactions differ from church to church and from ecclesial tradition to ecclesial tradition, whatever the phenomenological manifestations or ethnographic records. However, the basic scriptural marks ought to be discernible about how holiness sanctifies the church amid its relationship to the wider community, so its pursuit of perfection in love marks it as distinct from the norms and ways of the world (e.g., Butler 2007).

FIGURE 5.5

This was originally the first page of the Hours of the Holy Spirit *from a fifteenth-century illuminated prayer book. The text along the bottom of the image is the opening line of the evening prayer (vespers) for these Hours, which is in such prayer books almost always accompanied by an image of the outpouring of the Spirit on the day of Pentecost. The illumination artist for this prayer book, Jean Fouquet, follows this tradition but does so in unusual ways. Whereas most depictions of Pentecost place the scene inside a house (in accordance with Acts 2:2b), Fouquet situates the faithful neither in an upper room nor indoors at all but in a city—or rather on the outer margins of a city. This change of context has significant effects. (1) It emphasizes the radical implications of Pentecost for the city in which it takes place (see Acts 2:5-41): the outpouring of the Spirit is here not solely concerned with individual transformation but with the redemptive effect of this community in and for the city. (2) It also suggests ongoing reiterations of the Pentecost event: the Spirit is poured out in numerous subsequent communities spanning across diverse cultural-historical contexts. For both reasons, Fouquet sets the scene specifically in his own cultural and geographical context—the background is a topographically accurate depiction of medieval Paris—and he does so not out of disregard for the historical particularity of the original event but as a means of imagining and (visually) praying for the Spirit's presence and activity in his own historical moment. This artistic decision is especially appropriate to the words that the Hours will proceed to pray (always in the present tense): "Come O Holy Spirit, replenish the hearts of thy faithful, and kindle in them the fire of thy love."*

Fouquet's depiction of the outpouring of the Spirit into this tightly huddled community is visually subtle and understated (a thin golden beam "breaking into" the visible world), yet its effect is powerful, causing demons to scatter. This understated quality of the outpouring is significant: the demons scatter not by force but because of whose Spirit is present. This feature of the image is also important in the ways that it identifies the enemies of the faithful: their enemy is not the city (or "the world") to which they are marginal; their enemy is the demonic. ✦

Socially and cosmically, holiness involves the social expression of God's perfecting love as the church and its many members live in and bear witness to the world. This domain of holiness indicates that personal and spiritual holiness is not just for the self but for God and others and that ecclesial holiness is not just for the church but for the world (see Bretherton 2006). Ecclesial holiness without a corresponding social dimension is hypocritical. The first generation of Azusa Street renewalists, for instance, were convinced that the Spirit's baptism of love not only brought about a new spiritual unity that cut across denominational boundaries but also the capacity to overcome the racial and ethnic divides that permeated early twentieth-century American society in the Jim Crow era (see J. L. Thomas 2014). This mode of ordering a more inclusive ecclesial life had implications for attitudes and postures toward the wider society. Yes, the church is set off from and clearly demarcated from the world (e.g., Hauerwas and Willimon 1989, 1996). But the point of this distinctiveness is not just to be different but to bear witness of the love of God in Christ for and to the world. There is no doubt a tension, even a paradoxical one, between being *not of* but yet *in* the world. This means, for instance, that there is something unique about Christian love—its being found in God's self-sacrificial life in Christ—that the world does not possess. Yet there is also something universal to such love that will catch the world's attention, that will fuel its desires, and that may reorder its ways. In short, individuals called to holiness are being perfected in the company of others, the church as the locus of sanctification, amid but not of the world.

Hence, with regard to the path of sanctification, there is something inimitable about specifically *Christian* and *ecclesial* holiness—the abiding in Christ enabled by the Spirit—that is absent in the world. Yet there is also something universal to such sanctity that may be tapped into by indigenous and even world religious traditions (e.g., Organ 1970; Carmody and Carmody 1996). This may be why there are saints in many traditions, even exemplars from which Christians can learn about God's redeeming grace. This also explains how Christians can build bridges to other traditions of holiness also seeking the sanctification of individuals and of the world (e.g., Valantasis 2005). Yes, the christomorphic character of Christian holiness remains matchlessly distinctive and particular. Yet to debate holiness in a world of many faiths is itself unsanctified. Rather, the point about Christian holiness is bearing witness to others, to the world, of the perfect love of God manifest in Christ, by the power of the Spirit without denying that the Spirit's sanctifying effects may yet be displayed outside the church.

Later chapters will return to revisit some of these themes and important issues regarding the relationship between the gospel and culture, the church and the world, and Christianity and other religions. For the moment, however, our task is to reconsider how the Christian doctrine of sanctification can renew and empower Christian life in the late modern world. Our claim is that holiness is gift of God received in Christ and empowered by the Spirit to enable the embodying and living out of God's perfect love to and for others. The election of the people of God, then, involves not just separation from the world but the call to live out the love of God in the world, so others may come to experience the love of the

Father and the Son for themselves. Our next chapter burrows deeper into the formative processes of such divine encounter that radically inspire and revolutionize people's lives.

Discussion Questions

1. What are some aspects of your church's teachings about holiness and sanctification that are different from those discussed in the preceding discussion? Are these differences complementary or contradictory, and if the latter, what are possible responses to these divergent views?
2. What are highlights of your own experience of holiness or sanctification? Have these felt more instantaneous or progressive in your view? How might the preceding exposition provide you with some theological vocabulary to understand these experiences better?
3. Holiness, this chapter argues, involves becoming perfect in the love of God manifest in Christ and loving others in turn. How does this understanding of holiness as a verb and as a task helpful? What does it mean that holiness is to be lived out as a witness to others? How does this help us understand the relevance of holiness in the twenty-first century?

Further Reading

Barton, Stephen C., ed. 2003. *Holiness: Past and Present*. London: T&T Clark.
Brower, Kent E., and Andy Johnson, eds. 2007. *Holiness and Ecclesiology in the New Testament*. Grand Rapids: Eerdmans.
Burgess, Stanley M., ed. 1986. *Reaching Beyond: Chapters in the History of Perfectionism*. Peabody, Mass.: Hendrickson.
Coulter, Dale M. 2004. *Holiness: The Beauty of Perfection*. Cleveland, Tenn.: Pathway.
Demarest, Bruce A., ed. 2012. *Four Views on Christian Spirituality*. Grand Rapids: Zondervan.
Gundry, Stanley N., ed. 1987. *Five Views on Sanctification*. Grand Rapids: Zondervan.
Hyde, Michael J. 2010. *Perfection: Coming to Terms with Being Human*. Waco, Tex.: Baylor University Press.

6

Ordinances and Sacraments

Practicing the Christian Life

World Assemblies of God Fellowship Statement of Faith
—Article 7: The Ordinances of the Church

We believe that baptism in water by immersion is expected of all who have repented and believed. In so doing they declare to the world that they have died with Christ and been raised with Him to walk in newness of life (Matthew 28:19; Acts 10:47-48; Romans 6:4).

We believe that the Lord's Supper is a proclamation of the suffering and death of our Lord Jesus Christ, to be shared by all believers until the Lord returns (Luke 22:14-20; 1 Corinthians 11:20-34).

6.1 John the Baptist: In Water—and the Spirit?

Christian baptism has its most immediate antecedent in the baptism of John, Jesus' cousin from Elizabeth (section 3.1). As with other characters opening each chapter in this volume, deriving his narrative from the pages of the New Testament results less in a modern objective biography than in a thread of salvation history as mediated through the apostolic witness (Wink 1968; Taylor 1997). After all, John is consistently depicted not as one having his own identity but as one who bears witness to Christ (Conway 1999: 52–53). Yet the practices of John the Baptist, as he is called in the Synoptic Gospels, open up an important window for our topic at hand.

We know that John was born into a Levitical family, with his father Zechariah belonging "to the priestly order of Abijah" (Luke 1:5). His growing up in the wilderness (1:80) plus his baptizing activities have led more than a few scholars to explore the possibility that John may have been associated during at least part of this time with desert-based groups like the Essenes or the community at Qumran (Steinmann 1958; Badia 1980). There is no concrete evidence for such speculation, and there are distinctive elements to John's baptism. Yet he did see himself in accordance with an Isaianic text that was also central at Qumran—as "The voice of one crying out in the wilderness" (Luke 3:4 par. Matt 3:3; Mark 1:3; cf. Isa 40:3)—and his unconventional appearance and lifestyle (Matt 3:4; Mark 1:6; cf. Luke 1:15; 7:24-25) no doubt solidified a countercultural persona among those who came into the orbit of his ministry.

John finally appears in public not too long before his younger cousin Jesus (Luke 3:1-3). He preached "a baptism of repentance for the forgiveness of sins" (Mark 1:4), encouraging those who were waiting for the Messiah and challenging others who may have been more oblivious about that (see Luke 1:16-17, 76-79). His ministry began to gather large crowds, many of whom he baptized in the Jordan River (Luke 3:7; 7:29; John 3:23). Some of these became his followers (Matt 11:7; John 3:26), and we know that pockets of these disciples persisted into the region of Ephesus and other parts of Asia Minor (see Acts 18:24–19:1). Yet what is important is the audience John gained, even among tax collectors and soldiers (Luke 3:12-14), so much so that the Jewish historian Josephus (*Antiquities* 18.5.2; see Whiston 1991: 484) viewed him as being politically threatening to Herod Antipas (ca. 20 BCE–39 CE). What Josephus does not mention is well known from the Synoptic Gospels: John's prophetic voice was unafraid of challenging even the tetrarch of Galilee, not only for taking Herodias, his brother's wife, as his own, but also "because of all the evil things that Herod had done" (Luke 3:19; Matt 14:3-5; Mark 6:17-18). Eventually, at the behest of Herodias, John was beheaded (perhaps during the last year or two of Jesus' own public ministry).

These details are less our focus that what John did, which was baptize people, including Jesus. If John's baptism was for the forgiveness of sins, the theological question that has exercised many interpreters is why Jesus, viewed by the early Christian community as being without sin (Heb 4:15), sought out John's baptism. John also understood that he ought to have been baptized by Jesus instead, in particular with Jesus' fiery baptism of the Holy Spirit. Yet Jesus insisted: "Let it be so now; for it is proper for us in this way to fulfill all righteousness" (Matt 3:15). From here, Jesus began to gather a core group of disciples, and they also began baptizing in his name (John 3:26; 4:1-2; cf. Acts 2:38; 8:16; 10:48; 19:5).

While John's followers were no doubt concerned about their "competition," he himself seemed secure in his vocation of calling Israel to anticipate the revelation of the promised Messiah. He was not more than an echo in the desert and saw his task as only to baptize in water so the people could be cleansed from their sin and be ready for the messianic Day of the Lord. He recognized that "one who is more powerful than I is coming after me; I am not worthy to carry his sandals" (Matt 3:11

par. Mark 1:7; Luke 3:16), and he came to believe this was Jesus. Thus he denied to inquirers that he was even a prophet (John 1:19-26; 3:26-28), while continuously pointing to Jesus, saying, "He who comes after me ranks ahead of me because he was before me" (1:15), and "He must increase, but I must decrease" (3:30).

FIGURE 6.1

In this icon, the vertical form of the river and the descent of the Spirit from heaven become fused into a single downward flow that surrounds Christ's body and splits the composition into halves. In this fusion, John's baptism with water is taken up into the greater movement by which "God anointed Jesus of Nazareth with the Holy Spirit and with power" (Acts 10:38). In Eastern Orthodoxy, Christ's baptism is often referred to as the Epiphany ("revelation"), even Theophany ("revelation of God"), because it profoundly discloses Jesus' identity: "as he was coming up out of the water, he saw the heavens torn apart and the Spirit descending like a dove on him. And a voice came from heaven, 'You are my Son, the Beloved; with you I am well pleased'" (Mark 1:10-11). On the one hand, this can be interpreted as revealing Jesus' divine identity as the Son of God; on the other hand, when read in the context of the Isaianic prophesies (e.g. Isa 42:1-4, 64:1), Jesus is then more directly identified with Israel and is recapitulating Israel's history: both are referred to as God's son (Exod 4:22; Mark 1:11; cf. Ps 2:7), and after passing through the waters, both are sent into the wilderness, where they are tempted for forty years/days (Num 14:34; Mark 1:12-13).

Rublev's icon seems to merge all these readings together. The image is structured to suggest an Exodus passage through the waters. John, the forerunner of Christ, stands on the left (former) bank proclaiming "a baptism of repentance for the forgiveness of sins" (Mark 1:4), a message signified by a small tree and ax beside him (difficult to see in this damaged icon): "Even now the ax is lying at the root of the trees" (Matt 3:10). This call for repentance will ultimately point the people of Israel (and Gentiles) to this man standing in the river. John stands over Jesus but understands the impropriety of this position (Matt 3:14), so he bows even as he pours water over Christ's head. On the opposite (future) bank angels also bow, waiting to receive and clothe the baptized Christ. This implied movement from the left bank to the right suggests a passage through the waters reminiscent of the Exodus passage—and as in the Exodus an entire people will be called to follow this true Son of God through these waters by being baptized into him (cf. figs. 6.2 and 6.3). ✦

Two facets of John's baptism deserve final comment before proceeding. First, unlike the baptisms at the Qumran community, for instance, John's was nonsectarian, in that it did not initiate the masses into an exclusive group or way of life. To be sure, John expected that those baptized by him would "[b]ear fruit worthy of repentance" (Matt 3:8), and in that sense, that there would be observable changes in their lives. But there is no indication that he began a new community in the desert based on his own practices or convictions. Second, while John's baptism of repentance was intended for the forgiveness and thus ablution of sins, this was understood ritually (following ancient Jewish purification rites recorded in the Torah) rather than sacramentally (in the senses to be discussed momentarily). Cleansing from sin in John's view prepared the way for the coming of the Day of the Lord. John's baptism was therefore consistent with, if not central to, his announcements regarding the imminent unveiling of the Messiah. We shall see that the earliest followers of Jesus both built on and adapted these understandings for their own purposes.

6.2 The Great Tradition and Its Sacramental Tributaries

The title of article 7, "The Ordinances of the Church," already signals alignment on one side of an extremely contentious debate launched during the Reformation. The language of "ordinance" is used by Baptists and others in the Free Church tradition to refer to the rites of water baptism and the Lord's Supper believed to be instituted by Christ. What is being rejected on the other side are "sacraments," specific understandings of baptism and what Roman Catholic, Orthodox, and other established churches call *Eucharist*, in particular the notion that they mediate the salvific grace of God. Renewalists situated within the baptistic tradition thus oppose these sacramental interpretations and instead see both rites as symbolic or memorial activities performed in obedience to Christ's command (e.g., Warrington 1998: ch. 9).

Part of the contemporary challenge is that renewalists derive from across the spectrum of Christian churches. Many classical Pentecostals and others situated within evangelical and Free Churches know of nothing but "ordinances," while charismatics in mainline Protestant, Roman Catholic, Orthodox, and Anglican traditions are sacramentalists in many different senses (see Gunstone 1982: ch. 7; Hayes 1990). In order to navigate the philosophical, theological, and biblical issues, some historical perspective is essential. In this section, we will begin with practices of Christian initiation in the early church, focusing specifically on the baptismal rite, and then shift to medieval and Reformation disputes about the Lord's Supper. Because we see that early Christian initiation involved repentance, exorcism, and the renunciation of the devil (as a prelude to baptism), we will return in the third part of this section to explore this theme from a renewal perspective, in particular how it foregrounds deliverance from evil powers in the contemporary global context. Yet in each case we can do no more than provide a very cursory outline of developments in each arena. Interested readers will need to follow up on the references and the further reading list to fill in the many important gaps in our sketch.

One final caveat must be noted before proceeding. While the basic thrust of ordinance language deserves reaffirmation, the debates between ordinance and sacrament are tired and in need of fresh consideration. For that reason, although both terms will be used as appropriate within the context of the following discussion, we will talk periodically also about "the practices" of the church (see Yoder 2001). By doing so, a way forward may open that preserves what is biblical about both discourses while yet promulgating an alternative vocabulary more conducive for the present global conversation. The last part of this chapter will elaborate on how baptism and the Lord's Supper are central but nonexhaustive *practices* that define the church's identity and are central to its witness to the world.

6.2.1 Christian Initiation and Baptism

In some respects, Peter's response to the crowd's question—"What should we do?"—on the day of Pentecost became a template for Christian initiation, at least for the early church: "Repent, and be baptized every one of you in the name of Jesus Christ so that your sins may be forgiven; and you will receive the gift of the Holy Spirit" (Acts 2:37-38). One can break this down into either three or four components (depending on whether one separates baptism from the forgiveness of sins), but each is clearly discernible in initiation practices for the first few hundred years of the church.

For our purposes, we focus on the ancient document, *The Apostolic Tradition*, which many scholars link to Hippolytus (170–235), bishop of Rome. If correctly associated, this text reflects early third-century procedures for admitting converts into the church. Recall that during this period, Christians were periodically persecuted, so extra caution was taken to scrutinize candidates for conversion to determine their sincerity and readiness. After being subject to a period of instruction and catechesis for three years (*Trad. ap.* 17:1), catechumens finally were prepared for baptism through a week (or perhaps up to forty days) of prayer, fasting, and exorcistic and purificatory rites (see either "General Introduction" to the two volumes of Finn 1992).

On the morning of the fifth day of the week, the baptismal service would follow this sequence. First, under the guidance of the presiding presbyter, the candidate confesses: "I renounce you Satan, all your service and all your works," after which the presbyter responds with application of the "oil of exorcism," saying, "Let all evil spirits depart far from you" (*Trad. ap.* 21:9-10; see Stewart-Sykes 2001: 111; cf. Kelly 1985: part 2). Then, baptism by immersion follows, thrice according to the Matthean trinitarian formula (Matt 28:19). Subsequently the oil of thanksgiving is applied by the presbyter, who also invokes the Holy Spirit:

> Lord God, you have made them worthy to deserve the remission of sins through the laver of regeneration: make them worthy to be filled with the Holy Spirit, send your grace upon them that they may serve you in accordance with your will; for to you is glory, to the Father and the Son with the

Holy Spirit in the holy church both now and to the ages of the ages. Amen.
(*Trad. ap.* 21:21; Stewart-Sykes 2001: 112)

Interestingly, *The Apostolic Tradition* does not mention at this point that charismatic manifestations follow. Yet this is documented by innumerable witnesses East and West across the first few centuries (see McDonnell and Montague 1994: part 2). The initiates are finally confirmed through partaking of the oblation of the bread and cup, representing the body and blood of Christ. The new members of the body of Christ then join the existing community in taking the Lord's Supper together the next (Sabbath) day. Catechism, exorcism and renunciation of the devil, baptism, reception of the Holy Spirit, confirmation, and the Lord's Supper—each of these were integral moments to Christian initiation during this early period (Pocknee 1967).

After this early account, we come across an increasing variety of initiatory and baptismal practices and beliefs. For our purposes, however, two developments with St. Augustine deserve mention (see Ferguson 2009: ch. 52). First, against the Donatists, Augustine insisted that the efficacy of the baptismal rite depends not on the priest or minister but on the church's authority as given by Christ. Not only were the rebaptisms called for by Donatist apologists unnecessary, but such were schismatic in terms of their arbitrary distinctions between acceptable and unacceptable ministers and ritual practices. Second, against the Pelagians, Augustine defended the efficacy of infant baptism in dealing with the problem of original sin. The presumption here is that the sin nature is passed on to children by their parents through the sexual act of conception and that baptism is therefore salvifically regenerative for all, including those who die before growing to the age of accountability. During and after this time, however, what was once a part of a much more elaborate process of Christian initiation had become a focal moment associated with the new birth. Salvation, after all, was believed to be dispensed "through the water of rebirth and renewal by the Holy Spirit" (Tit 3:5b). If so, then baptism in water was concluded to be the divinely chosen instrument of regenerating human hearts.

Assuredly, the beliefs about and practices relating to Christian initiation as a whole as well as the rite of baptism specifically continued to evolve over the centuries (Johnson 1995, 1999). Within the Latin West, in particular the Roman tradition, not only was the period of catechism gradually separated from the rite of initiation, but the latter also developed to include four distinct sacraments: baptism, penance, Eucharist, and confirmation (see Kavanagh 1991: ch. 2). Among the Orthodox, baptism also remains a rite of Christian initiation that accomplishes the remission or forgiveness of sins, as affirmed in the Nicene Creed. More deeply than in many Protestant evangelical churches, however, the Orthodox emphasize baptismal participation in the death and resurrection of Christ—themes highlighted in Romans 6:1-4 and Colossians 2:11-13—by the Holy Spirit as integral to the believer's vision of or union with God (theosis or deification; see Schmemann 1974). The point is that these sacraments make available to believers the saving grace of God in Christ.

FIGURE 6.2   FIGURE 6.3

Throughout Christian tradition the shape and form of the church's baptismal waters have carried enormous symbolic significance. Following St. Paul, Christian baptism signifies a person's being "baptized into Christ Jesus," united with him in his death and resurrection (Rom 6:1-11; cf. Gal 3:26-27). For this reason, many early baptismal fonts were built in the form of a cross, such that immersion into the cruciform waters signified being "buried with him by baptism into death" (Rom 6:3), which also implies being resurrected into his life: "For if we have been united with him in a death like his, we will certainly be united with him in a resurrection like his" (Rom 6:4-5; cf. Col 3:3-4).

From this latter eschatologically oriented claim, there emerged a second (more pervasive) ancient convention: the octagonal baptismal font. Immersion into the eight-sided waters symbolized being baptized into the "eighth day": the new day of the coming week (age), the Easter on the other side of our own holy Saturday. And given that a Greek cross is easily inscribed within an octagon, the two symbolic structures were overtly held together: to be baptized into Christ's cruciform body is to be baptized into his resurrection body, which will return on the eschatological eighth day.

Whether the font was cruciform, octagonal, or otherwise, the baptizant would enter the waters after fully disrobing, stripping off his or her status and "old self" (Rom 6:6) and entering into Christ. The baptizant would exit the pool on the east side (the side of the new day), symbolically emerging as a new creation— "dead to sin and alive to God in Christ Jesus" (Rom 6:11)—and rerobed in a new white tunic, thus receiving a radically new identity: "As many of you as were baptized into Christ have clothed yourselves with Christ. There is no longer Jew or Greek, there is no longer slave or free, there is no longer male and female; for all of you are one in Christ Jesus" (Gal 3:27-28). And it is precisely here—in this formation of a new people who have passed through the waters (of death) into life—that baptism proclaims a new Exodus in Christ, an already-not-yet freedom from slavery to sin and death. Anticipating the other side of this Exodus, Paul thus urges us, "Present yourselves to God as those who have been brought from death to life. . . . For sin will have no dominion over you" (Rom 6:13-14). ✦

The Reformation introduced at least two additional perspectives on the baptismal rite. Within the specifically Reformed traditions, baptism was understood as a sign and seal of the new covenant and new birth, just as circumcision was such a sign and seal of the covenant with Israel. Baptism hence provided means of participation in Christ and of celebrating God's offering of Christ to the church (Riggs 2002). The practice of infant baptism by and large was retained, on the basis that the faith of the parents and of the church would suffice until such time as children would confirm their faith for themselves. For the Radical Reformers, however, baptism ought to follow the *confession* of faith and hence excluded those not old enough to understand the gospel. For these and later baptistic traditions, then, baptism was a public expression of the believer's faith confession. The result of these Reformation divergences, however, led to even further differences of thought and practice. The last few hundred years thus have spawned three groups: those who baptize infants, those who baptize believers only, and those who do both (Wright 2000).

Within the contemporary context, the variation of beliefs and practices continues to proliferate. One scholar suggests that there are generally eight distinct models (Haitch 2007). The value of this typology of Christian initiation is that it recognizes how the historic practice included rites of exorcism. Ironically, although there are various views of baptism among renewalists (Heath and Dvorak 2011: ch. 9), most disassociate Spirit Baptism from water baptism in particular and from Christian initiation in general—based on the subsequence notion (e.g., Ervin 1984)—while ignoring any formal role for the expulsion of evil spirits. Yet in the global context, wherein differences of opinion and particularly practice are also magnified due to processes of inculturation (see Best and Heller 1999), retrieving this exorcistic theme is important, even if that may exacerbate the differences rather than lead toward an ecumenical agreement on baptism. We will return to take up this thread later in this section.

6.2.2 The Eucharist/Supper as Sacrament and/or Ordinance?

The preceding mentioned that those newly initiated through baptism in the postapostolic period joined the local congregation in partaking of the bread and the cup. The earliest meal fellowships were more informal and festive occasions (Acts 2:42, 46). Hence the meal was partaken with thanksgiving, according to the spirit in which Jesus himself gave thanks for the bread and the cup (Matt 26:26-27 and parallels; also 1 Cor 11:24). Not unexpectedly, then, this supper of the Lord was called the Eucharist (initially in the late first-century or early second-century document *Didache*, or *Teaching of the Twelve Apostles*, 9:1), which simply means "to give thanks." Yet even by the third century, we see a liturgical shape emerging consistent with the widespread New Testament connection, not only in Paul (1 Cor 11:17-34) but also in the Gospels (Matt 26:17-30; Mark 14:12-26; Luke 22:7-23), of Christ's sacrificial life and death with the ancient Jewish Passover. And it was within this liturgical context that the Johannine teaching about the indispensability of Christ for eternal life as the eternally nourishing bread from heaven (John 6:25-59) was received.

Undoubtedly, this language in the New Testament about eating the body of Jesus and drinking his blood soon led to charges of cannibalism. Although a number of second-century apologists successfully defended Christians against such accusations, it is also fair to say that most Christians during the first few hundred years believed Christ to be present in their partaking of the liturgical meal (see Osborne 1987: ch. 10). Over the course of the centuries, debates evolved into more spiritual versus more realistic views of how Christ was present in the meal (e.g., McCracken and Cabaniss 1957: 90–148). The former were concerned that the latter depictions of Jesus' body and blood were grossly physicalistic and hence untenable, while the latter thought the former unable finally to account for Jesus' promised presence in any meaningful way.

The rediscovery of Aristotelian philosophy during the High Middle Ages, however, provided resources for theologians to proffer then a more satisfying intellectual explanation for Christ's real presence. Drawing on the Aristotelian distinction between substances and accidents, the doctrine of transubstantiation affirmed that when the elements are consecrated by the priest, they are (substantially) transformed into the body and blood of Christ while they retain their (accidental) texture for the communicant. This teaching of accidents coinhering in a new substance—of the bread and wine in the body of Christ—in the consecrated host was reaffirmed at the Roman Catholic Council of Trent in the sixteenth century and remains part of the Roman Catholic Church's official teachings: "By the consecration the transubstantiation of the bread and wine into the Body and Blood of Christ is brought about. Under the consecrated species of bread and wine Christ himself, living and glorious, is present in a true, real, and substantial manner: his Body and his Blood, with his soul and his divinity" (*Catechism of the Catholic Church*, §1413). Yet while Protestants focus on and (mostly) reject this idea, the Catholic view highlights instead not only Christ's real presence in the meal but also that the celebration of the Eucharist is at least *an* if not *the* "constitutive aspect of the Church" (LaVerdiere 1996: 187; cf. McPartlan 1993). Neither of these might be a major problem for mainline Protestants, but the doctrine of transubstantiation did become an issue during the Reformation. The major contested point, however, had to do with the sense that the transubstantiated presence of Christ in the elements meant that his sacrifice was repeated at each enactment of the Eucharist.

Focus on the details of the Roman Catholic Eucharist should not obscure the church's overarching sacramental vision. Briefly, the classical theology of the sacraments holds that God has chosen to reveal himself and save the world through certain material and visible realities, and that the church now remains the instrument through which such revelatory and salvific actions are mediated. This follows, in the Catholic account, a strictly incarnational logic, most forcefully articulated in the Johannine literature, that "the Word *became flesh* and lived among us, and we have seen his glory, the glory as of a father's only son, full of grace and truth" (John 1:14 [emphasis added]). The God who chose such an incarnational modality in Christ has continued to reveal himself in saving ways through the concreteness of the historical church and its divinely instituted practices (Tillard 2001). By the medieval period, seven such sacramental mediations were practiced—baptism, confirmation, Eucharist, penance (reconciliation), anointing of the sick, holy orders (ordination), and marriage—each of which provided palpable interfaces with divine salvific grace for historically embodied creatures (see Grün 2003).

The Reformation brought about two major alternative responses. On the one hand, the magisterial Reformers by and large accepted the medieval definition while delimiting the number of sacraments to the two that

Jesus himself underwent (baptism) and instituted (the Supper). In addition, they rejected the Catholic interpretation of the Eucharist as repeating the sacrificial death of Christ. But some in this tradition also began to talk about the proclamation of the word of God as having sacramental qualities in terms of its efficaciousness in bringing sinners to repentance and conversion. On the other hand, the Radical Reformers questioned the very notion that sacraments were efficacious in mediating God's saving grace. Hence, new vocabulary was needed, and the nomenclature of *ordinances* emerged in the wake of these developments.

With regard to the presence of Christ at the Supper, challenges to the Aristotelian philosophical synthesis gradually raised new concerns about the doctrine of transubstantiation. For Luther, Christ's *real presence* accompanies the elements not because of their transubstantiation but simply according to the gospel pronunciation: "this is my body" and "this is my blood of the covenant" (Matt 26:26, 28 and parallels; 1 Cor 11:24–25). This corporeal understanding was also undergirded by the distinctive Lutheran doctrine of the ubiquity of Christ's incarnational body, made possible by the communication of attributes of the divine nature of the Logos to Jesus' human nature, although uniquely to be found in the sacrament of the Supper following from Jesus' promise (Sasse 1959: 148–60). Other Reformers like Huldrych Zwingli (1484–1531), however, opposed the Lutheran view by distinguishing between the sign of the gifts and the reality of Christ's presence. "This is my body" means "this signifies my body" (Pipkin 1984: 139). From this, noting also that Jesus said, "Do this in remembrance of me" (Luke 22:19; cf. 1 Cor 11:24-25), Zwinglians have emphasized a commemorative or *memorial presence*—that Christ is remembered by his body, the church, in the Supper. Calvinists, however, think assertions about real presence inevitably beg irresolvable metaphysical assumptions and thus affirm only Christ's salvifically nourishing and *spiritual presence* in the Holy Spirit. These three Reformation perspectives, among others, have persisted to the present (Smith 2008; Smith and Taussig 1990), although the Zwinglian view has also led later baptistic and other low-church evangelical traditions to talk about Christ's *symbolic presence*.

More recently, however, a new appreciation regarding the central role of the Holy Spirit in the Supper is observable. This is occurring not only among Protestants (e.g., Oulton 1951) but also among Roman Catholics (e.g., Kizhakkeparampil 1995). Yet this ought not to be seen as a novel teaching, particularly in light of the close associations between reception of the Holy Spirit and Christian initiation into the meal of fellowship in the early church, and also in view of Calvin's pneumatological emphases. In addition, Orthodox theologians also have reminded us that the full scope of the eucharistic event is thoroughly pneumatological. It is not just that the epiclesis that calls on the Holy Spirit to transform the gifts into the body and blood of Christ is held to be "the summit of eucharistic celebration" (Schmemann 1987: 213). Rather the entire celebration—from entrance, to hearing of the word, the offering, the anaphora or prayer of offering up of the elements, thanksgiving, and remembrance—is an event of the Spirit. For many in the historic Christian tradition, then, the presence of Christ and the communion of the Holy Spirit are intimately intertwined and central to the Eucharist.

FIGURE 6.4

This image presents a meditation on the meaning of the Eucharist by superimposing multiple iconographical motifs onto one another. First, this image is a Last Supper: twelve disciples (including Judas, upper right) are present as Jesus presents bread and wine, proclaiming "This is my body that is for you . . . This cup is the new covenant in my blood. Do this, as often as you drink it, in remembrance of me" (1 Cor 11:24-25). Second, this also functions as a crucifixion scene: Christ stands cruciform while to his lower left—in accordance with most depictions of the crucifixion (cf. fig. 8.4)—Magdalene appears (holding a perfume jar) alongside Mary, who grieves with deep sorrow for her son (the centurion's declarative gesture might also be seen in the central figure on the right; Mark 15:39). Third, however, this is also clearly an image of the resurrected Christ, as designated by the title but also by the clean wounds in his hands and absence of a cross. This is the risen, ascended Lord presiding over his body, the church. And as his body the church's tasks are visually articulated in the figures immediately next to Christ: to the left, one of the five wise bridesmaids keeps an adequately supplied lamp, watchfully awaiting the bridegroom (Matt 15:1-13); and on the right, a disciple holds a fishing net, symbolic of the calling to be "fishers of people" (Matt 4:19). In the upper register, these vocations of watching and evangelizing are complemented by worship (upper left) and repentance (upper right).

All three of these holy week iconographies—Last Supper, crucifixion, and resurrection—converge in the bread and wine, which are precisely circumscribed within, and thus identified with, Christ's body. Jesus' proclamation of the new covenant on Maundy Thursday is thus carried through to the ongoing Eucharist celebration of the people of Easter Sunday: "For as often as you eat this bread and drink the cup, you proclaim the Lord's death until he comes" (1 Cor 11:26). Christ's form reaches all four edges of the composition, such that those shown here are in some sense included "in" Christ, or at least within reach of his cruciform embrace. The character of this "reach" remains at issue: these elements are a means of Christ's presence, but it is undecided whether this presence is best understood as real, memorial, symbolic, spiritual, or otherwise—in any case, it is necessarily pneumatological: a presence in and through the Spirit. ✦

Renewal theologians across the spectrum are beginning to add their own perspectives toward an ecumenical theology of the Supper. Finnish Pentecostal and ecumenical theologian Veli-Matti Kärkkäinen (2002a: ch. 10) highlights that the presence of the Spirit also makes available the healing power of Christ in the Supper. His Finnish colleague, writing from a Lutheran charismatic perspective, previously also had argued a closely related thesis (Antola 1998: 155–57), but more importantly established this connection on the basis of the charismatic experience in faith as achieving union with Christ's real (and healing) presence. Other charismatic theologians are also arguing that there can be authentic sacramental effects through the Supper by the power of the Holy Spirit (De Arteaga 2002). The Reformation gap between sacrament and ordinance appears to be closing (see Tomberlin 2010; Archer 2011: ch. 4; cf. Cross and Thompson 2003, 2008).

Further consideration of these foundational Christian practices is guaranteed when we expand our horizon to the contemporary global context. In this latter domain, there are innumerable variations, as the practice of the Supper has been inculturated in diverse contexts (Berger 2001; Tovey 2004). Inevitably, these variations illuminate very different assumptions about eating, the nature of food, what it means to be in communal relation, and how human beings encounter God liturgically and in daily life (see Costen 1993: ch. 5). Yet they also provide new opportunities to revisit old debates and assumptions given the dynamic liturgical transformations being enacted by renewal movements in the global south (e.g., Lindhardt 2011).

6.2.3 Renouncing the Devil: Deliverance and Discernment

Some of what is happening liturgically in the global renewal movement has to do with new rites of Christian initiation that hearken back to practices in the ancient church, except reappropriated in a nonbaptismal register. Recall that in *The Apostolic Tradition*, catechumens were led through purificatory rites of exorcism and that this culminated in an explicit renunciation of the devil right before baptism. What is comparatively different about contemporary global renewal praxis is the less-formalized rites of initiation, in some cases dissociated altogether from baptism. What is similar, however, is that full Christian initiation oftentimes involves deliverance from the powers of the devil (see Gifford 2004: ch. 4; Stålsett 2006). Such includes not merely prayers of renouncing the devil but also the exorcising of demonic forces related to physical illnesses and psychological torment, and to countering the debilitating effects of witchcraft and other sources of malevolence believed to oppress personal lives (see Davies 2010; Onyinah 2011).

In addition, beyond these rites of exorcism focused at the individual level, contemporary global renewal movements have developed elaborate cosmologies that identify spiritual powers behind geographic, regional, institutional, social, economic, and political phenomena. Renewalists who embrace this paradigm tend to engage in "spiritual warfare" (see Wagner 1996) against such forces. Intending to resist the forces hindering the promulgation of the gospel, "strategic-level warfare" involves congregational prayer, fasting, and other related activities (Holvast 2008). These ideas and their associated practices are undoubtedly controversial (e.g., Arnold 1997; Lowe 1998). Yet they reflect some of the ways in which, rightly or wrongly, the New Testament language of principalities and powers is being received by renewalists across the global south (e.g., Gatumu 2008).

In effect, however, some broader historical perspectives will indicate how these developments are not so innovative. Exorcisms were prevalent in the early church not just in the baptismal context but on the evangelistic and missionary frontier. Signs, wonders, healings, and miracles (see also ch. 8 of this volume) were as important, if not more so, than intellectual arguments, yet the repudiation of evil spirits should not be minimized in the successful expansion of the Christian message (MacMullen 1984: ch. 4; Sorensen 2002). A distinctive evangelistic witness was simultaneously being developed in the desert tradition. In this context, eremitic and cenobitic monastics cultivated the discernment of spirits as part of their spiritual practice of exemplifying their being *in but not of* the world (Rich 2007).

From this early Christian milieu, an ever-expanding range of models unfolded for understanding and dealing with the spiritual dimensions of Christian life. Medieval Christians wrestled with beliefs and practices related to the discernment of spirits amid the broader disputes pitting charismatic visionaries within local communities on the one side and the church hierarchy on the other (see Caciola 2003; Anderson 2011). During the Reformation period, the practice of Ignatian discernment was articulated from out of the contemplative tradition in order to orient Christian life and mission in an increasingly complex social world (Toner 1995). The Great Awakening revivals and other similar revitalization movements in the eighteenth and nineteenth centuries in turn motivated the discernment of true from misguided religious affections and related charismatic phenomena (see Howard 2000: ch. 2). In most instances these discernments of spirits were not directly tied in with Christian initiation per se. However, they certainly had implications for Christian fellowship, while they also reflected changing perceptions of how the spiritual dimensions of the world interfaced with and influenced the nexus of personal, interpersonal, and socioecclesial relationships.

In the contemporary global context, there is no consensus about how to understand or envision, much less engage, the devil and his minions. Modernistic impulses have sought to demythologize these notions, leading those in pastoral care contexts to psychologize, anthropologize, or sociologize their phenomenological manifestations (e.g., McCasland 1951; Davies 1995; Wink 1998; Capps 2008). In the global south context, the powers of the New Testament are sometimes mapped onto preexisting indigenous cosmologies involving ancestors and other spiritual beings, and for evangelicals and renewalists this often results in a more expansive

demonology that includes deliverance of believers from deceitful ancestral spirits (e.g., Oladipo 1996: ch. 4; Wulfhorst 2005). Within the wider
renewal context, of course, there is a gamut encompassing focus on individual exorcism on the one side to corporate spiritual warfare on the
other side (Collins 2009). Those on the former end of the spectrum are
more apt to model their ministries and practices according to the gospel accounts of Jesus' confrontations with demoniacs. Others are more
focused on the Pauline admonitions, in particular that regarding the waging of battle "against the rulers, against the authorities, against the cosmic
powers of this present darkness, against the spiritual forces of evil in the
heavenly places" (Eph 6:12).

The preceding is horribly truncated, but we need to return to the
issue at hand: that concerning a theology of sacramentality. The question
is if, how, or to what degree spiritual realities can be manifest through
material ones. Classical theologies of the sacraments explored specifically
how salvific grace could be communicated through the waters of baptism
or the elements of the Supper. Our discussion of exorcism and discernment of spirits may appear to be tangential in this context. While we
could have discussed them along with other spiritual gifts in chapter 3,
they have been taken up in the present due to their historical role in the
Christian practice of baptismal initiation. The question that arises in this
context is this: If divine grace can be given and received sacramentally,
is this limited only to the officially recognized channels, whether sacraments or ordinances? Or might it also be possible that a sacramental theology can illuminate spiritual dimensions of the material world, including
the workings of spiritual forces that are malign rather than salvific? In
other words, might a renewal theology of sacramentality clarify not only
how God saves embodied people through the life of Christ in the power
of the Holy Spirit, but also how such salvation involves deliverance from
the powers of evil that are destructive of human life?

6.3 The "Sacramentalism" of the Fourth Gospel

To begin answering these questions, we will turn to the gospel of John.
(We use here its traditional name without any presumptions about the
identity of the author; see also section 12.1.) In particular, if we start
with John's overarching cosmology, its dualism is arresting. Note, however, that Johannine dualism contrasts the light of God in Christ with the
darkness of the world. Little time is spent on the devil or on specifically
demonizing the powers of darkness. Without doubt, Jesus seems to agree
that people can be possessed by demons, but it is the antagonistic Jewish
leaders who accuse him of being so haunted (John 8:44-52). Jesus may

have precipitated this exchange by saying of his opponents that they were of the devil: "You choose to do your father's desires. He was a murderer from the beginning and does not stand in the truth, because there is no truth in him. When he lies, he speaks according to his own nature, for he is a liar and the father of lies" (8:44). The one instance in which Jesus does identify the devil—when he says to the Twelve: "Did I not choose you, the twelve? One of you is a devil" (6:70)—calls attention to its deceitful nature. But all the while that the devil had been working on and in Judas (13:2) and even after Satan was said to have entered him (see section 10.1), his colleagues were still unable to discern this devious presence (13:27-29). If authentic disciples by and large remain anonymous in the Fourth Gospel (Beck 1997), it seems also that those possessed by the devil are similarly unrecognizable.

The wider Johannine tradition, however, insisted both that the devil was sinful and devoid of love (1 John 3:8, 10) and that haters and murderers are discernible as being "from the evil one" (3:12). Rather than fearing the devil, "perfect love casts out fear" (4:18). Hence the light of God in Christ is manifest in deeds of love, while the darkness of the antichrist is evident in acts of hatred. More exactly, the ultimate criterion of discernment of spirits is christological: "By this you know the Spirit of God: every spirit that confesses that Jesus Christ *has come in the flesh* is from God, and every spirit that does not confess Jesus is not from God. And this is the spirit of the antichrist, of which you have heard that it is coming; and now it is already in the world" (4:2-3 [emphasis added]). For our purposes in this chapter, this normative standard for spiritual discernment is explicitly incarnational and, arguably, sacramental.

The centrality of the incarnational motif in John has long featured in the sacramental theology and exegesis of the church, both East and West (e.g., Patte 2004: 412–18; McDonnell 2011). We cannot provide any complete exposition of these matters across the span of the Fourth Gospel, so we focus our discussion on three aspects: the references to baptism, rebirth, and water, especially in the opening chapters; the feeding of the five thousand and the bread of life discourse in chapter 6; and the footwashing account in chapter 13. The goal throughout is to tease out the contours of what we might call the Johannine logic of sacramentality, albeit for purposes of renewing Christian theology and praxis in contemporary global context.

First, John's baptism at the forefront of the gospel is ceremonial and purificatory (John 3:25), but also thoroughly christocentric. In his own words, his baptism is related to the coming Christ: "I came baptizing with water for this reason, that he might be revealed to Israel" (1:31).

Yet John's baptism does not seem to be a prerequisite for reception of the Messiah. There is no reason to believe that Nicodemus, "a leader of the Jews" (3:1), was baptized by John even as Jesus' disciples were baptizing contemporaneous with John (4:2). But Jesus did instruct Nicodemus that "no one can see the kingdom of God without being born from above" (3:3). We are told only that this involved "being born of water and Spirit" and that "what is born of the Spirit is spirit" (3:5-6). To these cryptic remarks, Jesus later added, in dialogue with the Samaritan woman at the well: "Everyone who drinks of this water will be thirsty again, but those who drink of the water that I will give them will never be thirsty. The water that I will give will become in them a spring of water gushing up to eternal life" (4:13-14). In short, John's baptismal practices and related theological ideas in the Fourth Gospel can only be understood inferentially as supporting a sacramental theology. However, Jesus' linking of water—that of the new birth and that which he would give—to the reign of God and to eternal life invites us to press further.

The feeding of the five thousand (6:5-13) and Jesus' teaching the next day about the bread of life in a synagogue in Capernaum (6:25-69) lie together at the heart of the eucharistic tradition of theology. Although Jesus is recorded only as saying he will give the water of life to the thirsty, here he makes a clear affirmation, "I am the bread of life" (6:35, also 48), and then extends the parallel to include his capacity to quench thirst: "Whoever comes to me will never be hungry, and whoever believes in me will never be thirsty" (6:35). More specifically, in contrast to the manna from heaven with which Moses fed the Israelites in the wilderness, Jesus says of himself: "I am the living bread that came down from heaven. Whoever eats of this bread will live forever; and the bread that I will give for the life of the world is my flesh" (6:51). This is of course obscure, not only for the Jews but also for Jesus' followers (6:52, 60), although it fits with the Johannine theme of how Jesus' person and message shone a light that a dark world was unable to bear (see Blount 2007: 194). But instead of providing clarification, the ensuing discourse descends to a further level of density and opacity:

> Unless you eat the flesh of the Son of Man and drink his blood, you have no life in you. Those who eat my flesh and drink my blood have eternal life, and I will raise them up on the last day; for my flesh is true food and my blood is true drink. Those who eat my flesh and drink my blood abide in me, and I in them. Just as the living Father sent me, and I live because of the Father, so whoever eats me will live because of me. This is the bread that came down from heaven, not like that which your ancestors ate, and they died. But the one who eats this bread will live forever (6:53-58).

At this juncture, the link ought to be observed between the material nourishment of eating, which Jesus provides (e.g., for the five thousand), and the spiritual reception of eternal life, which is embodied in Jesus himself. This represents one of the foundational assertions of the Johannine community: that the living word of God had descended from heaven to take on human embodiment. Against an incipient Gnosticism that questioned how a holy God could take the form of what was presumed to be unholy and created materiality (see Anderson 1996: ch. 6), the Johannine tradition insisted on the audibility, visuality, and touchability of the Word made flesh (1 John 1:1). Yet the incarnational logic of the Fourth Gospel is wholly christological, personal, and relational, rather than magical. When with his small group of disciples, Jesus explains, "It is the spirit that gives life; the flesh is useless. The words that I have spoken to you are spirit and life" (John 6:63). Later, at the Feast of Tabernacles, when Jesus said, "Let anyone who is thirsty come to me, and let the one who believes in me drink" (7:37), it is clarified that this was "about the Spirit, which believers in him were to receive; for as yet there was no Spirit, because Jesus was not yet glorified" (7:39). Hence participation in the eternal life who is Christ is made possible only in the Spirit of Christ. This cautions against any enchanted view, such as the one thought operative at the pool by the Sheep Gate in Jerusalem (5:1). Whereas the paralytic believed that the first one to enter into the stirred waters would be healed (5:7), Jesus manifested the healing and saving power of God to the man through his word (see Bryan 2003). The point is that Johannine incarnational theology suggests a christocentric and pneumatologically mediated sacramentality. As Jesus also elucidated much earlier in the bread of life discourse, "all who see the Son and believe in him may have eternal life" (6:40).

Before leaving John's gospel, some brief observations are appropriate about Jesus' washing his disciples' feet, because that has motivated the practice among many different churches and groups throughout the history of Christianity (see Jeffery 1992: ch. 3). While Jesus clearly enjoined his disciples to continue the practice following his example (13:14-15), the emphasized point had to do with who washed whose feet. Peter's receiving a footwashing from his Lord and teacher thus established his calling to similarly serve others, even neophytes in the faith (a particularly poignant message in cultures wherein elders get their feet washed by those younger rather than the other way around; see Adeyemo 2005: 1308). But more relevant for thinking about sacramentality are the reasons for his actions: "Unless I wash you, you have no share with me" (13:8b). When Simon Peter then asks for his entire body to be cleansed, he shows he misunderstood the point: that "the footwashing symbolizes allowing

Jesus to serve his followers by embracing his death for them" (Keener 2003: 2.109). This cleansing and participation thus had to do with the degree to which Jesus' followers could identify with his purpose, mission, and even ultimate ends. Not incidentally, then, the rite of footwashing connects Jesus' sanctifying work with reception of the Holy Spirit or Paraclete announced in the Farewell Discourses given after the event (Thomas 1991). This empowerment of the Spirit was to be a bulwark for a threatened and harassed community, even while empowering that same community to bear witness to a hostile world through living out the new commandment to love one another (Moloney 1997: ch. 5). Would those who wash one another's feet in imitation of Christ thus experience the comforting presence of Christ and the empowering dynamic of the Spirit precisely in this act of fraternal solidarity?

It would be anachronistic to suggest that the Fourth Gospel presents a sacramental theology. Yet as received by the church and as meaningfully effective in the long ecclesial history of baptismal, eucharistic, and footwashing practices—even in renewal communities (see Green 2012: 179, 221–38)—the incarnational message of the gospel invites a sacramental interpretation of how God values the created world and what God has done to redeem the world precisely in and through that materiality. As the author of this treatise puts it, "these are written so that you may come to believe that Jesus is the Messiah, the Son of God, and that through believing you may have life in his name" (20:31). The incarnation of the Son of God unveils the heavenly world for earthly and enfleshed people. Thus do the invisible things of God become manifest in and through the creation's elements.

Yet the Johannine message, while apocalyptic, is not otherworldly. Yes, the gospel unveils what had before been hidden about the Son of Man—this is its apocalyptic dimension; but the point of the revelation of God in Christ is so that people can come to experience eternal life in the present (rather than a future) world (see B. E. Reynolds 2008). The Johannine narrative thus indicates how the heavenly realm is distinct from but yet fused with the earthly domain. This potentially helps us to begin moving beyond the older debates about sacramentality that depend on dualistic categorizations of nature and grace (Kysar 2005: ch. 16). Instead of explicating the sacramental dimension of God's salvific work according to ontological conceptions derived from Aristotelian philosophy, perhaps we might come to a fresh appreciation for how the sharing of life with one another in the name of Jesus—that is, in the baptizing that forgives sins and invites the forgiveness of sins, in the breaking and eating of bread, and in the washing of the feet of others—are interpersonal practices through which the Spirit is redemptively at work. If so, then the Christian practices of baptism, the Supper, and even footwashing become windows into the solidarity of ecclesial life, which identifies the people of God as different from the world but yet also empowers their witness of service to a present and loving deity in an otherwise selfish and hateful world.

FIGURE 6.5

In John 13, Jesus dramatically interrupts a meal with his disciples (presumably the Passover meal): he "got up from the table, took off his outer robe . . . and began to wash the disciples' feet and to wipe them with the towel that was tied around him" (13:4-5). This scene is shocking on many levels, particularly the extent to which Jesus seems to be humiliating himself, performing the duty of someone of low social status. He upsets the codes of decorum and the dignity deserving of a rabbi, and the only rationale given is that Jesus did this "knowing that the Father had given all things into his hands" (13:3). When given authority over all things, this is what he does with it (Whitacre 1999).

Understandably, Peter will not have any of this, and he bluntly announces "You will never wash my feet"—to which Jesus offers an equally blunt reply: "Unless I wash you, you have no share with me" (13:8). The icon shown here attempts to slow down our reading at this point and allow these words to ring in our ears. How can Peter's reverence for Jesus permit this—his rabbi stooping to wash the residual dust and dung of the roadways from his feet? Why would this kind of humility (humiliation) be intrinsic to having a share with Christ? The icon depicts Peter's response: he lets his feet drop into the water basin and leans forward touching his head: "Lord, not my feet only but also my hands and my head" (13:9). This must have been an extraordinary letting-go for Peter, and Jesus leans over, looks Peter in the face, and reaches gently for his hand (rather than feet). Peter has not yet understood the principle: this is not about washing; it is about receiving the radicality of Christ's love, which will reach a self-humiliation much deeper than footwashing (cf. fig. 8.4). The other disciples look on, stunned at what they see and hear. Jesus will proceed to wash all of their feet (including Judas') and then reason with them: "Do you know what I have done to you? . . . If I, your Lord and Teacher, have washed your feet, you also ought to wash one another's feet" (13:12-15). And by setting the scene outside, the artist implies that the disciples' repetition of this example of self-giving love might not have any clear boundaries as to who counts as "one another." ✦

6.4 Repent, Renounce, Be Baptized, Eat, and Drink: Practicing the Christian Life

What then ought to be said as we consider a renewed Christian theology of the sacraments? This section concludes with three overarching theological comments, followed by a series of brief meditations about God's salvific presence as manifest in the church's sacramental practices. The following elaborates on my earlier contribution to a pneumatological theology of the sacraments (Yong 2005: ch. 3) by expanding the scope of Christian practices and reflecting on their relational character in light of the preceding chapters.

First, the thoroughly trinitarian character of the sacraments as Christian practices needs to be underscored. This refers to the christological, pneumatological, and relational core of these practices. We have already seen that the ordinance of footwashing was explicitly instituted by Christ.

Similarly, Christians fellowship around the Supper not only because it was instituted by Christ as recorded in the Gospels, but because this institution was witnessed to by Paul, long before the Gospels appeared: "For I received from the Lord what I also handed on to you . . ." (1 Cor 11:23). Baptism is practiced on account of the apostolic injunction (i.e., Acts 2:38). Yet Jesus' own example is paradigmatic in this regard, in particular the descent of the Spirit upon him (Matt 3:16; Mark 1:10; Luke 3:22; John 1:32-34). Jesus' baptism and reception of the Spirit thus provides a model for Christian practice, consistent with his injunction to Nicodemus about the necessity of being born of water and the Spirit. More importantly, Jesus' own Spirit-baptized life is the reality into which his followers are invited, precisely through their own baptism in, with, and by the Holy Spirit.

Beyond these christological and pneumatological aspects, however, the trinitarian point to be underscored is that these practices are relational and semiotic means through which divine grace is communicated to undeserving creatures (Volf 1998). What is important here is identification of the trinitarian God as the one who has initiated such charismatic and redemptive encounters for human beings and has chosen to reveal himself in precisely these events. This means that the practices precede individual participation and in effect significantly shape such participation. It also means that these ecclesial practices of the body of Christ and the fellowship of the Spirit (see also ch. 7 of this volume) constitute the normal matrix within or through which people encounter God's saving actions. So there is something sacramental about these practices insofar as they are occasions through which salvific grace meets human creatures. However, such mediation occurs not merely because certain words are uttered or certain actions are performed. Rather, God's gracious saving power is manifest to the faith community insofar as these practices are enacted relationally in Christ by the power of the Spirit (see McKenna 1975: part 3). As speaking in tongues is an eschatological sign of the Holy Spirit's missional presence, so also these pneumatically infused enactments called sacraments or ordinances become signs that foreshadow the new creation and coming reign of God (Green 2012: esp. ch. 5). The gift or baptism of the Spirit thus opens up to the full scope of God's redeeming the material creation.

Yet while the Christian practices are initiated by the triune God, their relational character involves their reception by human creatures. There is therefore a performative dimension to the practices. By baptizing in the name of Jesus (as did the apostles; Acts 2:38; 8:16; 10:48; 19:5) or in the name of the triune God (as historically practiced; see Matt 28:19), breaking bread in the fellowship of the Spirit, or washing each other's feet according to the example of Jesus, and so on, Christians as historically embodied creatures are tangibly and kinesthetically both receiving from God and simultaneously bearing witness to the world. Hence there are both iconic and symbolic aspects to the practices. As Jesus himself is "the image [εἰκὼν/icon] of the invisible God" (Col 1:15) and "the exact imprint [χαρακτὴρ/character] of God's very being" (Heb 1:3), so also can the body of Christ be understood iconically as announcing the arrival of God's reign and mediating the good news of that reign through its various practices. The key to an iconic representation is that it facilitates access to what lies behind or beyond the icon. The point is not that this or that material element is iconic, because the world as created can always be a medium of revelation regarding the Creator (Davies 2004; Yong 2002: ch. 6). Instead, for any theology of sacraments, ordinances, or Christian practices, the point is more precisely christological and ecclesiological (Schillebeeckx 1963). As the Johannine incarnation reveals the heavenly word of God through the Holy Spirit, so also do the practices of those who believe and follow that word in the power of the Spirit connect to the God of Jesus Christ and reveal that God to a watching world. The symbolic dimension of these practices, then, consists neither in their inherent materiality nor even in their capacity to shape the church's self-understanding (although that is certainly present) but in how they locate the people of God through Christ in relationship to the world. Christian practices are thus signs of a church not closed in on itself but open to the future but yet coming and even present reign of God and to interaction with the world. The church as an icon of the triune God is thus in the world, but capable of transforming it also through the works of its members accomplished in the power of the Spirit (Segundo 1974). These performative elements will be briefly explicated through a contemporary retrieval of the practices of the early church.

We begin with catechesis, which we noted above as extending for up to three years among the early Christians. While there is an important place in contemporary evangelical and renewal praxis for saying the sinner's prayer, this ought to be viewed as an important moment in an ongoing process of conversion and discipleship. Such present-day conversion practices preserve the confession of and repentance from sin, which reflect the person's recognition that he or she has fallen short of the mark of God, has failed—intentionally or not—to love his or her neighbor, and is in need of a reorientation of life toward God and others. Such moments of initial confession and repentance are essential, but these ought to be followed by ongoing confession and repentance (Gelpi 1998), what some

Christian traditions have called penance. The grace of forgiveness is not magically conferred on these occasions but is made possible through them. Forgiveness thus emerges from the reconciling work of the Spirit that restores relationships otherwise broken by sin (Scanlan 1972).

The early Christian practice of exorcism and renunciation of the devil, as noted, has been recaptured as part of conversion and initiation in the global renewal landscape. This would be, as it was in the early church, an extension of repentance and involve reorientation of values, commitments, and goals toward the coming reign of God. What ought to be exorcised are the powers of selfishness, untruth, hatred, and destruction that are nurtured in human hearts and that entangle human creatures in a world of darkness, and the renunciation of the devil is an iconic symbolization and performative speech-act of the intention to be aligned with the love, truth, and eternal life of Christ. The practice of exorcism in some cases may be less formal, and in other cases may involve more intensive phenomenological interactions when dealing with those who are for various reasons more deeply under felt oppression. In the latter situations, ministers ought not to be hesitant to call on the aid of other professionals, both for ritual purposes but also for the ongoing pastoral care needed to enable people to transition into vibrant Christian faith. And while there is an undeniable personal dimension to the practice of exorcism, ultimate deliverance and healing will in the eschatological long run include the full church's discernment of and engagement with the principalities and powers of the various social systems that are broken and afflict human wholeness (see Yong 2010: ch. 4). At either the personal or ecclesial and social levels, the point is to emphasize Christ's eschatological victory over the principalities and powers (and thus not to give the devil any more than his due) but yet be pastorally sensitive to the complex webs of sinful relationship that have to be unraveled in the conversion process (Parker 1996; Warren 2012). Practices of exorcism and renunciation of the devil thereby achieve the healing work of the Holy Spirit as people turn away from the conventions of the world, especially insofar as such have come under the power of the evil one (1 John 5:19), and realign themselves through the fellowship of the Spirit with Christ as the light of the world. So if there are malevolent spiritual forces that threaten to destroy creaturely life, then the redemptive response of God is accomplished sacramentally first in Christ and then by the ongoing work of the Holy Spirit.

The preceding, as the early Christians understood, are important elements of initiation into faith in Christ and into the new people or community of God that is called the church. The central practice marking that transition, however, is baptism. Thus does baptism save people, "not as a removal of dirt from the body, but as an appeal to God for a good conscience, through the resurrection of Jesus Christ" (1 Pet 3:19). Salvific grace emerges as people confess their sins, repent of their ways, seek cleansing (through exorcism) from their distorted values and commitments, renounce the father of lies and all that he represents, and embrace their membership among the people of God—even as they are affirmed, welcomed, and embraced by the extant body of Christ in turn through the local community and its leadership (Gelpi 1976: ch. 5). In other words, baptism saves through repositioning or resituating people in a new matrix of relationships that is the body of Christ and the fellowship of the Spirit. Again, it is not that the baptismal formula or the waters of immersion achieve their salvific effects as if automatically. Rather, baptism into the name of Jesus and of the triune God identifies association with the life, death, and resurrection of Jesus (Rom 6:1-4; Col 2:12) and commits to solidarity with a new community that facilitates ongoing conversion, repentance, and salvation in the power of the Spirit (Brooks 1987) in anticipation of the full salvation to come (Witherington 2007:106–10).

Baptism in water was followed formally by the rite of baptism in the Holy Spirit. The ministerial laying on of hands and pronunciation to receive the Spirit reenact the impartation of the Spirit by Jesus: "When he had said this, he breathed on them and said to them, 'Receive the Holy Spirit'" (John 20:22). An Aristotelian substance metaphysics would lead to questions about whether or not this is the first instance of the Spirit's infilling or if the Spirit is somehow absent to the catechumen prior to this moment. Patristic accounts that charismatic signs, including that of glossolalia, would manifest themselves precisely at this moment provide supportive historical data for the initial evidence doctrine (see ch. 4 of this volume), even while the classical pentecostal theology of Spirit Baptism as subsequent to initiation can be understood as consistent with, rather than opposed to, this historic account in which reception of the Spirit is at least a logically distinct moment within the overall initiation rite. Hence without discounting the divergences in these perspectives, the relational dimension of this rite of initiation ought to be highlighted instead. The Johannine account of the giving of the Spirit has Jesus following with this invitation: "If you forgive the sins of any, they are forgiven them; if you retain the sins of any, they are retained" (20:23). Whatever the charismatic manifestations, the power of the Spirit forges new possibilities for broken and alienated relationships. Reception of the Spirit brings not only reconciliation with God but also healing between sinners wounded by others.

We can now perhaps better understand how in the early church baptism in water and in the Spirit also opened up to the formal rite of communion around the Lord's Table. Here it is important to distinguish between the more informal practice of meal fellowship (done daily and even from home to home; see Acts 2:46) and the more formal reenactment of the Holy Communion (which ought to occur separately from meals taken for bodily nourishment, according to Paul in 1 Cor 11:33-34). These both constitute the body of Christ, albeit in different ways. The former nurtures bonds of fraternal solidarity through the presence and activity of the Spirit. The latter focuses the people of God on the person and work of Christ in order to solidify through the Spirit their identification with his life, message, and mission. Both are essential to the saving work of God. To eat of the body of Christ and drink of the blood of Christ is an act of identification with the christomorphic and crucicentric character of the church's Lord (see Mark 10:38-39). Hence recognition of the Christ revealed in the breaking of the bread and the drinking of the cup (Luke 24:35) constitutes the Spirit's call toward brokenness and the willingness to be similarly poured out on behalf of a needy world. In that sense, partaking of the body and blood of Christ is salvific in reorienting people toward Christ in relationship with others, albeit in anticipation of the wholeness of the eschatological people of God to come (Vondey 2008: ch. 7). Yet particularly in light of this unfinished character, this more formal practice of the Supper ought not to be completely detached from the less formal meals of fellowship. Without the latter, the people of God remain strangers to one another and will eventually be incapable of living out the new commandment of love for the sake of the world.

The practice of footwashing confirms this last point. No, it does not save us through the removal of dirt from our feet. But yes, the washing of the feet of others, particularly by leaders of their followers, as with the example of Jesus, saves and sanctifies by enabling human participation in and manifestation of the trinitarian life amid a stratified world. It provides a particularly kinesthetic, relational, and incarnational window into how divine grace purifies embodied human creatures (see Albrecht 1999). Yet its Christian meaning derives from the exemplary service of Jesus so that "you are blessed if you do them" (John 13:17). If baptism is the initiatory practice marking the cleansing that transforms human beings and gives them ecclesial identities, then footwashing is the ongoing practice that renews and perfects the loving and egalitarian posture of the new commandment, apart from which the world will not recognize the gospel in Christ (13:34-35).

While the practices of repentance, exorcism/renunciation, baptism, reception of the Spirit, the Supper, and footwashing have normative significance, a pneumatological approach will always recognize the fluid sequence of the practices. The scriptural accounts also suggest that some-times baptism in water precedes reception of the Spirit (Acts 19:5-6), and sometimes the reverse happens (as in the case of Cornelius; see Acts 10:47-48). More important is that the dynamic character of Christian living means that aside from baptism in water, the other practices are repeated. The people of God are called to ongoing repentance, cleansing, renunciation of the devil, filling with the Holy Spirit, and ecclesial fel-lowship and solidarity. A pneumatological approach, however, stresses the relational nature of God's presence in Christ. These practices are effective in communicating divine salvation only because of faith made possible in Christ by the Spirit. Christ is present by the Spirit as believers in the Mes-siah gather in and submit to these practices in his name (see Matt 18:20). The fullness of Christ's outpouring of or baptizing with the Spirit—upon or including all flesh, no less—is thereby accomplished at least in part through these practices.

The preceding exposition highlights what article 7 identifies as the declaratory and proclamatory aspects of Christian practices. This gets us beyond the sacrament-versus-ordinance debate about whether or not sav-ing grace is mediated. This is a question that cannot be answered within conventional philosophical or metaphysical frameworks (see also Luke 20:3-6), precisely because the sign quality of these enactments is escha-tological, concerning present glimpses of or portals into the reign of God that is yet to fully arrive. My contribution is to highlight how these com-municative practices (Garrigan 2004) are not mere symbols but also per-formative icons through which participants eschatologically encounter God in Christ through the Spirit and are then empowered to bear witness to the world. Participation in the Christian practices effectively marks out an identity in which Jesus is Lord, not Caesar or any other earthly master. Thus baptism into Christ and the ongoing expression of these other practices have social and even political ramifications with regard to the Christian witness. Especially where Christians remain persecuted for their faith, persistence with these practices will involve service, suffering, and even martyrdom (see Ekka 2007). Our pneumatological, relational, and eschatological understanding of these Christian practices thus also illuminates the missional dimension of the church's witness announced in Acts 1:8.

This chapter has presented a relational—more precisely eschatologi-cal, pneumatological, and trinitarian—approach to thinking about how the heavenly and spiritual domains of God interface with the concrete and material world of human creatures. The ordinances or sacraments are signs of the presence of the Spirit and of the coming reign of God. But what then are the implications of such an approach for the renewal of the doctrine of the church (ecclesiology)? To that question we turn next.

Discussion Questions

1. What are some aspects of your church's teachings about baptism in water, and how do they compare with the preceding discussion? How is water baptism related to the baptism in the Holy Spirit, if at all? What are the implications of the connections between these two baptisms for Christian faith and practice

2. How does your church celebrate the Lord's Supper? What is or ought to be the role of the Holy Spirit in the Supper? How should the Supper and other Christian practices inform Christian relationships with those outside the church?

3. Have you ever experienced an exorcism or a deliverance (for yourself or someone else)? How important is the renunciation of the devil for Christian faith and practice and why? How might the discernment of such spirits be related to discernment of the Holy Spirit, and vice-versa?

Further Reading

Beilby, James K., and Paul Rhodes Eddy, eds. 2012. *Understanding Spiritual Warfare: Four Views*. Grand Rapids: Baker Academic.

Irwin, Kevin W. 2005. *Models of the Eucharist*. Mahwah, N.J.: Paulist.

Kay, William K., and Robin Parry, eds. 2011. *Exorcism and Deliverance: Multidisciplinary Studies*. Eugene, Ore.: Wipf & Stock.

Schreiner, Thomas R., and Matthew R. Crawford, eds. 2010. *The Lord's Supper: Remembering and Proclaiming Christ until He Comes*. Nashville: B&H Academic.

Wright, David F. 2007. *Infant Baptism in Historical Perspective: Collected Studies*. Milton Keynes, U.K.: Paternoster.

Wright, David F., ed. 2009. *Baptism: Three Views*. Downers Grove, Ill.: IVP Academic.

7

The Church and Its Mission

The Spirit of the Reconciling God

World Assemblies of God Fellowship Statement of Faith
—Article 6: The Church and Its Mission

We believe that the church is the body of Christ and the habitation of God through the Spirit, witnesses to the presence of the kingdom of God in the present world, and universally includes all who are born again (Ephesians 1:22-23; 2:22; Romans 14:17-18; 1 Corinthians 4:20).

We believe that the mission of the church is to (1) proclaim the good news of salvation to all humankind, (2) build up and train believers for spiritual ministry, (3) praise the Lord through worship, (4) demonstrate Christian compassion to all who suffer, and (5) exhibit unity as the body of Christ (Matthew 28:19-20; 10:42; Ephesians 4:11-13).

7.1 Stephen's Eschatological Vision of the People of God

Stephen is well known as the first Christian martyr. He is initially introduced among six others with Greek names as being full of wisdom, faith, and the Holy Spirit (Acts 6:3, 5a) who were chosen by the apostles to provide diaconal leadership for the growing numbers of Hellenistic Jews, including widows (6:1), among the early messianic community. It is safe to assume that, with the possible exception of Nicolas, who was identified as "a proselyte of Antioch" (6:5b), these deacons were Hellenized Jews from the Jewish diaspora across the Mediterranean seaboard. In this increasingly conflicted scenario involving Greek-speaking and Hebrew-speaking groups, the apostles were quickly realizing that there were linguistic and cultural dynamics already fracturing the budding messianic community.

We do not know Stephen's origins. However, as one "full of grace and power, [he] did great wonders and signs among the people" (6:8). This generated some opposition from "the synagogue of the Freedmen (as it was called), Cyrenians, Alexandrians, and others of those from Cilicia and Asia" (6:9). Consisting probably of ex-slaves from around the diaspora, members of this group appear to have been motivated, perhaps by their experience of slavery, to resist accommodation to the dominant Hellenistic culture and to uphold instead a strict Jewish piety (see Simon 1958). This involved zealous defense of the Law of Moses, the land of Israel, and the temple of Yahweh, understood as the dwelling place of God himself (7:46). From what they understood about what Jesus and his disciples were teaching, there was now no more need for sacrifices for sins (God seemingly has chosen to dispense forgiveness in Jesus' name), no need for a priesthood (the twelve apostles were not of the tribe of Levi), and perhaps no need for the temple at all. Stephen thus was charged with speaking against the temple and the Mosaic laws and customs and was brought before the Sanhedrin (6:13-15). His defense (7:2-53) confirmed for them his guilt and precipitated his death by stoning (7:57-58).

There has been much comment about Stephen's apology and its role in relationship to Luke's purposes in the wider Acts narrative (e.g., Penner 2004). While Stephen addressed the charges against him only in a very indirect sense, the substance of the accusations brought had some roots in Jesus' own actions and sayings. Jesus did destabilize local notions of Jewish identity (whether Sabbath keeping or observance of dietary laws), as well as predict that the temple would be destroyed (Matt 24:1-2; Mark 13:1-2; Luke 21:5-6). His teaching and way of life appeared to anticipate a reconfiguration of the identity of the people of God as a new family or kinship group with shared commitments to the values of the coming divine reign (Hellerman 2007). One way to understand the message recorded by Luke in Acts 7 is its illumination of how Hellenists like Stephen glimpsed through the teachings and actions of Jesus a more universal and inclusive vision of God's salvific intentions (see Yong 2011a: ch. 16).

Thus Stephen's speech reflects an appreciation of God's providential ways as already including the non-Jewish world from the very beginning. In response to fellow Hellenistic Jews, he begins by calling attention to the origins of Israel's "founding father," Abraham, a lifelong sojourner from Mesopotamia, Haran, and the land of the Chaldeans (Acts 7:2, 4). He himself never received the land promised to him and is even buried as a nomad in Shechem (7:16) on the Judean–Samarian border (perhaps anticipating the gospel's arrival in Samaria in Acts 8). Later, the patriarchs of Israel (Joseph, his brothers, and their descendants) were formatively shaped as "resident aliens" (7:6) for over four hundred years in the land of Egypt. Moses himself was "instructed in all the wisdom of the Egyptians" (7:22), even as he later spent forty years as a refugee in Midian

(7:23, 29-30), what is today known as the Sinai Peninsula. It is Moses, of course, who God used to lead Israel out of their Egyptian captivity back to the land of Canaan (promised to Abraham), although the people resisted his leadership variously (7:27-28, 39-40). Stephen's perspective can be understood certainly as a specifically "*Christian* interpretation of Jewish history" (Kilgallen 1976: 31 [emphasis in original]), but that is the point. Viewed through the lens of Christ and his own Hellenistic background, Stephen reenvisioned the story of Israel as being more inclusive, with universalistic horizons (thus Acts 3:25), at its very roots.

FIGURE 7.1

Near the center of this image, a man lifts a head-sized stone, preparing to crush St. Stephen's head with it. And this stone essentially divides the composition into two overlapping spaces. In the lower space, everything revolves violently around the vulnerable head of St. Stephen. Enraged members of the Sanhedrin raise heavy rocks to destroy a man they consider a blasphemer, and we find ourselves suspended in the moment before they shatter his body. While his attackers direct their attention downward toward him, Stephen directs his attention (and ours) upward into a second space, wherein he is offered a glimpse of "the glory of God" (Acts 7:55). In this higher (or deeper) space, everything pivots around the hand of Christ pouring onto Stephen the Holy Spirit (depicted here as a dove; cf. figs. 1.4, 3.4, 4.3, and 4.4). These two focal points—the head of Stephen and the hand of Christ—are situated on the central vertical axis of the image, where they form the organizing poles for these two spaces and in fact for two kinds of vision. The driving question here thus concerns the orientation and scope of one's vision—a question that would later dramatically confront Saul (fig. 2.1), who approved of and perhaps authorized the stoning of Stephen (7:58; 8:1; 22:20). The image encourages us to take seriously (perhaps quite personally) Stephen's stinging accusation: "You stiff-necked people, uncircumcised in heart and ears, you are forever opposing the Holy Spirit, just as your ancestors used to do" (7:51).

In the distant background, perched between these upper and lower spheres of activity, is the city of Jerusalem. In this position its significance doubles: on the one hand, the outskirts of Jerusalem provide the site of this murderous event: "they dragged him out of the city and began to stone him" (7:58). This is the holy city that violently rejected both Christ and his young disciple, Stephen. On the other hand, it also reads as the future Jerusalem (cf. figs. 1.4 and 12.1): the Holy City in which the dwelling of God will be with men and there will thus be one sphere of activity rather than two (Rev 21:2-3). Over against the brutality unfolding in the foreground, the city in the background anticipates a time in which "[d]eath will be no more; mourning and crying and pain will be no more" (Rev 21:4). ✦

Further, in contrast to the apostles who still seemed to have anticipated some kind of conventional restoration of Israel and the temple from Roman rule (Acts 1:6), the Hellenistic and cosmopolitan Stephen had come to a wider outlook. For him, the God of Israel was also the God of all nations—of Mesopotamians, Chaldeans, Egyptians, Midianites, among others—and God's "dwelling place" was not limited to a specific region or locale (whether Judea, Jerusalem, or even the temple; see John 4:21-24). Instead, all of heaven and earth belonged to the Lord (Acts 7:48-50). Stephen's citation here from Isaiah 66:1-2 indicates that he was well aware of the universal vistas of that passage (see Beale 2004: 218–22). In that case, the eschatological redemption and renewal of Israel, initiated in the life, death, and resurrection of Christ, also hinted at the possibility of salvation for Gentiles, not just the Jews. For this reason, Stephen harshly castigates his listeners as being the children of those who had persecuted the prophets and murdered Jesus in part to preserve their narrowly conscribed borders and traditions.

Stephen's life (and death) provides us with windows into the contested character of the early messianic mission and the self-understanding of those who considered themselves as the chosen and elect people of God. In a real sense, this was an intra-Jewish dispute. On the one side were traditionalists (i.e., the Freedmen here and the Judaizers later; see Gal 2:14) who felt that it was Stephen and those like him—including Saul/Paul, later (Acts 9:29)—who were compromising the traditional faith and thus needed to be opposed, even via drastic measures. On the other side, Hellenistic Jews like Stephen were comfortable in the wider Greco-Roman world and saw the possibility of Jewish faith being freed from some of its particularistic trappings in light of the person and work of Christ. To be clear, Stephen was not yet urging the full embrace of Gentiles (see Wilson 1973: ch. 5). But his speech in Acts 7 does present "the constitution for the formation of a new people of God for Jews and Gentiles" (Wiens 1995: ix). It also is indicative of why, as we shall see, the idea of the church was and remains a contested one, especially vis-à-vis its Jewish origins.

7.2 Contestations among/about the People of God

The claim that Pentecostals have yet to develop a cohesive ecclesiology (doctrine of the church) is partly true (see Kärkkäinen 2002c: ch. 6). This may apply also to the larger renewalist movement, concerned as it has been with doing what the church is supposed to do rather than with trying to define what it is. However, a recent contribution regarding a "fivefold" ecclesiology (Thomas 2010)—from the pentecostal fivefold gospel of Jesus as savior, sanctifier, Spirit Baptizer, healer, and coming king (see Yong 2010: ch. 3)—may point the way forward. Within the fivefold scheme, the church is understood as a redeemed, sanctified, empowered, healing, and eschatological community. Its correlative practices include baptism, footwashing, glossolalia, anointing with oil, and the Lord's Supper, even as its ministries are carried by apostolic, teaching, charismatic, pastoral, and evangelistic functions (the latter set following the fivefold ministries of Eph 4:11). The specifics of the fivefold correlations are of less interest than how they invite consideration about the doctrine of the church across multiple registers.

The following contextualization of the ecclesiological discussion will highlight the need for precisely such a pluralistic approach. The discussion will proceed by addressing, in order, three major ecclesiological fault lines: (1) the church's relationship to Israel; (2) the ecumenical nature of the one church constituted by its many forms; and (3) the post-Christendom global ecclesial and missiological ferment. Each subsection can only treat the issues briefly, so what gets included (or excluded) will be dictated by renewal interfaces, perspectives, and concerns. The objective is to identify the contested issues in contemporary ecclesiology, so we can appreciate the broader theological debates behind at least the first part of article 6.

One caveat before proceeding. Article 6 indicates that the church "includes all who are born again." This may suggest to some that being born again (salvation proper) precedes membership in the church. However, another reading is possible: that being born again involves nothing less than being incorporated into the church as the body of Christ and fellowship of the Spirit. If so, then ecclesiology (the doctrine of the church) rightly precedes—as in this volume (see also Pinnock 1996: chapters 4-5)—or at least encompasses, soteriology (the doctrine of salvation). So although we will return in chapter 9 to the latter, readers should be alert to the soteriological ramifications of the following ecclesiological considerations.

7.2.1 Israel and the Church: Whence the Temple of the Spirit?

The sixth article references the Ephesian description of the church as being "a dwelling in which God lives by his Spirit" (2:22, NIV). This pneumatological emphasis is in part what led pentecostal ecclesiologists to identify the church primarily as the charismatic fellowship of the Holy Spirit (Kärkkäinen 2002a: ch. 8). As we shall see in the next section, however, the broader context of this part of the Ephesian letter concerns the relationship between the church and Israel. Yet this connection opens up challenging issues not only for the doctrine of the church but also for Christian theology as a whole. In the following short discussion, we focus especially on contemporary renewal perspectives on Israel and set those against the wider backdrop.

There is no one view about Israel across the global renewal landscape. However, the most prominent are also perhaps the most pronounced, and these are often informed by dispensationalist perspectives that understand the present church age (the Common Era) to be followed by a millennial reign of Christ in which the covenant with Israel will finally be fulfilled and "all Israel will be saved" (Rom 11:26). In this framework, Jews are thought to be spiritually dull to the gospel of Christ (with appeals here to Stephen's analysis and also to Acts 28:23-28, Rom 11:7-10, 25, and elsewhere) even if there are signs, such as the twentieth-century reestablishment of Israel as a nation, that the time for fulfillment of God's covenant promises is at hand (according to one interpretation of Luke 21:24). Hence in many renewal circles, the fortunes of Israel are inextricably tied in with the coming eschatological redemption of the world. More fervent renewalist philo-Semitism is manifest in regular celebration of ancient Jewish feast days and festivals, as well as in public support for the nation-state of Israel (e.g., Helgesson 2006: ch. 8).

Interestingly, charismatic renewal since the 1960s has also touched contemporary Jewish–Christian communities. For instance, upward of two-thirds of messianic Jewish congregations—groups of more rather than less observant Jews who believe in Jesus as Messiah—are charismatic (see Hocken 2009: ch. 5). These charismatic believers, however, face opposition along at least three fronts: suspicions from some noncharismatic messianic Jews; rejection by contemporary Judaism across the spectrum (for having embraced Jesus as Messiah); and misunderstanding by Christians (e.g., some evangelicals think them too Jewish and other progressivists think them too Zionist). Part of the reason for their ambiguous status amid these and other contested theological, religious, and political matters pertains to responses of both Jews and Christians to the long history of anti-Semitism that has marked Jewish–Christian interfaces (see Cohn-Sherbok 2000).

There is certainly no space here to go into the details of the very complex history between Jews and Christians (see Perry and Schweitzer 1994). Any summary, however, ought to mention at least the following major factors. First, that the earliest followers of Jesus were all Jews, and the first generation of the messianic movement represented simply one strand of a much more complicated set of intra-Jewish struggles against Hellenistic and other Greco-Roman currents (e.g., Burtchaell 1992; Wilson 1995: 67–71). Second, succeeding generations underwent a contested, drawn-out, and arguably "painful parting of ways" (Dunn 1992; cf. Becker and Reed 2007, with increasingly hostile and polemical interactions between Jews and Gentiles. Third, the long history of Christian anti-Semitism ought to be acknowledged, culminating in the events of the Holocaust in the twentieth century (see Schoeps 1963; Carroll 2001). Much more ought to be said, but this minimally frames the historical arc amid which renewal perspectives on and responses to Judaism and Israel should be considered.

Post-Holocaust developments have opened up a range of Christian theologies of Israel and its relationship to the church. Far on the one side remain those who hold that the covenantal blessings promised to the Jews have been given to Christians and hence that ancient Israel has been superseded by the church. This view is advocated from a few recalcitrant texts in the New Testament (e.g., Matt 21:43, among some parables). For renewalists, one odd if also quite marginal version of this view is maintained by British Israelists (who insist that true Jews are descendants of the tribe of Judah found among certain European lineages) including Charles Fox Parham (see Goff 1988: 101–2). The mainstreams of both Judaism and Christianity, of course, have never been close to embracing such straightforwardly supersessionist ideas.

On the opposite end of the spectrum would be messianic Jews. Most of those of the charismatic and more evangelical variety would insist on the continued messianic mission to contemporary Jews (Cohn-Sherbok 2001), while others have been urging more recently a "postmissionary" posture (see Kinzer 2005, 2011). Advocates of the latter recognize a solidarity between Jews and Christians as bilaterally constituting the one people of God. But although they emphasize that messianic Jews and Christians ought to witness to Christ in ways that inspire Jewish covenantal faithfulness, such a "postmissionary" emphasis on Torah observance potentially alienates these messianic believers from the Gentile church (Harvey 2009: 183).

More conventionally, between these two extremes are three contemporary Christian theological positions. One, the already mentioned dispensationalist view (e.g., Larsen 1995), involves what might be understood as a temporary supersessionism: the political dimensions of God's promises to Israel remain in effect, in some respects even awaiting ultimate fulfillment in the coming age, although the spiritual elements of the covenant have been inaugurated in Christ and are now available through the church. Other more broadly evangelically oriented approaches might emphasize more the unity of the one people of God under one covenant as well as a commitment to contemporary Israel, even if they might still insist on the importance of evangelism to Jews in light of Christ's fulfilling work (De Ridder 1977; Ariel 2002). A third alternative, more prevalent among some mainline Protestant church segments, understands the Gentiles as being grafted into the trunk of the house of Israel (with Gentiles thereby not required to keep the Jewish laws; see Rom 11:13-24; Acts 15:14-17) and hence holds that the ongoing validity of the Jewish covenant undermines the rationale for Christian evangelization or proselytization of Jews (Williamson 1993). There are certainly variations within each of these positions, although these delineate the main options for our purposes. All agree, however, that God's covenant with Israel will be kept, at least in the future, if not also somehow persisting through the present age of the church (appealing to texts such as Rom 11:25-29 and Luke 22:28-29).

The preceding forces upon us the ecclesiological question that is the focus of this chapter: how ought the people of God be understood theologically in light of the salvation-historical testimony of Scripture? In terms of the New Testament witness itself, the issues are complicated, interwoven with the internecine rhetoric deployed by various communities located in different sociopolitical contexts (Donaldson 2010). The weight of a supersessionist history is not easily overcome, even if some are recognizing that Christian supersessionism was itself in a sense superseded by the Muslim version. On the contemporary horizon, however, there is increasing recognition of the need for finding ways to consider both Jews and Christians as people of God, whether distinctly or even in relationship (Braaten and Jenson 2003). Theological globalization has made the issues more complex rather than clarifying them (e.g., Ucko 1996).

Might renewalist instincts toward a pneumatological and trinitarian ecclesiology provide a way to cut through these various enigmas? Here Stephen's claim that "Most High does not dwell in houses made by human hands" (Acts 7:48) is filled out by other New Testament assertions regarding the actual people of God, rather than the buildings they erect, as constituting the temple of the Holy Spirit (1 Cor 3:16; 6:19; cf. 2 Cor 6:16). How would such a pneumatological theology of the people of God contribute to the renewal of Christian ecclesiology in the twenty-first century?

7.2.2 Reformist, Restorationist, Renewalist: What Body of Christ?

The preceding question is of course only one of a triad of challenging ecclesiological conundrums facing contemporary Christian theology. No less daunting is the broader ecumenical question, which is exacerbated in the renewal context. Article 6's reference to the body of Christ consisting of all who are "born again" implicitly privileges the baptistic notion of the church being constituted by individuals (through their confession of faith) over and against a more sacramental vision of the church's ontological primacy. The result is that most renewalists operate under the assumption that God's fundamental relationship is with individuals rather than mediated through the church, and "born again" spirituality reflects these radically democratizing sensibilities (see Chesnut 1997; Marshall 2009). Herein is a fundamental divide for considering the doctrine of the church.

Of course, there is too much in the New Testament on the unity of the church for renewalists, even with their individualistic proclivities, to ignore. On the matter of how to achieve Christian unity, classical pentecostal reactions have included a diversity of attitudes. On the one hand, there were "come-outers" (following their reading of 2 Cor 6:14-17), who, like other conservative Protestants at the turn of the twentieth century, were as much pushed out from their existing churches as they advocated separation from what they believed to be lukewarm (at best) or apostate (at worst) denominations. Over the course of the succeeding century, perhaps even more than other Christian streams, pentecostal churches following this trajectory have exhibited an impulse toward increasing fragmentation and in the process posed severe ecumenical challenges (see Crowe 1993; Moltmann and Kuschel 1996). A number of dispensationalist assumptions concerning the last days falling away (read from scriptural texts like Matt 24:12, 2 Thess 2:3, 2 Tim 3:1-5, and Rev 2:4, 3:1, 15-16) have driven these pentecostal assessments of other so-called (from their perspective) churches. Further, the ecumenical movement's perceived liberalism was seen as being part and parcel of the end-time apostasy. As a result, few pentecostal churches or denominations have been formally involved in ecumenical endeavors.

On the other hand, many of the early Pentecostals also were part of restorationist movements that yearned for the unity for which Jesus prayed (John 17) and that they believed would be accomplished through the breaking down of denominational barriers. For these Pentecostals, the baptism of the Spirit erased artificial distinctions and reminded the people of God of their fundamental equality and unity in Christ (see Vondey 2010b: ch. 1). Later, similar perspectives have informed charismatic visions of a spiritually unified church amid different traditions, expressions, and even practices (e.g., Au 2011). There is a sense in which the charismatic renewal has been catalytic for facilitating the realization that the unity of the church requires neither its uniformity nor, necessarily, its structural or organizational unanimity (see Kärkkäinen 2002a: part 1). A double-sided movement appears to be emerging: a kind of "ecumenical grace" is being received from across the global renewal movement (Hocken 1987), even as there is a growing recognition of the true church being both charismatic and pentecostal, in the Acts 2 sense (Afanasiev 2007: 5–6).

None of this suggests that the church catholic is over the ecumenical hump. Part of the remaining challenge involves how precisely to comprehend the ecumenical gifts of the renewal movement, and this question is interrelated both with pentecostal self-understandings of the church and Christian history and with pentecostal considerations of what gifts other Christian traditions, churches, or movements have to offer. Some of the more dispensationalistically inclined have been predisposed to see much of what happened after the third century in pejorative terms. Some with this perspective, traceable in part to the radical Reformation tradition, identify the fall of the church with the ascendency of Constantine.

Renewalists in this vein then have associated the Christendom project with the triumph of ecclesial institutions over charismatic dynamics, the latter left sputtering on the margins of the established church (Allen 1994: ch. 3; Hyatt 2002: ch. 4). Hence, the end-time pentecostal outpouring of the Spirit is intended to restore fully to the church catholic what institutionalized Christianity had neglected, subordinated, or lost.

FIGURE 7.2

The title of this work comes from the Greek word οἰκουμένη *(oikouménē), meaning "inhabited"—a term used in the Greco-Roman world as a general designation for all the populated, civilized regions of the known world. Alternatively spelled as "ecumene," this same word forms the root of our contemporary terms "ecumenical" and "ecumenism," which designate efforts to think in terms of a single, global church and to develop unity across Christian denominations.*

With this title, the image depicts a single ecumenical boat (the boat is an ancient symbol of the church) that carries six uniquely dressed figures: one for each of the six inhabited continents. A red cruciform mast stands in the center of the boat, stretching its arms over the group and visually unifying them. Two doves of peace meet at the center of the cross, and a rainbow arches across the sky. In the context of the boat and dove(s), the presence of the rainbow calls to mind God's global covenant symbol following the flood: "I have set my bow in the clouds, and it shall be a sign of the covenant between me and the earth. . . . I will see it and remember the everlasting covenant between God and every living creature of all flesh that is on the earth" (Gen 9:12-17). As such, the image presents a vision (or perhaps simply a hopeful yearning) for a unified Christian church situated within an even larger vision of God reconciling all of creation (cf. Col 1:20).

The global motif of this image is significant, but it also raises many questions. How might we responsibly conceptualize this kind of intercultural, interdenominational unity of the church? How should we imagine the extremely diverse Christians of the earth standing in solidarity with and mutual understanding of one another under the cross of Christ (when that cross seems have so many different meanings)? Any answers that might be proffered here are going to require a distinctly pneumatological imagination: the coherence of this global vessel is a unity only possible in the oneness of the Spirit (1 Cor 12:13; Eph 4:1-6). ✦

A less negative view of Christian history would see divine providence as activated especially with the Reformation to return the church to its apostolic and scriptural foundations. Connected to this, of course, would be the Pietist and Methodist movements, not to mention the Great Awakening revivals. These are believed to have returned to the church the scriptural call to holiness and a vibrant and affectively renewed Christian life (see Bernard 1996: ch. 11). Even into the eighteenth century, other calls for the restoration of New Testament–shaped and denominationally undivided Christianity can be heard, and the Holiness forebears of the pentecostal movement imbibed this vision for church unity (Ware 2004) and passed it on to their spiritual descendants. What emerged according to this perspective was a gradual refurbishing and renovation of the church from its medieval slumber, so in each succeeding century since the Reformation, important elements of authentic Christian faith have been regained. The culmination of this renewalist historiography, of course, is the reestablishment through the early twentieth–century pentecostal revival of the "full gospel," especially the "latter rain" baptism in the

Holy Spirit. Within this theological scheme, ecumenical unity involves the pentecostalization or charismatization of all churches, so the full gospel can be the embraced by the whole church for the world. Yet this way of approaching the issues glosses over the fact that it was precisely the Reformation's making the Bible available to the people—not to mention the roles of pietist, revivalist, and renewal movements to inspire individual initiative—that led to a proliferation and fragmentation of churches and the current ecumenical impasse.

The preceding account has said little about the many questions regarding the unity, catholicity, and apostolicity of the church being negotiated by those in the wider ecumenical and evangelical streams. For Protestants, there are important issues regarding the disunification of the church, disagreements regarding the sacraments, and the nature of ministry, among other matters, that many continue to work tirelessly to resolve, even as some lament such divisions as signifying the absence of the Spirit (Radner 1998). Between Protestants, Orthodoxy, and the Roman Catholic Church, historical disputes persist—about the *filioque* or the Council of Trent, just to name two—that cannot be ignored by those who take ecclesial doctrines seriously. Observations about "the winter of ecumenism" (Evans 1996: 1) and its imminent demise are probably premature. True, the role of formal ecumenical organizations may diminish going forward, but the issues of perennial concern regarding the church's organizational institutions, teachings, mission, and witness to the world will continue to be engaged, even if this occurs outside formal ecumenical venues (see Fitzgerald 2004). In each of these arenas, Pentecostals are latecomers to the ecumenical conversation but also slowly realizing that the maturation of renewal theology will necessitate consideration of these matters. The results are at present unpredictable. Pessimists might think that renewal perspectives merely complicate issues, adding one more "voice" to the table that needs to be adjudicated. Optimists, however, are buoyant that the renewal intervention provides a possible new approach, perhaps one that gets around the historic standoffs.

Might renewalist instincts regarding a pneumatological or spiritual unity of the church chart a way forward? If earlier we inquired about how the church as understood as the temple of the Spirit of God might provide some way to think theologically about the people of God, including both Jews and Gentiles in our time, might a similar perspective also open up fresh considerations about the fellowship of the Spirit constituted by many members and gifts? Is it possible for such a pneumatological theology of the people of God to contribute to the renewal of Christian ecclesiology in the present?

7.2.3 Between Israel and the Reign of God:
Whither Global Christianities?

If within article 6 questions related to the Jews and the wider church catholic are latent, the central reference to the coming reign of God opens up pertinent ecclesiological issues within a global horizon. These can be framed conceptually as three concentric circles related to ecclesial leadership, forms, and mission. We shall see that if the Jewish question reaches back to the first century (with present and ongoing relevance), and if the ecumenical question is a more recent modernist concern (again, with continuing implications), the eschatological dimension of the church presses matters related to its various mutations in global context.

In terms of ecclesial *leadership*, while renewal spirituality is inherently egalitarian in terms of recognizing the empowerment and call to ministry of male and female, young and old, well-to-do and less well off (my gloss on Acts 2:17-18; see Fettke 2011), for the same reasons it also long has been susceptible to valorization of charismatically gifted individuals (Lee 2005: ch. 6). Renewalist restorationism thus has been drawn especially to retrieval of the apostolic and prophetic functions of the fivefold ministry (Eph 4:11), the other three being acknowledged to have been operative in the wider church. More to the point, the episcopal notion of apostolic succession in the historic Christian tradition is redefined functionally according to the Spirit-empowered vocation of mission and church planting (Johnson 2009). Beyond this, the ongoing vitality of the church is not only established by but also relies on the continued expression of charismatically inspired apostolic and prophetic leadership (according to Eph 2:20). Often these work in tandem: apostolic visionaries exercise Spirit-empowered governance due in part to their having prophetic insight regarding the mission of the church (Beacham 2004).

On the one hand, such an apostolically and prophetically defined model of ecclesial leadership tends to be fiercely individualistic. Part of the result of this phenomenon, at least in the classical pentecostal tradition, has been the emergence of independent congregations headed by ministers with self-appointed apostolic, prophetic, and even episcopal ("Bishop this or that . . .") labels (see Harris 2010). Renewal movements centered around such charismatic leaders are liable to degenerate into hierarchical and authoritarian communities (Moore 2003). In patriarchal and gerontocratic cultures, such styles and forms of leadership potentially inhibit, even harm, rather than foster lay initiative and ministry.

On the other hand, more recently and riding the global networking capacities of the information age, apostolic and prophetic networks have appeared (e.g., Kay 2007). Usually gathered around charismatic and visionary leaders, such networks are more informal partnerships than structured organizations, operating in a more dynamic and relational modality to connect people and congregations but without the bureaucracy of denominations. In their most healthy expressions, apostolic and prophetic networks are missionally driven to establish churches and nurture vital congregational life in a globalizing world. This "network church" (Lord 2012)—to use a shorthand—can be understood as a twenty-first-century global iteration of the classical pentecostal mission networks at the beginning of the twentieth century (see Anderson 2007: ch. 3) and of the apostolically driven mission of the first-century church.

The advent of the network church in renewal circles is a symptom of, as well as a contributor to, wider shifts in ecclesial *forms* in a very fluid global context. Precisely what is coming into being is yet undetermined, except in terms of what is being left behind. Hence we are now living in a *post-Christendom* world, one in which the church is no longer linked politically to the (modern) state. The network church thrives on engaging in ecclesial mission and evangelism amid, but yet without getting their hands dirty with, the political domain. Further, we are also now inhabiting what some call a *postmodern* and *postcolonial* situation, one after the pretenses of Western universal rationality have been exposed and local cultural logics and languages are being welcomed into the global conversation. The network church consists not of one center but of many, with communicative nodes and influences emerging from and extending in multiple directions simultaneously, bringing north, south, East, and West into dynamic interaction. Last but not least, we also exploring what it means to be a *postdenominational* Christianity, one in which the Reformation confessions are viewed more as perpetuating ecclesial divisions than as providing viable Christian identity. While renewalists, long come-outers from established churches, have never been invested in denominational structures, the "equal opportunity" entrepreneurship of network church relations exhibits the capacity to revitalize even existing denominations, insofar as the latter are willing to collaborate in these relational forums (see Poloma and Green 2010).

The important point to register here is that the preceding ecclesial ferment is related to the shift of the Christian center of gravity from the Euro-American hemisphere to the global south. Established occidental and Reformation forms of the church are being gradually revisited if not superseded as those outside the modern West are taking ownership of their Christian faith. What the missionaries originally brought with them was tolerated for a while, but renewal movements generally have privileged charismatically charged leadership to shape local congregations under the (presumed) inspiration of the Holy Spirit. This explains not only the diversity of renewal in global context (e.g., Melloni 2003), but also the pluralism of ecclesial forms on the ground.

The evangelical emphases of renewal Christianity also will continue to catalyze ecclesial *mission* and, concomitantly, experimentation. This concerns not only the fact that local contextualization and inculturation (to use missiological terms) will lead to diversification, but also that the goal of the church's mission, usually understood in terms of proclaiming if not participating in the work of the Spirit, is to inaugurate the coming reign of God (van Engen 1991: ch. 7). Yet this overall missional objective raises both the theological question about the relationship between the church of the present age and that of the divine reign to come and the practical question about how the many forms of the present church antici-pate, if at all, the nature of the coming divine reign. Put more pointedly, in our present era when Christianity is for the first time a truly global or world religion, such diversity has to be accounted for missiologically, ecclesiologically, and eschatologically (Gaillardetz 2008).

In fact, it is even fashionable to talk these days not about Christian-ity in the singular but about *Christianities* in the plural (McLeod 2006; Phan 2011). The Latin American context, dominated for centuries by the Roman Catholic presence, is gradually diversifying amid the combination of Protestant influence, economic globalization, and political democratiza-tion. The emerging post-Western and postmodern Latina/o ecclesiology emphasizes a pluralistically constituted identity, an interrelationally and dynamically negotiated way of life, and an open-ended, liberatively, and hopefully oriented impulse (e.g., García-Johnson 2009). These are condu-cive to network church dynamics, even as they raise normative questions about the nature of the eschatological hope that is aspired to.

The Asian context defies description. On the one hand, the estab-lished churches are redefining what it means to be the church in Asia by emphasizing its pilgrim status (as a post-Christendom context); prioritiz-ing presence and dialogue rather than aggressive efforts of evangelism and proselytism (in a multicultural and multireligious context); and addressing the widespread challenges of classism, poverty, and the plight of women and children (Thoppil 1998; Massey 2008). The renewal in China, in the meanwhile, has a bit less of the historically established traditions of the church to contend with (than in India, for instance), and has almost instinctively imbided a kind of network format (Wesley 2004). The results are nevertheless convergent: there is a diversity of Asian Christiani-ties, with renewal and traditionalization working simultaneously toward unpredictable long-term configurations.

FIGURE 7.3

The book of Revelation is addressed to seven churches in seven different cities in what is now modern-day Turkey (see sections 12.1 and 12.3). Each of these churches found itself in unique circumstances with its own distinctive character, and as such each is uniquely addressed in the first three chapters of the book. And as we set Revelation within the broader New Testament canon, a further diversity of audiences and concerns emerges in the letters addressed to churches as different from one another as those in Rome, Corinth, Galatia, and Philippi, and to situations as dissimilar as those in Hebrews, Philemon, Timothy, and Titus. The church, from its very beginning, was composed of very diverse communities wrestling with a wide range of priorities, questions, and difficulties.

The image reproduced here depicts St. John addressing the seven churches in Revelation. These churches are represented as seven different structures, each of which has its own unique "angel" or spirit depicted above it (cf. Rev 1:20). Despite their diversity, there is also a kind of unity visually articulated here: these assorted buildings stand as one block as the angels pray over them in concert with one another (with hands upheld in orans posture).

Although this image is a very old illumination of a much older text, it maps onto the contemporary notion of the "network church" in interesting ways. There is no privileged center among the churches here, which instead consist of multiple centers, multiple structures, multiple locations. And in the global context of contemporary Christianity, perhaps we should reimagine these as churches from wildly different locations around the globe, all addressed by the revelation of

Jesus Christ (and united in him) even while speaking extremely varied languages within extremely varied local histories, traditions, and cultural contexts. The spectrum of angels–structures–languages along which Christ spoke to the churches of first-century Asia Minor has over the past two millennia widened into a spectrum truly global in scope, the entirety of which is still addressed by the one "who is and who was and who is to come" (Rev 1:8). ✦

The African situation has long featured prophetic forms of indigenously organized alternatives to the colonial mission churches. Renewal Christianities in Africa are simply part and parcel of this extremely heterogeneous and dynamic field (Kalu 2008). Yet within this continent, there are palpable indigenous traditions of community, strong existential concerns for salvation understood in terms of this-worldly health and well-being, and instinctive environmental and ecological sensitivities related to more holistic indigenous worldviews (see Ilo, Ogbonnaya, and Ojacor 2011). This matrix suggests that ecclesiological concerns are further complicated by cosmological, soteriological, and eschatological notions.

The preceding threatens to tear the fabric of the church from multiple directions: historically vis-à-vis Israel and the Jewish tradition; internally, in a sense, vis-à-vis the Orthodox and Roman Catholic traditions, not to mention Protestantism's diversity of churches; and missionally and eschatologically in terms of the triangulation between church, the world, and the coming reign of God. If indeed there are a plurality of Christianities, does this invite consideration of a kind of pluralistic ecclesiology? Is such desirable, even possible? Might it be that here the full-gospel vision of the people of God embedded within the renewal tradition could spark and renew ecclesiological reflection for the contemporary global church?

7.3 An Ephesian Ecclesiology

As with other doctrinal loci, there are many places we can consult in the New Testament in thinking about ecclesiology. In fact, given the preceding discussion, it is important also to note that there are arguably many ecclesiologies across the New Testament itself, not to mention ecclesiological images (Minear 1975; Collins 2004). For our purposes, however, and in keeping with our biblical-theological methodology, we focus here on one New Testament writing, the Letter to the Ephesians. This short epistle has long been viewed as providing an important point of entry for thinking about the nature of the church (e.g., Williamson 1971).

While there is currently no consensus among scholars about the Pauline authorship of Ephesians, this issue does not need to be resolved for our purposes. We will, however, refer to the author as Paul following the epistolary greeting (Eph 1:1), even if this is meant conventionally rather than as prejudging the debate. Our discussion will traverse three broad themes related to the divine character of the church, its human constitution, and its missional dimension, all motivated in part by the above discussion.

There are three aspects to the divine character of the church discernible in Ephesians: its being the body of Christ, the temple of the Holy Spirit, and the unveiled mystery of God. First, God has made Christ "the head over all things for the church, which is his body, the fullness of him who fills all in all" (1:22-23; cf. 4:15b). Second, the church is "marked with the seal of the promised Holy Spirit" (1:13; also 4:30), and said to be "a holy temple in the Lord; in whom you also are built together spiritually into [ἐν πνεύματι/*en pneumati*] a dwelling-place for God" (2:21-22). What is important to note, here anticipating our next discussion of the human constitution of the church, is that the church as the body of Christ and the temple of the Spirit has a trinitarian character. As Paul also writes: "through him [Christ] both of us [Jews and Gentiles] have access in one Spirit to the Father" (2:18).

This leads to a consideration of the Ephesian depiction of the church as the unveiling of the mystery of God. There is a spiritual aspect to this revelation that ought to be foregrounded in order to emphasize the divine nature of the church. On the one hand, "the God and Father of our Lord Jesus Christ . . . has blessed us in Christ with every spiritual blessing in the heavenly places" (1:3). Thus there is a cosmic horizon to the church's identity: God "has made known to us the mystery of his will, according to his good pleasure that he set forth in Christ, as a plan for the fullness of time, to gather up all things in him, things in heaven and things on earth" (1:9-10). On the other hand, not only is Christ seated at God's right hand "in the heavenly places, far above all rule and authority and power and dominion, and above every name that is named, not only in this age but also in the age to come" (1:20-21); but God has also "raised us up with him and seated us with him in the heavenly places in Christ Jesus" (2:6). In fact it is precisely the unveiling of this spiritual and heavenly reality to which the church witnesses: "so that through the church the wisdom of God in its rich variety might now be made known to the rulers and authorities in the heavenly places" (3:10). The point to be registered here is the nature of the church as theologically established (by the triune God) and spiritually manifest (to the powers; see Brannon 2011). Because any overemphasis on the spiritual character of the church tends toward an otherworldliness that is of no earthly good (see Segovia and Sugirtharajah 2007: 265–80), we will return in due course to take up this matter.

But of what exactly does the unfolded mystery of the church consist? Here we arrive at its human constitution, more precisely, Jews and Gentiles together. Many Christians have so domesticated this idea as to be unable to appreciate the nature of the church. Three points are highlighted from the letter itself. First, the Gentiles were before "without Christ, being aliens from the commonwealth of Israel, and strangers to the covenants of promise, having no hope and without God in the world. But now in Christ Jesus you who once were far off have been brought near by the blood of Christ" (2:12-13). Second,

> [Christ] is our peace; in his flesh he has made both groups into one and has broken down the dividing wall, that is, the hostility between us. He has abolished the law with its commandments and ordinances, so that he might create in himself one new humanity in place of the two, thus making peace, and might reconcile both groups to God in one body through the cross, thus putting to death that hostility through it. So he came and proclaimed peace to you who were far off and peace to those who were near (2:14-17).

Third then, Gentiles "are no longer strangers and aliens, but you are citizens with the saints and also members of the household of God, built upon the foundation of the apostles and prophets [see also 3:5], with Christ Jesus himself as the cornerstone" (2:19-20).

Ephesians 2 on its own might suggest that what were before two distinct groups have now been joined together, resulting in a third community. Yet Paul elsewhere is very specific that the Gentiles have been grafted into the covenant of God with Israel (Rom 11:17-24), and this is intimated as such later in the Ephesian letter: "the Gentiles have become fellow-heirs, members of the same body, and sharers in the promise in Christ Jesus through the gospel" (Eph 3:6). As Ephesians is addressed primarily to Gentiles, it is appropriate that they are called to remembrance of their former life, outside God's covenant with Israel (2:11-12). Yet this also presumes Jewish remembrance of the covenant promises. The important point is christological: that reconciliation of Jew and Gentile, with the latter grafted into the former, is thus possible and actualized only in Christ (Harrington 1980: 68–74).

This one Jewish and Gentile people of God suggests an inclusivist versus ethnocentric ecclesiology (see also 1 Cor 12:13). While the proposal that Ephesians 2 is about ethnic reconciliation (Yee 2005) is arguably anachronistic, the reception history of this text does indicate that it is pregnant with implications for overcoming ethnic and even racial hostilities. Yet the Jewish and Gentile differences, however, also invite consideration that "church unity does not mean uniformity" (Rader 1978: 249). Indeed, the one body of Christ and the one temple of the Spirit dyad is constituted by many members (Eph 4:16; 5:30), consistent with what we find elsewhere in Paul (e.g., 1 Cor 12:12-31). Hence, the ecclesial unity affirmed in this epistle is first and foremost spiritual and pneumatological: "making every effort to maintain the unity of the Spirit in the bond of peace" (Eph 4:3; see Hanson 1946: 148). The unity of the Spirit surely is in-exclusive of "one Lord, one faith, one baptism, one God and Father of all, who is above all and through all and in all" (4:5-6), but these unite Jews and Gentiles rather than divide them.

To what end, then, the church, and utilizing what means? Theologically, the people of God are formed "to be holy and blameless before him in love" (1:4), "to the praise of [God's] glorious grace" (1:6), and to "live for the praise of [Christ's] glory" (1:12). There is a cognitive dimension to the church's calling: that "you may know what is the hope to which he has called you, what are the riches of his glorious inheritance among the saints, and what is the immeasurable greatness of his power for us who believe, according to the working of his great power" (1:18-19); and "that you may have the power to comprehend, with all the saints, what is the breadth and length and height and depth, and to know the love of Christ that surpasses knowledge, so that you may be filled with all the fullness of God" (3:18-19). Yet beyond all that can be thought of or imagined (3:20), the church is called to work and bear witness. Those gifted for ministry (4:8-11) are to equip the saints, to build up the people of God, to disciple and bring to maturity each person (4:12-15), and to promote "the body's growth in building itself up in love" (4:16; see also Thurston 1993: ch. 8). In doing so, the people of God will live a Spirit-filled (5:18) and countercultural life in a pagan world (4:17-24), one marked by truthfulness, patience, honesty, hard work, edifying speech, lack of malice, kindness, forgiveness, sexual purity, wisdom, joy, and thankfulness (4:25–5:20). Gentiles may be exempt from having to maintain the ceremonial aspects of the law (see Acts 15:19-21), but they now live according to the higher law and light of Christ in a dark world.

At one level, the author's conceptualization of the new people of God does not enable him to rise above the patriarchal and cultural norms of his time with regard to his instructions regarding husbands and wives and masters and slaves. However, at another level, the call for the submission of wives is preceded by the insistence that male and female members of the body of Christ ought "[b]e subject to one another out of reverence for Christ" (Eph 5:21). Similarly, while slaves are urged to submit to and obey their masters, the latter are also admonished, "do the same to them!" (6:9). There is a reciprocity in both cases consistent with that relating Jews and Gentiles, as well as the Pauline dictum: "There is no longer Jew or Greek, there is no longer slave or free, there is no longer male and female; for all of you are one in Christ Jesus" (Gal 3:28; also Col 3:11).

These very concrete and practical guidelines inform the behavior and practices of the people of God not only before a watching world but also before the principalities and powers (Eph 3:10). So although Paul says that "our struggle is not against enemies of blood and flesh, but against the rulers, against the authorities, against the cosmic powers of this present darkness, against the spiritual forces of evil in the heavenly places" (6:12), yet the spiritual weapons of truth, righteousness, proclamation (not to mention embodiment) of the gospel of peace, faith, the word of God, prayer, and perseverance are essential to rather than distinct from practicing the Christian life as outlined above. Here the spiritual, missiological, teleological, eschatological, and theological dimensions of the church converge again (Efird 1980). The people of God who live out of the gospel bear witness to the world even as they receive the fulfillment of the Pauline prayer that they may realize their calling, identity, and hope in Christ.

7.4 Into All the World! The Church as *Missio Spiritus*

We have covered much ground, and it is time to pull the threads together toward the task of renewing the doctrine of the church for the twenty-first century. If prior systematic and dogmatic discussion has revolved around the traditionally understood four marks of the church—its unity, holiness, catholicity, and apostolicity (F. Sullivan 1988)—the following can be understood to provide a complementary set of renewalist inflections, perspectives that highlight the relational, dynamic, and activity-oriented character of the church. In some respects the next few pages can be viewed as just another model of the church alongside others (e.g., Dulles 1974). From another angle, however, perhaps such a renewalist ecclesiological sketch can inform other perspectives, even enrich the ecumenical discussion about the nature of the church and what it does. We proceed to explore four interrelated major theses, expand on the missional dimensions of the fourth thesis, and conclude by returning to the question of the church as the people of God in relationship to Israel and contemporary Judaism. That discussion will provide a very preliminary test case concerning the viability of the following ecclesiological proposal.

- Thesis 1: The church as the people of God must be understood christologically. The church as the new people of God is nothing less than the body of Christ, which also means that Christ is the head of the church (Eph 5:23). For historically embodied and social creatures, Christ is refracted, however dimly, through the institutions, confessions, canons, offices, and liturgies of the church (Chan 2011). According to his promises, in addition, he is also more clearly present sacramentally in the practices of the church, as discussed in the preceding chapter, even as he is made known concretely to the world in the love that his followers show to one another (John 13:35). Yet fundamentally for most pietists, restorationists, and renewalists, Christ's presence is mystical and spiritual: "where two or three are gathered in my name, I am there among them" (Matt 18:20). On the other hand, sometimes Christ is hidden altogether, most obscured in the cross (1 Cor 1:20-23), and following from this, also in the crucible of human life. Discernment and confession of Christ is thus difficult, even impossible, merely on human terms. It happens only with the Holy Spirit (1 Cor 12:3).
- Thesis 2: The church as the people of God must be understood pneumatologically. The Holy Spirit, poured out upon the world by Christ (Acts 2:17, 33), takes what is Christ's and makes it known to the world (John 16:15). This pneumatic dimension highlights the interpersonal and interrelational character of the people of God. Structures, institutions, organizations, and even confessions that do not facilitate the dynamic communion of the people of God inevitably betray (if left unchecked) the pneumatic and organic vitality of the church (McGuire 1982; Nichols 1997). For this reason, the church as the fellowship of the Spirit is also inherently charismatic (Küng 1967; Moltmann 1977): there are many members and many gifts, even as there are many congregations, movements, and historic ecclesial traditions, because every situation, region, time, and place needs each in distinctive design. On the one hand, then, discerning the people of God is simply christological: the people of God are those who confess Christ and do the works of Christ in the power of the Spirit. On the other hand, "Not everyone who says to me, 'Lord, Lord,' will enter the kingdom of heaven, but only one who does the will of my Father in heaven" (Matt 7:21), and sometimes there are those who do the will of God in Christ without even recognizing or knowing him (Matt

25:34-40; see section 11.3). The inherent ambiguity in the whence and whither of the Spirit (John 3:8) carries over in any efforts to recognize the people of God as communing in the Spirit.

• Thesis 3: The church as the people of God must be understood eschatologically. The eschatological, as discussed in chapter 2, is the already discernible but not yet completely present reign of God that will feature the dominion of Christ. Just as the sacraments are present gateways into the future reign of God (see section 6.4), so also the church is an eschatological sign— an incomplete, partial, and fragmented one, no less, but still an indication, for all that—of the divine shalom in the world between the first and second coming of Christ. This eschatological dimension when interwoven with the pneumatological dynamic of the church suggests the people of God be understood as *in via*, on the way to being fully formed (see Clifton 2009). There therefore will be an ongoing waxing and waning of the church's proclamation and embodiment of the rule of God, representing the fallible and finite character of its witness. Yes, "the gates of Hades will not prevail against it" (Matt 16:18), but this does not provide any guarantees apart from the eyes of faith that in any particular space or time, the church's confession or witness will faithfully present the message of the kingdom. There will be occasions when the church's actions and deeds will undeniably signal the shalom—the peace, justice, and righteousness—of the reign of God. But there will also be too many other times when the human element inhibits the redemptive work of the Spirit. Hence this eschatological character of the people of God invites an appropriate humility, one ready to repent of its failures so that its broken witness might be redeemed by the Spirit for the glory of God (Hocken 2009: ch. 6).

• Thesis 4: The church as the people of God must be understood missiologically. This claim in effect summarizes the effective missiological thrust of our constructive dogmatic argument so far: that renewing Christian theology—the specific doctrines considered above and the doctrine of the church in this chapter—is missiologically driven as eschatologically oriented toward the coming reign of God. Here, the church is less a noun than a verb. The church is not only those called and chosen but that organic people of God participating in and heralding the reign of God in the power of the Spirit (Pomerville 1985;

Lord 2005). Ecclesiology, as article 6 of the SF thus indicates, is missiology and vice versa (see also York 2000: ch. 4). Insofar as recent developments in the missiological literature have attempted to secure a further trinitarian grounding to the mid-twentieth-century consideration of the church as the mission of God—what has been called *missio Dei* in theology of mission and ecumenical circles (e.g., Schwanz and Coleson 2011)—it is easy enough to confuse the triune redemptive work with human efforts (Flett 2010). A renewal perspective insists that such includes a robust pneumatological dimension, one that recognizes the church does not initiate but only participates in the divine mission in the power of Christ's Spirit. Hence the church can be considered also as the *missio Spiritus*, that is, as being enabled to achieve the mission of the Spirit who seeks the reconciliation of all creation to the Father through the Son. This identity of the people of God as *missio Spiritus* can be further explicated along four axes.

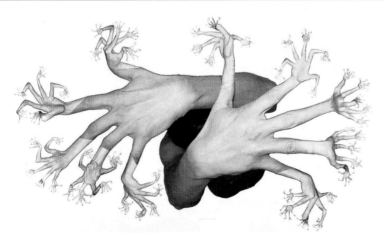

FIGURE 7.4

Contemporary artist Tim Hawkinson (cf. fig. 4.2) poetically renders his body as a tree of many hands, each hand branching into fingers that branch into further hands and fingers, and so on. This produces a striking human image that is simultaneously singular (one body) and plural (numerous hands performing numerous activities). And precisely because it is composed of hands, this body-tree reads as an image of accumulated human activity in the world: gestures suggestive of working, playing, grasping, pushing, building, breaking, worshipping, communicating (in visual art, figures often "talk" with their hands; e.g. figs. 2.2, 3.1, 5.2, and 8.4). Indeed, the "fruits" of this tree are the effects of these activities, whether for blessing or cursing.

But how might we interpret the relation between singularity and plurality in this body? Perhaps this image is best understood as a single person living and acting through time: it is a kind of self-portrait (constructed with photographs of the artist's body) that presents a human life as a "tree" of activity in the world, in which any given act grows from and makes possible further decisions and actions (cf. fig. 5.4). Another possibility is that we might see this image as a plurality of people (a community) collectively acting in the world. In this account, each individual hand is inextricably supporting and supported by the actions of other individuals, together comprising a semi-coordinated activity irreducible to the actions of individuals. And as with individual persons, the virtuous or vicious character of the "fruit" of collective activity cannot be understood simply in terms of discrete actions: there is an organic systemic unity at work within which these actions participate.

Intentionally or unintentionally, Hawkinson has created something that might stimulate our imaginations to think further about what it means to understand the body of the church christologically, pneumatologically, eschatologically, and missiologically. (The primary exception we need to make is for the racial homogeneity in this image, which is simply a by-product of the artist using his own body as the site for this visual experiment.) As a provisional image of the church, this artwork allows us to imagine the obscured image of Christ as being refracted through the actions of the church, and the fruit of the Spirit as being tangibly oriented toward the shalom of the world. And here we might also anticipate our discussion of soteriology in helpful ways (see ch. 9), insofar as the salvation that Christian theology points to is comprehensive, including the redemption of bodies, deeds, and social relationships. ✦

- Minor thesis 1: The *missio Spiritus* builds up the body of Christ. We have already seen, in our overview of the Ephesian letter, what is involved relationally among the people of God (see also Ma and Ma 2010: part 2). Part of what has been sought for here is to achieve a greater degree of unity than what is often felt, much less observed. This is, of course, first and foremost a unity of the Spirit around the person of Christ, rather than any structural or institutional unity. Yet such unity ought also to be visible in some way, in order that the world may know that the Father has sent the Son. The Acts narrative indicates that the Spirit-empowered people of God met regularly to break bread, for fellowship and worship, and to receive teaching and instruction, but that as a direct by-product, "day by day the Lord added to their number those who were being saved" (Acts 2:47). In short, the unifying activity of the body of Christ and edifying effects of the people of God living in the Spirit have a missional dimension and application.

- Minor thesis 2: The *missio Spiritus* declares the words of Christ. Classically and evangelically construed, the empowerment of the Spirit is to bear witness to the living Christ. "But how are they to call on one in whom they have not believed? And how are they to believe in one of whom they have never heard? And how are they to hear without someone to proclaim him?" Paul asks (Rom 10:14). The answer is that the people of God are to take the gospel of Christ in the power of the Spirit to the world. Central to this declaration is the forgiveness of sins available in Christ (Eph 1:7; Luke 1:77), which involves the giving and receiving of forgiveness within the body of Christ (Eph 4:32; Matt 18:21-22) and the readiness to grant forgiveness, without receiving it in turn, to others (John 20:23). Also essential is the timely capacity to speak forth the word of God into unjust real-world situations (Tyra 2011).

- Minor thesis 3: The *missio Spiritus* lives out the compassion of Christ. Article 6 of the SF clearly identifies the mission of the people of God as consisting of compassion, by which is meant both works of service on behalf of others (the poor, the hungry, the sick, those in prison, etc.) and engagement with the social, political, and economic structures that are oppressive rather than life-giving (see Kwon 2011: part 3). The former involves entering into solidarity with the marginalized, suffering, and outcasts of society, as will be elaborated upon later (see section 8.4). Addressing the latter, structural dimensions of human oppressiveness will always require, in the contemporary global context, discerning collaboration and partnerships with other ecclesial groups but also, more often than not, with those beyond the church (Ormerod and Clifton 2011). In some sociopolitical contexts, the verbal witness of the church ought to be subordinated to its ministries of compassion. In other contexts wherein there is greater freedom for traditional forms of evangelism, the people of God who do not exhibit the compassion of Christ will proclaim a very hypocritical message that will not be good news to their hearers. The point, however, is that regardless of what the church says, the world can always see how it behaves and what it does (cf. Phil 2:15; Tit 2:7-8; 1 Pet 2:12-20). The proper response then is not to neglect verbal witness, when possible, but to strive to develop compassionate ministries and mission initiatives that also facilitate social transformation in the power of the Spirit (Yong 2008: ch. 5; Augustine 2012). Full salvation, involving abundant life according to the gospel promise (John 10:10), cannot but also address, encourage, and empower these material domains of life.

- Minor thesis 4: The *missio Spiritus* engages "against the spiritual forces of evil in the heavenly places" (Eph 6:12) in the name of Christ. This calls attention to the cosmic horizon of God's redemptive plan, one that includes the gathering up of all things in and through Christ (Eph 1:10-11; 4:10). Hence there is a need to cultivate the armaments of the Spirit, but not at the expense of becoming no earthly good. Rather, such an approach prepares the people of God to make a difference in their world, in their relationships, their communities, their nations, even to the ends of the earth, precisely because it provides them with spiritual insight and perspective on the relational dynamics that are often beneath the surface of things. What fragments the church or inhibits authentic worship? What undermines the compassionate witness of the people of God or hinders reception of the gospel? These concern the spiritual dynamics of the church's life, which invite more intentional cultivation of a Spirit-empowered theology of mission that is contextual, dialogical, and liberative vis-à-vis the principalities and powers of this world (Kim 2003; Yong 2010: ch. 4).

This chapter closes via a return to the question percolating throughout, introduced first and registered starkly in our discussion of Stephen's martyrdom: How ought we to comprehend the relationship between the church and Israel? Four considerations are due, informed by the preceding discussion. First, there is no question that the church and Israel are neither completely one nor also yet absolutely two. On the one hand, there is a "double-consciousness" (Blount 2007: 348), even in the Ephesian letter, which recognizes an "us" of Jews and a "you" of Gentiles. On the other hand, there is also the grafting of Gentiles into the Jewish trunk (Hocken 2009: ch. 5). Both are messianically focused, although Jews reject that the Messiah has come in Jesus. For better or for worse, Jews and Gentiles are in this together, and we have to engage all of our differences, of which there are many, recognizing this paradoxical togetherness in distinction and vice versa. However, it is only through hearing and living with the other in all of their otherness that we might discern through the Spirit the possibilities for rapprochement, and perhaps such will turn out to present a joint witness to the truth of a covenant-making God.

Second, the eschatological framework presented for considering the people of God invites us to hold our convictions open. There is a real sense in which "Jews and Christians are called to prove that they are members of God's people and children of the same Father by performing the service entrusted to them" (Barth 1983: 71–72). Those Jews who live into the older covenant in anticipation of the messiah will bear truthful witness to the world, including to Christians. Simultaneously, to the degree that Christians live into the covenant with Christ, they will also bear truthful witness to the world, including to Jews. In both instances, the vocation of divine peoplehood involves less enjoying the benefits of such election than participating in the mission of the divine Spirit, which oftentimes involves suffering, to inaugurate the coming reign of God (Ucko 2000).

Third then, ought Christians to bear witness to and even seek the conversion of Jews? If Jews also ought to bear witness to Christians, even seeking to convert them, then why not vice versa? Yet for Christians, their witness is always to Christ and is eschatological, requiring their ongoing conversion until the Parousia. And as already indicated (see minor thesis 3 above), there are different forms of witness bearing. So in a post-Holocaust world, Christians ought to be discerning about the appropriateness of their mission strategies and activities when interacting with Jews. Most importantly, as the messianic Jewish example demonstrates, Christian conversion could also involve embrace of Christ without abandonment of Jewish commitments. In some cases, following Christ in the Spirit might lead Jews to Christian communities; but otherwise, Jews continue to await the Messiah whose appearance (reappearance, for Christians) will bring about their final conversion (Moltmann 1992a: 108). But in any case, Christians bear witness to Christ, even if only "so as to make Israel jealous" (Rom 11:11).

Last (due to space constraints) but not least (there is so much more to examine), any Christian philo-Semitism should not be exclusivistic. Some Christians, perhaps in order to make up for the centuries of anti-Semitism, have bent over backward to the point of embracing a form of pro-Israelism that undermines the witness of the gospel in the wider Middle Eastern context. Any love for Israel that includes less than loving attitudes or responses to that country's enemies still compromises the gospel message and the *missio Spiritus* (Newberg 2012: ch. 9). Surely, the issues are extremely complicated. Yet that is precisely what is entailed when we begin to inquire into the nature of the church as the people of God in relationship to Israel and the world.

Discussion Questions

1. What are some aspects of your church's teachings about Israel and how do they compare with the preceding discussion? How ought the biblical portrayal of Jews and Gentiles inform our thinking about what it means to be the people of God today? What are the practical and even political implications of these matters for Christian life and thought in the twenty-first century?

2. How might some see the many different types of churches to be a problem that needs resolution? How might others see such diversity as a blessing instead? How has your church encouraged you to view other churches? What if anything ought we to do differently about the plurality of churches going forward?

3. How much emphasis on missions exists in your church? What kinds of mission practices or activities are promoted, and which of these are you most/least comfortable with? Does mission define the church and vice versa—if so, how, and if not, why not? What are the implications, if any, of this chapter for further developing your church's implicit or explicit theology of mission?

Further Reading

Arrington, French L. 2008. *The Spirit-Anointed Church: A Study of the Acts of the Apostles.* Cleveland, Tenn.: Pathway.

Bosch, David J. 1991. *Transforming Mission: Paradigm Shifts in Theology of Mission.* Maryknoll, N.Y.: Orbis.

Fee, Gordon D. 1996. *Paul, the Spirit, and the People of God.* Peabody, Mass.: Hendrickson.

Kee, Howard Clark. 1995. *Who Are the People of God? Early Christian Models of Community.* New Haven: Yale University Press.

Kinnamon, Michael, and Brian E. Cope, eds. 1997. *The Ecumenical Movement: An Anthology of Key Texts and Voices.* Geneva: World Council of Churches.

Mortensen, Viggo, and Andreas Østerlund Nielsen, eds. 2010. *Walk Humbly with the Lord: Church and Mission Engaging Plurality.* Grand Rapids: Eerdmans.

Soulen, R. Kendall. 1996. *The God of Israel and Christian Theology.* Minneapolis: Fortress.

Vondey, Wolfgang. 2010-2013. *Pentecostalism and Christian Unity.* 2 vols. Eugene, Ore.: Pickwick.

Divine Healing

Salvation of the Body and Redemption of the World

World Assemblies of God Fellowship Statement of Faith
—Article 5: Divine Healing

We believe that deliverance from sickness is provided in the atonement and is the privilege of all believers (Isaiah 53:4-5; Matthew 8:16-17; James 5:14-16).

8.1 Legion: Deliverance and Healing

The church as the christological, pneumatological, eschatological, and missiological people of God is also a saving and healing community. There are many healing stories in the Bible. These are favored among renewalists for whom Jesus is savior precisely because he is also healer. In fact, many more renewalists, especially across the global south, became Christians as a result of experiencing or knowing someone who has experienced healing (Brown 2011). It might be that the more impoverished lack access to medical or health care and so respond instead to messages regarding the healing power of Jesus. Yet not everyone gets healed, or more precisely, to anticipate a distinction that we will be making in this chapter, not everyone gets physically cured. Many renewalists, as well as Christians in general, live with their infirmities and impairments. Some despair in these conditions and cease participating within their communities of faith. But what if curing were distinct from healing, and what if the latter also involved a communal (ecclesial) and social dimension, unlike the former? Against this backdrop, the story of the so-called Gerasene demoniac (Mark 5:1-20) proves particularly illuminating.

Our focus here is on an unnamed man, the only anonymous person featured in the introductory sections of this book's chapters. Although there is some question about the historicity of this account (e.g., Aus 2003: 89–92; but see also Pilch 2008), it is the Markan characterization that is of interest to us. In particular, how might this narrative invite consideration of a more multidimensional model of healing than some might be accustomed to working with?

What do we know about this afflicted life from the gospel account? First, as a man "with an unclean spirit" (Mark 5:2), he is already identified as impure, certainly in contrast to "Jesus, Son of the Most High God" (5:7, acknowledged here by the man himself), whom we know from earlier in Mark was alighted upon and driven by the *Holy* Spirit (1:10-12). The man's impurity is further heightened along three fronts. (1) He lived among tombs (5:2b), which are contaminated sites for ancient Jews. (2) His abode was adjacent to a grazing area for an extremely large herd of pigs, also considered by Jews as polluted. (3) The area of the Gerasenes and the surrounding Decapolis (5:1, 20) were historically centers of Greco-Roman culture and influence, with a majority Gentile population (no doubt only these were eligible to serve as pig-herders; 5:14). This eastern region is clearly identified as being on the "other side" (4:35, 5:1) of the Sea of Galilee from Capernaum, Jesus' primary location of ministry through the first four chapters of Mark. Even the demons appeared to have felt "at home" in this pagan and Gentile world, as they "begged [Jesus] earnestly not to send them out of the country" (5:10).

Second, this man was tormented in many ways. Life "among the tombs and on the mountains" (5:5) meant he was isolated, except of course from the pigs and their herders. This isolation, however, appears to have been intermittent, at least insofar as it appears repeated efforts had been made by the townspeople to restrain him, even using chains. But these endeavors had amounted to naught: "no one could restrain him *any more* . . . the chains he wrenched apart, and the shackles he broke in pieces; and no one had the strength to subdue him" (5:3-4 [emphasis added]), and so he was left on his own, perhaps self-quarantined in this rural area, certainly avoided by others. Yet even in this situation, after continuously "bruising himself with stones" (5:5b), the man had not succeeded in ending his life.

In the confrontation with Jesus, we find out that this man was possessed by a "legion" of demons (5:9), certainly enough, upon their exorcism from him, to destroy at least two thousand pigs (5:13). Whatever Mark's understanding or intent, the demonic name would have called to mind in this Greco-Roman outpost the Roman legion of upward of five thousand soldiers that was officially charged with keeping the regional peace, but unofficially at least perceived by the locals as an oppressive scourge. Maybe this man had internalized this sense of injustice, even perhaps the notion that he was the scapegoat for the Jewish residents of the Decapolis, all of whom longed for liberation but yet had to come to terms with the fact that the promised messiah had not arrived. This view (Newheart 2004: ch. 5; Myers 2008: 190–94) is not so far-fetched, given that even after his deliverance, the people were afraid rather than rejoiced (5:15) and "began to beg Jesus to leave their neighbourhood" (5:17). They had lost not only their pigs but also the one who bore the brunt of their collective resentment under the Roman regime. The man himself now felt doubly alone—belonging neither at the tombs nor in the cities—and "begged [Jesus] that he might be with him" (5:18b). Jesus, unlike other occasions in Mark where he silenced those who glimpsed his messianic identity, instructs the delivered one to bear witness.

FIGURE 8.1

Bible scholar Rikki Watts has argued that the threefold repetition of the terms "tombs" and "pigs" in Mark's telling of this story (5:1-17) is a means of connecting this passage to Isaiah 65, wherein God laments the adulterous unfaithfulness of his people, who "sit among the graves and . . . who eat the flesh of pigs" (Isa 65:4, NIV). These were conspicuously unclean under Mosaic law, but moreover they were emblematic of idolatrous worship. So in one sense, by emphasizing the narrative setting of Jesus' healing of the Gerasene demoniac amidst tombs and large-scale pig-herding, Mark poetically shows Jesus cutting to the heart of idolatry by overthrowing the oppressive demonic powers that potentially lurk behind the logic of the idols (Watts 2000: ch. 6).

In another sense, however, this is a deeply personal story of a desperate man being healed. In Tissot's depiction of the scene, the Gerasene's liberation from demonic oppression leads to—and is perhaps enacted in—interpersonal embrace. The newly healed/freed man reaches up toward Jesus, who in turn looks him squarely in the face and embraces him. At the same time, a disciple of Jesus begins to clothe the otherwise naked man, giving him basic material provision and the beginnings of a renewed social standing. What is thus depicted here is not only this man's freedom from demonic power but the first phase of social healing through direct personal acknowledgment, acceptance, and reinclusion into a community.

We might also notice that as the healed man reaches up toward Jesus in the foreground, his gesture is visually echoed by a pig-herder on the hill in the background, who reaches upward in panic and anger as his entire drove of pigs tumbles into the sea. We might wonder about this man: by visually rhyming the man of the tombs with the man of the pigs, Tissot prompts us to consider their possible connections and contrasts. What comes as tremendous relief to one man is at great cost to the other. The two emblems of idolatry in this narrative have been overthrown—a human person has been redeemed from the tombs, and the pigs have been driven into the sea (and both the effects of overthrowing the Legion)—but not without leaving scars. ✦

More recent readings of this text have noted the parallels between the man's symptoms and what modern societies call mental illness (Leslie 1965: ch. 10). Possessed by a legion of unclean spirits, this man no doubt exhibited multiple identities (named now variously as bipolar disorder, multiple personality disorder, schizophrenia, etc.). More striking is his loss of dignity, fractured social relations, and the palpable alienation and estrangement he felt from his community. Mental illness in contemporary parlance has two sides: a biochemical aspect that in some cases can be medically and pharmaceutically controlled (at least moderated), but also a social dimension that, when addressed, involves restoration and stabilization of communal relations (Avalos, Melcher, and Schipper 2007: ch. 9). In this case of the afflicted Gerasene, there is also a spiritual dimension, involving "Legion." It is unfortunate that this connection has had a long history of negative aftereffects, so those who have exhibited similar symptoms have been believed to be demon-possessed as well. The point here, however, is that the curing of the man through exorcism and deliverance deals only with the spiritual, psychical, and phenomenological features—that is, he is found "sitting there, clothed and in his right mind" (Mark 5:15)—but that social healing and reconciliation is delayed until he reengages the Decapolis community, now as an evangelist. Even then, however, the response of the people is ambivalent: "everyone was amazed" (5:20b). The demons may have been taken out of the man, but the Roman legion was still present in the midst of the people. Put otherwise, his mental health may have been restored, but their social wholeness was still lacking.

8.2 Healing, Miracles, and Disability: The Broader Conversation

At one level, according to the succinctly formulated terms of article 5, the narrative of the Gerasene demoniac is a success story. Testimonies of healing in renewal Christianity are believed to be extensions of the early Christian reports, especially in the Gospels and Acts. Jesus' authority over the "Legion" in the case above is part and parcel of his authority over sickness, disease, and even disabilities, which we also see in the gospel account. There are two major questions attending this correlation, however. First, if such healing is "the privilege of the believer," as the article stipulates, then the life stories of those who are not healed or who live with ongoing infirmity, impairment, and disability are implicitly marginalized. This has ill aftereffects, in particular by promoting only certain examples of a Spirit-filled life of faith (i.e., those who are cured) and suggesting thereby that those who do not measure up to these norms are somehow substandard Christians, if believers at all. Second, going beyond what the article explicitly states, within renewal circles the more spectacular the healing, the more impressive the testimony. This also suggests that an authentic Spirit-empowered life ought to be followed by signs and wonders of the more instantaneous and remarkable type. And this, once again, becomes the uninterrogated and problematic measure of faithfulness.

Our task in this chapter requires that we develop some historical perspective on these matters. The following treats healing in the Christian tradition; the contested notion of miracle, especially in the modern world of science and technology; and the questions related to more recent understandings of disability. Each discussion, of course, will need to be narrowly circumscribed, identifying the salient issues that interface with renewal Christianity and that any contemporary theology of healing will need to engage. Our overarching intention, the goal of this chapter, is to triangulate—in thinking about miraculous healing, modern science, and impairment or disability—toward a renewed theology of health, healing, wholeness, and salvation that will have traction for the global, evangelical, and ecumenical church of the twenty-first century.

8.2.1 Healing and Miracles: Unpredictable Traditions?

Healing has been central to modern renewal Christianity from its beginnings at the turn of the twentieth century. Fed in part by the emerging emphasis on divine healing that characterized Holiness, Keswick, and other pietist movements during the middle to late nineteenth century (Hardesty 2003; Curtis, 2007; Robinson 2011), Jesus was embraced as healer, besides being savior, sanctifier, Spirit Baptizer, and coming king (Dayton 1987). This renewalist expectation was further buttressed by a restorationist hermeneutic. Not only did Jesus heal the sick, but he also commissioned his disciples "to proclaim the kingdom of God and to heal" (Luke 9:2; 10:9). So if "God anointed Jesus of Nazareth with the Holy Spirit and with power; [and] he went about doing good and healing all who were oppressed by the devil, for God was with him" (Acts 10:38), it should not be unanticipated that his Spirit-filled apostles would do the same: "A great number of people would also gather from the towns around Jerusalem, bringing the sick and those tormented by unclean spirits, and they were all cured" (Acts 5:16). Jesus himself had promised: "the one who believes in me will also do the works that I do and, in fact, will do greater works than these, because I am going to the Father" (John 14:12), and the pentecostal revival was understood to be a last days realization of these promises. Pentecostal healing then gained even further momentum during the middle of the twentieth century, in part through the charismatic renewal movements and in part through the prominent ministries of healing evangelists like William Marion Branham, Oral Roberts, and Kathryn Kuhlman, among others (Harrell 1975). A variety of healing beliefs and practices have thus appeared (Hejzlar 2009), perhaps in response to the various types of physical, emotional, psychical, spiritual, and even demonic ailments (MacNutt 1974). Through all of this, healing has remained central to the renewal message of a Spirit-empowered Christianity.

In this, of course, the renewal emphasis on healing is a single current, even a turbulent if not torrential one, among others in the history of Christianity (e.g., Kelsey 1973: ch. 8). The early Christians of the second and third centuries were apologetically motivated to confirm the superiority of Christ's power over that of Jewish and pagan exorcists and healers (Daunton-Fear 2009). The apostolic signs, wonders, miracles, and gifts of healing eventually were passed on to saints (including those martyred before the time of Constantine), desert solitaries and abbés, and monastics (both cenobitic and eremitic), all of whom were recognized as holy persons. Over time, the cult of especially martyred saints emerged, shrines were established, the healing powers of their relics were extolled, and pilgrimages were undertaken to these shrines. To be sure, there were also failed shrines and unmet expectations. But here oral histories, folklore, and the stuff of legends converge (Koopmans 2011), and it is not so much what can be demonstrated but what can be hoped for and anticipated that is registered in the historical accounts. In effect, then, by the medieval period, the saints and their miraculous cures were thoroughly woven into the expectations of the Christian community. In hindsight, what is evident is the physiological, sociological, and psychological functions of the shrines as sources of healing, social coherence, and spiritual assurance (Finucane 1977). Yes, miraculous healings were signs of a transcendent deity, but they were immanent signs also, indications that the God of the heavens was also present on earth and involved in the lives of people. Hence for medieval Christians, "miracles were unanimously seen as part of the City of God [the coming heavenly realm] on earth, and whatever reflections men might have on their cause and their aim, they formed an integral part of ordinary life" (Ward 1982: 2).

The Renaissance and Reformation not only produced more critical postures and analytical approaches to miracle accounts but also brought about a more christological focus among Protestants. The Counter-Reformation rejoinder both reflected as well as inspired a more Marian-centered piety among Catholics, which in turn fed miraculous healing phenomena in relationship to visions of the Virgin Mother. On the one hand, this also precipitated a cautious approach to miracles and healings by the ecclesial hierarchy, and the Roman Catholic Church became more discerning in promoting popular claims related to local manifestations (Duffin 2009). On the other hand, the popularity of Marian-related miracles is indicative of broader historical trends that suggest the prevalence of healing accounts among women. Yet this gendered perspective only shows that such phenomena may be more important for women because their retelling (and testimony) nurtures compassion, empowers personal persistence, sustains communal suffering, enables confrontation with the stigmas of female corporeality, and propels the overcoming of felt oppression (Korte 2004). Together, then, miraculous healings display divine graciousness in extranormal ways, and these are important especially to women navigating a male-dominated world (see Mukonyora 2007).

In the contemporary global context, there is greater realization than ever that Christians do not own the copyright on miracles and healings. Surely, different religious traditions view and understand miraculous healings differently (Woodward 2000: 383–84; Weddle 2010; Twelftree 2011), whether as related to divine covenant (Judaism), as a manifestation of divine authority (Islam), as significant for spiritual liberation (Hinduism), or as a portal into transcendent wisdom (Buddhism), among other understandings. Of course, these generalizations mask the diversity of interpretations of miracles and healings within each tradition, even as we see that the different perspectives registered in the Christian tradition (above) both intersect with as well as diverge from these other accounts (Corner 2005). From a renewal perspective, one popular explanation for the presence of miraculous cures in non-Christian religions is that even "Satan disguises himself as an angel of light" (2 Cor 11:14), and thus has the capacity to accomplish signs and wonders to deceive religious others and blind them to the truth (2 Cor 4:4; 2 Thess 2:9). So similarly to how tradition indicates that "Jannes and Jambres opposed Moses" (2 Tim 3:8a) through their magical pagan (Egyptian) arts (see Exod 7:10-12, 22), there will be those in other religions who also exercise comparable powers. Without denying that the powers of this age are at work to close the hearts and minds of all people to the truth of the gospel, genuine healings in other religious contexts suggest that more may be going on than meets the (renewalist) eye. What Jesus said in response to those who believed he was doing the work of Satan remains applicable in our global context: "How can Satan cast out Satan? If a kingdom is divided against itself, that kingdom cannot stand. And if a house is divided against itself, that house will not be able to stand. And if Satan has risen up against himself and is divided, he cannot stand, but his end has come" (Mark 3:23-26 and parallels). Are there other ways of understanding the presence of miracles and healings in other religions without collapsing their differences from Christian healing?

This question is all the more important because taking up the discussion about healing in a world of many religions also invites consideration of indigenous or local traditions of health and wholeness (see Kinsley 1996). Within this wider context, natural remedies that define healing in social and environmental terms set in relief the theological question about how to understand God in relationship to the healing arts. Coming back full circle to the modern Western world, how is God related, if at all, to modern science, technology, and medicine?

8.2.2 Healing and Modern Science: Challenges or Opportunities?

We have seen already at various junctures above the need to think about Christian doctrines as they relate to our contemporary scientific understanding of the world. Modern science is particularly threatening to renewal spirituality, because its methodological naturalism often translates into a metaphysical naturalism along with a rather deistic notion of God as removed from human lives. While we will return in chapter 10 to discuss science and naturalism, here the concerns revolve around how advances in modern medicine may impinge on a renewal theology of healing. In its crassest forms, the ongoing march of science, pharmacology, and medical technology seems to have alleviated any need for a healing God.

The Newtonian cosmology developed in the early modern period was especially challenging for any theology of providence, much less divine healing. In such a cosmological framework, the world, while created by God, was a closed system of causes and effects. So if God acted in the world in general, or to heal people in particular, such could only occur indirectly, through the laws of nature already in place. This explains, at least in part, the emergence of the "Christian science" movement in the nineteenth century (later the Church of Christ Scientist), as well as other notions of spiritual or theosophical healing that claimed to see divine healing accomplished through scientifically identifiable natural laws. God's healing powers could be accessed through prayer, meditation, and other human actions congruent with the laws of health and wholeness embedded in the created order (Porterfield 2005: ch. 7).

Of course, it was a short step from here to be skeptical not just of divine healing but of divinity altogether. Cynics who were pessimistic about faith healing surely found more than enough "counterevidence"—not only through exposés of fraudulent claims but also through identification of natural healing processes underneath religious testimonies—to feed modernist incredulity toward miraculous cures (Nickell 1993). Indeed, from a naturalistic perspective, healing could be and was being reinterpreted by the neurobiological, psychological, and social sciences as an evolutionary phenomenon that conferred reproductive advantages on the human species (see McClenon 2002). Within this scientifically dominant environment, the Reformation dismissal of medieval superstition was taken to a whole new level: modernists now ought to be dismissive altogether of faith (Brown 1984).

At one level, modern science and medicine have given us understanding of germinal, genetic, and biochemical and neurological processes, so we are much less inclined to accept spiritual, moral, or demonic etiologies or explanations. Further, the development of penicillin (for germs), social and educational systems (to support families and individuals with congenital disabilities), and antidepressives and other similar medications (for mental health), among other interventions, also leave us less inclined to rely on "supernatural" divine intervention. In the wake of the modernist critiques, then, some Christians might not deny that God heals miraculously, although they might understand this less in terms of miraculous cures than in terms of divinely granted but still natural processes of communal health and restoration (e.g., Melinsky 1968: ch. 7). Alternatively, others may say that inexplicable occurrences identified as miraculous healings depend on rather than produce faith, or at least that they represent a call to faith. Such healings are therefore less empirically demonstrable than they are confessions of faith. They thereby have supportive rather than a coercive epistemic force, belonging to the order of redemption, rather than to the order of nature or creation (Theissen 1983; Brown 1985).

Yet to stop here would be too easy. The genius of modern science is that all claims, even those concerning religious experience, are open to empirical investigation. So while the scientific method can neither confirm nor deny the existence of God or say anything about divine action, the effects of religious life, including prayer, church attendance, and other forms of spiritual activity, can be and have been quantitatively measured and qualitatively assessed (e.g., Brown 2012). Along this front, the scientific data can indeed be understood as providing some empirical support that postures of faith are correlated with increased life satisfaction, longer marriages and life spans, ability to cope with stress, lower rates of depression and serious cardiovascular disease, more rapid recovery from certain illnesses, stronger immune systems, fewer expensive hospital stays, and other indications of well-being (Koenig 1999). Properly handled, scientific methods can be deployed to examine, if not substantiate, the efficacy of believers' life of faith (Lee and Yong 2012).

But if the scientific evidence is open to interpretations generally complementary to Christian views regarding divine healing, understood along other registers, it is also convergent with indigenous traditions of health and healing that are experiencing resurgence around the world. The emerging postmodern, postcolonial, and post-Enlightenment paradigm is now reconsidering Chinese acupuncture, Indian ayurveda, indigenous herbal medicines, and ritual healing involving alternative states of consciousness, among other meditative and psychotherapeutic techniques, all equally conducive to the achievement of holistic health and healing (McGuire and Kantor 1988; Sullivan 1989; McNeill and Cervantes 2008; Incayawar et al. 2009). Yet the rejuvenation of these traditional approaches is being conducted in light of, rather than being entirely opposed to, the latest developments in modern medicine. Thus medical surgeries are being performed as guided by psychic and spirit healers (Greenfield 2008); psychosomatic health is being nurtured with sensitivity to interpersonal, communal, and social relations (e.g., Csordas 2002; Freund, McGuire, and Podhurst 2003); and Western pharmacological prescriptions are expected to work alongside, rather than displace, natural and environmental medicines preserved by oral cultures and traditions. Clearly we are witnessing the end of the hegemony of Western medicine, although there is simultaneously no turning back the clock in terms of opposing what modern science and technology has to offer and will continue to generate for human health and well-being.

Christian responses, of course, have been mixed. On the one hand, indigenous Christian movements, particularly in the African context, have long attempted to combine what was perceived to be the best in Western medicine and traditional forms of healing (e.g., Oosthuizenet al. 1988; cf. Roth 2001). Healing has thus been understood multidimensionally (e.g., Lartey, Nwachuku, and Kasonga 1994), involving physical and bodily health, spiritual realities (perhaps counteracted through spirit-possession rituals), ancestral relations (thus addressing the question of human identity and relationship intergenerationally across time), emotional and mental aspects (treatable therapeutically through dance, music, etc.), socioeconomic connections (that are vulnerable to curses, ill will, and other invisible or structural forces), and environmental harmony (thereby promoting a more ecologically sustainable way of life). More evangelical approaches have developed theologies of shalom that include medical technologies, communal and interpersonal relations, economic development, sustainable environment practices, and even some forms of traditional practices—except those contrary to explicit scriptural teaching, like sorcery, witchcraft, shamanism, and spirit possession—all under a biblically informed approach attentive to contextual and indigenous cultural patterns (e.g., Long 2000; cf. Ram 1995).

What is clear is that human health is nurtured in multiple domains. On the one hand, without clean water and accessible basic health care, for instance, the threat of disease is maximized. On the other hand, more traditional approaches to healing are not closed to combining prayer and spiritual practices with a wide range of other kinds of activity, from forgiving others to taking sociopolitical action. The reality of globalization is constituted by multidirectional processes that can bring about sickness or foster health in places and times far removed from one another (Moe-Lobeda 2002).

Renewalists, of course, find themselves betwixt and between. On the one hand, especially in the Western context, most find themselves aligned against the materialism, naturalism, and skepticism urged by some so-called scientific voices ("so-called" because these are more informed by philosophical presuppositions than scientific data, as will be shown in ch. 10). On the other hand, despite their supernaturalistic rhetoric, many are also increasingly practicing what some might consider to be a para-doxical understanding of healing that presumes spiritual approaches work in tandem with medicinal, social, and other nature-based therapies (e.g., Droogers, van der Laan, and van Laar 2006: part 3).

8.2.3 Disability: Renewal Christianity's "Thorn in the Flesh"?

Renewal Christian emphases on healing are further challenged when confronted by the reality of persistent disability, in particular those who are prayed for but do not experience healing. This is related not only to the intimations in Scripture connecting impairing conditions with divine curses responding to human disobedience and sin (Deut 28:21-22, 27-29, 35, 58-61; cf. John 5:14 and Jas 5:14-16), but also to the links, tangential as they are, between evil spirits and certain disabling experiences (e.g., not only the case of the Gerasene demoniac discussed above, but also that of the epileptic boy in Mark 9:14-32; cf. Matt 9:32-33; 12:22). Further, if "deliverance from sickness is provided in the atonement," as article 5 of the SF affirms, and if the lines between sickness and disability are blurred, at least in some cases (e.g., that of chronic illness), then the persistence of such disabling sickness calls into question at least the faith of the afflicted, if not that of the entire (local) community. Then when renewal literature publicizes the testimonies of those who are cured from disabling condi-tions—for example, those delivered from wheelchairs, their sight restored, their deaf ears opened—others without such testimonies in time begin to internalize this dominant message, and even they begin to question why they are not recipients of the promised divine favor. It is thus not unexpected if people with disabilities are not obviously present in renewal churches (Monteith 2005).

Yet the World Health Organization estimates that up to 20 percent of the world's population lives with some kind of physical or mental impair-ment. The range and types of impairing conditions defy classification: from congenital (e.g., from mild to profound Down syndrome) to later onset (due to war or accidents); from visible (dependent on wheelchairs or guide dogs) to invisible (related to chronic pain, mental illness, or developmental delay); from that ameliorated by biomedical technologies (like cochlear implants) to that following the natural process of aging, among many others. That many disabilities are invisible suggests there are more people in churches with impairing conditions than is realized, but still many are reluctant to be open about their situations because of the associated stigma. Further, in a global context, whether impairments are disabling depends on whether there is access to affordable interventions (Kabue et al. 2011). Yet the flip side is that disability includes a social dimension, such that, for instance, a legally blind person with corrective lenses or whose vocation requires only nearsightedness is visually impaired but not disabled. On the negative end of this social perspective, many cultures continue to see disabilities as stigmatized conditions (with undergirding religious rationalization, as within Christian circles) that justify social ostracism that is marginalizing (at best) or even oppressive (at worst) for the lives of such people (Rao 2002; Schumm and Stoltzfus 2011).

FIGURE 8.2

Tim Lowly's artistic practice has been profoundly organized around his daughter Temma (b. 1985). When only days old, Temma stopped breathing and had a cardiac arrest, which resulted in severe brain damage: manifestations including cortical blindness, relatively little ability to communicate, and very limited volitional movement of her body. The Lowly family has insisted on caring for Temma in their home (vs. an institution) in resolute commitment to love her. As Lowly states: "Part of my fairly political agenda is to say that disabled children are a part of life. These are not freaks. What I'm saying is that we should advocate for eyes of compassion that see human beings as human beings, rather than separating them into the beautiful, the ugly, the normal, the freak" (Camper 2002: 17). In this context, he has painted images of Temma for nearly three decades in a powerful ongoing meditation on human dignity and compassion (cf. figs. 10.3 and 10.4).

In this large painting (8' × 12') Lowly places his daughter in visual continuity with the earth, the implications of which are multiplied through a double reading of the title: In one sense, "Temma on Earth" is a stark description of her vulnerable body lying on the soil. But the title might also refer to a limited perspective: that is, this is Temma as seen "on earth" through earthly frames of reference—as opposed to seeing Temma "in spirit," or "on the day of resurrection," or "as God knows her," or even "as she knows herself." In this frame of reference, Lowly places his daughter's disability in continuity with the groaning of the earth—here dry and drained of vivid color (cf. fig. 10.5)—calling to mind St. Paul's articulation of the cosmic and human groanings "while we wait for adoption, the redemption of our bodies" (Rom 8:22-23).

This image inhabits the traditional genre of "figure in landscape," but as John Brunetti notes, it entirely subverts the convention of an upright person standing against the horizon (Brunetti 2001). This has a remarkable effect, placing the figure in a visual field that has no horizon (no glimpse of the heavens), which alters the ways we experience gravity in this image. On the one hand, Temma lies inert on the ground, the earth's gravity pulling her body tightly against the soil. On the other hand, because of her placement in the upper half of the composition, and because there is no horizon to "ground" her, she appears to float. Brunetti describes this evocatively: "Despite her palpable inertia, she seems to have broken free of the earth's gravity. Traditional roles of land and sky have been reversed. The bleached, dried ground becomes luminously celestial . . . Physically one with the ground yet seeming to journey far away, weighted down while being lighter than air" (Brunetti 2001: 5). ✦

Christians have responded to disability with various theological views over the centuries. Augustinian traditions have typically understood disability as vestiges of a broken creation connected to the Adamic fall, yet as allowed by an omnipotent and omnibenevolent God to reveal human brokenness and need for divine grace, to provide occasions for the church to serve those in need, or to increase the human desire for heaven, when broken bodies will be perfected and disabilities will be erased (Beates 2012: 161–65). This last point overlooks the possibility that, as with Jesus, the marks of impaired bodies will be retained in the resurrection (Eiesland 1994: ch. 5). Others might agree that God's redemptive purpose works all things together "for good for those who love God, who are called according to his purpose" (Rom 8:28), even if they are more comfortable in seeing impairments related to the consequences of creaturely freedom and derived from the contingencies inherent in the created order than from God's (permissive or otherwise perplexing and apparently arbitrary) will.

Christians, however, have also been subject to wider cultural presuppositions. Thus the dominant views of the image of God, influenced historically by the philosophical tradition, as consisting of uprightness of physical form or of the spiritual, moral, and rational capacities lacking in nonhuman animals, have inclined some to call into question the *imago Dei* in those lacking these qualities. Similarly, the urbanization, industrialization, and medical advances characterizing the modern West, when combined with Enlightenment individualism, have also shaped contemporary understandings. Even Christians tend to reduce disability to individual bodily conditions and to seek cures either through divine curing or through biomedical or pharmaceutical technologies. But given these assumptions, the social, economic, and cultural aspects of disability are minimized, and the shame attached to those who appear or behave differently is perpetuated rather than interrogated as the discriminatory stereotypes that they are (see Yong 2007: chs. 3–4).

The emergence of the civil rights movement in America in the 1960s was soon followed by disability rights advocacy. People with disabilities have begun to speak out, thereby challenging traditional depictions of them merely as passive objects of pity or charity. Part of the result is the emergence of disability approaches to the Bible that have pointed out how much the received theological tradition has drawn scriptural conclusions thought to be "normal," but which have had inadvertent and detrimental consequences impacting people with disabilities, because they reflect perspectives uninformed by such life experiences (e.g., Avalos, Melcher, and Schipper 2007; Schipper and Moss 2011). Thus, for instance, a reading of the Bible from a blind person's perspective illuminates some of the stereotypes sighted people have about darkness (Hull 2001); other readings from the perspective of deaf culture indicate how the Bible can be redemptive for deaf people just as they are (e.g., Hitching 2003; Lewis 2007; W. Morris 2008); and an alternative approach from the perspective of those with intellectual disabilities challenges us to see how God's wisdom and glory can be revealed even through what the world considers foolishness (e.g., T. Reynolds 2008; Reinders 2008; Reimer 2009). While contemporary understandings of disability now more widely available should not be imposed anachronistically on the Bible, yet when read from the perspective of people with disabilities, Christians can come to better appreciate how God's grace is manifest in presumed weakness. This not only challenges the independence promulgated by modern individualism but also enables the church to be a healing, welcoming, and belonging community, one that includes those who live with their impairments (Block 2002; Carter 2007; Webb-Mitchell 2010).

Renewalists, among other Christians, may need to reconsider why there are not as many people with disabilities in their churches. This absence may be because they have, however unintentionally, propagated rather than questioned traditional views that are oppressive of people with disabilities. Yet the first "Christian" theologian—a fervent Jew, no less—was one who himself may well have been impaired (see Monteith 2010; Yong 2011b: ch. 4). Perhaps it was through living with his "thorn in the flesh" (2 Cor 12:7-10) that Paul was able to envision a theology of divine power manifest in weakness. This first charismatic theologian (or theologian of the *charismata*, as we saw in section 2.1) urged not only that the one body of Christ and fellowship of the Spirit had many members (1 Cor 12:12) but also that "the members of the body that seem to be weaker are indispensable, and those members of the body that we think less honourable we clothe with greater honour, and our less respectable members are treated with greater respect; whereas our more respectable members do not need this. But God has so arranged the body, giving the greater honour to the inferior member" (1 Cor 12:22-24). This invites the people of God to develop ministries *with* people with disabilities rather than only *to* or *for* them. If that happens, the church becomes a liberating community precisely by overcoming the traditional barriers that have divided the unimpaired "us" from the impaired "them." Is this message synthesizable with and conducive for renewing a Christian theology of healing?

8.3 Wholeness and Salvation in Mark

To begin to answer the questions emerging from the previous section, we turn here to the gospel of Mark. As in other chapters in this volume, we focus in this third section on one biblical text or book in order to see whether a deeper reading of it might be informative for the dogmatic locus at hand. Our wager is that this second and shortest gospel—traditionally ascribed to St. Mark, of whom we know little—will be insightful for a contemporary theology of healing. Read comparatively alongside other parallel synoptic passages, the Markan witness can help us take into account at least some of the heretofore raised issues.

If the theological character of the Fourth Gospel (section 6.3) is more overt and has long been recognized, that of the Synoptic Gospels, including Mark, is also increasingly acknowledged (e.g., Telford 1999). Yet by and large, the miracle accounts in the gospel are reliable, even if not always defensible according to contemporary criteria of historicity (Twelftree 1999). Broadly speaking, there are associated with the life and ministry of Jesus approximately three categories of miracles, some overlapping. We have already seen the exorcism of the Gerasene demoniac, one of a number in the gospel (e.g., the man with an unclean spirit in Mark 1:21-28; the daughter of the Syrophoenician woman in 7:24-30; and the epileptic boy in 9:14-32), that might be understood as healings involving spiritual deliverance. There are, further, what appear to be physical cures accomplished by Jesus (Peter's mother-in-law in 1:29-34; a leper in 1:40-45; a paralytic in 2:1-12; a man with a withered hand in 3:1-5; a woman with an issue of blood and the daughter of Jairus in 5:21-43; the deaf-mute in 7:31-37; and two different blind men in 8:22-26 and 10:46-52). Finally, there are what are best termed miracles of nature, such as Jesus' stilling a storm (4:35-41), walking on water (6:45-52), and feeding multitudes of people with minimal food sources (6:30-44, 8:1-9). The sweeping summary statement that wherever Jesus went, "into villages or cities or farms, they laid the sick in the market-places, and begged him that they might touch even the fringe of his cloak; and all who touched it were healed" (6:56), suggests divine healing dispensed through ordinary material.

A number of observations are noteworthy in and through these accounts. First, in one instance at Capernaum, it is said: "they brought to him *all* who were sick or possessed with demons. And the whole city was gathered around the door. And he cured *many* who were sick with various diseases, and cast out *many* demons" (1:32-34 [emphasis added]). It appears here that not *all* who were sick or possessed by demons were cured or delivered (cf. the case of Trophimus in 2 Tim 4:20). Later, in his hometown of Nazareth, "he could do no deed of power there, except that he laid his hands on a few sick people and cured them. And he was amazed at their unbelief" (Mark 6:5-6). Miraculous cures, here, are correlated with faith and belief, and their absence with the lack of faith and belief.

Second, in his narration concerning the commissioning of the Twelve, Mark says only that Jesus "began to send them out two by two, and gave them authority over the unclean spirits" (6:7), whereas Matthew adds: "gave them authority over unclean spirits, to cast them out, and to cure every disease and every sickness (Matt 10:1). Luke (9:1) parallels Matthew in his account of Jesus' sending out the Twelve but does not mention the authority to expel unclean spirits in the commissioning of the Seventy (Matt 10:1-12). Still, the Markan pericope concludes: "So they went out and proclaimed that *all* should repent. They cast out *many* demons, and anointed with oil *many* who were sick and cured them" (6:12-13 [emphasis added]). While not wishing to minimize that many were indeed delivered and cured, and while also not insisting that there is a direct equivalence between Jesus' healing ministry and that manifest in later and even contemporary times (Warrington 2000), the more important point is that all were invited to repentance. The links between healing and repentance, later connected, are more important than usually noted.

Third, at one point, Mark records the Pharisees looking for a sign from Jesus, "to test him"; "he sighed deeply in his spirit and said, 'Why does this generation ask for a sign? Truly I tell you, no sign will be given to this generation'" (8:11-12). Thus it appears that miraculous wonders are given as signs only to those whose hearts are already opened to the coming reign of God (Hurtado 1995: 124–25).

Fourth, on one other occasion, when instructing the disciples about the power of faith, Jesus says, "Whatever you ask for in prayer, believe that you have received it, and it will be yours"; immediately, however, he adds, "Whenever you stand praying, forgive, if you have anything against anyone; so that your Father in heaven may also forgive you your trespasses" (11:24-25). The links here are unmistakable. Faith may produce miracles, but these should not be divorced from the healing and saving power of forgiveness, both as received from God and as given to others.

Fifth, there are also some interesting connections, found only in the Synoptic Gospels, between some forms of impairment—in particular deafness, muteness, blindness, and epilepsy—and evil spirits. On these occasions, alleviation of the symptoms is achieved through exorcisms. We note though that the gospel accounts thereby do not assume that all such conditions are related to demonic oppression—Matthew explicitly distinguishes, for instance, "various diseases and pains, demoniacs, epileptics, and paralytics" (4:24). Further, it is interesting that two of the three exorcisms in Mark's gospel occur in Gentile territory (that of the Gerasenes and of Tyre; 7:24), with one of them on behalf of a pagan Gentile family (the Syrophoenician and her daughter). Matthew and Luke both note that Jesus' exorcisms are signs of the coming reign of God (Matt 12:28; Luke 11:20), which in these cases announce God's visitation dawning upon the Gentiles.

Sixth, social scientific perspectives from the field of medical anthropology can also illuminate the healing message of the gospel accounts (see Pilch 2000). Within the Mediterranean context, it is helpful to distinguish between *illnesses*, which refer to the underlying reality; *diseases*, which identify the perspective—not being at ease—of the afflicted persons; *sicknesses*, being the prognosis of others; *cures*, which have to do with removal of the symptoms of the illnesses; and *healings*, which in the New Testament relate to the salvation of God eschatologically inaugurated in the person and work of Christ. While English translations of these notions do not always capture the nuances involved, these insights clarify some important matters. Note for instance that Luke identifies Peter's mother-in-law's *illness* as a tormenting "great fever" (4:38), indicative of an oppressive force impinging from without (a *sickness* with spiritual connotations), to which Jesus responds with an exorcistic rebuke (4:39). That her symptoms are *cured* means that she is able to rise up from her *dis-eased* (dis-empowered) state. More important is that she is *healed* and thus restored to her social status of serving guests in her home. Mark sees only a sickness, but also notes both the cure and the restorative healing (1:31).

In other words, we ought to be careful about equating *curing* and *healing* as if they are completely synonymous. Illnesses are specific sociocultural states of value or disvalue, the healing of which may include the alleviation of felt *dis-ease* on the part of subjects (curing) but always involves the restoration of subjects as valued members of their communities. We therefore ought not to impose on the gospel narratives modern biomedical notions of curing related to viruses, germs, and psychosomatic and neurochemical disorders, none of which were known by the ancients. Healing can be accomplished even when physical cures (defined in contemporary terms) are not experienced (Patte 2004: 379–84). This is not to say that we need to dismiss all cures noted in Jesus' ministry. It is to say we ought to view healings in the New Testament more as accounts of God's saving work in the lives of people in their communities—this itself being more conducive to modern holistic notions of health—than as merely biomedical cures of individual bodies.

Within the wider scope of the gospel message, the question of miraculous healing ought also to be subordinated to that of the healer, "Jesus Christ, the Son of God" (Mark 1:1). The nature of Jesus' healings is less the issue than that it is he who has the power and authority over illnesses within the health-care systems of first-century Palestinian Judaism (see Wainwright 2010: 169–70). This is the one who will baptize with the Holy Spirit (1:8), and who comes "proclaiming the good news of God, and saying, 'The time is fulfilled, and the kingdom of God has come near; repent, and believe in the good news'" (1:14-15). Hence the works of Christ are signs announcing the arrival of the reign of God, and the gospel ought thus to be read within this eschatological horizon, as a tract written in apocalyptic times for what has been historically thought to be a perse-cuted and suffering people. Jesus thus emerges as one "whose apocalyp-tic revelation of God's kingdom shatters the institutions, laws, and codes that structure religious and political society in first-century Palestine" (Blount 1998: xi). His works both circumvent the health-care institutions and conventions of first-century Judaism and provide a glimpse of God's redemptive, restorative, and salvific work.

FIGURE 8.3

Throughout Scripture, blindness (and the loss of human senses in general) is symbolically connected with idolatry. It's not that blind people are considered idolaters but rather that blindness is metaphorically employed to articulate the deadening effects that idolatrous trust has on the human heart: "The idols of the nations . . . have mouths, but they do not speak; they have eyes, but they do not see; they have ears, but they do not hear, and there is no breath in their mouths. Those who make them and all who trust them shall become like them" (Ps 135:15-18; cf. Ps 115:3-8; Isa 42:17-20). The flip side of this metaphor is that imagery of eschatological redemption often specifically includes the healing of eyes and reenlivening of bodies: "Then the eyes of the blind shall be opened, and the ears of the deaf unstopped; then the lame shall leap like a deer, and the tongue of

*the speechless sing for joy" (Isa 35:3-10; cf. 29:18). It is therefore highly signifi-
cant that the Gospels give much attention to Jesus healing people in precisely the
terms anticipated by the prophets—in fact Jesus himself summarizes his ministry
as featuring exactly such healing (Luke 4:18; 7:21-22; Matt 11:2-5).*

*The fresco shown here offers a visual interpretation of John 9, in which Jesus
heals a man blind from birth: he makes mud with his saliva, spreads it on the
man's eyes, and tells him to wash in the pool of Siloam (9:7). The man sees
for the first time in his life, which initiates an extended controversy (9:8–10:21)
between Jesus, the Pharisees, and the community concerning the nature of true
sight and blindness. This fresco depicts Jesus in the manner of Pantokrator imagery, holding a scroll in his left hand—"all authority in heaven and on earth"
(Matt 28:18)—and blessing (healing) with his right hand. And as the man
turns to wash in the pool (suggestive of a baptismal font), Peter turns to address
us directly. He gestures to Jesus, urging those who see the image to also come, to
wash in the baptismal waters, and to have our eyes (and our idolatrous hearts)
opened that we might also truly see the one who is speaking to us (John 9:37).
In this sense, the artwork outstrips itself: this image of Peter points to an image of
Jesus that is provisional and makeshift, a dim pointing toward an eschatological
day in which we truly "will see his face" (Rev 22:4; 1 Cor 13:12). ✦*

More importantly, the glorious signs and wonders of Mark ought also
to be subordinated to the more encompassing theme of Jesus' suffering and
death. Whatever cures are accomplished are subservient to the narrative
of Christ as the suffering servant (Mackrell 1987; Farley 2004). Practically
the bulk of the gospel account is taken up with announcing the passion of
Christ and detailing his giving "his life a ransom for many" (Mark 10:45).
Arguably, Mark has more of a theology of the cross than a theology of
miracles, and this is to be expected, because his gospel has long been associated with the Apostle Paul, who lived with his own persisting "thorn in
the flesh" (Dawson 2008; also section 3.3). This indicates not only that
"the Kingdom will come in power in himself in his upcoming death"
(Maloney 2004: 105), but also that the passion and suffering of Christ is
the pattern of discipleship for his followers (Hurtado 1995: 10–11). Hence
the reign of God is already present in Christ, in his ministry, death, and
resurrection, but also, mysteriously, in and through his suffering! This call
toward sacrificial and suffering obedience will surely resonate with many
Christians of the global south, struggling as many are with nonaffluence
and its attending challenges. Yet Jesus' Spirit-empowered way of the cross

also challenges those who, like the Corinthian congregation, proclaim only a theology of glory marked by charismatic signs and wonders (Mansfield 1987).

We are not minimizing the curative power of God manifest in the gospel accounts. Yet similar to how postcolonial readings of the gospel have argued that we must get beyond either a pro- or anticolonial conclusion (which itself reads contemporary perspectives back too simplistically into the New Testament; see Samuel 2007), so also must we get beyond either curing or not (which itself reads contemporary medical notions back too naïvely into the Bible). A broader horizon is needed against which to understand the gospel message and to develop a theology of healing. This inevitably invites us to at least bracket our assumptions for a moment in order that other perspectives can emerge. These latter might be considered as contrary to, and hence threatening of, our cherished conventions; in the long run, however, they might enrich our theological views and empower our missional praxis.

It is with this in mind that we conclude this portion of our discussion with a brief reflection on what is now known as the "longer ending of Mark" (16:9-20). This passage is important, because its references to signs of especially exorcism, tongues-speech, and healing as following those who believe (16:17-18) have functioned canonically and authoritatively for renewalists (J. C. Thomas 2005: ch. 6). Yet most scholars believe that the existing manuscript evidence concludes with verse 8: "So they went out and fled from the tomb, for terror and amazement had seized them; and they said nothing to anyone, for they were afraid." There have been many efforts to explain this—that Mark was comfortable ending his story abruptly in order to invite his readers to live out the open-endedness of the Jesus story; that the original longer ending was lost; that Mark himself initially ended the narrative with verse 8 but then later changed his mind to include the longer version; or that the longer ending is the work of a later redactor—albeit there is no consensus (Black 2008). Two points are important. First, we as human beings are understandably desirous of a different conclusion. However, if in fact verse 8 originally concluded the gospel, one message might be that terror, amazement, and fear summarize widely divergent yet also appropriate responses to the good news that involves rather than dismisses suffering. But second, even if life might be characterized by suffering, such can be redemptive rather than debilitating. Whatever the provenance of the longer ending, there are good reasons for seeing it as not only legitimizing but also empowering the missionary advance of Christian faith (Kelhoffer 2000). Hence there is a missional dimension to the message of the longer ending, and this concerns more the heralding of the coming reign of God than the availability of biomedical cures. So following in the footsteps of the suffering servant surely undermines triumphalism even as it also inculcates the humility, trust, and dependence of God that Jesus himself prayed for in the garden of Gethsemane: "Father, for you all things are possible; remove this cup from me; yet, not what I want, but what you want" (Mark 14:36).

8.4 Be Healed! Saving the Church, Redeeming the World

Healing is an existentially palpable and extremely personal matter, especially for those who have experienced miraculous cures and for the afflicted who long for a divine touch in circumstances that seem hopeless. Yet what follows develops three aspects of a Christian theology of healing—the personal, the ecclesial, and the eschatological—in light of the preceding reflections. My major thesis is that authentic healing that includes but ought not be reduced to cures is always part of the salvific work of the Spirit of God in Christ, and as a "sign of the kingdom" (Ervin 2002), invites our inhabitation of the coming reign of God. We conclude by considering how such a theology of healing is nevertheless commensurate with what might be paradoxically called a renewal theology of disability.

We begin with the personal experience of divine healing manifest in miraculous cures to which many have testified. There is no question that God meets human beings in remarkable and inexplicable ways by touching and curing infirm bodies. Pastoral, evangelistic, and missionary agents also have been and will continue to be ministers of healing through which God provides medically unexplainable cures that bring about a saving knowledge of Christ (McGee 2010). An important caveat, however, bridges this personal element and the wider ecclesial and eschatological dimensions of healing. To insist that God's healing involves curing does not mean that modern medicine can be dispensed with or that we can ignore other domains of knowledge that affect human health and wholeness. Human beings are complex creatures constituted by spiritual, material, psychical, social, political, economic, and environmental aspects. Science, medicine, and the humanities provide windows into various aspects of the human condition, and we would be irresponsible to ignore these insights. As God enables the human advance of knowledge in these areas, we may be able to explain more and more of how the Spirit can inspire and bring about an even wider range of remedies for human ills. This should not undermine faith in a healing God. Medical doctors can be agents of divine healing just as well as healing evangelists. Yet because medical diagnoses and prescriptions always address local symptoms, holistic health and (for our purposes) final healing lie beyond even the most exhaustively delineated scientific accounts.

This leads us to the ecclesial aspect of healing. Any testimony to or affirmation of divine curing involves an explicitly theological layer of explanation above either incredulity ("I don't know how this happened!") or other lower-level assessments ("The expert surgeon and his team were successful in removing the cancer"). Yet the effectiveness of such theological accounts is ecclesiological and christological simultaneously: they derive from an overarching faith community that believes in Jesus as savior and healer. Without this broader theological framework, there will be either no need or desire to testify to divine healing ("Oh, it was just a coincidence"). Yet within a Christian interpretive framework, the God who sent Jesus Christ to declare good news to sick and oppressed sinners invites their reconciliation with God, which includes reconciliation with others. In other words, there is no such thing as a merely individualistic perspective on the healing that God accomplishes. Healing occurs only in relationship to the believing community and its exaltation of the living Christ.

More concretely, this ecclesial dimension of healing indicates that any physical cures are part of the larger redemptive work of the Spirit of Christ. Thus the WAGF SF affirms that "deliverance from sickness is provided in the atonement," but the atonement involves saving individuals in the community of the faithful, the church. So also, a text that suggests a link between the atonement and healing points to the relational character of health: "He himself bore our sins in his body on the cross, so that, free from sins, we might live for righteousness; by his wounds you have been healed" (1 Pet 2:24). Physical health and wholeness thus are supported and completed by, if not also requiring the repair of, interpersonal and social relations. The removal of sins in the cross of Christ allows human beings to forgive one another and to accept one another as forgiven in Christ. Cures, even miraculous ones, may not persist without such forgiveness and relational reconciliation. Interpersonal and social alienation will undermine the long-term efficacy of any physical cure. The witness to Christ thus nurtures new relationships within the body of Christ and the fellowship of the Spirit, and these enable the flourishing of bodily cures into the full salvation that individuals experience only with others.

FIGURE 8.4   FIGURE 8.4 (DETAIL)

Grünewald's Crucifixion *is the central exterior image of a huge polyptych altarpiece painted for the Monastery of St. Anthony in Isenheim, where for centuries monks devoted themselves to caring for those suffering from the plague and various skin diseases, particularly Saint Anthony's Fire (understood today as ergotism, erysipelas, or herpes zoster).*

In the center of this altarpiece the severely abused body of Christ is crucified with contorted arms and hands opening upward into a black sky. His massive scale in relation to the other figures signals that this is a theological meditation on what the crucifixion means, not just what it looked like: this is where all curses, sickness, dysfunction, deadness, and God-forsakenness were absorbed into a single body. And here, in the context of a hospital devoted to treating painful disease, those who looked upon this image (during the Eucharist) saw a fellow sufferer—the fellow sufferer. The skin of this emaciated Christ is pierced with thorns and covered with boils, taking up into himself all the suffering of humankind (both inside and outside the hospital) and thus evoking identification with the Isaianic Servant: "Surely he has borne our infirmities and carried our diseases" (Isa 53:3-5; cf. Matt 8:17).

On the left side of the image are those usually included in crucifixion imagery: the penitent Magdalene, the sorrowful Mary, the compassionate St. John. To the right, however, the scene is more unusual: John the Baptist anachronistically appears with one hand holding open the prophesies and with the other extending a long index finger toward the tortured body of Christ. Karl Barth (who had a reproduction of this image over his desk for his entire writing career) refers to this painting at several points in his writing; he was particularly impacted by

John's "prodigious index finger. Could anyone point away from himself more impressively and completely?" (Barth 2010a: I/1: 112). Between John's mouth and this pointing hand an inscription in red lettering declares, Illum oportet crescere, me autem minui *("He must increase, but I must decrease"—John 3:30), while at his feet a lamb stands over a communion chalice as a clear echo of John's pointing: "Behold, the Lamb of God who takes away the sin of the world!" (1:29). But Barth cautions: "Shall we dare turn our eyes in the direction of the pointing hand of Grünewald's John? We know whither it points. It points to Christ. But to Christ the crucified, we must immediately add. That is your direction, says the hand" (Barth 1928: 76).* ✦

Beyond the confines of local congregations, however, the ecclesial aspect of healing points also to the social dimension of health and wholeness. The church's message of healing interfaces with the role of the larger society in at least three ways. First, the church can and ought to come alongside other social, economic, and developmental initiatives focused on health and health care. Christian organizations like World Vision, among many others, have led the way in this regard. Second, this ministerial approach may also need to be accompanied by a more prophetic posture. There are often structural impediments that keep communities impoverished and perpetuate ill health, and the church ought to be at the forefront of calling attention to and engaging these matters, so structural changes can be effected for the common good (Freeman 2012). Last but not least, physical infirmities in many cases are variously symptomatic of and correlative with underlying moral, psychical, and most importantly, spiritual ailments. The last lies within the prerogative of the church and requires the full panoply of spiritual weapons from prayer and fasting to exorcism. Yet full healing will require that the social dimensions of ill health also be addressed.

This leads to healing's eschatological aspect, which, as has been consistently argued in this volume, is both already and not yet. Miraculous cures are present signs of the full reign of God, which is yet to be unveiled. The "natural laws" that operate within the divine rule that is coming now appear extraordinary according to our present understandings and expectations (cf. Bulgakov 2011: 51–53). Thus, those with gifts of healing—whether healing evangelists or medical doctors, just to name two types—are made participants through the Spirit of Christ in the eschatological work of heralding the coming domain of God. In the new heavens and new earth, we are told that the "leaves of the tree are for the healing of the nations" (Rev 22:2b). Herein is indication that the healing power of God in some sense resides within the divinely ordered creation. On the one hand, sin has both wracked God's creatures with brokenness and illness even as it has also retarded the curative and healing capacities of the created order (see ch. 10, this volume). Yet on the other hand, this also explains the discovery of the medicinal powers of the earth, of medical advances, and of healing traditions not specifically informed by the Christian theological vision. But with Christian healing, the works of the Spirit-anointed Christ as of those also now empowered with the Spirit accomplish bodily cures and nurture holistic health in the present life as signs of the full redemption to come.

Miraculous curing mediated through prayer, discernment, confession of sins, intercession, exorcism, and medicinal or other applications (Thomas 1998; Kydd 1998) provide humanity with a glimpse of the impending full salvation offered by God (Rom 13:11). On the one hand, then, we ought not to minimize the power of these curative signs for transforming lives and communities. On the other hand, we may also be seduced into seeking after miraculous signs and miss out on the fact that they are merely icons or windows into the eschatologically redemptive work of God that involves others, the world, even the whole creation. Bodily cures, from those affected more miraculously to those less extravagantly manifest, remain potent marks of the in-breaking of the reign of God.

How then does the preceding renewal theology of healing inform a theology of disability? There are many types of disabilities, for instance those derived from war, which we ought to avoid, as well as those resulting from contingent or accidental events. We now also know more about how chromosomal mutations occur that result in congenitally impairing conditions. Regardless of their source, disabilities need not be blamed on God. However, Christian faith can be hopeful that nothing lies beyond the pale of God's eschatologically redeeming work (cf. Gen). Jesus' response to the question about why the man was born blind does not answer the question, but it does point to how God can bring good out of any situation: "Neither this man nor his parents sinned; he was born blind so that God's works might be revealed in him" (John 9:3). An eschatologically oriented renewal theology of disability focuses less on trying to understand why there are disabling conditions than on how we might be open to experiencing God's saving work even in and through such impairing situations (Yong 2007: chs. 6 and 9).

Hence a renewal theology of disability will understand the temporal and even limited experience of physical cures in the present life within the larger perspective of salvific healing in the coming reign of God. Some renewalists who might emphasize the present "finished work" of Christ may be less comfortable with such an eschatological framework than others (Alexander 2006). Yet reception of divine favor in the form of physical cures now is no guarantee that full salvation follows, even as the latter—wholeness, health, and shalom—can indeed be experienced in the present life despite the absence of the former (Dawn 2008). Rather, the real miracle of healing is the receipt of the gift of the triune deity, incarnationally given in the Son and pentecostally poured out in the Spirit, for life abundant realized in the reconciliation of all creatures with God and each other. The following therefore need to be kept in mind.

First, faith-filled prayers for physical cures are never out of order in light of Jesus' eschatological works; however, such prayers also ought to invoke God's full salvific work (rather than merely focusing on the physical maladies) on behalf of others. Second, however, even when cures are delayed, those with disabilities or impairments ought not be presumed to be lacking faith, persisting in sin, or oppressed by the devil; people ought not to internalize a "second-class Christian citizenship" just because they have not experienced physical cures. Third, people with disabilities are, like Zacchaeus (see section 9.1) and the Ethiopian eunuch, among others, full members of the body of Christ *in* and *with* their impairments; ecclesial membership is a spiritual and sacramental condition (see chs. 6 and 7) distinct from our physical, sensory, or intellectual abilities or lack thereof. Fourth, full salvation will eventually involve physical cures (this is the point of the resurrection body), but such bodies will retain the marks of their impairments (as did Jesus' resurrected body). The retention of such marks, however, excludes the pain—both physical and social—accompanying disability in the present life, while potently testifying to the full salvation of individual lives in all their particularity and in relationship to others and the triune God.

Last but not least, the church continues its present ministry, in this time anticipating the Parousia, of ministry *to* people with disabilities and their families but also *with* those who are variously impaired. People with disabilities are not merely passive objects of pity needing the care of able-bodied people. Rather, all people, including those who are temporarily able-bodied ("normal" people come into the world dependent and if they are blessed to live long enough, they will exit the world in a similarly dependent state), are indispensable members of the body of Christ through whom the gifts of the Spirit can be manifest for the common good (1 Cor 12; Yong 2011b: ch. 4). Perhaps more importantly, believers in the Messiah from Galilee should not underestimate the degree to which Christ remains in solidarity with the weak, the sick, and even people with disabilities, so their reception of the ministries of compassion redounds to the salvation of those to serve in Jesus' name (Matt 25:31-46; cf. Yong 2011b: ch. 5; section 11.3).

Any theology of healing and of disability ought to inspire faith and hope in a curing but more importantly a healing and saving God, be linked to the forging of new personal identities in the body of Christ and the fellowship of the Spirit, and emphasize pastoral sensitivity and care, so people can be empowered to deal with and overcome the afflictions derived from various spiritual, physical, psychical, emotional, interpersonal, and environmental maladies. We have seen that these practical guidelines only make sense within a robust ecclesiology, a trinitarian Christology, and an overarching theology of creation and fall. The ecclesiological issues have already been discussed. The next two chapters further elaborate on the christological and creational aspects of a renewed Christian theology.

Discussion Questions

1. Have you had a personal experience of healing or do you know of someone who has? Compare these experiences with those of others. Is there room in the preceding construct for these various accounts?

2. What are some aspects of your church's teachings about miracles that are consistent with the preceding discussion? Are these differences complementary or contradictory to the idea presented that miracles can be understood as signs of the coming reign of God? What are the implications of either response for Christian ministry in the twenty-first century?

3. What are some aspects of your church's teachings about disability that are different from the preceding discussion? Are these differences complementary or contradictory, and if the latter, what are possible responses to these divergent views?

Further Reading

Brock, Brian, and John Swinton, eds. 2012. *Disability in the Christian Tradition: A Reader.* Grand Rapids: Eerdmans.

Ellens, J. Harold, ed. 2008. *Miracles: God, Science, and Psychology in the Paranormal.* 3 vols. Westport, Conn.: Praeger.

Grudem, Wayne, ed. 1996. *Are Miraculous Gifts for Today? Four Views.* Grand Rapids: Zondervan.

Keener, Craig S. 2011. *Miracles: The Credibility of the New Testament Accounts.* 2 vols. Grand Rapids: Baker Academic.

Sheils, W. J., ed. 1982. *The Church and Healing.* Oxford: Basil Blackwell.

Warrington, Keith. 2005. *Healing and Suffering: Biblical and Pastoral Reflections.* Milton Keynes, U.K.: Paternoster.

9

Salvation in Christ through the Spirit

An Eschatological Soteriology

World Assemblies of God Fellowship Statement of Faith
—Article 4: The Salvation of Man

We believe in salvation through faith in Christ, who died for our sins, was buried, and was raised from the dead on the third day. By His atoning blood, salvation has been provided for all humanity through the sacrifice of Christ upon the cross. This experience is also known as the new birth, and is an instantaneous and complete operation of the Holy Spirit whereupon the believing sinner is regenerated, justified, and adopted into the family of God, becomes a new creation in Christ Jesus, and heir of eternal life (John 3:5-6; Romans 10:8-15; Titus 2:11; 3:4-7; 1 John 5:1).

9.1 Zacchaeus and the Salvation of the Children of Abraham

We begin this chapter with a look at the character of Zacchaeus, mentioned (with no other synoptic parallels) at the beginning of Luke 19. That Zacchaeus is described as being "short in stature" (Luke 19:3) is especially relevant as a follow-up on the preceding discussion on healing and disability. More precisely, Jesus' pronouncement of salvation upon him and his house (19:9) allows exploration of the multidimensionality of salvation broached throughout this volume, but which emerged in a pressing manner in the previous chapter.

Canonically considered, Zacchaeus' short-staturedness provokes recollection of the dwarfism that is included among a list of impairments that disqualified priests in ancient Israel from offering the sacrificial food or approaching the altar in the holy of holies (Lev 21:16-24). More damagingly, first-century Hellenistic beliefs about the "science" of physiognomy—which understood outward bodily traits to be related to or manifestations of inward moral or spiritual characteristics—would have viewed his smallness not only as representative of lowly self-esteem, but also in a derogatory sense as indicative of small-mindedness and greediness (Parsons 2006: ch. 5). In fact, that Zacchaeus is later designated a sinner (Luke 19:7) would have provided further confirmation for his physical condition, because such congenital physical diminutiveness would also have been assumed to be the result of sin (see John 5:14; 9:1-2).

From a renewal perspective, however, Zacchaeus' physical stature deserves more extended comment. Although it would be anachronistic to think about Zacchaeus as fitting what in today's medical terminology is called pathological dwarfism, this assumption finds support in how Luke's description conjures up images of the crowd watching, in fascination or derision as the case may have been, Zacchaeus' less symmetrically proportioned body run or move awkwardly ahead of the crowd and climb a sycamore tree (Luke 19:4). And while Zacchaeus appears to be relatively healthy, shortness of stature across the centuries has brought with it a wide range of physical disabilities, mobility challenges, and intellectual deficiencies. The text is silent about the degree to which he may have been physically challenged above and beyond having to get around in a "tall" world. Yet socially there is no doubt his very visible condition elicited unfair caricatures and discriminatory attitudes wherever he went. One wonders if he became a tax collector, a despised position for a Jew because it required collusion with the hated Roman government, in desperation after failing to find employment because of his shortness. He may have been like many little people who despair about their plight. Regardless of how physically capable he might have been, he experienced firsthand what it meant to be a social outcast.

Yet although people with impairments, including short-statured people, are often thought of as "charity cases" in need of help from able-bodied people, Zacchaeus exercises personal initiative. He risks mockery because he wants to see Jesus. Perhaps he had heard of Jesus' miraculous healing abilities and of his compassion for the oppressed and afflicted. He welcomes Jesus into his home (19:6) and also repents of any sins he may have committed: "Look, half of my possessions, Lord, I will give to the poor; and if I have defrauded anyone of anything, I will pay back four times as much" (19:8). We know he was rich, no doubt the result of his tax collecting, although we do not know if his wealth was accumulated through exploitation of others through his official position. In any case, without incriminating himself, Zacchaeus recognized that acceptance by Jesus involved also getting right with those around him. He was thus prepared to bridge at least the economic gap that had opened up between him and his compatriots, and this would be costly indeed. Yet he does all of this before there is any indication of what, if anything, he expects to receive from Jesus. Perhaps it was too much to think that Jesus might cure him of his shortness; or was it?

FIGURE 9.1

Everyone in this image is in motion, except Jesus. The crowd has been moving through the trees, listening for whatever the provocative teacher might say next; and though the crowd continues to move, Jesus has stopped. His feet are planted against the centerline of the composition, and the crowd divides around him: those on the left stride onward, confused as to why he would stop here, and those on the right shift around the scandalizing exchange beginning to unfold.

Zacchaeus is making a fool of himself—a wealthy little man perched in a tree—while Jesus is making a fool of himself, stopping to greet this foul person who is believed to have extorted his countrymen in collusion with the occupying Roman Empire. And Jesus' folly compounds as he openly announces that he will excuse himself from this crowd of devotees in order to share a meal with this man in the very house financed by his faithless occupation. Indeed, "All who saw it began to grumble and said, 'He has gone to be the guest of one who is a sinner'" (Luke 19:7).

In his depiction of the scene Stevns seems to want us to empathize less with Jesus (the center of the offensive action) or Zacchaeus (who is quite peripheral) than with the crowd, particularly the foreground figure who turns toward us looking over his shoulder. Who is he? One of Jesus' dearest disciples (perhaps Peter) or a teacher of the law? Why does he turn away? Is this an embarrassed glance to see who has noticed his rabbi debasing himself like this? Is it defensive—perhaps this is the man who will later attack a servant of the high priest when he feels Jesus under threat (Luke 22:50)? Or is he disgusted, looking around to ensure that temple authorities are seeing this scandal? However we regard this figure, he provides a location for us to interrogate ourselves: In what ways does Jesus violate our own senses of propriety, godliness, and social inclusion/exclusion? How can we accept that almost immediately beforehand Jesus sent a righteous ruler away in sadness, charging him to give away everything (18:18-30), and yet he embraces this tax collector without any similar charge (19:1-10)? (On that question see 18:10-14.) When do we also find ourselves scandalized by Jesus' embrace of others? How might we too turn toward the man in the tree, joining Jesus as he ignores both fine clothes and short stature and looks Zacchaeus directly in the face? ✦

To what degree was Luke intentional about subverting the physiognomic assumptions of his day? With Jesus' pronunciation, "Today salvation [σωτηρία/*soteria*] has come to this house, because he too is a son of Abraham" (Luke 19:9), the (Levitical) prohibition against Zacchaeus and those like him from full participation in the liturgical cult of ancient Israel was thereby lifted (cf. Isa 56:3-5). Perhaps Zacchaeus and those around him were expecting to see a miraculous cure. Yet in an ironic and counterintuitive sense, what they saw instead was the saving good news of the gospel, not only for Zacchaeus but also for themselves. For those who believed Zacchaeus to be too much of a sinner, too short, or too impure for whatever reason to be included in the covenant community of Israel, Jesus declares otherwise. The prejudices of the people are thereby exposed, and to the degree that they believed in and accepted his proclamation, they also would have embraced Zacchaeus and thereby experienced their own salvation from conventional stereotypes and discriminatory behaviors.

There is one more point, however, to make of Zacchaeus' testimony. Jesus' acceptance of Zacchaeus just as he is undermined the expectations of normal people—those of his day and in ours—that those who are (abnormally) impaired and disabled will need to be "fixed" or cured in order to participate fully in the renewal and restoration of Israel. After all, Jesus' healing all of the sick who were brought to him (Luke 6:19; Acts 10:38) would have encouraged such beliefs. Yet Zacchaeus becomes a disciple of the Messiah without having to go through the process of literally being stretched from his diminutive condition. Certainly little people today need not undergo the various surgical procedures touted to increase the length of their limbs or their overall height just to fit in with the aesthetic sensibilities of taller people. So how might this also not apply to others with impairing physical and even intellectual conditions?

Most importantly for the immediate purposes of this chapter, salvation for Zacchaeus involved a sustained encounter with Jesus, in his home, over a meal. This brought with it a change of heart with concrete behavioral results. Zacchaeus' repentance was not merely ideal but real. His reconciliation to the God of Jesus included reconciliation with others, including his enemies (assuming he had them), and not merely interpersonally but also socially, politically, and economically, indicating these are not extraneous to the gospel. More precisely, he who was lost, perhaps listless and without a community (not even a community of faith), was now found, reinserted into the community of Abraham. In fact, he and members of his household, themselves also communally and socially ostracized because of his reputation, were now reconciled to the tradition from which they had been estranged. Jesus, as the Son of Man, through an incisive speech-act, had brought about a new set of salvific circumstances for an entire family and community in response to the hospitality and repentance of this household head. All of this was a part of the renewal and restoration of Israel (Acts 1:6). Might Zacchaeus' story, in particular his encounter with Jesus, inspire our thinking about Christian salvation today?

9.2 Salvation Histories and Christian Traditions

Article 4 of the SF focuses primarily on the *what* of Christian salvation, and less on the *how* or the *who* that brings about that saving reality. This is, at least in part, in keeping with renewal sensibilities, especially the role played by testimonies in renewal spirituality. The testimony accentuates the experience of Christ's intervention by the Spirit—as we have seen in the Zacchean story—presuming thus their divine identity and salvific potency. Our contextual elaboration in this chapter therefore will strictly follow this renewalist logic and sensibility. We will begin with the doctrine of salvation (the *what* of saving experience) and shift from there to the doctrines of atonement (the *how*) and Christology (the *who*).

Along the way in this tripartite section of the chapter, we will draw from the christological affirmations in article 2b of the WAGF SF that focus on the person and work of Christ. The rationale for explicitly including this material here instead of waiting until chapter 11 is both methodological and theological. The former includes constraints related to the extended length and multiple parts that constitute article 2. If we were to wait until then to address all of the topics referenced therein, chapter 11 would either be ridiculously simplistic (to remain within a comparably manageable length) or it would have to be two or three times the size of others in this volume (to do justice to the discussion). Neither of these are optimal options. More importantly, however, there are important theological reasons for including material from article 2b in our discussion here, because any Christian soteriology (doctrine of salvation) is essentially christological. More precisely, the renewal of soteriology proffered in this volume is trinitarian not only because it is christological but also because the doctrine of Christ and his atoning work is also thoroughly pneumatological and eschatological, the other consistent threads through our theological vision so far. So we begin our contextualization with the major thrusts of article 4 and then shift to article 2b in order to situate the renewal of the doctrine of salvation undertaken in the second half of this chapter within a broader christological, pneumatological, and trinitarian frame of reference.

9.2.1 The Many Encounters with the Saving Christ

Article 4 of the SF focuses on the new birth through the Holy Spirit and its effects. These are identified specifically as including regeneration, justification, adoption, and eternal life. Of the scriptural texts referenced, Titus 3:4-7 provides the most expansive set of categories, albeit without mentioning adoption, which the SF associates with embrace by the family or people of God. A more Reformed register would include within the *ordo salutis*—the order of salvation—divine foreknowing, predestining, calling, justifying, and glorifying (cf. Rom 8:29-30; see also Stoever 1978: ch. 7). Arminians, Wesleyans, and Holiness-Pentecostals would certainly not reject this particular Pauline formulation, although they would be more likely to insist that predestination (and election) is based on God's foreknowledge of human responses (to divine salvific initiatives), election is as much if not more corporate (about the church) than individualized, and sanctification ought not be overlooked.

More precisely, a Holiness-Pentecostal approach would highlight an additional set of reconsiderations about the traditional (Reformed) *ordo salutis*. First, any strict order of the specific moments of salvation would be deemphasized in light of the fluid and dynamic ways in which human beings encounter the redeeming work of the triune God. This means that the Pauline itemization in Romans 8 is less an exhaustive and rigidly progressive series than it is a contextual articulation open to various forms of systematization or understanding. In fact, the New Testament itself (see Colijn 2010; Talbert and Whitlark 2011) is suffused with a wide range of soteriological notions, both those more directly related to the classical *ordo salutis* (forgiveness, election, perfection, eternal life) and those more broadly construed (e.g., new covenant, new exodus, divine enablement, resurrection, rescue, healing, reconciliation, peace, transformation, perseverance). For Holiness-Pentecostals, one approach has been to talk instead about the *way of salvation* (Gause 1980) so as to avoid either the speculative debates or the seemingly arbitrary sequence of the major categories that have arisen regarding the *ordo salutis*. Further, shifting metaphors to highlight the *path* of salvation invites consideration also about human response crucial to holiness and renewal traditions. Thus not only is sanctification insisted upon between justification/adoption and glorification, but repentance—central to both Scripture and renewal experience—becomes essential to traversing God's saving pathway.

A renewalist soteriology would also retrieve the ancient dictum *lex orandi, lex credendi* methodology, which Latin can be loosely translated as "the law of prayer is the law of belief." The point here is that Christian confession arises out of Christian practices, and in that sense, Christian theology emerges as a second-order set of reflections on Christian life. A renewal parallel insists that Christian doctrine derives from Christian spirituality (Stephenson 2013: ch. 5). This perspective illuminates the renewal tradition's gravitation toward what might be called a fivefold soteriology.

Earlier the classical pentecostal fivefold gospel of Jesus as savior, sanctifier, baptizer in the Spirit, healer, and coming king was introduced (see section 7.2). While a technical interpretation of the fivefold gospel would parse only the first element of Jesus' work soteriologically, as already indicated (in chs. 4–6 and 8), there are also good reasons to understand the sanctifying, Spirit baptizing, and healing works of Christ in soteriological terms. It has also been argued from the beginning that the eschatological horizon of renewal spirituality ought to be understood not only futuristically but also as inaugurated in the incarnational and pentecostal events and hence as having relevance to our contemporary period between the time of Christ's first and second advents. Within this framework, then, the pentecostal fivefold gospel registers a multifaceted encounter with the living Christ that can be interpreted in at least two complementary ways. One would highlight how the one saving work of God includes sanctifying, empowering, healing, and eschatological aspects. The other would affirm that the pentecostal experience of Jesus as sanctifier, empowerer, healer, and coming king constitutes salvation, broadly construed. The point is that the fivefold formulation both emerges from the pentecostal encounter with the triune God along the way of salvation and is capable of accounting for a wider swath of the scriptural witness to God's saving actions. The good news of salvation includes, even if it cannot be reduced to, sanctification and healing (as specific aspects of the fivefold gospel), the forgiveness of sins (justification), adoption (into a new community), and new life (regeneration)—referenced in article 4—among other features witnessed to by the scriptural, theological, and dogmatic traditions.

Two more aspects of article 4 deserve comment: its individualistic understanding and its pneumatological emphasis. First, the saving work of God is focused on what happens with "believing sinners." Assuredly, any contemporary Christian theology of salvation must explicate what happens in individual hearts and lives. At the same time, the renewal experience of divine salvation is increasingly being understood in broader terms (e.g., Yong 2005: chs. 1–2, 2010: ch. 1). God saves people in families and communities, even while people are saved not only as souls but as embodied, as material, economic, social, and political creatures, and as environmentally and ecologically situated—hence the "full gospel." Thus we highlighted in chapter 7 that the church's emphasis on ministries of compassion should be understood not just in missional terms but also as defining the "good news of salvation" that article 6 affirmed.

Such a more expansive soteriological scope makes more sense not just of the global renewal movement but within the ecumenical theological discussion. The classical soteriological articulations focused on future salvation—eternal life (for Protestant traditions), the beatific vision (in the Catholic orbit), and theosis/deification (for Eastern Christians)—surely ought not to be minimized, and there are efforts underway to reconsider renewal soteriological impulses in light of these historic formulations (e.g., Rybarczyk 2004; Kärkkäinen 2005). At the same time, the good news of God's saving work is increasingly being considered in terms of what difference is made in the concrete realities of human lives. So yes, salvation includes the forgiveness of sins, but this reconciles people not only to God but also to others (interpersonally) and even to themselves (intrapersonally) (Shults and Sandage 2003). This means that salvation involves not only right standing before God but also the fruits of right attitudes and actions toward both God and others, our neighbors (Huang 2009). Beyond this, the fruits of salvation include doing what Jesus did in terms of entering into solidarity with the poor and in the contemporary global context, working to identify, name, and challenge existing systems of domination, oppression, and unjust death (Gutierrez 1973), and empowering human flourishing in such contexts. And if human beings are not merely atomized realities but also environmentally constituted, then salvation has a terrestrial and even cosmic dimension, one we are reminded about by the groaning creation (Rom 8:22-23; see also Boff 1995; Wessels 2003; Snyder and Scandrett 2011).

FIGURE 9.2A

FIGURE 9.2B

Shortly after achieving independence from Portugal in 1975, the Republic of Mozambique descended into extremely brutal civil war (1977–1992) between communist and anticommunist forces. Ultimately this war claimed one million lives, displaced millions more, and devastated the country's infrastructure, agriculture, and economy. In 1995, one year after the country's first free elections, Anglican Bishop Dinis Sengulane joined Christian Aid and the Mozambican Christian Council to establish the Transforming Arms into Tools (TAE) program ,with the mission of giving Mozambicans the opportunity to exchange guns and ammunition for tools and building materials. Over a nine-year period the project collected and decommissioned more than six hundred thousand weapons in exchange for plows, sewing machines, bicycles, roofing materials, even tractors.

In tandem with the TAE program, four Mozambican artists (collectively known as Nucleo de Arte) were commissioned by the British Museum to transform hundreds of these weapons into a sculptural image of Eden: a central Tree of Life surrounded by numerous creatures, all made entirely out of dismembered machine guns, pistols, and rocket-propelled grenade launchers—objects designed (and used) to kill. The retrieval and reconfiguration of these instruments of violence into an emblem of life creates a provocative tension: this image of life has countless violent and painful histories inscribed in its very materiality (cf. fig. 9.4). The kind of life this tree thus represents (and calls forth) is not a pristine state of being but, rather, a redeemed life that comes through disarmament, through the slow painful process of reconciliation, rebuilding, and the transformation of what has been. As such, it is an extraordinary contemporary visualization of Isaiah's eschatological vision of a time in which "many peoples . . . shall beat their swords into plowshares, and their spears into pruning hooks" (Isa 2:3-4).

This sculpture and the TAE initiative behind it give powerful form and testimony not only to the terrible groaning of creation under the weight of evil but also to the orientation of Christian hope, which proclaims that the wondrous works (Acts 2:11) of God in the world are organized around the redemption of all that is presently broken and dysfunctional in God's good creation. Indeed, at the center of Christian hope is the trinitarian movement of God in Christ through the Spirit "to reconcile to himself all things, whether on earth or in heaven" (Col 1:20). ✦

A global renewal soteriology also insists that salvation is never generic but particular. God saves men in some ways differently from how God saves women (Ruether 2012), for instance, because they face some similar but also many different challenges. Similarly, contextual theologians are reminding us that all theology, including Western theology, bears contextual witness to the saving work of God in Christ. Asian thinkers observe that the good news humanizes people in situations of dire poverty and enables and empowers Christian discipleship in a religiously pluralistic and extremely diverse world (Gnanakan 1992; cf. Coward 2003). African theologians likewise highlight that salvation in that context has important—even essential—socioeconomic dimensions, engages environmental degradation, and empowers women and children in a patriarchal world (Hoffmeister and Kretzschmar 1995). Any theology that fails to address these global contexts and concerns will remain parochial and ultimately fail to renew Christian theology today.

Our final set of comments in this subsection build off the pneumatological emphasis in article 4. Salvation is urged to be "an instantaneous and complete operation of the Holy Spirit." The discussion so far in this book suggests that such a pneumatological soteriology is more dynamic (without discounting this important moment of regeneration and conversion) and ought also to have a more expansive horizon. Here we are helped by renewal theologians in the global context. For instance, African theologians are urging that an African pneumatological soteriology, rather than promoting a naïve supernaturalism related to the sub-Saharan cosmology of many spirits, ought to draw from wisdom traditions, cultivate a creational scope, and engage the scientific rationality so urgent for the development of the continent (Ngong 2010). Simultaneously, Indian renewalists are exploring pneumatological soteriologies that engage with the poverty, cultural richness, and religious diversity that is the Indian context (Mathai 1999). The saving work of the Holy Spirit transforms human hearts and lives into the image of Jesus Christ so that they can bear adequate witness in their various contexts.

The point to be made is that any contemporary renewal soteriology ought also to be robustly pneumatological. Classical Reformation formulations have suggested that soteriology belongs primarily to the person of Christ, with the work of the Spirit being to apply the benefits of Christ's atonement to believers. In a sense, article 4 perpetuates this trinitarian division of labor. However, the article also contains within it the seeds of a more fully trinitarian soteriology, one that sees the work of the Spirit in relationship to the person and work of Christ, while also opening up, in a global context, to a more than individualistic rendition. Here the article rightly insists that it belongs to the work of the Spirit not only to sanctify (as classically delimited by some strands of the Reformation tradition) but to regenerate, justify, adopt, and bring about the new life in Christ. Yet new creatures in the Spirit of Christ can hardly be disentangled from the new creation as a whole.

9.2.2 The Many Theories of the Work of Christ

Similar to how article 4 opens up to creational perspectives, considerations regarding the atoning work of Christ also have included such cosmic horizons. In the following, we begin with the WAGF articles 4 and 2, navigate from there backward through the history of Christian thought, and then come forward again to map contemporary atonement theologies in a global perspective. What we ought to keep in mind in this overly brief discussion is our goal of formulating not a theology of the atonement per se, but a renewal soteriology rooted in the trinitarian work of God.

Article 4 references "salvation through faith in Christ, who died for our sins" and provided salvation through his atoning sacrifice on the cross. This builds on a sentence in article 2 that explicates the work of Christ in these terms: "We believe in His sinless life, miraculous ministry, substitutionary atoning death, bodily resurrection, triumphant ascension, and abiding intercession." The key notion here for atonement theology is the adjective "substitutionary."

The notion of a substitutionary atonement has a long history, particularly developed since the beginning of the second millennium (Holmes 2007). The basic idea is that "Christ died for our sins" (1 Cor 15:3, basically preserved in article 4), which is understood to mean that Christ died on behalf or in place of human sinners. This notion was most vigorously elaborated by Anselm (1033–1109) and developed by Calvin. The former reasons that divine honor had been tarnished with human disobedience, an offence that humans were incapable of rectifying. Hence God became human in Christ in order to live a sinless life in obedience to the divine mandate and to satisfy divine anger and placate divine wrath incurred because of sin. This Anselmian notion was expanded by Calvin and others to clarify that Christ suffered *for* human beings by taking on the punishment that was due to them (arguing from Isa 53:6-10, Rom 3:25-26, Heb 2:17, 1 Pet 3:18a, and 1 John 2:2, among other passages). Both accounts—Anselm's satisfaction and Calvin's penal substititionary theories—sought to justify how God could forgive sins, that is, through the innocent God-man's representative life and his substitutionary death on behalf of others. Put crudely, the atonement in this understanding responds to divine wrath against sin and divine justice condemning sin.

Of course, both explanations have been questioned. There is a sense in which the medieval regal and sixteenth-century legal backgrounds of Anselm and Calvin, respectively, provided an overarching template resulting in a limited forensic set of models that explicated atonement largely as a binitarian affair between the Father and the Son. At least those following in the footsteps of Calvin, if not he himself, were led, through the logic of a theology of particular election and predestination, to argue for a limited atonement: that Christ's death is efficacious for covering the sins of only the elect. Otherwise, if Christ died as a substitute for all sinners, their indebtedness would have been absolved, leading to universal salvation. Arminians and Wesleyans, among others, have counterargued for a universally applicable atonement that benefits only those who believe (from texts such as 1 John 2:2 and 1 Tim 4:10). More recently, looking back to the time prior to Calvin, there has been uproar, especially against Anselmian satisfaction. The complaints are wide-ranging (e.g., Weaver

2001; Love 2010): that this presumes a wrathful and retributive deity, the Father, who could be appeased only through the death of the Son; that such appeasement introduces a cleavage into the very heart of the trinitarian life of God; that such vicarious suffering sanctions divinely initiated violence—by the Father against the Son, for instance—which in turn valorizes and potentially perpetuates human violence, and so on. Any retention of either satisfaction or penal substitution notions will need to heed these criticisms rather than merely repeat these theories.

If we shifted back from this medieval and Reformational period to the early church, however, a whole range of atonement ideas come into focus (Turner 1952). Starting with Irenaeus of Lyons (d. 202 CE) in the second century and extending to many other third- and fourth-century church fathers, the saving work of Christ was thought about as not only reconciling humanity with God but as enabling participation of creatures in the life of God. Irenaeus introduced the fundamental terms of the discussion, urging that Christ as second Adam (Rom 5:12-17; 1 Cor 15:22, 45) accomplished what the first Adam had failed to do: he represented human beings in sinless obedience to God and thus healed, restored, and recapitulated all of creation to God through his life, death, resurrection, and ascension. The problem of sin was thus overcome through Christ's sinless life, while the problem of death, which came into the world through sin, was also conquered through Christ's resurrection from the dead. In effect, as the New Testament authors indicated (Matt 20:28; Mark 10:45; 1 Tim 2:6; 1 Pet 1:18; Rev 5:9), Christ's life and death constituted a ransom that redeemed and rescued creatures enslaved by sin, captive under the power of the law, and without escape from the stronghold of death. Yet the idea also emerged that insofar as, due to Adam's sin, "the whole world lies under the power of the evil one" (1 John 5:19) and human beings are "held captive by [the devil] to do his will" (1 Tim 2:26), Christ's ransom was also paid to the devil. However, the latter was tricked out of his presumed payment through the former's resurrection from the dead (McDonald 1985: ch. 12). Regardless of the mechanism, the point was clear: Christ was victorious over sin, death, and the devil (Aulén 1970; cf. Ray 1998), reconciling humans with God through his work.

Anselm was led to his satisfaction theory in part because he did not believe that the devil's lawless usurpation could ever amount to a just claim against human beings, much less the creation. His younger contemporary, Abelard (1079–1142), agreed with him on this point, adding that the tendency to personify sin, the law, death, and the devil opened up an untenable cosmic dualism. But in contrast to Anselm's more *objective* theory of atonement (focused on the work of Christ as appeasing divine wrath and satisfying the honor of God), Abelard provided a more *subjective* understanding about Christ's work, intended to accomplish a transformation of human hearts burdened by the guilt of sin. Thus Christ's was an exemplary life that revealed God's patient acceptance and forgiveness of guilty sinners (as imaged through the parable of the Prodigal Son), even as his death was designed to inspire human hearts by showing the depths to which God would descend in order to demonstrate his unconditional love for creatures. While there is every reason to be critical of articulating a theology of atonement only in subjective terms, this Abelardian motif is less controversial when seen not only in continuity with aspects of early (Irenaean) healing, recapitulationist, and representationalist theories, but also as anticipating more recent theologies of the love of God (see Schmiechen 2005: ch. 10).

FIGURE 9.3

The Apostles' Creed asserts that between Good Friday (in which Christ "suffered under Pontius Pilate, was crucified, died and was buried") and Easter Sunday ("he rose again from the dead") there was a Holy Saturday in which "he descended into hell" or "he descended to the dead" (see appendix 2). Whether or not Christ's literal descent into hell (or alternatively, Sheol) is supported by the Scriptures, it creates a visual metaphor with profound biblical resonance. In Orthodox iconography this descent is portrayed as an all-out assault and plundering (or "harrowing") of hell, in which Christ overcomes the power of Satan and death itself.

This scene came to be referred to in Greek as the anastasis, which might be translated as "raising up" or "recovery." In this scene Christ is shown in the center, forcefully striding over the doors of hell, which he has just knocked down. Beneath these broken doors a bound and incapacitated Satan writhes in protest. And as Jesus strides forward, with his right hand he grabs hold of a very elderly Adam and with his left he grabs hold of Eve, yanking both of them out of their respective tombs. And in the wake of this act, numerous other Old Testament figures emerge to follow Christ out of their own bondage to death: on the left David, Solomon, and several other righteous leaders are ushered toward Jesus by Elijah/John the Baptist (for the conflation of the two, see Mal 4:5-6 and Mark 1:2-9 and 11:20-30); and on the right, behind Eve, are gathered Abel (holding a shepherd's crook) and seven prophets.

While the details of this scene are extrabiblical, its visualization helpfully represents the work of Christ as an ultimate Exodus, in which the most ancient human captives are set free (Isa 61:1; Luke 4:18; Eph 4:7-10; 1 Pet 18-22) from the cruel slavery of sin and death and from the idolater more wicked than Pharaoh. In this context, the salvation offered in Christ is understood not only as a payment of debts or a release from legal culpability but as a radical bringing-to-life in his overthrowing of, and exodus through, death itself (cf. fig. 11.4). ✦

Unlike the doctrine of the person of Christ (to which we turn in a moment), there are no conciliar or ecumenical definitions of the atonement that are incumbent on Christian belief. This ought not be surprising, given the many soteriological themes even within the scriptural tradition (Tidball, Hilborn, and Thacker 2008). Arguably, the many different theories are related at least in part to the breadth of the biblical witness (Beilby and Eddy 2006). As we have seen, differences can be traced with regard to how sin is understood, whether its effects or offenses are defined primarily in relationship to human beings themselves, to cosmic powers (like the devil), or to God, and how Christ's atoning work is supposed to save.

Against this backdrop, we can now better understand why article 4 of the SF affirms a substitutionary atonement amid a broader understanding of Christ's work through his incarnational and postascension ministries.

While the article certainly emphasizes the work of the Spirit in accomplishing salvation in the hearts and lives of believers, a renewal perspective would also insist that the work of Christ—in his life and death—cannot be adequately understood apart from the work of the Spirit (see Stibbe 2001). If there are both objective and subjective aspects to the atoning work of Christ, a renewal approach would resist merely subjectivizing the work of the Spirit and relegating that to the application of an otherwise objectively wrought atonement achieved by Christ. Instead, both Christ's atoning work and the believer's experiences of such can and ought to be pneumatically mediated and pneumatologically understood. Is it possible that such a pneumatological perspective will also hold together multiple atonement theories in order that a more comprehensive and renewed soteriology might emerge for our time?

9.2.3 The Many Face(t)s of the Person of Christ

The foregoing discussion leads from the experience of the work of Christ to the nature of the person of Christ. Preceding the statement on the work of Christ in article 2b is this affirmation regarding the person of Christ: "We believe in the Lord Jesus Christ, the second person of the triune Godhead, who was and is the eternal Son of God; that He became incarnate by the Holy Spirit and was born of the virgin Mary." The statement clearly makes a trinitarian claim regarding Christ's person, but just as clearly defines the incarnation pneumatologically, as a work of the Spirit. The following discussion very quickly traces out these two aspects of Christ's person from the scriptural witness, through the early church, and into the contemporary arena in order to show the interrelationship between Christology, atonement, and soteriology.

The earliest christological confessions are possibly those of the Apostle Paul, close to the end of his first Letter to the Corinthians: "that Christ died for our sins in accordance with the Scriptures, and that he was buried, and that he was raised on the third day in accordance with the Scriptures, and that he appeared to Cephas, then to the twelve . . ." (1 Cor 15:3-5). Note that this is repeated, albeit not exactly and without reference, at the beginning of article 4 of the SF (although 1 Cor 15:4 is referenced in article 2b, to which we turn momentarily). What this statement also tells us is that Christ's person is inextricably tied in with his work; in fact, who Christ is in himself is less vital than who he is *as us* and what he has done *for us*.

Although writing later than Paul, Luke suggests that the Pauline connection of the work and person of Christ was of wider prevalence in this early post-Easter period. Peter's introduction of Christ to Cornelius emphasizes "how God anointed Jesus of Nazareth with the Holy Spirit and with power; how he went about doing good and healing all who were oppressed by the devil, for God was with him" (Acts 10:38). This is consistent with the Lukan portrayal of Christ as conceived and born of the Holy Spirit (Luke 1:35), full of the Holy Spirit in his life (4:1; 10:21), and missionally empowered by the Spirit throughout his public ministry (4:14-19). It turns out that not only is Jesus incarnate of the Spirit, as article 2 indicates, but that his entire life is Spirit-empowered, the point made earlier (chs. 3–4) about its exemplarity for his followers (cf. Hawthorne 1991). Additionally, however, this Lukan understanding clearly presumes Jesus' humanity. He accomplishes all he does under the inspiration of the Spirit, as a human person anointed and empowered by God. Surely, as God's representative, Jesus also acts with divine prerogative, forgiving sins, healing and curing the sick, and exorcising demons, for instance. All of this announces the arrival of God's reign and the deliverance of all oppressed by the evil one.

It is not until we get to later strands of the New Testament that Jesus' divine identity is more clearly enunciated. The Fourth Gospel, arguably the latest of the gospel accounts, begins not with Jesus' human birth but with his divine origins: "In the beginning was the Word, and the Word was with God, and the Word was God. . . . And the Word became flesh and lived among us, and we have seen his glory, the glory as of a father's only son, full of grace and truth" (John 1:1, 14). While Jesus is indicated as acknowledging "the Father is greater than I" (14:28), he also says, consistent with the Johannine prologue, "The Father and I are one" (10:30). His disciples bear further and clear witness to his divine status, as in Thomas' confession: "My Lord and my God!" (20:28). The point is that in contrast to the depiction of Jesus' humanity in the Synoptic Gospels, John begins with his divine character, from above, as it were. Yet it should be emphasized that the Johannine portrayal also connects the person and work of Christ. The point is not to speculate about *who* Jesus is, but "so that you may come to believe that Jesus is the Messiah, the Son of God, and that through believing you may have life in his name" (20:31).

In many respects, the history of christological reflection unfolds following these scriptural trajectories (see, e.g., O'Collins 1995: chs. 7–8). During the first few centuries, various articulations were deemed heretical precisely because they did not hold together both the human and divine aspects witnessed to by the apostolic writings. Ebionites, mostly Jewish believers in Jesus, were reluctant to affirm unambiguously his divinity for fear of compromising their monotheistic commitments, while docetists, more philosophically informed believers, were hesitant to acknowledge his humanity due to concerns that the carnality of creaturely fleshliness would tarnish the purity and holiness of divinity. Within the parameters of the early Christian tradition, broadly seen, Alexandrian Christians were alert to docetist errors but nevertheless prioritized Jesus' divine nature and adopted a complementary spiritualizing and allegorizing hermeneutic to make sense of his person and work. Antiochene Christians, by contrast, although wary of Ebionite aberrations, yet began with Jesus' humanity while deploying a more historical and typological approach to scriptural interpretation commensurate with their views. If the former then erred on the side of protecting the unity of God and thus minimizing the full extent of Jesus' humanity (as did the fourth-century bishop Apollinarius of Laodicea, for instance), the latter similarly stumbled on the side of either diminishing Jesus' fully divine status (Arianist tendencies) or fracturing the unity of his personhood (as was claimed of the theologian Nestorius [ca. 386–451], for example).

The christological debates of the third through fifth centuries came to a head with the Council of Chalcedon in 451 (see appendix 2). The fathers gathered there affirmed Christ as "truly God and truly man" (rather than siding with either the Alexandrian or Antiochene sides); "of a reasonable soul and body" (against Apollinarius' denial that Jesus' human soul was replaced by the Logos); and "acknowledged in two natures, inconfusedly, unchangeably, indivisibly, inseparably . . . not parted or divided into two persons, but one and the same Son" (against Nestorius' separation of the divine and human natures to the point of threatening the unity of Christ's person), among other elements. The council also recognized Jesus as being "born of the virgin Mary," which is registered in article 2 of the SF, but (and here again also contra Nestorius) then goes on to identify her as "the mother of God" (Greek: *theotokos*, lit. "God-bearer"), which becomes part of a long history of Marian doctrinal development. We have already suggested that any theology of Mary ought to serve our understanding of the redemptive work of Christ (see section 5.1). The point to be emphasized here is that all of these christological commitments are couched within the broader confession of Christ's work, "for us and for our salvation," consistent with the New Testament witness.

The preceding does not do justice to the protracted debates leading up to the Chalcedonian meeting, and we have no space to provide even cursory summaries of the history of christological ideas since then (see Kärkkäinen 2003: esp. part 2). What is important for our purposes, however, is to fast-forward to the present ferment in order to highlight global christological developments on the one hand and the reemergence of Spirit Christologies on the other. With regard to the former, the meaning of Christ *for us* looms large. Liberation and feminist Christologies, for instance, are less concerned about who Christ is in the abstract and more focused on what he means and has done for humans as historically embodied creatures (e.g., Boff 1978; Sobrino 1978; Ruether 1981; Schüssler Fiorenza 1994). Similarly, in a global context, scriptural and historical resources are being brought to bear on understanding the person of Christ in relationship to the saving work of God in concrete, impoverished, and culturally pluralistic societies (Levison and Pope-Levison 1992; Kuster 2001; Inbody 2002; Greene 2003). More contextually grounded articulations are emerging, especially in Africa, of Jesus Christ as brother and ancestor (Nyamiti 1984), as kin and guest (Udoh 1988), as humble king (Manus 1993), and as liberator in a situation of suffering (Mugambi and Magesa 1998; Stinton 2004). Last but not least, there is the currently almost frantic discussion about the meaning of Christ in a pluralistic world, in particular in relationship to the interreligious encounter and with regard to world religious traditions (e.g., Thangaraj 1994, Alangaram 1999, Muck and Gross 2000, Jensen 2001, Luz and Michaels 2006, Tsoukalas 2006, Singh 2008). One of the clear trends in the preceding is that while Jesus' divinity is not rejected (in most cases), it is Jesus' humanity that invites consideration about the concrete challenges that human beings encounter in the contemporary global ferment.

Similarly, the retrieval of Spirit-christological themes, grounded in the synoptic witness (noted above), also appears to connect contemporary human engagements with the fundamental question Jesus posed: "Who do you say that I am?" (Matt 16:15). It is not that emphases on Jesus' divinity do not respond to this question, nor is it that Spirit christologians desire to displace the Logos Christology of John (e.g., Del Colle 1994, Habets 2010b). But it does seem as if overemphasizing Jesus' transcendent identity is less meaningful in the contemporary theological and global climate. Understandings of Jesus of Nazareth as anointed by the Spirit to accomplish the works of God provide a more conducive framework for seeing Jesus' solidarity with human beings and project a springboard for envisioning missional discipleship in his footsteps (Moltmann 1989). Within contexts such as India, for instance, Spirit-christological categories are inspiring considerations of how incarnational theology compares and contrasts with the complex history of religious and philosophical ideas prevalent in the Hindu Indian subcontinent (Manohar 2009).

Renewal Christologies appear to be following suit. On the one hand, there is no concession of the Johannine-inspired high-Christology, a given for almost all renewalists (e.g., T. Norris 2009). On the other hand, Spirit-Christologies are emerging, focused particularly on how the Spirit-inspired and empowered Christ also translates into Christ accompanying us in and through the empowering Spirit (Dorries 2006; Alfaro 2010). Further, on the global scene, renewal understandings of Christ are connecting with the oral traditions of indigenous cultures, thus facilitating the translation of christological confession into vernacular languages for local contexts (Clarke 2011). In each of these cases, renewalism's christocentric piety and pneumatic spirituality provide orientations to the person and work of Christ that contrast with the more scholastic and speculative methodologies of some strands of the previous Spirit-christological discussion.

9.3 Once-and-for-All through Christ and the Spirit: Salvation for Hebrews and Gentiles

We now focus our scriptural reflections on the anonymously authored letter or exhortation to the Hebrews, in part because of its role in mediating both Alexandrian and Antiochene traditions during the patristic period (see Greer 1973). Additionally, the structure of the letter (Kroeger and Evans 2002: 765) addressing Christ's person (chs. 1–4), work (chs. 5–10), and human salvation (chs. 12–13) maps onto, at least in reverse order, the three doctrinal loci discussed in this chapter. Our goal will be not only to observe the way that Hebrews connects the person and work of Christ to salvation but also to notice if and how it addresses some of the issues raised in the preceding regarding the person of Christ, the nature of atonement, and the role of the Spirit in these matters. At some point we will also need to address the implications of this work for Christian–Jewish relations, a topic broached previously in chapter 7 and to be further elaborated in chapter 11.

Hebrews is certainly about the incomparable greatness of salvation in Christ (Stibbs 1970), at least when contrasted with the salvific potency of the covenant with Israel. Jesus' person and work is superior to, especially in the sense of completing and fulfilling, that of the prophets (Heb 1:1-3), the angels (1:4-2:13), Moses (ch. 3), Joshua (4:1-14), the high priesthood of Aaron (4:14-5:10) and Melchizadek (ch. 7), Abraham (6:13-20), the old covenant (ch. 8), the Mosaic ritual (ch. 9) and the sacrificial (10:1-18) systems, and the faith of the Old Testament saints (ch. 11). Hence its readers are repeatedly reminded that in Christ there is a "better hope" (7:19), a "better covenant" (7:22), "better promises" (8:6), a "better sacrifice" (9:23), and the promise of a "better country" (11:16) and a "better resurrection" (11:35). Surely here is "something better" (10:34, 11:40), a "better word" (12:24) that inspires the author's confidence of "better things in your case, things that belong to salvation" (6:9). What is it that undergirds the bold optimism of the letter?

The author certainly has a high Christology, pronounced from the start about the Son, "whom [God] appointed heir of all things, through whom he also created the worlds. He is the reflection of God's glory and the exact imprint of God's very being, and he sustains all things by his powerful word" (Heb 1:2-3). Yet this Son also entered into and experienced the depths of the human condition. As his brothers and sisters were constituted by flesh and blood, "he himself likewise shared the same things . . . [and became] like his brothers and sisters in every respect" (2:14, 17). More precisely, "[i]n the days of his flesh, Jesus offered up prayers and supplications, with loud cries and tears, to the one who was able to save him from death, and he was heard because of his reverent submission" (5:7). It was through his undeniable suffering that the Son "learned obedience" (5:8), and was perfected by God as "the pioneer of [human] salvation" (2:10). Hence the letter affirms Christ's solidarity with humankind (Koester 2001b: 106–09; McCruden 2008), albeit with an important difference: "For we do not have a high priest who is unable to sympathize with our weaknesses, but we have one who in every respect has been tested as we are, yet without sin" (4:15). Christ was perfected by God not in the sense of being purified from sin but in the sense of being enabled to persevere through his mission despite the suffering he endured at the hands of sinners. In this, Christ's impeccability grounds God's saving work, and this is seen not only in his death but also in his life of humiliation and exaltation.

Hebrews makes patently clear that Christ's death "made purification for sins" (1:3). More particularly, it declares: "it is by God's will that we have been sanctified through the offering of the body of Jesus Christ once for all. . . . But when Christ had offered for all time a single sacrifice for sins, 'he sat down at the right hand of God.' . . . For by a single offering he has perfected for all time those who are sanctified" (10:10, 12, 14). The "once-and-for-all" character of Christ's sacrificial offering is repeatedly insisted upon (7:27; 9:12, 26, 28). The problems to be dealt with are multiple: human priests are themselves beset with weakness, and their sins are also in need of atonement (5:1-3); the methods of the original covenant were not faultless (8:8), indeed they were "weak and ineffectual" (7:18) and "obsolete and growing old" (8:13); earthly sacrifices were necessarily repetitive but even then ineffectual in providing access to the heavenly sanctuary of God's presence (9:6-7, 23-28); and "it is impossible for the blood of bulls and goats to take away sins" (10:4). Yet, "under the law almost everything is purified with blood, and without the shedding of blood there is no forgiveness of sins" (9:22). Hence it was through offering his own blood that Christ procured the atonement for sins (9:22; 10:19; 12:24; 13:12).

Some have argued that Christ's sacrifice not only ended all sacrifice but also unmasked the violence of all sacrificial systems (e.g., Heim 2006; Jersak and Hardin 2007). While granting that there is an important and irreducible sense in which this is true, the related problem is that of death. Hebrews does not make the point that "the wages of sin is death" (Rom 6:23), but it recognizes the problem of death. Anticipating a more complete discussion in the next chapter, our focus here is christological and soteriological: Jesus died not only so "he might taste death for everyone" (Heb 2:9) but also "so that through death he might destroy the one who has the power of death, that is, the devil, and free those who all their lives were held in slavery by the fear of death" (2:14b-15). Jesus thus submits to the consequences of sin but yet destroys sin's power of death precisely through his perfected suffering and resurrection from the dead. Yet physical death is only a type of spiritual death, separation from God. Christ overcomes the power of fear accompanying physical death precisely in order to reconcile creation to the very presence of God. So, through "the power of an indestructible life" (7:16), Jesus "entered into heaven itself, now to appear in the presence of God on our behalf" (9:24b). Although not mentioned specifically in Hebrews, then, resurrection is presumed as a central aspect of Christ's full atoning work, which culminated in its repeated assertion that the living Christ has ascended to the "right hand of the Majesty on high" (1:3; cf. 1:13; 8:1; 10:12; 12:2; Moffitt 2011). Elsewhere we are told that it is the Spirit who is the power of the resurrection, both for Christ and for believers in him (Rom 1:4; 8:11).

Yet if the death, resurrection, and ascension of Christ render death impotent, how do they also accomplish the forgiveness of sins? Here Jesus' pronunciation, "Father, forgive them; for they do not know what they are doing" (Luke 23:34), empowered as are all his words and deeds by the Spirit (as we ought to recall in the Lukan narrative), is important. Not only as divine representative but also as "the exact imprint of God's very being" (Heb 1:3), Jesus pronounces divine forgiveness for the most heinous of crimes committed by humanity against God. Jesus' forgiving the sins of those who murdered him thus also amounts to a declaration of God's forgiveness of sins. In effect, Jesus "is able for all time to save those who approach God through him, since he always lives to make intercession for them" (7:25). Beyond this, while the blood of bulls and goats cannot heal the conscience of sinful people (9:9), Jesus' absolution assures that the sins of human beings will not be held against them. Hence Hebrews also declares jubilantly: "how much more will the blood of Christ, who through the eternal Spirit offered himself without blemish to God, purify our conscience from dead works to worship the living God!" (9:14). The role of the Spirit is thus central both to the death and resurrection of Christ, and to its capacity to address the guilt of sinners.

Yet the salvation secured by Christ is accomplished not only in his death, resurrection, and ascension, but in his entire life journey. We have already highlighted how the letter emphasizes Christ's passion and suffering. As representative of humankind, however, it is precisely Christ's life of persevering obedience that both enters into and enables for others entrance to the rest of God (Heb 3:7–4:11). Through his sinless life, Christ thus provides access to the holy of holies, the city and country of God (11:10, 16), indeed "to Mount Zion and to the city of the living God, the heavenly Jerusalem, and to innumerable angels in festal gathering" (12:22). It is thus his entire life of humiliation and exaltation that overcomes the powers of sin, death, and the devil, and reopens the pathway to eternal life in the presence of God (Cody 1960).

To be sure, the mechanisms of the old covenant promised such rest but were incapable of leading the people of God to that rest. The problem was not only that of sins committed, but the ongoing incapacity to live within the covenant provided by God. So while Jesus' passion atoned for sins committed, his obedience exemplified the path of righteousness for the forgiven. The difference now is that the law is written not only on tablets and stones but in human hearts (8:10; cf. 2 Cor 3:3). Under the old covenant, human hearts were perennially hardened (Heb 3:8, 15), constrained externally but also condemned by the law. But now:

> The Holy Spirit also testifies to us, for after saying, "This is the covenant that I will make with them after those days, says the Lord: 'I will put my laws in their hearts, and I will write them on their minds,'" he also adds, "I will remember their sins and their lawless deeds no more." Where there is forgiveness of these, there is no longer any offering for sin. (10:15-18)

While the author here quotes from Jeremiah's (31:33-34) pneumatologically grounded affirmation, the reference to the work of the Spirit hearkens also to a parallel passage in the prophet Ezekiel (36:26-27; 37:1-14), wherein God promises that the power to live in obedience will derive internally from the gift of the Spirit of God. So if the problem is not only the atonement for past sins but also the capacity, will, and ability to live into the rest of God, then the answer is both the forgiveness available in Christ's sacrifice and the exemplary solidarity of Christ with human beings through his Spirit, now empowering human lives from within to triumph over sin (Emmrich 2003).

Christ is thus both representative and "pioneer and perfecter of our faith" (Heb 12:2). As such, he is both object and model for faith. People are thus to believe in him and emulate him. That Christ beckons his followers from the right hand of the throne of God is consistent with Hebrews anticipating the eternal salvation to come (2:5; 5:9; 6:5; 9:11-12, 28; 13:14). Yet even presuming this (what scholars call) Jewish two-stage apocalyptic eschatology, the word of exhortation is directed to living faithfully in the present while anticipating the coming age (Mackie 2007). So while we ought to be wary that such a futuristic emphasis can devolve into an "ideology of the transcendent" (Segovia and Sugir-tharajah 2007: 351) that undermines Christian faith in the present life, the author urgently enjoins commitment to Christ and practical obedience. "Today" is the day of salvation (3:7, 13, 15; 4:7), and response to God's gracious offer in Christ brings about the requisite obedience (2:2; 4:6, 11; 5:9) in the power of the Spirit (Rhee 2001). Faith pleases God (11:6), which is what the heroes of old both attempted to do and, even in their failures, modeled as a life of obedience. How much more ought those who now have the example and companionship of Christ in the power of Spirit also persevere (12:1-17) and live in reconciliation with others (13:1-8).

The wrath of God in Hebrews is not on sins in general, these having been taken care of by Christ's once-and-for-all sacrifice. Instead, God's judgment is impending on those who have already tasted but then neglected the graciousness available in Christ and the Spirit (2:1-4; 6:4-8; 10:26-39; 12:25-29). Hence the enemies and adversaries of God are under divine judgment because they "have once been enlightened, and have tasted the heavenly gift, and have shared in the Holy Spirit . . . and then have fallen away" (6:4b, 5a). In short, they have "outraged the Spirit of grace" (10:29) by committing what other New Testament writers call "blasphemy against the Spirit" (Matt 12:31 par. Mark 3:29; Luke 12:10). God is thus a "consuming fire" (Heb 10:27; 12:29) not for sinners in general but for those who persist in ignoring and then despising the Spirit's work in Christ and human hearts. A final judgment therefore awaits all so-called believers and will separate the sheep from the goats.

Before moving on, we have to take up one final question: that related to the alleged anti-Semitic character of the exhortation of Hebrews. There is no question that, like other texts in the Christian New Testament, the historical effects of texts like Hebrews has included anti-Semitic beliefs and practices. Clearly its message about the superiority of Christ's work over the covenant with ancient Israel can be and has been taken in anti-Jewish directions. Yet it ought also be recalled that the overall polemic of the argument is not to do away with the faith of ancient Israel but—as a document arguably written by a Jew either for other Jewish followers of Jesus as Messiah or for Gentile Christians who were enamored with Jew-ish ideas and practices (Koester 2001b: 42–48)—to fulfill it. The goal of

Christ's ministry, as evinced in his encounter with Zacchaeus (discussed previously), was to complete, if not enlarge, those numbered among the children of Abraham. In this sense, one can affirm a "qualified supersessionism" (Kim 2006: 201) in Hebrews, one that recognizes its overarching commitments to Christ but does not perpetuate a disparaging anti-Jewish message (see section 7.4).

9.4 "Today If You Will Hear His Voice . . .": Receiving the Gift of Salvation

It is now time to thread together the disparate lines not only of this chapter but also of the entire argument of the book so far. The "big picture" of renewal soteriology that is emerging is christological, trinitarian, and eschatological. Salvation is available in Christ, with there being no bifurcation between his person and work. Further salvation in Christ essentially involves the work of the Spirit, both in his person and work. Last but not least, salvation in Christ by the Spirit is directed eschatologically toward the reign of God. The following expands on this trinitarian conception by focusing on what salvation addresses (traditionally understood as atonement, explicated in SF article 2b) and on how salvation is accomplished (historically labeled soteriology proper, the focus of SF article 4). As will be clear, the historical affirmations of the person of Christ are presumed in what follows, except that an interconnected Spirit-Christology and pneumatological soteriology will be privileged (cf. Yong 2005: ch. 2).

To understand what salvation addresses, we need to anticipate briefly the more complete discussion of the next chapter on the doctrine of sin. There it will be argued in further detail that the mystery of sin concerns human actions that "fall short of the glory of God" (Rom 3:23), resulting in hostility toward God, alienation from others, and brokenness and guilt in human creatures. The saving work of Christ, accomplished from first to last in the power of the Spirit, addresses these three interrelated dimensions of sin and its effects.

First, Christ's sinless life breaks the power of sin and its attendant guilt on human hearts. Human lives are distorted by sin; their wills are warped by sin; and their self-perception, affections, and hopes are disoriented by sin. Where Adam failed, Christ resists temptation in the power of the Holy Spirit (McKinley 2009: 290–98). This same Spirit is now given to humans, to enable triumph over sin in the footsteps of Christ. We return to this below.

Second, Christ's miraculous ministry cures human bodies wracked by sin, heals human souls oppressed by sin, and reconciles human communities ravaged by sin. Where human bodies are broken due to the effects of sin on nature's contingent processes, Christ enters by the Spirit into solidarity with human suffering, to the point that the marks of his earthly impairment are eternally imbedded even on his resurrection body. Where human souls are oppressed by sin, Christ, through the Holy Spirit, exorcses the demonic and delivers human beings from their fears, guilt, hatred, estrangement and other debilitating effects of sin. Where human communities are torn apart by sin, Christ's Spirit-empowered life and sacrificial death expose and resist the mechanisms of violence that drive human hostilities, thus opening up the possibility of an eschatological peace (Heb 12:11, 14; 13:20). Christ's resurrection from the dead for human justification (Rom 4:25) seals once-and-for-all his solidarity with the weak, marginalized, excluded, and oppressed victims of history and empowers reconciliation with their oppressors in anticipation of the shalom—justice, righteousness, and peace—to come (Tamez 1993).

FIGURE 9.4

Trees provide several of the most important visual-symbolic motifs in the Bible, precisely because of the ways that they function as images of creaturely life. The biblical canon is bookended by the tree of life (Gen 2; Rev 22), and everywhere in between tree imagery and allusions are deployed to interpret human life in relationship to the Gardener who ordered the world for flourishing and who cultivates it continuously. Human individuals and societies are repeatedly presented as plants dependent for life from outside themselves (light, water, and soil are loaded biblical symbols) and whose health and dysfunctions are understood through the logic of fruit-bearing (cf. figs. 5.4 and 7.4). Tree language is used for both blessing and cursing, virtue and wickedness, judgment and restoration, human hearts and kingdoms, Israel and the church, among other symbolic pairings. And in this context, it is deeply significant that Christ's cross—in all of its cursedness—is and perhaps must be a tree (Gal 3:13; 1 Pet 2:24; Acts 5:30; 10:39; cf. Deut 21:22-23). In Christian thought, this hideous wooden instrument of execution becomes a tree of life.

In the late Middle Ages, a visual tradition emerged that understood soteriology in precisely these terms, merging the crucifixion and the tree of life into a single image. Such a merger causes the image to teeter on the edge of cognitive dissonance: the Son of God, "the heir of all things" (Heb 1:2-3), is shown executed on the most ancient symbol of fully flourishing life. The offensiveness and foolishness of such an image would not have been lost on St. Paul, who saw in the difficult "rhetoric of the cross" the very "power of God" offering "righteousness and sanctification and redemption" (1 Cor 1:18-31).

Redemption is conceptualized in this image on at least two scales. Narrowly, this tree of life is an image of the church, as stated in the Latin inscription along the bottom: "The Church of Christ is likened to this vine—the Law made it wither but the Cross made it bloom." More broadly, this tree also clearly has cosmic proportions: though planted in Eden (note the four rivers at the base; Gen 2:10), its luxuriant branches fill the entire apse, enfolding all kinds of people, animals, and vegetation. The whole of creation (see ch. 10), including the diverse organic systems of nature and culture alike, is implicated in the life-giving power of this cruciform man, through whom God was pleased to "reconcile to himself all things, whether on earth or in heaven, by making peace through the blood of his cross" (Col 1:20). ✦

Third, Christ's "substitutionary atoning death, bodily resurrection, triumphant ascension, and abiding intercession" are the culmination and extension of his sinless life and miraculous ministry, not to be separated from the latter. Christ embraced the full extent of the human condition; "through the eternal Spirit [he] offered himself" (Heb 9:14) and "became obedient to the point of death—even death on a cross" (Phil 2:8). But death could not hold him, and the resurrecting power of God's Spirit vindicated his life of obedient suffering. More precisely, as the second Adam, Christ restores human beings, alienated from the presence of God since their fall from grace, to their "place" in the holy sanctuary. Thus the God who so loved the world entered into the world through his Son and suffered death at the hands of sinners in order that the world might be reconciled to God's eternal life through the Spirit's resurrecting power (Daly 2009). God's unconditional forgiveness of sinners pronounced by Christ is thus reaffirmed in the resurrection. Sinners no longer have to suffer under guilt or persist in alienation from God.

We see then that the redemptive work of Christ is thoroughly trinitarian in character. It is pneumatological in being empowered by the Spirit and also entirely focused on accomplishing reconciliation with God from beginning to end. As a work of the triune God, then, the incarnational dimension is thereby also intrinsically pentecostal. This is not a reversion to the traditional distinctions about "objective" (related to Christ) and "subjective" (related to human beings) salvation. Rather, both the incarnational and pentecostal aspects of salvation are eschatological, both objectively grounded in history and yet anticipating the full salvation to come. The *how* of salvation thus calls attention to human participation in Christ's life and resurrection by the power of the Spirit in heralding the coming reign of God. Again, we elaborate on this notion at the personal, interpersonal, and cosmic levels.

Jesus' forgiveness of his enemies in the power of the Holy Spirit is not only the authoritative expression of the Father's unconditional forgiveness but also the exemplary manifestation that empowers human forgiveness, of ourselves and of others. Part of the problem of sin is that it produces a marred self-understanding and a deformed perception of others. If the greatest commandments are to love God fully and to love our neighbors as ourselves (Luke 10:27), then the forgiveness of sins makes this possible. Thus did Jesus say to and breathe upon his disciples at his reappearance after his resurrection, "Peace be with you. As the Father has sent me, so I send you. . . . Receive the Holy Spirit. If you forgive the sins of any, they are forgiven them; if you retain the sins of any, they are retained" (John 20:21-23). The retention of sins of others certainly includes the persistence of the unforgiven's existential guilt; yet it could also include the sense that those who do not forgive remain tormented as victims. Freedom, peace, and abundant life—in effect, new life, what article 4 calls regeneration and new creation—come when humans receive their acceptance before God and also refuse to hold the sins they have suffered at the hands of others against their perpetrators. The forgiveness of sins is thereby not merely a juridical matter involving our standing before God but a performative matter involving redemption of our attitudes to and reorientation of our interactions with others. This is the peaceful path of Jesus (1 Pet 2:21), made possible by the Holy Spirit.

Hence new life in Christ is never a solo or individual affair, but involves what article 4 defines as adoption into the family of God. This highlights the relational dimension of salvation, thereby indicating that it is an essential rather than incidental aspect of triune redemption. In this case, salvation transforms human beings into human doers, persons who interface with others. The point is that Christology and atonement—doctrines regarding the person and work of Christ—are not speculative but practical (Wilson 2001; Tilley 2008). The salvation of God both resituates human beings into redemptive communities and inspires and empowers redemptive, liberative, and healing social action. Forgiveness must go beyond either mental assent or existential release to include the hard work of organizing and sustaining communities of reconciliation and shalom that transform victims and oppressors in the power of the Spirit (Park 2009). Salvation thus includes not just the vertical and internal dimension of experiencing peace with God but also the horizontal and interpersonal nexus of reconciling with others as the body of Christ and fellowship of the Spirit. There is no Christian salvation without human response, appropriation, and transformation by the Spirit's power.

Last but not least, article 4 defines salvation in terms of sinners becoming "a new creation in Christ." Insofar as human beings are never merely individuals, their new creaturehood also involves, rather than is abstracted from, the renewal of the creation as a whole. Thus are the intrapersonal and interpersonal dimensions of salvation cosmically situated. Death, as we shall see further in the next chapter, is not merely an individual or interpersonal reality, but affects all creatures. The defeat of death therefore involves an explicitly eschatological horizon. Similarly, the defeat of the devil, especially in the patristic articulation of Christ's salvific work, involves also the defeat of the principalities and powers, both their destruction and subjugation (1 Cor 15:24-25). Not only does the heavenly city feature the multitudes of angels, but through Christ, "God was pleased to reconcile to himself all things, whether on earth or in heaven, by making peace through the blood of his cross" (Col 1:20). While Christians are not by themselves responsible for the renewal of the whole of creation, they are called both to engage in God's resistance against the powers of darkness, death, and destruction (Yong 2010: part 2), and to participate in the divine mandate to care for creation (Studebaker 2012: ch. 7). We will further explicate this theme in the next chapter.

The preceding sketches the main lines of a renewal soteriology as christological, pneumatological, eschatological, and performative, each being intricately related to the others. Of course, we have not provided a full exposition of the doctrines of either the person or the work of Christ (Christology or atonement)—in fact, multivolumed discussions could not do justice to either topic—but only situated these within a renewal-soteriological matrix. Our basic framework—the WAGF SF—constrains but also provides helpful and rich parameters for our discussion. Within this SF context, there is no denying that the saving power of God in Christ by the Spirit works instantaneously, as article 4 insists. From a narrative perspective, this spotlights the many testimonial accounts that bear witness to the powerfully transformative effects of conversion. Renewalists may enumerate these as first, second, and even third works of grace. Argument over the exact number and sequence is distracting, precisely as inconclusive as debates regarding the *ordo salutis* in the wider Reformation traditions. The important point to be carried forward, however, is that Christian salvation is never an abstract transaction but is palpably experiential and personal, with wider effects. When lives are touched redemptively by God, things are changed, behaviors are redirected, and salvific transformation unleashed. The eschatological horizon of salvation means that each redemptive encounter makes an eternally relevant difference while also anticipating the next thing that God intends to accomplish and that the Spirit is working out.

The final point to be addressed before moving on has to do with the images of violence inherent in at least some versions of classical models of atonement (see section 9.2.2). There is no minimizing the fact that God's unconditional, recapitulative, and eschatological welcome and generosity are made possible by the preferential and cruciform hospitality revealed in Israel and Christ, which goes beyond the world's economy of strict tit-for-tat exchange (Boersma 2004). What this means is that while violence was clearly a part of the passion of Christ, it is more accurate to say that God uses and exposes its mechanisms rather than sanctions them. As Joseph recognized with regard to his brothers' evil intentions—"Even though you intended to do harm to me, God intended it for good" (Gen 50:20)—so also does God redeem the world despite the violence of evil people. Thus the sacrificial death of Christ, with whom God identifies, reveals a God of peace who submits to the violence of sinners in order to redeem the world from its spiral of violence. The salvation procured by the God of Jesus Christ thus ought to inspire not acts of violence but prophetic resistance in the power of the Spirit (cf. Yong 2012: ch. 4). Doing so in the shadow of the cross of Christ, as we shall see in the next chapter, will further lay bare the violence of sin and the fall and undermine its destructive powers.

Discussion Questions

1. How does the preceding account of a Spirit-inspired Christ compare and contrast with the Logos Christology prevailing in the Christian tradition? What are the advantages and shortcomings of each model by itself? How are they complementary? How ought our understanding of the person of Christ inform our discipleship as Christians?

2. Do your church's teachings about the atoning work of Christ preserve the various scriptural data presented in the preceding discussion? Is seeing the role of the Spirit in the work of Christ helpful? How should our understanding of the doctrine of the atonement make a difference in our Christian lives?

3. What does it mean to say that salvation is from God but yet also involves human response? Which of the various aspects, facets, and dimensions of salvation developed in this chapter are important for Christian belief and practice? How is salvation instantaneous while also having ongoing and even lasting effects?

Further Reading

Christensen, Michael J., and Jeffery A. Wittung, eds. 2008. *Partakers of the Divine Nature: The History and Development of Deification in the Christian Traditions.* Grand Rapids: Baker Academic.

Gelpi, Donald L. 2000. *The Firstborn of Many.* 3 vols. Milwaukee: Marquette University Press.

Green, Joel B., and Mark D. Baker. 2000. *Recovering the Scandal of the Cross: Atonement in New Testament and Contemporary Contexts.* Downers Grove, Ill.: InterVarsity.

Lanooy, Rienk, ed. 1994. *For Us and Our Salvation: Seven Perspectives on Christian Soteriology.* Utrecht, The Netherlands: Interuniversitait Instituut voor Missiologie en Oecumenica.

Stackhouse, John G., Jr. 2001. *What Does It Mean to Be Saved? Broadening Evangelical Horizons of Salvation.* Grand Rapids: Baker Academic.

Van der Watt, Jan Gabriël, ed. 2005. *Salvation in the New Testament: Perspectives on Soteriology.* Leiden: Brill.

10

Creation and Fall

Natural History and the Redemptive Ends of God

World Assemblies of God Fellowship Statement of Faith
—Article 3: The Fall of Man

> We believe that humankind was created good and upright. However, volun-
> tary transgression resulted in their alienation from God, thereby incurring
> not only physical death but spiritual death, which is separation from God
> (Genesis 1:16-27; 2:17; 3:6; Romans 5:12-19).

10.1 Judas, the Son of Perdition

How do people who are created good and begin well transgress into
alienation from God and incur not only physical death but perhaps even
ultimate separation from God? This chapter invites consideration on some
of the big questions of life in relationship to creation and the fall. The
life of Judas, the infamous disciple, sets in relief the difficult issues before
us. Rather than merely unfolded chronologically, his story will be told
through six contradictions or paradoxes, aspects of his life that appear to
admit of two conflicting sides or perspectives.

First, Judas the son of Iscariot was both chosen and elect as an apostle
and yet condemned as a traitor, in effect, *the* traitor of all time. Among the
Synoptic Gospels, in each case it is clear that Judas was numbered among
the Twelve, but yet described by the qualifying phrase "who betrayed
him" (Mark 3:19; also Matt 10:4; Luke 6:16; cf. John 6:64). Judas walked
with Jesus for as long as the other disciples did. He appears to have gained
the trust of the group and was put in charge of their finances and made
responsible for distribution to the poor (John 12:29b). Yet it comes out
later that "he was a thief; he kept the common purse and used to steal
what was put into it" (John 12:6). Perhaps he was, however inexplicably,
one of the many who were called, yet despite all of his exposure to the
presence, goodness, love, and teaching of Jesus, not of the few who are
finally chosen (Matt 20:16; 22:14).

Second, Judas was the recipient of Jesus' sanctifying influences and actions, but yet this did not protect him from the destructive lures of Satan. John's (12:12) gospel indicates that Jesus served Judas at the Last Supper and washed his feet, along with the rest of the Twelve, and Matthew (26:50) affirms that Jesus continued to accept him, even until the very last moment, as "friend." Yet perhaps satanic betrayal is possible only amid real relationship, even developed friendship (Anderson 1991). Even before the Supper, Satan had already entered Judas (Luke 22:3; John 13:2). One would have thought that such prolonged exposure to Jesus as Judas experienced would have inhibited the possibility of his life being taken over by the nefarious forces of darkness. But go out into the night he did (John 13:30).

To do what? To finalize plans he had made with the chief priests and temple police about handing Jesus over to them (Matt 26:14-16; Mark 14:10-11; Luke 22:4). Herein we come to the third paradox: Judas conspired to betray Jesus into the hands of his enemies, but yet we are told this supposed conspiracy was also the doing of God. There has been much speculation about what Judas might have been thinking. Perhaps he had been inspired by Jesus' messianic actions and teachings to think even he, as Jesus' follower, had a part to play in Yahweh's deliverance of Israel from the hands of the Roman oppressors and that this involved facilitating a meeting between Jesus and the leaders of Israel that could lead to the deliverance of the people (Meyer 2007). Whatever Judas thought he was doing, however, there were even larger cosmic purposes and forces in play than that of Satan. God himself appeared to have been at work. More precisely, as Luke recounts Peter's day of Pentecost sermon to the crowd: "this man [Jesus], handed over to you according to the definite plan and foreknowledge of God, you crucified and killed by the hands of those outside the law" (Acts 2:23; cf. Acts 3:13). Aside from Judas, then, we have the Jews who clamored for Jesus' crucifixion; we have the collaborating Roman government ("those outside the law"); and we also have God, including the divinity's "definite plan and foreknowledge" (cf. Rom 4:25), not to mention Jesus, who says, "No one takes [my life] from me, but I lay it down of my own accord" (John 10:18; see also Klassen 1996). In the bigger scheme of things, actually, God's plan appears to have included "the Lamb slain from the foundation of the world" (Rev 13:8b, KJV). No wonder, then, that much of Judas' betrayal appears to have been scripted by messianic anticipations in the First Testament (Matt 27:6-10; John 13:18; Acts 1:18-20). Is Judas therefore no more than a pawn in the large cosmic wheel? Perhaps in the end is he no more than a faithful even if profoundly misguided disciple (Rollins 2008: ch. 1).

FIGURE 10.1

Within this long panoramic scene, Judas stands alone in the left half of the composition, clutching his ears as if to refuse the sound of the large torch-bearing crowd that moves into the background in the right half of the image. Whereas most artistic depictions of the arrest of Christ focus on the moment of Judas' betrayal (his profoundly disturbing kiss), this artist is imaginatively constructing Judas' experience of the minutes immediately following his act of betrayal. Judas has betrayed the Son of Man with a kiss, and he is left standing utterly alone as the large, well-armed crowd (Matt 26:47) ushers its prisoner back toward the city to face an illegal trial in the house of the high priest (Mark 14:53-65). The city walls loom in the distance, and as the sun begins to set over the city, it casts most of Judas' figure into shadow, as well as the entire slope behind (and visually surrounding) him. In contrast to the torches that zealously burn in the distance, Judas stands motionless in the foreground as a darkness slowly overtakes him. This is the Judas of Matthew's gospel, who is so profoundly "seized with remorse" that he eventually unburdens himself of the blood money and hangs himself (Matt 27:3-5, NIV).

Judas stands with his back to Jerusalem, the unfaithful city of God, and he faces a vast, parched desert. It is a barren place, lifeless and difficult—an image of the created order made barren under the curse of human sin, a place of thorns and thistles (Gen 3:17-18; cf. fig. 10.5). This is the desert into which Jesus was led by the Spirit to confront the temptations of the devil (Matt 4:1); and here we see Judas overcome and overthrown by that tempter. He stands alone in the desert, clutching his head: he just committed the profoundest betrayal in history and now finds himself in a horrifying kind of barrenness: "It would have been better for that one not to have been born" (Matt 27:24). ✦

We have indications this may have been the case, leading us to our fourth point. Judas, upon realization that he had contributed to the execution of an innocent man (contrary to his original intentions), repented of his deeds—but this may have come too little too late. So deep was his repentance and remorse (Matt 27:3), so it would seem, that when he saw the dastardly effects of his deeds, "he went and hanged himself" (Matt 27:5). Later Christians—if indeed we think, as we have good reason to, that Luke followed rather than preceded Matthew—eliminated any trace of Judas' contrition, suggesting instead that he fell to his death as if strangled by the devil (Halas 1946: 156–57) or as if condemned by the hand of divine retribution (Acts 1:18; see D. MacDonald 2011). Did or did not Judas experience sorrow, shame, and penitence, and if yes, what sort of compunction was this? Or perhaps was it only a self-damning regret, as he may have been like Esau, who "was rejected, for he found no chance to repent, even though he sought the blessing with tears" (Heb 12:17)?

Still, perhaps, and here we come to point five, if the Lukan intimations are correct, Judas was called but "elected to rejection" instead (McGlasson 1991: 146)! This is a hard teaching indeed, as centuries of wrestling with the Calvinist doctrine of double predestination have unequivocally demonstrated. But it is said of Judas that he is as a devil (John 6:70) and that "It would have been better for that one not to have been born" (Mark 14:21), and he is identified, in no uncertain terms, as "the one destined to be lost" (John 17:12), even "the son of perdition" (KJV)! Yet is the traditional teaching correct that suicide (as noted in the Matthean account) signals the epitome of faithlessness and hence "worthiness" of everlasting damnation? Or is there room for understanding self-murder as indicative of the agony of sorrow and despair that leaves no other options than that of turning oneself over to the one who is the final judge over life and death? Even if the "son of perdition" is associated elsewhere with Satan (2 Thess 2:3, 9), we ought not forget that others like Peter had been identified with Satan who nevertheless were not doomed to eternal destruction (Matt 16:23; see Anderson 2005: 66).

Sixth and last for our purposes, in acting of his own accord in betraying Jesus, Judas appears to have opened up to greater goods. Here we are referring not only to the salvation God chose to bring about through the handing over of the Son, but also to the apostleship opened up to Paul through the slot vacated by Judas. Both Judas and Paul are the rejected who are elected in Christ, even if perhaps differently (see Barth 2010b: 477–501). Which raises the question: Is not each one of us also rejected like Judas but elected in Christ? Judas's life has been presented according to these six contradictions not only because six is the number of humanity

(Rev 13:18) but also because Judas' life lays open the incomprehensibility of creation and fall, foregrounds the mystery of sin and death at work in us, and highlights the impenetrability of divine sovereignty and its interface with creaturely freedom.

10.2 Creation and Fall: So What Is the Problem?

Article 3 of the SF focuses primarily on the doctrine of humanity, called theological anthropology in the guild. Even more accurately stated, its primary focus is less on human nature, central to theological anthropology, than on the human condition in its fallen state, alienated from God and anticipating, without intervention otherwise, eternal death. This is in part because renewalist pragmatism is missionally focused (and clarity of the ills that plague humanity also help identify the remedies) rather than concerned about peering into the "secret things [that] belong to the Lord" (Deut 29:29a). Hence the bulk of this chapter will be focused on clarifying the doctrine of humanity in its fallen condition. However, the article does state that "humankind was created good and upright," the only reference to the doctrine of creation in the SF. The three subsections to follow therefore explicate the fortunes of theological anthropology within the broader doctrine of creation, with regard to death and the effects of sin, and in terms of the image of God. This relatively short SF thus opens up the big questions of theology, indeed the perennial questions of human life, so this chapter will be one of the longest of this book.

This is in part because, as previously anticipated at various places in our discussion so far, this is the chapter in which we turn to engage with modern science most directly and extensively. The argument throughout has presumed the importance of renewing Christian theology in light of contemporary realities, including those related to modern scientific advances, and we have had opportunities to do so already, especially with regard to the notion of divine action vis-à-vis miracles and healings (see ch. 8, this volume). Yet the doctrines of creation, fall, and theological anthropology are particularly under pressure when scrutinized in light of contemporary scientific perspectives. Hence any adequate understanding of the present global theological context cannot avoid engaging the most pressing of scientifically induced questions. For that reason, the following discussion correlates each doctrinal locus with a set of theological problems: that of creation with the problem of divine providence, that of death and the fall with the problem of evil, and that of humanity with the problem of sin. Throughout, however, we will focus particularly on matters more germane to renewal understandings, largely because the field of discussion would otherwise stretch out too wide for us to handle adequately

within the scope of a chapter. Our constructive considerations for renewing theological anthropology in the latter half of this chapter will depend
on clearly delineating the relevant challenges and how to navigate them.
Yet our destination nevertheless will refocus on the important renewalist
questions: What then should we do and how then ought we live?

10.2.1 Creation and Modern Science: The Problem of Providence

The SF begins the article affirming "that humankind was created good
and upright." This is clearly based on the seven divine declarations in the
Genesis 1 narrative that creation "was good" (1:4, 10, 12, 18, 21, 25).
Indeed, the final evaluation at the end exclaims: "God saw everything
that he had made, and indeed, *it was very good*" (1:31 [emphasis added]).
Humankind was created good, in part because they were a part of a larger
world that was also good. The question is: What does it mean that the
original creation was good, even very good?

The plainest understanding of an originally good creation begins by
following the basic sense of the Genesis narrative. God created the world
in seven days, with human beings formed on the sixth. The world was
good, in fact an Edenic paradise (Gen 2:8-14). But not too long hence,
Adam and Eve disobeyed God's command, fell from grace, and were
expelled from the Garden. Their disobedience resulted in death (3:3),
in the woman's pain of childbirth and subordination to the male (3:16),
and in the male's toiling a cursed ground (3:17-19). In this traditional
account, Adam's sin not only brings death into the world (cf. Rom 5:12-
14 and 1 Cor 15:21-22) but also disrupts the goodness of the cosmos as a
whole. Whereas previously life, harmony, and beauty were evident, the
fall of humankind introduced death, dissonance, and destruction into the
human, animate, and sentient domains of the world (Terreros 1994; in this
reading, as we shall see later in this chapter, the fall of humanity brings
about not just human death but creaturely death). Hence the garden of
Eden itself is no longer to be found, whether because God is protecting it
from discovery (Gen 3:24) or because it too has decayed under the burden
of sin (cf. Scafi 2006).

Early twentieth-century renewalists thus aligned themselves, by and
large, with conservative evangelicals and similarly minded Christians in
embracing a fairly literal—they would say "biblical"—understanding of
the Genesis creation days that include a young earth and a literal fall from
grace by a historical Adam and Eve (e.g., Kulikovsky 2009). How young
the earth is for these groups varies, although there is a centuries-long tradition that suggests, based on calculations drawn from the genealogies of
the Bible, it is not more than a few thousand years old. In the latter half

of the twentieth century, a movement called scientific creationism arose, a group of mostly Christians (although there are some Muslim young earth creationists as well) dedicated to developing an alternative scientific paradigm not prejudiced by old earth or evolutionary ideas. Many scientific or young earth creationists today are not tied to the genealogical numbers and thus are willing to consider the earth to be even tens of thousands of years old, although this remains far short of the 4.6 billion years promulgated by mainstream science. Still, like many in the global evangelical world (see Roberts 2008: ch. 7), large numbers of renewalists continue to embrace a recent earth understanding of creation and the science that supports such a perspective, believing these to be most faithful to the biblical message (see Smith and Yong 2010: ch. 5).

Yet there have also emerged within evangelical and renewal circles alternative interpretations of the Genesis narrative. Part of the freedom to explore these options has arisen from the recognition that the Christian tradition itself includes interpretive models, such as Augustine's (see Doody, Goldstein, and Paffenroth 2013), which can be viewed as compatible with the modern scientific consensus. Yet the driving forces behind the emergence of alternatives to the young earth position are awareness that the geological and paleontological evidence is suggestive of a much older earth and that astronomical data points to an even older universe. Early in the twentieth century, renewalists (among others) read the notes of the *Scofield Reference Bible* (1909), which presented what has since been called the "gap theory" regarding an indeterminate amount of time between Genesis 1:1 and 1:2, during which the fall of angels occurred, leading an originally good creation to devolve into "a formless void [when] darkness covered the face of the deep" (1:2). Later, the *Dake Annotated Reference Bible* (1963) added to this "gap" the "day-age theory," wherein each of the six creation days was an indefinite period of time. If an old earth was supported in the former gap-theory by positing a distinction between the original (1:1) and re-creative (1:2) works of God, it was promoted through the latter day-age view by making possible a concord between the six days and the emerging understanding of a very old universe. Both of these ideas have had venerable histories within the Christian tradition. In the contemporary evangelical and renewal scene, however, those advocating either or both have little tolerance for any alleged scientific data that allows for macroevolutionary developments (evolution from one species to another), because these are thought to be contrary to the biblical record that God distinctly created each species of animals, including human beings, according to its kind (Gen 1:21, 24, 25). A good number of evangelicals are thus "progressive creationists" in embracing an old earth while insisting on the successive appearance of discrete forms of life by divine intervention (e.g., Ross 1994; Whorton 2005).

Yet over the last few centuries, the tide has been gradually if not inexorably turning against the young earth view in particular, and even more recently against a merely old earth perspective (see Yong 2011c: 134–44). Besides geological and paleontological data, radiometric dating instruments have become more and more precise over time in securing estimates regarding an earth billions of years old. Further, the astronomical and cosmological sciences now show that, based on the speed of light traveling at 186,000 miles per second, we can see back as far as 13 billion years, indicating the universe itself is at least that old. Last but not least, the anthropological and biological sciences, especially the neo-Darwinian synthesis and its notion of evolution via mutation and natural selection, have produced an impressive theory of life's aquatic and terrestrial development. More recently, the genomic sciences' confirmation that human beings share 96 percent or more of their genetic sequences with their closest relatives has bolstered the sense that there is at present nothing with more scientific explanatory power than the theory of evolution. (Note: "theory" here means not just merely hypothetical but, in scientific terms, an overarching account that makes the most sense of data from disparate fields of inquiry.) In the face of these developments, old earth advocates still hold to an ancient cosmos, but reject evolution and the claim that all living creatures descend from a common ancestor (citing, for instance, Acts 17:26). Yet many evangelicals (e.g., Alexander 2001; Falk 2004; Collins 2006; Lamoureux 2009a; McGrath 2011; Poe and Davis 2012) are now convinced evolutionary creationists who believe that God has guided the processes of world history and human development and that this understanding is compatible with the biblical message of salvation and redemption. This would be in opposition to atheistic, materialistic, and purely naturalistic views of evolution on the one side, as well as to young earth creationism, which is deemed less capable of providing a comprehensive and coherent account of modern genetics, anthropology, paleontology, geology, astronomy, and cosmology.

Yet it would also appear that old earth advocates, especially evolutionary creationists, are not off the hook with regard to understanding how such a world can be considered a primordially good creation as affirmed in the book of Genesis. There are at least two interrelated levels of questions. First, there is the issue of natural disasters and the pain and suffering these inflict on human beings. Within a young earth framework, of course, it is the curse of creation related to the human fall that opens the doors to calamities in the natural world. An ancient cosmos, not to mention an evolutionary perspective, however, indicates that mass extinctions are caused by planetary upheavals related to meteorite impacts, among other natural phenomena, and these raise the following dilemma. Either God originally created a world with its constraints and constants that have produced just these kinds of tragedies, in which case we end up with a deistic God who is uncaring or incapable of friendship with human creatures; or God could have or has intervened in human affairs to ameliorate the effects of natural history, but his interventions have nevertheless resulted in massive suffering and death, so he appears to be insufficiently powerful or inadequately good. Either way, God as traditionally understood cannot be defended and is in any case unworthy of worship. This is certainly not to say that young earth or nonevolutionary frameworks are any more successful in resolving the problem of natural evil. It is to say that for conservative evangelicals these traditional questions about the goodness, power, and providence of God appear to be exacerbated outside of a recent creation framework (Rosenhouse 2012).

Second, with regard to the evolutionary process itself, it is clear that there are hundreds if not millions of years of animal predation, disease, parasitism, death, and even the extinction of whole species to be accounted for (Watson 1995). In fact, if the prevailing estimates are right, more than 99.9 percent of all species believed to have evolved are also now extinct (Korsmeyer 1998: 79–82). How can the world be considered good in light of this long history of struggle and death? In particular, how can we understand the prevalence of death in the world long before the emergence of the first human beings, much less the fall of any putative Adam and Eve? And how can we affirm human beings as created good and in the image of God if we are the result of a long evolutionary process? These questions will be taken up in the next two sections.

10.2.2 Evolution and Death: The Problem of Evil

The traditional view, already noted, sees evil as derivative from Adam's historical fall into sin. In the following we shall consider a supplement to this established account, analyze further how the theory of evolution impacts these classical formulations, and explore a range of what might be called evolutionary theodicies—that is, attempts to square the origins and persistence of evil with the existence of a good and powerful God. Most importantly, we will observe how these various theodicies interface with renewal sensibilities and commitments.

Figure 10.2

When Rembrandt took up the subject of the temptation of Adam and Eve, he depicted them not as young people (as was common) nor as idealized Greek heroes or demigods (also common). Instead, he portrayed them as if they were his middle-aged neighbors; he wants us to engage their deep moral crisis in the same terms that we wrestle with our own confusions and conflicted priorities.

In the upper right corner of the composition the serpent is perched in the tree of the knowledge of good and evil. The serpent is presented as a dragon, an intertextual interpretive move derived from reading Genesis 3 alongside Revelation 12, wherein the "ancient serpent . . . the deceiver of the whole world" appears as a great dragon (Rev 12:9; cf. 20:1-3). From its position in the upper corner, the serpent reaches its head forward until its mouth is positioned on the central vertical axis of the composition—and, provocatively, the image is structured so that the entire narrative unfolds from the mouth of the serpent downward along this central axis. The serpent whispers to the woman, challenging her memory and reframing God's declaration of freedom (Gen 2:16-17) into one of prohibition (3:1). Exchanging glances of confusion with the man, she holds the fruit up into the light: this is the deeply questionable focal point around which everything in the composition revolves. As we proceed downward past this point, everything on the central axis falls into dark shadow, alluding to the great sorrows that unfold from this event and plague the most vital God-given human vocations: sorrows in childbearing (3:16) and sorrows in cultivating the earth (3:17-18).

The illuminated fruit might be the visual focus, but the very center of the composition—visually and conceptually—is the darkened womb of the woman. The great horror that Rembrandt attempts to visualize is a devastating historical rupture that casts deathly shadows over all human generations—shadows that haunt the woman's name (given to her after the curses): "The man named his wife Eve, because she was the mother of all living" (3:20). And not only humanity but the earth itself—the womb from which the man and woman were taken (2:7, 3:19)—is cast into this same shadow. When placed within the evolutionary scaffolding of this chapter, this image poignantly articulates difficult questions arising from our persistent sense that things are not as they should be: the operations of evil and death in our lives are somehow invasions, ruptures that curse creation and human history alike. ✦

If there has been any attempt at all to look back to the time prior to Adam's sin in classical theology, the most obvious and immediate recourse is to the serpent in the garden of Eden, which has always been associated with the "great dragon . . . who is called the Devil and Satan" (Rev 12:9; cf. Rev 20:2). The serpent who deceived Eve (2 Cor 11:3) is thus also connected with the primordial fall of Satan from heaven, taking a third of the angels with him (Luke 10:18; Rev 12:3-4). The origins of evil in this account are traced back to the freedom given to nondivine but yet nonterrestrial or nonmaterial creatures (Boyd 2001). However, even if this locates the source of Adam and Eve's deception, it is less helpful clarifying from whence Satan, if a creature of God then himself originally good, in turn conceived of the idea of rebellion against God. The mythological explications pointing to pride (Isa 14:9-21; Ezek 28:12-19) are not clearly connected to the Satan figure, not to mention that such notions perhaps have more to do with how ancient Jews understood themselves as refracted through the mirror of their pagan oppressors than with articulating foundational explanations regarding the origins of evil (see Reed 2005). While scientifically informed moderns also have difficulty accepting these notions, renewalists are often more inclined toward these explanations for obvious reasons connected to their supernaturalistic sensibilities. Yet if the root of the matter has to do with creaturely freedom, do we need to look beyond the evil wrought by human agents?

But the question pressed by modern science concerns what appear to be the evil of death and species extinction long before the arrival of Adam and Eve. Strictly speaking, an evolutionary account does not need a theodicy. There is need to acknowledge neither God nor "evil," because the evolutionary process is what it is, bringing with it life that is good but also death apart from which life would not be (Anders 1994). Some theologians have followed suit, saying that there is neither a historical Adam and Eve nor a primordial fall from grace (Williams 2001). Instead, nature is as it is, and original sin is no more or less than the sociobiological matrix responsible for the evolution of self-conscious human beings in all of their tragedy but, intertwined with that, also all of their capacity to experience truth, goodness, and beauty, as well as their opposites.

Others might be more inclined to a more concordist explication of the human experience of pain, suffering, and evil with the biblical witness. Going down this road, the self-preservation inherent in the process of natural selection is correlated with the original selfishness that alienates creatures from one another and from God (Domning 2006) and that comes to moral consciousness as sin in human beings (Tennant 1902). More abstractly and cosmologically, the second law of thermodynamics has also been correlated with the processes of entropy (the natural tendency of things to fall into disorder), equilibrium, and, for sentient creatures, death (see King 1970). Understood theologically, this is seen as the best of all possible worlds (Southgate 2008). The world is rightly declared to be good in the sense that an evolutionary creation has given rise to the values human beings hold. Yet the extensive death found in the evolutionary process is intrinsic to the emergence and expansion of life itself.

Still, a number of other explicit theodicy strategies have emerged, each of which presents important elements for any viable theology of creation in the twenty-first century. One approach draws from the symbol of the primordial chaos of the Bible (Niditch 1985; Anderson 1987; Levenson 1988; Warren 2012), perhaps a spiritually derivative but otherwise inexplicable disorder out of which God ordered the creation, which he has since sought to resist and contain. This has also been related historically to the fall of angels motif, particularly in terms of its central symbol of the Leviathan or ancient dragon creature, but it ultimately trades more on impersonal than personified symbolism. There is a long even if minor theological tradition, most recently promulgated by process theologians

(Korsmeyer 1998; Keller 2003; cf. Williams 1927), that has observed how the primordial chaos has been opposed to, if not even constrained by, God's creative and providential activity. Beyond connections to process theology, this move has the benefit of providing symbolic, analogical, and metaphysical bridge points for the contemporary theology and science discussion, particularly with regard to exploring the relevance of chaos theory for theological considerations (Huchingson 2001; Bonting 2005). In this view, God works persuasively to adjust initial conditions of dynamical systems in order to mitigate outcomes that will negatively impact human life (which evolves later). The question here, in process, relational, or any other theological perspective that may presume a kind of ontological notion of "chaos" distinct from the divine, is whether God can ultimately bring about God's preferred results or ends.

Many evolutionary theodicies, as observable above, dispense with a historical Adam. As we shall see momentarily, evangelicals are reluctant to demythologize Adam and Eve and dismiss a historical fall into sin. Nineteenth-century Christian geologists responded to Darwin's theory about the descent of humanity by considering whether the Adamic fall, understood in evolutionary perspective, could have had retroactive effects, and this notion has recently been retrieved by evangelicals as well (Dembski 2009). Parallels have historically been drawn to the benefits of the cross of Christ having similar application backward in historical time. If such conceptions include material or efficient causal connections (between Adam's fall and the preceding natural history of the world) or are set within a strong doctrine of divine determinism (that suggests God's creation thereby is purposefully defective), as is often the case in at least Reformed evangelical circles, their advantages may be undermined. A viable historical fall from grace will need to show how death and extinction anticipate the emergence of Adam without depending on any theory of retroactive causality or minimizing the goodness of creation.

From a theological and renewal point of view, the most promising theodicies are less those that attempt to account for the origins of evil (and pain, suffering, and death) than those that reinterpret existing evil in light of the Christian drama of redemption. The most obvious place to begin is the incarnation and passion of Christ, which reveals a God not aloof from the suffering of the world but in solidarity with it. From this, an approach emerges that foregrounds, for instance, the Lutheran theology of the cross, so God is to be found, mysteriously and hidden, in the suffering, pain, and death of the creation's evolutionary processes (Murphy 2003; see also section 3.3). On the eschatological side of the redemption story, the suffering of the world will be transformed by God's future renewal of all things, itself foreshadowed in the resurrection of Jesus from the dead (Kropf 1984). There might appear to be evolutionary progress, but this is not evident within the natural order of things; it is only visible to the eyes of faith, inspired by the resurrection of the Son and the pentecostal outpouring of the Spirit.

It should be noted here that what the popular imagination conceives as horrendous pain and suffering, the biological and ecological sciences view as a marvelous process of life coming from death. In fact, death is inherent to life as we know it, even as creatures who come from the dust of the ground return to that same ground to renew the earth and give life to the next generation. The finitude of creation is not necessarily evil in this perspective. Creation's finite resources mean that creatures need to be "recycled" in some way (Heinrich 2012). Even biblically, God appears to have intended a natural world that produces life out of death, red in tooth and claw, to use this well-known saying (see Job 38-41; cf. Osborn 2014). Jesus himself said, "Unless a grain of wheat falls into the earth and dies, it remains just a single grain; but if it dies, it bears much fruit" (John 12:24). Might it be that the husks of wheat must die, so the seeds of life can be released for another season? Is it possible in this perspective to understand death not merely in negative terms but as always in anticipation of life to come? Rather than instrumentalizing any living creature, however, perhaps this helps us to value the particularity of each life in its own sphere. More precisely, from a theological perspective, it may open up venues for thinking about the life, death, and resurrection of Jesus as transforming and redeeming death once-and-for-all toward eternal life. We will develop these ideas later in this chapter.

The preceding has taken up the historic problem of evil not over its panoramic scope but as focused on the doctrine of creation unfolded within a modern scientific and evolutionary horizon. Even within this scheme of things, the discussion is exceedingly wide and horribly shallow. Our objective, however, is not to cover exhaustively the existing landscape but to set out the basic parameters for a constructive theology of creation in the twenty-first-century context.

Renewalists have only recently begun to engage the discussions of both theology of creation and the theology and science conversation (Yong 2009; Smith and Yong 2010). Even if it turns out that evolution via common descent is false, the problem of evil will not go away. But if anything like the current evolutionary hypothesis holds forth going forward, any efforts to renew the Christian doctrine of creation in the third millennium will need to provide coherent, if not convincing, accounts of the prevalence of suffering and death before the appearance of human beings and for their resolution. Central to both will be how to understand Adam, the image of God, and human uniqueness in biblical perspective, subjects to which we now turn.

10.2.3 The Imago Dei and the Fall: The Problem of Sin

There is, again, much ground to cover here. We will move rapidly from the question of when the human image of God appeared, to understanding it, especially vis-à-vis the notion of original sin. We will also work to consider interfaces, real and potential, with renewal views.

The main question that the evolutionary sciences raise for traditional theological anthropology is that regarding human uniqueness in relationship to the animal kingdom. In the young earth and progressive creationist depictions, there is no blurring of human and higher animal identities: God created the former de novo (uniquely and separately) and replete with the spiritual, psychical, intellectual, and moral capacities lacking in the latter. This is in part why acknowledgment of the distinctiveness of the historical Adam and Eve is important—to preserve human dignity and distinctiveness (Collins 2011: ch. 4).

Yet human uniqueness is by no means presumed to be compromised within an evolutionary framework. Official Roman Catholic teaching, for instance, is willing to consider human evolution, so long as human souls, the core of the image of God, are held (on the basis of faith) to be "immediately created by God" and the doctrine of polygenism—the theory asserting that the present human species derives from different genetic lineages—is rejected in favor of a monogenetic unity of all humanity from a primordial couple (Humani Generis §§36–37, in Cotter 1952: 41). The rationale for at least the latter is that polygenesis fails to square with the biblical pronouncements regarding both Adamic ancestorship (Acts 17:26) and the inevitability of death for all under Adam. Scientifically, however, anthropologists and paleontologists disagree about when and where modern humans are distinguishable from their ancestors and also about whether a primordial couple or many of them were involved. Thus it is too much to expect theological agreement about matters related to this heretofore unresolved scientific matter. Some evangelical scientist-theologians are comfortable with affirming that at a particular time in evolutionary history, God visited a couple or even small group of perhaps Neolithic farmers and entered into a covenantal relationship with them then (Pearce 1987; D. Alexander 2008: ch. 10). Other evangelical scientist-theologians think that any efforts to render modern science concordant with a more or less literal interpretation of the first few chapters of Genesis misses and thereby obfuscates the important theological points being made in the biblical text (e.g., Lamoureux 2009b). Rather, the Genesis narratives are literary devices intended by God to teach important but nonscientific truths, albeit accommodated to specific cultural assumptions at various points in time. If so, there is no need to posit either a historical Adam or fall from grace, as these are instead about all people caught in the grip of sinfulness and in need of redemption. Yet all evangelical scholars, including those who accept evolutionary creationism, affirm human uniqueness from animals.

FIGURE 10.3   FIGURE 10.4

The ways we depict other people carry extraordinary significance, not only for how we understand the persons pictured but also for how we understand what it means to be a human person per se. Portraits are (intentionally or not) sites in which we explore and negotiate our understanding of humanness in the faces of another. In theological terms, we might say that images of people are always in some sense begging questions about the image of God in people.

These two portraits are poignant and complicated examples. On the left is an example of Fayum mummy portraiture—an ancient Greco-Egyptian tradition in which strikingly naturalistic painted portraits were used as burial masks (installed over the faces of mummies). Evidence suggests that such portraits (nearly one thousand are still extant) were usually painted from observation of living persons, although made for the event of their deaths. Thus the lifelikeness of this image was from the beginning haunted by the mortality of the woman pictured. And ultimately this is true of all human images: we see the image of the immortal God in the faces of those mortal others who are inexorably passing away. The image on the right is attributed to a noted Scottish abolitionist, who went on to become principal painter to the king of England. This portrait probably depicts Ignatius Sancho (ca. 1729–1780), a man born into slavery who was eventually emancipated and became a powerful voice against the cruelties of slavery. After teaching himself to read and write, Sancho became an eloquent poet, playwright, actor, composer, and epistler (his posthumously published letters would be particularly influential in the abolitionist cause). In 1773, he and his wife opened a grocery shop, making him an independent male householder and thus legally qualifying him as the first black man to vote in British parliamentary elections, which he did in both 1774 and 1780.

It is worth noting that although we might see both images as conveying the beauty and dignity of two individuals, these also serve as memorials to the profoundly dysfunctional notions of otherness that surely plagued the lives of both individuals. Throughout large portions of human history neither of these persons—a woman on the one hand and a black man on the other—would have been accorded the dignity and standing of being fully human (with rights as such). There is thus a palpable, lamentable violence that haunts these images of male and female persons made in the image of God (cf. Gen 1:27). ✦

What then constitutes the image of God? Renewalists have long presumed a tripartite anthropological constitution according to the Pauline reference to "spirit and soul and body" (1 Thess 5:23), alongside other biblical extrapolations. They have been influenced in this regard by the best-selling works of authors like Watchman Nee (1903–1972), including his tripartite understanding of the human person made in the image of God (see Wu 2012). In today's scientifically informed climate, however, such triadic conceptualizations have few advocates, understandably so, because science has few, if any, resources to investigate the spiritual domain. Even more traditional dualist construals—of human beings as constituted by minds/souls and bodies—are in the minority (e.g., Moreland and Rae

2000), taking a backseat to holist perspectives that see each of these dimensions as intertwined with rather than disparate from the other. The prevailing argument is that contemporary biological, psychological, and neuroscientific models of the human person are convergent more with the body–soul unity of the ancient Hebrews than with dualist conceptions either received from the legacy of neoplatonism or developed during the modern period (e.g., Green 2004, 2008).

Interestingly, aspects of the traditional notion of the image of God have also been corrected in the last few generations. Although Genesis clearly indicates that God created both male and female in his image (1:27), the long legacy of Aristotelian philosophy combined with some New Testament passages (e.g., 1 Cor 11:7-7; 1 Tim 2:13-14) perpetuated the view of female inferiority (see Becking and Hennecke 2010). This has been corrected by feminist scholarship (Graff 1995; Gonzalez 2007; Stephenson 2012: part 2), although in some cases such corrections have devolved into an ideology of misandry (Young and Nathanson 2010). Similarly, while never elevated to any authoritative level, the view of human beings as upright, whole, intelligent, and able-bodied has marginalized the bent over, intellectually impaired, and disabled from consideration as reflecting the full image of God (Yong 2007: ch. 2). As already noted (section 8.2.3), such ableist presumptions also have been challenged and persist less widely. Shifting from the arena of popular opinion to aspects of early modern scientific developments, however, even up through the late nineteenth and early twentieth centuries, polygenist ideas about multiple lineages for premodern and modern humans were deployed to defend racist attitudes and perspectives, even to the point of justifying slavery (Livingstone 2008; Brown 2010). Although the scientific issue of monogenism or polygenism is unresolved, racism ought to be rejected on theological terms (Teel 2010). Last but not least, the contemporary global conversation is challenging the notion of human individualism as too narrowly conscripted by Western ideas of the self. Instead of the Cartesian "I think, therefore I am," those from the global south are responding with a more communal understanding of the image of God: "we are, therefore I am" (Ng'weshemi 2002: 14). Yet human community is not merely anthropocentric but also environmentally, terrestrially, and cosmically situated and defined (Kamalu 1998; Ranger 2007; Paper 2007).

These considerations suggest that our understanding of the image of God is intertwoven at least in part with what we think sin is. To put it crassly, if sin is associated with femaleness, impairments, and racial or ethnic phenotypes, then the image of God is presumed to be male, able-bodied, and Caucasian. Of course, in reality, things are never said quite that simply. Instead, the nature of sin is complex, multidimensional, even mysterious (Braaten and Jenson 2000), "humanity's unnatural nature" (Schwarz 1977: 205), as one commentator put it. Yet its primordiality, pervasiveness, and universality have led to its identification not merely as sin but as *original sin* (Wiley 2002). But what, then, is original sin?

Irenaeus suggested that the fall distorted but did not efface the image of God in humanity, thus allowing human beings to grow into the moral likeness of God, a process that traverses the full scope of the world's history, albeit one that is also recapitulated in the life, death, and resurrection of Christ. Augustine was less sanguine about humankind's moral journey toward the divine image, fundamentally tarnished as it was by the concupiscence transmitted to each soul conceived through the lustful act of sexual intercourse. While Augustine's ideas linking original sin with concupiscence have largely been abandoned, the contemporary science of genetics suggests that our genes may have much more to do with perpetuating sinful dispositions and passing on the effects of sin than we might want to admit (Peters 1994: ch. 10). Regardless of the possible scientific correlations, that human sin is constituted by universal propensities suggests that it thoroughly infects the human condition (Cherbonnier 1955).

The preceding already suggest that original sin is less an individual reality than a relational, social, and even structural one (Ryan 1998; Nelson 2009). As has been variously intimated in previous chapters, sin exists not only radically in human hearts but also pervasively in lives, between lives, in social structures. In effect, sin is generative of the constant struggle (Isasi-Díaz 1993; Fernandez 1994) in and amid which humans live, move, and have their being. A relational understanding of sin emphasizes its self-obsessiveness to the point of either disregard for or, more damagingly, exploitation of others (Jenson 2006). Others have also conceptualized sin as the promulgation of violence (Suchocki 1994), perhaps perpetuated and aggravated by a mimetic collective mechanism operative in human evolution (Schwager 2006). If there is violence, then there are perpetrators, but there are then also victims, so the universality of sin calls attention to the primordial victimhood by which every single human being—as infant, child, and adult—is wounded, if not scarred (Ormerod 2007: 79–84; cf. Park 1993; Park and Nelson 2001). From this perspective, sin becomes nothing less than a "cosmic terrorist" (Gaventa 2007: 130), a destructive force that overpowers, oppresses, victimizes, and haunts the human condition. It is indeed at the roots of what we might call a coercive "kingdom of evil" that resists the impending reign of God.

While the reality of sin is everywhere open to empirical confirmation (even in global context; see Iloanusi 1984; Boureux and Theobald 2004), theologically sin is only understood, even if opaquely, in the light of the Christ event. Irenaeus indicated that only in Christ can we see the full image and likeness of God (Steenberg 2009: ch. 1), and more recently, Karl Barth (1956) has insisted that we can know the truth about authentic human nature only in Christ, not the other way around. Following this christological key, perhaps it is more appropriate to distinguish, as did the early church fathers, between a fallen human nature, which Christ assumed, and a sinful or sinfully predisposed human will, which Christ did not exercise (McFarland 2010). The point of God's saving work in Christ and the Spirit is to restore human creatures, so they grow into the likeness of Christ, who is "the image of the invisible God" (Col 1:15; cf. 2 Cor 4:4; Rom 8:29; see also Maloney 1973). Such a christological understanding also opens up to a trinitarian or relational anthropology (Shults 2003, Powell 2003). Human beings are not only thinkers (believing creatures) but also lovers (hence fundamentally relational) and hopers (anticipators of something more) (Kelsey 2009). Sin in turn distorts our noetic, relational, and affective capacities. As shall be developed later in this chapter, God's work in Christ and the Spirit is to renew human minds, reconcile human hearts, and reorient human hopes and desires in anticipation of the immanent divine reign that is nevertheless yet to come.

10.3 The Groaning of the Spirit: Romanizing Creation and Fall

It is impossible to provide an exhaustive commentary of the richness of Paul's Letter to the Romans. Our very selective reading will focus on gleaning insights related to the doctrinal themes of this chapter: creation, the fall, and theological anthropology. Yet even such a partial reading is both appropriate and holds promise of paying great dividends, because this epistle is where Paul's theological vision is most comprehensively laid out. As will be shown, Romans provides a trinitarian, pneumatological, and eschatological set of lenses to guide our considerations on these important cosmic matters. The following thus seeks to build a scriptural bridge between the broader contextual parameters sketched in the preceding discussion and the constructive reflections to follow. While there are many ways to approach this letter (e.g., Yong 2012: ch. 7), for the sake of following Paul's own argument as carefully as possible, we will commence where he does.

Almost at the very beginning of this letter, we are introduced to the created world as revelatory of God's "eternal power and divine nature" (Rom 1:20). Rather than then proceeding to developing a theology of creation, however, this is merely a springboard into a prolonged argument that human beings are without excuse (1:20; 2:1). Even with the clear knowledge of God pronounced in creation, "they did not honour him as God or give thanks to him, but they became futile in their thinking, and their senseless minds were darkened" (1:21). From here, Paul goes on to recount humanity's persistent depravity, wickedness, and sinfulness, all of which justify the visitation of God's wrath. Jews are no less exempt from God's judgment, because they have the law (in contrast to Gentiles) but yet have also broken it (2:17-29). Thus "all, both Jews and Greeks, are under the power of sin" (3:9), and "[t]here is no one who is righteous, not even one" (3:10). Humanity may not even be capable of enjoying God's goodness as revealed in the creation: "Claiming to be wise, they became fools; and they exchanged the glory of the immortal God for images resembling a mortal human being or birds or four-footed animals or reptiles" (1:22-23).

Any minimization of the dire condition of human sinfulness will lack similar appreciation for God's salvific response provided in Christ. God's answer to a species whose divine image has been distorted to the point of unrecognizability is to call out for himself a people—Israel, headed by Abraham (Rom 4)—that would, "hoping against hope" (4:18), believe in God's capacity to save a world condemned by its own evil. As Abraham believed in one "who gives life to the dead and calls into existence the things that do not exist" (4:17), even to the point of receiving life both from "his own body, which was already as good as dead" and from that of his barren wife (4:19), so also did this anticipate God's raising Jesus from the dead. The latter was "handed over to death for our trespasses and was raised for our justification" (4:25). Earlier, Paul had referenced, as if in passing, the Spirit as the power of divine resurrection (1:4), and he later makes explicit this connection: "If the Spirit of him who raised Jesus from the dead dwells in you, he who raised Christ from the dead will give life to your mortal bodies also through his Spirit that dwells in you" (8:11).

The point is that even when humanity was weak and ungodly (Rom 5:6), sinners (5:8), and enemies of and hostile to God (5:10), Christ died for them. And it is at this point that Paul broaches the discussion of Adam and Christ. Augustine's Vulgate-influenced reading of 5:12—"just as sin came into the world through one man, and death came through sin, and so death spread to all, *in quo omnes peccaverunt* (in whom all have sinned)" (cited in Ormerod 2007: 70)—suggested to him that all die, because *all have sinned in Adam*. It is but a short step from here to seeing death entering the world as a whole, not only for humans but also for animals, through Adam. Yet a more accurate translation of the extant Greek manuscripts would be: "so death spread to all because all have sinned." This explicitly connects human

death with human sin and leaves aside the death of animals, not to mention plant and bacterial death—each explicable on its own terms (Munday
1992)—which predate humanity (Bruner 1966). It is also consistent with
the opening chapter of Romans, which indicates that humanity's "bondage
to sin was not simply a result of a single act of Adam but a collective suppressing of the truth by the human race" (Collins 2003: 481).

Surely, taken on its own and in isolation from the rest of the epistle,
the author of Romans 5 can be assumed to presume a historical Adam
through whom sin and death came into the world and spread at least to all
other human beings. So if humans existed before Adam, then their death
would be impossible according to this reading. Alternatively, of course,
if taken historically, Adam (and Eve) could have been the first of their
kind, and in that sense, death before them would have struck prehominids
instead. In any case, Paul is here consistent with apocalyptic literature
in early Judaism that connects death with Adam's transgression. Yet it
should also be mentioned that Jewish wisdom literature from this period
presumes mortality to be a built-in feature of creaturely finitude uncon-
nected to Adam's fall (Levison 1988), and this opens up another perspective consistent with the evolutionary hypothesis.

But what if we read Romans 5 christologically rather than as foregrounding a clear teaching about the human fall into sin? If so, then we
note that Paul says Adam "is a type of the one who was to come" (5:14),
pointing to Christ. Even if it does not exclude historical literalness, typological thinking does not require such. Read thus, this text then explains
not the whence of death but its universal hold on humanity. Paul is thereby
to be understood as using the conceptual resources available to him to
make this point (Enns 2012: part 2). In that sense, there is an Adamic
representation of, even headship over, all others (Blocher 1997), and the
race is unified not necessarily biologically—the question of monogenism
or polygenism being left open—but with regard to sinfulness and death,
both in anticipation of Christ, especially his resurrection. Adam anticipates
sinful humanity, even sinful Israel (Barth 1956). More precisely, in the
Romans context, Adamic humankind in Christ overcomes the fragmentation, fracturedness, and alienation between Jews and Gentiles (Rom 9–11;
see also van Kooten 2008 and the section 7.3 discussion of Jew and Gentiles in Ephesians). And this reconciliation is universally available, because,
as in the former case, all humanity is spiritually in solidarity with but not
carnally related to the second Adam (Kasujja 1986: 194–95).

And that is precisely the good news: the unity of the race condemned
under Adam also allows for its salvation under Christ. Four times in this
passage we are told that as potent as was Adam's sin in spreading the power

of death, "much more" (Rom 5:9, 10, 15, 17) effective is the salvation, reconciliation, grace, justification, and life available through Christ. More to the point, the causality described by Paul here is neither biological nor historical, rather it is representative:

> just as one man's trespass led to condemnation for all, so one man's act of righteousness leads to justification and life for all. For just as by the one man's disobedience the many were made sinners, so by the one man's obedience the many will be made righteous. But law came in, with the result that the trespass multiplied; but where sin increased, grace abounded all the more, so that, just as sin exercised dominion in death, so grace might also exercise dominion through justification leading to eternal life through Jesus Christ our Lord. (Rom 5:18-21)

The question is: Can Adam be a representative figure without being literally the first human being? Saint Paul's parallel references toward the end of his first Corinthian letter suggests *yes*. There he speaks specifically about the "first man, Adam" and Jesus as the "last Adam" (1 Cor 15:45). Clearly Christ is not the last human, which suggests there is no need to think of the first Adam as the initial *Homo sapiens* either (I owe this point to conversations with one of my students, Dick Fischer). If so, then Adam and his type (Rom 5:14) tell us not about the first or last human being but about the fallen human condition and God's saving response. We shall see later if and how such representation thinking suggests a way forward for a constructive consideration of such matters in an evolutionary framework while also addressing the question of death before Adam.

Romans 5 provides the pivot of the salvation history narrative of the triune God, which involves not only the resurrection life of Christ but also the love of God "poured into our hearts through the Holy Spirit that has been given to us" (5:5). Moving forward with Paul, the eternal life obtained in Christ is now also available to all through the Spirit. Yes, human beings continue to die in Adam; but as Christ also tasted death and triumphed over it, it is also now possible to be "buried with him by baptism into death, so that, just as Christ was raised from the dead by the glory of the Father, so we too might walk in newness of life" (6:4). And yes, human beings will continue to struggle with sin, but they will no longer be slaves of sin (6:15–7:25). Rather, "we are discharged from the law, dead to that which held us captive, so that we are slaves not under the old written code but in the new life of the Spirit" (7:6).

All of this leads to the crescendo of Pauline theology and pneumatology, which is Romans 8 (see Wood 1963). Yet the pneumatological themes of this chapter are thoroughly woven in with the soteriological, the eschatological, and the cosmological. The Spirit has delivered frail and fallen human beings from the bondage of the law, the curse of death, and the weakness of the sin nature, thereby reconciling humanity to God (8:1-17). The Spirit also inspires human groaning with the creation in anticipation of its full and glorious redemption (8:18-25). And last but not least, the Spirit "helps us in our weakness; for we do not know how to pray as we ought, but that very Spirit intercedes with sighs too deep for words. And God, who searches the heart, knows what is the mind of the Spirit, because the Spirit intercedes for the saints according to the will of God" (8:26-27). The centrality of the work of the Spirit in this culminating section on God's saving work invites a rereading of the first part of the letter in this light (see Cimpean 2004). A few comments are in order from this perspective.

First, Paul refers to the people of God as those "who have the first fruits of the Spirit" (Rom 8:23; cf. 2 Cor 5:5; Eph 1:13b). We are also those who groan with the creation. Hence, the Spirit is not only in human hearts (Rom 5:5) but also in "radical solidarity with fallen creation" (Szypula 2007: 362). Creation is not neutral, as if merely "the natural world" (Jackson 2010). It is fallen and laden with sin, even if it is not itself sinful. But it continues to be the "place" that is sustained by the wind, breath, and Spirit of God (cf. Gen 1:2). Similarly, regardless of how far humanity has fallen—and the depth of such a fall should not be minimized in light of the apostle's description in the first three chapters of this missive— the presence of the Spirit is never far, albeit always groaning through vessels that allow such. What begins apocalyptically (focused on sin and its destructive effects) opens up to the resourcefulness of God's redemptive power, beauty, and glory, all captured in Romans 8 (see Johnson 1989). Meaningful human life is eschatologically possible now, even if it is marked by stammering tongues, groans, and cries in the Spirit in anticipation of the full salvation of God to come.

Second, Paul also indicates that "creation was subjected to futility, not of its own will but by the will of the one who subjected it" (Rom 8:20). This assertion about creation "subjected to futility" is consonant with at least one side of the evolutionary process as described by modern science (see Horrell, Hunt, and Southgate 2010: 134–36). However, curiously from another side, the futility of creation can be seen both as wondrously life-giving (from a biological and ecological perspective, as previously discussed) even as it also is ordained at least in some respects by God. Yet such ordination is carried out "in hope, that the creation itself will be set free from its bondage to decay and will obtain the freedom of the glory of the children of God" (8:20b-21). There is a sense that redemption is not just to a pre-fall state. Rather, in line with Irenaeus' theological vision of Christ's recapitulating work, "Creation will gain more in the new age than it lost due to the fall of Adam," as befitting the "much more" of Christ's life-giving work compared to Adam's death-dealing sin (Hahne 2006: 208). We will have to see in the final part of this chapter how the futility of creation is on the one hand the result of human sin but on the other hand permitted of God in hope.

Third, consistent with the apocalyptic mentality of first-century Judaism, death is related in this letter both to legal, penal, and forensic matters, and to cosmic forces and realities. Romans 5 and 8 describe the overcoming of both aspects of the power of death, so in the end there is no dualism between physical/legal and spiritual/cosmic death (de Boer 1988). In both cases, the cross and resurrection of Christ in the power of the Spirit are the final answer, indeed not only as the resolution to the problem but as pointing to the goal of creation. The creation and all its creatures, human beings included, are thus caught up in this cosmic renewal of the triune God.

We have space only to make one last point before moving on. The justifying, sanctifying, and redeeming work of God so central to the Letter to the Romans not only has cosmic implications, as we have now seen, but is also eminently practical. Thus Paul turns in the final third of the epistle to urge: "I appeal to you therefore, brothers and sisters, by the mercies of God, to present your bodies as a living sacrifice, holy and acceptable to God, which is your spiritual worship. Do not be conformed to this world, but be transformed by the renewing of your minds, so that you may discern what is the will of God—what is good and acceptable and perfect" (12:1-2). The redemption of the world is therefore interconnected with the renewing of our minds. Such creaturely renewal will inspire loving behavior (12:9-21; 13:8-14), has political relevance (13:1-7), and looks out for those who are weaker (ch. 14). Salvation is coming, in fact, "is nearer to us now than when we became believers" (13:11). Creation itself, if not also human nature, anticipates the eschatological transformation into the image and likeness of Christ. Are human hearts so incorrigible that they persist in resembling "birds or four-footed animals or reptiles" (1:23) instead?

10.4 Renewing the Cosmos: A Trinitarian Theology of Creation, Cross, and Culmination

We have covered much ground in this chapter and have to pull many threads together. In line with the overall thrusts of the renewal theology being developed in this volume, a trinitarian—by which is meant christological, pneumatological, and eschatological—theology of creation and fall is articulated that responds to the major questions raised by the preceding. Whole chapters, even volumes, can and ought to be written on almost each paragraph to come. Consider this as no more than a sketch of what a coherent theology of creation and of the human problem in the global context of twenty-first-century science ought to address. We begin with some general thoughts on how to understand theology in relationship to science.

FIGURE 10.5   FIGURE 10.6

In the curses of Genesis 3, human sorrows are joined to the groaning of the earth: "Cursed is the ground because of you; in toil you shall eat of it all the days of your life; thorns and thistles it shall bring forth for you" (Gen 3:17-18). The thorns and thistles in Laura Lasworth's painting (fig. 10.5) allude to both sides of this cursedness. On the one hand, they connote the harshness and scarcity of an arid landscape—they are a kind of counterimage to the tree of life in the garden-temple of Eden. On the other hand, these thistles are also emblems of human fruitlessness, both in Adam and in Israel (note the twelve stems). Although appointed by God to be "a luxuriant vine" (Hos 10:1; Ps 80:7-19; Jer 2:21), Israel deadened and turned sour, and the curse recapitulated: "Thorn and thistle shall grow up on their [idolatrous] altars" (Hos 10:8).

In the center of these thistles—in fact in the center of the composition—appears a single white lily, a symbol of purity and peace often associated with the annunciation of Christ's incarnation. As the thistles vocalize the groaning of creation and humanity, Christ appears in their midst "as a lily among brambles" (Song 2:2) inaugurating new life in and for both (cf. fig. 9.4). We must notice that (profoundly) there is only one vase: the lily appears in the center of human history in the same bloody water as the thistles—suggestive of the blood of human violence crying out from the ground (Gen 4:10) as well as the "blood mingled with water" that flowed from Jesus' side (John 19:34). We might also notice that a strange double light casts shadowy images across a sky-blue background. The christological imagery of the vase is thus cast into eschatological dimension, wherein we glimpse (albeit in shadows) a reality in which blood is separated from water and in which thistles become animated with a different kind of life.

In the end, we might posit that the Christology of this image (the vase) and its eschatology (the shadows) presuppose and demand a pneumatology (the light that unites them). The light in this painting, by which we see the image of Christ in history and by which that history is cast toward a redemptive future, might be understood (theologically and iconographically) as the work of the Spirit.

Challenge to the reader: with all of this in mind, compare the visual logic of Lasworth's painting with that of Aitchison's Crucifixion (fig. 10.6). ✦

There are a number of standard options for if and how to relate theology and science. One classic response, dominant in many popular circles, is that these are antithetical to one another (see Giberson 1993). Young earth creationism implies such "warfare," as do naturalistic, materialistic, and atheistic scientific voices. The former seems hard-pressed to provide models of science acceptable to the scientific establishment, while the latter are philosophical and ideological extrapolations rather than legitimate scientific conclusions. Evangelicals in general thus either are prone to suggest that theology and science are independent domains of knowledge or that they are somehow convergent with or complementary to one another (Carlson 2004). The importance of dialogue cannot be understated, and there are many viable models about how to proceed (Van Huyssteen and Gregersen 1998; Peters and Hewlett 2003; Stenmark 2004). This is particularly true in global context, wherein what counts as "theology" or "religion" and as "science" is rather a bit broader than how these are understood in the Western Hemisphere (Brooke and Numbers 2011).

My own view is to accept a present complementarity between theology and science as mutually illuminating (e.g., Padgett 2003), albeit from distinctive perspectives, and to anticipate an ultimate (eschatological) convergence that reveals a unified narrative of the whole (see Yong 2011c). God's two books—of Scripture and of nature (see Berry 2003)—cannot be finally contradictory, so any appearances of conflict are the results of either mistaken scriptural interpretations, or incomplete scientific data or understanding, or both. Sure, the scientific data can be interpreted variously, including atheistically (e.g., Stenger 2011), but such can also be approached in a theological vein. The key from a renewal perspective is to develop a trinitarian account, one that is not only christological but also robustly pneumatological. Hence what emerges will be resolutely theological—a theology of nature or a theology of creation—rather than pretending to be scientific. Yet theological reflections in our time must also be aware of and about to account for rather than ignore the range of plausible hypotheses promulgated by mainstream science (Clayton 1989).

Of course, what science says is more contested than what its "mainstream" might have us believe. As I am not a scientist, I will not attempt here to adjudicate matters that in the long run only science can resolve. I do think that even among evangelicals the big bang cosmology is largely uncontested, even if there is less agreement on its significance; from this, for instance, there is a much wider range of opinions among evangelicals regarding the evolutionary account of natural history and human origins. Yet as evangelicals are increasingly considering the compatibility of the evolutionary thesis with Christian faith (see Yong 2011c: ch. 5), renewal Christians ought to at least explore what it means to live faithfully in a world where we otherwise enjoy the many medical, electronic, technological, transportation, communicative, and other benefits of modern science.

A pneumatological approach will treat the many sciences as different voices that bear witness to the truth of God's creation, even if such tongues—as all utterances—demand interpretation, discernment, and critical assessment. But science, framed by questions and curiosity, is driven as much by its own internal criticisms, even as it is also open, in principle, to any hard questions theologians can generate. Hence patient and learned dialogue is in order. The following both presumes and attempts to illustrate this perspective vis-à-vis, in order, theological anthropology and the doctrines of the fall and creation.

Our understanding of humanity is refracted through the salvation historical narrative of the biblical revelation. What we can say is that as created in the image of God, human beings are male and female (Gen 1:27—which has normative implications for understanding human sexuality, albeit we have neither time nor space for this detour), and hence intrinsically social creatures. Further, as formed "from the dust of the ground" (Gen 2:7a), human beings are also essentially embodied and environmentally, terrestrially, and cosmically constituted (see also Simkins 1994). Last but not least, as recipients of the divine breath (Gen 2:7b), human beings are also essentially and spiritually related to God (Murphy 2006), although how uniquely so compared with other sentient creatures (Gen 1:30) is open to ongoing exploration both theologically (e.g., Levison 2009) and scientifically. In fact, these basic features of theological anthropology are illuminated also by the biological, cognitive, psychological, anthropological, and sociological sciences, and we neglect them to our ignorance. What is undeniable is that the intellectual, moral, and spiritual capacities of humans are far above and arguably qualitatively different from those of other animals.

From a theological perspective, we might thus agree with the Roman Catholic hierarchy (and its promulgation in *Humani Generis*, referred to above) that human souls are uniquely implanted into human lives by God. From a scientific perspective, any kind of "emergent anthropology" (Yong 2007: ch. 6; 2011c: ch. 5) would suffice that sees these intellectual, moral, and psychical capacities as arising unpredictably from out of a sufficiently complex nexus of constituent parts, but once having emerged, being irreducible to the sum of such parts (like how the features of water, H_2O, are novel and are unforeseeable merely as hydrogen and oxygen taken separately). Both the theological and scientific views are, to varying degrees, postures of faith, complementary in outcome but derived from different starting points.

But whatever is refracted dimly about humanity in a fallen world grows in brilliance when illuminated in the light of Christ. Life in Adam reveals the frailty of the present human condition; life in Christ projects and even makes present what is possible, what is emerging, what is promised in the gospel. Thus Irenaeus' instincts are sound, indicative of the fact that we know about the image of God not necessarily from what we see presently in ourselves, but from what is revealed eschatologically in Christ: "Just as we have borne the image of the man of dust, we will also bear the image of the man of heaven" (1 Cor 15:49). "Of heaven" refers not merely to a transcendental, otherworldly, and spiritualized "existence" to come, but to what is manifest in the incarnational—and thereby always and forever also human—and resurrection life of Jesus. Human beings are thus truly in search of the image of God (Micks 1982), albeit that image has appeared already in Christ. In that sense, theological anthropology not only opens up to but essentially involves eschatology as well (see Phan 1988: esp. ch. 2).

The fall of humanity into sin is therefore also part of the Christian statement of faith, not a scientific claim. Yes, there is from one perspective plenty of empirical evidence for human depravity and sinfulness, but our understanding of such as people of faith derives from the scriptural witness, not from the social sciences. As such, any claims about a historical Adam and Eve, whether as a couple or a (Neolithic) group of people, will be similarly theological, not scientific. One might even essay that the garden of Eden is similarly a historical place, a paradisiacal "dome" that sets apart the specific hominids with whom God chose to enter into a covenantal relationship (e.g., Webb 2010). But this is again a theological perspective, as is the set of views that reads the Genesis narrative literarily as a contrasting creation story to that of other ancient Near Eastern accounts or even liturgically as being about God's hallowing himself as the focal point of the cosmic temple that is creation (e.g., Walton 2009). Thus the Genesis narrative is open to a range of hermeneutical approaches, the main points of which are not scientific (as measured by modern standards) but are intended to show that creation is dependent on the God of Israel and how sinfulness is endemic to the human condition (Coats 2009). It is better therefore to opt for those interpretations of the primeval creation that are least dissonant with other realms of knowledge, including science, unless there are compelling reasons to do otherwise, while always realizing that such theological interpretation, no less than scientific knowledge, is dynamic rather than static.

What then does the doctrine of the fall into sin entail? Article 3 of the SF says that humanity's "voluntary transgression resulted in their alienation from God, thereby incurring not only physical death but spiritual death, which is separation from God." The doctrine of the fall is less dependent on some historical sequence of events than it is a description of the present human condition that involves both physical and spiritual death, ultimately separation from God. The Genesis narrative, wherein God warns *ha adam*, "for in the day that you eat of it you shall die" (2:17), clearly refers not to physical death but rather to alienation from God, symbolized by the eviction from Eden, the presence of God. As we have seen previously (section 10.3), however, physical death and spiritual death are intertwined. Human experience confirms that beyond the physical cessation of life, death is experienced existentially as aloneness, forsakenness, and abandonment (von Speyr 1988: 39), ultimately, from God! But God's response is an eschatological redemption that involves a holistic and even "embodied" and social reconciliation. Yes, "flesh and blood cannot inherit the kingdom of God, nor does the perishable inherit the imperishable" (1 Cor 15:50), but "this perishable body must put on imperishability, and this mortal body must put on immortality. When this perishable body puts on imperishability, and this mortal body puts on immortality, then the saying that is written will be fulfilled: 'Death has been swallowed up in victory'" (1 Cor 15:43-54). Death in this life is thus anticipatory of eternal life with God.

More precisely, death in this world has to be illuminated not only in the human confrontation with death but in the cruciform death of Christ. The New Testament witness refers to, as already indicated, "the Lamb slain from the foundation of the world" (Rev 13:8b, KJV). An alternative, grammatically consistent, translation of this phrase is "everyone whose name has not been written from the foundation of the world in the book of life of the Lamb that was slaughtered" (NRSV), which parallels the later "whose names have not been written in the book of life from the foundation of the world" (17:8), which omits reference to the slain Lamb. Yet there are other scriptural references to Christ's incarnation and death as "destined before the foundation of the world" (1 Pet 1:20). While the precise sense of "from" or "before" is open to dispute, what is clear is that God's plan to send Christ to live and die was resolved from the beginning. Similarly, the salvific plan to redeem the people of God was also set in motion from the beginning, in Christ: "just as he chose us in Christ before the foundation of the world to be holy and blameless before him in love" (Eph 1:4; cf. Matt 25:34b; John 17:24). (This does not need to entangle us with the Reformed tradition's speculative debate about whether God logically decreed creation, incarnation, and fall [traditionally called *supralapsarianism*] or creation, allowance of the fall, and incarnation [traditionally called *infralapsarianism*]. Either will involve an eschatological resolution [e.g., van Driel 2008], so whatever God's logical order, the divine response ultimately resolves the associated conundrums.)

The death of Adam, not to mention of all creatures before and after such a primordially understood fall, thus needs to be viewed in light of the death of Christ. In fact, the two are intertwined: Adam's death leads to Christ's death, and Christ's death begins the redemption of Adam's death. Either way, the meaning of the world, including that of death in all its forms, finds its illumination in Christ, in the cross and the resurrection. The resurrection of Christ, which points forward to the eschatological overcoming and redemption even of death, cannot but be understood pneumatologically. Hence, creation as a whole—its goodness, fallenness, and even the death that ravages it—is both cruciform in accordance with what is revealed in the cross (Murphy 2003) and pneumatically illuminated in accordance with the Spirit's resurrecting power wrought from out of death (Dabney 1997). The pain of human death as well as the apparent meaninglessness of animal death, not to mention that of other sentient forms of life, therefore find both their fulfillment and hope in the life, death, and resurrection of Christ in the Spirit.

The role of death in this trinitarian light can perhaps now be better understood. From the foundations or the beginning of the world, God in his wisdom and foreknowledge already anticipated the fallen sinfulness of a free humanity (in Adam) and the perfect obedience of his Son (the second Adam). This Adamic sinfulness binds humanity and the world with which humans are in rebellious solidarity into a "singularity" of selfishness, unrighteousness, and disobedience (see Rice 2009). Perhaps such a singularity is conceptualizable as something like the big bang, albeit not necessarily so, particularly as cosmologists and physicists are divided about how to understand and conceptualize this first "moment" of our present universe. In any case, speaking theologically, God thus actualizes this kind of world that allows for the fall, a world in which evolutionary predation and death is part of the "fine-tuning"—not only with regard to the physical constants underlying cosmic evolution and star formation but also vis-à-vis the environmental niches, fitness spaces, and functional convergences—that make possible the appearance of *Homo sapiens* capable of goodness and sin (see Corey 1993; S. Morris 2008; McGrath 2009). If biologists wonder at the life-giving propensities of death, theologians declare that death has been and will finally be redeemed by the God of life.

An evolutionary naturalism would indeed be merely materialistic and, most worrisome, nihilistic apart from God, precisely because of the central role of death. However, an evolutionary creation highlights that the world in its dynamism, including death, is in the hands of a saving God, precisely because death is followed by resurrection, beginning with Jesus' raising from the dead by the Holy Spirit. While the standard mechanism of random mutations and natural selection suggests that only death reigns and there is neither design nor direction in the evolutionary scheme of things, even mainstream biologists acknowledge that the issues are much more complicated. So although there are some scientists who think that replaying the evolutionary history of the world would produce vastly different creatures, others suggest that there are evolutionary parameters, niches, and convergences that indicate something very close to human beings will eventually appear (Morris 2004). This teleological dimension will continue to be debated, but there is no getting around it, because the ubiquity of death has not derailed the evolution of life. Intelligent design theorists are right to call attention to this issue, although to equate the intelligent designer with God involves a theological stance of faith that goes beyond science. The point here, however, is that it is possible to talk about a direction of the evolutionary trail in and through death, and this opens up to and invites commentary from the perspective of the eschatological horizons of Christian faith understood through the cross, resurrection, and Pentecost.

Viewing the creation in light of the cross and resurrection suggests that an evolutionary world should be understood not only in faith but also from a moral point of view (e.g., Murphy and Ellis 1996). This latter horizon of judgment exposes ethical goodness and sin, not only the conditions that make them possible but also the choices that reflect creaturely embrace of and rebellion against God. The cross unveils, among other truths, God's judgment on sin, and in this vein becomes the central symbol of God's purifying love that judges and refines the world in preparation for the shalomic reign to come. Hence, in anticipation of the realm of righteousness revealed in Christ, God "breaks into" this singularity of sin and selfishness and by doing so creatively sets in motion a plan to redeem what was and is meant for evil. The entry of death into the world thereby can be accounted for in terms of an Adamic fall, not with the latter having retroactive causal powers, but in terms of human sin and death both being potently in the primordial womb—or "big bang"—of creation (as Levi is said to have been, before his birth, at work in the loins of Abraham; Heb 7:9-10) and then actually redefining and giving decisive meaning to the prior death of animals and other sentient forms of life. In particular, Adam's death unveils death's power to separate creatures from their Creator, not just physically but spiritually. But Adam's death, juxtaposed with Christ's death and resurrection, invites an eschatological understanding of the evolutionary history of the cosmos: the natural world's anticipation of evolving free human creatures with the capacity for good and evil finds new meaning in Adam's fall and full meaning in God's eschatological judgment, which condemns sin and reveals all that is good, true, and beautiful (see Peters 2006). Thus Christ's death provides the ultimate and redemptive response to creaturely death: God intends to overcome the power of death through the renewing, redeeming, and resurrecting power of the Holy Spirit.

In this eschatological sense we can affirm the world as primordially good but also as now fallen. The goodness of the present world is that it is capable of bringing forth and has brought forth human creatures and an incarnate deity, the former being able to appreciate, create, and yearn for beauty, truth, and goodness, and the latter manifesting their fulfillment. Creation's fallenness reflects the subjection of the world and all its creatures to the contingencies of finitude, the struggle for (self-) preservation, and the consequences of sinful and wicked choices. Yet the subjection of the world would be unfathomable apart from the hope of new life and of ultimate redemption, a hope that involves divine judgment on all that inspires sin, brings about destruction, and spreads death. Concomitantly, this judgment also involves the restoration of what sin destroys, the revitalization of what life's struggle terminates, and the renewal of a finite creation through the Spirit's baptism and filling of the cosmos (Macchia 2010). (Note, though, that God's final response in Christ and the Spirit does not necessitate universal salvation, because free creatures may nevertheless resist and reject God's saving offer [see section 2.2.2].)

So if human nature and the fall can only be understood in light of the trinitarian and redemptive ends of God, so also the creation itself. Any theological account of the world is thus necessarily christological and pneumatological. "All things came into being through [the Logos]" (John 1:2). More elaborately:

> For in him all things in heaven and on earth were created, things visible and invisible, whether thrones or dominions or rulers or powers—all things have been created through him and for him. He himself is before all things, and in him all things hold together. He is the head of the body, the church; he is the beginning, the firstborn from the dead, so that he might come to have first place in everything. For in him all the fullness of God was pleased to dwell, and through him God was pleased to reconcile to himself all things, whether on earth or in heaven, by making peace through the blood of his cross. (Col 1:16-20)

Similarly, if all things are to be reconciled, restored, and renewed through the blood of the cross, these are accomplished through the life-giving Spirit (Job 34:14-15; Ps 104:29-30; Isa 32:15; cf. Moltmann 1992b; Löning and Zenger 2000: ch. 14). This means that from the standpoint of Christian faith there is no "natural world" in and of itself, only a creation shaped by what Irenaeus called the "two hands of the Father" (see Yong 2002: ch. 2.1)—the Son and the Spirit—that "waits with eager longing for the revealing of the children of God" (Rom 8:19) and groans for such through unutterable human gasps enabled by the Spirit. Creation and new creation are thus two sides of the one coin (see Welker 2012).

A trinitarian theology of creation therefore makes three interrelated affirmations. First, the world is neither self-originating nor self-sustaining. Rather, its ultimate origins, even its fallen character, are anticipated by the God of Jesus Christ, even from the foundations of the world. That is the theological significance of the creation narratives, not what can be rendered concordant with scientific perspectives. Second, the Christian doctrines of creation and providence are also intertwined. Christian theodicy is most successful explicating not the whence of evil but the whither of evil (Fretheim 2010), especially its eschatological redemption in Christ by the Spirit (Wright 2009). In fact, nature's constancy itself, within which human life evolves and flourishes, cannot be understood except as central to the Christian doctrine of providence. And the same constancy also undergirds the scientific enterprise. From a pneumatological perspective, the many scientific disciplines can all illuminate various (important) facets of human life and the (even tragic) processes of the world, even as the evolutionary sciences themselves provide a range of perspectives on the multifaceted nature of human tragedy. But it is theology that provides understanding of significance and meaning—both proximate and ultimate—amid the human condition. Finally, the goal of creation is redemption and community with the fellowship of the triune God (Buxton 2005). The answer to the questions of suffering, evil, and death depends ultimately on human inquirers finding their lives mapped on to the divine story of the Father sending the Son to be reconciled with the world through the Spirit. Hence it is human response and action inspired by the manifest Spirit-empowered Son of God that is most central for generating and sustaining hope in the face of pain, suffering, and tragedy (Tilley 1991; Swinton 2007). These are the basic elements of the whence, why, and whither of a trinitarian theology of creation.

We must now turn, even if briefly, to the performative aspects of a renewal theology of creation. Prior to this we discussed how the creation of the world can be comprehended as a dramatic exposé of sin and righteousness. The former is symbolized most vividly but paradoxically in the singularity of sin and selfishness of Adam anticipated in the natural history of the world before the arrival of *Homo sapiens* but actualized out of the sinfulness of all humans since. The latter is what is made possible in the light of God's creative, providential, and redemptive works in Christ and the Spirit. So whatever the historical Adam turns out to be, "the Adam in whom all men die lives on, the creation and the creator of history, a moral being whose every intellectual triumph is at once a temptation to evil and a power for good" (Greene 1959: 339). The meaning of the doctrines of creation and theological anthropology has little to do with understanding *how* God created the world or human beings—that is a question that science is best equipped to tell in the long run. Instead, these doctrines are invitations to free creatures like us to exercise choices that will ultimately be revealed, and judged, as either God-glorifying or self-obsessed. Human freedom is not absolute, constrained as it is by our finitude, creatureliness, sinfulness, and original victimhood, as previously asserted. We are all caught in Judas' predicament, himself a negative anti-type of Adam, somehow wishing to accomplish God's will but yet finding ourselves hopelessly, tragically, and destructively entangled in the cosmic forces of original sin and circumstances that strangle our lives. At the same time, we are now also open to the intervention of the other Adamic anti-type, that of Christ, whose yes to our befuddled and transgressive nos opens up the destructive singularities of our self-absorbed lives to the redemptive possibilities of the Spirit of God. As evolutionary predation and death produce ever-increasingly complex forms of life, so also do the saving and sanctifying works of the Spirit renew and recreate sinners in the image of Christ, as a new people of God.

Three avenues for living out the preceding trinitarian theology of creation thus recommend themselves. First, both testaments enjoin: "you shall love your neighbour as yourself" (Lev 19:18; cf. Matt 19:19; Mark 12:31; Luke 10:27; Rom 13:9; Gal 5:14; Jas 2:8). Ironically, it is precisely the evolutionary instincts of self-preservation that open up the self to the neighbor. Self-love includes, besides the potential of self-regard, self-concern, and selfishness, also cooperativeness, altruism, and benevolence (see Yong 2012: ch. 2). What is exemplary of the latter is particularly the cruciform life of Christ, which itself was fully subjected to the world with all its contingencies and evils, but precisely in order to redeem nature's processes of death and violence. The stakes are all the higher in an evolutionary world that includes earthquakes, tsunamis, and hurricanes, among other natural but yet destructive phenomena. On this stage, human responses and choices are all the more ethically charged, capable of unveiling the depths of human self-centeredness but also making possible the revelation of a crucified but also resurrecting power. Hence there is something to those soul-making theodicies (Corey 2000) that urge the capacity of God to bring something good out of what is otherwise wanton and gratuitous. When bad things happen, then the moral law written into human hearts judges each response (Rom 2:12-16). Creation and history are thereby the combined stage on which the ethical trajectories of human lives are sorted out. History itself will judge the consequences of our actions, whether they love only the self or also the other as well, and eternity will separate out the other-oriented sheep and the self-consumed goats in the light of God's loving and purifying judgment (Matt 25:31-46; 1 Cor 3:12-15). Simultaneously, we are not alone: the crucified and risen one who is in solidarity with the human condition has sent his Spirit to enable emergence of such self-sacrificial and self-giving lives for others out of an evolutionary cosmos.

Besides responding to our neighbors, with whose lives ours are irrevocably intertwined, there is a level of ethical response also to our environment, to the dust of the ground, which ultimately derives from the cosmic dust itself, with and through which we are symbiotically constituted. Human groaning that is inspired by the Holy Spirit echoes that of the creation itself across the inanimate–animate spectrum (see Gen 4:11; cf. Park 2009: 94–108). The Scripture that says "the elements will be dissolved with fire, and the earth and everything that is done on it will be disclosed" (2 Pet 3:10b) refers not to the ultimate destruction of this world, as some dispensationalist accounts suggest, but to the disclosure of God's judgmental fire. Hence the world and our human environment are not to be neglected as if they were to be finally discarded, but are rather to be cared for, appropriate to the divine stewardship with which humans have been entrusted and mandated (Gen 1:26; cf. Swoboda 2013). What is redemptive is human participation in the creational work of God in Christ by the power of the Spirit (Fulljames 1993: ch. 7; Hefner 2000: esp. ch. 15). Herein, then, is social justice inextricably linked to environmental and ecological justice, not because we have an overly realized eschatological imagination, but precisely because the cruciform cosmology and pneumatology of the cross developed in this chapter open up to what might also be called an eschatology of the cross (Chester 2006: ch. 15) that works patiently in the present in anticipation of the cosmic reign to come.

Most importantly, the goal of human lives, along with the entire creation, is to become the temple of the living God (see Walton 2009). As such, the eschatological point is for God to be enthroned not only in human hearts and minds or even "on the praises of Israel" (Ps 22:3) but "above" the creation itself. Hence any theology of creation, besides inspiring human ethics and motivating care for the earth, ought to inculcate the reverence that precedes authentic worship (Dawn 2009), precisely what the first chapters of Romans tells us that human sin has incapacitated. The psalmist observed, "The heavens declare his righteousness, for God himself is judge" (Ps 50:1). The world is the stage upon which its various creatures are designed to reveal, adore, and worship God, each in its own way. So also with human creatures; as multidimensional and multifaceted as we are, our end is to give glory to God in a multitude of ways (see Harrison 2010).

Discussion Questions

1. What are some aspects of your church's teachings about the Christian doctrine of creation, including its relationship to modern science, that are different from the preceding

discussion? Are these differences complementary or are they contradictory, and if the latter, what are possible responses to these divergent views?

2. How do your church's teachings about the problem of evil, sin, and death compare and contrast with the preceding discussion? Is the kind of trinitarian and eschatological framework presented here adequate for contemporary theology? Why or why not?

3. The preceding has suggested that human nature needs to be understood as unfinished, although revealed normatively and theologically in Christ. How is such a view viable for a twenty-first-century theological anthropology? What else is missing that is important for such Christian thought and practice?

Further Reading

Badger, Steve, and David Bundrick, eds. 2012. *Proceedings of the Inaugural Faith & Science Conference, Springfield, Missouri, June 27–28, 2011.* Springfield, Mo.: Gospel Publishing House.

Bennett, Gaymon, et al., eds. 2008. *The Evolution of Evil.* Göttingen: Vandenhoeck & Ruprecht.

Berry, R. J., and Thomas A. Noble, eds. 2009. *Darwin, Creation and the Fall: Theological Challenges.* Nottingham, U.K.: Apollos.

Creegan, Nicola Hoggard. 2013. *Animal Suffering and the Problem of Evil.* Oxford: Oxford University Press.

Hayes, Zachary. 1980. *What Are They Saying about Creation?* New York: Paulist.

Moreland, J. P., and John Mark Reynolds, eds. 1999. *Three Views on Creation and Evolution.* Grand Rapids: Zondervan.

Oord, Thomas J. 2010. *The Nature of Love: A Theology.* St. Louis, Mo.: Chalice.

11

The Eternal Godhead

The Mystery of the Triune God in a World of Many Faiths

World Assemblies of God Fellowship Statement of Faith
—Article 2: The Eternal Godhead

We believe in the unity of the one true and living God who is the eternal, self-existent One, and has revealed Himself as one being in three persons: Father, Son, and the Holy Spirit (Matthew 3:16-17; 28:19).

a. God the Father

We believe in God the Father, the first person of the triune Godhead, who exists eternally as the Creator of heaven and earth, the Giver of the Law, to whom all things will be subjected, so that He may be all in all (Genesis 1:1; Deuteronomy 6:4; 1 Corinthians 15:28).

b. The Lord Jesus Christ

We believe in the Lord Jesus Christ, the second person of the triune Godhead, who was and is the eternal Son of God; that He became incarnate by the Holy Spirit and was born of the virgin Mary.

We believe in His sinless life, miraculous ministry, substitutionary atoning death, bodily resurrection, triumphant ascension, and abiding intercession (Isaiah 7:14; Hebrews 7:25-26; 1 Peter 2:22; Acts 1:9; 2:22; 10:38; 1 Corinthians 15:4; 2 Corinthians 5:21).

c. The Holy Spirit

We believe in the Holy Spirit, the third person of the triune Godhead, who proceeds from the Father and the Son, and is ever present and active in the work of convicting and regenerating the sinner, sanctifying the believer, leading into all truth and empowering for ministry (John 14:26; 16:8-11; 1 Peter 1:2; Romans 8:14-16).

11.1 Cornelius the Just

The Cornelius story marks one of the axes (the account of the Ethiopian eunuch in Acts 8:26-40 arguably being another) upon which the shift of focus from Jews to Gentiles turns in the Acts narrative (see also Yong 2011a: ch. 23). What might this tell us about the nature of God, including God's relationship with Jesus and the Spirit? Further, how does Cornelius' encounter with Peter unveil a global God of all nations?

Luke's sketch provides precious few details about Cornelius' life and character. He seems to have lived awhile—at least long enough to have had relatives and close friends in the immediate vicinity (Acts 10:25)—in Caesarea, a Roman outpost on the north side of Judea, working there as "a centurion of the Italian Cohort" (10:1). This means that besides personal servants, he had at least a hundred men under his command, among whom were "devout" soldiers (10:7). This devotion may have been motivated at least in part by his own exemplary piety, one manifest not just in himself but through "all his household"; further, "he gave alms generously to the people and prayed constantly to God" (10:2), so much so that he was "well spoken of by the whole Jewish nation" (10:22). Last but not least, although he wielded the authority and power of a centurion, an authentic humility also is evident, especially in his reverent prostration before Peter at their meeting (10:25). Clearly the one who ruled over men also recognized his place before others, particularly those who served the God that he also feared and sought to worship.

Cornelius' piety as a God-fearer sympathetic to the Jewish religion stands in stark contrast to Roman civil religiosity, which demanded steadfast acknowledgment of Caesar as lord. Hence while Cornelius exercises all of the authority of Roman centurions, he also displays obeisance to the God of Israel (who appears through his angelic servant; Acts 10:3-7), his all-too-human servant Peter, and even the Spirit of God himself, at least in acquiescing to the Spirit's enabling his "speaking in tongues and extolling God" (10:46). As such, rather than participating in or extending Roman brutality through subjugation of local residents, he was known for his generosity and kindness throughout the occupied territory under his administration. To what degree does Cornelius not only provide a countercultural model of masculinity for first-century followers of Jesus as Messiah (see Flessen 2011), but also, through the normative Lukan portrayal, illuminate the divine character that does not lord it over others? This is an important question in light of the fact that the God who Cornelius worshipped also comes to be revealed as the God of not only Cornelius but of all the nations.

The preceding discussion opens up to two sets of affirmations regarding Cornelius that are relevant for our considerations. First, his men introduced him to Peter as "an upright and God-fearing man" (Acts 10:22a), among other descriptions. Note that the word translated "upright" is *dikaios* (δίκαιος), which is the same root word used in the rest of the New Testament, including the Pauline Epistles and Romans, to refer to the justness and righteousness by which people are saved. This ascription is importantly rendered of Cornelius even before he is evangelized by Peter. Whatever the condition of his soul vis-à-vis the next world prior to meeting Peter, here was one whose devoutness was noticed even by God (mentioned twice: 10:4, 31).

Second, upon meeting first Cornelius' men and then their master, Peter came to understand that the vision of the animals (Acts 10:9-16) applied also to his understanding of the distinctions separating Jews from Gentiles. Whereas before he would have categorized Gentiles as impure pagans with whom Jews ought not to associate, now "God has shown me that I should not call anyone profane or unclean" (10:28b). More pointedly, "I truly understand that God shows no partiality, but in every nation anyone who fears him and does what is right is acceptable to him" (10:34-35). Note here that it is Cornelius' accepted standing before God that brings Peter to him, rather than vice versa. God's impartiality means not that Cornelius has no sin (as we saw in the previous chapter, all humans are sinners) but that God is able to see through the sins to the piety, devotion, and rectitude that also characterized the centurion's life. Peter proceeds to tell Cornelius and his household of Jesus the Messiah, and midway through this, the Gentiles are given the gift of the Holy Spirit, leading to their baptism in water (10:44-48).

So on the one hand, that Cornelius himself was drawn to the God of the Jews reflects that there was a universalizing stream in first-century Judaism amid which his own faith was being nurtured. On the other hand, Peter himself had to be introduced to this universalizing trajectory (Parsons 2007: 160–86). Hence what ought to be noted is not only Cornelius' conversion as a God-fearer to a Jesus follower, but also Peter's conversion as a Jewish exclusivist to one willing to be in fellowship with Gentiles. In this meeting of strangers, both were transformed: minds were changed and hearts were altered. Peter's revolution ought not to be minimized, even if we realize that this intellectual change of mind brought about a full transformation of heart not immediately but only over a prolonged period of time, as his relapse into his old ways of thinking later in Antioch reflects (see Gal 2:11-13; cf. section 4.1). The sequence of events coming out of this episode in the apostolic community reveals how deeply entrenched beliefs, behaviors, and habits persisted over time, dividing the earliest Jewish followers of Jesus into two groups over whether and/or how Gentiles ought to be accepted as Jesus' disciples. Non-Jews had simply been categorized as the excluded "other" for too long, and the possibility of communion between Jews and Gentiles was unimaginable. If Gentiles finally were accepted as followers of Jesus as Messiah, it was less because they had come to peace with Jews than because the two would eventually go their separate ways.

FIGURE 11.1

On the tanner's rooftop in Joppa, Peter's prayers give way to revelatory visions: "He saw the heaven opened and something like a large sheet coming down, being lowered to the ground by its four corners. In it were all kinds of four-footed creatures and reptiles and birds of the air. Then he heard a voice saying, 'Get up, Peter; kill and eat'" (Acts 10:11-13). This image depicts this vision in the upper right but primarily concentrates our attention on Peter's response. Over against the teeming prodigality of the vision Peter holds out his hands in refusal: "By no means, Lord; for I have never eaten anything that is profane or unclean" (10:14). And as he straightens his arms, he looks past the animals toward the open heavens: How could this be the voice of God? Does this not upend the sacred law itself?

The voice speaks again: "What God has made clean, you must not call profane" (10:15). It is precisely this moment that the image isolates: Peter's resistance seems to melt somewhat, his straightened arms dropping toward the horizon until his gesture of refusal begins to look more like a gesture of blessing toward the world around him. From this rooftop position, Peter's vision of heaven will give way to a deeply revised vision of the earth. As the sheet is "suddenly taken up," the scene opens outward onto the city and toward the rest of the world (including those lands beyond the horizon on the other side of the sea). In the wake of this event, Peter finds himself "greatly puzzled" (10:17) but oriented toward the entire (Gentile) world around him in radically new ways.

And in this light we might speculate that the conspicuous appearance of the vine immediately beside him is meant to draw subtle parallels (and contrasts) between Peter and Jonah (see Jonah 4:5-11). At the center of both stories are sharp questions regarding Israel's orientation toward its Gentile neighbors, and in fact in both stories Joppa provides a significant point of departure for the narrative (cf. Jonah 1:3). By placing Peter under a shade-providing vine, overlooking a city, this artist cleverly renders Acts 10 as a recapitulation of Jonah 4—only this time the man of God will look at the city before him quite differently: "God has shown me that I should not call anyone profane or unclean. . . . I truly understand that God shows no partiality, but in every nation anyone who fears him and does what is right is acceptable to him." (Acts 10:28, 34-35). ✦

11.2 The Triune God: Pentecostal, Ecumenical, and Interreligious Perspectives

We already began a discussion of part of article 2 (§2b on the "Lord Jesus Christ") in chapter 9, which will make it a bit easier to handle this longest article of the SF within the scope of one chapter. However, rather than leaving the christological confession aside, we assume the prior discussion in what follows and build on that. Yet the structure of the article subsumes Christology under the broader rubric of the doctrine of God. More precisely, Christology plus pneumatology and the doctrine of God the Father are threads within an overall theology of the triune God. The rationale for this dogmatic structure, as we shall see momentarily, traces to the split between trinitarian and non-trinitarian, or oneness, Pentecostals during the embryonic phase of the movement in the second decade of the twentieth century.

We proceed as follows. First, we review the early modern pentecostal debate between oneness and trinitarian believers and the lens that provides insight into the patristic disputes and the development of orthodox trinitarianism. We then shift to a consideration of contemporary developments in the doctrines of God, Trinity, and pneumatology, especially as these have unfolded globally. Finally, we will broaden the contextual discussion in this chapter to include the question about Christian theology in a world of many faiths. While this complicates the issues considerably within the scope of a single chapter, it concerns matters that have been with us since the beginning of this book and that any contemporary theology in global context cannot avoid. Further, as the Cornelius narrative unveils, if indeed God does not show partiality, then the God of the Jewish and Christian faiths begs to be understood not only as the God of all nations but also as the God of all cultures and even of all religious traditions. How might the God revealed in Christ and the Spirit also be such a God, and what does that mean?

11.2.1 Oneness and Trinity: Foundational Issues

During the second decade of the modern pentecostal movement, a "new issue" broke out—beyond the "finished work" debate (discussed in ch. 5)—which diverged into two separate streams, one classically trinitarian and the other not. Decisions of the nascent Assemblies of God general council meetings from 1914 to 1916 effectively served to exclude from fellowship those "Jesus only" Pentecostals who rejected the received doctrine of the Trinity (Menzies 1971: ch. 6). On the other side, members of the new non-trinitarian group, more positively self-identifying as "oneness" because of their strict monotheism, believed that they were simply being more biblical not only about the doctrine of God but also about reception of God's saving work through water baptism for the forgiveness of sins in Jesus' name (Butler 2004: ch. 6).

There are three foundational tenets undergirding the distinctive oneness pentecostal witness (e.g., Bernard 1983). First, oneness Pentecostals affirm what they understand to be a biblical monotheism, one anchored by an uncompromising Jewish declaration of the oneness or unity of God (e.g., Deut 6:4), defined in part by a rejection of the classical affirmation of God in three persons. Yet unlike those in the Unitarian tradition who have then proceeded to reject the divinity of Christ, oneness believers insist on a high Christology: in the man Jesus Christ of Nazareth, "the whole fullness of deity dwells bodily" (Col 2:9). Hence Jesus and the Father are one (John 10:30) in essence, although Jesus in his human and incarnate form is subordinate to his deity (John 14:29). Second, and by extension then, Christian initiation involves baptism into the one covenant of God through Jesus, and following the apostolic witness, ought to be done in

Jesus' name (e.g., Acts 8:16; 10:48; 19:5). The singular name of Jesus is not only the name of God but also the one "name [also singular, they note] of the Father and of the Son and of the Holy Spirit" in the Matthean Great Commission (Matt 28:19). Last but not least, also claiming to follow apostolic precedent, Christian regeneration climaxes with the reception of the Holy Spirit (Acts 2:38), which according to the Acts narrative is evidenced by tongues speech (Bernard 1984). The combined force of these oneness distinctives has effectively pushed it, for at least classical pentecostal believers, beyond the bounds of trinitarian orthodoxy (see Dalcour 2005).

In some respects, oneness pentecostal theology and praxis represent the logical culmination of the Protestant Reformation. The Radical Reformers, for instance, believed that the Reforming impulse ought to have looked back not only to the time prior to the medieval church but even before the fourth-century "Constantinian settlement." Oneness Pentecostals, however, not only question the creedalism represented by such collusion between church and state but also reject the trinitarian doctrine ensconced in the Nicene and Constantinopolitan confessions. Similarly, many restorationist groups since the sixteenth century have sought to recapture such apostolic "primitivism" and ecclesiality. Yet oneness Pentecostals have also insisted on the thoroughly Jewish, and hence strictly monotheistic, character of the early Jesus movement, almost as if in anticipation, long before the end of the twentieth century, of those who affirm such, like advocates of the "new perspective" in biblical and theological scholarship. And finally (for now), the earliest modern Pentecostals surely sought to rehabilitate the apostolic spirituality of spiritual gifts and tongues speech. But oneness Pentecostals go further and see the latter not only as a second or third work of grace and empowerment for witness but as being at the core of entrance into the new covenant secured in Christ.

But what about the trinitarian consensus that emerged from out of the fourth-century ecumenical councils? Oneness Pentecostals are not the first ones to aver that Christian theology took a number of wrong turns related to adoption of nonbiblical—by which they mean Hellenistic, Greek, and Platonic, in particular—categories of thinking that came into increasing prominence throughout the third century (see Bernard 1991). By the time of the fourth-century debates, both sides presumed the neoplatonic notions of time and eternity and thus were forced to reinterpret the biblical data within this foreign framework (see Yong 2005: ch. 5). Thus one side (the Arians) sought to protect the Father's transcendence and so ended up rejecting the Son being of the same substance (*homoousios*) as the Father. But the other side (the Athanasians) could only defend the soteriological significance of the Son by resorting to philosophical distinctions (i.e., between "nature" or *ousia* and "substance" or *hypostasis*). From the oneness perspective, the triumph of the latter in the Christian tradition—not uncontested as debates raging into the seventh century testify (see, e.g., de Margerie 1982: part 1; Dünzl 2007)—twisted beyond recognition the biblical witness to the one and only true God of Jesus Christ.

The approved oneness genealogy, therefore, travels partway back through the modalist and monarchian traditions of the second and third centuries, then interfaces also with aspects of the Antiochene school of thought in the fourth and fifth, albeit not without important differences. Part of the challenge is that much of the thinking of especially the earlier theologians is only preserved in the writings of their opponents, those who belonged to the orthodox tradition that (later) triumphed. In any case, the oneness claim is that it was modalists like Praxeas, Noetus, and perhaps Sabellius who preserved the unity of God without lapsing into the "three-person" language drawn (it is maintained) from the philosophical tradition. The difference is that any notion of "successive modalism"—the idea that God is revealed *first* as Creator and Father, *then* as incarnate in Christ, and *last* as the Holy Spirit—is dismissed. Instead, the one God is both revealed in Christ incarnationally and in the Spirit pentecostally and ecclesiastically; God is revealed in three *modes*, but these are fundamentally neither sequential nor only historical.

Then in order to clarify the relationship between the Father and the incarnate Son, a Nestorian-type distinction is made between the divine and the human natures in Jesus. "Nestorian-type" is suggested because oneness Pentecostals neither appeal to Nestorius nor accept the Nicene-Constantinopolitan confession presumed by the fifth-century theologian. Yet oneness thinking runs parallel to Antiochene instincts, in which tradition Nestorius was a significant member, taking seriously the humanity of Jesus and recognizing that this was distinguishable from the divine nature. Jesus therefore ate and slept, for instance, as a man, but he did miracles or arose from the dead as divine. In each of these ways and more, oneness Pentecostals claim to be more biblical, logical, and historically true to the God of Israel revealed finally in Jesus Christ (see D. Norris 2009).

The historical polemics on both sides of the oneness–trinitarian divide have resulted in estranged relations within the renewal family. Of course, to even suggest that the "renewal family" includes both oneness followers and trinitarian believers presumes some kind of valid relationship that some Pentecostals and surely more than a few evangelicals will contest. Yet the oneness tradition is by no means demographically marginal to the renewal movement across the global south (French 1999). They also are, like many other Pentecostals, more pragmatically oriented, more consciously contextually situated in their various locales, and often carried by diasporic or immigrant dynamics. These apostolics are noncompromising about their theological and doctrinal commitments, although they are also less predisposed to making apologetic arguments because the biblical narrative seems, from their perspective, both so obviously oneness in overall commitments and yet accommodating of triune language in its overall message.

As oneness scholars have begun to emerge from within the ranks, then, assessments from the broader renewal academy have also become more nuanced and dialogical. More recent analysts have thus called for a moratorium on antagonistic declarations of the "oneness heresy" and instead note that the oneness position may be historically nonorthodox but is surely understandable as a contextual adaptation of the biblical message across the global renewal landscape (see Gill 1994). In fact, when read in the first-century Jewish context, as oneness advocates urge, oneness views emerge as a contemporary expression of the ancient Jewish theology of the name of the one true God (see Reed 2008: part 3). In the global context, the apostolic–trinitarian divide goes beyond these prominent theological disputes and involves negotiations of race and inculturation in an increasingly post-Western, postcolonial, and post-Christendom world (see Gerloff 1992). So although scholarly dialogue between oneness and trinitarian Pentecostals is now underway, it may take another generation or two before formal ecclesiastical conversations ensue. While theological and doctrinal agreement between these two renewal streams may be elusive, the issues certainly cannot be ignored.

11.2.2 Toward a Twenty-First-Century Trinitarian Faith

It should be noted that oneness anxieties about trinitarianism lapsing into tritheism have perennially been concerns of, as well as temptations to, the orthodox Christian tradition (Holmes 2012). The classical doctrine of the Trinity was forged on the mantra "not three Gods," as explicitly argued by Gregory of Nyssa (335–394), one of the dominant fourth-century theological voices (see Swindal and Gensler 2005: 84–86). In view of this history, the oneness faithful worry that three persons cannot mean anything other than three deities ignores important clarifications of trinitarian thinking over the centuries. First, the tri-person language was designed to take seriously both the plain sense of the biblical narrative and the soteriological thrust of the scriptural witness to Christ. Second, the divine persons have always been understood monotheistically in the sense that they subsist inherently within, rather than exist outside or alongside, each other, with the one amplification that the triune persons were distinguished by the Son's begottenness by and the Spirit's procession from the Father. Third, such subsisting divine personhood, along with the Father's originality, the Son's generation, and the Spirit's spiration, is thereby also significantly divergent from the dominant models of human personhood—whether the classical sense of individual substances with a rational nature (Boethius, c. 480–524/525), the early modern notion of self-aware souls or minds distinct from bodies (René Descartes, 1596–1650), or the later modern idea of autonomous rational subjects (Immanuel Kant, 1724-1804)—on offer. Father, Son, and Spirit are "perichoretically" interrelated, meaning, according to the tradition, coindwelling and mutually interpenetrating each other (see Prestige 1985: ch. 14). For all of these reasons, then, the triune persons ought not to be merely equated with human persons, and this has warded off some confusion of the Trinity as three separate deities. This discussion is meant neither to argue against oneness views nor to apologize for the trinitarian construct, but simply to indicate that oneness monotheistic concerns have also driven trinitarian reflection historically.

Another angle into the issues is the doctrine of the Holy Spirit (pneumatology). The early fourth-century discussion at Nicaea (325) focused on clarifying christological matters and only affirmed belief "in the Holy Spirit." Over the next two generations, however, further discussion led to an elaboration at the Council of Constantinople (381): "We believe in the Holy Spirit, the Lord, the giver of life, who proceeds from the Father [and the Son]. Who with the Father and the Son is worshiped and glorified. Who has spoken through the prophets" (see appendix 2). That the Spirit was also worshipped with the other two persons was central to the argument for the Spirit's coequal divinity with the Father and the Son (see Yong 2008: 39–46). Note though that the bracketed phrase, "and the Son" (Latin: *filioque*) was not in the original version of the creed and was added later (to Latin translations) by the Western Church. Eastern Christians have long resisted this revision to and expansion of the Nicene confession of faith, in part for theological and in part for ecclesiastical and procedural reasons, and Westerners have been no less unwavering on these issues (Siecienski 2010).

The WAGF SF, following the lead of the Assemblies of God, a Western-based renewal church, includes the *filioque* clause in article 2c regarding the derivation of the Spirit. If the question regards what is biblical about the matter, scriptural arguments can be marshaled for both versions. Trinitarian renewalists so far seem to have followed either Eastern or Western tradition, depending on where they are located, rather than thinking matters through themselves. For oneness theology, however, there is no conceptual space for the debate to even arise, because there are no personal distinctions between Father, Son, and Holy Spirit.

FIGURE 11.2

FIGURE 11.3

Conceptualizing trinitarian theology has been a massive (sometimes massively problematic) topic in verbal and written theology, and so too has it been in visual theology. How does one visually articulate the perichoresis of the triune God, the mutual indwelling of the Father, Son, and Spirit? Icons like Rublev's Holy Trinity *(fig. 1.3) offer profound trinitarian mediations, but they also do so in ways that potentially lend themselves to subtle tritheistic misunderstandings. Other artists, including those represented here, have attempted to avoid these misunderstandings by emphasizing the oneness of the trinitarian God. The first of these (fig. 11.2) attempts to present the three divine persons as a single royal entity: one throne, one cloak, one crown, one halo—interestingly, a cruciform halo (which is usually reserved only for Jesus).*

The eighteenth-century image from Peru (fig. 11.3) goes a step further, attempting to entirely avoid tritheism by rendering one figure with three faces. Trifacial depictions of the Trinity such as this were controversial among European ecclesiastical authorities, and in fact were officially condemned by the Roman Catholic Church three times: in 1628, 1658, and 1745. Despite this, it was widely adopted in South America as an effective means of understanding trinitarian doctrine in contradistinction to indigenous polytheisms. Given the singularity of the one God with three "faces," this image might be interpreted as strictly modalist but for the diagrammatic Scutum Fidei *(or "shield of the Trinity") in the center of the image, which identifies each of the three divine persons as God (e.g.* Pater est Deus, Filius est Deus, Spiritus Sanctus est Deus*), while also differentiating them from one another (*Pater non est Filius, Filius non est Pater, *and so on).*

It is possible that the entire project of visually representing the Trinity is inherently and hopelessly problematic, given that visual forms are generally mutually exclusive: three forms cannot occupy the very same space without displacing or deforming one another. For this reason, visual conceptions of the Trinity are able to emphasize the three-ness of God but have great difficulty emphasizing the three-in-oneness of God. Jeremy Begbie has argued that perhaps musical space is more conducive to artistically understanding Trinitarian doctrine—or is at least a helpful supplement—because in sonic space three sounds can remain wholly distinct and yet entirely mutually indwell one another in a single sound, as in the case of a musical chord (Begbie 2007; cf. fig. 4.2). ✦

Yet what are some of the implications of this pneumatological and trinitarian discussion? Western protests notwithstanding, Eastern theologians have suggested that saying the Spirit derives also from the Son subordinates the economy of the Spirit to that of the Son and perhaps limits the work of the Spirit to the realm of the church and undercuts the more cosmic work of the Spirit attested to in the Bible. Thus some Orthodox theologians are comfortable saying that "we can only know with some assurance where the Spirit is, rather than where the Spirit is not" (cited in Yong 2003: 187), which allows for a broader understanding of the Spirit's work in culture and society at large and even among the religions. Yet Catholic theologians are no less open to thinking about the work of the Spirit in these spheres, even with the addition of the *filioque* to the creed (see Congar 1986: chs. 7–8).

The *filioque* dispute as it related to the broader question of pneumatology does cut through the global renewal movement along similar registers. On the one hand, more classical pentecostal churches with deeper roots in the Western tradition have also imbibed a more ecclesiocentric perspective on the work of the Spirit and hence place more emphasis on the missional empowerment of the Spirit in the church's work of evangelism and evangelization. This is not to deny the cosmic work of the Spirit, but it is to distinguish carefully between the Spirit's convicting work among those yet "outside" the church from the Spirit's "converting" activity that brings about the new birth in the body of Christ (see Chan 2011: ch. 1).

On the other hand, more indigenous renewal movements, especially in the global south, appear to presume a less ecclesially defined pneumatology. The alleged "primal spirituality" (Cox 1995) that emphasizes ecstatic speech, mystical piety, and wondrous healing has been posited as facilitating the unprecedented growth and expansion of the movement outside the Euro-American hemisphere. Even if many renewal churches explicitly reject the claim that their spiritual practices draw from or are shaped by indigenous cultural or religious notions, there is no denying that the adaptability and flexibility of renewalism is meeting the spiritual needs of non-Westerners on their own less-rationalized terms (e.g., Cho 2010). So renewalists by and large do not question the received cosmologies of indigenous traditions, replete as they are with many levels or layers of spiritual beings and realities; yet more classical pentecostal groups demonize these traditional "principalities and powers" and subordinate them to the liberating power of the Spirit through exorcisms and other deliverance ministries (see section 6.2.3; cf. Kalu 2008: ch. 9). Still, there is also no denying that there is a very rich and vibrant pneumatological cosmology operative among renewalists that enables inculturation in non-Western idioms and allows for integration of indigenous beliefs and practices with Christian faith (Rasmussen 1996; Park 1998; Anderson 2001). These elements suggest that there may be more to pneumatology than many renewal theologians may want to recognize (e.g., Kärkkäinen, Kim, and Yong 2013), even as they also highlight the attendant difficulties will be no less contested than those of the East–West *filioque* dispute.

Clearly, the current ferment in pneumatology has implications for contemporary discussions both in trinitarian theology and in the doctrine of God. In fact, it is clear that the present renaissance in pneumatology is indexed in more than one way to the post-Barthian resurgence in trinitarian theology in general (see Kärkkäinen 2002b, 2004a, 2007). A robust doctrine of the Trinity needs nothing less than an equally robust doctrine of the Holy Spirit; simultaneously, the development of pneumatology also pushes forward the discussion of trinitarian theology. Developments along both pneumatological and trinitarian fronts have also spurred further thinking in other theological arenas and doctrinal loci. If Barth's legacy was to urge a thoroughgoing christological reconsideration of any received theological topic, the post-Barthian landscape is filled with those building on the legacy of the Swiss grandmaster of Basel. Pneumatological theologies that revisit familiar doctrines in light of the person and work of the Spirit, and trinitarian theologies that do similarly by deploying perichoretic and other related notions, both understand the present theological task to involve reformulation of older ideas in light of these distinctive logics.

The case of feminist theology participates in and exemplifies both trajectories. The sexism of patriarchal language has always been the major hurdle for the doctrine of God, although alternative proposals have not gained much traction, especially at the liturgical level (see Greene-McCreight 2000: ch. 6). Yet the task is less that of discovering new nomenclature than it is thinking through issues both trinitarianly and pneumatologically. The former opens up to a relational logic, while the latter invites an emphasis on divine immanence. Feminists have deployed both approaches in reconsidering the doctrine of the Trinity (Johnson 1992). On the doctrine of the Holy Spirit, immanence motifs have been foregrounded (e.g., Prichard 1999), but so has trinitarian relationality (Victorin-Vangerud 2000) and perichoresis (Marshall 2003).

Within the global context the ferment is further heightened. Feminist concerns are now especially mapped onto liberationist, postcolonial, and even interfaith discourses. One recent proposal in the Indian context, as a case in point, engages with Hindu traditions in part, in order to fill out neglected feminine dimensions in the doctrines of God, Trinity, and the Spirit that are latent in the Christian tradition (Rani 2003). Here as well, revisiting the tradition invites reconsideration on both pneumatological and trinitarian fronts, usually simultaneously. Consistent also with one-ness commitments, there is no segregation of either from the other: to do pneumatology is to do trinitarian theology, and vice versa (Kim 2007).

The Indian example is not an isolated one. Especially on the trinitarian register, efforts to reconsider the theology of the Trinity vis-à-vis south Asian dialogue partners have been percolating for the last few hundred years (see Mattam 1975). Beyond the Hindu Indian context, recontextualizations and reconstructions of trinitarian theology have also been attempted in engagement with east Asian traditions (Lee 1996; Miyahira 2000), African indigenous traditions (Ogbonnaya 1994; Kombo 2007), and even Islam (Walters 2002). Can Christian theology, even in its trinitarian forms, maintain its distinctive witness in the multicultural and interfaith global context of the twenty-first century?

11.2.3 Renewal Theology in a Pluralistic World

Although Christianity has always existed alongside many faiths, only in the last few hundred years has the challenge of doing theology in interfaith mode come to be recognized (Plantinga 1999; Dupuis 2002). Renewal traditions are even more recent latecomers to the task, having accentuated a missional emphasis for much of the last century. In this evangelistic mode, dialogical interaction with other faith traditions has always been deemphasized in favor of more kerygmatic and proclamation-based approaches. After all, non-Christian cultural realities, much less religious traditions, were suspect and were to be domesticated or, even better, replaced by the Christian faith (e.g., Dombrowski 2001). Interest in non-Christian others could lead, however inadvertently, to syncretism that compromised Christian commitments and identity. In opposition to such tendencies, renewal Christians have, as others before them in the Christian tradition, hitched their missionary fervor to the ancient rhetorical tactic of demonizing other religions and even their adherents (see Kalu 2008: ch. 12; cf. McDermott 2007).

These more traditional renewal attitudes and approaches toward other faiths are consistent with the ethos of the broader global evangelical movement. Certainly evangelicals have historically taken what has been labeled a more exclusivistic posture, one that insists not only that Christ and Christianity are the only ways to salvation (Acts 4:12) but also that those in other or no faith traditions need to hear the gospel and believe and confess it to be saved (understood according to Rom 10:9-14; see also Sookhdeo 1978; Erickson 1996; Jones 1996; Piper 2010). This emphasis on intellectual assent can be understood as a Protestant variation of the older Catholic teaching that salvation is mediated by the church and its sacraments (see Sullivan 1992). Yet such an exclusivistic approach has come under increasing strain in the global context, particularly when the question of the unevangelized stretches back through time across the centuries (Marshall 1993; Twesigye 1996). More recently, then, evangelicals have begun to distinguish the question of salvation (always in Christ) from that of how those in other faiths ought to be engaged. More dialogical and relational approaches have been emerging through which evangelicals have begun to express a desire to listen to those in other faiths (Tennent 2002; Muck and Adeney 2009). In fact, some are also advocating learning, as Christians, *from* their neighbors in other faiths (e.g., McDermott 2000; Metzger 2012). And beyond learning either about or from those in other traditions, a few are also suggesting that there may be important ways not only in which other faiths point to Christ but also in which Christ fulfills aspects of other faith traditions (Pinnock 1992; Sanders 1992). In none of these evangelical models, however, is the centrality of Christ dismissed. If any are saved, this happens because of the person and work of Christ, even for the unevangelized.

Beyond the evangelical horizon, of course, there are so-called pluralist models that relativize Christ vis-à-vis other faiths (Hick and Knitter 1987; Hick 1989). For these, either Christ saves only Christians (with other salvific means available for those in other paths) or Christ is known as such only among Christians (while the christic reality is known by other names in other traditions). Against these types of pluralist theologies, others have emerged insisting on an even more radical pluralism, one that recognizes the diversity of ends in the various faiths, few if any of which are reducible to or even commensurable with Christian understandings (Dinoia 1992). This so-called "incommensurability thesis" is consistent with, if not based on, the recently promulgated "postliberal" presupposition that each faith tradition operates according to a different religious grammar nurtured by a distinctive history and set of practices (see Lindbeck 1984). This postliberal understanding of religions and their doctrines has given impetus to a new form of exclusivist theology of religions, albeit one that highlights the distinctiveness of each faith as opposed to merely asserting Christian superiority.

The predominant theological interfaces with religious pluralism currently appear to be riding on two parallel tides: the postliberal approach that remains at a more normative theological level and a comparative approach that attempts actual interfaith explorations. The former in many ways builds where Karl Barth left off: there is an undeniable christological and trinitarian uniqueness to the Christian faith that nevertheless has universal (if not soteriologically universalistic) significance, so much so that Christ can be seen as the greater light through which the lesser lights of all other faiths shine, perhaps even as "secular words" of the reign of God (e.g., Chestnutt 2010; Greggs 2011). This reaffirms Christian particularity while leaving open the question of interfaith commensurability, thus inviting interreligious dialogue and exploration. The latter, dubbed the "new comparative theology" in some circles (Clooney 2011)—as opposed to the older efforts that proceeded on presumed commensurabilities that ultimately were not sustainable—does not prejudge the question of salvation in other faiths one way or another. Rather, the new comparativists pay close attention to developing adequate categories that facilitate not only comparisons but also contrasts, and provide in-depth readings of multiple religious traditions (including their scriptural texts, dominant theologians, and dynamic sets of practices). Specialists in the new comparativism are usually trained in multiple religious traditions as well as their relevant languages, and it will be some time before the implications, not to say results, of such undertakings become clear (e.g., Neville 2001).

To be sure, the major questions regarding the historic and contemporary encounters between Christianity and other faiths are both soteriological (how are people saved, especially those in other religions) and theological (how is the one true God related to all people, including those in other traditions). Along the latter front, the question about the nature of God is most pointed, and many of the trinitarian issues reemerge here in even more complicated forms. In fact, trinitarian faith encountering other religions has developed in many directions. One has seen in the Trinity an archetype through which triune vestiges or symbols are identified in other traditions (e.g., Panikkar 1970), while another has argued from God revealed in triadic form to one revealed in many other names (e.g., Hick 1982). A third proposal, more indebted to postliberal currents, has emphasized the diversity of religious ends but attempts to correlate these with the inexhaustible trinitarian nature of God (Heim 2001). Here we see the fertility of trinitarian theological speculation in a pluralistic world, although for many the concreteness and specificity of Christ and Christian faith is jeopardized (Johnson 2011).

The aforementioned intertwined tasks of trinitarian and pneumato-logical theology can also be observed in the theology of religions enter-prise. If, as the preceding indicates, trinitarian proposals threaten to become dislodged from their christocentric anchor, so also should pneu-matological theologies of religions be similarly admonished. While the intent of some to explore the viability of a distinctive cosmic-wide econ-omy of the Holy Spirit is commendable, such an approach can be taken in directions that risk unhinging pneumatology from Christology and thereby lead to a devolution of trinitarian faith into a problematic trithe-ism. Still, the potential of a pneumatological approach to the interfaith dialogue and theologizing should not be minimized (Pinnock 1996: ch. 6; Yun 2012). The promise of a pneumatologically vigorous and hence trinitarianly robust theology of religions is still on the horizon, inviting consideration of how Christian doctrines about religious others intersect with Christian practices in relationship to and even with those in other faiths (D'Costa 2000).

Renewal theologies in the present time are also seeking alternative formulations more conducive to global interfaith engagement. What-ever else they might be, renewal theologies of religion will be no less christocentric, evangelical, and missional than before. What needs to be addressed, however, is the triumphalism characteristic of large segments of the tradition, as well as the tendency to demonize other cultural and religious traditions (Clarke and Yong 2011). Renewal theologians who live in pluralistic cultures wherein Christianity is a minority rather than dominant tradition are seeing the importance of articulating more sophis-ticated theologies of culture, society, and the polis in order to open up new avenues for approaching and engaging those in other faiths (see Yong 2003, 2008; George 2006; Tan Chow 2007; Lee 2011: 87–115). After all, renewalists are still in the end concerned with missional praxis, and whatever does not contribute to that task eventually falls by the wayside. Toward this end, then, more dialogical theologies of interfaith encoun-ter are being honed in renewal circles, in particular those highlighting the roles that mutual testimony (a practice central to renewal spirituality) can play in facilitating interreligious relations in the twenty-first century (Richie 2011). Still, the fundamentally theological and even trinitarian questions cannot be forever avoided, and renewal theologians also are slowly beginning to take up these tasks (e.g., Kärkkäinen 2004b; Studebaker 2012: ch. 6; Richie 2013).

At present, however, there are many more questions than answers at this intersection where theology and Trinity meet the many religions (Vanhoozer 1996). Three levels of inquiry persist: the epistemological, the theological, and the practical. First, the modernist quest for assurance remains pressing in a global multifaith context. How can anyone know with certainty that his or her religious beliefs are true as opposed to those in other traditions? Postliberal approaches appear to have the most traction epistemologically at present. However, this option severely stresses the ultimate truth questions, which can only provide a certain degree of existential confirmation for practitioners of any tradition, to the degree that such traditions shape functional religious lives. But even if Christianity "works" pragmatically, what theological guarantee do we have that the God of Christian faith exists, much less the triune God? Last but not least, even if such more theoretical or abstract questions could be satisfactorily answered, or even if they were to be set aside, how ought Christians to posture themselves, approach, and interact with adherents of non-Christian traditions in a post-Christian world?

11.3 From Israel to the Nations: Matthew's Narrative of the Triune God

As a scriptural springboard toward our constructive reflections, we begin with the first book of the New Testament. The overarching initial statement of SF article 2 on the triune God references two Matthean texts: that related to the Spirit's alighting on the Son at his baptism (3:16-17), and the Great Commission text, which reads: "Go therefore and make disciples of all nations, baptizing them in the name of the Father and of the Son and of the Holy Spirit" (28:19). Our conversation with the First Gospel will therefore begin with the trinitarian question and shift from there to address Matthew's "universalism" and his criteria for salvation, with both of the latter themes potentially shedding light on the Christian encounter with other faiths.

While higher critical scholars have in many cases developed extended arguments for why the trinitarian reference at the end of Matthew is a later interpolation, no solid textual evidence exists to support this claim (Hubbard 1974: appendix 2). The later-redaction argument is not necessarily a rejection of Nicene orthodoxy, but is perhaps even consistent with the overall view, agreed upon by many across the conservative–liberal spectrum, that not only is the word "Trinity" not in the Bible but that trinitarian faith is at best scripturally implicit, only fully developed later. Oneness interpreters accept the textual witness at face value and emphasize two points in response. First, the passage is strongly christological, not only asserting that the disciples worshipped the risen Christ (Matt 28:17) but also that cosmic authority rightfully belonging to God was under Jesus' prerogative (28:18). Second, the command is for baptism to be performed "in the name [note the singular rather than plural] of the Father and of the Son and of the Holy Spirit," which thus invites understanding the divine triad as a synonymous expression of the one true God named Jesus. My claim, however, is that we ought to accept the trinitarian nature of the Matthean (and by extension New Testament) witness according to its own narrative arc (So 2006: esp. chs. 3–4), rather than on the tri-person categories and terms of the fourth-century councils, and that doing so facilitates dialogue between rather than exacerbates oneness–trinitarian relations.

Trinitarian faith is fundamentally about the Father–Son–Spirit relation (see Scaer 2004: ch. 6). Jesus refers to the Father in heaven thirty-eight times in the gospel, fifteen of them in the Sermon on the Mount alone. More significantly, on thirteen occasions Jesus refers to "my Father," and in three he addresses the Father in prayer. Jesus not only is in communion with the Father but also knows he reveals the Father: "All things have been handed over to me by my Father; and no one knows the Son except the Father, and no one knows the Father except the Son and anyone to whom the Son chooses to reveal him" (Matt 11:27). Yet Jesus is also not merely an emissary or revelatory conduit. The angelic pronouncement to Joseph indicates that he is conceived "from the Holy Spirit"; that he will "save his people from their sins"; and that his name is both Jesus and Emmanuel, "which means, 'God is with us'" (1:20-23). Thus Jesus exercises divine authority not only in his risen and exalted state (as per 28:18) but in his forgiving sinners (9:2), raising the dead (9:18-26), healing the sick, and exorcising demons (the last two discussed in earlier chapters). Similarly, the worship due only to God is given to Jesus not only as resurrected lord (28:9, 17) but throughout his life and ministry, beginning as an infant (2:11; 8:2; 9:18; 14:33; 15:25; 20:20; 21:16; see Powell 1995: 56–57). Oneness Pentecostals rightly caution against resorting to personalistic notions of the Father–Son relation, especially when these bring with them later philosophical connotations that are not essential to explicating the scriptural narrative. But the high Christology that they observe in the gospel accounts depends upon a Father–Son relation that invites trinitarian (not tritheistic) reflection.

And so with the Holy Spirit. Not only is Jesus conceived of the Spirit, but he is visited by the Spirit at his baptism (Matt 3:16), is led and empowered by the Spirit (4:1, 12:18), and exorcises demons by the Spirit (12:28). The Spirit is recognized as the one who inspired the prophets (22:43) and their message, which is fulfilled in Jesus. Within the larger scheme of Matthew's gospel, Jesus fulfills the law and the prophets (5:17) and heralds the eschatological reign of God (Chae 2006). In that sense, the Spirit is the divine power and presence of this restorative work (Charette 2000). Going forward, Jesus will be the baptizer with the Holy Spirit (3:11), and the people of God are urged to be receptive to the Spirit's work: "Whoever speaks a word against the Son of Man will be forgiven, but whoever speaks against the Holy Spirit will not be forgiven, either in this age or in the age to come" (12:32).

All this is to say that the thrust of Matthew invites consideration of the Father, Son, and Spirit as triunely related. This means only that the triadic baptismal formula at the end is coherent with the Matthean narrative, not that Matthew believes God exists "in three persons." In fact, it is just as plausible, if not even more so, to see the triad in 28:19 as developing out of triads in the background of the Jewish apocalyptic ideas prevalent in the centuries before Christ, even as the same argument notes Matthean adjustments that temper the cataclysmic elements of that tradition by emphasizing how Jesus' exaltation and transcendence over death now also have positive cosmic ramifications for all nations (Schaberg 1980). So even if Matthew's apocalypticism can be understood as already manifest in the judgment on Israel and the temple (24:3-25), presuming he wrote after the Jewish revolt in 70 CE (see Sim 1996), his christologically and messianically inaugurated eschatology does not overly determine a dualistic hostility between the people of God and the present world. Rather, the arising of the Son from the dead means that the Father's work through the Son by the Spirit confronted and triumphed over mortality. Early Christian "trinitarianism," then, was believed to have universal relevance, at least as understood by the First Gospel author.

Much of the discussion of Matthew's "universalism"—meaning his "all nations" (Matt 28:19) horizons, not the belief that all will be saved—has had to negotiate the question of the thoroughly Jewish character of the gospel and its argument. If Matthew, one of the twelve disciples, is the author of the First Gospel, as tradition attests, we know little about him except that he was a tax collector (9:9; 10:3) and hence perhaps felt alienated in some ways from his fellow Jews. Be that as it may, current scholarly consensus is that the gospel was written to a community of Jewish Christians who were either estranged from or in the process of separating from

Jewish synagogues. So on the one hand, Jesus has come to fulfill the law (5:17) and even directed his public ministry to Israel (10:5). But on the other hand, the rejection of Jesus by the Jewish leadership (20:1-16; 21:28-44; 22:1-14; 23:1-39; 25:1-30) opens up the doors of the coming divine reign to Gentiles (Tisera 1993). Thus the Great Commission is the logical culmination of the broad thrust of the gospel account that "this good news of the kingdom will be proclaimed throughout the world, as a testimony to all the nations; and then the end will come" (24:14; cf. 10:18).

FIGURE 11.4

The larger scenes in the upper two-thirds of each panel of this altarpiece entail and make possible those in the lower third. The centerpiece is the enthroned madonna and child, which throughout Christian history symbolizes the mystery of the incarnation: "when the fullness of time had come, God sent his Son, born of a woman, born under the law" (Gal 4:4). The Christ child holds a small white Book of Life in his left hand and a staff-scepter in his right, gesturing toward the left panel (to which we will return). Mary holds a mappula (royal ceremonial handkerchief) in one hand, and with the other she points from the child to the adult Christ. Here we see Jesus blessing and teaching his followers (fourteen rather than the expected twelve) and offering them the white book held by the Christ child. The teaching of the adult Jesus points toward the right panel, where we witness his crucifixion and burial. And here the crucifixion is directly connected to Eucharist: angels catch the blood from Jesus' hands and feet in chalices, and two disciples (John 19:39) present the wrapped body.

Whereas the adult Christ points toward the crucifixion (cf. Mark 8:31), the child Christ points toward the left panel, where the resurrected Jesus carries a victory banner and pulls an elderly Adam and Eve from their graves (cf. fig. 9.3). Below this image of resurrection (and in light of it) the archangel tramples and slays the satanic dragon (cf. fig. 10.2). This conquering of death and evil is the end to which the child in the central panel is pointing: this is the telos of the incarnation. And, interestingly, of the four depictions of Christ, only this one—the resurrected Christ—makes direct eye contact with us the viewers, as if prompting us to consider the implications: "If the Spirit of him who raised Jesus from the dead dwells in you, he who raised Christ from the dead will give life to your mortal bodies also through his Spirit that dwells in you" (Rom 8:11).

Here we must note the trinitarian logic of this image. It is not that the three panels should each be associated with one person of the Trinity. Rather, in these three scenes—incarnation, crucifixion, and resurrection—Christ exhibits the actions of the trinitarian God (cf. fig. 4.3). This theological imagination is thoroughly christocentric (as much so as any oneness doctrine) at the same time that it is pneumatological and eschatological, presenting the one who "was declared to be Son of God with power according to the Spirit of holiness by resurrection from the dead" (Rom 1:4). ✦

Of course, the Matthean trajectory from Israel to the world is consistent with the broad sweep of the Old Testament witness to the covenant of Abraham opening up to include the Gentiles (LaGrand 1995). Matthew himself cites this prophetic line of thought (4:15; 12:18-21), even beginning his account with Jesus' genealogy, including four Gentile women (Tamar, Rahab, Ruth, and "Uriah's wife" or Bathsheba; 1:3, 5, 6). The "wise men from the East" (2:1) may have been of Judean origin (Teres 2002: 74–75) but are nevertheless clearly portrayed as deploying pagan (astrological) arts otherwise condemned in the Jewish tradition. Other Gentile outsiders are favorably mentioned, including a centurion and a Canaanite woman. Of the former, Jesus said, "In no one in Israel have I found such faith" (8:10). (Note that the parallel Lukan passage

[7:1-10] provides a gospel counterpart anticipating the faith of Cornelius in Acts; cf. section 11.1.) The plight of the latter woman is heightened when compared with the Markan parallel (7:24-30). Mark's more neutral "Syrophoenician woman" becomes the more despicable "Canaanite woman," and she is rebuffed not once but thrice (by the crowd, disciples, and Jesus; Matt 15:21-28). Yet Matthew's point may have been that even according to the most stringent interpretation of laws governing Jewish and Gentile relations, the latter are not excluded from access to the benefits of the covenant (Jackson 2002). Yes, there are disparaging comments made of Gentiles by Jesus (e.g., 5:47; 6:7-8, 31-32), but in that context Jews are not exempt from negative assessments either (5:46; 6:5; see Paschke 2012: 131). All in all then, the preceding suggests that the universal horizon with which the gospel closes is not out of character for Matthew. Consistent with the message of the Old Testament, the God of Israel is also the God of the nations, and Israel's Messiah is the Lord of the nations as well.

Yet *that* the gospel is for the nations says little about other faiths. Of course, Matthew addresses only Jewish–Gentile relations, not other religions. We shall return toward the end of this section to pick up on the former idea, but for the latter, we have to adopt another line of Matthean investigation. The question regarding what Matthew sees as the criteria for salvation suggests itself as fruitful for consideration in this context.

There are four sets of texts that are relevant in this regard. First, the Sermon on the Mount has historically been a springboard for interfaith discussion, in large part because its ethical maxims find parallels in the world's great religious traditions (see Patte 2004: 361–66). Further, the fact that the sermon was given in the region of the Decapolis (Matt 4:25) suggests that Gentiles were to be found in the audience and invites a more universalistic (rather than narrowly Jewish) understanding (Paschke 2012). In this framework, the Beatitudes (5:3-10) suggest basic ethical guidelines for inheriting the reign of God. Yet it is also precisely in this context that Jesus cautions, "Enter through the narrow gate; for the gate is wide and the road is easy that leads to destruction, and there are many who take it. For the gate is narrow and the road is hard that leads to life, and there are few who find it" (7:13-14). Although there is a case to be made for seeing the emphasis here on the stark duality of choosing one of two roads—anticipating being identified later with *either* the sheep *or* the goats (see 25:31-46)—there is also no minimizing that at least in this context of discussing messianic discipleship, Jesus does not inspire confidence that salvation is easily accessed (see Martin 2012). This pessimism is certainly consistent with Jesus' cautioning against false prophets by admonishing against complacency: "Not everyone who says to me, 'Lord, Lord,' will enter the kingdom of heaven, but only one who does the will of my Father in heaven. On that day many will say to me, 'Lord, Lord, did we not prophesy in your name, and cast out demons in your name, and do many deeds of power in your name?' Then I will declare to them, 'I never knew you; go away from me, you evildoers' " (7:21-23). "Insiders" are here forewarned that knowledge and confession are insufficient without the relevant behavioral fruit (7:24-28).

Second, Jesus identifies "the greatest in the kingdom of heaven" (Matt 18:1) with children (cf. 19:14), saying "unless you change and become like children, you will never enter the kingdom of heaven" (18:3; par. Mark 9:33-37; Luke 9:46-48). Childlike trust is here more important than either knowing or doing. Further, their preciousness is doubly emphasized: "in heaven their angels continually see the face of my Father in heaven" (18:10), and "it is not the will of your Father in heaven that one of these little ones should be lost" (18:14). It may be that, as the Third Evangelist writes in another context: "From everyone to whom much has been given, much will be required; and from one to whom much has been entrusted, even more will be demanded" (Luke 12:48). The point may be that greater knowledge makes more difficult, not easier, salvific faith and trust in God.

Third, in Jesus' response to the straightforward question from a rich young man, "What good deed must I do to have eternal life?" (Matt 19:16) and ensuing discussion, a number of salvific criteria emerge. One is keeping the commandments (9:17-19), while another is divesting oneself of possessions and giving to the poor as acts of discipleship in the way of Christ (19:21). While one point of this exchange may have been that "it is easier for a camel to go through the eye of a needle than for someone who is rich to enter the kingdom of God" (19:24), another is also that "[f]or mortals it [salvation] is impossible, but for God all things are possible" (19:26). And yet to cap this off, the warning of Jesus is that "many who are first will be last, and the last will be first" (19:30). Again the message is somewhat paradoxical: for those most worried about salvation, things do not look good; yet when things do look impossible, salvation is God's business, something that God is not only interested in but has resources for realizing.

Finally for our purposes is the parable of the sheep and the goats (Matt 25:31-46). Space constraints prohibit the kind of analysis that ought to be given (e.g., as found in Yong 2011b: 136–41), even as we have already had occasion in preceding chapters to reference this important parable. These very brief comments must suffice. It is clear that salvation (for sheep) comes because of their ethical activity—which includes feeding the hungry, being hospitable to strangers, clothing the naked, and caring for the sick—toward "one of the least of these who are members of my family" (25:40, 45), while damnation (for goats) follows their lacking the same. There is broad scholarly consensus, however, that at least in the Matthean context, the "least of these" (the hungry, etc.) refer to Christians in general and Christian missionaries in particular (see 10:42; cf. Gray 1989: 359; Luz 1995: 129–30; Wilson 2004: 245–46). In that case, rather than teaching a humanitarian ethic through which the world will be judged, the parable provides a christological criterion that acceptance or judgment follows from whether or not those from the nations personally accept Christ, at least in the form of his followers and their message. While this is an important interpretation of the parable, within the broader universalistic horizon of the gospel, its ethical message ought not be minimized. So even if the "charitable works used in the passage originally referred to the treatment of Christian missionaries, it nevertheless also serves well Matthew's own more universalistic concerns" (Luomanen 1998: 190). Further, in its more immediate context (Matt 19–25), wherein "insiders" are denounced because of their unbelief, this parable also suggests that the new people of God drawn from the nations "is defined along ethical and not ethnic lines" (Olmstead 2003: 165). Even if we were to stay with the scholarly consensus on the parable, then, it would only address those whose paths encounter "the least of these," but in that case would not address the unevangelized. But in any case, there is also a viable, even if minority, stream within Christian tradition that understands the "least of these" as referring to the needy in general, which renders it both permissible and orthodox (see Bullivant 2012: ch. 5). This line of thinking opens up the possibility that the unevangelized meet the mystical body of Christ in and through the least of the world.

11.4 Worshipful Witness to the God of Jesus Christ in the Spirit

Two overarching topics need to be addressed in concluding this chapter: those concerning the trinitarian nature of God and how to understand such in a pluralistic world. Can the Christian confession of God as triune be both more biblically faithful and more conducive to interfaith evangelism, dialogue, and relationship than has been previously considered? We will argue this thesis in what follows.

At the intrarenewal level, the most contentious oneness-trinitarian matter has to do not with the doctrine of God or even the baptismal formula but the soteriological implications of tongues-speech in relationship with receiving the Holy Spirit (as understood by oneness interpretations of Acts 2:38). It is hoped that the more expansive theology of Spirit Baptism and the dynamic and eschatological soteriology developed in earlier chapters of this volume provide bridges over which further oneness-trinitarian dialogue can be held on pneumatology in relationship to the doctrine of salvation. The key may be to observe, as with the baptismal formula, that the apostolic witness provides for multiple perspectives that validate practices on both sides. On this point, it is only insistence that there is one right mode of baptism that stalls conversation. But if both sides were to remain faithful to the scope of Scripture, then there is no need to dismiss those baptized either in Jesus' name (in Acts) or in the name of the triune God (in Matthew). This is especially the case if God's triunity is understood narratively according to the gospel witness, precisely what has been suggested here (section 11.3), rather than according to later (fourth century or other) formulations. The gospel narratives invite a triadic, triune, or trinitarian understanding of God. Using these terms adjectivally rather than as nouns avoids conveying tritheistic connotations to the uninitiated.

However, the intrapentecostal debate interfaces with the broader Christian tradition. Most Reformation traditions affirm the primacy of Scripture not instead of, but alongside accepting the fourth-century ecumenical achievements. For many of the historic churches, then, the resoluteness with which oneness believers hold their anti-trinitarian conviction is not only a hindrance to dialogue but a scandalous heterodoxy. While a full proposal to bridge the gap is beyond the scope of this chapter (for further proposals in this vein, see Yong 2005: ch. 5), four lines of response can be sketched.

First and most simply, oneness modalism is distinctively Christian, in contrast with, for instance, Unitarian anti-Trinitarianism. The former insists on a high Christology, while the latter tends to reject the divinity of Christ. The oneness position thus may be said to affirm the spirit of the ecumenical creeds (Jesus Christ's deity and lordship), albeit deploying pre-Nicene rationales and categories of thinking, whereas many across the diffuse Unitarian spectrum, arguably, would reject the substance of the tradition's christological confessions.

Second, might oneness renewalists be open to more sympathetically engaging with the ecumenical achievements of the church and providing alternative understandings of and perhaps even additional insights into these affirmations? This would be possible if two assumptions were clarified: ecumenical creeds are historically situated declarations that provide limited, albeit no less true, perspective, understood in certain important respects, and as such, they are always open to further interpretation (with regard to what they may have meant for their original context) and supplementation (by later developments). These are operative presuppositions for the WAGF SF undergirding this theological exercise, and those in other churches are invited to view their own confessions in similar terms. Would oneness theologians also be able to view not only their statements of faith in this way but also those of the fourth and fifth centuries? That would enable dialogue with the Christian tradition: those later ones can provide charitable readings of prior confessions, embracing what can be affirmed while pointing out the limitations inherent in any theological or doctrinal construct.

A third line of response builds on the narrative approach recommended in this chapter and on the eschatological orientation of this volume as a whole. The movements suggested here are twofold: backward from the gospel narratives toward the narrative of ancient Israel (thus gaining further insight into God the Father) and forward from the narrative of the Son to the narrative of the church and the eschaton (thus anticipating the full revelation of the resurrection power of God the Spirit). This is not to then canonize oneness modalist instincts, because that remains a pre-Nicene stance in terms of affirming only that God is revealed successively (modally) as Father, Son, and Spirit. Rather, it is to pay attention to the life of the triune God as unveiled in the full scope of the scriptural narrative and to anticipate that God is always the redemptive good news to come in the power of the Spirit of Jesus (e.g., Jenson 1982; cf. Tomlin 2011). It also invites oneness believers and Trinitarians who have encountered the Spirit of Pentecost to revisit the Christian drama of redemption and build on their common charismatic experiences in rereading and interpreting these texts afresh.

The advantages here are at least twofold. Initially, such an approach drives Christian theology back to the biblical narrative and seeks from there to think through a biblically informed theology and metaphysics about God's relationship to the world and about the nature of time and eternity. From this, then, the historic Christian trinitarian tendency to lapse into binitarianism (relating Father and Son) can be avoided, so a fully trinitarian theology can continue to emerge that takes seriously the person of the Spirit as the possibility and future of God (e.g., Jenson 1997: esp. ch. 9). The future is not yet actual, because saying this would be to adopt a neoplatonic notion of time in relationship to eternity, rather than following out the plot line of hope laid out in the biblical narrative. But simultaneously, the future also does not have its own ontological grounding, as if it is what makes God possible. Rather, it is the resurrecting power of the Spirit of Christ that makes the future possible, so the tri-une God is unveiled, according to the biblical story, as the Lord of time (Padgett 1992: ch. 6). God as triune is revealed in the Father, as source; in the begotten Son, as taking up history into the divine life; and in the proceeding or spirating Spirit from the Father and the Son, as holding forth and bringing about the promise of future redemption.

Yet from the latter eschatological vantage point, it is the Spirit of the Father poured out by the Son who brings creation back through the Son to the Father (e.g., Coffey 1999). This perspective foregrounds not the mysteries of creation but the hopes anticipating the salvation to come. The latter thereby become the promises that secure the identities of Spirit, Son, and Father. The Spirit makes present God's future promises in Christ (proleptically) and in the church (anticipatorily); the Son's incarnation and resurrection, both through the Spirit, open history up to God's future; and the Father creates and renews according to the image of and out of love for the Son, albeit both via the fullness of the divine breath. What results is a triune monotheism that is faithful to the biblical story line from creation to eschaton, and even more so when it is read in reverse. This would allow for metaphysical speculation (human beings are speculative creatures as well) while hesitating about making commitments in this domain beyond what is necessarily scriptural.

Such a strategic approach to metaphysical theology is also consistent with the pragmatism central to renewal spirituality. And this leads to our fourth line of response: the performative and pragmatic dimension of trinitarian theological thinking. Starting with worship and liturgy, for instance, both oneness and trinitarian renewalists imbibe a christocentric piety yet are energized by a pneumatic spirituality. Hence, "Trinity" in this case is not an abstract idea but a mode of authentic worship, one that consists in our creaturely adoration of God through Jesus Christ in the Spirit (see Parry 2005). Trinitarian theology also highlights the perichoretic nature of divine relationality, which in turn provides a map for human communion. This reorders ecclesial and other relationships interpersonally (Volf 1998; Smail 2005; T. Norris 2009) and inspires missional models of mutuality (Seamands 2005; Treier and Lauber 2009). The point is that at least the more speculatively inclined will perennially debate the fine points of the theological tradition—not least those relating to the triune mystery—but Christian life is structured by an inescapable trinitarian rhythm: life in the Spirit shaped according to the image of Christ and directed to the glory of the Father. This does not need tri-person explication reducible to or exhausted by fourth-century Nicene categories, although there is no need to diminish the important contributions of the early ecumenical achievements. But it does inspire human persons to worshipful witness to the God of Christ in the Holy Spirit.

To be sure, such witness now unfolds in a pluralistic world to which Christians are becoming more sensitized. How might the triune and eschatological God of the biblical narrative be understood in relationship to the many religions? More importantly, how can trinitarian faith inspire worshipful witness for those of other traditions? Article 2 of the SF includes four clauses that confess God the Father as "Creator of heaven and earth, the Giver of the Law, to whom all things will be subjected, so that He may be all in all." Each clause provides a springboard for thinking about these questions.

As "Creator of heaven and earth," God the Father is the source of all things by the Word and Spirit. People are created in the image of God, in anticipation of the fully manifest image in Christ (as discussed in ch. 10), and imbued with the divine breath. Human sociality and culture, similarly, reflect the triune relationality, however distorted by sin, although the church does so now as abiding in Christ and being filled with the Spirit. So while fully recognizing the fallen character of human relationships, institutions, cultures, and traditions, the church also recognizes that these are nevertheless also purveyors of common and life-sustaining goods, truths, and beauty. Insofar as religious traditions are also constituted by and intertwined with the various economic, political, social, cultural, and historical strands around which human life is woven, to that same degree they are also conduits of the goods, truths, and beauty that enable human flourishing. This is not to baptize everything that happens in the name of religion, or even in the space of culture or in the global economy or in the realm of the political. It is to say that to the degree that these are life producing, they are providential gifts of the triune God, whose Logos enlightens every person (John 1:9) and whose Spirit has been poured out on all flesh (Acts 2:17). On the other hand, to the degree that these are life-destroying, they anticipate divine judgment and await eschatological redemption.

As "the Giver of the Law," God provides the Mosaic covenant to Israel in anticipation of the new covenant in Christ. Yet the Mosaic covenant itself follows after both the universal human covenant made with Noah (Gen 9:1-17) and the particular Abrahamic covenant, the blessings of which were nevertheless intended for "all the families of the earth" (Gen 12:3). Further, even as the Mosaic law was given to guide Israel, so also were the laws of the heart given to the Gentiles (Rom 2:12-15). So even if the covenant with Israel is unique and without parallel in other religious traditions (see Sparks 2010), the latter can be derived at least in part from the laws of conscience, even as they are also potentially caught up in the universal blessings enfolded within the Abrahamic covenant. Hence Jesus can be said to be in precise continuity with and have come in order to fulfill only the law of Moses. But insofar as the full unfolding of the law culminates with the reign of God, it establishes the domain of Christ and the Spirit across every human arena, from the political to the economic to the cultural to the social and even to the religious. Hence the eschatological fulfillment of the law will find the rule of Christ judging the ugliness, falsehoods, and evils on the world but redeeming whatever is good, true, and beautiful. In that case, the lawful aspects of the world's faiths will be similarly fulfilled, even as their deepest spiritual aspirations that are noble and redeemable because of common or prevenient grace will be transfigured in the light of Christ.

FIGURE 11.5

Traditionally, depictions of Christ Enthroned in Majesty function as eschatological visions of the reign of God, drawing heavily from the visions of the throne of God in the book of Revelation (cf. fig. 1.4). And in this, Laura James' triptych is traditional: Christ is enthroned in the center, and behind him "something like a sea of glass" (Rev 4:6) extends outward and upward to the top of the composition. The throne is surrounded by the "four living creatures" (4:6-8), who iconographically double as the four gospel writers (see fig. 2.3). These creatures sing without ceasing: "Holy, holy, holy, the Lord God the Almighty, who was and is and is to come" (Rev 4:8), and as they sing, twenty-four elders fall before the throne in worship (4:9-10). James portrays these elders in the side panels of the painting, gathered from all ethnicities and regions of the earth, all worshipping the Lord of life: "for you created all things, and by your will they existed and were created" (4:11).

The expansiveness of this "all things" must be felt as this image opens outward toward us with an indeterminate multitude of people and creatures standing on our side of the picture plane. As the scene in Revelation unfolds, the songs of worship grow in scale until the author finally hears "every creature in heaven and on earth and under the earth and in the sea, and all that is in them, singing, 'To the one seated on the throne and to the Lamb be blessing and honor and glory and might forever and ever!'" (5:13; cf. 19:6-7). This eschatologically orients us to regard images of Christ's enthronement in at least three ways: First, images like this are reminders to remain "open" to the cosmic scope of Christ's work as God reconciles to himself "all things, whether on earth or in heaven" (Col 1:20), ultimately "so that God may be all in all" (1 Cor 15:28). Second, this image is itself a call to join the elders in worshipping and enthroning Christ in our lives (from this side of the picture plane). Third, this worship occurs in and through the life-giving Spirit: the one who raised Jesus from the dead also dwells in you (Rom 8:11). ✦

Christian faith proclaims faith in the one "to whom all things will be subjected, so that He may be all in all" (1 Cor 15:28). In a pluralistic world, this will be viewed as a triumphalist assertion that has had a long history of destructive, even demonic, effects enacted in the name of Christ (e.g., the Crusades, slavery, colonialism, the Holocaust). Hence while the future orientation of this clause—". . . will be . . ." and ". . . may be . . ."—invite the performative commitment of those who embrace this hope in their hearts, such ought to be conducted in the humility of spirit that recognizes humans can only participate in rather than dictate God's redemptive work. Yet simultaneously, such future orientation is not otherworldly. In fact, Christian mission and evangelism according to the New Testament are motivated not by the fear of eternal damnation (which is inculcated to admonish the faithful, not to scare the pagan) but in response to the empowering work of the Spirit. Hence the eschatological future opens up life abundant (John 10:10), beginning now, and thereby inspires Christian mission for the sake of the present world.

Aspects of such a trinitarian and *worshipful witness*—as opposed to haughty domination—engaging with others humbly before God can be delineated along three lines (see also Yong 2008).

First, the Great Commission is not an option but an imperative for followers of Christ. Yet there are a multitude of ways to evangelize, missionize, and make disciples, even if all of these involve at the appropriate moment, baptism into the death of Christ (section 6.4), and resurrection into the body of Christ and the fellowship of the Spirit (section 7.4). While a renewal perspective has historically emphasized traditional modes of proselytism, in an interfaith context worshipful witness ought also to involve interpersonal testimony, itself peculiarly central to renewal spirituality (Richie 2011, 2013). Mission and evangelism in such a testimonial mode is unavoidably dialogical. Christians testify to the works of God in Christ by the Spirit in their lives, but such Spirit-empowered witness emerged out of a relational matrix within which they also listen to and even receive the testimonies of those of other or no faith. Even authentic missional and evangelistic encounter thus involves the sharing of stories across alien lines, as well as the mutual transformation of the testifiers. Peter learned as much from Cornelius as the latter did from him, and the Matthean account of Jesus' encounter with the Canaanite woman also reflects that the Messiah became convinced by her side of the story. In short, Christian proclamation in a multifaith context will need to be driven by diverse modes of worshipful and interpersonal witness.

Second, the Great Commission involves the making of disciples according to the relational life of the triune God. Discipleship is inherently ecclesial, so there is an element of growth in faith according to the liturgical fellowship of the church as the body of Christ. But as we have also seen (ch. 7), ecclesial life is diaconal and missional. Hence discipleship inherently involves interface with, ministry amid, and service to the world in all of its dimensions. There is thus a liberative thrust in search of justice and shalom at these civil, social, political, economic, environmental, and other levels that can only be tackled collaboratively with people of other or no faith. This does not require the church to give up its distinctive witness. On the contrary, its discipleship in the public square is more starkly registered, precisely because its compassionate witness (see ch. 7) is cruciform and Spirit-empowered, directed to the glory of the Father. Worshipful witness in this arena participates perseveringly and steadfastly in the Spirit's work of renewing the creation in anticipation of the eschatological lordship of Christ.

Third, beyond the interpersonal and the public spheres, there is also the encounter between religions in the present age. A pentecostal or Acts 2 theology of human languages here opens up also to a theology of culture (languages and cultures are intertwined). This in turn is suggestive for a theology of religions, because there is an undeniable cultural dimension to religion, even as religion can be understood as the depth dimension of culture (Tillich 1959, 1969; Yong 2005: chs. 4 and 6). Again, this is not to say that all aspects of all religions are redeemed, even as it is not to say that all aspects of every culture or all parts of every language are thereby sanctified by the Spirit. Eschatologically, the redemptive judgment of God will expose and reject all that is evil, false, and ugly, while purifying and preserving what is good, true, and beautiful in each case. In the meantime, however, every language, culture, and even religious tradition potentially bears, however haltingly because of finite and fallen character, witness to the one under whom all things will be finally subject.

So on the one hand, Christian faith will invariably involve making distinctions, clarifying commitments to the triune God and their entailments, condemning lies, and prophetically opposing all things that undermine God-given life. And in many cases, such resisting activities will come vis-à-vis other faiths. However, in other cases, Christians ought to embrace the good, true, and beautiful in other faiths when this is discerned. Perhaps the Christian reception of the witness of those in other faiths will bring about repentance, involve a deeper conversion to the God of Jesus Christ, and transform what remains needful of purification. On the one hand, then, there is a boldness and confidence in Christian proclamation; on the other hand, there is a humility that resists triumphalist attitudes toward religious others, imperialistic interpretations of their ideas, and colonialist practices in interacting with them. Knowing which is which requires Christians not only to proclaim the gospel but also to listen to and learn from their neighbors in other faiths. That is the proper posture of worshipful witness in this in-between time, in anticipation of the final redemption to come.

In contrast to the Jewish witness during the Second Temple period, which was not overtly aggressive in seeking proselytes (McKnight 1990), Christians have almost from the beginning been an active missionary faith. Yet depending on the context, there is an equal amount of urging within the apostolic witness of leading quiet and peaceable lives before a watching world (e.g., Matt 5:13-16; 1 Thess 4:11-12; 1 Tim 2:2; 1 Pet 2:11-12). Christian witness, in other words, does not have to be antagonistic to those in other faiths, especially not when it is realized that God "has not left himself without a witness" to the nations (Acts 14:17), and that "[i]n him [all people] live and move and have [their] being" (Acts 17:28). Here the Matthean community may be suggestive as a model for how to live amid the differences of two increasingly dissimilar faith communities. Thus Matthew makes a distinction between moral and ritual law, not rejecting the latter for Jews but yet insisting on the import of the former for Gentiles. Might living in a pluralistic world today involve making similar distinctions that respect and honor the living witness of those in other faiths on the one hand and yet also hold forth an olive branch in a posture of worshipful witness in anticipation of the coming reign on the other?

Discussion Questions

1. How does the preceding discussion of the doctrine of the triune God compare and contrast with your church's teachings? How much should we try to clarify the mystery of God based on divine revelation? To what degree is our worship of God in Christ and the Spirit sufficient to express the trinitarian character of Christian faith?

2. Should Christian theology focus more attention on resolving the ancient *filioque* dispute? How is the doctrine of the Holy Spirit a unifying feature for contemporary Christian theology on the one hand, but how might it be a divisive doctrine for the church on the other hand?

3. What aspects of the preceding discussion of theology of religions and interreligious encounter compare or contrast with your church's views on these topics? Is the Christian understanding of God as triune a barrier to interfaith relations, or does it have the potential to facilitate positive Christian relationships with those in other faiths? What does it mean for you and your church to be engaged in worshipful witness in a pluralistic world?

Further Reading

Atkinson, William. 2013. *Trinity after Pentecost*. Eugene, Ore.: Pickwick.

Hunt, Anne. 1998. *What Are They Saying about the Trinity?* Mahwah, N.J.: Paulist.

Kärkkäinen, Veli-Matti. 2003. *An Introduction to the Theology of Religions: Biblical, Historical and Contemporary Perspectives*. Downers Grove, Ill.: IVP Academic.

Knitter, Paul F. 2002. *Introducing Theologies of Religions*. Maryknoll, N.Y.: Orbis.

Macchia, Frank D. 2010. *The Trinity: Practically Speaking*. Downers Grove, Ill.: InterVarsity.

Ockholm, Dennis L., and W. Gary Phillips, eds. 1996. *Four Views on Salvation in a Pluralistic World*. Grand Rapids: Zondervan.

Shults, F. LeRon, and Andrea Hollingsworth. 2008. *The Holy Spirit*. Grand Rapids: Eerdmans.

12

The Spirit-Inspired Scriptures

*Biblical Authority and Theological Methods
for Us and Our Salvation*

World Assemblies of God Fellowship Statement of Faith
—Article 1: The Inspiration of the Scriptures

We believe that the Scriptures, both the Old and New Testaments, are verbally inspired of God and are the revelation of God to man, the infallible, authoritative rule of faith and conduct. Divine inspiration extends equally and fully to all parts of the original writings, insuring their entire trustworthiness (2 Timothy 3:15-17; 2 Peter 1:21).

12.1 John—One Name, Many Voices

Many Christians know that the Bible consists of many books (sixty-six to be exact) and many authors. This chapter begins with one of the contributors to the New Testament: John. The problem is that we are not sure if "John" was one person or many, and we are not even sure if "he" represents the literary achievements of a group of people or even a school of writers (see Culpepper 1994). Yet even if the latter is the case, the various traditions related to "John" are almost harmonious in affirming that each has received its inspiration from one such individual. In the following, I want to present the various "faces" associated with that name in the New Testament. If they are all related, they provide a conglomerate kaleidoscope to the richness of God's self-revelation through a personal life. If they are not, then it is still as remarkable that the coherence of the witness to Christ nevertheless comes through the polyphony of these apostolic testimonies.

The most well-known John is surely one of the twelve disciples of Jesus, the son of Zebedee and Salome, and the brother of James. The brothers were raised as fisherman by their father, who appears to have had an established business (Mark 1:19-20), and nurtured by a mother who urged them on in their ambitions (Matt 20:20-21; cf. Mark 10:35-37).

Thus they seemed not to have lacked confidence, perhaps indicated by the name Jesus gave them: "Boanerges, that is, Sons of Thunder" (Mark 3:17), even as John gives an impression of himself as an overzealously motivated student (see Luke 9:49-55). Still, they found themselves, along with Peter, in Jesus' inner circle (e.g., Matt 17:1; Mark 5:37; 9:2; 13:3; 14:33; Luke 8:51; 9:28). Christian tradition stretching back to the second century asserts that this disciple of Jesus is the author of the gospel, three short letters, and the Revelation of the New Testament, although there is no scholarly unanimity about these matters.

The Fourth Gospel is anonymous as to its authorship. There is a dominant tradition, however, that equates the enigmatic "beloved disciple" (John 13:23; 20:2; 21:7, 20) with John the apostle. If this association is correct, then the one of whom his own mother had high aspirations was charged by Jesus to care for Mary: "When Jesus saw his mother and the disciple whom he loved standing beside her, he said to his mother, 'Woman, here is your son.' Then he said to the disciple, 'Here is your mother.' And from that hour the disciple took her into his own home" (19:26-27). It is intriguing to note, if this is the case, that the one who cared for the mother of Jesus perhaps the rest of her life—tradition also indicated (following 21:23) he lived a long life himself—mentions nothing about Jesus' extraordinary birth in his gospel.

The Johannine letters, as already noted (section 5.3), are anonymous. The two shorter epistles both begin with greetings from "the elder" (2 John 1; 3 John 1), while the first opens with a clear claim to an eyewitness relationship with Jesus as the Word of life (1 John 1:1-3). External evidence from the postapostolic period suggests the early church viewed "John the elder" as the apostle, and there may be little reason to doubt the equation. If so, then besides caring for the mother of the Lord, he also took on pastoral responsibilities with dexterity and passion eminently portrayed in each of these epistles.

Interestingly, of the New Testament writings attributed to John, only the Apocalypse is nominally specific. Rather than clarifying himself as the "apostle John," however, the author self-identifies only as "his [Jesus Christ's] servant John" (Rev 1:1). Beyond servanthood, John's vision leads him to prostrate himself before the divine presence on more than one occasion (1:17, 22:8). From this posture, he addresses "the seven churches that are in Asia" (1:4), which suggests, perhaps related to the eldership mentioned in 2 and 3 John, pastoral and even apostolic oversight for a number of churches in a region. As "your brother who shares with you in

Jesus the persecution and the kingdom and the patient endurance, was on the island called Patmos because of the word of God and the testimony of Jesus" (Rev 1:9), there is a long tradition assuming the letter was written under conditions of exile, perhaps during the years of intermittent persecution of Christians (Blount 2009: x) under the emperor Domitian (r. 81–96). If so, then the fact that only those of higher social standing would have suffered banishment suggests that John had attained a certain reputation (Thomas 2012: 43–44). Yet "because of the word of God and the testimony of Jesus" also can suggest that John came to Patmos to evangelize. This is consistent with his renown as "John the evangelist." It is certainly also possible that the expatriated émigré made the best of his plight and received it as a missionary opportunity (Bournis 1968).

There are three more noteworthy aspects of John's character to be gleaned from his book that closes the Christian canon. First, while he does not call himself a prophet, he surely understands what he has written as a prophecy (e.g., Rev 1:3; 22:7, 10). Second, whatever his personality dispositions, John is clearly a visionary and a mystic. Revelation is written from all that John sees and hears, which he received as one "in the Spirit" (1:10; 4:2; 17:13; 21:10; see Barr 2003: ch. 9). Third, in one of his visions, he is given a little scroll and invited to consume it: "So I took the little scroll from the hand of the angel and ate it; it was sweet as honey in my mouth, but when I had eaten it, my stomach was made bitter" (10:10). The bitterness no doubt reflects the apocalyptic contents of the scroll, while the consumption of the scroll itself is a fulfillment of Old Testament prophetic types wherein the word of God was ingested (Jer 15:16; Ezek 2:8–3:3). Revelation is steeped in Old Testament symbols and imagery. Each of these aspects of the Apocalypse will receive further comment below.

If there is one John behind each of these New Testament documents who is the disciple of Jesus, then the composite picture that emerges is of a Judean fisherman turned prophet and visionary who crosses linguistic (Aramaic to Greek), cultural (Palestinian to Mediterranean), and even religious (ancient Israelite to Greco-Roman) worlds (see González 1999: ch. 4). If John refers to two or more distinct individuals, they still may be related through the so-called "Johannine school" posited by many scholars. Regardless, the Johannine witness sounds out a multifaceted set of testimonies to Jesus Christ. How might this Johannine set of voices inspire our thinking theologically and doctrinally about Scripture and the divine revelatory word?

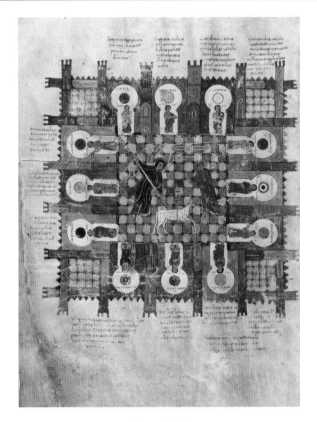

FIGURE 12.1

The numerous visions recorded in Revelation—all richly evoking and ringing with Old Testament allusions—ultimately push toward John's vision of the New Jerusalem, wherein heaven and earth are "married" such that "the home of God is among mortals. He will dwell with them; they will be his peoples, and God himself will be with them" (Rev 21:3). And at the center of this vision, as throughout the book, John sees the Lamb (cf. fig. 1.4).

The image shown here (from a medieval illuminated commentary on Revelation) visualizes several significant details of John's vision. The City of God is depicted as having "a great, high wall with twelve gates, and at the gates twelve angels" (Rev 21:12); and although these gates are inscribed with the tribes of Israel, they open outward in every direction, calling in (and here representing) many regions and ethnicities, culminating in "a great multitude that no one could count, from every nation, from all tribes and peoples and languages" (7:9). This image also presents something of the overall structure of the city: John describes it as an enormous cubic structure, approximately 1,400 miles (2,200 km) in each direction (21:16), which an angel calculates using a golden measuring rod (21:15). These dimensions are astonishing in two ways: (1) the only other struc-ture in the biblical canon that is a cube is the holy of holies (1 Kgs 6:20; 2 Chr 3:4-8; Ezek 41:4), and (2) this holy of holies is utterly awesome in size—for an ancient person it simply would have encompassed the entire known world. John's vision audaciously points toward an eschatological day in which the entire earth, including diverse peoples and languages, will be the dwelling of the holy, enlivening Spirit of God.

All of this has implications for how we think about divine revelation. John's imagery is presented to have striking affective impact: the revelation is sensually, visually, and audibly received and is passed on to us in terms intended to gener-ate an imaginative sensory experience. Indeed, the massiveness and audacity of this image are an invitation into a mysterium tremendum et fascinans, a mystery before which we both tremble and are fascinated. ✦

12.2 Divine Revelation/s: Many Interpretations

Article 1 of the WAGF SF focuses on the doctrine of Scripture. It functions foundationally for the entire SF by providing the authoritative ground for its various claims. The need for such epistemic underpinning has been more palpable, especially in light of the Enlightenment's emphasis on rea-son over tradition, including religious traditions. Ecclesial confessions in the wake of the Enlightenment are thus much more likely to begin by securing the epistemic criteria for belief, which are usually derived from the Bible for Reformation traditions. This stands in stark contrast to the early ecumenical confessions, for instance (see appendix 2), which were formulated under entirely different circumstances with alternative needs, warrants, and purposes.

Like Protestants in general, renewalists also have always been people of the book (Hollenweger 1972: ch. 21). Yet in some important senses, while authoritative, Scripture functions less cerebrally for renewalists than for other conservative Protestants. Instead, as we shall see, Scripture is authoritative for renewalists precisely because they find it provides a vital map for their spiritual and daily lives. There is therefore an experien-tial dimension to their Bible-reading that invites a distinctive renewal approach not only to the doctrine of Scripture but also to the theology of revelation and even to theological method. Some historical perspective on these three themes will frame the discussion in this final chapter of our book.

12.2.1 Sola Scriptura *and the Word of God: Reformed and Always Reforming*

Many renewalists, while not vocal proponents of the Reformation slogan *sola scriptura*, are nevertheless pietistic practitioners of the doctrine. The Reformers called for a return to Scripture to correct abuses accreted by tradition over the centuries. "Scripture alone" thus meant not that no other sources could be consulted but that the church was to be reformed under the norm and supreme authority of biblical revelation (see Payton 2010: ch. 6). Renewalists generally are confirmed Protestants in both of these senses: the Bible alone is to be the ultimate authority, and the church always ought to be reformed and reforming (*semper reformanda*)—even renewed and renewing—through its subjection to Scripture and "by the life giving, sanctifying work of the triune God" (Allen 2010: 179). Yet emphasizing the priority of Scripture has spurred reflection about its nature, and this in turn has led to the development of a theology of the Bible as revelation. The ensuing centuries have seen critical questions posed, and defenders of the Bible have arisen in response.

Three phrases in the SF article 1 provide windows into this broader Protestant wrestling with and about the Bible. First, the Scriptures are "verbally inspired of God." This means that each of the biblical words, not just its basic message, has been superintended by God, albeit without denying the unique contributions of the human authors God used. This doctrine of verbal inspiration thus usually straddles between either a dictation theory that minimizes if not altogether eliminates the human role (as in some Muslim theories of Qur'anic inspiration) or a range of less conservative views that emphasize the human element and downplay if not outwardly reject divine authorship (thus the Bible is just like other sacred scriptures, if not like any other book, and is to be read in conjunction with other scriptures and texts; e.g., Smith 1993; Coward 2000; Lee and Yoo 2009). The more recent trend among evangelicals presumes the inspired character of Scripture but seeks to clarify the nature of the human contribution (Enns 2005; Sparks 2008). Others have sought to explore how God can adopt and has adopted human discourse as God's own in order to reveal himself (Wolterstorff 1995; Vanhoozer 2002: part 2). The issue has to do with the reliability of Scripture: If merely of human provenance, then how can it be God's word? If divinely derivative, then how can the Bible be studied like other books, deploying literary, critical, and hermeneutical methods?

FIGURE 12.2

When Jordaens portrays the four gospel writers, he renders them as thoroughly ordinary men. He withholds their traditional symbolic associations (Luke with the ox, Mark the lion, John the eagle, and Matthew the angel), as well as their usual haloes; they are portrayed in the most common human terms possible. In fact, these men are so removed from traditional iconography that some art historians wonder whether we have correctly identified the subject matter at all (the title is not traceable to Jordaens).

Assuming that this is indeed an image of the evangelists (which seems to be the best explanation and is still the general consensus), their activity is also quite striking. It is common to depict the evangelists writing their texts in private conversation with angels or sometimes even with Christ himself (perhaps suggesting dictation theories of inspiration), but it is unusual in Christian art history to picture them immersed in hermeneutic conversation with each other. Such an image reimagines the extent to which the gospels emerged from intense discourse grounded in careful readings and rereadings of the (Old Testament) Scriptures.

This helpfully highlights the thoroughly polyphonic character of the Christian Scriptures. Jesus did not write any extant texts himself but rather is testified to through multiple witnesses, multiple gospels. Matthew, Mark, and Luke are referred to as Synoptic Gospels, because of the ways they share narrative material and see Jesus along similar points of view—and yet they are certainly not "monoptic." Each one accounts for the significance of Jesus' life and ministry with different emphases, different concerns (with the Fourth Gospel being even more divergent), and each is differently situated in relation to the Law and Prophets. The Christian gospel emerges from plurivocal, intertextual practices and then produces plurivocal, intertextual practices; and it is precisely this interconnected plurality of texts that Christians hold to be authoritative.

We should note one final detail of Jordaens' painting: one of the apostles has conspicuously pulled back the background curtain to reveal a glimpse of the world beyond this scene, as if to suggest that the implications of this discourse will extend radically outward. Indeed, this is a message of good news about and for all the world. ✦

The concerns regarding verbal inspiration thus open up to the claim that the Bible is "the infallible, authoritative rule of faith and conduct." The latter assertion regarding the normativity of the Bible is itself scripturally derived: "All scripture is inspired by God and is useful for teaching, for reproof, for correction, and for training in righteousness, so that everyone who belongs to God may be proficient, equipped for every good work" (2 Tim 3:16-17). The reference to scriptural infallibility, however, while an equally ancient conviction, has in more recent times been compared and contrasted with claims regarding the Bible's inerrancy (see Davis 1977). The former stays focused on the Bible's soteriological and ethical message, while the latter insists further that all scriptural avowals—whether historical, anthropological, or even scientific—are equally truthful and without inaccuracies. Many renewalists, like other evangelicals (e.g., Bovell 2007), embrace infallibility without insistence also on inerrancy. Inerrantists, however, counter that if the Bible can be mistaken on any matter, how can it be trustworthy about the important things related to salvation?

Article 1 may have included two nods toward an inerrant Bible. One is discerned in the final sentence, which insists on Scripture's "*entire trustworthiness*" (emphasis added). Yet many renewalists are not enamored by the apologetic maneuvers needed to defend inerrancy on every detail (e.g., Archer 2001), because for them, the dependability of the Bible derives from "demonstration of the Spirit and of power, so that your faith might rest not on human wisdom but on the power of God" (1 Cor 2:4b-5). Hence the Bible can be entirely trustworthy without holding to inerrancy in its modern epistemic sense. Or, if the Bible is indeed error-free—and few renewalists think it problematic that an omnipotent God can produce an inerrant Bible—then, as is the usual strategy among their conservative Protestant cousins (e.g., Geisler 1980), such inerrancy applies "fully to all parts of the original writings." Of course, as none of the original manuscripts are extant, this article of faith is immune to critical inquiry, and hence similarly without much apologetic foundation or urgency.

Of course, the underlying worry in all of this is that the rise of modern biblical criticism has often undermined rather than inspired faith. For theological and doctrinal purposes, then, searching critical analysis of the Bible in all of its details seems to be undertaken in a skeptical rather than a believing posture. An infallible if not inerrant Bible is important not only for human salvation but for understanding God, surely the whole point of divine revelation. It is to be expected, then, that conservative Protestants have spent much time and effort in waging "the battle for the Bible" (Lindsell 1978). In this view what is important are the scriptural propositions themselves, because they communicate essential truths about the world, salvation, and God.

Yet this contemporary preoccupation minimizes many other aspects of the Bible. The diversity of the scriptural genres—narrative, poetry, law, prophecy, letter, and so on—means that biblical truths are communicated variously other than merely propositionally. Further, the many modes of interaction with and reception of Scripture—certainly through reading and studying but even more important historically: singing, chanting, recitation, preaching—suggest that the message of the Bible "works" not only cognitively but also affectively and synesthetically, differentiated according to human sight and hearing. Additionally, Scripture's various functions—not only informing but also correcting, encouraging, guiding, and inspiring, among other purposes—suggest that divine revelation is multifaceted rather than reducible to any one register. Last but not least, the media of Scripture itself have been dynamic: from the oral traditions of ancient Israel finally preserved by scribes, to papyri accessible only to the very small percentage of literate church leaders, to bound versions since the fifteenth-century introduction of the printing press in Europe, and to Internet proliferation in our contemporary cyber age (see O'Donnell 1998). Each of these aspects of what we call Scripture invites a more nuanced theological understanding than those driven by the epistemic requirements of the modern world.

Ironically, by and large and without overarching intentionality, renewalists have engaged with the Bible in all of these ways through what may be appropriately termed a "precritical" approach (e.g., Archer 2004: chs. 2–3; Grey 2011: chs. 4–5). This means both that they are less inclined to explore the historical world behind the text and more likely to collapse the distance between the world of the text and their own world. Renewalists love the Bible, because it is not just a book about what God has done in the past but is first and foremost about God's direct and immediate word for their lives in the present (cp. Dulles and Martin 1979; Jenkins 2006). In fact, in some extreme cases, renewalists are committed to the word of God not in its textual but oral character (Engelke 2007). "Scripture" as the living word of God is passed on orally via memory, recitation, song, and testimony. While this specific form of scriptural traditioning is not prevalent across the renewal landscape, its underlying assumptions about God's word mediated by the power of the Holy Spirit are widespread. Thus has emerged in pentecostal biblical scholarship and hermeneutics articulation of both pneumatic and aural approaches to the Bible (Kärkkäinen 2002a: ch. 1; and Martin 2008, respectively): "the word of God is living and active" (Heb 4:12), because the Holy Spirit makes Scripture come alive to human ears, hearts, and lives. Hence while not privy to all of the details behind the Reformation motto *semper reformanda*, the renewalist, love of and commitment to Scripture as the living word of God have driven their own version of an always-reforming church. Yet many evangelicals in the classical Reformed tradition think these renditions are misguided. Why?

12.2.2 Christ and/as Divine Revelation: From Canon to Tradition

Part of the concern registered in Reformation traditions has been that renewalists bring too many of their own assumptions to Scripture rather than being subjected to *sola scriptura*. Such subjectivism is particularly problematic, because in the wake of historical criticism, the objectivity of divine revelation has itself come under siege. While numerous theories of revelation have been propounded in response, the renewal rejoinder seems strikingly like other more subjective approaches, such as those developed by modern pietists and others influenced by the post-Kantian turn to the subject (see McDonald 1959). Evangelicals certainly affirm the role of the Spirit, but they usually understand such in relationship to the inspiration of the biblical authors or the illumination of readers of the Bible to apprehend and then apply divine truths (e.g., Brown 2002; Ward 2009). The absoluteness of biblical truth, however, is once-and-for-all established by the words of the scriptural text, so its original verbally inspired and divinely intended meaning is believed to be unchanging and secure.

The role of believers and readers so central to renewal spirituality is not easily accommodated to this evangelical framework (see Wyckoff 2010: ch. 3). Can the original scriptural message take on new significance given by the Spirit that goes beyond, even if it does not contradict, what the text meant for its original authors and hearers? Is human response to the text important to its ongoing meaning and relevance? Did not the apostolic writers under the Spirit's guidance reinterpret the Old Testament message in light of their new experiences of Christ, and if so, are not Spirit-filled believers since similarly invited to follow not only the apostles' words but also their example? The question is, in part, how God's word can be authoritative and trustworthy if revelation involves—as renewal spiritual-ity assumes—the Spirit's mediating the reception of the biblical message according to the needs, assumptions, and horizons of later generations of readers and followers of Christ (Pinnock and Callen 2006).

Yet there are two further sets of issues underlying these questions, one related to the fundamental mode of divine revelation encoded in Scrip-ture and the second to the means of its propagation since. With regard to the former, when the genres of the Bible are closely examined, at least four candidates emerge (cf. Dulles 1992). First, revelation can be under-stood fundamentally as emerging from out of human experience, whether God's visitation to Abraham, Job's mystical encounter, or Paul's visionary journey, and so on (cf. Ward 1994: part 2). Yet none of these on their own seem to suffice without proper interpretation. Hence, a second view of revelation emerges, one related to the more specifically didactic portions of Scripture: the law given, even dictated, to Israel; Jesus' actual teach-ings; and the doctrinal portions of the apostolic letters. However, the significance of such teachings only emerges within a broader narrative that identifies origins (where we have come from) and goals (where we are headed). Thus, revelation as experience or as teaching expands to revela-tion according to the full scope of the salvation or redemption history of Israel and the church together, as preserved in the biblical canon. What is revelatory is neither this nor that personal encounter or doctrinal proposi-tion but the totality of God's interactions with Israel and the church. From a Christian perspective, all of this culminates in Christ: "Long ago God spoke to our ancestors in many and various ways by the prophets, but in these last days he has spoken to us by a Son, whom he appointed heir of all things, through whom he also created the worlds" (Heb 1:1-2). If that is the case, then revelation is fundamentally personal and about Jesus Christ, who is "the way, and the truth, and the life" (John 14:6), and as such is irreducible to any experience or proposition.

If this is the case, then when thinking about the means of propagating divine revelation, the question that presses itself is this: How can personal encounters with Jesus Christ be facilitated? What are the means through which people can meet with and be transformed by the living Christ? For much of Christian history, then, with the masses being basically illiterate, Scripture was heard (through proclamation, song, etc.) and seen (through the church's iconography) rather than read individually. In the early church period, Scripture was thus understood as a central but not the sole means of grace that mediated the living presence of Christ (see Abraham 1998: esp. ch. 2; Abraham, Vickers, and Van Kirk 2008). Alongside and intertwined with the canon of Scripture were the sacraments, rules of faith, rites of initiation, liturgies, icons, spiritual/devotional practices, elders/saints/teachers (episcopate of persons), councils, and creeds. This broader canonical heritage was revelatory of Christ, even as the church was discerning which of the alleged apostolic writings were authoritative and trustworthy (Lienhard 1995; Metzger 1997: part 2). The contours of the biblical canon have been contested periodically over the centuries. However, the power of Scripture to reveal the living Christ amid the church as the people of God persists.

In reality, then, there is a paradoxical sense in which the church has always been subject to Scripture even while Scripture has also always been the book of the church, canonized, interpreted, and sustained via its traditions (e.g., Work 2002: part 3; Rush 2009). The Roman Catholic and Orthodox churches thus perennially have never seen a chasm between Scripture and church tradition, even as the priority of Scripture is generally upheld and even if there remain disputes about which traditions are more or less authoritative. Reformation churches, of course, emphatically subordinated tradition to the Bible in their insistence upon *sola scriptura* even as most of the Reformers—with the exception of a few Anabaptist groups—embraced the important role of the early church for defining the Christian life of faith. Yet the Reformation *sola scriptura* was conjoined with other *solas*—*sola Christo*, signifying the centrality of Christ, and *sola gratia* and *sola fide*, referring to salvation by grace through faith alone rather than also through works (Eph 2:8–9). The *sola scriptura/sola Christo* combination ensured that biblical revelation, even if complemented by tradition, is fundamentally christomorphic in character.

Since the Reformation, the supporting role played by tradition has been revised and even expanded. The Church of England, historically an attempt to carve out a via media between Catholic and Protestant emphases, emerged from the Enlightenment period with its own distinctive synthesis, which has come to be known as the "Anglican triad" of Scripture, tradition, and reason (see McAdoo 1965; Thompson 1997). Within the Anglican tradition itself, the pietistic sensitivies of the Wesleys launched the Methodist revival in the eighteenth century, and over time the crucial role of experience was added to the Anglican triad. The result has since come to be labeled the "Wesleyan quadrilateral," with tradition, reason, and experience—the last linked to the heart religiosity central to Wesley's piety—being nevertheless subservient to Scripture (see Thorsen 1990; Gunter et al. 1997). Evangelicals within these Anglican and Wesleyan streams inevitably are shaped by these sensibilities, even as there are emerging others seeking to rehabilitate the role of tradition, especially the traditions of the early church (e.g., Webber 1999; Oden 2004; Williams 2005).

Renewalists in the Holiness-pentecostal line are intuitively Wesleyan once they are introduced to these views of revelation, while Keswickian or more Reformed Pentecostals remain more inclined to reaffirm the *sola scriptura* commitment. Yet across the renewal spectrum, there remains a strong impulse to understand the power of Scripture pneumatically. Divine revelation through Scripture climaxes in Christ through the power of the Holy Spirit. Growing attention has also been given in the wider theological academy to the role of the Spirit in revelation (e.g., Gorringe 1990; Habets 2010a). How might a renewalist contribution to this topic unfold?

12.2.3 The Spirit and Theological Method: Renewed and Always Renewing

From the perspective of the task of theology in the twenty-first century, precisely the burden of this book, theologies of Scripture and tradition (above) open up to considerations about theological method. Christian theology has predominantly entailed reflection on the primordial Christian sources, which is the apostolic testimony that is understood to have been preserved primarily if not exclusively in the scriptural canon. Yet as we have seen, theological reflection has also always recognized its traditioned character, namely, its reliance on prior interpreters of the apostolic message. While it is unlikely that consensus will be reached about theological method anytime soon, what are the major options available to renewal theologians?

FIGURE 12.3

Eastman Johnson painted this small work shortly after Lincoln's Emancipation Proclamation on New Year's Day, 1863—a context that makes this modest image extremely politically charged. Johnson portrays a young black man (possibly a former slave) reading the Bible by himself and for himself. Slaves were strategically forbidden to read or write; as an editorialist bluntly stated the matter in 1867: "The alphabet is an abolitionist. If you would keep a people enslaved, refuse to teach them to read" (Editorial 1867: 706). And thus this painting is an emblem of liberation: this man's literacy is in itself a declaration of independence and intellectual dignity, directed specifically toward the holiest text in Western culture.

The painting's title comes from the opening words of Psalm 23, that famous declaration of God's enduring care and provision in the midst of darkness: "The Lord is my shepherd; I shall not be in want." We initially assume this to be the passage the man peacefully reads as his dinner simmers behind him (subtle attestations to God's provision). However, he holds the Bible open not to the middle, where one would find the Psalms, but to the front of the canon: the book of Exodus. The Exodus narrative of a people who "groaned under their slavery" vibrates with significance amidst similar groaning in this man's own historical moment: "Out of the slavery their cry for help rose up to God" (Exod 2:23). Johnson keenly recognizes that the hymn to the shepherd in Psalm 23 and the story of Exodus are in fact tightly linked, as Psalm 78 makes clear: "He led out his people like sheep, and guided them in the wilderness like a flock. He led them in safety, so that they were not afraid" (Ps 78:52-53; cf. Ps 77:20; 79:13; Deut 2:7). This nineteenth-century man reads these ancient texts as someone yearning for the same gracious, liberating power of the Good Shepherd (cf. figs. 1.1 and 1.2).

This example strongly suggests that reading is not merely cognitive but practical: it makes claims on the shape of our lives in the present. It also suggests that reading is historically situated: a black Union soldier (note the blue Union Army blanket draped over his chair) interpreting Scripture in Virginia in 1863 inevitably reads with different concerns, sensitivities, and points of reference than does a German monk from three centuries earlier. With a text as thick with meaning as the Bible, a plurality of (faithful) readers might produce a plurality of (faithful) readings. ✦

Nonspecialists can easily get lost in the maze of (surely important) technicalities that constitute discussion of theological method (i.e., Lonergan 1979; Mueller 2004). The crucial issues to consider are the variables introduced in the time since the Reformation when the Scripture-tradition dialectic has been complicated by recognition of the roles of reason and experience. Even non-Anglicans and non-Wesleyans cannot dismiss what the triad and quadrilateral proffer. If before there was at least awareness that Scripture and tradition were inherently intertwined—so that any efforts to understand Scripture apart from tradition were doctrinally and theologically perilous, if not impossible—the present era has brought to full consciousness that human beings as knowing creatures engage what is unknown through what is known, what is unfamiliar through what is familiar. Hence, reason and experience, even if intentionally subordinated to Scripture (if not to Scripture and tradition), nevertheless play indispensable roles in the theological task. In short, there is no shortcut that brings readers directly into the scriptural horizon. Rather, Scripture is always interpreted by individuals or communities (of faith) from out of their own situatedness and perspective. Scripture may still be affirmed as having a foundational role for theology, but its substance is approached, interpreted, and understood from many other vantage points (see Shults 1999; Smith 2000; Grenz and Franke 2001).

Further, even if Scripture (and tradition) was to be prioritized, doing so in our late modern and postmodern contexts amounts to a sort of fideism and unquestioning faith (Farley 1982). This is because ancient authorities no longer provide indubitable foundations for moderns, who are aware not only of fissures within traditions (the ecumenical level) but also of alternatives without (the intercultural and interfaith domains). In a pluralistic and global context, for instance, there are other scriptural traditions—Islamic, Buddhist, Confucian, and others—that Christian theologians will have to consider (e.g., Ward 1994). Further, the Enlightenment has also ushered in irrevocably the age of science, and human rationality since has been indissolubly linked with, if not reduced to, scientific rationality (see ch. 10, this volume). Human thinking in global context is thus deeply rooted in multiple scriptural and discursive traditions and informed by diverse experiences. Can contemporary theology account for, much less effectively engage, such plurality?

Renewalists are fairly recent arrivals on the scene of theological academia and thus have just barely begun reflecting on matters related to theological method. In practice, they often do not think about doing theology but about living into and out of the scriptural narrative in general and the apostolic message in particular. With regard to the book of Acts, then, their own lives are but an extension of the apostles, the twenty-ninth chapter of an open book in fact, through which they are continuing and fulfilling what was begun by the first followers of Jesus (see Kling 2004: ch. 7). What is needed is not theological construction but faithful obedience and openness to the Spirit making the Bible come alive in the present.

Yet of course, renewalists have also written theological texts, and when doing so, they have been basically evangelical in their approach, which means committed practically (if not formally) to *sola scriptura*, utilizing an inductive approach to the Bible in order to organize and explicate theological and doctrinal truths (see also section 1.2). More recently, renewalists have been appreciating the importance of tradition, in particular the early modern or first-generation pentecostal movement and its theological contributions (e.g., Jacobsen 2003, 2006). The role of experience is also slowly being recognized (e.g., Neumann 2012). All of this, however, is framed pneumatologically, recognizing the vital work of the Spirit in engaging Scripture, thinking with the tradition, discerning experience, and enabling critical, creative, and constructive theological reflection (e.g., Oliverio 2012: esp. ch. 7; Stephenson 2013). It is precisely the Holy Spirit who makes present and real the resurrected and living Christ to people in and through the particularities of their situations. Scripture remains normative, even if its meaning and application allow for a practically unpredictable number of interpretations and applications through which the Spirit communicates the personal truth that is Jesus Christ. In that sense, renewal theological method emphasizes the Spirit's constantly renewing role in revealing Jesus Christ to those who are near "and for all who are far away, everyone whom the Lord our God calls to him" (Acts 2:39b). Here the bibliocentrism and christocentrism of renewal piety converge.

For evangelicals to whom "tradition" is less attractive as a major category for thinking about revelation, the work of the Spirit is important, despite the many worries about subjectivism rightfully registered. Thus evangelicals who have sought to do full justice to the contributions of Anglicans and Wesleyans have been open to thinking about divine revelation and theological method in terms of Word and Spirit (e.g., Bloesch 1992). Generally speaking, part of the problem with this construct is that the Word has been equated with an objective scriptural revelation, while the Spirit has been associated with the subjective or merely applicational aspects of divine revelation. Yet this ignores both the multivocality of Scripture itself and the relationship between the Spirit and Scripture (e.g., 2 Pet 1:19-21). Such objective/subjective bifurcations also overlook the dynamic nature of tradition as it mediates the revelatory message of Scripture across space and time to different communities and recipients. More pointedly, the entire debate about objectivity and subjectivity is driven by modernist modes and habits of thought that are presently being called into question. Pneumatological and trinitarian theologies of revelation, for instance, are bypassing these binary categories and are instead discussing how the Spirit enables creaturely participation in the trinitarian life and work of God (e.g., Watts 2005: ch. 6). How might such pneumatologically rich considerations revitalize contemporary thinking about Scripture, revelation, and theological method in a posttextual (cybernetic), post-Christian (pluralistic), and postmodern (relativistic) age?

12.3 The Apocalyptic Revelation: One Christ, Many Images and Resonances

We begin our constructive reflections by going to the end of the Bible. At the conclusion of his prophecy, John warned, "I warn everyone who hears the words of the prophecy of this book: if anyone adds to them, God will add to that person the plagues described in this book; if anyone takes away from the words of the book of this prophecy, God will take away that person's share in the tree of life and in the holy city, which are described in this book" (Rev 22:18-19). Many renewalists, like other Christians before them, read this admonishment as applying not just to the Apocalypse, but to the biblical canon as a whole. Doing so provides an aura to the scriptural text that safeguards its distinctiveness from other merely human writings. Understanding these verses in this way, of course, ignores the fact that such warnings were routinely included in Jewish and apocalyptic writings (Smalley 2005: 584; Fee 2011: 314; cf. Deut 4:2; 12:32). Still, the point is forcefully made: do not tamper with God's holy writ!

And it is precisely as prophetic holy writ that the Apocalypse unveils the nature of Scripture and of divine revelation. Ultimately, the revelation of God in this book specifically and in the Bible as a whole, read from a Christian perspective, is about Jesus Christ (Rev 1:1). John bears witness "to the word of God and to the testimony of Jesus Christ" (1:2) and brings greetings "from him who is and who was and who is to come, and from the seven spirits who are before his throne, and from Jesus Christ, the faithful witness, the firstborn of the dead, and the ruler of the kings of the earth" (1:4b-5). He sees and brings a message from "one like the Son of Man" (1:13), one who says, "I am the first and the last, and the living one. I was dead, and see, I am alive for ever and ever; and I have the keys of Death and of Hades" (1:17b-18). Yet, as we shall see, John's testimony to Christ comes through the Spirit and is not merely eschatological but also assuredly this-worldly and practical.

It was mentioned above (section 12.1) that John received his revelation of Jesus in the Spirit. In the Apocalypse, the Holy Spirit is depicted not merely in unitary terms but as the "seven spirits who are before his [God's] throne" (Rev 1:4; cf. 3:1, 4:5). Indeed, in one instance, "the seven spirits of God" are equated with "the seven horns and seven eyes" of the Lamb (5:6). Hence the Spirit of God who bears witness to Christ is also the Spirit of Christ. In fact, the identity of the Spirit wholly distinct from God and Christ is inconceivable in Revelation: "For the testimony of Jesus is the spirit of prophecy" (19:10; cf. Waddell 2006: 160, 182). Yet precisely as given in and through the Spirit, then, Christ is unveiled not merely propositionally but imagistically, audibly, and synesthetically, replete with the emotional pathos correlative with pneumatic unveiling not of an idea but of a person (see deSilva 2009: chs. 7–8).

Note first that what is read as text is given to John in visions (Rev 1:11, 19). On almost seventy different occasions John is instructed to see or reports seeing. Twelve of these involve angels and their activities, and another dozen are images of the beast and other creatures related to the "unholy trinity" (Satan, the beast, and the false prophet). John also observes the martyrs and survivors of the faith (6:9; 15:2; 20:4), the throne of God and the final judgment (20:11, 12), and heaven (4:1; 15:5; 19:11; 21:1-5). Most importantly, throughout John envisions the many faces and aspects of Jesus Christ, the "Lion of the tribe of Judah" (5:5) and slaughtered Lamb (5:6), as well as what emanates from his right hand (1:20; 5:1).

But on one occasion, John "turned to see whose voice it was that spoke to me" (1:12). John was a mystic who not only saw visions but also heard voices. Again, there are more than seventy references either commanding him to listen or describing what he hears. Numerous general heavenly voices as well as those of angels and of other divine creatures are recorded. John also hears the voices of saints, martyrs, and their representatives (6:10; 16:7; 19:1, 6), and pronouncements of significant numbers (7:4; 9:16). In fact, the entire disclosure is framed by the utterance of Christ, whose "loud voice like a trumpet [says], 'Write in a book what you see and send it to the seven churches, to Ephesus, to Smyrna, to Pergamum, to Thyatira, to Sardis, to Philadelphia, and to Laodicea'" (1:10-11). Thus is the final revelation given to "one who heard and saw these things" (22:8). Whereas reading and understanding are primarily an intellectual affair, visual and audible perceptions are imagistic and dynamic, suggesting that divine disclosure, while including a cognitive component, is also imaginative, rhythmic, and affective. Hence the "word of God" addresses not only human heads but also embodied human beings located in space and time. Divine revelation not only discloses information but contributes to human formation, shapes human hearts, and addresses human hopes.

That Revelation is in part about the future there can be no doubt. Jesus directed John: "Now write what you have seen, what is, and what is to take place after this" (Rev 1:19). Historically, dispensationalists (see section 2.2.1) believe this command structures the book itself. "What you have seen" is the vision of Christ (ch. 1); "what is" concerns the letters to the seven churches (chs. 2–3); and "what is to take place after this" is reintroduced immediately after the seven letters by a voice from heaven saying, "Come up here, and I will show you what must take place after this" (4:1), which refers to the rest of the book (chs. 4–22). The key for dispensationalists, however, is that much of Revelation concerns the future indeed, things that remain unfulfilled and ahead not only of all recipients in the past almost two thousand years but also of contemporary readers (Gregg 1997: 61). Yet such a futurist reading exacerbates the delay of the fulfillment of the prophecy, especially in light of Jesus' prior blessing that introduces the book as a whole: "Blessed is the one who reads aloud the words of the prophecy, and blessed are those who hear and who keep what is written in it; *for the time is near*" (1:3 [emphasis added]). Less problematic is to understand "what must take place after this" as simply what is revealed later (Skaggs and Benham 2009: 30), even as it is important to realize that for John, the past, present, and future are intertwined under the lordship of Christ in ways not easily segregated (Wall 1991: 64; Keener 2000: 98). Put another way, the revelation of Jesus Christ in the Spirit—as is the word of God as divine revelation generally—is prophetic not merely in the sense of forecasting the future but of inspiring faithful witness in the present, whenever and wherever its readers or hearers may be found.

Thus while there is much to be observed about the similar structures of the seven letters (Rev 2–3), for our purposes what is important is the refrain in each: "Let anyone who has an ear listen to what the Spirit is saying to the churches" (2:7, 11a, 17a, 29; 3:6, 13, 22). The injunction to listen here suggests that the text is both to be read and heard and that its readers and hearers are urged to be attentive to both the warnings and the promises (see Wilson 2007). Read across the Apocalypse as a whole, however, the invitation to listen extends to the entire message of the "Spirit of prophecy." In that case, "what must take place after this" (4:1), while perhaps involving things yet to come for any generation, nevertheless is pertinent for the testimony of Christ in the lives of his followers.

The point is that if the bulk of Revelation were to concern the last days in the technical sense of the events leading up to the Parousia of Jesus, then much of it remains opaque and irrelevant to most readers, because there will only ever be one generation that lives out the events of that epoch. For this reason, many who believe themselves living in such days eventually become disabused of their speculative interpretations about the future, in which case, then, this book is neither living nor active as the divine word (Newton 2009). On the contrary, whereas other apocalyptic scrolls were kept sealed and shut (e.g., Dan 12:4, 9), those in Revelation continue to be opened, indicating their ongoing relevance (Koester 2001a: 202–4).

Hence each generation approaching the text in the Spirit through which it was written can find divine revelation for their lives. Biblical scholars and interpreters of Revelation across a range of renewal traditions (e.g., Priscilla Benham, Gordon Fee, Ronald Herms, Jon Newton, Rebecca Skaggs, John Christopher Thomas, Robby Waddell, Mark Wilson) by and large agree that even if the future horizon of the text recedes beyond any generation, the Apocalypse as Scripture has the power to perennially address contemporary realities. The letters to the seven churches and the larger Apocalypse of which they were a part were originally intended to comfort, admonish, encourage, and inspire (see Boesak 1987). That these functions are transgenerational is a mark of their divinely inspired character. Further, if, for its original audiences, Revelation proclaimed Christ as lord over the Roman Empire (Bauckham 1993), such a message remains pertinent in every age dominated by different national, imperial, political, and socioeconomic powers. Read in postcolonial context, for example, "Revelation is wrath and punishment for the oppressors, but good news (gospel) for those excluded and oppressed by the empire of the beast" (Richard 1995: 4). To be sure, Revelation could also be used by imperial powers to justify or legitimate in the name of God (see Segovia and Sugirtharajah 2007: 452), so even here its message ought to be appropriated cautiously.

Yet in the end, the Spirit who inspires many tongues, languages, and cultures (see chs. 3–4, this volume) also empowers many acts of imperial resistance in this eschatological period between the first and second comings of Christ (see Rhoads 2005). The prophecy concerns "many peoples and nations and languages and kings" (Rev 10:11). Surely many follow the beast (11:7-9) or whore after the seductions of the empires of this world (17:15). However, as already mentioned, the testimonies of the martyrs and the marginalized are given voice by the Spirit. Despite persecution or suffering, the redemptive word of God gathers "a great multitude that no one could count, from every nation, from all tribes and peoples and languages, standing before the throne and before the Lamb, robed in white, with palm branches in their hands" (7:9). The many voices are given prominence not only in this heavenly vision but also in the image of the new Jerusalem: "The nations will walk by its light, and the kings of the earth will bring their glory into it. . . . People will bring into it the glory and the honour of the nations" (21:24, 26). Whereas "peoples and multitudes and nations and languages" run after the great whore (17:15), the new heavens and new earth (21:1) will include "the river of the water of life . . . [and] the tree of life with its twelve kinds of fruit . . . the leaves of the tree are for the healing of the nations" (22:1-2). Thus the final revelation expands, confirms, and culminates the vision for the nations initially given to Abraham.

The point is the Apocalypse as the word of God provides windows into the multifaceted character of divine revelation. God reveals himself in Christ and the Spirit in multisensory ways, through a range of sights, sounds, images, and genres (just in Revelation alone: letters, hymns, narrative, vision, prophecy), providing information surely, but also assuring, emboldening, and inspiring. Divine revelation lodges itself not only in our heads but in our hearts, motivating worshipful witness (Waddell 2006: 191; Newton 2009: 50–51). Divine revelation connects human beings with the past work of Christ in anticipation of the triune unveiling that is both on its way and yet also beyond the horizon. Christ comes by the Spirit to judge and purify, not only at the end of the age but also in the present—whenever and wherever such "present" may be—in order that God's redemptive work can be accomplished. Divine revelation is therefore not merely communicative but evocative, transformative, and salvific.

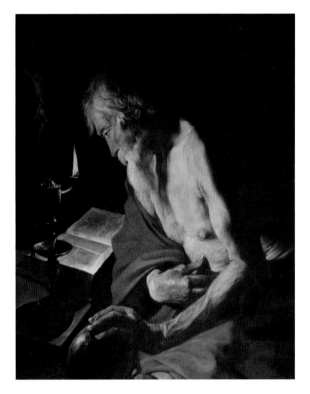

FIGURE 12.4

This painting is a meditation on scriptural hermeneutics, concisely posing several difficult hermeneutical questions with which thoughtful Scripture readers must grapple. The image presents the fourth-century doctor of the church St. Jerome as his aged body leans over a thick biblical codex that he reads intently. He has spent his life poring over this text: absorbing, digesting, translating it. His hands provide points of entry into the image. His right hand gestures toward his gut, his appetite: this renowned ascetic cautions us against the ways that desire might deform one's reading. But questions persist: In what ways and to what extent might our readings of the Scriptures be positively oriented and fueled by our human needs and longings? What kinds of desire might in fact be necessary for faithful reading? Meanwhile, Jerome's left hand rests squarely upon a human skull, a forthright reminder of the fragility and finitude of the human body, heart, and mind. Together these two hands signify competing—but yet also complementary—reading principles: desire and restraint, searching and humility.

As Jerome reads, a crucifix stands over the text: To what extent does a faithful reading demand that the entirety of the Scriptures be read christologically? What about eschatologically or pneumatologically? A single light is positioned between the reader, the text, and the crucifix—it is in fact the sole light by which Jerome reads and by which everything in the space is illuminated. By what light(s) are we to read: the light of reason? conscience? tradition? the Holy Spirit? On the wall behind him hangs (anachronistically) a cardinal's hat, which has a double connotation: signifying his humility on the one hand (he simply presents himself to the text without donning his symbol of status and stature) and church tradition on the other (he reads in light of past scholars and exegetes).

What is missing here is any indication of Jerome's own immediate social-historical context: In what environment is he reading? He appears to have withdrawn from the world in order to read: there are no windows, no outside, no others. Does he presume to have transcended the location from which he reads? And is it perhaps precisely this that causes him to read "in the dark"? Without context, is our reading in danger of becoming abstract, impotent, and even untrue? ✦

12.4 Knowing, Loving, and Serving God: One Spirit, Many Tongues

This final set of deliberations about theology of Scripture, theology of revelation, and theological method not only pulls together the threads of this chapter but also summarizes explicitly the methodological approaches to Scripture and theology manifest throughout this volume in service of articulating a renewal theology and of renewing the Christian theological enterprise. The trinitarian-performative-eschatological rhythm that structures the constructive reflections in the previous chapters should here be easily recognized. We begin with the theology of Scripture and revelation together in six interrelated dimensions before turning in the last few paragraphs to explicit comments on theological methodology.

Renewing Christian theology of Scripture and revelation begins with a resolutely christological character. The Christian revelation is ultimately not about a book but about the living Christ, the Spirit-anointed Messiah. The memory of Christ is surely preserved in the biblical canon. Yet even the portrait of Christ is explicitly multiple—there are four gospels, not one, among sixty-six books—even as there are innumerable other genres in both testaments that communicate the various faces of Christ's person and message. As the living Christ, then, he remains known only in part: "What we will be has not yet been revealed. What we do know is this: when he is revealed, we will be like him, for we will see him as he is" (1 John 3:2-3). Thus just as human persons grow in their knowledge of one another, followers of Christ grow in the grace, truth, and knowledge of Christ. This is mediated normatively through the biblical canon but is no less assuredly open toward the eschatological horizon.

Renewing Christian theology of Scripture and revelation next involves a thoroughly pneumatological aspect. The Holy Spirit of God is the Spirit of Christ, empowering his saving work and unveiling the many aspects of his living person. So also does the Spirit anticipate the living Christ in the ancient history of Israel, even as the Spirit extends the person and work of Christ in the church as the body of Christ. Revelation of the person of Christ in the Spirit thus is rich and multifaceted, because the Spirit speaks through many voices. Yet the Spirit not only inspires the polyphonic testimony of the human encounter with this triune God but also illuminates this witness to many others near and far off. Scripture thus comes alive with the message of Christ in the Spirit to people in many different times and places who are ready to receive this in faith. But divine revelation of Christ also breaks through in the Spirit to those who are otherwise aliens and strangers to—even unevangelized by—the covenantal story. Because revelation takes place in the Spirit, it remains God's prerogative and cannot be humanly manipulated or controlled.

Yet third, renewing Christian theology of Scripture and revelation insists on a a robust ecclesiology. The personal aspect of Christ as revelation does not mean that divine disclosure is merely individualistic. Human creatures are undeniably social (as argued throughout this book), so personal encounters with the living Christ take on essential meaning and relevance in the church as the body of Christ. The church preexisted the scriptural canon but not the word of God in Christ by the Spirit. Hence the church received the scriptural witness in response to the word of God in the Spirit of Christ, producing the biblical canon. But because the church, unlike Christ, is not infallible—to say that "the gates of Hades will not prevail against [the church]" (Matt 16:18) is not to affirm its infallibility—the people of God will continue to disagree about many things, including the shape of the canon (as do Protestants and Catholics). Yet while confirming the canonical corpus (in its rough outline) and providing a liturgical and ecclesial shape for interpreting and understanding that corpus, the church also abides in subjection to the word of Christ as the Spirit speaks through the Scriptures (e.g., Swain 2011: chs. 4–5). What all of this means, however, needs to be discerned afresh in every generation, because different times and places invite fresh receptions of the living word of Christ in the power of the Holy Spirit. And it is the church that discerns, even if dialogically, following the footsteps of Peter in response to and interaction with Cornelius.

Fourth, renewing Christian theology of Scripture and revelation affirms Scripture's verbal inspiration is part and parcel of God's ongoing speech and human proclamatory response. We finally arrive at the authority of Scripture, because this cannot be understood apart from the living Christ, the power of the Spirit, and the faithful people of God. This is not to minimize the textual character of Scripture, although we need to be open to new discursive modes and forms as attested to in the history of the reception of the sacred writings themselves. Yet the verbal character of Scripture means that God speaks—which means always through the divine breath, the Spirit—formerly through prophets, unsurpassingly through Christ, and now continually through the church and even other divinely chosen media. This occurs through evangelical proclamation, liturgical practices, and other communicative means, such that Scripture witnesses to the living Christ in the Spirit. Those who are visually impaired hear (or feel) the word; the hearing impaired receive the signs of the word; the intellectually impaired are caught up in the iconography of the word and participate in the ecclesial fellowship of the Spirit, and so on. The point is that precisely because Scripture is verbally inspired by God, it is eminently translatable into many tongues, which means not just languages but discursive practices. This is all the more the case given that its communicative idioms, even propositions, such as they are, point to the living Christ, whose reality transcends what is written (or read, chanted, said, etc.) but nevertheless becomes personally real and available through the verbalizations of the triune revelation.

Fifth, there is a performatively practical component to a renewed theology of Scripture and revelation. The message of the gospel is not merely for intellectual understanding but meets human hearts, inspires human hands, and transforms human lives. Again, while there is no need to minimize the historical, cognitive, and even scientific (understood broadly) aspects of the biblical canon, all of this translates into the valuable biblical and theological scholarship that enriches human understanding. Yet knowledge of Scripture is not for its own sake but for reforming humans as worshippers in the image of God, renewing them as servants in the image of Christ, and redeeming them as witnesses in the power of the Spirit. Reading Scripture, reciting the liturgy, and studying the text are practices, among others, that lead both to theological understanding and to worshipful witness that participates in and facilitates God's saving and sanctifying work in Christ (see Webster 2003; Treier 2008).

Last but not least is the dynamically eschatological dimension of a renewed theology of Scripture and revelation. This "eschatological sense" (see Greene-McCreight 1999: 241) points to the excessive and inexhaustible character of Scripture's communicative power, as the word of God is translated and interpreted across space and time in anticipation of the full revelation of the triune God. Yet it also points to Scripture's capacity to herald and inaugurate the reign of God in making present the living Christ in the power of the Spirit. Finally, it invites ongoing reception of the scriptural message rather than any absolutization of either its words or any particular interpretive clarification. This is not to deny the real and essential value of the latter, for instance in creedal or confessional explications of the biblical witness. But it is to say that any efforts to perpetuate these rules of faith without appreciating their historically particular character risk idolizing certain articulations and transmitting mere words. Hence Scripture as the word of the triune God is living and active in history precisely because there are no limits to its capacity to tutor creaturely understanding.

In short, renewing Christian theology involves understanding Scripture and revelation in christological, pneumatological, ecclesiological, verbal, performative, and eschatological terms. These scriptural aspects point to the way in which a supremely personal God encounters human persons: in dynamic, situated, and never-ending ways. As the Apostle Paul indicated about the new covenant written not on tablets but on human hearts: "for the letter kills, but the Spirit gives life" (2 Cor 3:6b).

Such a renewed theology of Scripture and revelation begs for an equally dynamic theological method. Renewalists who have begun thinking about theological hermeneutics and method have tentatively developed triadic schemes prioritizing the role of the Holy Spirit: Spirit–Scripture–theology (Stronstad 1995) or Spirit–Scripture–community (Archer 2004). My own prior formulation of these matters—Spirit–word–community (Yong 2002)—also foregrounds the work of the Spirit in relationship to the living word of God in Christ as received and construed by the various communities of faith-seeking-understanding.

The preceding pages illustrate concretely how such a methodology functions. The renewing of Christian theology is inherently biblical, although there is no one approved hermeneutical approach but potentially as many as have "seemed good to the Holy Spirit and to us" (Acts 15:28a; cf. J. C. Thomas 2005: 233–47). The theological task also has to be attentive to the challenges of its context, which presently is the late modern, global, and pluralistic world of the twenty-first century. Yet even if every generation has to theologize afresh, its work builds on its predecessors (the historical aspect), even as it empowers the Christian witness (the performative and eschatological dimension). This constellation of sources, horizons, and goals invites consideration of three methodological dynamics for a renewed Christianity.

First, a theological methodology that is renewed and always seeking the renewal of the church in its mission embraces the hermeneutical circle or spiral (Osborne 2006). This means there is a fundamental commitment to Scripture, although there is yet also no question that the scriptural message has to be interpreted and translated afresh to every generation, and that readers, interpreters, and translators always enter into the scriptural world from their own times and places. Scriptural priority, authority, and normativity do not alleviate but actually accentuate the hard and always contested work of engaging Scripture and receiving its witness for a new situation. Yet the "conflict of interpretations" (Ricoeur 1974; cf. Vanhoozer 1990) that follows almost any theological/doctrinal proposition or claim, while potentially debilitating in some contexts, also is indicative of the illuminating power of Scripture to speak into many different situations, to address many contesting communities, and to heal many hurting lives. Human beings thus engage with the scriptural message from many different places or starting points. Or, perhaps better put, they are encountered by or arrested through Scripture in many different situations. There is an inexhaustive power of Scripture to be the word of the living God and mediate the presence of the resurrected Christ through the Spirit.

Second, a methodology that is renewed and always seeking the renewal of the church in its mission embraces the ecumenical, intercultural, and interdisciplinary character of the theological task. The ecumenical aspect highlights the diverse historical and confessional traditions of the church. The intercultural facet points to the global context in its dizzying plurality. The interdisciplinary feature insists on the many realms of knowledge that theology has to navigate and, sometimes, adjudicate. Thus theology is inherently and unavoidably dialogical (see Yong 2014a). Scripture is normative, yet its horizon is always open to ecumenical, intercultural, and interdisciplinary engagements. Thus the lines between general and special revelation, while helpful in some respects, are also more modernistic than biblical in other respects. The special character of God's saving work in Christ is theologically specified in dynamically shifting ways in new ecumenical, cultural, and dialogical contexts.

Finally, a methodology that is renewed and always seeking the renewal of the church in its mission not only embraces the hermeneutical circle and is fundamentally dialogical but is also essentially communicative. Theology is thus not merely theoretical but is performative. This practicality is not just an incidental add-on that clarifies the application of preestablished scriptural, theological, or doctrinal ideas. Rather, theology and even doctrinal truths emerge from out of the life and practices of the church carried by the Spirit (e.g., Hütter 1999; cf. Yong 2008: ch. 2). The on-the-ground aspect of Christian life drives theological reflection, and in that sense, theology always strives to keep up, interpret, and understand Christian discipleship in ever-changing contexts. Hence this performative aspect of the theological task cannot be merely marginalized as an afterthought. Rather, it is part and parcel of the hermeneutical circle wherein we encounter and confront Scripture and of the dialogical matrix wherein the many voices of our past meet and mesh with the many tongues and discursive practices that constitute our present lives. Yet such pluralism is disciplined by the eschatological horizon of the triune God who calls us forward to love, to faith, and to hope (e.g., Clark 2003). The performative aspect of the theological task thus ought to shape human loving of God and others, empower human acting, and inspire human hoping. Understood in this way, this practical dimension is not only concerned with our present lives but reframes what we think and do in God's eschatological time and place.

Theology is or should thus be exciting, having to navigate as it does the diversity of our past, the pluralism of our present, and the dim but no less discernible future of God that has already invaded history in Christ and the Spirit. There is no curtailing the theological reflection of the many tongues, yet not every utterance is equal. The church in renewal insists: "Let two or three prophets speak, and let the others weigh what is said" (1 Cor 14:29). This presumes that there is a group of prophets, which translated into theological idiom means that for the theological task, there are those who are more rather than less trained in the practices needed to bridge church and academy. But it also assumes that once the theologians of the church speak in their many voices, others will weigh, sift through, and discern whether what is said is of God, is faithful to the words God already has spoken, is meaningful and relevant for empowering the church's witness in the present, and inspires anticipation of and participation in God's future and yet present acts. And then the prophets—or theologians—respond to that judgment of the communities of faith, and the work of theology continues until "there will be no more night [and] they need no light of lamp or sun, for the Lord God will be their light, and they will reign for ever and ever" (Rev 22:5).

Discussion Questions

1. What are some aspects of your church's teachings about Scripture, and how do they compare with the preceding discussion? Are these differences complementary or are they contradictory, and if the latter, what are possible responses to these divergent views? What are the implications for Christian theology of Scripture in an electronic age?

2. What are some aspects of your church's teachings about the doctrine of revelation, and how do they compare with the preceding discussion? Is it more helpful to think of revelation in more objective terms or more open-ended terms? What are the advantages, disadvantages, and implications for Christian theology in either case?

3. Does or should theological method follow a clearly delineated set of operations or steps, or is it as "circular," dialogical, and dynamic as outlined in the preceding discussion? Are such recommendations perhaps only appropriate for renewal communities, or are they part and parcel of all Christian theologizing? Why or why not?

Further Reading

Allen, Paul L. 2012. *Theological Method: A Guide for the Perplexed*. London: T&T Clark.

Bloesch, Donald G. 1994. *Holy Scripture: Revelation, Inspiration and Interpretation*. Downers Grove, Ill.: InterVarsity.

Callahan, Allen Dwight. 2006. *The Talking Book: African Americans and the Bible*. New Haven, Conn.: Yale University Press.

Fackre, Gabriel J. 1997. *The Doctrine of Revelation: A Narrative Interpretation*. Edinburgh: Edinburgh University Press.

Graham, Elaine, Heather Walton, and Frances Ward. 2005. *Theological Reflections: Methods*. London: SCM Press.

Herms, Ronald. 2006. *An Apocalypse for the Church and for the World: The Narrative Function of Universal Language in the Book of Revelation.* Berlin: De Gruyter.

McDonald, Lee Martin. 2007. *The Biblical Canon: Its Origin, Transmission, and Authority.* Rev. 3rd ed. Peabody, Mass.: Hendrickson.

Wilson, Mark. 2007. *Charts on the Book of Revelation: Literary, Historical, and Theological Perspectives.* Grand Rapids: Kregel.

Epilogue

This book has not undertaken the task of providing an explicit apology for or defense of the WAGF's Statement of Faith. It has presumed the faithfulness of such a statement—which affirms neither its exhaustiveness nor its infallibility—and attempted to explicate such in the present context. In fact, it is precisely the level of generality of the WAGF SF that has opened up theological and conceptual space for such an unabashedly evangelical but no less generously ecumenical reconsideration. In the spirit of the early modern pentecostal revival focused on empowering a viable and collaborative Christian witness across the ecclesial spectrum, the SF can be understood as providing a platform for doctrinal unity without insisting on uniformity of thinking. The point of the SF is thus to undergird Christian life and mission, rather than foreclose Christian confession across evangelical or even ecumenical lines.

As such, the foregoing assumes that confessional statements, such as the SF, bear approximate but yet also appropriate and faithful witness to the Christian faith as understood in specific places and times. This volume provides one interpretation of the SF while recommending its consideration to the church evangelical, ecumenical, and global. Its thesis is that the theological task emerges afresh in every age and that for the present, renewal Christianity in its global manifestation inspires a way forward for Christian life and thinking. Any theological proposal ought minimally to indicate how the biblical and historical witness illuminates present-day realities and yet also charts a normative path forward in response to contemporary challenges.

As already intimated, other renewalists outside the WAGF orbit, and even those not specifically part of the global renewal movement, can use this text as an example for renewing Christian theology in their own (confessional) traditions and contexts now and, hopefully, in the future.

What it presents is not only a set of concrete theological proposals but also an example of theological thinking. Many other theological doctrines ought to be treated but are not in this book. Further, of the doctrines that are discussed, each can be greatly expanded, even to a book of its own. (A twelve-volume, WAGF SF-inspired renewal theology begs to be written to complement—maybe extend—Barth's *Church Dogmatics*!) This volume also invites further biblical consideration of each theme or topic, as already indicated, not only across the New Testament but with the Scriptures of ancient Israel. Last but not least, each of the ecumenical, intercultural, and interdisciplinary dimensions of this work can be much more fully explicated vis-à-vis distinctive doctrinal and scriptural elaboration.

All this to say that *Renewing Christian Theology* is no more than a modest and even preliminary contribution, one designed to introduce theology students to the richness of the biblical and Christian traditions and also to showcase the capacity of a Spirit-inspired Christian faith to empower life amid the complexities of our twenty-first-century global village. This textbook also registers the distinctive contributions of renewal Christianity but precisely thereby aspires to renew global Christian theological reflection. Readers and students ought to have been weighing each aspect of the discussion along the way, and now some may be motivated to correct and improve upon the proceeding. Such is the appropriate response to the task of theological renewal, one that is, hopefully, always being enabled by the Holy Spirit.

Appendix 1

The World Assemblies of God Fellowship Statement of Faith

The following derives from the WAGF "Constitution and Bylaws," adopted by the General Assembly in August 2000 in Indianapolis, Indiana; and revised in May 2005 in Sydney, Australia, and again in February 2011 in Chennai, India.

Article II—Statement of Faith

Preface

This Statement of Faith is intended simply as a basis for belief, fellowship, and cooperation among us. The phraseology employed in this statement is not inspired, but the truth set forth is held to be essential to a truly Pentecostal ministry. No claim is made that it contains all biblical truth, only that it covers our need for these essential doctrines.

1. The Inspiration of the Scriptures

We believe that the Scriptures, both the Old and New Testaments, are verbally inspired of God and are the revelation of God to man, the infallible, authoritative rule of faith and conduct. Divine inspiration extends equally and fully to all parts of the original writings, insuring their entire trustworthiness (2 Timothy 3:15-17; 2 Peter 1:21).

2. The Eternal Godhead

We believe in the unity of the one true and living God who is the eternal, self-existent One, and has revealed Himself as one being in three persons: Father, Son, and the Holy Spirit (Matthew 3:16-17; 28:19).

a. God the Father

We believe in God the Father, the first person of the triune Godhead, who exists eternally as the Creator of heaven and earth, the Giver of the Law, to whom all things will be subjected, so that He may be all in all (Genesis 1:1; Deuteronomy 6:4; 1 Corinthians 15:28).

b. The Lord Jesus Christ

We believe in the Lord Jesus Christ, the second person of the triune Godhead, who was and is the eternal Son of God; that He became incarnate by the Holy Spirit and was born of the virgin Mary.

We believe in His sinless life, miraculous ministry, substitutionary atoning death, bodily resurrection, triumphant ascension, and abiding intercession (Isaiah 7:14; Hebrews 7:25-26; 1 Peter 2:22; Acts 1:9; 2:22; 10:38; 1 Corinthians 15:4; 2 Corinthians 5:21).

c. The Holy Spirit

We believe in the Holy Spirit, the third person of the triune Godhead, who proceeds from the Father and the Son, and is ever present and active in the work of convicting and regenerating the sinner, sanctifying the believer, leading into all truth and empowering for ministry (John 14:26; 16:8-11; 1 Peter 1:2; Romans 8:14-16).

3. The Fall of Man

We believe that humankind was created good and upright. However, voluntary transgression resulted in their alienation from God, thereby incurring not only physical death but spiritual death, which is separation from God (Genesis 1:16-27; 2:17; 3:6; Romans 5:12-19).

4. The Salvation of Man

We believe in salvation through faith in Christ, who died for our sins, was buried, and was raised from the dead on the third day. By His atoning blood, salvation has been provided for all humanity through the sacrifice of Christ upon the cross. This experience is also known as the new birth, and is an instantaneous and complete operation of the Holy Spirit whereupon the believing sinner is regenerated, justified, and adopted into the family of God, becomes a new creation in Christ Jesus, and heir of eternal life (John 3:5-6; Romans 10:8-15; Titus 2:11; 3:4-7; 1 John 5:1).

5. Divine Healing

We believe that deliverance from sickness is provided in the atonement and is the privilege of all believers (Isaiah 53:4-5; Matthew 8:16-17; James 5:14-16).

6. The Church and Its Mission

We believe that the church is the body of Christ and the habitation of God through the Spirit, witnesses to the presence of the kingdom of God in the present world, and universally includes all who are born again (Ephesians 1:22-23; 2:22; Romans 14:17-18; 1 Corinthians 4:20).

We believe that the mission of the church is to (1) proclaim the good news of salvation to all humankind, (2) build up and train believers for spiritual ministry, (3) praise the Lord through worship, (4) demonstrate Christian compassion to all who suffer, and (5) exhibit unity as the body of Christ (Matthew 28:19-20; 10:42; Ephesians 4:11-13).

7. The Ordinances of the Church

We believe that baptism in water by immersion is expected of all who have repented and believed. In so doing they declare to the world that they have died with Christ and been raised with Him to walk in newness of life (Matthew 28:19; Acts 10:47-48; Romans 6:4).

We believe that the Lord's Supper is a proclamation of the suffering and death of our Lord Jesus Christ, to be shared by all believers until the Lord returns (Luke 22:14-20; 1 Corinthians 11:20-34).

8. Sanctification

We believe that sanctification is an act of separation from that which is evil, and of dedication unto God. In experience, it is both instantaneous and progressive. It is produced in the life of the believer by his appropriation of the power of Christ's blood and risen life through the person of the Holy Spirit. He draws the believer's attention to Christ, teaches him through the Word and produces the character of Christ within him (Romans 6:1-11; 8:1-2,13; 12:1-2; Galatians 2:20; Hebrews 10:10, 14).

9. The Baptism in the Holy Spirit

We believe that the baptism in the Holy Spirit is the bestowing of the believer with power for life and service for Christ. This experience is distinct from and subsequent to the new birth, is received by faith, and is accompanied by the manifestation of speaking in tongues as the Spirit gives utterance as the initial evidence (Luke 24:49; Acts 1:8; 2:1-4; 8:15-19; 11:14-17; 19:1-7).

10. The Gifts of the Holy Spirit

We believe in the present day operation of the nine supernatural gifts of the Holy Spirit (1 Corinthians 12) and the ministry gifts of Christ (Ephesians 4:11-13) for the edification and expansion of the church.

11. The End of Time

We believe in the premillennial, imminent, and personal return of our Lord Jesus Christ to gather His people unto Himself. Having this blessed hope and earnest expectation, we purify ourselves, even as He is pure, so that we may be ready to meet Him when He comes (John 14:1-3; Titus 2:13; 1 Thessalonians 4:15-17; 1 John 3:2-3; Revelation 20:1-6).

We believe in the bodily resurrection of all humanity, the everlasting conscious bliss of all who truly believe in our Lord Jesus Christ, and that everlasting conscious punishment is the portion of all whose names are not written in the Book of Life (John 5:28-29; 1 Corinthians 15:22-24; Revelation 20:10-15).

Appendix 2

Early Ecumenical Creeds

Apostles' Creed

(Patristic period, from The Catechism to the Catholic Church, *2nd ed. [Vatican City: Libreria Editrice Vaticana, 1997], 49–50)*

I believe in God the Father almighty, creator of heaven and earth. I believe in Jesus Christ, his only Son, our Lord. He was conceived by the power of the Holy Spirit and born of the Virgin Mary. He suffered under Pontius Pilate, was crucified, died, and buried. He descended to the dead. On the third day he rose again. He ascended into heaven and is seated at the right hand of the Father. He will come again to judge the living and the dead. I believe in the Holy Spirit, the holy catholic Church, the communion of saints, the forgiveness of sins, the resurrection of the body, and the life everlasting. Amen.

Nicene-Constantinopolitan Creed (325/381)

We believe in one God, the Father, the Almighty, maker of heaven and earth, of all that is seen and unseen. We believe in one Lord, Jesus Christ, the only Son of God, eternally begotten of the Father, God from God, light from light, true God from true God, begotten, not made, one in Being with the Father. For us and for our salvation he came down from heaven, by the power of the Holy Spirit he was born of the Virgin Mary and became truly human. For our sake he was crucified under Pontius Pilate; he suffered, died and was buried. On the third day he rose again in fulfillment of the Scriptures; he ascended into heaven and is seated at the right hand of the Father. He will come again in glory to judge the living and the dead, and his kingdom will have no end. We believe in the Holy Spirit, the Lord, the giver of life, who proceeds from the Father [and the Son]. Who with the Father and the Son is worshiped and glorified.

Who has spoken through the prophets. We believe in one holy catholic and apostolic Church. We acknowledge one baptism for the forgiveness of sins. We look for the resurrection of the dead, and the life of the world to come. Amen.

Chalcedonian Creed (451)

We, then, following the holy Fathers, all with one consent, teach men to confess one and the same Son, our Lord Jesus Christ, the same perfect in Godhead and also perfect in manhood; truly God and truly man, of a reasonable soul and body; consubstantial with us according to the manhood; in all things like unto us, without sin; begotten before all ages of the Father according to the Godhead, and in these latter days, for us and for our salvation, born of the virgin Mary, the mother of God, according to the manhood; one and the same Christ, Son, Lord, Only-begotten, to be acknowledged in two natures, inconfusedly, unchangeably, indivisibly, inseparably; the distinction of natures being by no means taken away by the union, but rather the property of each nature being preserved, and concurring in one Person and one Subsistence, not parted or divided into two persons, but one and the same Son, and only begotten, God the Word, the Lord Jesus Christ, as the prophets from the beginning have declared concerning him, and the Lord Jesus Christ himself taught us, and the Creed of the holy Fathers has handed down to us.

Glossary

ANNIHILATIONISM: A belief that the wicked will be completely destroyed, instead of suffering from everlasting torment, after the final judgment.

ANTHROPOLOGY: The discipline that studies human nature.

ARMINIANISM: Named after Jacob Arminius (1560–1609), a Dutch theologian who emphasized humanity's freedom to respond to the gracious initiative of God in salvation.

BEATIFIC VISION: A direct perception of God (because of God's self-communication) in the life to come.

CALVINISM: Named after John Calvin (1509–1564), a French theologian who led the Swiss Reformation and emphasized the sovereignty and majesty of God.

CANONICAL CRITICISM: The method of studying the Bible that begins with the final form or received version of the Old and New Testament Scriptures.

CESSATIONISM: The view that the miraculous gifts of the Holy Spirit ceased by the time the canon of Scripture was closed.

CHARISMATA: The spiritual gifts as given by the Holy Spirit.

CHARISMOLOGY: The study of the spiritual gifts of the Holy Spirit.

CHRISTENDOM/POST-CHRISTENDOM: Christendom refers to the times and places of history where and when Christians have had social, cultural, economic, and political influence and power. Post-Christendom refers to the decline of Christian influence, denoting Christianity's minority rather than majority status in the society.

CHRISTOMORPHISM: The quality of being like Christ, of being in his image.

COGNITIVISM: In psychology, it is the study of how the mind influences, if not dominates, human behavior and development.

COLONIALISM/POSTCOLONIALISM: Colonialism is the territorial expansion by one people-group that has involved exploitation of another people-group and their land; historically this has referred to the period from the 1500s to the mid-1900s, when several European nations settled in parts of Asia, Africa, and Latin America. Postcolonialism refers primarily to the academic discipline that studies the consequences of colonialism after European withdrawal allowed for self-governance.

CREATIONISM: The belief that the universe is created by God; some creationists understand the seven days of creation in Genesis to refer to events that took place within a relatively recent time (a few thousand years ago rather than a few million or billion years ago).

CRUCIFORMITY: The quality of being conformed to the Christ in his passion or being in the image of the crucified Christ.

DISPENSATIONALISM: A view of history and eschatology (the study of the end times) that sees God dealing with human beings differently in different periods in time and in particular, envisions that the present period, when salvation is available to Gentiles, will be followed by a distinct period when God will complete the salvation of Jews.

DOCETISM: The belief that Jesus only appeared to be a person and that his physical and historical existence was illusory.

ECCLESIOLOGY: The theological study of the Christian church.

ECUMENISM: Initiatives designed to promote Christian unity among denominations or churches separated by institutional, practical, or doctrinal divergences.

ESCHATOLOGY: The study of the events that will happen at the end of historical and cosmic time and that concern the eternal fate of humanity and the world.

EVANGELICALISM: The historical movement, especially in Anglo-America, emphasizing biblical piety, Christ and cross-centeredness, Christian conversion, and an active life of faith.

EVOLUTION: The belief that living systems and creatures have adapted and developed in complexity over time; evolutionary creationism holds that such adaptation and development are guided by God.

EXCLUSIVISM: The doctrine that only one single worldview, belief system, or religion is true; Christian exclusivism sometimes refers to the belief that only those who have heard of, converted to, and confessed Christ will be saved.

FILIOQUE CLAUSE: Literally means "and from the Son," affirming that the Holy Spirit proceeds not only from the Father but also from the Son.

FIVEFOLD GOSPEL: A teaching within the renewal movement that Jesus is savior, baptizer, sanctifier, healer, and coming king.

HELLENISTIC CULTURE: The Greek way of life, often syncretized with local cultures, throughout the Roman Empire after the time of Alexander the Great.

HISTORICAL CRITICISM: The study of the historical and cultural background of a text in order to determine its original meaning.

HOLINESS MOVEMENT: A Christian movement that emerged from nineteenth-century Methodism that emphasized the teachings of holiness, sanctification, and Christian perfection, including the view that it is possible to live free from voluntary sin through an instantaneous experience of God's second work of grace.

INCARNATION: The belief that the second hypostasis of the triune God, the Logos or Word, took on a human body and appeared in history as Jesus Christ. He is regarded as both God and man in most Christian traditions.

INDIGENOUS VIEWS OF TIME: Some native cultures do not perceive time in linear terms of past, present, and future, but rather see time as a cycle or a repetitive set of seasons.

KESWICKIAN SPIRITUALITY: The spirituality developed through the Keswick movement in England in the nineteenth century, which emphasized cleansing from sin and leading a Spirit-empowered life for Christian service and ministry.

LATE MODERNITY: Used by some scholars to designate the present period of time, when human societies enjoy the fruits of modern science and technology even as modernist forms of Enlightenment thinking are increasingly seen as passé, although there is also a reaction to embracing too quickly the "postmodern" nomenclature.

LIBERATION THEOLOGY: A theological movement, originating in Latin America in the 1960s, that emphasizes the connections between Christian belief/doctrine and praxis, the latter including the task of responding to unjust political, economic, and cultural conditions as part of the Christian mission.

MILLENNIALISM: The eschatological doctrine that there will be one thousand years of peace on earth as promised by Scripture.

MISSIOLOGY: The study of the mission of the Christian church.

MODERNITY: Descriptively, refers to the period of time after the Reformation, which featured the emergence of industrialization, capitalism, and the contemporary nation-state; ideologically, this includes the form of Enlightenment thinking that European colonizers imposed as a universal standard around the world.

OBJECTIVITY/SUBJECTIVITY: Objectivity assumes that human knowledge can be attained of mind-independent realities without any bias, personal, or other influences; subjectivity assumes that all such knowledge is perspectival, related to the knower's perceptions and points of view.

OLD EARTH CREATIONISM: The belief that the earth is millions or even billions of years old; a concomitant belief is that different species of animals, and *homo sapiens*, were created specifically and specially by God.

ONENESS: The teaching among renewal (classical pentecostal) groups that God is indivisibly one (as opposed to the trinitarian teaching of the Godhead of three persons: the Father, the Son, and the Spirit), that Jesus is God's name, and that believers should be baptized in Jesus' name only (as opposed to the trinitarian formula); also describes the group of Pentecostals who hold these beliefs and practices.

ORDO SALUTIS: Literally means "the order of salvation," which refers to the conceptual steps that constitute the sequence of Christian salvation.

PALEONTOLOGY: The study of fossils and what they can inform us about prehistoric life.

PAROUSIA: A Greek term referring to the second coming of Christ.

PIETISM: A term referring to post-Reformation religious movements that emphasize the importance of personal devotion to Christ in Christian living, oftentimes in reaction to rationalistic trends in their traditions.

PLURALISM: The belief that there are diverse viewpoints or approaches to a certain subject.

POSTLIBERALISM: A contemporary theological movement that, in reaction to to the Bible first and foremost as either propositionally constituted (associated with theological conservatism) or experientially engaged (aligned with theological liberalism), insists on its narrative quality.

POST-CHRISTIANITY: Used adjectivally (post-Christian) to designate the feature of the contemporary pluralistic world, which highlights Christianity as no longer the dominant religious or cultural tradition.

PRAGMATISM: A philosophical school emphasizing that beliefs are best understood according to their practical consequences; used more colloquially, it refers to the sensibilities and commitments that foreground real-life application over abstract or speculative thinking.

PURGATORY: In Roman Catholic teaching, a place for the dead to receive purification before they go to heaven.

PURITANISM: A movement within English Protestantism seeking to promote religious piety and Calvinistic doctrinal teachings.

RATIONALISM: The dependence on reason as the major instrument for establishing knowledge or judgment.

REFORMED THEOLOGY: The theological tradition associated with John Calvin (1509–1564) and his legacy.

REIGN OF GOD: A teaching of Jesus referring to the transformation of humanity, social institutions, and the whole earth in anticipation of the coming millennial rule or kingdom of God.

REINCARNATION: The religious or philosophical belief that life after death takes on new forms as conditioned by the thoughts and actions of the previous life.

RENEWAL: An all-inclusive term referring to pentecostal, charismatic, and other related groups and movements.

REVELATION: The means through which God reveals special knowledge to human beings; also refers to the content of such disclosures perceived as from God.

SANCTIFICATION: The process of becoming holy or the work of holiness in Christian life.

SCHOLASTICISM: The medieval theological school influenced by Aristotle and featuring dialectical reasoning in theological studies.

SHAMANISM: Indigenous cultural practices in which specialists enter alternative states of consciousness to access the spirit world for the a wide range of religious, spiritual, and communal purposes.

SOLA SCRIPTURA: Literally means "Scripture alone." The teaching that the Bible has sufficient knowledge to guide individuals to salvation and a Christian way of life; in some Christian circles, this emphasis includes the rejection or minimization of other sources of theological knowledge, such as tradition, reason, or experience.

SOTERIOLOGY: The theological study of the doctrine of salvation.

SUBSTITUTIONARY ATONEMENT: The teaching that Jesus died in the place of humanity, suffering on their behalf, enabling human beings to be free from the consequences of their sin and reconciled with God.

SUPERSESSIONISM: The view that the Christian covenant with God replaces the Mosaic covenant that God made with the Jewish people.

TELEOLOGY: The study of the final causes that provide the rationale for any phenomenon.

TRINITY: The doctrine of God as three persons: Father, Son, and Holy Spirit.

UNIVERSALISM: The belief that all people will be saved, regardless of their beliefs, practices, or way of life.

WESLEYANISM: Named after John Wesley (1703–1791), who led the Methodist revival and emphasized the importance of Christian holiness or sanctification.

WESTMINSTER CONFESSION OF FAITH: A Reformed confession written up in 1646 that is widely recognized as a clear articulation of Reformed theology.

YOUNG EARTH CREATIONISM: The belief that the earth and even the universe are less than ten thousand years old (or at least not more than one hundred thousand years old), and thus relatively young.

ZIONISM: A Jewish nationalistic movement beginning in the late nineteenth century that later contributed to the establishment of the modern Jewish state in Palestine. It takes its name from Mount Zion, a place near Jerusalem that can be used symbolically to refer to Jerusalem.

References

Abraham, William. 1998. *Canon and Criterion in Christian Theology: From the Fathers to Feminism.* Oxford: Oxford University Press.

Abraham, William J., Jason E. Vickers, and Natalie B. Van Kirk, eds. 2008. *Canonical Theism: A Proposal for Theology and the Church.* Grand Rapids: Eerdmans.

Ackerman, David A., ed. 2002. *The Challenge of Culture: Articulating and Proclaiming the Wesleyan-Holiness Message in the Asia-Pacific Region.* Manila: Asia-Pacific Nazarene Theological Seminary.

Adeyemo, Tokunboh, ed. 2005. *African Bible Commentary.* Repr., Grand Rapids: Zondervan, 2010.

Afanasiev, Nicholas. 2007. *The Church of the Holy Spirit.* Michael Plekon, ed.; Vitaly Permiakov, trans. Notre Dame, Ind.: University of Notre Dame Press.

Alangaram, A. 1999. *Christ of the Asian Peoples: Towards an Asian Contextual Christology Based on the Documents of Federation of Asian Bishops' Conferences.* Bangalore, India: Asian Trading.

Albrecht, Daniel. 1999. *Rites in the Spirit: A Ritual Approach to Pentecostal/Charismatic Spirituality.* Sheffield, U.K.: Sheffield Academic.

Alexander, Denis. 2001. *Rebuilding the Matrix: Science and Faith in the 21st Century.* Grand Rapids: Zondervan.

———. 2008. *Creation or Evolution: Do We Have to Choose?* Oxford: Monarch.

Alexander, Donald L., ed. 1989. *Christian Spirituality: Five Views of Sanctification.* Downers Grove, Ill.: IVP Academic.

Alexander, Estrelda Y. 2005. *The Women of Azusa Street.* Cleveland, Ohio: Pilgrim.

———. 2008. *Limited Liberty: The Legacy of Four Pentecostal Women Pioneers.* Cleveland, Ohio: Pilgrim.

Alexander, Estrelda Y., and Amos Yong, eds. 2009. *Philip's Daughters: Women in Pentecostal Charismatic Leadership.* Eugene, Ore.: Pickwick.

Alexander, Kimberly Ervin. 2006. *Pentecostal Healing: Models in Theology and Practice.* Blanford Forum, U.K.: Deo.

Alfaro, Sammy. 2010. *Divino Compañero: Toward a Hispanic Pentecostal Christology.* Eugene, Ore.: Pickwick.

Allen, David. 1994. *The Unfailing Stream: A Charismatic Church History in Outline.* Tonbridge, U.K.: Sovereign World.

Allen, R. Michael. 2010. *Reformed Theology.* London: T&T Clark.

Allison, Dale C., Jr. 1985. *The End of the Ages Has Come: An Early Interpretation of the Passion and Resurrection of Jesus.* Philadelphia: Fortress.

Althouse, Peter F. 2003. *Spirit of the Last Days: Pentecostal Eschatology in Conversation with Jürgen Moltmann.* London: T&T Clark.

Althouse, Peter, and Robby Waddell, eds. 2010. *Perspectives in Pentecostal Eschatologies: World without End.* Eugene, Ore.: Pickwick.

Anders, Timothy. 1994. *The Evolution of Evil: An Inquiry into the Ultimate Origins of Human Suffering.* Chicago: Open Court.

Anderson, Allan H. 2001. *African Reformation: African Initiated Christianity in the 20th Century.* Trenton, N.J.: Africa World.

———. 2004. *Introduction to Pentecostalism: Global Charismatic Christianity.* Cambridge: Cambridge University Press.

———. 2007. *Spreading Fires: The Missionary Nature of Early Pentecostalism.* Maryknoll, N.Y.: Orbis.

Anderson, Bernhard W. 1987. *Creation versus Chaos: The Reinterpretation of Mythical Symbolism in the Bible.* Philadelphia: Fortress.

Anderson, Paul N. 1996. *The Christology of the Fourth Gospel: Its Unity and Disunity in the Light of John 6.* Valley Forge, Pa.: Trinity International.

Anderson, Ray S. 1991. *The Gospel according to Judas.* Colorado Springs: Helmers & Howard.

———. 2005. *Jesus and Judas: Amazing Grace for the Wounded Soul.* Eugene, Ore.: Cascade.

Anderson, Wendy L. 2011.*The Discernment of Spirits: Assessing Visions and Visionaries in the Late Middle Ages.* Tübingen: Mohr Siebeck.

Antola, Markku. 1998. *Experience of Christ's Real Presence in Faith: An Analysis on the Christ-Presence-Motif in the Lutheran Charismatic Renewal.* Helsinki: Luther-Agricola-Society.

Archer, Gleason L., Jr., ed. 1996. *Three Views on the Rapture: Pre-, Mid-, or Post-Tribulation?* Grand Rapids: Zondervan.

Archer, Gleason L., Jr. 2001. *New International Encyclopedia of Bible Difficulties.* Grand Rapids: Zondervan.

Archer, Kenneth J. 2004. *A Pentecostal Hermeneutic for the Twenty-First Century: Spirit, Scripture, and Community.* London: T&T Clark.

———. 2011. *The Gospel Revisited: Towards a Pentecostal Theology of Worship and Witness.* Eugene, Ore.: Pickwick.

Ariel, Yaacov. 2002. *Philosemites or Antisemites? Evangelical Christian Attitudes toward Jews, Judaism, and the State of Israel.* Jerusalem: Hebrew University of Jerusalem.

Arnold, Clinton E. 1997. *3 Crucial Questions about Spiritual Warfare.* Grand Rapids: Baker.

Arrington, French L. 1978a. *Divine Order in the Church: A Study in I Corinthians.* Repr., Grand Rapids: Baker, 1981.

———. 1978b. *Paul's Aeon Theology in I Corinthians*. Washington, D.C.: University Press of America.

———. 1992–1994. *Christian Doctrine: A Pentecostal Perspective*. 3 vols. Cleveland, Tenn.: Pathway.

———. 2008. *The Spirit-Anointed Jesus: A Study of the Gospel of Luke*. Cleveland, Tenn.: Pathway.

Arthur, William. 1856. *The Tongue of Fire; or the True Power of Christianity*. New York: Harper & Brothers.

Asamoah-Gyadu, J. Kwabena. 2005. *African Charismatics: Current Developments within Independent Indigenous Pentecostalism in Ghana*. Leiden: Brill.

Ashton, John, and Tom Whyte. 2001. *The Quest for Paradise: Visions of Heaven and Eternity in the World's Myths and Religions*. New York: HarperCollins.

Au, Connie Ho Yan. 2011. *Grassroots Unity in the Charismatic World*. Eugene, Ore.: Pickwick.

Augustine, Daniela C. 2012. *Pentecost, Hospitality, and Transfiguration: Toward a Spirit-Inspired Vision of Social Transformation*. Cleveland, Tenn.: CPT.

Aulén, Gustaf. 1970. *Christus Victor: An Historical Study of the Three Main Types of the Idea of the Atonement*. A. G. Hebert, trans. London: SPCK.

Aus, Roger David. 2003. *My Name Is "Legion": Palestinian Judaic Traditions in Mark 5:1-20 and Other Gospel Texts*. Lanham, Md.: University Press of America.

Austin, Gerard. 1985. *The Rite of Confirmation—Anointing with the Spirit*. New York: Pueblo.

Avalos, Hector, Sarah J. Melcher, and Jeremy Schipper, eds. 2007. *This Abled Body: Rethinking Disabilities in Biblical Studies*. Atlanta: Society of Biblical Literature.

Badia, Leonard F. 1980. *The Qumran Baptism and John the Baptist's Baptism*. Lanham, Md.: University Press of America.

Baker, Sharon L. 2010. *Razing Hell: Rethinking Everything You've Been Taught about God's Wrath and Judgment*. Louisville, Ky.: Westminster John Knox.

Barr, David L. 2003. *Reading the Book of Revelation: A Resource for Students*. Atlanta: Society of Biblical Literature.

Barth, Karl. 1928. *The Word of God and the Word of Man*. Douglas Horton, trans. London: Hodder & Stoughton.

———. 1956. *Christ and Adam: Man and Humanity in Romans 5*. T. A. Smail, trans. Edinburgh: Oliver & Boyd.

———. 2010a. *Church Dogmatics*, vol. I/1: *The Doctrine of the Word of God*. G. W. Bromiley and T. F. Torrance, eds. Repr., Peabody, Mass.: Hendrickson. Engl. trans./ed., T&T Clark, 1936; 2nd ed., T&T Clark, 1975.

———. 2010b. *Church Dogmatics*, vol. II/2: *The Doctrine of God*. G. W. Bromiley and T. F. Torrance, eds. Repr., Peabody, Mass.: Hendrickson. English trans./ed. T&T Clark, 1957.

Barth, Markus. 1983. *The People of God*. Sheffield, U.K.: JSOT Press.

Bassett, Paul M., ed. 1997. *Holiness Teaching: New Testament Times to Wesley*. Kansas City, Mo.: Beacon Hill.

Bassett, Paul M., and William M. Greathouse. 1985. *Exploring Christian Holiness*, vol. 2: *The Historical Development*. Kansas City, Mo.: Beacon Hill.

Bauckham, Richard. 1993. *The Theology of the Book of Revelation*. Cambridge: Cambridge University Press.

————. 2007. *The Testimony of the Beloved Disciple: Narrative, History, and Theology in the Gospel of John*. Grand Rapids: Baker Academic.

Baxter, J. Sidlow. 1973. *A New Call to Holiness: A Restudy and Restatement of New Testament Teaching Concerning Christian Sanctification*. Grand Rapids: Zondervan.

Beacham, Doug. 2004. *Rediscovering the Role of Apostles and Prophets*. Rev. ed. Franklin Springs, Ga.: LifeSpring Resources.

Beale, G. K. 2004. *The Temple and the Church's Mission: A Biblical Theology of the Dwelling Place of God*. Downers Grove, Ill.: IVP Academic.

Beates, Michael S. 2012. *Disability and the Gospel: How God Uses Our Brokenness to Display His Grace*. Wheaton, Ill.: Crossway.

Beck, David R. 1997. *The Discipleship Paradigm: Readers and Anonymous Characters in the Fourth Gospel*. Leiden: Brill.

Becker, Adam H., and Annette Yoshiko Reed, eds. 2007. *The Ways That Never Parted: Jews and Christians in Late Antiquity and the Early Middle Ages*. Minneapolis: Fortress.

Becking, Bob, and Susanne Hennecke, eds. 2010. *Out of Paradise: Eve and Adam and Their Interpreters*. Sheffield, U.K.: Sheffield Phoenix.

Begbie, Jeremy S. 2007. *Resounding Truth: Christian Wisdom in the World of Music*. Grand Rapids: Baker Academic.

Beilby, James, and Paul R. Eddy, eds. 2006. *The Nature of the Atonement: Four Views*. Downers Grove, Ill.: IVP Academic.

Beker, J. Christiaan. 1982. *Paul's Apocalyptic Gospel: The Coming Triumph of God*. Philadelphia: Fortress.

Berding, Kenneth. 2006. *Spiritual Gifts: Rethinking the Conventional View*. Grand Rapids: Kregel.

Berger, Teresa, ed. 2001. *Dissident Daughters: Feminist Liturgies in Global Context*. Louisville, Ky: Westminster John Knox.

Bernard, David K. 1983. *The Oneness of God*. Hazelwood, Mo.: Word Aflame.

————. 1984. *The New Birth*. Repr., Hazelwood, Mo.: Word Aflame, 1995.

————. 1991. *Oneness and the Trinity, AD 100–300: The Doctrine of God in Ancient Christian Writings*. Hazelwood, Mo.: Word Aflame.

————. 1996. *A History of Christian Doctrine*, vol. 2: *The Reformation to the Holiness Movement, A.D. 1500–1900*. Hazelwood, Mo.: Word Aflame.

Berry, R. J. 2003. *God's Book of Works: The Nature and Theology of Nature*. London: T&T Clark.

Best, Thomas F., and Dagmar Heller, eds. 1999. *Becoming a Christian: The Ecumenical Implications of Our Common Baptism*. Geneva: WCC.

Bevans, Stephen B. 2009. *An Introduction to Theology in Global Perspective*. Maryknoll, N.Y.: Orbis.

Bigger, Andreas, ed. 2010. *Release from Life, Release in Life: Indian Perspectives on Individual Liberation*. New York: Peter Lang.

Billingsley, Scott. 2008. *It's a New Day: Race and Gender in the Modern Charismatic Movement*. Tuscaloosa: University of Alabama Press.

Black, David Allen, ed. 2008. *Perspectives on the Ending of Mark: Four Views*. Nashville: Broadman & Holman.

Blocher, Henri. 1997. *Original Sin: Illuminating the Riddle*. Downers Grove, Ill: InterVarsity.

Block, Jennie Weiss. 2002. *Copious Hosting: A Theology of Access for People with Disabilities*. New York: Continuum.

Bloesch, Donald G. 1992. *A Theology of Word and Spirit: Authority and Method in Theology*. Downers Grove, Ill.: InterVarsity.

Blomberg, Craig. 2005. *Contagious Holiness: Jesus' Meals with Sinners*. Downers Grove, Ill.: IVP Academic.

Blount, Brian K. 1998. *Go Preach! Mark's Kingdom Message and the Black Church Today*. Maryknoll, N.Y.: Orbis.

———, ed. 2007. *True to Our Native Land: An African American New Testament Commentary*. Minneapolis: Fortress.

———. 2009. *Revelation: A Commentary*. Louisville, Ky: Westminster John Knox.

Boersma, Hans. 2004. *Violence, Hospitality, and the Cross: Reappropriating the Atonement Tradition*. Grand Rapids: Baker Academic.

Boesak, Allan A. 1987. *Comfort and Protest: Reflections on the Apocalypse of John of Patmos*. Philadelphia: Westminster.

Boff, Leonardo. 1978. *Jesus Christ Liberator: A Critical Christology for Our Time*. Patrick Hughes, trans. Maryknoll, N.Y.: Orbis.

———. 1995. *Cry of the Earth, Cry of the Poor*. Philip Berryman, trans. Maryknoll, N.Y.: Orbis.

Bogart, John. 1977. *Orthodox and Heretical Perfectionism in the Johannine Community as Evident in the First Epistle of John*. Missoula, Mont.: Scholars Press.

Bonnefoy, J.-Fr. 1967. *The Immaculate Conception in the Divine Plan*. Michael D. Meilach, trans. Paterson, N.J.: St. Anthony Guild.

Bonting, Sjoerd L. 2005. *Creation and Double Chaos: Science and Theology in Discussion*. Minneapolis: Fortress.

Boureux, Christophe, and Christoph Theobald, eds. 2004. *Original Sin: A Code of Fallibility*. London: SCM Press.

Bournis, Theodoritos. 1968. *"I Was in the Isle Patmos. . . ."* 2nd ed. Athens: n.p.

Bovell, Carlos R. 2007. *Inerrancy and the Spiritual Formation of Younger Evangelicals*. Eugene, Ore.: Wipf & Stock.

Bowie, Fiona, and Christopher Deacy, eds. 1997. *The Coming Deliverer: Millennial Themes in World Religions*. Cardiff: University of Wales Press.

Boyd, Gregory A. 2001. *Satan and the Problem of Evil: Constructing a Trinitarian Warfare Theodicy*. Downers Grove, Ill.: IVP Academic.

Boyer, Paul. 1992. *When Time Shall Be No More: Prophecy Belief in Modern American Culture*. Cambridge, Mass.: Belknap Press of Harvard University Press.

Braaten, Carl E., and Robert W. Jenson, eds. 2000. *Sin, Death, and the Devil.* Grand Rapids: Eerdmans.

———, eds. 2003. *Jews and Christians: People of God.* Grand Rapids: Eerdmans.

Brannon, M. Jeff. 2011. *The Heavenlies in Ephesians: A Lexical, Exegetical, and Conceptual Analysis.* London: T&T Clark.

Bretherton, Luke. 2006. *Hospitality as Holiness: Christian Witness amid Moral Diversity.* Aldershot, U.K.: Ashgate.

Bridge, Steven L. 2003. *Where the Eagles Are Gathered: The Deliverances of the Elect in Lukan Eschatology.* London: Sheffield Academic

Brodeur, Scott. 1996. *The Holy Spirit's Agency in the Resurrection of the Dead: An Exegetico-Theological Study of 1 Corinthians 15,44b-49 and Romans 8,9-13.* Rome: Editrice Pontificia Università Gregoriana.

Brooke, John Hedley, and Ronald L. Numbers, eds. 2011. *Science and Religion around the World.* Oxford: Oxford University Press.

Brooks, Oscar S. 1987. *The Drama of Decision: Baptism in the New Testament.* Peabody, Mass.: Hendrickson.

Brown, Alexandra R. 1995. *The Cross and Human Transformation: Paul's Apocalyptic Word in 1 Corinthians.* Minneapolis: Fortress.

Brown, B. Ricardo. 2010. *Until Darwin: Science, Human Variety and the Origins of Race.* London: Pickering & Chatto.

Brown, Candy Gunther, ed. 2011. *Global Pentecostal and Charismatic Healing.* Oxford: Oxford University Press.

———. 2012. *Testing Prayer: Science and Healing.* Cambridge, Mass.: Harvard University Press.

Brown, Colin. 1984. *Miracles and the Critical Mind.* Grand Rapids: Eerdmans.

———. 1985. *That You May Believe: Miracles and Faith Then and Now.* Grand Rapids: Eerdmans.

Brown, Paul E. 2002. *The Holy Spirit: The Spirit's Interpreting Role in Relation to Biblical Hermeneutics.* Fearn, U.K.: Christian Focus.

Bruner, Frederick Dale. 1970. *A Theology of the Holy Spirit: The Pentecostal Experience and the New Testament Witness.* Grand Rapids: Eerdmans.

Bruner, Frederick Dale, and William Hordern. 1984. *Holy Spirit: Shy Member of the Trinity.* Minneapolis: Augsburg.

Bruner, William T. 1966. *Children of the Devil: A Fresh Investigation of the Fall of Man and Original Sin.* New York: Philosophical Library.

Brunetti, John. 2001. "Peripheral Vision: The Paintings of Tim Lowly." Catalogue essay, Elgin Community College, Elgin, Ill.

Bryan, Steven M. 2003. "Power in the Poor: The Healing of the Man at Bethesda and Jesus' Violation of the Sabbath (Jn. 5:1-18)." *Tyndale Bulletin* 54 (2): 7–22.

Bulgakov, Sergius. 2011. *Relics and Miracles: Two Theological Essays.* Boris Jakim, trans. Grand Rapids: Eerdmans.

Bulkeley, Kelly. 2008. *Dreaming in the World's Religions: A Comparative History.* New York: New York University Press.

Bullivant, Stephen. 2012. *The Salvation of Atheists and Catholic Dogmatic Theology.* Oxford: Oxford University Press.

Bundy, David. 2009. *Visions of Apostolic Mission: Scandinavian Pentecostal Mission to 1935.* Uppsala, Sweden: Uppsala Universiteit.

Burgess, Stanley M., ed. 2011. *Christian Peoples of the Spirit: A Documentary History of Pentecostal Spirituality from the Early Church to the Present.* New York: New York University Press.

Burtchaell, James Tunstead. 1992. *From Synagogue to Church: Public Services and Offices in the Earliest Christian Communities.* Cambridge: Cambridge University Press.

Butler, Anthea. 2007. *Women in the Church of God in Christ: Making a Sanctified World.* Chapel Hill: University of North Carolina Press.

Butler, Daniel L. 2004. *Oneness Pentecostalism: A History of the Jesus Name Movement.* Bellflower, Calif.: International Pentecostal Church.

Buxton, Graham. 2005. *The Trinity, Creation and Pastoral Ministry: Imaging the Perichoretic God.* Milton Keynes, U.K.: Paternoster.

Caciola, Nancy. 2003. *Discerning Spirits: Divine and Demonic Possession in the Middle Ages.* Ithaca, N.Y.: Cornell University Press.

Callen, Barry L. 2011. *Heart of the Matter: Frank Conversations among Great Christian Thinkers on the Major Subjects of Christian Theology.* Wilmore, Ky.: Emeth.

Calvin, John. 1965. *Institutes of the Christian Religion.* 2 vols. John T. McNeill, ed. Ford Lewis Battles, trans. Philadelphia: Westminster.

Camper, Fred. 2002. "Temma Lowly and the Meaning of Life." *Chicago Reader,* November 21, 1, 14–20.

Capps, Donald. 2008. *Jesus the Village Psychiatrist.* Louisville, Ky: Westminster John Knox.

Carlson, Richard F., ed. 2004. *Science & Christianity: Four Views.* Downers Grove, Ill.: IVP Academic.

Carmody, Denise Lardner, and John Tully Carmody. 1996. *Serene Compassion: A Christian Appreciation of Buddhist Holiness.* Oxford: Oxford University Press.

Carroll, James. 2001. *Constantine's Sword: The Church and the Jews, A History.* Boston: Houghton Mifflin.

Carroll, John T. 1988. *Response to the End of History: Eschatology and Situation in Luke-Acts.* Atlanta: Scholars Press.

Carson, D. A. 1987. *Showing the Spirit: A Theological Exposition of 1 Corinthians 12-14.* Grand Rapids: Baker.

Carter, Erik W. 2007. *Including People with Disabilities in Faith Communities: A Guide for Service Providers, Families, and Congregations.* Baltimore: Paul H. Brookes.

Carter, J. Kameron. 2008. *Race: A Theological Account.* Oxford: Oxford University Press.

Cartledge, Mark J. 2007. *Encountering the Spirit: The Charismatic Tradition.* Maryknoll, N.Y.: Orbis.

Castelo, Daniel. 2012. *Revisioning Pentecostal Ethics: The Epicletic Community.* Cleveland, Tenn.: CPT.

Chae, Young Sam. 2006. *Jesus as the Eschatological Davidic Shepherd: Studies in the Old Testament, Second Temple Judaism, and in the Gospel of Matthew.* Tübingen: Mohr Siebeck.

Chan, Simon. 2011. *Pentecostal Ecclesiology: An Essay on the Development of Doctrine.* Blandford Forum, U.K.: Deo.

Chance, J. Bradley. 1988. *Jerusalem, the Temple and the New Age in Luke-Acts.* Macon, Ga.: Mercer University Press.

Charette, Blaine. 2000. *Restoring Presence: The Spirit in Matthew's Gospel.* Sheffield, U.K.: Sheffield Academic.

Cherbonnier, E. La B. 1955. *Hardness of Heart: A Contemporary Interpretation of the Doctrine of Sin.* Garden City, N.Y.: Doubleday.

Chester, Tim. 2006. *Mission and the Coming of God: Eschatology, the Trinity and Mission in the Theology of Jürgen Moltmann and Contemporary Evangelicalism.* Milton Keynes, U.K.: Paternoster.

Chesnut, R. Andrew. 1997. *Born Again in Brazil: The Pentecostal Boom and the Pathogens of Poverty.* New Brunswick, N.J.: Rutgers University Press.

Chestnutt, Glenn A. 2010. *Challenging the Stereotype: The Theology of Karl Barth as a Resource for Inter-religious Encounter in a European Context.* Oxford: Peter Lang.

Chidester, David. 2000. *Christianity: A Global History.* New York: HarperSanFrancisco.

Cho, Chuong Kwon. 2010. "*Han* and the Pentecostal Experience: A Study of the Growth of the Yoido Full Gospel Church in Korea." Ph.D. thesis, University of Birmingham, Birmingham, U.K.

Cimpean, Florin T. 2004. "From Margins to Center: Pentecostal and Orthodox Readings of Romans 8 in Romania." In Yeo Khiok-khng, ed., *Navigating Romans through Cultures: Challenging Readings by Charting a New Course,* 31–53. London: T&T Clark.

Clark, David K. 2003. *To Know and Love God: Method for Theology.* Wheaton, Ill.: Crossway.

Clarke, Clifton R. 2011. *African Christology: Jesus in Post-missionary African Christianity.* Eugene, Ore.: Pickwick.

Clarke, Clifton R., and Amos Yong, eds. 2011 *Global Renewal, Religious Pluralism, and the Great Commission: Toward a Renewal Theology of Mission and Interreligious Encounter.* Lexington, Ky.: Emeth.

Clayton, Philip. 1989. *Explanation from Physics to Theology: An Essay in Rationality and Religion.* New Haven: Yale University Press.

Cleary, Edward L. 2011. *The Rise of Charismatic Catholicism in Latin America.* Gainesville: University of Florida Press.

Clifton, Shane. 2009. *Pentecostal Churches in Transition: Analysing the Developing Ecclesiology of the Assemblies of God in Australia.* Leiden: Brill.

Clooney, Francis X., ed. 2011. *The New Comparative Theology: Interreligious Insights from the Next Generation.* London: T&T Clark.

Coakley, John W., and Andrea Sterk, eds. 2004. *Readings in World Christian History,* vol. 1: *Earliest Christianity to 1453.* Maryknoll, N.Y.: Orbis.

Coats, John R. 2009. *Original Sinners: A New Interpretation of Genesis*. New York: Free Press.

Cody, Aelred. 1960. *Heavenly Sanctuary and Liturgy in the Epistle to the Hebrews: The Achievement of Salvation in the Epistle's Perspective*. St. Meinrad, Ind.: Grail.

Coffey, David. 1999. *Deus Trinitas: The Doctrine of the Triune God*. Oxford: Oxford University Press.

Cohn, Norman Rufus. 1957. *The Pursuit of the Millennium: Revolutionary Millenarians and Mystical Anarchists of the Middle Ages*. Rev. and enl. ed. 1970. Repr: New York: Oxford University Press, 1977.

Cohn-Sherbok, Dan. 2000. *Messianic Judaism*. London: Cassell.

———, ed. 2001. *Voices of Messianic Judaism: Confronting Critical Issues Facing a Maturing Movement*. Baltimore: Lederer.

Colijn, Brenda B. 2010. *Images of Salvation in the New Testament*. Downers Grove, Ill.: IVP Academic.

Collins, C. John. 2011. *Did Adam and Eve Really Exist? Who They Were and Why You Should Care*. Wheaton, Ill.: Crossway.

Collins, Francis. 2006. *The Language of God: A Scientist Presents Evidence for Belief*. New York: Free Press.

Collins, James Michael. 2009. *Exorcism and Deliverance Ministry in the Twentieth Century: An Analysis of the Practice and Theology of Exorcism in Modern Western Christianity*. Milton Keynes, U.K.: Paternoster.

Collins, Raymond F. 2004. *The Many Faces of the Church: A Study in New Testament Ecclesiology*. New York: Crossroad.

Collins, Robin. 2003. "Evolution and Original Sin." In Keith B. Miller, ed., *Perspectives on an Evolving Creation*, 469–501. Grand Rapids: Eerdmans.

Congar, Yves M. J. 1986. *The Word and the Spirit*. David Smith, trans. London: Geoffrey Chapman.

Conway, Colleen M. 1999. *Men and Women in the Fourth Gospel: Gender and Johannine Characterization*. Atlanta: Society of Biblical Literature.

Conzelmann, Hans. 1961, *The Theology of St. Luke*. Geoffrey Buswell, trans. Repr., Philadelphia: Fortress, 1982.

Cook, L. Stephen. 2011. *On the Question of the "Cessation of Prophecy" in Ancient Judaism*. Tübingen: Mohr Siebeck.

Corey, M. A. 1993. *God and the New Cosmology: The Anthropic Design Argument*. Lanham, Md.: Rowman & Littlefield.

Corey, Michael A. 2000. *Evolution and the Problem of Natural Evil*. Lanham, Md.: University Press of America.

Corner, Mark. 2005. *Signs of God: Miracles and Their Interpretation*. Aldershot, U.K.: Ashgate.

Costen, Melva Wilson. 1993. *African American Christian Worship*. Nashville: Abingdon.

Cotter, A. C. 1952. *The Encyclical "Humani Generis," with a Commentary*, 2nd ed. Weston, Mass.: Weston College Press.

Cotton, Ian. 1996. *The Hallelujah Revolution: The Rise of the New Christians.* Amherst, N.Y.: Prometheus.

Coward, Harold G., ed. 2000. *Experiencing Scripture in World Religions.* Maryknoll, N.Y.: Orbis.

———. 2003. *Sin and Salvation in the World's Religions.* Oxford: Oneworld.

Cox, Harvey G. 1995. *Fire from Heaven: The Rise of Pentecostal Spirituality and the Reshaping of Religion in the 21st Century.* Reading, Mass.: Addison-Wesley.

Cross, Anthony R., and Philip E. Thompson, eds. 2003. *Baptist Sacramentalism.* Carlisle, U.K.: Paternoster.

———, eds. 2008. *Baptist Sacramentalism 2.* Milton Keynes, U.K.: Paternoster.

Crowe, Terrence Robert. 1993. *Pentecostal Unity: Recurring Frustration and Enduring Hopes.* Chicago: Loyola University Press.

Csordas, Thomas J. 2002. *Body/Meaning/Healing.* New York: Palgrave Macmillan.

Culpepper, R. Alan. 1994. *John, the Son of Zebedee: The Life of a Legend.* Columbia: University of South Carolina Press.

Curtis, Heather D. 2007. *Faith in the Great Physician: Suffering and Divine Healing in American Culture, 1860–1900.* Baltimore: Johns Hopkins University Press.

Dabney, D. Lyle. 1997. *Die Kenosis des Geistes: Kontinuität zwischen Schöpfung und Erlösung im Werk des Heiligen Geistes.* Neukirchen-Vluyn: Neukirchener Verlag.

Dalcour, Edward L. 2005. *A Definitive Look at Oneness Theology: Defending the Tri-Unity of God.* Lanham, Md.: University Press of America.

Daly, Robert J. 2009. *Sacrifice Unveiled: The True Meaning of Christian Sacrifice.* London: T&T Clark.

Daunton-Fear, Andrew. 2009. *Healing in the Early Church: The Church's Ministry of Healing and Exorcism from the First to the Fifth Century.* Milton Keynes, U.K.: Paternoster.

Davies, Oliver. 2004. *The Creativity of God: World, Eucharist, Reason.* Cambridge: Cambridge University Press.

Davies, Steven L. 1995. *Jesus the Healer: Possession, Trance, and the Origins of Christianity.* New York: Continuum.

Davies, Wilma Wells. 2010. *The Embattled but Empowered Community: Comparing Understandings of Spiritual Power in Argentine Popular and Pentecostal Cosmologies.* Leiden: Brill, 2010.

Davis, Stephen T. 1977. *Debate about the Bible: Inerrancy versus Infallibility.* Philadelphia: Westminster.

Dawn, Marva J. 2001. *Powers, Weakness, and the Tabernacling of God.* Grand Rapids: Eerdmans.

———. 2008. *Being Well when We're Ill: Wholeness and Hope in Spite of Infirmity.* Minneapolis: Augsburg.

———. 2009. *In the Beginning God: Creation, Culture, and the Spiritual Life.* Downers Grove, Ill.: InterVarsity.

Dawson, Audrey. 2008. *Healing, Weakness and Power: Perspectives on Healing in the Writings of Mark, Luke, and Paul.* Milton Keynes, U.K.: Paternoster.

Dayton, Donald W., ed. 1985. *Late Nineteenth Century Revivalist Teachings on the Holy Spirit*. New York: Garland.

———. 1987. *Theological Roots of Pentecostalism*. Peabody, Mass.: Hendrickson.

D'Costa, Gavin. 2000. *The Meeting of Religions and the Trinity*. Maryknoll, N.Y.: Orbis.

———. 2009. *Christianity and World Religions: Disputed Questions in the Theology of Religions*. Oxford: Wiley–Blackwell.

De Arteaga, William L. 2002. *Forgotten Power: The Significance of the Lord's Supper in Revival*. Grand Rapids: Zondervan.

de Boer, Martinus C. 1988. *The Defeat of Death: Apocalyptic Eschatology in 1 Corinthians 15 and Romans 5*. Sheffield, U.K.: JSOT Press.

de Margerie, Bertrand. 1982. *The Christian Trinity in History*. Still River, Mass.: St. Bede's.

De Ridder, Richard R. 1977. *God Has Not Rejected His People*. Grand Rapids: Baker.

de S. Cameron, Nigel M., ed. 1992. *Universalism and the Doctrine of Hell*. Carlisle, U.K.: Paternoster.

Deal, William S. 1978. *The March of Holiness through the Centuries: A Brief History of Holiness Doctrine*. Kansas City, Mo.: Beacon Hill.

Deere, Jack. 1996. *Surprised by the Voice of God: How God Speaks Today through Prophecies, Dreams, and Visions*. Grand Rapids: Zondervan.

Del Colle, Ralph. 1994. *Christ and the Spirit: Spirit-Christology in Trinitarian Perspective*. Oxford: Oxford University Press.

Dembski, William A. 2009. *The End of Christianity: Finding a Good God in an Evil World*. Nashville: B&H Academic.

Dempster, Murray W., Byron D. Klaus, and Douglas Petersen, eds. 1991. *Called and Empowered: Global Mission in Pentecostal Perspective*. Peabody, Mass.: Hendrickson.

deSilva, David A. 2009. *Seeing Things John's Way: The Rhetoric of the Book of Revelation*. Louisville, Ky: Westminster John Knox.

DeYoung, Curtiss Paul, et al., eds. 2010. *The Peoples' Companion to the Bible*. Minneapolis: Fortress.

Dinoia, J. A. 1992. *The Diversity of Religions: A Christian Perspective*. Washington, D.C.: Catholic University of America Press.

Dombrowski, Kirk. 2001. *Against Culture: Development, Politics, and Religion in Indian Alaska*. Lincoln: University of Nebraska Press.

Domning, Daryl P. 2006. *Original Selfishness: Original Sin and Evil in the Light of Evolution*. Burlington, Vt.: Ashgate.

Donaldson, Terence L. 2010. *Jews and Anti-Judaism in the New Testament: Decision Points and Divergent Interpretations*. Waco, Tex.: Baylor University Press.

Doody, John, Adam Goldstein, and Kim Paffenroth, eds. 2013. *Augustine and Science*. Lanham, Md.: Lexington.

Dorries, David. W. 2006. *Spirit-Filled Christology: Merging Theology and Power*. San Diego: Aventine.

Droogers, André, Cornelis van der Laan, and Wout van Laar, eds. 2006. *Fruitful in This Land: Pluralism, Dialogue and Healing in Migrant Pentecostalism*. Zoetermeer, Netherlands: Uitgeverij Boekencentrum.

Du Plessis, Paul Johannes. 1959. *ΤΕΛΕΙΟΣ: The Idea of Perfection in the New Testament*. Kampen, Netherlands: J. H. Kok.

Duffin, Jacalyn. 2009. *Medical Miracles: Doctors, Saints, and Healing in the Modern World*. Oxford: Oxford University Press.

Dulles, Avery. 1974. *Models of the Church*. Garden City, N.Y.: Doubleday.

———. 1992. *Models of Revelation*. Maryknoll, N.Y.: Orbis.

Dulles, Avery, and George Martin, eds. 1979. *Scripture and the Charismatic Renewal: Proceedings of the Milwaukee Symposium, December 1–3, 1978*. Ann Arbor, Mich.: Servant.

Dunn, James D. G. 1970. *Baptism in the Holy Spirit: A Re-examination of the New Testament Teaching on the Gift of the Spirit in Relation to Pentecostalism Today*. Philadelphia: Westminster.

———, ed. 1992. *Jews and Christians: The Parting of the Ways A.D. 70 to 135*. Tübingen: J.C.B. Mohr (Paul Siebeck).

Dünzl, Franz. 2007. *A Brief History of the Doctrine of the Trinity in the Early Church*. London: T&T Clark.

Dupuis, Jacques. 2002. *Toward a Christian Theology of Religious Pluralism*. Maryknoll, N.Y.: Orbis.

Editorial. 1867. "Education in the Southern States." *Harper's Weekly*, November 9.

Efird, James M. 1980. *Christ, the Church, and the End: Studies in Colossians and Ephesians*. Valley Forge, Pa.: Judson.

Eiesland, Nancy L. 1994. *The Disabled God: Toward a Liberatory Theology of Disability*. Nashville: Abingdon.

Ekka, Jhakmak Neeraj. 2007. *Christ as Sacrament and Example: Luther's Theology of the Cross and Its Relevance for South Asia*. Minneapolis: Lutheran University Press.

Ellis, E. Earle. 1972. *Eschatology in Luke*. Philadelphia: Fortress.

Emmrich, Martin. 2003. *Pneumatological Concepts in the Epistle to the Hebrews: Amtscharisma, Prophet, and Guide of the Eschatological Exodus*. Lanham, Md.: University Press of America.

Engelke, Matthew. 2007. *A Problem of Presence: Beyond Scripture in an African Church*. Berkeley: University of California Press.

Enns, Peter. 2005. *Inspiration and Incarnation: Evangelicals and the Problem of the Old Testament*. Grand Rapids: Baker Academic.

———. 2012. *The Evolution of Adam: What the Bible Does and Doesn't Say about Human Origins*. Grand Rapids: Brazos.

Erickson, Millard J. 1996. *How Shall They Be Saved? The Destiny of Those Who Do Not Hear of Jesus*. Grand Rapids: Baker.

Ervin, Howard M. 1984. *Conversion-Initiation and the Baptism in the Holy Spirit: A Critique of James D. G. Dunn, Baptism in the Holy Spirit*. Peabody, Mass.: Hendrickson.

———. 1987. *Spirit Baptism: A Biblical Investigation.* Peabody, Mass.: Hendrickson.

———. 2002. *Healing: Sign of the Kingdom.* Peabody, Mass.: Hendrickson.

Evans, G. R. 1996. *Method in Ecumenical Theology: The Lessons So Far.* Cambridge: Cambridge University Press.

Evans, Robert Maxwell. 1968. *Eschatology and Ethics: A Study of Thessalonica and Paul's Letters to the Thessalonians.* Doctor of Theology dissertation, University of Basel, Switzerland. Princeton, N.J.: McMahon Printing.

Fackre, Gabriel. 1984. *The Christian Story: A Narrative Interpretation of Basic Christian Doctrine.* Rev. ed. Grand Rapids: Eerdmans.

Falk, Darrell. 2004. *Coming to Peace with Science: Bridging the Worlds between Faith and Biology.* Downers Grove, Ill.: InterVarsity.

Farley, Edward. 1982. *Ecclesial Reflection: An Anatomy of Theological Method.* Philadelphia: Fortress.

Farley, Lawrence R. 2004. *The Gospel of Mark: The Suffering Servant.* Ben Lomond, Calif.: Conciliar.

Faupel, David W. 1996. *The Everlasting Gospel: The Significance of Eschatology in the Development of Pentecostal Thought.* Sheffield, U.K.: Sheffield Academic.

Fee, Gordon D. 1991. *Gospel and Spirit: Issues in New Testament Hermeneutics.* Peabody, Mass.: Hendrickson.

———. 1994. *God's Empowering Presence: The Holy Spirit in the Letters of Paul.* Peabody, Mass.: Hendrickson.

———. 2011. *Revelation: A New Covenant Commentary.* Eugene, Ore.: Cascade.

Ferguson, Everett. 2009. *Baptism in the Early Church: History, Theology, and Liturgy in the First Five Centuries.* Grand Rapids: Eerdmans.

Fernandez, Eleazar S. 1994. *Toward a Theology of Struggle.* Maryknoll, N.Y.: Orbis.

Fettke, Steven M. 2011. *God's Empowered People: A Pentecostal Theology of the Laity.* Eugene, Ore.: Wipf & Stock.

Finger, Thomas N. 1985. *Christian Theology: An Eschatological Approach.* Vol. 1. Nashville: Thomas Nelson.

———. 1989. *Christian Theology: An Eschatological Approach.* Vol. 2. Scottdale, Pa.: Herald.

Finn, Thomas M. 1992. *Early Christian Baptism and the Catechumenate.* 2 vols. Collegeville, Minn.: Liturgical.

Finucane, Ronald C. 1977. *Miracles and Pilgrims: Popular Beliefs in Medieval England.* Totowa, N.J.: Rowman & Littlefield.

Fitzgerald, Thomas E. 2004. *The Ecumenical Movement: An Introductory History.* Westport, Conn.: Praeger.

Flessen, Bonnie J. 2011. *An Exemplary Man: Cornelius and Characterization in Acts 10.* Eugene, Ore.: Pickwick.

Flett, John G. 2010. *The Witness of God: The Trinity, Missio Dei, Karl Barth, and the Nature of Christian Community.* Grand Rapids: Eerdmans.

Flew, R. Newton. 1934. *The Idea of Perfection in Christian Theology.* Repr., New York: Humanities, 1968.

Foakes-Jackson, F. J. 1927. *Peter: Prince of Apostles—A Study in the History and Tradition of Christianity*. New York: George H. Doran.

Forbes, Christopher. 1995. *Prophecy and Inspired Speech in Early Christianity and Its Hellenistic Context*. Repr., Peabody, Mass.: Hendrickson, 1997.

Freeman, Dena, ed. 2012. *Pentecostalism and Development: Churches, NGOs and Social Change in Africa*. New York: Palgrave Macmillan.

French, Talmadge L. 1999. *Our God Is One: The Story of Oneness Pentecostals*. Indianapolis: Vision & Vision.

Fretheim, Terence E. 2010. *Creation Untamed: The Bible, God, and Natural Disasters*. Grand Rapids: Baker Academic.

Freund, Peter E. S., Meredith B. McGuire, and Linda S. Podhurst. 2003. *Health, Illness, and the Social Body: A Critical Sociology*. 4th ed. Upper Saddle River, N.J.: Prentice Hall.

Fudge, Edward William, and Robert A. Peterson. 2000. *Two Views of Hell: A Biblical and Theological Dialogue*. Downers Grove, Ill.: IVP Academic.

Fulljames, Peter. 1993. *God and Creation in Intercultural Perspective: Dialogue between the Theologies of Barth, Dickson, Pobee, Nyamiti, and Pannenberg*. New York: Peter Lang.

Furnish, Victor Paul. 1999. *The Theology of the First Letter to the Corinthians*. Cambridge: Cambridge University Press.

Gaillardetz, Richard R. 2008. *Ecclesiology for a Global Church: A People Called and Sent*. Maryknoll, N.Y.: Orbis.

García-Johnson, Oscar. 2009. *The Mestizo/a Community of the Spirit: A Postmodern Latino/a Ecclesiology*. Eugene, Ore.: Pickwick.

Garrigan, Siobhán. 2004. *Beyond Ritual: Sacramental Theology after Habermas*. Aldershot, U.K.: Ashgate.

Gatumu, Kabiro wa. 2008. *The Pauline Concept of Supernatural Powers: A Reading from the African Worldview*. Milton Keynes, U.K.: Paternoster.

Gause, R. Hollis. 1980. *Living in the Spirit: The Way of Salvation*. Cleveland, Tenn.: Pathway.

Gaventa, Beverly Roberts. 2007. *Our Mother Saint Paul*. Louisville, Ky: Westminster John Knox.

Geisler, Norman L., ed. 1980. *Inerrancy*. Grand Rapids: Zondervan.

Gelpi, Donald L. 1976. *Charism and Sacrament: A Theology of Christian Conversion*. New York: Paulist.

———. 1998. *The Conversion Experience: A Reflective Process for RCIA Participants and Others*. New York: Paulist.

Gentle, Judith Marie, and Robert L. Fastiggi, eds. 2009. *De Maria Numquam Satis: The Significance of the Catholic Doctrines on the Blessed Virgin Mary for All People*. Lanham, Md.: University Press of America.

George, Geomon K. 2006. *Religious Pluralism: Challenges for Pentecostalism in India*. Bangalore, India: Centre for Contemporary Christianity.

Gerloff, Roswith I. H. 1992. *A Plea for British Black Theologies: The Black Church Movement in Britain in Its Transatlantic Cultural and Theological Interaction with*

Special References to the Pentecostal Oneness (Apostolic) and Sabbatarian Movements. Repr., Eugene, Ore.: Wipf & Stock, 2010.

Giberson, Karl. 1993. *Worlds Apart: The Unholy War between Religion and Science.* Kansas City, Mo.: Beacon Hill.

Gifford, Paul. 2004. *Ghana's New Christianity: Pentecostalism in a Globalizing African Economy.* Bloomington: Indiana University Press.

Gifford, Paul, Steve Brouwer, and Susan D. Rose. 1996. *Exporting the American Gospel: Global Christian Fundamentalism.* New York: Routledge.

Gilbertson, Richard. 1993. *The Baptism of the Holy Spirit: The Views of A. B. Simpson and His Contemporaries.* Camp Hill, Pa.: Christian Publications.

Gill, Kenneth D. 1994. *Toward a Contextualized Theology for the Third World: The Emergence and Development of Jesus' Name Pentecostalism in Mexico.* New York: Peter Lang.

Gnanakan, Ken. 1992. *Salvation: Some Asian Perspectives.* Bangalore, India: Asia Theological Association.

Goff, James R., Jr. 1988. *Fields White unto Harvest: Charles F. Parham and the Missionary Origins of Pentecostalism.* Fayetteville: University of Arkansas Press.

González, Justo L. 1999. *For the Healing of the Nations: The Book of Revelation in an Age of Cultural Conflict.* Maryknoll, N.Y.: Orbis.

Gonzalez, Michelle A. 2007. *Created in God's Image: An Introduction to Feminist Theological Anthropology.* Maryknoll, N.Y.: Orbis.

Goodman, Felicitas D. 1972. *Speaking in Tongues: A Cross-Cultural Study of Glossolalia.* Chicago: University of Chicago Press.

Gorringe, Timothy J. 1990. *Discerning Spirit: A Theology of Revelation.* London: SCM Press.

Graff, Ann O'Hara, ed. 1995. *In the Embrace of God: Feminist Approaches to Theological Anthropology.* Maryknoll, N.Y.: Orbis.

Gray, Sherman W. 1989. *The Least of My Brothers: Matthew 25:31-46—A History of Interpretation.* Atlanta: Scholars.

Greathouse, William M. 1979. *From the Apostles to Wesley: Christian Perfection in Historical Perspective.* Kansas City, Mo.: Beacon Hill.

Green, Chris E. W. 2012. *Toward a Pentecostal Theology of the Lord's Supper: Foretasting the Kingdom.* Cleveland, Tenn.: CPT.

Green, Joel B., ed. 2004. *What about the Soul? Neuroscience and Christian Anthropology.* Nashville: Abingdon.

———. 2008. *Body, Soul, and Human Life: The Nature of Humanity in the Bible.* Grand Rapids: Baker Academic.

Green, Joel B., and Max Turner, eds. 2000. *Between Two Horizons: Spanning New Testament Studies and Systematic Theology.* Grand Rapids: Eerdmans.

Greene, Colin. 2003. *Christology in Cultural Perspective: Marking Out the Horizons.* Carlisle, U.K.: Paternoster..

Greene, John C. 1959. *The Death of Adam: Evolution and Its Impact on Western Thought.* Ames: Iowa State University Press.

Greene-McCreight, Kathryn E. 1999. *Ad Litteram: How Augustine, Calvin, and Barth Read the "Plain Sense" of Genesis 1–3*. New York: Peter Lang.

―――. 2000. *Feminist Reconstructions of Christian Doctrine: Narrative Analysis and Appraisal*. New York: Oxford University Press.

Greenfield, Sidney M. 2008. *Spirits with Scalpels: The Culturalbiology of Religious Healing in Brazil*. Walnut Creek, Calif.: Left Coast.

Greenman, Jeffrey P., and Gene L. Green, eds. 2012. *Global Theology in Evangelical Perspective: Exploring the Contextual Nature of Theology and Mission*. Downers Grove, Ill.: IVP Academic.

Greer, Rowan A. 1973. *The Captain of Our Salvation: A Study in the Patristic Exegesis of Hebrews*. Tübingen: Mohr Siebeck.

Gregg, Steve, ed. 1997. *Revelation: Four Views—A Parallel Commentary*. Nashville: Thomas Nelson.

Greggs, Tom. 2011. *Theology against Religion: Constructive Dialogues with Bonhoeffer and Barth*. London: T&T Clark.

Grenz, Stanley J. 1992. *The Millennium Maze: Sorting Out Evangelical Options*. Downers Grove, Ill.: IVP Academic.

Grenz, Stanley J., and John R. Franke. 2001. *Beyond Foundationalism: Shaping Theology in a Postmodern Context*. Louisville, Ky: Westminster John Knox.

Gresham, John L., Jr. 1987. *Charles G. Finney's Doctrine of the Baptism of the Holy Spirit*. Peabody, Mass.: Hendrickson.

Grey, Jacqueline. 2011. *Three's a Crowd: Pentecostalism, Hermeneutics, and the Old Testament*. Eugene, Ore.: Pickwick.

Grider, J. Kenneth. 1980. *Entire Sanctification: The Distinctive Doctrine of Wesleyanism*. Kansas City, Mo.: Beacon Hill.

Grudem, Wayne A. 1994. *Systematic Theology: An Introduction to Biblical Doctrine*. Grand Rapids: Zondervan.

Grün, Anselm. 2003. *The Seven Sacraments*. John Cumming, trans. New York: Continuum.

Gunstone, John. 1982. *Pentecostal Anglicans*. London: Hodder & Stoughton.

Gunter, W. Stephen, et al. 1997. *Wesley and the Quadrilateral: Renewing the Conversation*. Nashville: Abingdon.

Guthrie, Steven R. 2011. *Creator Spirit: The Holy Spirit and the Art of Becoming Holy*. Grand Rapids: Baker Academic.

Gutiérrez, Gustavo. 1973. *A Theology of Liberation: History, Politics, and Salvation*. John Eagleson, trans. Maryknoll, N.Y.: Orbis.

Habets, Myk, ed. 2010a. *The Spirit of Truth: Reading Scripture and Constructing Theology with the Holy Spirit*. Eugene, Ore.: Pickwick.

Habets, Myk. 2010b. *The Anointed Son: A Trinitarian Spirit Christology*. Eugene, Ore.: Pickwick.

Hahne, Harry Alan. 2006. *The Corruption and Redemption of Creation: Nature in Romans 8:19-22 and Jewish Apocalyptic Literature*. London: T&T Clark.

Haire, James, Christine Ledger, and Stephen Pickard, eds. 2007. *From Resurrection *to Return: Perspectives from Theology and Science on Christian Eschatology.* Hindmarsh and Adelaide, Australia: ATF.

Haitch, Russell. 2007. *From Exorcism to Ecstasy: Eight Views of Baptism.* Louisville, Ky.: Westminster John Knox.

Halas, Roman B. 1946. *Judas Iscariot: A Scriptural and Theological Study of His Person, His Deeds, and His Eternal Lot.* Washington, D.C.: Catholic University of America Press.

Hanson, Stig. 1946. *The Unity of the Church in the New Testament: Colossians and Ephesians.* Uppsala, Sweden: Almqvist & Wiksells Boktryckeri Ab.

Hardesty, Nancy. 2003. *Faith Cure: Divine Healing in the Holiness and Pentecostal Movements.* Grand Rapids: Baker Academic.

Häring, Hermann, and Johannes Baptist Metz, eds. 1993. *Reincarnation or Resurrection?* London: SCM Press.

Harrell, David Edwin, Jr. 1975. *All Things Are Possible: The Healing and Charismatic Revivals in Modern America.* Bloomington: Indiana University Press.

Harrington, Daniel J. 1980. *God's People in Christ: New Testament Perspectives on the Church and Judaism.* Minneapolis: Fortress.

Harris, Antipas L. 2010. *For Such a Time as This: Re-imagining Practical Theology for Independent Pentecostal Churches.* Wilmore, Ky.: Emeth.

Harrison, Nonna Verna. 2010. *God's Many-Splendored Image: Theological Anthropology for Christian Formation.* Grand Rapids: Baker Academic.

Hart, Larry D. 2005. *Truth Aflame: Theology for the Church in Renewal.* Grand Rapids: Zondervan.

Harvey, Richard. 2009. *Mapping Messianic Jewish Theology: A Constructive Approach.* Milton Keynes, U.K.: Paternoster.

Hauerwas, Stanley, and William H. Willimon. 1989. *Resident Aliens: Life in the Christian Colony.* Nashville: Abingdon.

———. 1996. *Where Resident Aliens Live: Exercises for Christian Practice.* Nashville: Abingdon.

Hawthorne, Gerald F. 1991. *The Presence and the Power: The Significance of the Holy Spirit in the Life and Ministry of Jesus.* Waco, Tex.: Word.

Hayes, Stephen. 1990. *Black Charismatic Anglicans: The Iviyo loFakazi bakaKristu and Its Relations with Other Renewal Movements.* Pretoria: University of South Africa.

Heath, Gordon L, and James D. Dvorak, eds. 2011. *Baptism: Historical, Theological, and Pastoral Perspectives.* Eugene, Ore.: Pickwick.

Hefner, Philip. 2000. *The Human Factor: Evolution, Culture, and Religion.* Minneapolis: Fortress.

Heim, S. Mark. 2001. *The Depth of the Riches: A Trinitarian Theology of Religious Ends.* Grand Rapids: Eerdmans.

———. 2006. *Saved from Sacrifice: A Theology of the Cross.* Grand Rapids: Eerdmans.

Heinrich, Bernd. 2012. *Life Everlasting: The Animal Way of Death.* Boston: Houghton Mifflin Harcourt.

Hejzlar, Pavel. 2010. *Two Paradigms for Divine Healing: Fred F. Bosworth, Kenneth E. Hagin, Agnes Sanford, and Francis MacNutt in Dialogue.* Leiden: Brill.

Helgesson, Kristina. 2006. *"Walking in the Spirit": The Complexity of Belonging in Two Pentecostal Churches in Durban, South Africa.* Uppsala, Sweden: Department of Cultural Anthropology and Ethnology.

Heinrich, Bernd. 2012. *Life Everlasting: The Animal Way of Death.* New York: Houghton Mifflin.

Hellerman, Joseph H. 2007. *Jesus and the People of God: Reconfiguring Ethnic Identity.* Sheffield, U.K.: Sheffield Phoenix.

Hengel, Martin. 2010. *Saint Peter: The Underestimated Apostle.* Translated by Thomas H. Trapp. Grand Rapids: Eerdmans.

Hick, John. 1982. *God Has Many Names.* Philadelphia: Westminster.

———. 1989. *An Interpretation of Religion: Human Responses to the Transcendent.* New Haven, Conn.: Yale University Press.

Hick, John, and Paul F. Knitter, eds. 1987. *The Myth of Christian Uniqueness: Toward a Pluralistic Theology of Religions.* Maryknoll, N.Y.: Orbis.

Hickey, James Cardinal. 1988. *Mary at the Foot of the Cross: Teacher and Example of Holiness and of Life for Us.* San Francisco: Ignatius.

Hinchliff, Peter. 1982. *Holiness and Politics.* Grand Rapids: Eerdmans.

Hirsch, Alan, and Tim Catchim. 2012. *The Permanent Revolution: Apostolic Imagination and Practice for the 21st Century Church.* San Francisco: Jossey-Bass.

Hitching, Roger. 2003. *The Church and Deaf People: A Study of Identity, Communication and Relationships with Special Reference to the Ecclesiology of Jürgen Moltmann.* Milton Keynes, U.K.: Paternoster.

Hocken, Peter D. 1987. *One Lord One Spirit One Body: Ecumenical Grace of the Charismatic Movement.* Exeter, U.K.: Paternoster.

———. 2009. *The Challenges of the Pentecostal, Charismatic and Messianic Jewish Movements.* Aldershot, U.K.: Ashgate.

Hoffmeister, Desmond, and Louise Kretzschmar, eds. 1995. *Towards a Holistic, Afro-centric and Participatory Understanding of the Gospel of Jesus Christ.* Johannesburg: Baptist Convention of South Africa.

Hollenweger, Walter J. 1972. *The Pentecostals: The Charismatic Movement in the Churches.* R. A. Wilson, trans. Minneapolis: Augsburg.

———. 1997. *Pentecostalism: Origins and Developments Worldwide.* Peabody, Mass.: Hendrickson.

Holman, Charles L. 1996. *Till Jesus Comes: Origins of Christian Apocalyptic Expectation.* Peabody, Mass.: Hendrickson.

Holmes, Stephen R. 2007. *The Wondrous Cross: Atonement and Penal Substitution in the Bible and History.* London: Paternoster.

———. 2012. *The Quest for the Trinity: The Doctrine of God in Scripture, History and Modernity.* Downers Grove, Ill.: IVP Academic.

Holvast, Rene. 2008. *Spiritual Mapping in the United States and Argentina, 1989–2005: A Geography of Fear.* Leiden: Brill.

Hong, Christopher C. 1976. *Eschatology of the World Religions.* Washington, D.C.: University Press of America.

Horrell, David G., Cherryl Hunt, and Christopher Southgate. 2010. *Greening Paul: Rereading the Apostle in a Time of Ecological Crisis.* Waco, Tex.: Baylor University Press.

Horton, Stanley M. 1995. *Systematic Theology: A Pentecostal Perspective.* Springfield, Ky.: Logion.

Hovenden, Gerald. 2002. *Speaking in Tongues: The New Testament Evidence in Context.* London: Sheffield Academic.

Howard, Evan B. 2000. *Affirming the Touch of God: A Psychological and Philosophical Explication of Christian Discernment.* Lanham, Md.: University Press of America.

Huang, Paulos. 2009. *Confronting Confucian Understandings of the Christian Doctrine of Salvation: A Systematic Theological Analysis of the Basic Problems in the Confucian-Christian Dialogue.* Leiden: Brill.

Hubbard, Benjamin Jerome. 1974. *The Matthean Redaction of a Primitive Apostolic Commissioning: An Exegesis of Matthew 28:16-20.* Missoula, Mont.: Society of Biblical Literature.

Huchingson, James E. 2001. *Pandemonium Tremendum: Chaos and Mystery in the Life of God.* Cleveland, Ohio: Pilgrim.

Hull, John M. 2001. *In the Beginning There Was Darkness: A Blind Person's Conversations with the Bible.* London: T&T Clark.

Hummel, Charles E. 1994. *Fire in the Fireplace: Charismatic Renewal in the Nineties.* 2nd rev. ed. Downers Grove, Ill.: InterVarsity.

Hunt, Stephen. 2009. *A History of the Charismatic Movement in Britain and the United States of America: The Pentecostal Transformation of Christianity.* 2 vols. Lewiston, N.Y.: Edwin Mellen.

Hunter, Harold D. 2009. *Spirit-Baptism: A Pentecostal Alternative.* Rev. ed. Eugene, Ore.: Wipf & Stock.

Hurtado, Larry W. 1995. *Mark.* Peabody, Mass.: Hendrickson.

Hütter, Reinhard. 1999. *Suffering Divine Things: Theology as Church Practice.* Grand Rapids: Eerdmans.

Hvidt, Niels Christian. 2007. *Christian Prophecy: The Post-Biblical Tradition.* Oxford: Oxford University Press.

Hyatt, Eddie L. 2002. *2000 Years of Charismatic Christianity.* Lake Mary, Fla.: Charisma House.

Ilo, Stan Chu, Joseph Ogbonnaya, and Alex Ojacor, eds. 2011. *The Church as Salt and Light: Path to an African Ecclesiology of Abundant Life.* Eugene, Ore.: Pickwick.

Iloanusi, Obiakoizu A. 1984. *Myths of the Creation of Man and the Origin of Death in Africa: A Study in Igbo Traditional Culture and Other African Cultures.* New York: Peter Lang.

Inbody, Tyron L. 2002. *The Many Faces of Christology.* Nashville: Abingdon.

Incayawar, Mario, Ronald Wintrob, Lise Bouchard, and Goffredo Bartocci, eds. 2009. *Psychiatrists and Traditional Healers: Unwitting Partners in Global Mental Health.* Chichester, U.K.: Wiley-Blackwell.

Ingalls, Monique, and Amos Yong, eds. Forthcoming. *The Spirit of Praise: Music and Worship in Global Pentecostal-Charismatic Christianity.* University Park: Penn State University Press.

Irvin, Dale T., and Scott W. Sunquist. 2001. *History of the World Christian Movement: Earliest Christianity to 1453.* Maryknoll, N.Y.: Orbis.

Isasi-Díaz, Ada María. 1993. *En la Lucha: In the Struggle—A Hispanic Women's Liberation Theology.* Minneapolis: Fortress.

Jackson, Glenna S. 2002. *"Have Mercy on Me": The Story of the Canaanite Woman in Matthew 15.21-28.* London: Sheffield Academic.

Jackson, T. Ryan. 2010. *New Creation in Paul's Letters: A Study of the Historical and Social Setting of a Pauline Concept.* Tübingen: Mohr Siebeck.

Jacobsen, Douglas G. 2003. *Thinking in the Spirit: Theologies of the Early Pentecostal Movement.* Bloomington: Indiana University Press.

———, ed. 2006. *A Reader in Pentecostal Theology: Voices from the First Generation.* Bloomington: Indiana University Press.

Jeffery, Peter. 1992. *A New Commandment: Toward a Renewed Rite for the Washing of Feet.* Collegeville, Minn.: Liturgical.

Jenkins, Philip. 2002. *The Next Christendom: The Coming of Global Christianity.* Oxford: Oxford University Press.

———. 2006. *The New Faces of Christianity: Believing the Bible in the Global South.* Oxford: Oxford University Press.

Jennings, Willie James. 2010. *The Christian Imagination: Theology and the Origins of Race.* New Haven, Conn.: Yale University Press.

Jensen, David H. 2001. *In the Company of Others: A Dialogical Christology.* Cleveland, Ohio: Pilgrim.

Jenson, Matt. 2006. *The Gravity of Sin: Augustine, Luther and Barth on "Homo Incurvatus in Se."* London: T&T Clark.

Jenson, Robert W. 1982. *The Triune Identity: God according to the Gospel.* Philadelphia: Fortress.

———. 1997. *Systematic Theology.* Vol. 1. Oxford: Oxford University Press.

Jersak, Bradley. 2010. *Her Gates Will Never Be Shut: Hell, Hope, and the New Jerusalem.* Eugene, Ore.: Wipf & Stock.

Jersak, Brad, and Michael Hardin, eds. 2007. *Stricken by God? Nonviolent Identification and the Victory of Christ.* Grand Rapids: Eerdmans.

Johnson, Alan R. 2009. *Apostolic Function in 21st Century Missions.* Pasadena, Calif.: William Carey Library/Assemblies of God Theological Seminary.

Johnson, E. Elizabeth. 1989. *The Function of Apocalyptic and Wisdom Traditions in Romans 9–11.* Atlanta: Scholars Press.

Johnson, Elizabeth A. 1992. *She Who Is: The Mystery of God in Feminist Theological Discourse.* New York: Crossroad.

Johnson, Keith E. 2011. *Rethinking the Trinity and Religious Pluralism: An Augustinian Assessment.* Downers Grove, Ill: IVP Academic.

Johnson, Maxwell E., ed. 1995. *Living Water, Sealing Spirit: Readings on Christian Initiation.* Collegeville, Minn.: Liturgical.

————. 1999. *The Rites of Christian Initiation: Their Evolution and Interpretation.* Collegeville, Minn.: Liturgical.

Johnson, Todd M., and Kenneth R. Ross, eds. 2009. *Atlas of Global Christianity 1910–2010.* Edinburgh: Edinburgh University Press.

Jones, Hywel R. 1996. *Only One Way: Do You Have to Believe in Christ to Be Saved?* Kent, U.K.: Day One Publications.

Jungkuntz, Theodore R. 1983. *Confirmation and the Charismata.* Lanham, Md.: University Press of America.

Kabue, Samuel, Esther Momba, Joseph Galgala, and C. B. Peter, eds. 2011. *Disability, Society and Theology: Voices from Africa.* Limuru, Kenya: Zapf Chancery.

Kalu, Ogbu U. 2008. *African Pentecostalism: An Introduction.* New York: Oxford University Press.

Kamalu, Chukwunyere. 1998. *Person, Divinity and Nature: A Modern View of the Person and the Cosmos in African Thought.* London: Karnak House.

Kärkkäinen, Veli-Matti. 2002a. *Toward a Pneumatological Theology: Pentecostal and Ecumenical Perspectives on Soteriology, Ecclesiology, and Theology of Mission.* Amos Yong, ed. Lanham, Md.: University Press of America.

————. 2002b. *Pneumatology: The Holy Spirit in Ecumenical, International, and Contextual Perspective.* Grand Rapids: Baker Academic.

————. 2002c. *An Introduction to Ecclesiology: Ecumenical, Historical & Global Perspectives.* Downers Grove, Ill.: IVP Academic.

————. 2003. *Christology—A Global Introduction: An Ecumenical, International and Contextual Perspective.* Grand Rapids: Baker Academic.

————. 2004a. *The Doctrine of God: A Global Introduction.* Grand Rapids: Baker Academic.

————. 2004b. *Trinity and Religious Pluralism: The Doctrine of the Trinity in Christian Theology of Religions.* Aldershot, U.K.: Ashgate.

————. 2005. *One with God: Salvation as Deification and Justification.* Collegeville, Minn.: Liturgical.

————. 2007. *The Trinity: Global Perspectives.* Louisville, Ky: Westminster John Knox.

————, ed. 2010. *Holy Spirit and Salvation: The Sources of Christian Theology.* Louisville, Ky.: Westminster John Knox.

Kärkkäinen, Veli-Matti, Kirsteen Kim, and Amos Yong, eds. 2013. *Interdisciplinary and Religio-Cultural Discourses on a Spirit-Filled World: Loosing the Spirits.* New York: Palgrave Macmillan.

Kasujja, Augustine. 1986. *Polygenism and the Theology of Original Sin Today: Eastern African Contribution to the Solution of the Scientific Problem, the Impact of Polygenism in Modern Theology.* Rome: Pontificia Universitas Urbaniana.

Kavanagh, Aidan. 1991. *The Shape of Baptism: The Rite of Christian Initiation.* Collegeville, Minn.: Liturgical.

Kay, William K. 2002. *Pentecostals in Britain.* Carlisle, U.K.: Paternoster.

———. 2007. *Apostolic Networks in Britain: New Ways of Being Church.* Milton Keynes, U.K.: Paternoster.

Keener, Craig S. 2000. *The NIV Application Commentary: Revelation.* Grand Rapids: Zondervan.

———. 2001. *Gift Giver: The Holy Spirit for Today.* Grand Rapids: Baker Academic.

———. 2003. *The Gospel of John: A Commentary.* 2 vols. Peabody, Mass.: Hendrickson.

Kelhoffer, James A. 2000. *Miracle and Mission: The Authentication of Missionaries and Their Message in the Longer Ending of Mark.* Tübingen: Mohr Siebeck.

Keller, Catherine. 2003. *Face of the Deep: A Theology of Becoming.* London: Routledge.

Kelly, Henry Ansgar. 1985. *The Devil at Baptism: Ritual, Theology, and Drama.* Ithaca, N.Y.: Cornell University Press.

Kelsey, David. 2009. *Eccentric Existence: A Theological Anthropology.* 2 vols. Louisville, Ky: Westminster John Knox.

Kelsey, Morton T. 1973. *Healing in Christianity: In Ancient Thought and Modern Times.* New York: Harper & Row.

———. 1974. *God, Dreams, and Revelation: A Christian Interpretation of Dreams.* Minneapolis: Augsburg.

Kieckhefer, Richard, and George D. Bond, eds. 1988. *Sainthood: Its Manifestations in World Religions.* Berkeley: University of California Press.

Kilgallen, John. 1976. *The Stephen Speech: A Literary and Redactional Study of Acts 7,2-53.* Rome: Biblical Institute.

Kim, Kirsteen. 2003. *Mission in the Spirit: The Holy Spirit in Indian Christian Theologies.* Delhi: ISPCK.

———. 2007. *The Holy Spirit in the World: A Global Conversation.* Maryknoll, N.Y.: Orbis.

Kim, Lloyd. 2006. *Polemic in the Book of Hebrews: Anti-Semitism, Anti-Judaism, Supersessionism?* Eugene, Ore.: Pickwick.

King, Rachel H. 1970. *The Creation of Death and Life.* New York: Philosophical Library.

Kinsley, David. 1996. *Health, Healing, and Religion: A Cross-Cultural Perspective.* Upper Saddle River, N.J.: Prentice Hall.

Kinzer, Mark S. 2005. *Postmissionary Messianic Judaism: Redefining Christian Engagement with the Jewish People.* Grand Rapids: Brazos.

———. 2011. *Israel's Messiah and the People of God: A Vision for Messianic Jewish Covenant Fidelity.* Jennifer M. Rosner, ed. Eugene, Ore.: Cascade.

Kizhakkeparampil, Isaac. 1995. *The Invocation of the Holy Spirit as Constitutive of the Sacraments according to Cardinal Yves Congar.* Rome: Editrice Pontificia Università Gregoriana.

Klassen, William. 1996. *Judas: Betrayer or Friend of Jesus?* Minneapolis: Fortress.

Kling, David W. 2004. *The Bible in History: How the Texts Have Shaped the Times.* Oxford: Oxford University Press.

Knight, Douglas H. 2006. *The Eschatological Economy: Time and the Hospitality of God.* Grand Rapids: Eerdmans.

Knox, Ronald A. 1950. *Enthusiasm: A Chapter in the History of Religion, with Special Reference to the XII and XVIII Centuries.* New York: Oxford University Press.

Koenig, Harold G. 1999. *The Healing Power of Faith: Science Explores Medicine's Last Great Frontier.* New York: Simon & Schuster.

Koester, Craig R. 2001a. *Revelation and the End of All Things.* Grand Rapids: Eerdmans.

———. 2001b. *The Anchor Bible.* Vol. 36: *Hebrews.* New York: Doubleday.

Kombo, James Henry Owino. 2007. *The Doctrine of God in African Christian Thought: The Holy Trinity, Theological Hermeneutics and the African Intellectual Culture.* Leiden: Brill.

Koopmans, Rachel. 2011. *Wonderful to Relate: Miracle Stories and Miracle Collecting in High Medieval England.* Philadelphia: University of Pennsylvania Press.

Korsmeyer, Jerry D. 1998. *Evolution and Eden: Balancing Original Sin and Contemporary Science.* New York: Paulist.

Korte, Anne-Marie, ed. 2004 *Women and Miracle Stories: A Multidisciplinary Exploration.* Leiden: Brill.

Kroeger, Catherine Clark, and Mary J. Evans, eds. 2002. *The IVP Women's Bible Commentary.* Downers Grove, Ill.: InterVarsity.

Kropf, Richard W. 1984. *Evil and Evolution: A Theodicy.* London: Associated University Presses.

Kulikovsky, Andrew S., 2009. *Creation, Fall, Restoration: A Biblical Theology of Creation.* Fearn, U.K.: Mentor.

Küng, Hans. 1967. *The Church.* Ray and Rosaleen Ockenden, trans. New York: Sheed & Ward.

Kuster, Volker. 2001. *The Many Faces of Jesus Christ: Intercultural Christology.* London: SCM Press.

Kwon, Jin Kwan. 2011. *Theology of Subjects: Towards a New Minjung Theology.* Taiwan: Programme for Theology and Cultures in Asia, Chang Jung Christian University.

Kydd, Ronald A. N. 1984. *Charismatic Gifts in the Early Church.* Peabody, Mass.: Hendrickson.

———. 1998. *Healing through the Centuries: Models for Understanding.* Peabody, Mass.: Hendrickson.

Kysar, Robert. 2005. *Voyages with John: Charting the Fourth Gospel.* Waco, Tex.: Baylor University Press.

Ladd, George Elson. 1974. *The Presence of the Future: The Eschatology of Biblical Realism.* Grand Rapids: Eerdmans.

LaGrand, James. 1995. *The Earliest Christian Mission to "All Nations": In the Light of Matthew's Gospel.* Atlanta: Scholars Press.

Lamoureux, Denis. 2009a. *I Love Jesus and I Accept Evolution*. Eugene, Ore.: Wipf & Stock.

————. 2009b. *Evolutionary Creation: A Christian Approach to Evolution*. Eugene, Ore.: Wipf & Stock.

Land, Steven J. 1993. *Pentecostal Spirituality: A Passion for the Kingdom*. Sheffield, U.K.: Sheffield Academic.

Larsen, David L. 1995. *Jews, Gentiles and the Church: A New Perspective on History and Prophecy*. Grand Rapids: Discovery House.

Lartey, Emmanuel, Daisy Nwachuku, and Kasonga Wa Kasonga, eds. 1994. *The Church and Healing: Echoes from Africa*. Frankfurt am Main: Peter Lang.

Latourette, Kenneth Scott. 1941. *The Great Century, A.D. 1800–A.D. 1914 in Europe and the United States of America*. New York: Harper.

LaVerdiere, Eugene. 1996. *The Eucharist in the New Testament and the Early Church*. Collegeville, Minn.: Liturgical.

Lederle, Henry I. 1988. *Treasures Old and New: Interpretations of "Spirit Baptism" in the Charismatic Renewal Movement*. Peabody, Mass.: Hendrickson.

————. 2010. *Theology with Spirit: The Future of the Pentecostal-Charismatic Movements in the 21st Century*. Tulsa: Word & Spirit.

Lee, Edgar R., ed. 2005. *He Gave Apostles: Apostolic Ministry in the 21st Century*. Springfield, Mo.: Assemblies of God Theological Seminary.

Lee, Jung Young. 1996. *The Trinity in Asian Perspective*. Nashville: Abingdon.

Lee, Matthew T., and Amos Yong, eds. 2012. *The Science and Theology of Godly Love*. DeKalb: Northern Illinois University Press.

Lee, Samuel. 2011. *A New Kind of Pentecostalism: Promoting Dialogue for Change*. Amsterdam: Foundation University Press.

Lee, Yeong Mee, and Yoon Jong Yoo, eds. 2009. *Mapping and Engaging the Bible in Asian Cultures: Congress of the Society of Asian Biblical Studies 2008 Seoul Conference*. Seoul: Christian Literature Society of Korea.

Leies, John A. 1963. *Sanctity and Religion according to St. Thomas: A Study of the Angelic Doctor's Identification of Sanctity with the Virtue of Religion*. Fribourg, Germany: St. Paul's.

Lennartsson, Gøran. 2007. *Refreshing and Restoration: Two Eschatological Motifs in Acts 3:19-21*. Lund, Sweden: Lund University Centre for Theology and Religious Studies.

Leslie, Robert C. 1965. *Jesus and Logotherapy: The Ministry of Jesus as Interpreted through the Psychotherapy of Viktor Frankl*. Nashville: Abingdon.

Levenson, Jon D. 1988. *Creation and the Persistence of Evil: The Jewish Drama of Divine Omnipotence*. San Francisco: Harper & Row.

Levison, John R. 1988. *Portraits of Adam in Early Judaism: From Sirach to 2 Baruch*. Sheffield, U.K.: JSOT Press.

————. 2009. *Filled with the Spirit*. Grand Rapids: Eerdmans.

Levison, John R., and Priscilla Pope-Levison. 1992. *Jesus in Global Contexts*. Louisville, Ky: Westminster John Knox.

Lewis, Hannah. 2007. *Deaf Liberation Theology*. Burlington, Vt.: Ashgate.

Lienhard, Joseph T. 1995. *The Bible, the Church, and Authority: The Canon of the Christian Bible in History and Theology.* Collegeville, Minn.: Liturgical.

Lilley, A. L. 1925. *Prayer in Christian Theology: A Study of Some Moments and Masters of the Christian Life from Clement of Alexandria to Fenelon.* London: Student Christian Movement.

Lindbeck, George A. 1984. *The Nature of Doctrine: Religion and Theology in a Post-liberal Age.* Philadelphia: Westminster.

Lindberg, Carter. 1983. *The Third Reformation? Charismatic Movements and the Lutheran Tradition.* Macon, Ga.: Mercer University Press.

Lindhardt, Martin, ed. 2011. *Practicing the Faith: The Ritual Life of Pentecostal-Charismatic Christians.* New York: Berghahn.

Lindsell, Harold. 1978. *The Battle for the Bible.* Grand Rapids: Zondervan.

Livingstone, David N. 2008. *Adam's Ancestors: Race, Religion, and the Politics of Human Origins.* Baltimore: Johns Hopkins University Press.

Lonergan, Bernard. 1979. *Method in Theology.* 2nd ed. New York: Seabury.

Long, W. Meredith. 2000. *Health, Healing and God's Kingdom: New Pathways to Christian Health Ministry in Africa.* Oxford: Regnum.

Löning, Karl, and Erich Zenger. 2000. *To Begin with, God Created . . . : Biblical Theologies of Creation.* Omar Kaste, trans. Collegeville, Minn.: Liturgical.

Lord, Andy. 2005. *Spirit-Shaped Mission: A Holistic Charismatic Missiology.* Milton Keynes, U.K.: Paternoster.

———. 2012. *Network Church: A Pentecostal Ecclesiology Shaped by Mission.* Leiden: Brill.

Love, Gregory Anderson. 2010. *Love, Violence and the Cross: How the Nonviolent God Saves Us through the Cross of Christ.* Eugene, Ore.: Cascade.

Lowe, Chuck. 1998. *Territorial Spirits and World Evangelisation: A Biblical, Historical and Missiological Critique of Strategic-Level Spiritual Warfare.* Fearn, U.K.: Mentor.

Luckensmeyer, David. 2009. *The Eschatology of First Thessalonians.* Göttingen: Vandenhoeck & Ruprecht.

Luhrmann, T. M. 2012. *When God Talks Back: Understanding the American Evangelical Relationship with God.* New York: Knopf.

Luomanen, Petri. 1998. *Entering the Kingdom of Heaven: A Study on the Structure of Matthew's View of Salvation.* Tübingen: Mohr Siebeck.

Luz, Ulrich. 1995. *The Theology of the Gospel of Matthew.* J. Bradford Robinson, trans. Cambridge: Cambridge University Press.

Luz, Ulrich, and Axel Michaels. 2006. *Encountering Jesus and Buddha: Their Lives and Teachings.* Linda M. Maloney, trans. Minneapolis: Fortress.

Ma, Julie C., and Wonsuk Ma. 2010. *Mission in the Spirit: Towards a Pentecostal/Charismatic Missiology.* Oxford: Regnum.

MacArthur, John F., Jr. 1992. *Charismatic Chaos.* Grand Rapids: Zondervan.

Macchia, Frank D. 2006. *Baptized in the Spirit: A Global Pentecostal Theology.* Grand Rapids: Zondervan.

———. 2010. *Justified in the Spirit: Creation, Redemption, and the Triune God*. Grand Rapids: Eerdmans.

MacDonald, Dennis R. 2011. "Luke's Use of Papias for Narrating the Death of Judas." In Steve Walton et al., eds., *Reading Acts Today: Essays in Honour of Loveday C. A. Alexander*, 43–62. London: T&T Clark.

MacDonald, Gregory, ed. 2011. *"All Shall Be Well": Explorations in Universal Salvation and Christian Theology from Origen to Moltmann*. Eugene, Ore.: Wipf & Stock.

MacGregor, Geddes. 1992. *Images of Afterlife: Beliefs from Antiquity to Modern Times*. New York: Paragon.

Mack, Phyllis. 2008. *Heart Religion in the British Enlightenment: Gender and Emotion in Early Methodism*. Cambridge: Cambridge University Press.

Mackie, Scott D. 2007. *Eschatology and Exhortation in the Epistle to the Hebrews*. Tübingen: Mohr Siebeck.

Mackrell, Gerard. 1987. *The Healing Miracles in Mark's Gospel: The Passion and Compassion of Jesus*. Slough, Australia: St. Paul.

MacMullen, Ramsay. 1984. *Christianizing the Roman Empire (A.D. 100–400)*. New Haven, Conn.: Yale University Press.

MacNutt, Francis. 1974. *Healing*. Notre Dame, Ind.: Ave Maria.

Magnuson, Norris A. 1977. *Salvation in the Slums: Evangelical Social Work, 1865–1920*. Metuchen, N.J.: Scarecrow Press/American Theological Library Association.

Mahan, Asa. 1870. *The Baptism of the Holy Spirit*. New York: W. C. Palmer Jr.

Maloney, Elliott C. 2004. *Jesus' Urgent Message for Today: The Kingdom of God in Mark's Gospel*. New York: Continuum.

Maloney, George A. 1973. *Man the Divine Icon: The Patristic Doctrine of Man Made according to the Divine Image*. Pecos, N.M.: Dove.

Mann, Mark H. 2006. *Perfecting Grace: Holiness, Human Being, and the Sciences*. New York: T&T Clark.

Manohar, Christina. 2009. *Spirit Christology: An Indian Christian Perspective*. Delhi: ISPCK.

Mansfield, M. Robert. 1987. *Spirit and Gospel in Mark*. Peabody, Mass.: Hendrickson.

Manus, Ukachukwu Chris. 1993. *Christ, the African King: New Testament Christology*. New York: Peter Lang.

Markham, Paul N. 2007. *Rewired: Exploring Religious Conversion*. Eugene, Ore.: Pickwick.

Marshall, Molly T. 1993. *No Salvation Outside the Church? A Critical Inquiry*. Lewiston, N.Y.: Mellen.

———. 2003. *Joining the Dance: A Theology of the Spirit*. Valley Forge, Pa.: Judson.

Marshall, Ruth. 2009. *Political Spiritualities: The Pentecostal Revolution in Nigeria*. Chicago: University of Chicago Press.

Martin, David. 2002. *Pentecostalism: The World Their Parish*. Oxford: Blackwell.

Martin, Francis. 1998. *Baptism in the Holy Spirit: Reflections on a Contemporary Grace in the Light of Catholic Tradition.* Petersham, Mass.: St. Bede's.

Martin, Lee Roy. 2008. *The Unheard Voice of God: A Pentecostal Hearing of the Book of Judges.* Blandford Forum, U.K.: Deo.

Martin, Ralph P. 1984. *The Spirit and the Congregation: Studies in 1 Corinthians 12–15.* Grand Rapids: Eerdmans.

Martin, Ralph. 2012. *Will Many Be Saved? What Vatican II Actually Teaches and Its Implications for the New Evangelization.* Grand Rapids: Eerdmans.

Mason, John P. 1993. *The Resurrection according to Paul.* Lewiston, N.Y.: Mellen Biblical.

Massey, James, ed. 2008. *Ecumenism in India Today: A Search for a Relevant Ecclesiology and Church and Theological Education in India.* Bangalore, India: Board of Theological Education of the Senate of Serampore College and South Asia Theological Research Institute.

Mathai, Varghese. 1999. *Paraclete: The Experience of the Holy Spirit.* Thiruvalla and Kottayam, India: Christhava Sahithya Samithi.

Mattam, Joseph. 1975. *Land of the Trinity: A Study of Modern Christian Approaches to Hinduism.* Bangalore: Theological Publications in India.

Mbiti, John S. 1971. *New Testament Eschatology in an African Background: A Study of the Encounter between New Testament Theology and African Traditional Concepts.* London: Oxford University Press.

McAdoo, Henry R. 1965. *Spirit of Anglicanism: A Survey of Anglican Theological Method in the Seventeenth Century.* New York: Scribner.

McBirnie, William Steuart. 1973. *The Search for the Twelve Apostles.* Wheaton, Ill.: Tyndale.

McCasland, S. Vernon. 1951. *By the Finger of God: Demon Possession and Exorcism in Early Christianity in the Light of Modern Views of Mental Illness.* New York: Macmillan.

McClendon, William James, Jr. 1974. *Biography as Theology: How Life Stories Can Remake Today's Theology.* Nashville: Abingdon.

McClenon, James. 2002. *Wondrous Healing: Shamanism, Human Evolution, and the Origin of Religion.* DeKalb: Northern Illinois University Press.

McCracken, George E., and Allen Cabaniss, eds. 1957. *Early Medieval Theology.* Philadelphia: Westminster.

McCruden, Kevin B. 2008. *Solidarity Perfected: Beneficent Christology in the Epistle to the Hebrews.* Berlin: De Gruyter.

McDermott, Gerald R. 2000. *Can Evangelicals Learn from World Religions? Jesus, Revelation, and Religious Traditions.* Downers Grove, Ill.: InterVarsity.

———. 2007. *God's Rivals: Why Has God Allowed Different Religions?* Downers Grove, Ill.: IVP Academic.

McDonald, H. D. 1959. *Ideas of Revelation: An Historical Study, A.D. 1700 to A.D. 1860.* London: Macmillan.

———. 1985. *The Atonement of the Death of Christ: In Faith, Revelation, and History.* Grand Rapids: Baker.

McDonald, Suzanne. 2010. *Re-imaging Election: Divine Election as Representing God to Others and Others to God.* Grand Rapids: Eerdmans.

McDonnell, Kilian, ed. 1980. *Presence, Power, Praise: Documents on the Charismatic Renewal.* 3 vols. Collegeville, Minn.: Liturgical.

McDonnell, Kilian, and George T. Montague. 1994. *Christian Initiation and Baptism in the Holy Spirit: Evidence from the First Eight Centuries.* 2nd rev. ed. Collegeville, Minn.: Liturgical.

McDonnell, Rea. 2011. *From Glory to Glory: Spirit and Sacrament in the Writings of Paul and John.* Hyde Park, N.Y.: New City.

McFarland, Ian A. 2010. *In Adam's Fall: A Meditation on the Christian Doctrine of Original Sin.* Malden, U.K.: Wiley-Blackwell.

McGee, Gary B. 2010. *Miracles, Missions, and American Pentecostalism.* Maryknoll, N.Y.: Orbis.

McGlasson, Paul. 1991. *Jesus and Judas: Biblical Exegesis in Barth.* Atlanta: Scholars Press.

McGrath, Alister E. 2009. *A Fine-Tuned Universe: The Quest for God in Science and Theology.* Louisville, Ky: Westminster John Knox.

———. 2011. *Darwinism and the Divine: Evolutionary Thought and Natural Theology.* Oxford: Wiley-Blackwell.

McGuire, Meredith B. 1982. *Pentecostal Catholics: Power, Charisma, and Order in a Religious Movement.* Philadelphia: Temple University Press.

McGuire, Meredith B., and Debra Kantor. 1988. *Ritual Healing in Suburban America.* New Brunswick, N.J.: Rutgers University Press.

McKenna, John H. 1975. *Eucharist and Holy Spirit: The Eucharistic Epiclesis in Twentieth Century Theology (1900–1966).* Great Wakering, U.K.: Alcuin Club.

McKinley, John E. 2009. *Tempted for Us: Theological Models and the Practical Relevance of Christ's Impeccability and Temptation.* Milton Keynes, U.K.: Paternoster.

McKnight, Scot. 1990. *A Light among the Gentiles: Jewish Missionary Activity in the Second Temple Period.* Minneapolis: Fortress.

McLeod, Hugh, ed. 2006. *The Cambridge History of Christianity: World Christianities c. 1914–c. 2000.* Cambridge: Cambridge University Press.

McNeill, Brian, and Joseph Michael Cervantes, eds. 2008. *Latina/o Healing Practices: Mestizo and Indigenous Perspectives.* New York: Routledge.

McPartlan, Paul. 1993. *The Eucharist Makes the Church: Henri de Lubac and John Zizioulas in Dialogue.* Edinburgh: T&T Clark.

McQueen, Larry R. 2012. *Toward a Pentecostal Eschatology: Discerning the Way Forward.* Blandford Forum, U.K.: Deo.

Melinsky, M. A. H. 1968. *Healing Miracles.* London: A. R. Mowbray.

Melloni, Alberto, ed. 2003. *"Movements" in the Church.* London: SCM Press.

Menzies, Robert P. 1994. *Empowered for Witness: The Spirit in Luke-Acts.* Sheffield, U.K.: Sheffield Academic.

———. 2013. *Why I Am a Pentecostal.* Springfield, Mo.: Gospel.

Menzies, William W. 1971. *Anointed to Serve: The Story of the Assemblies of God.* Springfield, Mo.: Gospel Publishing House.

Menzies, William W., and Robert P. Menzies. 2000. *Spirit and Power: Foundations of Pentecostal Experience*. Grand Rapids: Zondervan.

Merk, Frederick, and Lois Bannister Merk. 1963. *Manifest Destiny and Mission in American History: A Reinterpretation*. Repr., Cambridge, Mass.: Harvard University Press, 1995.

Metzger, Bruce M. 1997. *The Canon of the New Testament: Its Origin, Development, and Significance*. Oxford: Oxford University Press.

Metzger, Paul Louis. 2012. *Connecting Christ: How to Discuss Jesus in a World of Diverse Paths*. Nashville: Nelson.

Meyer, Marvin W. 2007. *Judas: The Definitive Collection of Gospels and Legends about the Infamous Apostle of Jesus*. New York: HarperOne.

Michaels, J. Ramsey, ed. 2003. *The Spirit of Prophecy Defended*. Leiden: Brill.

Micks, Marianne H. 1982. *Our Search for Identity: Humanity in the Image of God*. Minneapolis: Fortress.

Milne, Garnet Howard. 2007. *The Westminster Confession of Faith and the Cessation of Special Revelation: The Majority Puritan View on Whether Extra-Biblical Prophecy Is Still Possible*. Milton Keynes, U.K.: Paternoster.

Minear, Paul S. 1975. *Images of the Church in the New Testament*. Philadelphia: Westminster.

Mittelstadt, Martin W. 2004. *Spirit and Suffering in Luke-Acts: Implications for a Pentecostal Pneumatology*. New York: Continuum.

Miyahira, Nozomu. 2000. *Towards a Theology of the Concord of God: A Japanese Perspective on the Trinity*. Carlisle, U.K.: Paternoster.

Miyamoto, Ken Christoph. 2007. *God's Mission in Asia: A Comparative and Contextual Study of This-Worldly Holiness and the Theology of* Missio Dei *in M. M. Thomas and C. S. Song*. Eugene, Ore.: Pickwick.

Moe-Lobeda, Cynthia D. 2002. *Healing a Broken World: Globalization and God*. Minneapolis: Fortress.

Moffitt, David M. 2011. *Atonement and the Logic of Resurrection in the Epistle to the Hebrews*. Leiden: Brill.

Moloney, Francis J. 1997. *A Body Broken for a Broken People: Eucharist in the New Testament*. Rev. ed. Peabody, Mass.: Hendrickson.

Moltmann, Jürgen. 1967. *Theology of Hope: On the Ground and the Implications of a Christian Eschatology*. James W. Leitch, trans. New York: Harper & Row.

———. 1977. *The Church in the Power of the Spirit: A Contribution to Messianic Ecclesiology*. Margaret Kohl, trans. London: SCM Press.

———. 1989. *The Way of Jesus Christ: Christology in Messianic Dimensions*. Margaret Kohl, trans. Minneapolis: Fortress.

———. 1992a. *History and the Triune God: Contributions to Trinitarian Theology*. John Bowden, trans. New York: Crossroad.

———. 1992b. *The Spirit of Life: A Universal Affirmation*. Margaret Kohl, trans. Minneapolis: Fortress.

Moltmann, Jürgen, and Karl-Josef Kuschel, eds. 1996. *Pentecostal Movements as an Ecumenical Challenge*. London: SCM Press.

Montague, George T. 1976. *The Holy Spirit: Growth of a Biblical Tradition*. Repr., Peabody, Mass.: Hendrickson, 1994.

Monteith, W. Graham. 2005. *Deconstructing Miracles: From Thoughtless Indifference to Honouring Disabled People*. Glasgow: Covenanters.

————. 2010. *Epistles of Inclusion: St Paul's Inspired Attitudes*. Guildford, U.K.: Grosvenor.

Moore, David George. 1995. *The Battle for Hell: A Survey and Evaluation of Evangelicals' Growing Attraction to the Doctrine of Annihilationism*. Lanham, Md.: University Press of America.

Moore, S. David. 2003. *The Shepherding Movement: Controversy and Charismatic Ecclesiology*. New York: T&T Clark.

Moreland, J. P., and Scott B. Rae. 2000. *Body and Soul: Human Nature and the Crisis in Ethics*. Downers Grove, Ill.: IVP Academic.

Morris, Simon Conway. 2004. *Life's Solution: Inevitable Humans in a Lonely Universe*. Cambridge: Cambridge University Press.

————, ed. 2008. *The Deep Structure of Biology: Is Convergence Sufficiently Ubiquitous to Give a Directional Signal?* West Conshohocken, Pa.: Templeton Foundation.

Morris, Wayne. 2008. *Theology without Words: Theology in the Deaf Community*. Burlington, Vt.: Ashgate.

Muck, Terry C., and Frances S. Adeney. 2009. *Christianity Encountering World Religions: The Practice of Mission in the Twenty-First Century*. Grand Rapids: Baker Academic.

Muck, Terry C., and Rita M. Gross, eds. 2000. *Buddhists Talk about Jesus, Christians Talk about the Buddha*. New York: Continuum.

Mueller, J. J. 2004. *What Are They Saying about Theological Method?* Mahwah, N.J.: Paulist.

Mugambi, J. N. K., and Laurenti Magesa, eds. 1998. *Jesus in African Christianity: Experimentation and Diversity in African Christology*. Nairobi: Acton Publishers.

Mühlen, Heribert. 1978. *A Charismatic Theology: Initiation in the Spirit*. Edward Quinn and Thomas Linton, trans. London: Burns & Oates.

Mukonyora, Isabel. 2007. *Wandering a Gendered Wilderness: Suffering and Healing in an African Initiated Church*. New York: Peter Lang.

Munday, John C., Jr. 1992. "Creature Mortality: From Creation or the Fall?" *Journal of the Evangelical Theological Society* 35 (1): 51–68.

Murphy, George L. 2003. *The Cosmos in the Light of the Cross*. Harrisburg, Pa.: Trinity International.

Murphy, Joseph M. 1994. *Working the Spirit: Ceremonies of the African Diaspora*. Boston: Beacon.

Murphy, Nancey. 2006. *Bodies and Souls, or Spirited Bodies?* Cambridge: Cambridge University Press.

Murphy, Nancey, and George F. R. Ellis. 1996. *On the Moral Nature of the Universe: Theology, Cosmology, and Ethics*. Minneapolis: Fortress.

Murray, Andrew. 1898. *The Two Covenants and the Second Blessing*. New York: Fleming H. Revell.

Myers, Ched. 2008. *Binding the Strong Man: A Political Reading of Mark's Story of Jesus.* 20th anniv. ed. Maryknoll, N.Y.: Orbis.

Ndubuisi, Luke. 2003. *Paul's Concept of Charisma in I Corinthians 12: With Emphasis on Nigerian Charismatic Movement.* Frankfurt am Main: Peter Lang.

Nelson, Derek R. 2009. *What's Wrong with Sin? Sin in Individual and Social Perspective from Schleiermacher to Theologies of Liberation.* London: T&T Clark.

Neumann, Peter D. 2012. *Pentecostal Experience: An Ecumenical Proposal.* Eugene, Ore.: Pickwick.

Neville, Robert Cummings, ed. 2001. *The Comparative Religious Ideas Project.* 3 vols. Albany: State University of New York Press.

Newberg, Eric Nelson. 2012. *The Pentecostal Mission in Palestine: The Legacy of Pentecostal Zionism.* Eugene, Ore.: Pickwick.

Newheart, Michael Willett. 2004. *"My Name Is Legion": The Story and Soul of the Gerasene Demoniac.* Collegeville, Minn.: Liturgical.

Newton, Jon. 2009. *Revelation Reclaimed: The Use and Misuse of the Apocalypse.* Milton Keynes, U.K.: Paternoster.

Ngong, David Tonghou. 2010. *The Holy Spirit and Salvation in African Christian Theology: Imagining a More Hopeful Future for Africa.* New York: Peter Lang.

Ng'weshemi, Andrea M. 2002. *Rediscovering the Human: The Quest for a Christo-Theological Anthropology in Africa.* New York: Peter Lang.

Nichols, Terence L. 1997. *That All May Be One: Hierarchy and Participation in the Church.* Collegeville, Minn.: Liturgical.

Nickell, Joe. 1993. *Looking for a Miracle: Weeping, Icons, Relics, Stigmata, Visions and Healing Cures.* Amherst, N.Y.: Prometheus.

Niditch, Susan. 1985. *Chaos to Cosmos: Studies in Biblical Patterns of Creation.* Chico, Calif.: Scholars Press.

Niebuhr, Reinhold. 1934. *Moral Man and Immoral Society: A Study in Ethics and Politics.* New York: Scribner.

Njiru, Paul Kariuki. 2002. *Charisms and the Holy Spirit's Activity in the Body of Christ: An Exegetical-Theological Study of 1 Corinthians 12,4-11 and Romans 12,6-8.* Rome: Editrice Pontificia Università Gregoriana.

Noll, Mark A. 2009. *The New Shape of World Christianity: How American Experience Reflects Global Faith.* Downers Grove, Ill.: IVP Academic.

Norris, David S. 2009. *I Am: A Oneness Pentecostal Theology.* Hazelwood, Mo.: WAP Academic.

Norris, Thomas J. 2009. *The Trinity: Life of God, Hope for Humanity—Towards a Theology of Communion.* Hyde Park, N.Y.: New City.

Nyamiti, Charles. 1984. *Christ as Our Ancestor: Christology from an African Perspective.* Gweru, Zimbabwe: Mambo.

O'Collins, Gerald O. 1995. *Christology: A Biblical, Historical, and Systematic Study of Jesus.* Oxford: Oxford University Press.

O'Donnell, James J. 1998. *Avatars of the Word: From Papyrus to Cyberspace.* Cambridge, Mass.: Harvard University Press.

O'Malley, J. Steven. 1995. *Early German-American Evangelicalism: Pietist Sources on Discipleship and Sanctification*. Lanham, Md.: Scarecrow.

Obilor, John Iheanyichukwu. 1994. *The Doctrine of the Resurrection of the Dead and the Igbo Belief in the "Reincarnation": A Systemico-Theological Study*. New York: Peter Lang.

Oden, Thomas C. 2004. *The Rebirth of Orthodoxy: Signs of New Life in Christianity*. San Francisco: HarperSanFrancisco.

Ogbonnaya, A. Okechukwu. 1994. *On Communitarian Divinity: An African Interpretation of the Trinity*. New York: Paragon.

Oladipo, Caleb Oluremi. 1996. *The Development of the Doctrine of the Holy Spirit in the Yoruba (African) Indigenous Christian Movement*. New York: Peter Lang.

Oliverio, L. William. 2012. *Theological Hermeneutics in the Classical Pentecostal Tradition: A Typological Account*. Leiden: Brill.

Olmstead, Wesley G. 2003. *Matthew's Trilogy of Parables: The Nation, the Nations, and the Reader in Matthew 21.28–22.14*. Cambridge: Cambridge University Press.

Omenyo, Cephas N. 2006. *Pentecost Outside Pentecostalism: A Study of the Development of Charismatic Renewal in the Mainline Churches in Ghana*. Zoetermeer, Netherlands: Boekencentrum.

Onyinah, Opoku. 2011. *Pentecostal Exorcism: Witchcraft and Demonology in Ghana*. Blandford Forum, U.K.: Deo.

Oord, Thomas Jay, and Michael Lodahl. 2005. *Relational Holiness: Responding to the Call of Love*. Kansas City, Mo.: Beacon Hill.

Oosthuizen, G. C., S. D. Edwards, W. H. Wessels, and I. Hexham, eds. 1988. *Afro-Christian Religion and Healing in Southern Africa*. Lewiston, N.Y.: Edwin Mellen.

Organ, Troy Wilson. 1970. *The Hindu Quest for the Perfection of Man*. Athens: Ohio University Press.

Ormerod, Neil J. 2007. *Creation, Grace, and Redemption*. Maryknoll, N.Y.: Orbis.

Ormerod, Neil J., and Shane Clifton. 2011. *Globalization and the Mission of the Church*. New York: T&T Clark.

Osborn, Ronald E. 2014. *Death before the Fall: Biblical Literalism and the Problem of Animal Suffering*. Downers Grove,Iii.: IVP Academic.

Osborne, Grant R. 2006. *The Hermeneutical Spiral: A Comprehensive Introduction to Biblical Interpretation*. Rev. and exp. ed. Downers Grove, Ill.: IVP Academic.

Osborne, Kenan B. 1987. *The Christian Sacraments of Initiation: Baptism, Confirmation, Eucharist*. New York: Paulist.

Ott, Craig, and Harold A. Netland, eds. 2006. *Globalizing Theology: Beliefs and Practices in an Era of World Christianity*. Grand Rapids: Baker Academic.

Oulton, J. E. L. 1951. *Holy Communion and Holy Spirit: A Study in Doctrinal Relationship*. London: SPCK.

Outler, Albert C., and Richard P. Heitzenrater, eds. 1991. *John Wesley's Sermons: An Anthology*. Nashville: Abingdon.

Padgett, Alan G. 1992. *God, Eternity and the Nature of Time*. New York: St. Martin's.

————. 2003. *Science and the Study of God: A Mutuality Model for Theology and Science.* Grand Rapids: Eerdmans.

Palmer, Phoebe. 1859. *Promise of the Father; or, a Neglected Specialty of the Last Days, Addressed to the Clergy and Laity of All Christian Communities.* Boston: H. V. Degen.

Panikkar, Raymond. 1970. *The Trinity and World Religions: Icon—Person—Mystery.* Madras: Christian Literature Society.

Pannenberg, Wolfhart. 1977. *Jesus: God and Man.* 2nd ed. Lewis L. Wilkins and Duane A. Priebe, trans. Philadelphia: Westminster.

Paper, Jordan D. 2007. *Native North American Religious Traditions: Dancing for Life.* Westport, Conn.: Praeger.

Park, Andrew Sung. 1993. *The Wounded Heart of God: The Asian Concept of Han and the Christian Doctrine of Sin.* Nashville: Abingdon.

————. 2009. *Triune Atonement: Christ's Healing for Sinners, Victims, and the Whole Creation.* Louisville, Ky: Westminster John Knox.

Park, Andrew Sung, and Susan L. Nelson, eds. 2001. *The Other Side of Sin: Woundedness from the Perspective of the Sinned-Against.* Albany: State University of New York Press.

Park, Jong-Chun. 1998. *Crawl with God, Dance in the Spirit: A Creative Formation of Korean Theology of the Spirit.* Nashville: Abingdon.

Parker, Stephen E. 1996. *Led by the Spirit: Toward a Practical Theology of Pentecostal Discernment and Decision Making.* Sheffield, U.K.: Sheffield Academic.

Parry, Robin A. 2005. *Worshipping Trinity: Coming Back to the Heart of Worship.* Milton Keynes, U.K.: Paternoster.

Parry, Robin A., and Christopher H. Partridge, eds. 2004. *Universal Salvation? The Current Debate.* Grand Rapids: Eerdmans.

Parsons, Mikeal C. 2006. *Body and Character in Luke and Acts: The Subversion of Physiognomy in Early Christianity.* Grand Rapids: Baker Academic.

————. 2007. *Luke: Storyteller, Interpreter, Evangelist.* Peabody, Mass.: Hendrickson.

Paschke, Boris. 2012. *Particularism and Universalism in the Sermon on the Mount: A Narrative-Critical Analysis of Matthew 5–7 in the Light of Matthew's View on Mission.* Münster: Aschendorff.

Patte, Daniel, ed. 2004. *Global Bible Commentary.* Nashville: Abingdon.

Payton, James R., Jr. 2010. *Getting the Reformation Wrong: Correcting Some Misunderstandings.* Downers Grove, Ill.: IVP Academic.

Pearce, E. K. Victor. 1987. *Who Was Adam?* 3rd ed. Walkerville, South Africa: Africa Centre for World Mission.

Pelikan, Jaroslav. 1989. *Mary through the Centuries: Her Place in the History of Culture.* New Haven: Yale University Press.

Penner, Todd. 2004. *In Praise of Christian Origins: Stephen and the Hellenists in Lukan Apologetic Historiography.* London: T&T Clark.

Pentecost, J. Dwight. 1958. *Things to Come: A Study in Biblical Eschatology.* Grand Rapids: Academie.

Perkins, Pheme. 1994. *Peter: Apostle for the Whole Church.* Repr., Minneapolis: Fortress, 2000.

Perry, Marvin, and Frederick M. Schweitzer, eds. 1994. *Jewish-Christian Encounters over the Centuries: Symbiosis, Prejudice, Holocaust, Dialogue.* New York: Peter Lang.

Perry, Tim. 2006. *Mary for Evangelicals: Toward an Understanding of the Mother of Our Lord.* Downers Grove, Ill.: IVP Academic.

Peters, Ted. 1994. *Sin: Radical Evil in Soul and Society.* Grand Rapids: Eerdmans.

———. 2000. *God—The World's Future: Systematic Theology for a Postmodern Era.* 2nd ed. Minneapolis: Fortress.

———. 2006. *Anticipating Omega: Science, Faith, and Our Ultimate Future.* Göttingen: Vandenhoeck & Ruprecht.

Peters, Ted, and Martinez J. Hewlett. 2003. *Evolution from Creation to New Creation: Conflict, Conversation, and Convergence.* Nashville: Abingdon.

Peters, Ted, Robert John Russell, and Michael Welker, eds. 2002. *Resurrection: Theological and Scientific Assessments.* Grand Rapids: Eerdmans.

Petersen, Norman R. 1993. *The Gospel of John and the Sociology of Light: Language and Characterization in the Fourth Gospel.* Valley Forge, Pa.: Trinity International.

Peterson, David G. 1995. *Possessed by God: A New Testament Theology of Sanctification and Holiness.* Grand Rapids: Eerdmans.

Phan, Peter C. 1985. *Culture and Eschatology: The Iconographical Vision of Paul Evdokimov.* New York: Peter Lang.

———. 1988. *Eternity in Time: A Study of Karl Rahner's Eschatology.* London: Associated University Presses.

———, ed. 2011. *Christianities in Asia.* Malden, U.K.: Wiley-Blackwell.

Pilch, John J. 2000. *Healing in the New Testament: Insights from Medical and Mediterranean Anthropology.* Minneapolis: Fortress.

———. 2004. *Visions and Healing in the Acts of the Apostles: How the Early Believers Experienced God.* Collegeville, Minn.: Liturgical.

———. 2008. *Stephen: Paul and the Hellenist Israelites.* Collegeville, Minn.: Liturgical.

Pinnock, Clark H. 1992. *A Wideness in God's Mercy: The Finality of Jesus Christ in a World of Religions.* Grand Rapids: Zondervan.

———. 1996. *Flame of Love: A Theology of the Holy Spirit.* Downers Grove, Ill.: InterVarsity.

Pinnock, Clark H., and Barry L. Callen. 2006. *The Scripture Principle: Reclaiming the Full Authority of the Bible.* 2nd ed. Grand Rapids: Baker Academic.

Piper, John. 2010. *Jesus the Only Way to God: Must You Hear the Gospel to Be Saved?* Grand Rapids: Baker.

Pipkin, H. Wayne, trans. 1984. *Huldrych Zwingli: Writings.* Vol. 2. Allison Park, Pa.: Pickwick.

Plantinga, Richard J., ed. 1999. *Christianity and Plurality: Classic and Contemporary Readings.* Oxford: Blackwell.

Plevnik, Joseph. 1997. *Paul and the Parousia: An Exegetical and Theological Investigation.* Peabody, Mass.: Hendrickson.

Pocknee, Cyril Edward. 1967. *Water and the Spirit: A Study in the Relation of Baptism and Confirmation.* London: Darton, Longman & Todd.

Poe, Harry Lee, and Jimmy H. Davis. 2012. *God and the Cosmos: Divine Activity in Space, Time and History.* Downers Grove, Ill.: IVP Academic.

Poewe, Karla O., ed. 1994. *Charismatic Christianity as a Global Culture.* Columbia: University of South Carolina Press.

Polkinghorne, John, and Michael Welker, eds. 2000. *The End of the World and the Ends of God: Science and Theology on Eschatology.* Grand Rapids: Eerdmans.

Poloma, Margaret M., and John C. Green. 2010. *The Assemblies of God: Godly Love and the Revitalization of American Pentecostalism.* New York: New York University Press.

Pomerville, Paul A. 1985. *The Third Force in Missions: A Contemporary Pentecostal Contribution to Contemporary Mission Theology.* Peabody, Mass.: Hendrickson.

Pope, Robert G. 1969. *The Half-Way Covenant: Church Membership in Puritan New England.* Princeton: Princeton University Press.

Porterfield, Amanda. 2005. *Healing in the History of Christianity.* New York: Oxford University Press.

Powell, Mark Allan. 1995. *God with Us: A Pastoral Theology of Matthew's Gospel.* Minneapolis: Fortress.

Powell, Samuel M. 2003. *Participating in God: Creation and Trinity.* Minneapolis: Fortress.

Prestige, G. L. 1985. *God in Patristic Thought.* 2nd ed. 1952. Repr., London: SPCK.

Prichard, Rebecca Button. 1999. *Sensing the Spirit: The Holy Spirit in Feminist Perspective.* St. Louis, Mo.: Chalice.

Prior, Michael. 1995. *Jesus the Liberator: Nazareth Liberation Theology (Luke 4.16-30).* Sheffield, U.K.: Sheffield Academic.

Prosser, Peter E. 1999. *Dispensationalist Eschatology and Its Influence on American and British Religious Movements.* Lewiston, N.Y.: Edwin Mellen.

Quanstrom, Mark R. 2004. *A Century of Holiness Theology: The Doctrine of Entire Sanctification in the Church of the Nazarene, 1905–2004.* Kansas City, Mo.: Beacon Hill.

Rabens, Volker. 2010. *The Holy Spirit and Ethics in Paul: Transforming and Empowering for Religious-Ethical Life.* Tübingen: Mohr Siebeck.

Rader, William Harry. 1978. *The Church and Racial Hostility: A History of Interpretation of Ephesians 2: 11-22.* Tübingen: J. C. B. Mohr (Paul Siebeck).

Radner, Ephraim. 1998. *The End of the Church: A Pneumatology of Christian Division in the West.* Grand Rapids: Eerdmans.

Rah, Soong-Chan. 2009. *The Next Evangelicalism: Freeing the Church from Western Cultural Captivity.* Downers Grove, Ill.: InterVarsity.

Ram, Eric, ed. 1995. *Transforming Health: Christian Approaches to Healing and Wholeness.* Monrovia, Calif.: Mission Advanced Research and Communications.

Ranger, Shelagh. 2007. *The Word of Wisdom and the Creation of Animals in Africa.* Cambridge: James Clarke.

Rani, T. Mercy. 2003. *Assailants of the Spirit and the Upholders of "Sakti": An Indian Feminist Assessment of the Holy Spirit*. Bangalore, India: South Asia Theological Research Institute.

Rao, Anand. 2002. *Soteriologies of India and Their Role in the Perception of Disability: A Comparative Transdisciplinary Overview with Reference to Hinduism and Christianity in India*. Münster: LIT.

Rappaport, Roy A. 1999. *Ritual and Religion in the Making of Humanity*. Cambridge: Cambridge University Press.

Rasmussen, Ane Marie Bak. 1996. *Modern African Spiritualities: The Independent Holy Spirit Churches in East Africa, 1902–1976*. London: British Academic.

Ratzinger, Joseph. 1988. *Eschatology: Death and Eternal Life*. Michael Waldstein and Aidan Nichols, trans. Washington, D.C.: Catholic University of America Press.

Rausch, Thomas P. 2012. *Eschatology, Liturgy, and Christology: Toward Recovering an Eschatological Imagination*. Collegeville, Minn.: Liturgical.

Ray, Darby Kathleen. 1998. *Deceiving the Devil: Atonement, Abuse, and Ransom*. Cleveland, Ohio: Pilgrim.

Reed, Annette Yoshiko. 2005. *Fallen Angels and the History of Judaism and Christianity: The Reception of Enochic Literature*. Cambridge: Cambridge University Press.

Reed, David A. 2008. *"In Jesus Name": The History and Beliefs of Oneness Pentecostals*. Blandford Forum, U.K.: Deo.

Reid, Barbara E. 1996. *Choosing the Better Part? Women in the Gospel of Luke*. Collegeville, Minn.: Liturgical.

Reimer, Kevin S. 2009. *Living L'Arche: Stories of Compassion, Love, and Disability*. Collegeville, Minn.: Liturgical.

Reinders, Hans S. 2008. *Receiving the Gift of Friendship: Profound Disability, Theological Anthropology, and Ethics*. Grand Rapids: Eerdmans.

Reynolds, Benjamin E. 2008. *The Apocalyptic Son of Man in the Gospel of John*. Tübingen: Mohr Siebeck.

Reynolds, Thomas E. 2008. *Vulnerable Communion: A Theology of Disability and Hospitality*. Grand Rapids: Brazos.

Rhee, Victor. 2001. *Faith in Hebrews: Analysis within the Context of Christology, Eschatology, and Ethics*. New York: Peter Lang.

Rhoads, David M., ed. 2005. *From Every People and Nation: The Book of Revelation in Intercultural Perspective*. Minneapolis: Fortress.

Rice, Martin J. 2009. "Ethical Encounter Theology: An Interdisciplinary Consonance." Ph.D. thesis, Griffith University, Queensland, Australia.

Rich, Antony D. 2007. *Discernment in the Desert Fathers: Διάκρισις in the Life and Thought of Early Egyptian Monasticism*. Milton Keynes, U.K.: Paternoster.

Richard, Pablo. 1995. *Apocalypse: A People's Commentary on the Book of Revelation*. Maryknoll, N.Y.: Orbis.

Richie, Tony. 2011. *Speaking by the Spirit: A Pentecostal Model for Interreligious Encounter and Dialogue*. Wilmore, Ky.: Emeth.

———. 2013. *Toward a Pentecostal Theology of Religions: Encountering Cornelius Today.* Cleveland, Tenn.: CPT.

Ricoeur, Paul. 1974. *The Conflict of Interpretations.* Don Ihde, ed. Evanston, Ill.: Northwestern University Press.

Riggs, John W. 2002. *Baptism in the Reformed Tradition: A Historical and Practical Theology.* Louisville, Ky: Westminster John Knox.

Robeck, Cecil M., Jr., ed. 1984. *Charismatic Experiences in History.* Peabody, Mass.: Hendrickson.

———. 1992. *Prophecy in Carthage: Perpetua, Tertullian, and Cyprian.* Cleveland, Ohio: Pilgrim.

———. 2006. *The Azusa Street Mission and Revival.* Nashville: Nelson Reference.

Robert, Dana Lee. 2008. *Converting Colonialism: Visions and Realities in Mission History, 1706–1914.* Grand Rapids: Eerdmans.

Roberts, Michael. 2008. *Evangelicals and Science.* Westport, Conn.: Greenwood.

Robinson, James. 2011. *Divine Healing: The Formative Years, 1830–1890.* Eugene, Ore.: Pickwick.

Rollins, Peter. 2008. *The Fidelity of Betrayal: Towards a Church beyond Belief.* Brewster, Mass.: Paraclete.

Rook, Russell, and Stephen R. Holmes, eds. 2008. *What Are We Waiting For? Christian Hope and Contemporary Culture.* Milton Keynes, U.K.: Paternoster.

Rosenhouse, Jason. 2012. *Among the Creationists: Dispatches from the Anti-evolutionist Front Line.* Oxford: Oxford University Press.

Ross, Hugh. 1994. *Creation and Time: A Biblical and Scientific Perspective on the Creation-Date Controversy.* Colorado Springs: NavPress.

Roth, Ron. 2001. *Holy Spirit for Healing: Merging Ancient Wisdom with Modern Medicine.* Carlsbad, Calif.: Hay House.

Ruether, Rosemary Radford. 1981. *To Change the World: Christology and Cultural Criticism.* New York: Crossroad.

———. 2012. *Women and Redemption: A Theological History.* 2nd ed. Minneapolis: Fortress.

Runyon, Theodore, ed. 1981. *Sanctification and Liberation: Liberation Theologies in Light of the Wesleyan Tradition.* Nashville: Abingdon.

Rush, Ormond. 2009. *The Eyes of Faith: The Sense of the Faithful and the Church's Reception of Revelation.* Washington, D.C.: Catholic University of America Press.

Russell, Jeffrey Burton. 1968. *A History of Medieval Christianity: Prophecy and Order.* New York: Thomas Y. Crowell.

Ruthven, Jon. 1993. *On the Cessation of the Charismata: The Protestant Polemic on Postbiblical Miracles.* Sheffield, U.K.: Sheffield Academic.

Ryan, Patrick, ed. 1998. *Structures of Sin, Seeds of Liberation.* Nairobi: Paulines Publications Africa.

Rybarczyk, Edmund. 2004. *Beyond Salvation: Eastern Orthodoxy and Classical Pentecostalism on Becoming Like Christ.* Milton Keynes, U.K.: Paternoster.

Sampson, R. V. 1956. *Progress in the Age of Reason: The Seventeenth Century to the Present Day*. Cambridge, Mass.: Harvard University Press.

Samuel, Simon. 2007. *A Postcolonial Reading of Mark's Story of Jesus*. London: T&T Clark.

Sanders, Cheryl J. 1996. *Saints in Exile: The Holiness-Pentecostal Experience in African American Religion and Culture*. New York: Oxford University Press.

Sanders, John. 1992. *No Other Name: An Investigation into the Destiny of the Unevangelized*. Grand Rapids: Eerdmans.

Sanneh, Lamin O. 1989. *Translating the Message: The Missionary Impact on Culture*. Maryknoll, N.Y.: Orbis.

―――. 2008. *Disciples of All Nations: Pillars of World Christianity*. Oxford: Oxford University Press.

Sasse, Hermann. 1959. *This Is My Body: Luther's Contention for the Real Presence in the Sacrament of the Altar*. Minneapolis: Augsburg.

Savage, Timothy B. 1996. *Power through Weakness: Paul's Understanding of the Christian Ministry in 2 Corinthians*. Cambridge: Cambridge University Press.

Scaer, David P. 2004. *Discourses in Matthew: Jesus Teaches the Church*. St. Louis, Mo.: Concordia.

Scafi, Alessandro. 2006. *Mapping Paradise: History of Heaven on Earth*. Chicago: University of Chicago Press.

Scanlan, Michael. 1972. *The Power in Penance: Confession and the Holy Spirit*. Notre Dame, Ind.: Ava Maria.

Schaberg, Jane. 1980. *The Father, the Son and the Holy Spirit: The Triadic Phrase in Matthew 28:19b*. Chico, Calif.: Scholars.

Schatzmann, Siegfried S. 1987. *A Pauline Theology of the Charismata*. Peabody, Mass.: Hendrickson.

Schillebeeckx, E. 1963. *Christ the Sacrament of the Encounter with God*. Kansas City, Mo.: Sheed, Andrews & McMeel.

Schipper, Jeremy, and Candida R. Moss, eds. 2011. *Disability Studies and Biblical Literature*. New York: Palgrave Macmillan.

Schmemann, Alexander. 1974. *Of Water and Spirit: A Liturgical Study of Baptism*. Crestwood, N.Y.: St. Vladimir's Seminary.

―――. 1987. *The Eucharist, Sacrament of the Kingdom*. Crestwood, N.Y.: St. Vladimir's Seminary.

Schmiechen, Peter. 2005. *Saving Power: Theories of Atonement and Forms of the Church*. Grand Rapids: Eerdmans.

Schoeps, Hans Joachim. 1963. *The Jewish-Christian Argument: A History of Theologies in Conflict*. David E. Green, trans. New York: Holt, Rinehart & Winston.

Schumm, Darla, and Michael Stoltzfus, eds. 2011. *Disability in Judaism, Christianity, and Islam: Sacred Texts, Historical Traditions, and Social Analysis*. New York: Palgrave Macmillan.

Schüssler Fiorenza, Elisabeth. 1994. *Jesus: Miriam's Child, Sophia's Prophet—Critical Issues in Feminist Christology*. New York: Continuum.

Schwager, Raymund. 2006. *Banished from Eden: Original Sin and Evolutionary Theory in the Drama of Salvation*. James Williams, trans. Leominster, U.K.: Gracewing.

Schwanz, Keith, and Joseph Coleson, eds. 2011. Missio Dei: *A Wesleyan Understanding*. Kansas City, Mo.: Beacon Hill.

Schwarz, Hans. 1977. *Our Cosmic Journey: Christian Anthropology in Light of Current Trends in the Sciences, Philosophy and Theology*. Minneapolis: Augsburg.

Seamands, Stephen. 2005. *Ministry in the Image of God: The Trinitarian Shape of Christian Service*. Downers Grove, Ill.: InterVarsity.

Segovia, Fernando F., and R. S. Sugirtharajah, eds. 2007. *A Postcolonial Commentary on the New Testament Writings*. London: T&T Clark.

Segundo, Juan Luis. 1974. *A Theology for Artisans of a New Humanity*, vol. 4: *The Sacraments Today*. John Drury, trans. Maryknoll, N.Y.: Orbis.

Sharma, Arvind, ed. 2000. *Women Saints in World Religions*. Albany: State University of New York Press.

Shaw, Mark. 2010. *Global Awakening: How 20th-Century Revivals Triggered a Christian Revolution*. Downers Grove, Ill.: IVP Academic.

Shelton, James B. 1991. *Mighty in Word and Deed: The Role of the Holy Spirit in Luke-Acts*. Peabody, Mass.: Hendrickson.

Shelton, Sally. 2015. "Overshadowed by the Spirit: Mary, Mother of Our Lord, Prototype of Spirit-Baptized Humanity." Ph.D. diss., Regent University School of Divinity, Virginia Beach, Virginia.

Shults, F. LeRon. 1999. *The Postfoundationalist Task of Theology: Wolfhart Pannenberg and the New Theological Rationality*. Grand Rapids: Eerdmans.

———. 2003. *Reforming Theological Anthropology: After the Philosophical Turn to Relationality*. Grand Rapids: Eerdmans.

Shults, F. LeRon, and Steven J. Sandage. 2003. *The Faces of Forgiveness: Searching for Wholeness and Salvation*. Grand Rapids: Baker Academic.

Siecienski, A. Edward. 2010. *The Filioque: History of a Doctrinal Controversy*. Oxford: Oxford University Press.

Sim, David C. 1996. *Apocalyptic Eschatology in the Gospel of Matthew*. Cambridge: Cambridge University Press.

Simkins, Ronald A. 1994. *Creator and Creation: Nature in the Worldview of Ancient Israel*. Peabody, Mass.: Hendrickson.

Simon, Marcel. 1958. *St Stephen and the Hellenists in the Primitive Church*. London: Longmans, Green.

Singh, David Emmanuel, ed. 2008. *Jesus and the Cross: Reflections of Christians from Islamic Contexts*. Oxford: Regnum.

Skaggs, Rebecca, and Priscilla C. Benham. 2009. *Revelation: The Pentecostal Commentary Series*. Blandford Forum, U.K.: Deo.

Smail, Tom. 2005. *Like Father, Like Son: The Trinity Imaged in Our Humanity*. Milton Keynes, U.K.: Paternoster.

Smalley, Stephen S. 2005. *The Revelation to St. John: A Commentary on the Greek Text of the Apocalypse*. Downers Grove, Ill.: InterVarsity.

Smart, Ninian, and Steven Konstantine. 1991. *Christian Systematic Theology in a World Context*. Minneapolis: Fortress.

Smith, Dennis E., and Hal E. Taussig. 1990. *Many Tables: The Eucharist in the New Testament and Liturgy Today*. London: SCM Press.

Smith, Gordon T., ed. 2008. *The Lord's Supper: Five Views*. Downers Grove, Ill.: IVP Academic.

Smith, James K. A. 2000. *The Fall of the Interpretation: Philosophical Foundations for a Creational Hermeneutic*. Downers Grove, Ill.: InterVarsity.

———. 2009. *Desiring the Kingdom: Worship, Worldview, and Cultural Formation*. Grand Rapids: Baker Academic.

———. 2010. *Thinking in Tongues: Pentecostal Contributions to Christian Philosophy*. Grand Rapids: Eerdmans.

———. 2013. *Imagining the Kingdom: How Worship Works*. Grand Rapids: Baker Academic.

Smith, James K. A., and Amos Yong, eds. 2010. *Science and the Spirit: A Pentecostal Engagement with the Sciences*. Bloomington: Indiana University Press.

Smith, Timothy L. 1957. *Revivalism and Social Reform in Mid-19th-Century America*. Nashville: Abingdon.

Smith, Wilfred Cantwell. 1993. *What Is Scripture? A Comparative Approach*. Minneapolis: Fortress.

Snyder, Howard A., with Joel Scandrett. 2011. *Salvation Means Creation Healed: The Ecology of Sin and Grace*. Eugene, Ore.: Cascade.

So, Damon W. K. 2006. *Jesus' Revelation of His Father: A Narrative-Conceptual Study of the Trinity with Special Reference to Karl Barth*. Milton Keynes, U.K.: Paternoster.

Sobrino, Jon. 1978. *Christology at the Crossroads: A Latin American Approach*. John Drury, trans. Maryknoll, N.Y.: Orbis.

———. 1988. *Spirituality of Liberation: Toward Political Holiness*. Robert R. Barr, trans. Maryknoll, N.Y.: Orbis.

Solivan, Samuel. 1998. *The Spirit, Pathos, and Liberation: Toward an Hispanic Pentecostal Theology*. Sheffield, U.K.: Sheffield Academic.

Sookhdeo, Patrick, ed. 1978. *Jesus Christ the Only Way: Christian Responsibility in a Multicultural Society*. Trowbridge, U.K.: Paternoster.

Sorensen, Eric. 2002. *Possession and Exorcism in the New Testament and Early Christianity*. Tübingen: Mohr Siebeck.

Southgate, Christopher. 2008. *The Groaning of Creation: God, Evolution, and the Problem of Evil*. Louisville, Ky: Westminster John Knox.

Sparks, Adam. 2010. *One of a Kind: The Relationship between Old and New Covenants as the Hermeneutical Key for Christian Theology of Religions*. Eugene, Ore.: Pickwick.

Sparks, Kenton L. 2008. *God's Word in Human Words: An Evangelical Appropriation of Critical Biblical Scholarship*. Grand Rapids: Baker Academic.

Stålsett, Sturla, ed. 2006. *Spirits of Globalization: The Growth of Pentecostalism and Experiential Spiritualities in a Global Age*. London: SCM Press.

Steenberg, Matthew C. 2009. *Of God and Man: Theology as Anthropology from Irenaeus to Athanasius*. London: T&T Clark.

Steinmann, Jean. 1958. *Saint John the Baptist and the Desert Tradition*. Michael Boyes, trans. New York: Harper & Brothers.

Stenger, Victor J. 2011. *The Fallacy of Fine-Tuning: Why the Universe Is Not Designed for Us*. Amherst, N.Y.: Prometheus.

Stenmark, Mikael. 2004. *How to Relate Science and Religion: A Multidimensional Model*. Grand Rapids: Eerdmans.

Stephanou, Eusebius. 1997. *The Baptism in the Holy Spirit: An Orthodox Understanding*. Destin, Fla.: St. Symeon the New Theologian Orthodox Brotherhood and Renewal Center.

Stephenson, Christopher A. 2013. *Types of Pentecostal Theology: Method, System, Spirit*. Oxford: Oxford University Press.

Stephenson, Lisa. 2012. *Dismantling the Dualisms for American Pentecostal Women in Ministry: A Feminist-Pneumatological Approach*. Leiden: Brill.

Stewart-Sykes, Alistair, ed. 2001. *Hippolytus: On the Apostolic Tradition*. Crestwood, N.Y.: St. Vladimir's Seminary.

Stibbe, Mark. 2001. *Fire and Blood: The Work of the Spirit, the Work of the Cross*. London: Monarch.

Stibbs, Alan Marshall. 1970. *So Great Salvation: The Meaning and Message of the Letter to the Hebrews*. Exeter, U.K.: Paternoster.

Stinton, Diane B. 2004. *Jesus of Africa: Voices of Contemporary African Christology*. Maryknoll, N.Y.: Orbis.

Stoever, William K. B. 1978. *A Faire and Easie Way to Heaven: Covenant Theology and Antinomianism in Early Massachusetts*. Middletown, Conn.: Wesleyan University Press.

Strickling, Bonnelle Lewis. 2007. *Dreaming about the Divine*. Albany: State University of New York Press.

Stronstad, Roger. 1984. *The Charismatic Theology of St. Luke*. Peabody, Mass.: Hendrickson.

———. 1995. *Spirit, Scripture and Theology: A Pentecostal Perspective*. Baguio City, Philippines: Asia Pacific Theological Seminary.

———. 1999. *The Prophethood of All Believers: A Study in Luke's Charismatic Theology*. Sheffield, U.K.: Sheffield Academic.

Studebaker, Steven M. 2012. *From Pentecost to the Triune God: A Pentecostal Trinitarian Theology*. Grand Rapids: Eerdmans.

Suchocki, Marjorie. 1994. *The Fall to Violence: Original Sin in Relational Theology*. New York: Continuum.

Sullivan, Clayton. 1988. *Rethinking Realized Eschatology*. Macon, Ga.: Mercer University Press.

Sullivan, Francis A. 1982. *Charisms and Charismatic Renewal: A Biblical and Theological Study*. Ann Arbor, Mich.: Servant.

———. 1988. *The Church We Believe In: One, Holy, Catholic, Apostolic*. New York: Paulist.

———. 1992. *Salvation outside the Church: Tracing the History of the Catholic Response.* New York: Paulist.

Sullivan, Lawrence E., ed. 1989. *Healing and Restoring: Health and Medicine in the World's Religious Traditions.* New York: Macmillan.

Suurmond, Jean Jacques. 1994. *Word and Spirit at Play: Towards a Charismatic Theology.* John Bowden, trans. Grand Rapids: Eerdmans.

Swain, Scott R. 2011. *Trinity, Revelation, and Reading: A Theological Introduction to the Bible and Its Interpretation.* London: T&T Clark.

Swindal, James, and Harry J. Gensler, eds. 2005. *The Sheed & Ward Anthology of Catholic Philosophy.* Lanham, Md.: Rowman & Littlefield.

Swinton, John. 2007. *Raging with Compassion: Pastoral Responses to the Problem of Evil.* Grand Rapids: Eerdmans.

Swoboda, A. J. 2013. *Tongues and Trees: Towards a Pentecostal Ecological Theology.* Blandford Forum, U.K.: Deo.

Synan, Vinson. 1997. *The Holiness-Pentecostal Tradition: Charismatic Movements in the Twentieth Century.* Grand Rapids: Eerdmans.

———. 2001. *The Century of the Holy Spirit: 100 Years of Pentecostal and Charismatic Renewal, 1901–2001.* Nashville: Thomas Nelson.

Szypula, Wojciech. 2007. *The Holy Spirit in the Eschatological Tension of the Christian Life: An Exegetico-Theological Study of 2 Corinthians 5,1-5 and Romans 8,18-27.* Rome: Editrice Pontificia Università Gregoriana.

Talbert, Charles H., and Jason A. Whitlark, eds. 2011. *Getting "Saved": The Whole Story of Salvation in the New Testament.* Grand Rapids: Eerdmans.

Tamez, Elsa. 1993. *The Amnesty of Grace: Justification by Faith from a Latin American Perspective.* Sharon H. Ringe, trans. Nashville: Abingdon.

Tan Chow, Mayling. 2007. *Pentecostal Theology for the Twenty-First Century: Engaging in Multi-Faith Singapore.* Aldershot, U.K.: Ashgate.

Taylor, Joan E. 1997. *The Immerser: John the Baptist within Second Temple Judaism.* Grand Rapids: Eerdmans.

Taylor, John V. 1972. *The Go-Between God: The Holy Spirit and Christian Mission.* London: SCM Press.

Taylor, Richard S. 1985. *Exploring Christian Holiness.* Vol. 3: *The Theological Formulation.* Kansas City, Mo.: Beacon Hill.

Teel, Karen. 2010. *Racism and the Image of God.* New York: Palgrave Macmillan.

Telford, William. 1999. *The Theology of the Gospel of Mark.* Cambridge: Cambridge University Press.

Tennant, Frederick Robert. 1902. *The Origin and Propagation of Sin.* Cambridge: Cambridge University Press.

Tennent, Timothy C. 2002. *Christianity at the Religious Roundtable: Evangelicalism in Conversation with Hinduism, Buddhism, and Islam.* Grand Rapids: Baker Academic.

———. 2007. *Theology in the Context of World Christianity: How the Global Church Is Influencing the Way We Think.* Grand Rapids: Zondervan.

Teres, Gustav. 2002. *The Bible and Astronomy: The Magi and the Star in the Gospel.* 3rd ed. Oslo: Solum Forlag.

Terreros, Marco T. 1994. "Death before the Sin of Adam: A Fundamental Concept in Theistic Evolution and Its Implications for Evangelical Theology." Ph.D. diss., Andrews University, Berrien Springs, Mich.

Thangaraj, M. Thomas. 1994. *The Crucified Guru: An Experiment in Cross-Cultural Christology.* Nashville: Abingdon.

Theissen, Gerd. 1983. *The Miracle Stories of the Early Christian Tradition.* Francis McDonagh, trans. John Riches, ed. Philadelphia: Fortress.

Thomas, John Christopher. 1991. *Footwashing in John 13 and the Johannine Community.* Repr., Sheffield, U.K.: Sheffield Academic, 1991.

————. 1998. *The Devil, Disease and Deliverance: Origins of Illness in New Testament Thought.* Sheffield, U.K.: Sheffield Academic.

————. 2005. *The Spirit of the New Testament.* Blandford Forum, U.K.: Deo.

————, ed. 2010. *Toward a Pentecostal Ecclesiology: The Church and the Fivefold Gospel.* Cleveland, Tenn.: CPT.

————. 2012. *The Apocalypse: A Literary and Theological Commentary.* Cleveland, Tenn.: CPT.

Thomas, Joseph L. 2014. *Perfect Harmony: Interracialism in Early Holiness-Pentecostalism, 1880–1909.* Wilmore, Ky.: Emeth Press.

Thompson, Matthew K. 2010. *Kingdom Come: Revisioning Pentecostal Eschatology.* Blandford Forum, U.K.: Deo.

Thompson, Ross. 1997. *Is There an Anglican Way? Scripture, Church and Reason— New Approaches to an Old Triad.* London: Darton, Longman & Todd.

Thoppil, James. 1998. *Towards an Asian Ecclesiology: Understanding of the Church in the Documents of the Federation of Asian Bishops' Conferences (FABC) 1970–1995 and the Asian Ecclesiological Trends.* Rome: Pontifica Universitas Urbaniana.

Thorsen, Donald A. D. 1990. *Wesleyan Quadrilateral: Scripture, Tradition, Reason and Experience as a Model of Evangelical Theology.* Wilmore, Ky.: Francis Asbury.

Thurston, Bonnie Bowman. 1993. *Spiritual Life in the Early Church: The Witness of Acts and Ephesians.* Minneapolis: Fortress.

Tidball, Derek, David Hilborn, and Justin Thacker, eds. 2008. *The Atonement Debate: Papers from the London Symposium on the Theology of the Atonement.* Grand Rapids: Zondervan

Tillard, J.-M.-R. 2001. *Flesh of the Church, Flesh of Christ: At the Source of the Ecclesiology of Communion.* Collegeville, Minn.: Liturgical.

Tilley, Terrence W. 1991. *The Evils of Theodicy.* Washington, D.C.: Georgetown University Press.

————. 2008. *The Disciples' Jesus: Christology as Reconciling Practice.* Maryknoll, N.Y.: Orbis.

Tillich, Paul. 1959. *Theology of Culture.* Robert C. Kimball, ed. New York: Oxford University Press.

————. 1969. *What Is Religion?* New York: Harper & Row.

Tisera, Guido. 1993. *Universalism according to the Gospel of Matthew*. Frankfurt: Peter Lang.

Tomberlin, Daniel. 2010. *Pentecostal Sacraments: Encountering God at the Altar*. Cleveland, Tenn.: CPT.

Tomlin, Graham. 2011. *The Prodigal Spirit: The Trinity, the Church and the Future of the World*. Oxford: Lion.

Toner, Jules J. 1995. *Spirit of Light or Darkness? A Casebook for Studying Discernment of Spirits*. St. Louis, Mo.: Institute of Jesuit Sources.

Tovey, Phillip. 2004. *Inculturation of Christian Worship: Exploring the Eucharist*. Aldershot, U.K.: Ashgate.

Treier, Daniel J. 2008. *Introducing Theological Interpretation of Scripture: Recovering a Christian Practice*. Grand Rapids: Baker Academic.

Treier, Daniel J., and David Lauber, eds. 2009. *Trinitarian Theology for the Church: Scripture, Community, Worship*. Downers Grove, Ill.: IVP Academic.

Trevett, Christine. 1996. *Montanism: Gender, Authority, and the New Prophecy*. Cambridge: Cambridge University Press.

Tsoukalas, Steven. 2006. *Krsna and Christ: Body-Divine Relation in the Thought of Sankara, Ramanuja, and Classical Christian Orthodoxy*. Milton Keynes, U.K.: Paternoster.

Turner, H. E. W. 1952. *The Patristic Doctrine of Redemption: A Study of the Development of Doctrine during the First Five Centuries*. London: Mowbray.

Turner, Max. 1996. *Power from on High: The Spirit in Israel's Restoration and Witness in Luke-Acts*. Sheffield, U.K.: Sheffield Academic.

Twelftree, Graham H. 1999. *Jesus the Miracle Worker: A Historical and Theological Study*. Downers Grove, Ill.: InterVarsity.

———, ed. 2011. *The Cambridge Companion to Miracles*. Cambridge: Cambridge University Press.

Twesigye, Emmanuel K. 1996. *African Religion, Philosophy, and Christianity in Logos-Christ: Common Ground Revisited*. New York: Peter Lang.

Tyra, Gary. 2011. *The Holy Spirit in Mission: Prophetic Speech and Action in Christian Witness*. Downers Grove, Ill.: IVP Academic.

Ucko, Hans, ed. 1996. *People of God, Peoples of God: A Jewish-Christian Conversation in Asia*. Geneva: WCC.

———. 2000. *The People and the People of God: Minjung and Dalit Theology in Interaction with Jewish-Christian Dialogue*. Münster: LIT.

Udoh, Enyi Ben. 1988. *Guest Christology: An Interpretative View of the Christological Problem in Africa*. New York: Peter Lang.

Vähäkangas, Mika, and Andrew A. Kyomo. 2003. *Charismatic Renewal in Africa: A Challenge for African Christianity*. Nairobi: Acton.

Valantasis, Richard. 2005. *Centuries of Holiness: Ancient Spirituality Refracted for a Postmodern Age*. New York: Continuum.

van Driel, Edwin Chr. 2008. *Incarnation Anyway: Arguments for Supralapsarian Christology*. Oxford: Oxford University Press.

Van Dusen, Henry P. 1958. *Spirit, Son, and Father: Christian Faith in the Light of the Holy Spirit*. New York: Scribner.

van Engen, Charles. 1991. *God's Missionary People: Rethinking the Purpose of the Local Church*. Grand Rapids: Baker.

Van Huyssteen, J. Wentzel, and Niels Henrik Gregersen, eds. 1998. *Rethinking Theology and Science: Six Models for the Current Dialogue*. Grand Rapids: Eerdmans.

van Kooten, George H. 2008. *Paul's Anthropology in Context: The Image of God, Assimilation to God, and Tripartite Man in Ancient Judaism, Ancient Philosophy and Early Christianity*. Tübingen: Mohr Siebeck.

Vanhoozer, Kevin J. 1990. *Biblical Narrative in the Philosophy of Paul Ricoeur: A Study in Hermeneutics and Theology*. Cambridge: Cambridge University Press.

———, ed. 1996. *The Trinity in a Pluralistic Age: Theological Essays on Culture and Religion*. Grand Rapids: Eerdmans.

———. 2002. *First Theology: God, Scripture and Hermeneutics*. Downers Grove, Ill.: IVP Academic.

———, ed. 2003. *The Cambridge Companion to Postmodern Theology*. Cambridge: Cambridge University Press.

Victorin-Vangerud, Nancy M. 2000. *The Raging Hearth: Spirit in the Household of God*. St. Louis, Mo.: Chalice.

Voaden, Rosalynn. 1999. *God's Words, Women's Voices: The Discernment of Spirits in the Writing of Late-Medieval Women Visionaries*. Suffolk, U.K.: York Medieval Press.

Volf, Miroslav. 1998. *After Our Likeness: The Church as the Image of the Trinity*. Grand Rapids: Eerdmans.

von Campenhausen, Hans. 1969. *Ecclesiastical Authority and Spiritual Power in the Church of the First Three Centuries*. Stanford: Stanford University Press.

von Speyr, Adrienne. 1988. *The Mystery of Death*. Graham Harrison, trans. San Francisco: Ignatius.

Vondey, Wolfgang. 2008. *People of Bread: Rediscovering Ecclesiology*. Mahwah, N.J.: Paulist.

———. 2010a. *Beyond Pentecostalism: The Crisis of Global Christianity and the Renewal of the Theological Agenda*. Grand Rapids: Eerdmans.

———, ed. 2010b. *Pentecostalism and Christian Unity: Ecumenical Documents and Critical Assessments*. Eugene, Ore.: Pickwick.

Wacker, Grant. 2001. *Heaven Below: Early Pentecostalism and American Culture*. Cambridge, Mass.: Harvard University Press.

Waddell, Robby. 2006. *The Spirit of the Book of Revelation*. Blandford Forum, U.K.: Deo.

Wagner, C. Peter. 1996. *Confronting the Powers: How the New Testament Church Experienced the Power of Strategic-Level Spiritual Warfare*. Ventura: Regal.

Währisch-Oblau, Claudia. 2009. *The Missionary Self-Perception of Pentecostal/Charismatic Leaders from the Global South in Europe: Bringing Back the Gospel*. Leiden: Brill.

Wainwright, Elaine M., ed. 2010. *Spirit Possession, Theology, and Identity: A Pacific Exploration.* Hindmarsh, Australia: ATF.

Walker, Andrew. 1985. *Restoring the Kingdom: The Radical Christianity of the House Church Movement.* London: Hodder & Stoughton.

Wall, Robert W. 1991. *New International Biblical Commentary: Revelation.* Peabody, Mass.: Hendrickson.

———. 2011. "John's John: A Wesleyan Theological Reading of 1 John." *Wesleyan Theological Journal* 46 (2): 105–41.

Walls, Andrew F. 1996. *The Missionary Movement in Christian History: Studies in the Transmission of Faith.* Edinburgh: T&T Clark.

Walls, Jerry L. 1992. *Hell: The Logic of Damnation.* Notre Dame, Ind.: University of Notre Dame Press.

———. 2002. *Heaven: The Logic of Eternal Joy.* Oxford: Oxford University Press.

———. 2012. *Purgatory: The Logic of Total Transformation.* Oxford: Oxford University Press.

Walters, Albert Sundararaj. 2002. *We Believe in One God? Reflections on the Trinity in the Malaysian Context.* Delhi: ISPCK.

Walters, John R. 1995. *Perfection in New Testament Theology: Ethics and Eschatology in Relational Dynamic.* Lewiston, N.Y.: Mellen Biblical.

Walton, John H. 2009. *The Lost World of Genesis One: Ancient Cosmology and the Origins Debate.* Downers Grove, Ill.: IVP Academic.

Ward, Benedicta. 1982. *Miracles and the Medieval Mind: Theory, Record and Event, 1000–1215.* Philadelphia: University of Pennsylvania Press.

Ward, Keith. 1994. *Religion and Revelation: A Theology of Revelation in the World's Religions.* Oxford: Oxford University Press.

Ward, Timothy. 2009. *Words of Life: Scripture as the Living and Active Word of God.* Downers Grove, Ill.: IVP Academic.

Ware, Steven L. 2004. *Restorationism in the Holiness Movement in the Late 19th and Early 20th Centuries.* Lewiston, N.Y.: Edwin Mellen.

Warfield, Benjamin B. 1918. *Counterfeit Miracles.* Repr., Edinburgh: Banner of Truth Trust, 1972.

Wariboko, Nimi. 2012. *The Pentecostal Principle: Ethical Methodology in New Spirit.* Grand Rapids: Eerdmans.

Warren, E. Janet. 2012. *Cleansing the Cosmos: A Biblical Model for Conceptualizing and Counteracting Evil.* Eugene, Ore.: Pickwick.

Warrington, Keith, ed. 1998. *Pentecostal Perspectives.* Carlisle, U.K.: Paternoster.

———. 2000. *Jesus the Healer: Paradigm or Unique Phenomenon?* Carlisle, U.K.: Paternoster.

———. 2008. *Pentecostal Theology: A Theology of Encounter.* London: T&T Clark.

Watson, Lyall. 1995. *Dark Nature: A Natural History of Evil.* New York: HarperCollins.

Watts, Graham J. 2005. *Revelation and the Spirit: A Comparative Study of the Relationship between the Doctrine of Revelation and Pneumatology in the Theology of Eberhard Jüngel and Wolfhart Pannenberg.* Milton Keynes, U.K.: Paternoster.

Watts, Rikki E. 2000. *Isaiah's New Exodus in Mark*. Grand Rapids: Baker Academic.

Weaver, J. Denny. 2001. *The Nonviolent Atonement*. Grand Rapids: Eerdmans.

Webb, Stephen H. 2010. *The Dome of Eden: A New Solution to the Problem of Creation and Evolution*. Eugene, Ore.: Cascade.

Webber, Robert E. 1999. *Ancient-Future Faith: Rethinking Evangelicalism for a Postmodern World*. Grand Rapids: Baker Academic.

Webb-Mitchell, Brett. 2010. *Beyond Accessibility: Toward Full Inclusion of People with Disabilities in Faith Communities*. New York: Church Publishing.

Weber, Eugen. 1999. *Apocalypses: Prophecies, Cults, and Millennial Beliefs through the Ages*. Cambridge, Mass.: Harvard University Press.

Webster, John B. 2003. *Holy Scripture: A Dogmatic Sketch*. Cambridge: Cambridge University Press.

Weddle, David L. 2010. *Miracles: Wonder and Meaning in World Religions*. New York: Palgrave Macmillan.

Welker, Michael, ed. 2012. *The Spirit in Creation and New Creation: Science and Theology in Western and Orthodox Realms*. Grand Rapids: Eerdmans.

Wesley, John. 1872. *A Plain Account of Christian Perfection*. Repr., Kansas City: Beacon Hill, 1971.

Wesley, Luke. 2004. *The Church in China: Persecuted, Pentecostal, and Powerful*. Baguio City, Philippines: Asia Journal of Pentecostal Studies.

Wessels, Cletus. 2003. *Jesus in the New Universe Story*. Maryknoll, N.Y.: Orbis.

Westhelle, Vitor. 2012. *Eschatology and Space: The Lost Dimension in Theology Past and Present*. New York: Palgrave Macmillan.

Whiston, William. 1991. *The Works of Josephus: Complete and Unabridged*. New updated ed. Peabody, Mass.: Hendrickson.

Whitacre, Rodney A. 1999. *John*. IVP New Testament Commentary Series 4. Downers Grove, Ill.: InterVarsity.

Whorton, Mark S. 2005. *Peril in Paradise: Theology, Science, and the Age of the Earth*. Milton Keynes, U.K.: Authentic Media.

Wiens, Delbert. 1995. *Stephen's Sermon and the Structure of Luke-Acts*. North Richland Hills, Tex.: BIBAL.

Wiley, Tatha. 2002. *Original Sin: Origins, Developments, Contemporary Meanings*. Mahwah, N.J.: Paulist.

Williams, D. H. 2005. *Evangelicals and Tradition: The Formative Influence of the Early Church*. Grand Rapids: Baker Academic.

Williams, J. Rodman. 1996. *Renewal Theology: Systematic Theology from a Charismatic Perspective*. 3 vols. Grand Rapids: Zondervan.

Williams, Norman Powell. 1927. *The Ideas of the Fall and of Original Sin: A Historical and Critical Study*. London: Longmans, Green.

Williams, Patricia A. 2001. *Doing without Adam and Eve: Sociobiology and Original Sin*. Minneapolis: Fortress.

Williamson, Clark M. 1993. *A Guest in the House of Israel: Post-Holocaust Church Theology*. Louisville, Ky: Westminster John Knox.

Williamson, Lamar, Jr. 1971. *God's Work of Art: Images of the Church in Ephesians*. Richmond: CLC/M. E. Bratcher.

Wilson, Alistair I. 2004. *When Will These Things Happen? A Study of Jesus as Judge in Matthew 21–25*. Milton Keynes, U.K.: Paternoster.

Wilson, Jonathan R. 2001. *God So Loved the World: A Christology for Disciples*. Grand Rapids: Baker Academic.

Wilson, Mark. 2007. *The Victor Sayings in the Book of Revelation*. Eugene, Ore.: Wipf & Stock.

Wilson, Stephen G. 1973. *The Gentiles and the Gentile Mission in Luke-Acts*. Cambridge: Cambridge University Press.

———. 1995. *Related Strangers: Jews and Christians, 70–170 C.E.* Minneapolis: Fortress.

Wink, Walter. 1968. *John the Baptist in the Gospel Tradition*. Cambridge: Cambridge University Press.

———. 1998. *The Powers That Be: Theology for a New Millennium*. New York: Doubleday.

Witherington, Ben III. 1992. *Jesus, Paul, and the End of the World: A Comparative Study in New Testament Eschatology*. Downers Grove, Ill.: InterVarsity.

———. 2007. *Troubled Waters: Rethinking the Theology of Baptism*. Waco, Tex.: Baylor University Press.

Wolterstorff, Nicholas. 1995. *Divine Discourse: Philosophical Reflections on the Claim That God Speaks*. Cambridge: Cambridge University Press.

Wood, A. Skevington. 1963. *Paul's Pentecost: Studies in the Life of the Spirit from Romans 8*. Exeter: Paternoster.

Wood, Laurence W. 1980. *Pentecostal Grace*. Wilmore, Ky.: Francis Asbury.

Woodward, Kenneth L. 2000. *The Book of Miracles: The Meaning of Miracle Stories in Christianity, Judaism, Buddhism, Hinduism, Islam*. New York: Simon & Schuster.

Work, Telford. 2002. *Living and Active: Scripture in the Economy of Salvation*. Grand Rapids: Eerdmans.

Wright, David F., ed. 2000. *Baptism: Three Views*. Downers Grove, Ill.: IVP Academic.

Wright, N. T. 2008. *Surprised by Hope: Rethinking Heaven, the Resurrection, and the Mission of the Church*. New York: HarperOne.

Wright, Terry J. 2009. *Providence Made Flesh: Divine Presence as a Framework for a Theology of Providence*. Milton Keynes, U.K.: Paternoster.

Wu, Dongsheng John. 2012. *Understanding Watchman Nee: Spirituality, Knowledge, and Formation*. Eugene, Ore.: Wipf & Stock.

Wulfhorst, Ingo, ed. 2005. *Ancestors, Spirits and Healing in Africa and Asia: A Challenge to the Church*. Geneva: Lutheran World Federation.

Wyckoff, John W. 2010. *Pneuma and Logos: The Role of the Spirit in Biblical Hermeneutics*. Eugene, Ore.: Wipf & Stock.

Wynkoop, Mildred Bangs. 1972. *A Theology of Love: The Dynamic of Wesleyanism*. Kansas City, Mo.: Beacon Hill.

Yee, Tet-Lim N. 2005. *Jews, Gentiles, and Ethnic Reconciliation: Paul's Jewish Identity and Ephesians.* Cambridge: Cambridge University Press.

Yoder, John Howard. 2001. *Body Politics: Five Practices of the Christian Community before the Watching World.* Scottdale, Pa.: Herald.

Yong, Amos. 2002. *Spirit-Word–Community: Theological Hermeneutics in Trinitarian Perspective.* Aldershot, U.K.: Ashgate.

———. 2003. *Beyond the Impasse: Toward a Pneumatological Theology of Religions.* Grand Rapids: Baker Academic.

———. 2005. *The Spirit Poured Out on All Flesh: Pentecostalism and the Possibility of Global Theology.* Grand Rapids: Baker Academic.

———. 2007. *Theology and Down Syndrome: Reimagining Disability in Late Modernity.* Waco, Tex.: Baylor University Press.

———. 2008. *Hospitality and the Other: Pentecost, Christian Practices, and the Neighbor.* Maryknoll, N.Y.: Orbis.

———, ed. 2009. *The Spirit Renews the Face of the Earth: Pentecostal Forays in Science and Theology of Creation.* Eugene, Ore.: Pickwick.

———. 2010. *In the Days of Caesar: Pentecostalism and Political Theology.* Grand Rapids: Eerdmans.

———. 2011a. *Who Is the Holy Spirit? A Walk with the Apostles.* Brewster, Mass.: Paraclete.

———. 2011b. *The Bible, Disability, and the Church: A New Vision of the People of God.* Grand Rapids: Eerdmans.

———. 2011c. *Spirit of Creation: Modern Science and Divine Action in the Pentecostal-Charismatic Imagination.* Grand Rapids: Eerdmans.

———. 2012. *Spirit of Love: A Trinitarian Theology of Grace.* Waco, Tex.: Baylor University Press.

———. 2014a. *The Dialogical Spirit: Christian Reason and Theological Method for the Third Millennium.* Eugene, Ore.: Cascade Books.

———. 2014b. *The Missiological Spirit: Christian Mission Theology for the Third Millennium Global Context.* Eugene, Ore.: Cascade Books.

York, John V. 2000. *Mission in the Age of the Spirit.* Springfield, Mo.: Logion.

Young, Katherine K., and Paul Nathanson. 2010. *Sanctifying Misandry: Goddess Ideology and the Fall of Man.* Montreal: McGill-Queen's University Press.

Yun, Koo Dong. 2003. *Baptism in the Holy Spirit: An Ecumenical Theology of Spirit Baptism.* Lanham, Md.: University Press of America.

———. 2012. *The Holy Spirit and Ch'i (Qi): A Chiological Approach to Pneumatology.* Eugene, Ore.: Pickwick.

Zuesse, Evan M. 1979. *Ritual Cosmos: The Sanctification of Life in African Religions.* Athens: Ohio University Press.

Scripture Index

Old Testament

Genesis

1	260
1:1	261, 293
1:2	261, 278
1:4	260
1:10	260
1:12	260
1:16-27	255
1:18	260
1:21	260, 261
1:24	261
1:25	260, 261
1:26	291
1:26-28	53
1:27	271, 272, 283
1:30	283
1:31	260
2	248
2:7	265, 283
2:8-14	260
2:10	249
2:16-17	264
2:17	255, 284
3	106, 264, 280
3:1	264
3:3	260
3:6	255
3:16	260, 265
3:17-19	260
3:17-18	257, 265, 280
3:19	265
3:20	265

3:23-24	106
3:24	260
4:10	281
4:11	291
9:1-17	321
9:12-17	172
12:3	321
18:1	13
18:7-8	14
49:24	3
50:2	219
50:20	252

Exodus

2:23	341
4:22	134
7:10-12	200
7:22	200
24:10	47

Leviticus

19:18	290
21:16-24	223

Numbers

14:34	134

Deuteronomy

2:7	341
4:2	344
6:4	293, 298
12:32	344
21:22-23	249
28:21-22	204
28:27-29	204
28:35	204
28:58-61	204

29:18	120
29:29	259
1 Kings	
6:20	331
2 Chronicles	
3:4–8	331
Job	
34:14–15	288
38–41	268
Psalms	
1:3	120
2:7	134
22:3	291
23	340, 341
23:1	3
50:1	291
52:8	120
77:20	341
78	341
78:52–53	341
78:70–71	4
79:13	341
80:7–19	21, 281
104:29–30	288
104:30	14
115:3–8	212
135:15–18	212
Proverbs	
11:28–30	120
Song of Songs	
2:2	281
Isaiah	
2:3–4	232
7:14	106, 293
9:2	71
9:6	13
11:2	63
14:9–21	265
29:18	213
32:15	288
35:3–10	213
40:3	132
40:11	3
42:1–4	134
42:17–20	212
49:6	4
53:3–5	217
53:4–5	193

53:6–10	234
56:3–5	226
59:21	100
61:1	237
64:1	134
65	196
65:4	196
66:1–2	164
66:1	40
Jeremiah	
2:21	21, 281
15:16	329
23:1–8	4
31:10	3
31:33–34	245
Ezekiel	
1:4–28	47
1:26–28	47
2:8–3:3	329
28:12–19	265
34	4
36:24–27	125
36:26–27	245
37:1–14	245
41:4	331
Daniel	
12:2	38
12:4	346
12:9	346
Hosea	
10:1	281
10:1–2	21
10:8	281
Jonah	
1:3	297
4	297
4:5–11	297
Zechariah	
10:2–3	4
Malachi	
4:5–6	237

New Testament

Matthew	
1:3	314
1:5	314
1:6	314
1:18	104

1:19	105	10:1-12	210
1:20-23	311	10:1	209
1:20	104	10:3	112, 312
2:1	314	10:4	255
2:11	311	10:5	313
2:13-20	104	10:18	313
3:3	132	10:28	39
3:4	132	10:42	161, 317
3:8	134	11:2-5	213
3:11	93, 132, 312	11:7	132
3:15	132	11:27	311
3:16-17	293, 310	12:18	312
3:16	154, 312	12:18-21	314
4:1	257, 312	12:22	204
4:15	314	12:28	45, 210, 312
4:18	81	12:31	246
4:19	144	12:32	312
4:25	315	13:31-33	35
5:3-10	315	13:40	38
5:13-16	325	14:3-5	132
5:17	312, 313	14:33	311
5:46	315	15:1-13	144
5:47	315	15:15	82
5:48	87, 113	15:21-28	315
6:5	315	15:25	311
6:6	13	16:15	241
6:7-8	315	16:17	81
6:31-32	315	16:18-19	83
7:13-14	315	16:18	184, 350
7:15-19	120	16:23	258
7:19	38	17:1	328
7:21-23	52, 75, 316	17:24	83
7:21	183	18:1	316
7:24-28	316	18:3	316
8:2	311	18:10	316
8:10	314	18:12-14	4
8:14-15	82	18:14	316
8:16-17	193	18:20	159, 183
8:17	217	18:21-22	187
8:20	107	18:21	82
9:2	311	19:14	316
9:7	213	19:16	316
9:8-10:21	213	19:19	290
9:9	112, 312	19:21	316
9:17-19	316	19:24	316
9:18-26	311	19:26	316
9:18	311	19:27	82
9:32-33	204	19:30	316

20:1-16	313	Mark	
20:16	255	1:1	211
20:20-21	327	1:2-9	237
20:20	311	1:3	132
20:28	235	1:4	132, 134
21:16	311	1:6	132
21:28-44	313	1:7	133
21:43	168	1:8	93, 211
22:1-14	313	1:10-12	194
22:14	255	1:10-11	134
22:43	312	1:10	154
23:1-39	313	1:11	134
24	34	1:12-13	134
24:1-2	162	1:14-15	211
24:3-25	312	1:19-20	327
24:12	34,170	1:21-28	209
24:14	35, 36, 313	1:21	81
25:1-30	313	1:29	81
25:1-13	50	1:29-34	209
25:31-46	53, 221, 290, 315, 316	1:29-31	82
25:34-40	184	1:31	211
25:34	285	1:32-34	209
25:40	317	1:40-45	209
25:41	38, 40	2:1-12	209
25:45	317	3:1-5	209
25:46	38	3:10	134
26:14-16	256	3:14	134
26:17-30	140	3:17	328
26:26-27	140	3:19	255
26:26	142	3:23-26	200
26:28	142	3:29	246
26:33-35	82	4:24	210
26:40	82	4:35-41	209
26:47	257	4:35	194
26:50	256	5:1-20	193
26:64	47	5:1-17	195
27:3-5	257	5:1	194
27:3	258	5:2	194
27:5	258	5:3-4	194
27:6-10	256	5:5	194
27:24	257	5:7	194
28:9	311	5:9	194
28:17	311	5:10	194
28:18	47, 213, 311	5:13	194
28:19	3, 131, 136, 154, 293, 299, 310, 312	5:14	194
		5:15	195, 197
28:19-20	161	5:17	195
		5:18	195

5:20	194, 197	1:7	58
5:21-43	209	1:13	58
5:37	328	1:15	57, 132
6:3	104	1:16-17	132
6:5-6	209	1:16	95
6:7	209	1:18	58
6:12-13	210	1:25	58
6:17-18	132	1:26	103
6:30-44	209	1:28	124
6:45-52	209	1:29	104, 105
6:56	209	1:30	106
7:24	210	1:31	105
7:24-30	209, 315	1:32-33	60
7:31-37	209	1:35	57, 80, 95, 104, 107, 239
8:1-9	209	1:37	104
8:11-12	210	1:38	104, 106
8:22-26	209	1:39	104
8:31	314	1:40	59
9:2	328	1:41	58
9:14-32	204, 209	1:42-45	59
9:33-37	316	1:43	60
9:48	38	1:46-55	103
10:35-37	327	1:48-52	58
10:38-39	158	1:48	104
10:45	213, 235	1:50	104
10:46-52	209	1:51-53	104
11:20-30	237	1:54	95
11:24-25	210	1:67	95
12:31	290	1:76-79	132
13:1-2	162	1:77	45, 187
13:3	82, 328	1:79	71
14:10-11	256	1:80	131
14:12-26	140	2:19	106
14:21	258	2:32	48
14:33	328	2:35	106
14:36	215	2:38	48
14:53-65	257	2:41-50	104
14:67	84	2:48-51	106
14:68	84	2:51	106
14:71	84	3-4	239
15:39	144	3:1-3	132
16:7	82	3:4	60, 132
16:8	214	3:6	48
16:9-20	214	3:7	48, 132
16:17-18	214	3:12-14	132
Luke		3:16	80, 93, 133
1:5	131	3:19	132
1:6	58	3:22	154

4:1	239	15:3-7	4
4:14-19	239	17:20-21	46
4:18-19	95	17:28-35	48
4:18	45, 213, 237	18:10-14	226
4:19	48	18:18-30	226
4:38-39	82	18:28	82
4:38	211	19:1-10	226
4:39	211	19:3	223
5:1	81	19:4	224
5:2-3	81	19:6	224
5:8	84	19:7	224, 226
5:34-35	50	19:8	224
6:16	255	19:9	223, 226
6:19	227	19:11	47
7:1-10	315	20:3-6	159
7:21-22	213	20:35-36	48
7:24-25	132	21:5-6	162
7:29	132	21:8	47
8:45	82	21:12	49
8:51	82, 328	21:14	48
9:1	209	21:23	48
9:2	198	21:24	167
9:28	328	21:28	48
9:46-48	316	22:3	256
9:49-55	328	22:4	256
9:58	107	22:7-23	140
10:9	46, 198	22:14-20	131
10:11	46	22:19	142
10:12-16	48	22:28-30	48
10:18	265	22:28-29	168
10:20	48	22:29-30	51
10:21	239	22:31-32	82
10:27	250, 290	22:50	226
11:2	49	22:69	47
11:13	49	23:34	244
11:20	45, 210	24:35	158
11:31-32	48	24:47	3, 45
11:48	96	24:48	96
12:5	48	24:49	81, 83
12:10	246	24:50-51	45
12:40	48	John	
12:41	82	1:1	239
12:46	48	1:2	288
12:48	316	1:4	21, 239
13:18-21	49	1:9	321
13:28-30	48	1:14	141
14:14	48	1:15	133
14:15-24	48	1:18	13

1:19-26	133	9:3	219
1:29	218	9:22	122
1:31	148	9:37	213
1:32-34	154	10:1-21	4
1:33	93	10:10	4, 21, 188, 323
1:40	81	10:18	256
1:42	81	10:30	239, 298
1:44	81	12:6	255
2:1-5	107	12:12	256
3:1	149	12:24	268
3:3	149	12:29	255
3:5-6	149, 223	12:42	122
3:8	74, 184	13	151
3:16	39, 101, 122	13:2	148, 256
3:23	132	13:3	153
3:25	148	13:4-5	151
3:26-28	133	13:8	150, 153
3:26	132	13:9	153
3:30	133, 218	13:12-15	153
4:1-2	132	13:14-15	150
4:2	149	13:17	158
4:13-14	149	13:18	256
4:21-24	164	13:23	328
5:1	150	13:27-29	148
5:7	150	13:30	256
5:14	204, 224	13:34-35	123, 158
5:26	21	13:35	183
5:28-29	29, 38	14:1-3	29
6:5-13	149	14:2	13, 29
6:8	81	14:6	338
6:25-69	149	14:12	198
6:25-59	140	14:26	293
6:35	149	14:28	239
6:40	150	14:29	298
6:48	149	15	20
6:51	149	15:1	21
6:52	149	15:4	21
6:53-58	149	15:6	38
6:60	149	15:9	21
6:63	150	15:10	21
6:64	255	15:12	21
6:70	148, 258	15:17	21
7:37	150	16:2	122
7:38	101	16:8-11	293
7:39	150	16:15	183
8:44-52	147	17:12	258
8:44	148	17:24	285
9:1-2	224	19:25	103

19:26-27	328	2:33	45, 93, 94, 183
19:27	104	2:36	45
19:34	281	2:37-38	136
19:39	314	2:38	30, 45, 132, 154, 299, 318
20:2	83, 328	2:39	48, 101, 343
20:21-23	250	2:42	140
20:22	157	2:46	140, 158
20:23	157, 187	2:47	187
20:26	53	3:1-6	82
20:28	239	3:6	82
20:31	151, 239	3:13	256
21:3	81	3:15	45, 96
21:7	328	3:19	45
21:18-23	82	3:20-21	48
21:20	328	3:21	16
21:23	328	3:25	48, 163
Acts		4:2	45
1-2	70	4:8	82
1:5	80, 93	4:10	45
1:6	164, 227	4:12	307
1:7	49	4:13	81
1:8	1, 4, 48, 49, 67, 73, 80, 81,	4:31	100
	92, 95, 96, 107, 159	4:33	45
1:9	45, 293	5:1-11	82
1:11	47, 48	5:15	82
1:14	104, 107	5:16	198
1:15	82	5:30	60, 249
1:18-20	256	5:31	45
1:18	258	5:32	96
2	70, 84, 88	5:34	30
2:1-4	81, 92	6:1	161
2:1	67	6:3	161
2:2	128	6:5	161
2:3	99	6:8	161
2:4	82, 97, 99, 107	6:9	30, 162
2:5-41	128	6:13-15	162
2:11	71, 98, 232	7	162, 165
2:12	91	7:2-53	162
2:14-36	84	7:2	162
2:17-18	45, 58, 64, 76, 101, 174	7:4	162
2:17	45, 48, 183, 321	7:6	162
2:20	48	7:16	162
2:22	293	7:22	162
2:23	256	7:23	162, 163
2:27	45	7:27-28	163
2:29-36	30	7:29-30	162, 163
2:31	45	7:39-40	163
2:32	45, 96	7:46	162

7:48-50	164	11:14-17	81
7:48	169	11:15-17	92
7:51	164	11:16	93
7:55-56	45	11:26	1
7:55	100, 164	13:26-37	30
7:56	30, 47	13:31	96
7:57-60	30	13:38	30
7:57-58	162	13:47	4
7:58	96, 164	13:52	100
8	162	14:17	325
8:1	30, 164	14:22	49
8:15-19	81	14:34-35	76
8:16	132, 154, 299	15	82
8:20-23	82	15:14-17	168
8:26-40	1, 293	15:16-17	48
9	70	15:19-21	181
9:13	30	15:28	353
9:21	30	17:3	30
9:29	165	17:6	58, 73
9:32-42	82	17:18	30
9:43	82	17:26	262
10	88, 297	17:28	325
10:1	294	17:31	30, 48
10:2	294	18:24–19:1	132
10:3-7	294	19:1-7	81, 88
10:4	295	19:2	92
10:6	82	19:5	132, 154, 299
10:7	294	19:5-6	159
10:9-16	295	19:6	92
10:11-13	296	22:3	30
10:14	82, 296	22:4	30
10:15	297	22:6-8	30
10:17	297	22:6	30, 31
10:22	294	22:20	164
10:25	294	23:6	30
10:28	84, 295, 297	24:15	30
10:31	295	24:21	30
10:32	82	24:25	48
10:34-35	295, 297	25:19	30
10:34	58, 76	26:6-8	30
10:38	45, 134, 198, 227, 239, 293	26:10-11	30
10:39	60, 96, 249	26:12-15	30
10:43	45	26:13	30, 31
10:44-48	295	26:18	30
10:44-45	92	26:23	30
10:46	294	26:28	1
10:47-48	131, 159	28:20	30
10:48	132, 154, 299	28:23-28	166

Romans		8:1-17	278
1:4	45, 244, 275, 314	8:1-2	103
1:20	274, 275	8:5-6	120
1:21	275	8:11	32, 45, 94, 244, 275, 314, 323
1:22-23	275	8:13	103
1:23	279	8:14-16	293
1:24	40	8:18-28	53
2:1	275	8:18-25	278
2:12-16	290	8:18-22	125
2:12-15	321	8:19	288
2:17-29	275	8:20-21	278
3:9	275	8:20	278
3:10	275	8:22-23	206, 231
3:23	125, 247	8:23	98, 277
3:25-26	234	8:26-27	278
4	275	8:28	207
4:17	275	8:29-30	228
4:18	275	8:29	274
4:19	275	8:34	47
4:25	248, 256, 275	8:39	41
5	276, 277, 279	9–11	276
5:5	15, 101, 277, 278	10:8-15	223
5:6	275	10:9-14	307
5:8	275	10:14	187
5:9	277	11:7-10	166
5:10	275, 277	11:11	189
5:12-21	41	11:13-24	168
5:12-19	255	11:17-24	180
5:12-17	235	11:25-29	168
5:12-14	260	11:25	166
5:12	275	11:26	36, 166
5:14	276, 277	11:33	16
5:15	277	11:36	41
5:17	277	12	76
5:18-21	277	12:1-2	103, 124, 279
6:1-11	103, 138	12:5	71
6:1-4	138, 157	12:6-8	71
6:3	138	12:9-21	279
6:4-5	32, 138	12:9	71
6:4	131, 277	12:10-21	71
6:6	139	12:11	248
6:11	21, 139	12:14	248
6:13-14	139	13:1-7	279
6:15–7:25	277	13:8-14	279
6:23	244	13:9	290
7:4	32	13:11	219, 279
7:6	277	13:20	248
8	229, 277, 278, 279	14	279

14:11	41	13:8	71
14:17-18	161	13:12	54, 72, 213
16:26	3	13:13	71
1 Corinthians		14	77, 92, 98
1:7	32	14:1	71
1:17	72	14:3	71
1:18–2:5	73	14:5	71
1:18-31	249	14:12	71
1:20-23	183	14:17	71
1:26	69	14:26	71
1:31	73	14:27	72
2:4-5	335	14:29-31	76
2:9-16	74	14:29	72, 354
3:12-15	40, 126, 290	14:31	71
3:16	94, 169	14:33	75
4:20	161	14:40	75
6:2	51	15	72
6:14	32	15:3-5	238
6:19	169	15:3	234
7:29	32	15:4	238, 293
8:6	14	15:12-19	30
11:7	272	15:12	72
11:17-34	140	15:20	37
11:20-34	131	15:21-22	260
11:23	154	15:22-24	29
11:24-25	142, 143	15:22	235
11:24	140	15:24-25	251
11:26	144	15:28	38, 293, 323
11:33-34	158	15:31	126
12	57, 69, 72, 76, 92, 221	15:35-49	54
12:3	72, 183	15:43-54	285
12:4-6	69	15:45-49	126
12:4	61	15:45	235, 277
12:7	61	15:49	283
12:8-10	61	15:50-56	32
12:11	58, 61, 69	15:50	285
12:12-31	181	15:54	55
12:12	208	2 Corinthians	
12:13	172, 180	3:6	352
12:22-24	208	4:4	200, 274
12:22	73	4:14	32
12:23	73	5:1-5	37
12:24	69, 73	5:1	13
12:25	73	5:4	55
12:28	61	5:5	278
12:31–13:3	69	5:15	32
12:31	61, 71	5:17	21, 112, 126
13:2-3	71	5:21	293

6:14–17	169	2:12–13	180
6:16	169	2:14–17	180
7:1	113	2:18	179
11:3	265	2:19–20	180
11:14	200	2:20	174
11:30	73	2:21–22	179
12:5	73	2:22	94, 161, 166
12:7–10	208	3:5	180
12:9–10	73	3:6	180
13:4	73	3:10	179, 182
13:9	73, 113	3:18–19	181
13:13	123	3:20	181
Galatians		4	72, 76
1:13	30	4:1–6	172
2:11–14	85	4:3	181
2:11–13	295	4:5–6	181
2:14	165	4:5	7
2:20	103, 126	4:7–10	41, 237
3:13	14, 60, 249	4:8–11	181
3:26–27	138	4:10	188
3:27–28	139	4:11–13	57, 161
3:27	21	4:11	165, 174
3:28	101, 181	4:12–15	181
4:4	313	4:12	71
5:14	290	4:15	179
5:25	98	4:16	181
6:7–9	53	4:17–24	181
6:8	120	4:24	112
Ephesians		4:25–5:20	181
1:1	179	4:30	179
1:3	179	4:32	187
1:4	181, 285	5:18	98, 181
1:6	181	5:21	182
1:7	187	5:22–33	50
1:9–10	179	5:23	183
1:10–11	188	5:30	181
1:10	41	6:9	182
1:12	181	6:12	147, 182, 188
1:13	86, 179, 278	Philippians	
1:18–19	181	1:28	39
1:20–21	179	2:5–8	73
1:20	47	2:8	249
1:21–23	41	2:10–11	41
1:22–23	161, 179	2:12–13	97
2	180	2:15	188
2:1	125	3:5–6	29
2:8–9	338	3:10–11	33
2:11–12	180	3:19	39

3:20-21	32	3:4-7	228
Colossians		3:5	137
1:15	13, 112, 155, 274	Hebrews	
1:16-20	288	1:1-3	242
1:20	41, 172, 232, 249, 251, 323	1:1-2	62, 337
1:27	29	1:2-3	243, 249
2:9	298	1:3	13, 112, 155, 243, 244
2:11-13	138	1:4–2:13	242
2:12	157	1:13	244
3:1	47	2:1-4	246
3:3-4	138	2:2	246
3:5	126	2:5	246
3:10	112	2:9	244
3:11	182	2:10	243
3:17	27, 39	2:14-15	244
1 Thessalonians		2:14	243
1:10	32	2:17	234, 243
3:13	32	3	242
4:11-12	325	3:7–4:11	245
4:13-18	32	3:7	246
4:14-17	36	3:8	245
4:15-17	29, 32	3:13	246
5:16-18	113	3:15	245, 246
5:23	271	4:1-14	242
2 Thessalonians		4:6	246
1:9	39	4:7	246
2:3	170, 258	4:11	246
2:9	200, 258	4:12	336
1 Timothy		4:14–5:10	242
1:13	30	4:15	132, 243
2:2	325	5:1-3	243
2:6	235	5:7	243
2:13-14	272	5:8	243
2:26	235	5:9	125, 246
3:16	45	6:1	87, 113
4:10	234	6:4-8	246
6:16	13, 38	6:4	246
2 Timothy		6:5	246
3:1-5	170	6:8	38
3:8	200	6:9	242
3:15-17	327	6:13-20	242
3:16-17	334	7	242
4:20	209	7:9-10	287
Titus		7:16	244
2:7-8	188	7:18	243
2:11	223	7:19	242
2:13	29	7:22	242
3:3-7	223	7:25-26	293

7:25	244	12:29	38, 246
7:27	243	13:1–8	246
8	242	13:12	243
8:1	47, 244	13:14	246
8:6	242	13:20	4
8:8–13	125	James	
8:8	243	2:8	290
8:10	245	3	97
8:13	243	3:1	97
9	242	3:5–8	98
9:6–7	243	3:9–10	98
9:9	244	3:12	20
9:11–12	246	5:7	32
9:12	243	5:9	51
9:14	125, 244, 249	5:14–16	193, 204
9:22	243	1 Peter	
9:23–28	243	1:1–2	96
9:23	242	1:2	293
9:24	244	1:15	112
9:26	243	1:18	235
9:27	41	1:19	16
9:28	32, 243, 246	1:20	285
10:1–18	242	1:21	327
10:4	243	2:11–12	325
10:10–14	123	2:12–20	188
10:10	103, 243	2:20–25	96
10:12	243, 244	2:21	251
10:14	103, 243	2:22	293
10:15–18	245	2:24	14, 60, 216, 249
10:19	243	2:25	4
10:26–39	246	3:14	96
10:27	38, 246	3:18–20	41
10:29	246	3:18	45, 234
10:34	242	3:19	157
10:39	39	3:22	47
11	242	4	76
11:6	246	4:1	96
11:10	245	4:6	41
11:16	242, 245	4:7	72
11:35	242	4:10–11	72
11:40	242	4:12–19	96
12:1–17	246	4:16	1
12:2	47, 244, 245	5:7–10	96
12:5–11	40	5:14	126
12:17	258	2 Peter	
12:22	245	1:19–21	343
12:24	242, 243	3:3–9	50
12:25–29	246	3:7	39

3:10	291	5:19	156, 235
3:11-12	32	2 John	
1 John		1	328
1:1-3	328	3 John	
1:1	150	1	328
1:8	118	5–8	126
1:9	118	Jude	
1:10	118	6	38
2:1-2	118	Revelation	
2:2	122, 234	1:1	328, 344
2:4	119	1:2	344
2:5	113, 119	1:3	329, 345
2:9-10	119	1:4-5	344
2:10	119	1:4	328, 344
2:16	126	1:8	50, 178
2:20-27	119	1:9	329
3:2-3	29, 51, 118, 350	1:10-11	345
3:2	75	1:10	329
3:6	118	1:11	344
3:8-10	118	1:12	345
3:8	148	1:13	344
3:9	118	1:17-18	344
3:10	148	1:17	328
3:11	119	1:19	344, 345
3:12	148	1:20	177, 345
3:14	119	2–3	346
3:15	119	2:4	170
3:16-17	126	2:7	14, 60, 346
3:16	119	2:11	346
3:18	119	2:17	346
3:23	119	2:29	346
3:24	119	3:1	170, 344
4:1-6	119	3:2	113
4:2-3	148	3:6	346
4:7	119	3:10	36
4:8	119	3:13	346
4:11-12	119	3:15-16	170
4:12	87	3:20	51
4:13	119	3:22	346
4:16	119	4:1	345, 346
4:17	87, 119	4:2-3	47
4:18	113, 148	4:2	329
4:19	119	4:5	344
4:20	119	4:6–6:8	47
5:1	119, 223	4:6-8	322
5:2	119	4:6	322
5:16-21	126	4:8	323
5:18	118	4:9-10	323

4:11	323
5:1	345
5:5	345
5:6	16, 344, 345
5:9-13	17
5:9	98, 235
5:13	323
6:9	344
6:10	345
7:4	345
7:9-14	17
7:9	330, 347
7:11	47
7:14	36
7:15-16	4, 17
7:17	4, 16, 17
9:16	345
10:10	329
10:11	347
11:7-9	347
12	264
12:3-4	265
12:9	264, 265
13:8	256, 285
13:18	259
14:3	47
14:11	38
15:2	344
15:5	345
15:7	47
16:7	345
17:3	329
17:8	285
17:15	347
19	34
19:1	345
19:4	47
19:6-7	323
19:6	345
19:7-8	50
19:10	344
19:11	345

20	34
20:1-6	29
20:1-3	264
20:2	265
20:4	344
20:10-15	29
20:10	38
20:11-12	345
20:12	53
21–22	75
21:1-5	345
21:1	347
21:2-5	47
21:2-3	164
21:2	50
21:3	330
21:4	164
21:5	55
21:8	53
21:9	50
21:10	53, 329
21:12	330
21:15	330
21:16	331
21:24	347
21:26	98, 347
21:27	53
22	248
22:1-2	347
22:1	17
22:2	219
22:4	213
22:5	355
22:7	329
22:8	328, 345
22:10	329
22:13	50
22:14-15	53
22:14	60
22:17	17, 55
22:18-19	344

Index of Names

Abelard, 235–36
Adeyemo, Tokunboh, 24, 150
Aitchison, Craigie, 280
Albrecht, Daniel, 158
Alexander, Denis, 262, 269
Althouse, Peter F., 50
Anderson, Allan H., 5–6, 175, 305
Angelico, Fra, 105
Anselm, 234–35
Appollinarius of Laodicea, 240
Aquinas, Thomas, 7, 109–10, 126
Archer, Kenneth J., 145, 335–36, 352
Aristotle, 110
Arrington, French L., 9–10, 71–72, 190
Arthur, William, 87
Augustine, 34–35, 109, 261, 273, 275

Barth, Karl, 8, 12, 14, 41, 189, 217–18,
    258, 274, 276, 305, 308, 358
Bauckham, Richard, 122, 347
Beatus of Liébana, 330
Begbie, Jeremy, 304
Beker, J. Christiaan, 32
Bernard, David K., 172, 298–99
Bevans, Stephen B., 6
Blocher, Henri, 276
Bloesch, Donald G., 56, 343, 355
Blount, Brian K., 24, 149, 188, 212, 329
Boethius, 302
Bosch, David J., 190
Branham, William Marion, 198
Bundy, David, 5
Burgess, Stanley M., 62, 130
Byrne, Kati, 231

Calvin, John, 8, 64, 86, 110, 142, 234
Cano Villalobos, Mandy, 54
Caravaggio, Michelangelo Merisi da, 31,
    111–12
Carter, J. Kameron, 2
Cartledge, Mark J., 62, 102
Chinnawong, Sawai, 66
Cleary, Edward L., 5
Clifton, Shane, 184

Clooney, Francis X., 308
Cohn-Sherbok, Dan, 167–68
Conrad of Hirsau, 120
Constantine, 2, 34, 109, 170, 199
Conzelmann, Hans, 44
Coppo di Marcovaldo, 39
Cox, Harvey, 68, 304

Dawn, Marva J., 74, 220, 291
Dayton, Donald W., 15, 87, 198
D'Costa, Gavin, 41, 309
De Arteaga, William L., 144
Descartes, René, 302
DeYoung, Curtiss Paul, 24
Dulles, Avery, 182, 336–37
Dunn, James D. G., 91, 167
Dyck, Anthony van, 79

Enns, Peter, 276, 332
Erickson, Millard, 8
Ermengau, Matfre, of Béziers, 303
Ervin, Howard M., 91, 140, 215
Eyck, Hubert van, 16
Eyck, Jan van, 16

Fackre, Gabriel, 25, 355
Farley, Edward, 19
Faupel, David W., 383
Fee, Gordon D., 48, 91, 190, 344, 346
Finger, Thomas N., 15
Finney, Charles Grandison, 86–87
Fletcher, John, 88
Fouquet, Jean, 127

García-Johnson, Oscar, 6
Gelpi, Donald L., 155, 157, 253
Gifford, Paul, 5
Gordon, A. J., 86
Green, Chris E. W., 154
Green, Joel B., 25, 253
Gregory of Nyssa, 301
Grenz, Stanley J., 34, 342
Grudem, Wayne, 10, 80, 221
Grünewald, Matthias, 217

Guthrie, Steven R., 100
Gutiérrez, Gustavo, 231

Hart, Larry, 10
Hawkinson, Tim, 90, 185
Heim, S. Mark, 244, 309
Hippolytus, 136–37
Hocken, Peter D., 167, 170, 184, 189
Hodge, Charles, 8
Hollenweger, Walter J., 5, 331
Honthorst, Gerrit van, 83
Horton, Stanley M., 10
Hunter, Harold D., 91
Hurtado, Larry W., 210, 213

Irenaeus, 235, 273–74, 279, 283
Irvin, Dale T., 2

Jacobsen, Douglas G., 107
James, Laura, 313
Jenkins, Philip, 4, 336
Jennings, Willie James, 2
Jenson, Matt, 38
Jenson, Robert W., 319
Johnson, Eastman, 340
Jordaens, Jacob, 333
Josephus, 132

Kalu, Ogbu U., 178, 305, 307
Kant, Immanuel, 302
Kärkkäinen, Veli-Matti, 96, 144, 165–66,
    170, 230, 240, 305, 310, 326, 336
Kay, William K., 6, 33, 160, 174
Keener, Craig S., 97, 151, 222, 346
Kelsey, Morton T., 68, 198
Kim, Kirsteen, 188, 305–6
Kinzer, Mark S., 168
Knox, Ronald A., 65
Kroeger, Catherine Clark, 24, 242
Kuhlman, Kathryn, 198
Kydd, Ronald A. N., 62

Ladd, George Eldon, 51
Lamoureux, Denis, 270
Land, Steven J., 22
Lasworth, Laura, 280
Latourette, Kenneth Scott, 5
Lederle, Henry I., 15, 86, 89
Levison, John R., 241, 276, 283

Lindbeck, George A., 308
Lindberg, Carter, 65
Lonergan, Bernard, 341
Lord, Andy, 185
Lowly, Tim, 205
Luhrmann, T. M., 68
Luther, Martin, 110, 116

Macchia, Frank D., 50, 81, 288, 326
MacDonald, Gregory, 41
MacGregor, Geddes, 43
Mahan, Asa, 87
Maius, 332
Marshall, Molly T., 306–7
Maurus, Rabanus, 94
Mbiti, John S., 43
McClendon Jr., James William, 24
McDermott, Gerald R., 307
McDonnell, Kilian, 5, 137
McGee, Gary B., 102, 25
McGrath, Alister E., 262, 286
McKenna, John, 154
McQueen, Larry R., 15, 33
Menzies, Robert P., 57, 85
Menzies, William W., 91, 298
Michelangelo Buonarroti, 31, 111–12
Mittelstadt, Martin W., 96
Moltmann, Jürgen, 15, 56, 170, 183, 189,
    241, 288
Montague, George T., 62, 137
Moody, D. L., 86
Moreland, J. P., 271, 292
Morelli, Domenico, 257
Morris, Simon Conway, 286
Mühlen, Heribert, 77
Murphy, George L., 286
Murphy, Nancey, 283, 287
Myers, Ched, 195

Nee, Watchman, 271
Nestorius, 240, 300
Netland, Harold A., 6
Neville, Robert Cummings, 308
Newberg, Eric Nelson, 190
Niebuhr, Reinhold, 125
Noetus, 300
Noll, Mark A., 5
Northrop, Henry Davenport, 296

Oden, Thomas, 8
Ormerod, Neil J., 187, 273, 275

Palmer, Phoebe, 87
Panikkar, Raymond, 309
Pannenberg, Wolfhart, 8, 37
Parham, Charles Fox, 88, 168
Parry, Robin A., 41, 160, 320
Patte, Daniel, 24, 148, 211, 315
Pelagius, 109
Pelikan, Jaroslav, 107
Peters, Ted, 15, 44, 273, 281, 287
Phan, Peter C., 15, 176, 284
Pilch, John J., 68, 193, 210,
Pinnock, Clark H., 14, 166, 307, 309, 337
Polkinghorne, John, 44
Praxeas, 300

Qi, He, 143

Rah, Soong-Chan, 3
Raj, P. Solomon, 20
Ramsay, Allan, 270
Ratzinger, Joseph, 41
Rembrandt Harmenszoon van Rijn, 264
Robeck Jr., Cecil M., 5, 62
Roberts, Oral, 198
Rose, David, 231
Rublev, Andrej, 13, 133, 303
Ruether, Rosemary Radford, 232
Russell, Jeffrey Burton, 63
Russell, Robert John, 44

Sabellius, 300
Sanneh, Lamin O., 2, 4
Schillebeeckx, Eduard, 155
Schleiermacher, Friedrich, 8
Schmemann, Alexander, 138, 143
Segovia, Fernando F., 24, 121, 180, 246, 347
Segundo, Juan Luis, 155
Sengulane, Dinis, 231
Shelton, James B., 91
Shults, F. LeRon, 230, 274, 326, 342
Smith, James K. A., 98, 261, 268, 342
Solivan, Samuel, 22
Soulen, R. Kendall, 191
Sparks, Kenton L., 332

Stackhouse Jr., John G., 253
Stevns, Niels Larsen, 225
Stronstad, Roger, 57, 76, 92, 352
Sugirtharajah, R. S., 24, 121, 180, 246, 347
Sullivan, Francis A., 89, 182, 307
Sunquist, Scott W., 2
Suurmond, Jean Jacques, 74
Synan, Vinson, 5, 116

Taylor, John V., 14
Tennent, Timothy C., 6
Thomas, John Christopher, 151, 165, 214, 219, 329, 346, 353
Tillich, Paul, 8, 325
Tissot, James Jacques Joseph, 195
Torrey, R. A., 86
Trevett, Christine, 63
Turner, Max, 80
Twelftree, Graham H., 209

Van Dusen, Henry P., 14
Vanhoozer, Kevin J., 310, 332, 353
Vasari, Giorgio, 163
Volf, Miroslav, 154, 320
von Campenhausen, Hans, 63
Vondey, Wolfgang, 22, 158, 170, 191

Wacker, Grant, 22
Währisch-Oblau, Claudia, 3
Walls, Andrew F., 2–4
Walls, Jerry L., 38, 41, 56
Walton, John H., 284, 291
Warfield, Benjamin B., 65
Wariboko, Nimi, 74
Warrington, Keith, 6, 135, 210, 222
Watanabe, Sadao, 171
Watts, Rikki, 195–96, 343
Webb, Stephen H., 284
Welker, Michael, 44, 288
Wesley, John, 87–88, 112–13, 117–19, 125
Westhelle, Vitor, 48
Weyden, Rogier van der, 59
Williams, J. Rodman, 8–10
Wink, Walter, 131, 146
Witherington III, Ben, 48, 157
Wolffort, Artus, 348
Wolterstorff, Nicholas, 332

Wood, Laurence, 89
Wright, N. T., 38, 48, 56
Wright, Terry J., 289
Wynkoop, Mildred Bangs, 114

Yoder, John Howard, 136
Yun, Koo Dong, 89, 309

Zuesse, Evan M., 116–17
Zwingli, Huldrych, 142

Subject Index

*[Note: **bolded** pages refer to whole sub-section discussions of those subjects]*

Abel, 237
ableism, 272
abolition, 270–71, 340
Abraham, 13, 40, 162, 275, 337–38; children of, 227, 247
acupuncture, 202
Adam, 112, 120–21; first, 75, 235, 277; historical, 260, 266–67, 269–70, 276, 284, 289; second, 75, 106, 111–12, 120–21, 126, 235, 248–50, 276–77, 286
Adam and Eve, 106, 237, 260, 263–67, 269, 276, 284, 314
Adam and Eve (Rembrandt), 264
adoption, 228, 230, 233, 251
Adoration of the Mystic Lamb (Eyck), 16
Africa, 171, 178, 231–32, 306
African cultures, 116–17
Alexandrian school, 109, 240, 242
alienation, 284
altar, 13–14, 16–17, 143–44, 217
altruism, 290
amillennialism, 35–36
Amsterdam Bible, 257
Anabaptism, 35, 338
anaphora, 143
anastasis, 236–37
Anastasis (Kariye), 236
ancestors, 146, 203
ancestral spirits, 147
angels, 13–14, 16–17, 46–47, 104, 120–21, 133–34, 177–78, 296–97, 303–4, 330–31, 344–45

Anglican Church, 18, 135, 339, 343; *see also* Church of England
Anglican triad, 339, 341
animal, 269
animal predation, 263
annihilationism, 38–39
annunciation, 105–6, 280–81
Annunciation (Angelico), 105
anointing, 141, 165
anthropology, 114, 262; communal, 115; emergent, 283; medical, 210; relational, 114, 274; trinitarian, 274; *see also* theological anthropology
antichrist, 119, 148
antinomianism, 6, 65, 86
Antiochene school, 242, 300
anti-Semitism, 167, 190, 246
apocalyptic, 29, 32, 34, 37, 44, 47–48, 62, 151, 212, 246, 276, 278–79, 312, 329, 343–44, 346 apocalypticism, 48, 312
Apollo, 4
apologist, 140
apostasy, end-time, 170
apostles, 16–17, 46–47, 66–67, 70, 79–80, 90–91, 94–95, 99–100, 127–28, 143–44, 225–26, 313, 330–31, 333–34
Apostles' Creed, 7, 97, 236, 363
apostolic networks, 6, 174
apostolic succession, 63, 174
Arianism, 240, 299
Aristotelianism, 7, 109–10, 114, 140, 142, 151, 157, 272

Arminianism, 228, 234

arts, pagan, 200, 314

ascension, 39–40, 46–47, 234, 245

Ascension of Christ (Rabbula), 46

Asia, 66, 115, 171, 176, 232, 306

assurance, theology of, **85–88**

astronomy, 262

Athanasius, 299

atonement, 110, 122, 125, 216, **233–38**, 242–43, 245, 251–53; penal substitutionary theory, 234–35, 249; ransom theory, 235; satisfaction theory, 234–35

Augustinianism, 34–35, 109–10, 206, 261

authority, 39–40, 46–47, 70–71, 94–95, 111–12, 213, 348–49

ayurveda, 202

Azusa Street revival, 5, 101, 128

Babylon, 121

barrenness, 257, 163–64, 280–81

baptism, 16–17, **135–40**, 141, 151, 156–60, 165, 298, 324; of love, 71, 128; of repentance, 132, 134; theology of, 138–39; *see also* Spirit Baptism

Baptism of Christ (Rublev), 133

baptismal font, 16–17, 39, 138–39, 212–13

baptismal formula, 312

baptismal rite, 135, 137

Baptist church, 135

Baptistery of San Giovanni (Florence, Italy), 39

beatific vision, 52, 110, 126, 230

Beatitudes, 315

beauty: *see* transcendentals

begottenness, 301

benevolence, 290

betrayal, 256

biblical criticism, 335

bibliocentrism, 343

Big Bang cosmology, 44, 286–87

binitarianism, 319

biology, 262, 286

bipolar disorder, 196

blessing, 13–14, 39–40, 59–60, 94–95, 120–21, 143–44, 152–53, 195–96, 212–13, 248–49, 296–97

blindness, 31, 205, 207, 210, 212–13

blood, 16–17, 96, 103, 137, 140–43, 149,

158, 180, 223, 243–44, 249, 251, 288, 360–61

Body of Christ, 16–17, 20–21, 39–40, 46–47, 90, 94, 99–100, 143–44, **169–73**, 177–78, 185–86, 217, 248–49, 313–14

body-soul unity, 272

Book of Life, 16, 313–14

born again, 161, 166, 169, 361

breaking bread, 155, 187; *see also* Lord's Supper

Breviary of Love (Ermengau), 303

British Israelism, 168

Buddhism, 42, 66, 200, 342

call (vocational), 228

Calling of Saint Matthew (Caravaggio), 111

Canaanite woman, 314–15, 324

canon, scriptural, **336–39**, 351

Cartesianism, 272

Catacomb of Domitilla (Rome), 3

catechesis, 136, 155

Catechism of the Catholic Church, 141

Catholic apostolics, 65

causality, retroactive, 267

cessationism, 64–65, 75

charismata: *see* spiritual gifts

charismatic renewal, 5, 167, 170

charismatic spirituality, 68

charismology, 75–80; christological, 72–73; ecclesiological 75, 77 ; missiological, 77; Pauline, **69–74**

chaos theory, 266–67

childbirth, 260, 265

children, 176

China, 176

Christ Child as the Good Shepherd (Indian), 3

Christ Enthroned (James), 313

Christ Healing the Man Born Blind (Sant'Angelo), 212

Christ, presence of: *see also* Eucharist; healing, 144; memorial, 142; real, 141–42, 44; spiritual, 142; symbolic, 142

Christendom, 35, 171, 175–76

Christian Aid, 231

Christian practices, 136, 151–52, **153–60**, 182–83, 229; communicative, 159; eschatological, 159; liturgical, 351;

missional, 159, 190; pneumatology of, 158–59
Christian Science, 65, 201
christocentrism, 343
Christology, **238–42**, 297, 309, 344; African, 241; eschatological, 228; feminist, 241; high, 242, 311, 318; interreligious, 241; liberation, 115, 205, 241; Logos, 239, 241, 253; pneumatological, 228; *see also* Spirit Christology
chronic illness, 204
church, **166–69**; apostolicity, 173, 182; catholicity, 173, 182; eschatological, 174; fellowship of the Spirit, 23, 123, 125, 154–57, 166, 177, 183, 208, 216, 221, 251, 324, 351; healing community, 193; holiness, 182; and Israel, 188–89; leadership, 174; marks of, 182; mission of, **182–90**; service, 324; unity of, 170, 173, 181–82; *see also* ecclesiology
Church of Christ Scientist, 201
Church of England, 112, 338; *see also* Anglican Church
circumcision, 139
civil religiosity, 294
civil rights movement, 207
clothing, clothed, 54–55, 59–60, 111–12, 133–34, 138–39
cognitive science, 114, 272
colonialism, 2, 178, 323
come-outers, 169, 175
common good, 78
common descent, 262, 268–69
communication of attributes, 142
communion of saints, 16–17, 20–21, 39–40
comparative theology, 308
compassion, 71, 121, 161, 187–88, 199, 206, 221, 224, 230, 324, 361
concordism, 266, 269
concupiscence, 273
conditional immortality: *see* annihilationism
confession of sin, 155, 157, 219
confessions (statements), 299, 357
confirmation, 89, 137, 141
Confucianism, 342
conscience, 244, 322
contextual theology, 232, 242

contingency, 290
conversion, 31–32, 77, 87, 100, 110–12, 135, 155–56, 252, 325; of Jews, 189
Conversion of Saint Paul (Caravaggio), 31
Cornelius, 92, 159, 238, **293–97**, 315, 324, 351
corporeality, 199
"Cosmos," 70–71
cosmology, 53, 262, **279–92**; African, 117; Big Bang, 282; Einsteinian, 114; indigenous, 146; Johannine, 147; Newtonian, 114, 201; physical, 44
Council of Chalcedon, 451
Council of Constantinople, 302
Council of Ephesus, 103
Council of Nicea, 302
Council of Trent, 141, 173
covenant, 48, 167–68, 189, 243, 245, 269; Abrahamic, 48, 314, 321–22; Israel, 139, 166, 168, 180, 242, 246, 321; Mosaic, 321; old, 245
creation, **260–63**, 274; care of, 251; doctrine of, 268; goodness of, 267; materiality, 154–55; renewal of, 251, 324; temple of God, 291; theology of, 221, 266, 268, 274–75, **279–92**
Creation of Adam (Buonarroti), 111
creationism: old earth, 261–62; progressive, 269; scientific, 260; young earth, 261–62, 269, 281; *see also* evolutionary creation
Creator, 321
creedalism, 299
creeds, 338; ecumenical, 318–19
crucifixion, 143–44, 217–18, 248–49, 280–81, 256
Crucifixion (Grünewald), 217
Crusades, 323
cult of martyrs, 199
curse, 98, 105–6, 120–21, 203, 217, 249, 257, 264–65, 280–81

darkness, 31, 70–71, 83, 111–12, 138–39, 217, 236–37, 257, 264–65, 280–81
David (king), 60, 237
day-age theory, 261
Deaf culture, 207
deafness, 210

death, 39–40, 54–55, 138–39, 163–64, 231–32, 235, 244, 249, 251, 259–60, **263–68**, 271, 275, 286–90, 348–49; of Adam, 287; of animals, 276; biological, 268; cosmic, 279; legal, 279; physical, 279, 284; spiritual, 279, 284; universal, 276

deification: *see* union with God

deism, 65, 201, 263, 342

deliverance, 113, 135, **145–47**, 156, 160, **193–97**, 204, 209, 216, 239, 256, 305, 361

demoniacs, 147, 204

demonology, 39–40, 120–21, 128, 147, 194–96, 201, 210; *see also* evil spirits

demon-possession, 197

demythologization, 146

Denial of St. Peter (Honthorst), 83

denominations, 170

depravity, 110, 274, 284

Descent of the Holy Spirit (Russian), 70

desert solitaries, 199

destruction, eternal, 258, 323

determinism, 267

devil, 118, 135, 137, 145–48, 156, 159–60, 198, 220, 235, 237, 239, 244–45, 251, 257–58, 265; *see also* Satan

dialogue, 307–9, 324

Didache, 140

disability, 197, **204–8**, 212–13, 217–18, 221; ministry, 208; rights of, 207; social model of, 205; theology of, 215, 219–21; *see also* impairment; intellectual disability

discernment, 76, **145–47**, 148, 156, 160, 183, 219, 282; communal, 86; Ignatian, 146; of spirits, 61, 146–48, 160

discipleship, 21, 77, 155, 181, 213, 227, 232, 241, 253, 315–16, 324, 354

discrimination, 226

disease, 209–11, 217

dispensationalism, 36, 50, 166, 168, 170, 291, 345

divine action, 259

divine healing, 198, 201; *see also* healing

Docetism, 122

Donatism, 137

double predestination, 258

dove, 16–17, 79–80, 94, 105–6, 133–34, 163–64, 171–72, 280–81

Down syndrome, 204

drama of redemption, 319

dreams and visions, 63–64, 68, 77, 80

dualism, 151; anthropological, 271–72; cosmic, 235, 279; Johannine, 147

dwarfism, 223–24

Easter, 138, 144, 236, 280–81, 313–14

Eastern Orthodoxy, 5, 18, 104, 135, 137–38, 142, 173, 338–39

Ebionism, 239

ecclesiology, 72, 75; christological, 183; Ephesian, 166, **179–82**, 186, 188; eschatological, 184; missiological, 184–85; pluralistic, 178; pneumatological, 183; trinitarian, 179; *see also* church

ecumenism, 16–17, 171–173, 177–78

egalitarianism, 101, 174

Egypt, 2, 104, 162–64, 200, 271

"eighth day," 16–17, 39–40, 138, 322–23, 330–31

elders, 16–17, 322–23

election, 85–86, 110, 129, 165, 228–29, 234, 258

Elizabeth (sister of Mary), **57–61**, 71, 76, 103–4, 123, 131

Emancipation Proclamation, 340

Enlightenment, 2, 19, 64–65, 76, 207, 331, 339, 342

enlightenment, religious, 42–43

enthusiasm, 65

entropy, 266

environment, 117, 232; theology of, 203, 291

epiclesis, 143

epilepsy, 210

Epiphany, 134; *see also* Theophany

epistemology, 310

Esau, 258

eschatology, 72; final-state, 37; historic, 33; realized, 47; signs of, 154

Essenes, 131

eternal life, 32, 41, 53–54, 119, 122, 140, 149–51, 156, 223, 228–30, 245, 250, 268, 277, 285, 316, 360

eternity, 38, 54–55, 290, 299, 319

ethical goodness, 287
ethics, 119, 315, 317
Ethiopian eunuch, 2, 220, 293
Eucharist, 13–14, 16–17, 135, 137, **140–45**, 217–18, 313–14; see also Lord's Supper
Eucharistic theology, 144
Evangelical churches, 6, 135, 138, 167, 343
Evangelical theology, 9–10, 12, 24, 26, 36, 40–41, 51
evangelism, 176, 188, 304, 323–24; to Jews, 168
evangelization, 168, 304, 324; see also proselytization
evil, problem of: see theodicy; see also natural evil
evil spirits, 136, 140, 146, 204; see also demonology
evolution, 201, 261, **262–68**, 278, 282, 286–87, 289; human, 273; Roman Catholic teaching, 259
evolutionary cosmology, 290
evolutionary creation, 261–62, 286
evolutionary naturalism, 286
exclusivism, 307
exodus, 133–34, 138–39, 195–96, 236–37, 340–41
exorcism, 45, 105–6, 135–37, 139, 145–47, 156–58, 160, 194–99, 209–10, 214, 218–19, 239, 248, 264–65, 305, 312
experience, 339, 341–42

faith, 210, 220, 246
faith-cure movements, 65
faith-seeking-understanding, 353
fall (of creation), 206, 266, 274, 282, 284
fall of angels, 261, 266
false prophets, 315
fasting, 136, 145, 218
fellowship, 85, 158, 159, 187
filioque, 173, 302, 304, 325
fine tuning (cosmology), 286
finished work (of Christ), 107, 116, 220, 298
finitude, 268, 276, 288, 290, 349
fire, 66–67, 99, 257
fivefold, 230; ecclesiology, 165; gospel, 15, 50, 229–30; ministry, 61, 165; soteriology, 229

flesh, 53, 108–10, 114, 120, 123, 126, 150
footwashing, 122, 150–54, 158, 165
foreknowledge, 228, 256, 286
forgiveness, 53, 121, 156, 162, 181, 187, 210, 216, 229, 234, 239, 244–45, 251; of enemies, 250; of sins, 30, 45, 125, 129, 132, 134, 136, 138, 151, 157, 187, 230, 243–44, 250, 298, 363; of sinners, 236, 250, 311; unconditional, 250
Four Evangelists (Jordaens), 333
four living creatures, 46–47, 322–23
Free churches, 12, 135
Freedmen, 30, 161, 165
freedom, creaturely, 207, 250, 259, 287, 289, 290
freewill, 114
French Prophets, 65
friendship, 256
fruit, fruitfulness, 20–21, 120, 185–86, 248–49, 264–65
full gospel, 172–73, 178, 230
fundamentalism, 66
future, 319–20

Gabriel, Archangel, 79, 104–6
gap theory, 261
Garden of Eden, 65, 105–6, 249, 260, 264–65, 284
gender, 101
generation, 302
genetics, 262
Gentiles, 314–15
geology, 261
Ghent Altarpiece (Eyck), 16
globalization, 203
glorification, 228
glory, theology of, 214
glossolalia, 81, 85, 88, 89, 90–92, 97–98, 102, 157, 165; actual languages (xenolalia), 89; see also tongues
Gnosticism, 150
God the Father, 13–14, 18, 20, 27, 45, 49, 94–96, 101, 106, 112–13, 118, 124–26, 130, 133–34, 136, 149, 153, 164, 179, 181, 183, 185, 187, 189, 198, 210, 215, 234–35, 239, 244, 250, 277, 288–89, 293, 297–304, 310–12, 316, 319–21, 324, 327, 359–60, 363–64

God-fearer, 294–95
good and evil, 287
good news, 3, 7, 18, 35, 95, 155, 161, 188, 211, 230
Good Shepherd, 3–4, 248–49, 340–41
Good Shepherd (Roman), 3
goodness: *see* transcendentals
gospel and culture, 129
grace, 154, 159, 277; common, 322; preserving, 86; prevenient, 322; *see also* Christian practices
Great Awakening, 35, 65, 86, 146, 172
Great Commission, 299, 310, 313, 324
great tribulation, 36
guilt, 45, 236, 247–48, 250

Halfway Covenant, 86
hand of God, 94, 99–100, 105–6, 111–12, 248–49
hands of Christ, 20–21, 111–12, 152–53, 164, 185–86, 195–96
healers, psychic, 203
healing, 68, 89, 144, 146, 156, **193–98, 198–200, 201–4**, 205–6, 212–13, 221, 229–30, 259; ecclesiological, 215–16, 218; gifts of, 218; Pentecostal, 198; social, 218; theology of, 198, 214, **215–21**; traditional forms of, 203; women and, 199–200
health, holistic, 200, 216
health and wealth, 96
healthcare, 193, 211–12
heaven, 30–31, 33, 36–37, 40–41, 45, 47–48, 53, 55, 56, 75, 79, 83, 98, 109, 115, 133–34, 140, 147, 149–51, 159, 164, 179, 182–83, 188, 199, 206–7, 210, 213, 232, 243–46, 249, 251, 265, 283, 288, 291, 293, 296–97, 311, 316, 321, 323, 330, 345, 347, 360, 363
hell, 39–40, 236–37
Hellenistic Jews, 30, 161–62, 165
herbal medicines, 202
heresy, 62, 301
hermeneutical circle, 353–54
hermeneutics, 24–26, 333, 348–49; allegorical, 240; inductive, 93, 342; restorationist, 198
Hermes Kriophoros, 4

Herod, 104
Herod Antipas, 132
Herodias, 132
heterodoxy, 30, 318
Higher Life, 87; *see also* Keswick
Hinduism, 42, 200, 241, 306
historical criticism, 336
historiography, 172
history of religion, 116
holiness, 112; christological, 123; cultic, 108; ecclesial, 108, 124, 126, 129; eschatological, 108; mystical, 108; performative aspects of, 126; political, 115; social, 108, 115, 128; trinitarian, 125
Holiness tradition, 9, 85, 87–88, 93, 96–97, 100, 198, 228–29, 339; *see also* Wesleyan-Holiness tradition
Holocaust, 167, 189, 323
Holy Communion, 158; *see also* Lord's Supper
Holy of Holies, 330–31
holy orders, 141
Holy Saturday, 236
Holy Spirit, 13–14, 16–17, 47, 66–67, 70–71, 79–80, 90–91, 94–95, 99–100, 105–6, 127–28, 133–34, 163 –64, 171–72, 280–81, 303; economy of, 304; inner witness of, 86; procession/spiration of, 301, 302; and prophecy, 346; reception of, 158; temple of, 169, 181
Holy Trinity (Ermengau), 303
Holy Trinity (Peruvian), 303
Holy Trinity (Rublev), 13
homoousios, 299
hospitality, 126, 227, 252, 317
Hours of Étienne Chevalier (Fouquet), 127
house of God, 13–14, 40, 94–95, 330–31
human dignity, 269
human nature, 259
human origins, 282; *see also* common descent
human portraits, 270–71
human rights, 115
human uniqueness, 269–70
humility, 104–5, 114, 121, 153, 184, 215, 294, 323, 325, 349
husbands and wives, 181
hypostasis, 300

icon, 13, 70, 133–34, 152–53

iconography, 13, 67, 70, 133–34, 143–44, 153, 155–56, 159, 219, 237, 281, 303, 323, 333, 338, 351

idolatry, 111–12, 120–21, 196, 212–13, 281

illness, 211

image of God, 94, 112, 205–6, 212–13, **269–74**

imitation of Christ, 110

immaculate conception, 124

Immanuel (God with us), 105–6

impairment, 193, 197, 219; *see also* disability

impartiality, divine, 295

impeccability, 243

imputation, 113

"in Christ," 20–21, 70–71, 120–21, 138–39, 143–44, 153, 185–86, 248–49, 280–81

incarnation, 16, 41, 79, 91, 104, 106, 141–42, 148, 150–51, 155, 158, 220, 229, 237, 238, 241, 250, 267, 281, 283, 285, 300, 313, 314, 320

inclusivism, 307

India, 2, 3–4, 20, 42–43, 176, 202, 233, 241, 306

indigenizing principle, 4

indigenous cultures, 2–6, 43, 53, 242, 303, 305; African, 116–17

indigenous principle, 5

indigenous religions and traditions, 68, 305, 200, 202–3

indigenous renewal movements, 304

individualism, 207–8, 272

inerrancy, 334–35

infallibility, 334–35

infant baptism, 137, 139

infralapsarianism, 285

initiation, Christian, 89, 92, 100, 135, **136–40**, 145–45, 156; rites of, 338

intellectual disability, 52, 207, 220, 351

intelligent design, 287

intercession, 219, 234

interfaith dialogue, **306–10**

interfaith encounter, 69, 117, 241, 297, 308, 310, 324–26

intertextuality, 16–17, 105–6, 264, 334, 348–49

Irvingites: *see* Catholic apostolics

Isaac, 40

Isenheim Altarpiece (Grünewald), 217

Islam, 200, 306, 342

Israel, 20–21, 134, **166–69**, 280–81, 330; and the church, 188–90; judgment of, 312; nation-state of, 167; renewal/restoration of, 78, 95, 98, 164, 227

Italy, 2, 39, 138, 212, 248

Jacob, 40

Jerusalem, 67, 164, 257

Jesus Christ, 3, 20, 39, 46, 94, 111, 133, 143, 152, 195, 217, 225, 236, 248, 322; baptism of, 16–17, 79–80, 94, 133, 154; cross of, 16, 60, 112, 138, 172, 216, 217–18, 248–49, 252, 267, 280–81, 287; death of, 217–18, 236–37, 243, 280–81, 287; exaltation, 243, 245; exorcisms, 195–96, 209; and healing, 197–98, 211–13; humiliation, 242, 245; ministry of, 247; miracles, 211; moral exemplar, 110, 114; morality of, 287, 290; obedience of, 245, 250; passion of, 188, 213, 245, 252, 267; resurrection of, 30, 32–33, 37, 39–40, 45, 50, 54–55, 138, 143–44, 157, 165, 213, 234–36, 244–45, 248, 250, 268, 273, 276–77, 279, 284–87, 293, 313–14, 320, 360, 363; sacrifice of, 118, 122, 141, 223, 234, 243–46, 360; sanctifier, 15, 165, 198, 230; Spirit baptizer, 15, 50, 93, 95–96, 165, 198; suffering of, 213, 217

Jewish-Christian relations, 167, 242

Jews and Gentiles, 1, 48, 165, 167, 173, 179–82, 189–90, 276, 295–96, 315

Jim Crow era, 129

John, 217, 330–31, 333; beloved disciple, 328; brother of James, 327; son of Zebedee, 327; the elder, 328; the evangelist, 324

John the Baptist, 57–58, 93, 131–35, 217, 237

John's baptism, 148–49

Jonah, 297

Joppa, 82, 296–97

Joseph, 104, 162

joy, 59

Judaism, 200

Judaizers, 165

Judas, 143, 148, 153, **255–59**, 290

judgment, 34, 40, 42, 48, 53, 119, 126, 246, 249, 275, 288, 290–91, 321, 325; final, 34, 38–40, 41–42, 46–47, 52, 246, 287, 345

justice, 248, 324

justification, 110, 113, 223, 228–30, 233–34, 248, 275, 277, 279, 360

Kariye Camii (Chora Church) (Istanbul, Turkey), 236

karma, 42–43, 52

Keswick, 87, 107, 198, 339; *see also* Higher Life

kingdom of God: *see* reign of God

kingdom of heaven, 316

lamb (of God), 3–4, 13–14, 16–17, 217–18, 248–49, 280–81, 330

Last Judgment (Coppo), 39

Latin America, 171, 176, 303

latter rain, 172

law and gospel, 110, 116

laws of nature, 201, 218

leadership, church, 174

Leviathan, 266

lex orandi, lex credenda, 229

liberalism, 66, 170

liberation, 42

light, 13–14, 16–17, 30, 39–40, 79, 83–84, 105–6, 111, 12, 249, 280–81, 349

Lily among the Thistles (Lasworth), 280

liturgy, 320, 352

Lord Is My Shepherd (Johnson), 340

Lord's Supper, 135, **140–45**, 154–55, 158, 160, 165; *see also* Eucharist

love commandments, 122

love of God, 14, 41, 101, 119, 121, 126, 129–30, 236, 277

love of neighbor, 126, 155

loving God, 108, 250

loving neighbor, 119, 121, 250, 290

Ludwig III 1 (*Dyson Perrins Apocalypse*), 177

Luke (evangelist), 70, 333–34

macroevolution, 261

mappula, 314

male and female, 271–72, 283

Mamre, 13–14

Marian piety, 199

Mark (evangelist), 70, 330–34

marriage, 141; *see also* sacraments

martyrdom, 34, 63, 73, 82, 96, 102, 109, 115, 159, 161, 188, 199, 344–45, 347

Mary (mother of Jesus), 57, 59–60, 71, 79, **103–7**, 123–24, 144, 199, 217, 238, 240, 313, 328; virginal conception of, 104

Mary Magdalene, 3–4, 144, 217

masculinity, 294

masters and slaves, 181

materialism, 204

Matthew (Gospel of), 112, 333–34

Maundy Thursday, 144

medical technology, 201, 203

medicine, 215, 219

meditation, 42, 201

mental illness, 196, 204

messianic Judaism, 167–68, 189

metaphysics, 157, 319–20

method: *see* theological method

Methodism, 65, 87, 172

millennialism, **34–37**; *see also* eschatology

millennium, 33–34, 42, 166

ministry, 174, 181, 220, 324; apostolic, 174; nature of, 173; prophetic, 174

miracles, 77, 146, **198–200**, 221, 259; of Jesus, 209; of nature, 209

misandry, 272

missio Dei, 185

missio Spiritus, 185–88, 190

mission, 2, 176, 323–24; holistic, 115; theology of, 185, 188, 190

missionaries, 317

modalism, 300, 318–19

modernism, 202, 343

moksha, 42, 52

monarchianism, 300

monasticism, 109, 146, 199

monogenism, 272

monotheism, 298–99, 301, 320

Montanism, 63–64

Mosaic law, 162, 321–22

Moses, 162–63

Mount of Transfiguration, 82
Mozambican Christian Council, 231
Muslims, 332
multiple personality disorder, 196
multiverse, 44
Mummy Portrait: Head of a Woman
    (Fayum), 270
mutuality, 320
mutations (genetic), 286
mystery, 52, 75, 78, 100, 247, 259, 293,
    313, 320, 326, 331; of God, 179; of the
    church, 180
mysticism, 63–64
mystics, 329, 345

nativity, 79–80
natural disasters, 262
natural evil, 263, 290
natural history, 267, 282, 289
natural selection, 262, 266, 286
natural-supernatural dichotomy, 76–77
naturalism, 204, 262; metaphysical, 201;
    methodological, 201
nature and grace, 151
neo-Darwinism, 262
Neolithic period, 269, 284
neoplatonism, 37–38, 109, 114, 272, 299,
    319
"network church," 175–77
neuroscience, 114, 272
new birth, 32, 81, 85, 89, 93, 119, 137,
    139, 149, 223, 228, 304, 360–61
new covenant, 139, 229, 321
new creation, 16–17, 54–55, 105–6, 111–
    12, 212–13, 248–49, 250–51, 330–31
new heavens and earth, 34, 50, 53–54, 98,
    219, 347
new Jerusalem, 16–17, 53, 164, 330
New World, 2, 35
Nicene Creed, 7, 14, 18, 138, 299
Nicodemus, 149, 154

oikouménē, 171
Oikoumene (Watanabe), 171
Old School Presbyterianism, 86
Oneness Pentecostalism, 89, **297–301**,
    311, 320
Oneness-trinitarian dialogue, 318

ontology of persons, 114
oral cultures and traditions, 203, 242, 335
ordination, 141; *see also* holy orders
ordo salutis, 108, 110, 228–29, 252
original sin, 109–10, 124, 137, 266, 272,
    290
orthodoxy, 19–21, 212–13, 217–18, 248–
    49, 296–97, 333–34, 340–41
orthopathy, 16–17, 19–21, 83–84, 120–21,
    152–53, 217–18, 248–49
orthopraxy, 19–21, 120–21, 152–53, 185–
    86, 213–13, 231–32, 248–49, 344
Orpheus, 4
ousia, 200

Pacific Rim, 117
paleontology, 261, 269
Pantokrator, 39–40, 46–47, 94, 212–213,
    303–4
papacy, 63
Paraclete, 62, 151
Paris, 128
parousia, 50, 56, 220, 346
pastoral care, 156
patriarchy, 174, 181, 232, 305
Paul (apostle), **29–33**, 47, 70, 120, 138,
    258; *see also* Saul
peace, 229, 248, 250, 252
Pelagianism, 137
penance, 137, 141, 155
Pentecost, day of, 19, 66–67, 70, 79–80,
    90–91, 94, 99–100, 127–28
Pentecost (Chinnawong), 66
Pentecost (Dyck), 79
Pentecost (Hawkinson), 90
Pentecost (Winchester), 99
Pentecostalism, 5–6, 9, 89, 116, 170, 303,
    339
perfect love, 112–14, 119, 123, 129, 148
perfection, **87–88**, 229; eschatological,
    118; Wesleyan-Holiness, **87–88**, 97, 100
perichoresis, 302
persecution, 1, 11, 30, 32, 34, 49, 96, 109,
    115, 159, 329, 347
perseverance, 229
persons, ontology of, 114
Peter (apostle), **81–85**, 112, 153, 213, 226,
    295–97, 324

Peter's Vision on the Housetop (Northrop), 296

pharmacology, 201

philo-Semitism, 167, 189

physiognomy, 223, 226

Pietism, 65, 110, 172, 183, 198

pilgrimages, 199

Platonism, 299; *see also* neoplatonism

pluralism, 3–4, 16–17, 20–22, 66–67, 171–72, 177–78, 185–86, 232, 241, 296–97, 307, 330–31, 333–34, 340–41, 343, 353–54

pneumatology, 297–98, 302, 305, 309

polygenism, 269, 272

Portrait of an African (Ramsay), 270

postascension, 237

post-Christendom, 301

postcolonialism, 121, 175, 214

postdenominationalism, 175

postmillennialism, 35–36, 43

postmodernism, 175–76, 343

poverty, 176, 218, 232–33

practices, Christian: *see* Christian practices

pragmatism, 22, 259, 320

prayer, 43, 51, 56, 58, 84, 127–28, 136, 143, 145, 155, 182, 201–3, 210, 218–20, 229, 243, 278, 296, 311

predation, 290

predestination, 228, 234

pregnancy, 59–60

premillennialism, 33, 36, 50–51

Presbyterian churches, 9

priesthood, 162

primitivism, 299

principalities and powers, 145–47, 156, 182, 188, 251, 305

process theology, 266–67

proclamation, 325, 351

Prodigal Son, 236

promises, 36, 45, 55, 58, 61–62, 86, 167–68, 180, 183, 198, 242, 245, 320, 346

prophecy, 61, 74, 77

prophets, 16–17, 106, 213, 236–37, 334, 354–55

proselytism, 168, 176, 324, 325

prosperity, 68

Protestantism, 5–6, 18, 135, 138, 168, 173, 307, 331, 338

providence, 162, 172, 201, **259–63**, 289

punishment, 347; everlasting, 33, 38, 41, 52, 54, 362

purgatory, 38, 40–41

Puritanism, 35, 97, 100

Quakers, 65

Qumran, 62, 131–32, 134

Qur'an, 332

Rabbula Gospels, 46

race and ethnicity, 128

racism, 272

Radical Reformation, 35, 64, 139, 142, 299

rapture, 36, 50

rationalism, 19, 64–65, 76

reason, 339, 341

rebaptism, 137; *see also* baptism

recapitulation, 236, 252, 279

reconciliation, 19, 30, 101, 106, 141, 157, 185, 197, 216, 220, 227, 229–30, 232, 235, 246, 248, 250, 276–77; communities of, 251; ethnic, 180; of Jews and Gentiles, 180; social, 285

redemption, 9, 41, 48, 75, 125, 186, 202, 206, 219, 232, 249, 262, 267, 270, 278–79, 319, 337; cosmic, 101, 288; eschatological, 48, 98, 164, 167, 212, 267, 285, 289, 320, 321, 325; triune, 251

Reformed theology, 10, 107, 115

regeneration, 91, 100, 110, 113, 125, 136–37, 223, 228, 230, 233, 250, 293, 299, 360

reign of God, 7, 9, 15, 33–34, 36, 45–46, 48–49, 51, 72–73, 75, 78, 97–98, 115, 149, 154–56, 159, 162, **174–78**, 184, 189, 210–11, 213–15, 218–21, 239, 247, 250, 273, 287, 308, 312, 315, 322, 352

reincarnation, 52–53

relationality, 306, 320, 324; trinitarian, 306, 321

relativism, 343

relics, 199

religions, 42; diversity of, 233; pluralism of, 308, 321–23; theology of, 307, 310, 325–26

Renaissance, 199

repentance, 77, 88, 95, 135, 142, 144, 155–59, 210, 227, 229, 258, 325

restorationism, 169–70, 172, 174, 183, 198, 299

resurrection of the dead, 29, 37–40, 43–45, 49, 52–55, 72, 138, 206–7, 220, 229, 242, 244, 248–50, 275, 280–81, 286–87, 313–14, 319, 324, 362–64

revelation, 31–32, 39–40, 105–6, 296–97, 333–34, **336–39**, 355; christological, 336–38, 350; ecclesiological, 350–51; Jesus Christ, 344; new, 75; objective, 343; pneumatological, 343, 350; renewal perspective on, 346; subjective, 343; theories of, 336; trinitarian, 343

Right Hand of God Protecting the Faithful (Fouquet), 127

righteousness, 294–95

Risen Lord (Qi), 143

Roman Catholic Church, 5, 7, 18, 22, 35, 40, 64, 109, 135, 141, 173, 199, 303, 307, 338–39; theology of, 89, 283

Roman Empire, 1–2, 225, 229, 347

Rome, 1, 2–3, 82, 136, 177

rule of God, 78, 184; *see also* reign of God

Russia, 14

sacraments, 137, 173, 184, 307, 338; theology of, 141, 147, 149, 151, 153, 155

sacrifice, 116, 243–44, 279; for sins, 162, 243

saints, 17, 52, 63, 71, 98, 116, 129, 180–81, 199, 242, 278, 338, 345, 363

salvation, 166, 226–27; cosmic, 231; criteria, 315–17; eschatological, 48, 211, 251–52; history of, 93, 95, 104, 169, 277, 283, 320, 337; liberative, 251, 324; multidimensionality of, 223; relational, 251; *see also* soteriology

Saint Jerome Reading (Flemish), 348

Samaria, 49, 67, 92, 162

San Clemente Basilica (Rome), 248

Sancho, Ignatius, 271

sanctification, 10, 23, 41, 52–53, 62, 86–88, 93, 95–96, 101, 103, 106–10, 113–17, 121, 123–27, 129–30, 158, 228–30, 243, 249, 325, 361; entire, 87, 108, 114, 119

Sanhedrin, 257

Sant'Angelo in Formis (Capua, Italy), 212

Satan, 39–40, 136, 148, 200, 236–37, 256–58, 264–65, 313–14, 344; *see also* devil

Saul, 31–32, 164; *see also* Paul (apostle)

schizophrenia, 196

scholasticism, 64, 65

science, 97, **201–4**, 259, **260–63**, 278, 282, 342; rationality of, 342; *see also* theology and science

Scofield Reference Bible, 261

Scripture: as living word, 336; authority of, 331, 351; function of, 335; genres of, 335, 337; inspiration of, 332–34, 351; means of grace, 338; media of, 335; normativity of, 343, 353; orality of, 336; primacy of, 318; reception of, 335; theology of, 332, 355; *see also* canon, scriptural

Scutum Fidei, 303

second blessing, 5, 35, 87, 168, 304

second law of thermodynamics, 266

second work of grace, 88, 113–14, 299

selfishness, 266, 286–87, 289–90

Sermon on the Mount, 311, 315

Seven Churches of Asia Minor (Ludwig III), 177

Shakers, 65

shalom, 184, 186, 203, 220, 248, 287, 324; communities of, 251

shamanism, 68, 77, 203

shame, 115, 258

shrines, 199

sickness, 211

signs and wonders, 146, 197, 199, 210

signs of the kingdom, 215

sin, 118, 204, 219, 244, 247–48, 259, 272, 275, 287; eradication of, 87, 114, 125; multidimensionality of, 273; problem of, **269–74**; relational theory of, 273; social aspects of, 125, 273; structural, 273; theology of, 114

singularity, 286–88, 290

sinlessness, 118

sinthao, 66–67

Sistine Chapel (Vatican City), 111

skepticism, 204

slavery, 2, 270–72, 323, 340–41

social action, 251

social justice, 291

sociobiology, 266

sociology, 114

sola Christo, 338

sola fide, 338

sola grata, 338

sola scriptura, 64, **332–36**, 338–39, 342

solidarity, 221

Solomon, 237

Son of God, 59–60, 105–6, 112, 134, 249

Son of Man, 30, 48, 59–60, 120–21, 149, 151, 227, 248, 257, 312, 344

sorcery, 203

sorrow, 258

soteriology, 166, **228–33**, 308; eschatological, 228, 250; pneumatological, 233; trinitarian, 228, 233, 250; *see also* salvation

soul, 37–38, 109, 230, 240, 247–48, 269, 271–72, 283, 295, 302, 364

sovereignty, 69, 259

speaking in tongues: *see* tongues

species, extinction of, 263, 266

Speculum Virginum, 120

speed of light, 262

Spirit Baptism, 9–10, 22, 68, 78, 82, **85–92,** 93–96, 98, 100–102, 123, 139, 157, 318

Spirit Christology, 239, 241–42, 247, 253, 312

spiritual gifts, **61–69**

spirituality (pentecostal/renewal), 22–23, 337

spirit-possession, 68, 91–92, 203

spiritual warfare, 145, 147, 188, 218

star formation, 286

Stephen, saint, **161–65**, 166

stereotypes, 226

Stoning of St. Stephen, with the Trinity Above (Vasari), 163

subjectivism, 66, 336, 343

subsequence, 89, 91, 93, 98, 100, 113, 116, 140, 157

suffering, 96, 212, 262–63, 268, 289, 347; redemptive, 214

suicide, 258

supernaturalism, 65, 233

supersessionism, 167–68, 247; Islamic, 169

superstition, 201

Supper: *see* Lord's Supper

supralapsarianism, 285

Swine Driven into the Sea (Tissot), 195

syncretism, 307

synergy, 97

synoptic gospels, 334

tarrying, 88

teleology, 287

Temma on Earth (Lowly), 205

temple, 58, 94, 98, 104, 106, 162, 164, 166, 169, 173, 179, 181, 226, 256, 280, 284, 291, 312, 325, 330; *see also* Holy Spirit, temple of

temptation, 83–84, 120–21, 257

testimony, 30, 34–35, 75, 81, 84, 87, 95–96, 98, 125, 169, 197, 199, 216, 227, 232, 309, 313, 324, 329, 336, 344, 346, 350; apostolic, 327, 339

The Apostolic Tradition, 145

The Repentance of Judas (Morelli), 257

The Twelve, 255

theodicy, **263–68**, 289, 292; soul-making, 290; *see also* evil, problem of

theologians, 333, 354–55

theological anthropology, 114, 259, 269, 272, 282, 289, 292; christological aspects of, 283; eschatological aspects of, 284

theological method, 339–43, 349, 353; dialogical, 353–55; ecumenical, 353–54; eschatological, 352, 354; intercultural, 353–54; interdisciplinary, 353–54; performative, 354

theology: countercultural, 11; ecological/environmental, 178; eschatological, 15, 17, 74–75, 189, 287; feminist, 24, 272, 305–6; global, 24, 26–27, 145, 232, 306, 358; incarnational, 150, 241; liberation, 115, 205; non-Western, 11, 22; performative, 100, 154–55, 251, 351; pneumatological, 14, 15, 19; postcolonial, 24, 306; postliberal, 308–10; relational, 159 theology and science, 268, 281–82; complementarity, 282; warfare, 281

theology of the cross, 73, 213, 267, 286; eschatological, 291; pneumatological, 291

theology of culture, 325

theology of nature, 282

Theophany, 134

theosis: *see* union with God

theotokos, 103, 123, 240

third wave, 6

third work of grace, 88, 252, 299; *see also* second work of grace

thorns and thistles, 257, 264–65, 280–81

Three Angels at Mamre (Holy Trinity) (Rublev), 13

throne of God, 16–17, 39–40, 46–47, 303, 322–23

time and eternity, 299, 319

Tityrus, 4

tongues, 66–68, 89, 91, 99, 101, 154, 214, 299; evidential tongues, 85, 97; *see also* glossolalia

tradition, ecclesial, **336–39**, 341–43

traducianism, 125

trance, 92

transcendence, 53, 68, 299, 312

transcendentals, 52, 266, 287–88, 321–22, 325

transformation, 229; eschatological transformation, 279; social transformation, 188

Transforming Arts into Tools (TAE) program, 231–32

transubstantiation, 141–42

tree of life, 13–14, 120–21, 217–18, 248–49, 231–32, 248–49, 280–81

Tree of Life (Nucleo de Arte), 231

Tree of Life (San Clemente), 248

Tree of Vice and *Tree of Virtue* (German), 120

trees, 13–14, 20–21, 31–32, 90–91, 120–21, 134, 185–86, 217–18, 225, 231–32, 249, 264

tribulation, 36, 50

trinitarian relationality, 306, 321

trinitarian theology, 17, 115, 153–54, **279–92**, 298, 299, 301, 305, 320

Trinity, 13–14, 94–95, 164, 303–4, 310, 320

Trinity and the Apostles (German), 94

tritheism, 301, 303, 309, 311

triumphalism, 215, 309, 325

triune vestiges, 308

true vine, 20–21, 120, 249, 280–81, 296–97

truth: *see* transcendentals

two books, 275

urbanization, 207

Undone (Cano Villalobos), 54

unevangelized, 307, 317, 350

union with Christ, 144

union with God, 38, 109, 116, 138, 230

Unitarianism, 298, 318

unity, ecumenical, 173

universal restoration, 48

universalism, 33, 41, 310, 312, 288

Untitled (Hawkinson), 185

verbal inspiration, 332, 351

vernacular languages, 242

victimhood, 273, 290

victims, 248, 250–51, 273

Vine and the Branches (Raj), 20

violence, 232, 235, 244, 248, 252–53, 271, 273, 281, 290

Virgin and Child with Archangels, Scenes from the Life of Christ, and Saints (Ethiopian), 313

virtues, 110

Vision of the Heavenly Jerusalem (Maius), 330

visionaries, 146, 329

visions, 47, 170, 199, 296, 322, 329, 330, 344–45

Visitation of Mary to Elizabeth (Weyden), 59

Washing of the Feet (Egyptian), 152

water of life, 3–4, 16–17, 133–34, 249

way of salvation, 229

weakness, 208; theology of, 73

Wesleyan churches/theology, 112, 339

Wesleyan-Holiness tradition, 116, 343; *see also* Holiness tradition

Wesleyan quadrilateral, 339, 341

Westminster Confession, 64
wilderness, 257
Winchester Pontifical, 99
witchcraft, 145, 203
witness, empowerment for, 92, 96, 98,
    299; *see also* worship, and witness
women, 62, 76, 101, 176
word of God, 345; *see also* Scripture
word of knowledge, 74
word of wisdom, 74
works of grace, 100, 125, 252

World Vision, 218
worship, 52, 92, 101, 144, 161, 186–88,
    196, 244, 263, 279, 291, 294, 302, 311,
    317, 320–21, 323–26, 347, 352, 361,
    363; and witness, 324–26, 347, 352
wrath, divine, 234, 246, 275, 347

Zacchaeus, 220, **223–27**, 247
Zacchaeus (Stevns), 225
Zechariah, 58–60
Zionism, 167